# Fodor's

# TURKEY

8th Edition

Fodor's Travel Publications · New York, Toronto, London, Sydney, Auckland

www.fodors.com

# FODOR'S TURKEY

**Contributors:** Jennifer Hattam, Vanessa Larson, Scott Newman, Vildan Yahni

**Editors:** Caroline Trefler (lead editor), Stephen Brewer, Joanna G. Cantor

**Production Editor:** Jennifer DePrima
**Maps & Illustrations:** Mark Stroud and David Lindroth, *cartographers;* Rebecca Baer, *map editor;* William Wu, *information graphics*
**Design:** Fabrizio La Rocca, *creative director;* Tina Malaney, Chie Ushio, Jessica Walsh, *designers;* Melanie Marin, *associate director of photography;* Jennifer Romains, *photo research*
**Cover Photo:** Man carrying tray of tea: Zubin Shroff/The Image Bank/Getty Images
**Production Manager:** Angela L. McLean

## SPECIAL SALES

This book is available at special discounts for bulk purchases for sales promotions or premiums. Special editions, including personalized covers, excerpts of existing books, and corporate imprints, can be created in large quantities for special needs. For more information, write to Special Markets/Premium Sales, 1745 Broadway, MD 3-1, New York, NY 10019, or e-mail specialmarkets@randomhouse.com.

## AN IMPORTANT TIP & AN INVITATION

Although all prices, opening times, and other details in this book are based on information supplied to us at press time, changes occur all the time in the travel world, and Fodor's cannot accept responsibility for facts that become outdated or for inadvertent errors or omissions. So **always confirm information when it matters,** especially if you're making a detour to visit a specific place. Your experiences—positive and negative—matter to us. If we have missed or misstated something, **please write to us.** Share your opinion instantly through our online feedback center at fodors.com/contact-us.

PRINTED IN COLOMBIA

10 9 8 7 6 5 4 3 2 1

# CONTENTS

# ABOUT THIS BOOK

## Our Ratings

As travelers we've all discovered a place so wonderful that its worthiness is obvious. And sometimes that place is so unique that superlatives don't do it justice: you just have to be there to know. These sights, properties, and experiences get our highest rating, **Fodor's Choice**, indicated by orange stars throughout this book. Black stars highlight sights and properties we deem **Highly Recommended**. By default, there's another category: any place we include in this book is by definition worth your time, unless we say otherwise. And we will. Disagree with any of our choices? Care to nominate a place or suggest that we rate one more highly? Visit our feedback center at www.fodors.com/feedback.

> For expanded hotel reviews, visit **Fodors.com**

## Hotels

Hotels have private bath, phone, TV, and air-conditioning, and do not offer meals unless we specify that in the review. We always list facilities but not whether you'll be charged an extra fee to use them.

## Restaurants

Unless we state otherwise, restaurants are open for lunch and dinner daily. We mention dress only when there's a specific requirement and reservations only when they're essential or not accepted—it's always best to book ahead.

## Credit Cards

We assume that restaurants and hotels accept credit cards. If not, we'll note it in the review.

## Budget Well

Hotel and restaurant price categories from ¢ to $$$$ are defined in the opening pages of the respective chapters. For attractions, we always give standard adult admission fees; reductions are usually available for children, students, and senior citizens.

| Listings | | Hotels & Restaurants | Outdoors |
|---|---|---|---|
| ★ Fodor's Choice | ✎ E-mail | 🛏 Hotel | 🏌 Golf |
| ★ Highly recommended | 🎟 Admission fee | ⬠ Number of rooms | 🏕 Camping |
| ⊠ Physical address | ◷ Open/closed times | ☖ Facilities | **Other** |
| ⊹ Directions or Map coordinates | Ⓜ Metro stations | 🍽 Meal plans | ☺ Family-friendly |
| ⌖ Mailing address | ⊟ No credit cards | ✗ Restaurant | ⇨ See also |
| ☎ Telephone | | ⟋ Reservations | ⊠ Branch address |
| 🖶 Fax | | 🏛 Dress code | ☞ Take note |
| ⊕ On the Web | | ⟍ Smoking | |

# Experience
# Turkey

# 1

# WHAT'S WHERE

*The following numbers refer to chapters.*

**2 Istanbul.** Straddling Europe and Asia, Istanbul is the undisputed cultural, economic, and historical capital of Turkey. There are enough monuments and attractions, as well as enticing restaurants, shops, and museums, to keep you busy for days.

**3 The Sea of Marmara and the North Aegean.** The battlefields of Gallipoli are one of the main reasons travelers visit this part of Turkey, but the area is also a destination for beach lovers and those looking for pleasant places to hike. The archaeological site of ancient Troy is here, too.

**4 The Central and Southern Aegean Coast.** The heart of what was once known by the ancient Greeks as Asia Minor, this area has been drawing visitors since the time of, well, Homer. The heavyweight attraction these days is the Roman city of Ephesus but there are also many beach destinations, ranging from glitzy to relaxed.

**5 The Turquoise Riviera.** The beaches along Turkey's Mediterranean shores— dubbed the Turquoise Riviera—are some of the best in the country, and the ruins here are spectacular. With unspoiled seaside villages and charming hotels and *pansiyons,* this is very close to paradise. Steer clear of the megaresorts though, which have started to invade, particularly around Antalya.

**6 Cappadocia and Central Turkey.** In magical Cappadocia, wind and rain have shaped soft volcanic rock into a fairy-tale landscape, where conical outcroppings were centuries ago turned into churches and homes. Southwest of Cappadocia is Konya, home to a museum and tomb dedicated to the 13th-century founder of the whirling dervishes. Ankara, Turkey's capital, is also here, though it ranks fairly low on most visitors' itineraries.

**7 The Far East and Black Sea Coast.** It may not have the resorts, boutique hotels, and upscale restaurants of western Turkey, but there are impressive sites—both natural and man-made—including picturesque mountain villages; historic monasteries and churches; the ancient city of Ani and the towering Mt. Ararat, believed by some to be the resting place of Noah's Ark; and the fascinating Mt. Nemrut. In all these places, you're certain to get a taste of a different and rewarding Turkey.

# TURKEY TODAY

## Politics

In June 2011, the Justice and Development Party (AKP) won a decisive victory, giving the conservative party, led by Prime Minister Recep Tayyip Erdoğan and President Abdullah Gül, a third term. Since its accession to power in 2002, the AKP has sparked alarm among diehard secularists who assert that the party seeks to erode the secular legacy of Mustafa Kemal Atatürk. Some even contend that the AKP seeks to impose Sharia (strict Islamic day-to-day religious law) on the country, pointing to its efforts to remove restrictions on headscarf wearing and Erdoğan's vocal opposition to alcohol and tobacco use, though party leadership denies this.

Under the AKP, Turkey has moved toward greater political and economic engagement with the Arab world, as well as with developing countries in other regions, though the government says it remains committed to joining the EU. Most member states are in favor of Turkey's accession, but there are some strong opponents, and the talks have made only halting progress as Turkey faces criticism on several issues. Continued Turkish occupation of Northern Cyprus (which only Turkey recognizes as a sovereign nation) is one stumbling block; another is the Turkish government's refusal to label the deaths of several hundred thousand Armenians during World War I as genocide. Domestically, critics cite Turkey's headscarf ban and criminal laws that punish anyone found guilty of insulting "Turkishness" (amended in 2008 to insulting the Turkish nation) as further obstructions.

## The Economy

The AKP's greatest bargaining chip in recent elections has been the upsurge of the Turkish economy since the aftermath of the 1999 Marmara earthquake, a trend that largely continued in 2011 despite the economic crisis in Europe. The country enjoys a diverse economy: self-sufficient agricultural production, a massive textile industry, and a growing electronics sector. Turkish annual GDP growth, averaging more than 6% throughout most of the 2000s and hitting 8.9% in 2010, is among the fastest in the world. Interest in Turkey has been steadily growing over the past decade, as evidenced by the number of foreign tourists nearly tripling between 2000 and 2010. International faith in the economy has driven considerable foreign investment, which has strengthened the Turkish lira. Inflation, which for 30 years led to the counting of the lira in millions, has dropped to single-digit levels and allowed the government to lop six zeroes from the old lira in 2005. Inflation began to rise again in 2011, while the lira's value dropped, though neither to degrees seen in the past. These trends, combined with Turkey's greatest economic liability—a sizable trade deficit, driven largely by the country's need to import foreign oil—and concerns about an overheating economy, have caused some renewed jitters among foreign investors.

## Religion

In Istanbul they sell a T-shirt with the name of the city spelled using a crescent, a cross, and a Star of David. Turks pride themselves on their tolerance of other religions, a legacy of the Ottoman Empire, which governed people of all faiths. Turkey is a secular republic, however: the population is overwhelmingly (99%) comprised of Muslims; the remaining 1% are Christians (Greek Orthodox and Armenian Apostolic) and Jews. One reason for the relative harmony between people of different faiths may be the relaxed

approach that many Turks take toward religion. In addition to having a secular government, many Turks drink alcohol and smoke cigarettes, and on any given day in Istanbul you're as liable to find as many scantily clad fashionistas walking down the street as women wearing head-scarves (many of whom are plenty stylish themselves).

## The Arts

Turkey has made many recent contributions to the art world—no surprise from a country that boasts such stunning antiquity—and Istanbul was chosen as a 2010 European Capital of Culture, drawing attention to its vibrant fine arts, music, and film scenes. The Istanbul Film Festival will be in its 31st year as of 2012: Held every April, the festival awards prizes for both Turkish and international films. The country's most well-known creative mind may be novelist Orhan Pamuk, who garnered Turkey's first Nobel Prize in 2006 for his dreamy yet historical novels, though the stars of other authors—as well as filmmakers, designers, and musicians—are beginning to rise as well. Additionally, Turkey's status as a large textile exporter has helped ensure the nation a place in fashion design, and Istanbul's Nişantaşı district is a maze of small boutiques selling imported and Turkish clothing. In the visual arts, Turkey is most famous for its ceramics and porcelain, especially hand-made Kütahya and İznik tiles.

## Sports

Turkey is a diehard soccer nation (they call it football), and heated rivalries run strong. Turkey's clubs boast lots of homegrown talent along with some players imported from Europe and South America. The Turkish national football team has enjoyed sporadic success in international play. In the last decade, the team reached the semifinals in the 2002 World Cup and 2008 European Cup. Basketball is also an increasingly popular sport in Turkey, which hosted the 2010 FIBA World Championship—and cheered its national team of "12 giant men" to a second-place finish.

## Media

Turkish media seems always to be on people's lips, mainly because of Article 301 and the Turkish government's penchant for closing down outlets that offend its sensibilities or offer criticism that is deemed too harsh. Until 2008, Article 301 forbade anyone from insulting "Turkish-ness," under pain of criminal prosecution (as above, the crime has now been changed to insulting the Turkish nation). Most cases are dropped but many notable Turks, including Orhan Pamuk, have been prosecuted. Frequent shutdowns of popular Internet sites, most prominently YouTube, have raised concerns about freedom of speech, as have recent detentions of journalists and the 2007 murder of Armenian-Turkish journalist Hrant Dink. Despite these controversies, the Turkish press remains large and vibrant, with a variety of voices represented.

## Smoking

In an effort to curb rampant tobacco addiction, the Turkish government introduced a ban on smoking in enclosed public places, which took effect in May 2008. Some bars and clubs simply ignore the ban, but the government estimates that Turks are smoking 10 to 15 percent fewer cigarettes each year, and that more than 2 million people have kicked the habit since the ban went into effect.

# TURKEY PLANNER

## When to Go

Most tourists visit Turkey between April and the end of October but July and August are the busiest—and hottest—months. April through June and September to October offer more temperate weather, and crowds are smaller; hotel prices usually lower, too.

Istanbul tends to be hot in summer, cold and rainy in winter. The Mediterranean (Turquoise) and Aegean coasts have mild winters and hot summers; you can swim along either coast from late April into October. The Black Sea coast is mild and damp, with a rainfall of 90 inches per year. Central and eastern Anatolia can be extremely cold in winter, with roads and mountain passes closed by snow; summers bring hot, dry weather, but cool evenings.

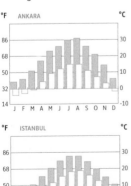

## Getting Around

In Turkey you can travel by plane, car, bus, or train. With the advent of several new domestic airline companies in recent years, competition has increased and the cost of domestic flights has come down, so if your aim is to see several different areas of the country in a short time, you may want to fly between destinations.

Turkey has an extensive bus network, with buses serving all the major cities and even the smallest towns. Buses are generally safe, reliable, and surprisingly comfortable, making them an excellent way to travel around the country.

Renting a car allows you greater flexibility than traveling by bus and the chance to see places that are more off the beaten path, as well a glimpse of small-town Turkish life. Although major roads are generally in good condition, minor roads can be rough and badly paved, and it's wise to avoid driving at night. Traffic in large cities, particularly Istanbul, can be nightmarish. If you don't want a stick shift, reserve well in advance and specify automatic transmission.

Although cheaper than buses, trains tend to be far slower and do not serve many areas of the country. High-speed rail lines run between Ankara and Konya and Ankara and Eskişehir, but for other routes it's not usually worth taking the train. *For more detailed information, see the Travel Smart chapter and the specific regional chapters.*

## What to Pack

For women, it's advisable to bring a scarf or shawl that will cover the hair (and shoulders, if you are wearing a sleeveless shirt) when entering mosques. If you're planning to visit Cappadocia, a flashlight can be useful for exploring cave churches and underground cities. If you're going anywhere with beaches or archaeological ruins, it's wise to bring sunscreen. An umbrella is a good idea if you're visiting Istanbul in the rainy winter months, though cheap ones are readily available for sale on city streets.

## Hotels in Turkey

Turkey has a variety of different types of accommodation, from simple inns to boutique hotels and luxury international chains. *Pansiyons,* found especially throughout the coastal areas and in small towns, tend to be small, family-run, and offer inexpensive but clean lodgings, usually including a Turkish breakfast. The designation of "special-class hotels" includes restored Ottoman mansions and villas, cave hotels in Cappadocia, and other establishments with unique historical, cultural, and/or architectural character.

Hotels in Turkey are officially classified on a one- to five-star system. These designations can be misleading though, as they're based on quantity of facilities rather than quality of service and décor; a lack of restaurant or lounge automatically relegates the establishment to the bottom of the ratings. In reality, a lower-grade hotel may be far more charming and comfortable than one with a higher rating.

## Restaurants in Turkey

Turkey has restaurants to suit your every mood and budget.

*Büfe.* These stands are great for cheap and simple *döners* (meat grilled on a vertical spit), *tost* (panini-like grilled cheese sandwiches), or packaged snacks.

*Lokanta.* This name is given to a range of traditional restaurants that serve homey dishes like soups, stews, and casseroles. Most *lokantalar* offer a variety of fresh food that's displayed in long steam tables. Point to what looks good and a waiter will bring it to your table.

*Meyhane.* Tavernlike *meyhanes* are the place to go for mezes, to drink rakı, and perhaps sing the night away with your fellow diners. *Meyhanes* usually also serve fish.

*Balıkçı. Balık* means "fish" in Turkish, and seafood restaurants tend to be more sedate than *meyhanes.* Though they serve many of the same mezes as *meyhanes,* these restaurants will have a larger selection of fish and more creative ways to cook them.

*Kebabcı.* Kebab restaurants, also known as *ocakbaşı* (grill room), typically stick to the basics: skewered meat (usually lamb, beef, and chicken), and a few sides.

*Muhallebici/Pastane. Muhallebicis* specialize in milk-based desserts like *sütlaç,* a rich rice pudding. *Pastanes* have European-style cakes and cookies, as well as some savory baked snacks.

## Mosque Etiquette

The Turks are quite lenient about tourists visiting mosques and most are open to the public during the day, but there are some rules of etiquette:

It's best not to enter a mosque during the five daily prayer sessions, especially at midday on Friday, when attendances are higher.

Immodest clothing is not allowed but an attendant by the door will lend you a robe if he feels you aren't dressed appropriately. For women, bare arms and legs aren't acceptable, and men should avoid wearing shorts. Women should cover their heads before entering a mosque, though this is sometimes overlooked.

Shoes must be removed before entering a mosque; there's usually an attendant who watches over them, or you can put them in your backpack or handbag, or use the plastic bags often provided near the entrance.

It's considered offensive for a non-Muslim to sit down in a mosque.

It's also advisable to show respect by talking only in whispers.

Don't take photographs inside the mosque, particularly of people praying.

A small donation is usually requested for the upkeep of the mosque. The equivalent of about $3 is appropriate.

# TURKEY
# TOP ATTRACTIONS

### Topkapı Sarayı

**(A)** Topkapı Palace was the home of the Ottoman Sultans and the heart of the empire. Its grassy courtyards once buzzed with the comings and goings of soldiers, ambassadors, eunuchs, and Pashas, while in the private chambers of the Harem, dripping with lovely blue tiles, the Sultan's women schemed to bring a son to the throne. Former storerooms overflow with gold thrones, gigantic diamonds, and the holiest relics of Islam.

### Aya Sofya

**(B)** Aya Sofya was, for nearly a thousand years, the greatest church in Christendom. Built by the emperor Justinian in the 6th century, it's one of the few buildings of its age, size, and grandeur to survive today. Its giant dome shelters numerous historic artworks, from Byzantine mosaics to Islamic calligraphy.

### Yerebatan Sarnıcı

**(C)** Dark basements with serious damp problems aren't normally tourist attractions, unless they happen to be evocative Byzantine cisterns, held up by ancient columns that are reflected in water teeming with fish. Built 1,500 years ago to preserve the city's water supply through siege and drought, it's a peaceful, surreal escape from the heat of an Istanbul summer.

### The Blue Mosque

**(D)** Elegant, cascading curves and a central location make the Blue Mosque (aka Sultan Ahmet Camii) the most famous mosque in Istanbul. Inside is a spectacular coating of blue İznik tiles, which gives it its nickname.

### Ephesus

**(E)** Ephesus was the metropolis of Asia Minor and archaeologists have revealed a treasure trove of ancient streets once walked by Alexander the Great and St. Paul. The houses, theaters, temples,

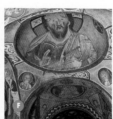

toilets, even a brothel, and the columned facade of the Library of Celsus are in remarkably good condition.

## Göreme Open-Air Museum

(F) The unique lunar landscape of Cappadocia is honeycombed with Byzantine churches cut from the rock in the Middle Ages, many decorated with beautiful frescoes. The most famous and easily accessible place to visit is the collection of churches and dwellings known as the Göreme Open-Air Museum.

## Pamukkale

(G) Stunning white travertine pools of water cascade down a hillside in the hinterland of the Aegean coast: this unique rock formation was created over eons by mineral-rich water and has attracted tourists for millennia, although the rock pools are smaller, and not as pristine as they once were.

## Mt. Nemrut

(H) Atop a lonely mountain overlooking the Euphrates, this ancient shrine to the megalomania of one man is an extraordinary archaeological site. The oversize heads of King Antiochos and a pantheon of gods litter the ground beside a great burial mound.

## Olympos

These jungle-entangled ruins in a valley by one of the Mediterranean's most beautiful beaches are overlooked by the natural eternal flame of the Chimaera. Few places combine so many of Turkey's many attractions as does Olympos.

# TOP TURKEY EXPERIENCES

### Take a Boat up the Bosphorus

A boat ride along the Bosphorus is one of the most enjoyable ways to see the sprawling, magnificent city of Istanbul. From the ferry's vantage point, you'll see landmarks like the Dolmabahçe and Çırağan Palaces; Ortaköy Mosque, perched right on the water's edge; and exquisite waterfront mansions, called *yalıs*, that were summer homes for the Ottoman elite. You'll also pass under the waterway's two suspension bridges, which connect Asia and Europe. While onboard, sip a glass of Turkish tea and listen to the calls of the seagulls as you contemplate this beautiful meeting of two continents.

### Scrub Down in a Turkish Bath

Before the era of indoor plumbing, going to a hammam, or public bath, was a central element of Turkish life. Today many beautiful centuries-old hammams are still in use, by both locals and tourists. Nearly all have either separate facilities, or different hours, for men and women. In the hammam's steam room, you can relax on the heated marble platform in the center and rinse yourself at one of the marble washbasins. If you choose, you'll also be lathered, scrubbed, and massaged by a hammam attendant, whose goal seems to be to remove every last dry skin cell from the surface of your body. You'll emerge ultraclean, refreshed, and having taken part in an age-old Turkish tradition.

### Stay in a Cave Hotel

Where but in Cappadocia can you sleep like the Flintstones while having all of your creature comforts? Few of Cappadocia's inhabitants still live in traditional homes carved out of the soft tufa stone, so in recent years the area's hoteliers have been converting more and more of these "cave" dwellings into hotels, which range from basic inns for backpackers to upscale lodgings with plush furnishings, modern lighting, and fully equipped bathrooms, some even with Jacuzzis. Surrounded by Cappadocia's magical landscape, tucked cozily into your cave room at night, you'll feel almost as if you're on another planet.

### Watch the Dervishes Whirl

Turkey is famous for its "whirling dervishes," a sect of Sufi mystics, the Mevlevi, who believe that ritual spinning in circles will bring them to union with God. This trancelike whirling is just one element of the *sema*, a highly symbolic religious ceremony that also includes music and Koranic recitation. Despite the fact that these dervish ceremonies have become increasingly tourist-oriented in recent years, attending a *sema* is still a powerful and mesmerizing experience. Seeing the dervishes whirl is one of the main draws of the festival commemorating Rumi in Konya each December; there are also regular dervish performances in Istanbul and elsewhere in Turkey.

### Take a Blue Cruise

One of the most popular and relaxing ways to experience Turkey's Aegean and Mediterranean coasts is to take a Blue Cruise aboard a *gulet,* or wooden fishing vessel. Usually lasting several days (or longer), these cruises take passengers along the rugged coastline, with stops to visit ruins or villages. Away from the beach crowds, you'll enjoy the simple pleasures of swimming in remote coves, eating fresh-caught fish, and sleeping on your boat in a wooded inlet.

### Quench Your Thirst Like the Locals

A trip to Turkey isn't complete without sampling certain quintessentially Turkish beverages. You can barely go anywhere without being offered a glass of çay, or tea:

The lubricant for every social and business encounter, it's consumed in Turkey at one of the world's highest rates per capita. The famous Turkish coffee, a thick brew made with extremely finely ground coffee beans, is in fact drunk far less often: primarily just on special occasions and as a digestive after meals. For something cold, try the ubiquitous *ayran,* a frothy, salted, yogurt drink that's a refreshing accompaniment to a spicy meal of kebabs. Another unique beverage is *sahlep,* a sweet, milk-based hot drink served during the winter months. And don't forget to taste the anise-flavored national liquor, rakı.

## See Cappadocia from Above

Taking a trip in a hot-air balloon is a thrilling way to see the amazing scenery of Cappadocia; for many people this is a highlight of their visit to the area. As your balloon follows the natural contours of the terrain, you'll look down into scenic valleys and sail right past "fairy chimneys" and unusual rock formations that seem almost close enough to touch. Flights leave at dawn, when the air is calmest and safest for flying, and end with a champagne toast.

## Wander Among Ruins

With so many civilizations having occupied the land that is now Turkey, it's no surprise that the country is sprinkled with ancient ruins. The remains of Roman and Greek cities, with their impressive theaters, temples, stadiums, and colonnaded streets, compete with even older sites dating back to the Hittites. From beachside Patara and Olympos, to Termessos high up in the mountains, to the inland Aphrodisias, each spot is uniquely picturesque. At the best-preserved sites like Ephesus and Troy, you'll be among many visitors marveling at the ruins, but at places that are more off the beaten path, you'll be free to wander and explore with virtually no one else around.

## Travel the Country by Bus

Taking an intercity bus in Turkey is a lot like taking an airplane in other countries. Since most Turks travel this way, bus terminals are as heavily trafficked as airports, and house a myriad of different companies with buses departing around the clock for every corner of the country. Seats are assigned, with unrelated males and females usually not seated together. During the ride, a uniformed bus attendant will regularly come around distributing snacks, water, and tea and coffee for no extra charge; he'll also offer you lemon-scented cologne to refresh your face and hands. To entertain passengers, films are shown en route—though don't expect subtitles.

## Experience and Appreciate Different Religions

Turkey is a cultural crossroads where the world's three major religions have coexisted for centuries, and one of the most surprising things for many visitors is the way these religions are juxtaposed. Particularly in Istanbul, but in other places as well, you'll see ancient churches and synagogues right around the corner from mosques. This is an excellent opportunity to learn about different religious traditions as you listen to the Muslim call to prayer, visit Istanbul's Jewish Museum, or gaze at Eastern Orthodox iconography in a Byzantine church.

# QUINTESSENTIAL TURKEY

## Markets and Bargaining

A highlight of any trip to Turkey is a stroll through one of the country's markets; they provide the chance to experience the country at its most vibrant and colorful. The granddaddy of them all is, of course, Istanbul's Grand Bazaar, a must-see simply for its size and historical significance. Though touristy, this is the most convenient place to stock up on souvenirs—inlaid wood backgammon sets, colorful ceramic bowls, and, of course, rugs.

Remember, in all of Turkey's markets, bargaining is the norm. Every vendor (and every buyer, as you will soon discover) has his or her own style, but some general rules govern the interaction. The seller will undoubtedly offer you a high initial price, so don't feel embarrassed to come back with a price that's much lower—try half, for starters. And remember, it's your money that's being spent, so feel free to walk out at any time—though it's both

bad manners and bad business to bargain aggressively or to decline to buy once the seller has accepted your offer. And don't shop in a rush: bargaining takes time.

## Mezes

Good things come in small packages, and the Turkish tradition of serving appetizers known as mezes—Turkey's version of tapas—is proof. Mezes originated when simple dishes—usually a slice of tangy, fetalike sheep's milk cheese with honeydew melon and fresh bread—were brought out to accompany rakı, the anise-flavored spirit that is Turkey's national drink. From its humble origins, though, the meze tradition has developed into something quite elaborate. Today, in the *meyhanes* (literally "drinking places") of Istanbul and other restaurants throughout Turkey, waiters will approach your table with a heavy wooden tray loaded down with sometimes more than 20 different kinds of small dishes—smoky eggplant

For many Westerners, visiting Turkey is an exotic experience, but it's incredibly easy to get drawn into the everyday rituals that make life here such a pleasure. Eat, drink, shop . . . you'll quickly understand the allure of the country and why the Turks are renowned for their hospitality.

puree, artichoke hearts braised in olive oil, slices of cured fish, perhaps—for you to choose from. Just point at whatever looks good and the dish will be placed on your table.

## Tea

Visitors who come to Turkey expecting to be served thick Turkish coffee at every turn are in for a surprise—tea is the hot beverage of choice and you'll be offered it wherever you go: when looking at rugs in the Grand Bazaar or when finishing your meal in even the humblest restaurant. Tea, called *çay*, is grown domestically along the slopes of the Black Sea coast. Flavorful and aromatic, it's not prepared from tea bags, a concept that horrifies most Turks; instead, it's made in a double boiler that has a larger kettle on the bottom for heating up the water and a smaller kettle on top where a dark concentrate is made using loose tea leaves. The resulting brew—strong and rust-color—is usually served in a small, tulip-shape glass, with two or more cubes of sugar (but never, Allah forbid, with milk or lemon). If you want your tea weak (light), ask for an *açık çay*.

Most teahouses will also carry a range of herbal teas, which are also popular, especially *ada çayı* (sage tea) and *ıhlamur çayı* (linden flower tea). *Elma çayı* (apple tea), usually made from a synthetic powder, is often served to tourists.

# IF YOU LIKE

## Ancient Sites

Turkey, a sort of bridge between Europe and Asia, has been a cultural crossroads for thousands of years. Numerous civilizations—Greeks from the west and Mongols from the east—settled or moved through the (vast) area at one point or another, leaving lasting and impressive reminders of their sojourns. As a result, virtually every region in Turkey has a bounty of stunning ancient ruins.

**Ani:** The abandoned former capital of a local Armenian kingdom, this haunting city in the middle of nowhere is filled with the ruins of stunning churches.

**Cappadocia's underground cities:** A marvel of ancient engineering, these subterranean cities—some reaching 20 stories down and holding up to 20,000 people—served as a refuge for Christians under siege from Arab raiders.

**Ephesus:** This remarkably well-preserved Roman city has a colonnaded library that seems as if it could still be checking out books and an amphitheater that appears ready for a show.

**Mt. Nemrut:** At the top of a desolate mountain, this 2,000-year-old temple—a collection of larger-than-life statues facing the rising and setting sun—is a testament to the vanity of an ancient king.

**Termessos:** This impregnable ancient city is set dramatically high up in the mountains above Antalya; even Alexander the Great and the Romans found it too difficult to attack.

## Beaches

With 8,000 km (5,000 mi) of coastline, it's no wonder that Turkey is home to several world-famous beaches, and you can find all kinds: from pristine, remote coves to resort hotel beaches with water sports and all sorts of amenities.

With its frigid waters and sometimes rocky shores, the Black Sea is not usually considered a beach destination, but it has some stretches of lovely, sandy shoreline. The beaches at **Kilyos** and **Şile,** both just outside Istanbul, are among the nicest and are easy to get to, although you may find them crowded on the weekends.

The Aegean has crystal clear waters and a mix of resorts and quieter seaside spots, although its beaches tend to be pebbly. Exceptions to that are **Altınkum,** near Çeşme, a series of undeveloped coves with glorious golden sand beaches, and the long stretch of sand at **Sarımsaklı,** near Ayvalık.

Turkey's Mediterranean coast has turquoise waters that stay warm well into October and an abundance of picture-perfect beaches, although overdevelopment has become a problem in some parts. Thankfully, there are still a good number of unspoiled beaches left. Dalyan's **İztuzu Beach** (a nesting ground for sea turtles) stretches for 5 sandy kilometers (3 mi), with a freshwater lagoon on one side and the Mediterranean on the other. Near Fethiye is **Ölüdeniz,** a stunning lagoon of azure waters backed by white sand. The beach at **Patara** is one of Turkey's best, an 11-km (7-mi) stretch with little but fine white sand and dunes.

**Olympos,** near Antalya, is another top spot, with a long crescent-shape beach that is backed by spectacular mountains and ancient ruins.

## Monuments

The Byzantine and Ottoman empires may be long gone, but they left behind some truly striking monuments: churches, mosques, and palaces that still hold the power to take your breath away.

As the former capital of both empires, Istanbul has the lion's share of Turkey's most famous structures, but there are also impressive ones to be found in every other part of the country. **Aya Sofya**, the monumental church built by the emperor Justinian some 1,500 years ago, continues to be an even more awe-inspiring sight— arguably the most impressive one in Istanbul or Turkey. The **Kariye Museum**, in what was the Chora Church, is much smaller and not as famous as the Aya Sofya, but this 12th-century Byzantine church on the periphery of Istanbul's Old City is filled with glittering mosaics and stunning frescoes that are considered among the finest in the world.

**Topkapı Sarayı**, the former home of the Ottoman sultans, is a sumptuous palace with stately buildings, tranquil gardens, and the must-see Harem. Also in Istanbul is the **Blue Mosque**: with its cascading domes and shimmering tiles, this exquisite mosque is one of the Ottomans' finest creations.

Edirne, not far from Istanbul, was the Ottoman capital before Istanbul. It's home to **Selimiye Camii**, the mosque that was the real masterpiece of the sultans' favorite architect, Mimar Sinan. Its massive dome has made many a jaw drop.

In Turkey's far east, near the legendary Mt. Ararat, is **Ishak Paşa Sarayı**, an 18th-century palace that seems as if it was transported straight out of a fairy tale.

## Museums

The country's wealth and depth of history guarantee that Turkey has lots of artifacts for its museums—even if there has been a problem with other countries shipping the booty off to foreign lands. The best and biggest museums are in Istanbul, where you can spend your days hopping from one fascinating exhibit to the other. The sprawling **Archaeology Museums**, near Topkapı Palace, hold finds from digs throughout the Middle East. Nearby is the excellent **Museum of Turkish and Islamic Art**, housed in an old Ottoman palace, which displays carpets, ceramics, paintings, and folk art. For a taste of something more up-to-date, visit the stylish **Istanbul Modern**, which has a good collection of modern Turkish art and a stunning waterfront location. Also worth visiting is the **Rahmi M. Koç Industrial Museum**, an old factory that is now used to display a quirky collection of cars, trains, ships, airplanes, and other industrial artifacts that will pique the interests of children and adults.

Istanbul doesn't have a monopoly on the museum business, though. The **Gaziantep Zeugma Mosaic Museum**, in Turkey's southeast, is one of the country's best, with a world-class collection of Roman-era mosaics. Ankara's **Museum of Anatolian Civilizations**, found in a restored 15th-century covered market, holds masterpieces spanning thousands of years of local history. Konya, in central Turkey, is home to the fascinating **Mevlâna Museum**, dedicated to the founder of the whirling dervishes and located inside what used to be a dervish lodge. The unusual **Museum of Underwater Archaeology**, in a 15th-century castle in Bodrum on the Aegean coast, displays booty found in local shipwrecks.

# ISLAM

### Islam and Muhammad

Islam is an Abrahamic religion—one of the three largest (and somewhat interrelated) monotheistic religions in the world. The prophet Muhammad is believed to be descended from Ishmael, son of Abraham, through a union with his wife Sarah's handmaiden, Hagar. Abraham also sired Isaac, who was one of the patriarchs of Judaism and Christianity. Thus, many of the prominent figures in Judaism and Christianity—Adam, Moses, and Jesus—are also revered as prophets in Islam.

Muhammad was born in Mecca on the Arabian Peninsula (near the Red Sea in present-day Saudi Arabia). He became a religious figure in 610 AD when, according to Islamic tradition, while meditating in solitude he began to receive visions from the angel Gabriel. The words of these visitations became the *shuras* (verses) of the Koran, the holy book of Islam. When Muhammad first began preaching the new religion he was met with hostility by pagan tribesmen and forced to flee to Medina (also in Saudi Arabia) in 622 AD. After converting the people of Medina to Islam, Muhammad returned to Mecca and converted his hometown, and by the end of the 6th century, Islam was the dominant religion in Arabia. In the subsequent centuries Muslim armies would sweep across North Africa and into Spain, throughout the Levant and eastward into Central Asia and Persia. Turkic peoples were converted to Islam sometime during their journey across Asia, and when the Seljuks swept through Byzantine territory in Asia Minor, they brought Islam with them. After the rise of the Ottoman Empire, Muslims crossed the Dardanelles into Eastern Europe, where the Turks conquered as far as Vienna. Today there are 1.6 billion Muslims throughout the world.

### Islam Today

Islam is a comprehensive religion and its tenets touch all aspects of life. Devout Muslims pray five times a day: at sunrise, midday, in the afternoon, at sunset, and in the early evening—exact times are determined by the sun's passage. One of the first things visitors to Istanbul notice is the sound of the call to prayer—called the *ezan*—wafting from the minarets of local mosques. The focal point of Muslim prayer is the Sacred Mosque in Mecca, at the center of which is the Kabaa, a shrine said to have been built by Abraham and rebuilt by Muhammad. One duty of able-bodied Muslims is to make the pilgrimage, or *hajj*, to Mecca at least once in their lifetime.

Despite a lot of praying, modern Turks tend to have a relaxed approach to their religion. Many drink alcohol and smoke cigarettes—both of which are forbidden by strict interpretations of Islam. They don't, however, eat pork. While the Koran expressly forbids eating all carnivores and omnivores, pigs are especially abhorrent. Turkish men can be shameless flirts and modern women often dress in contemporary and revealing couture, though such behavior is not in keeping with Islamic ideas of modesty. There are, however, a great many conservative folks, too, and in the modern Turkey, the role of religion in society is hotly debated as the political old guard fights with the young, often more religious majority, over Atatürk's definition of secularism.

### Islam and Art

Turkey enjoys a proud tradition of contributing to Islamic art. Ottoman mosque architecture incorporated many of the

Byzantine design elements that Mehmet II's armies found in Constantinople. Ottoman mosques with their spacious courtyards and mammoth domes, notably Sultanahmet Mosque are essentially variations on Aya Sofya. Ottoman art also boasts some of the most elaborate and colorful tile designs in the world. The best Ottoman tiles were created in İznik during the 16th and 17th centuries. Ottoman tiles sport dazzling geometric and floral designs, which adhere to the Islamic prohibition on depicting human figures. This ban (which scholars believe inspired the iconoclastic period during which the Byzantines actually destroyed their own icons), came out of a desire to discourage idolatry. When Mehmet II conquered Istanbul, the first things to go were the mosaics and frescoes. He recognized, however, that the Christian images were works of art created by talented artists and, rather than having the images scratched out, he merely had them painted over. The Sultan's foresight has allowed restorers to uncover many of the Byzantine images that adorned the walls of the city's churches before 1453.

## Ramadan

The Islamic holy month of Ramadan, called "Ramazan" in Turkish, lasts for 30 days and is an especially pious time. During it, observant Muslims abstain from eating, drinking, smoking, and sexual relations, from dawn to sunset; this self-denial teaches restraint and humility and is meant to bring one closer to God. Those who are fasting start each day with a predawn meal called *sahur*. At sundown, the fast is broken with a meal called *iftar*, which traditionally includes dates, soup and bread, olives, and other foods. Many restaurants offer special *iftar* fixed menus during Ramadan. In small towns and conservative parts of Turkey it may be hard to find restaurants open during the day during Ramadan, but in most cities and tourist areas it's not an issue. Though it's understood that non-Muslims will not be fasting, it's respectful to avoid eating in public (e.g., on the street or on public transportation) during Ramadan. You should also be prepared for the fact that in many places, even touristy areas like Sultanahmet in Istanbul, it's customary for drummers to walk around in the wee hours of the morning to wake people for the *sahur*—which can make for a rather startling, and early, awakening. The end of Ramadan is celebrated with a three-day holiday called Ramazan Bayramı or Şeker Bayramı ("sugar holiday"), during which people visit family and friends and plentifully consume sweets.

Another festival, Kurban Bayramı (feast of the sacrifice), requires Muslims to sacrifice an animal—typically a sheep or a cow—for their faith, honoring Abraham's willingness to sacrifice his firstborn son to God and God's last-minute substitution of a ram for the boy. Today, many Turks purchase vouchers that empower a professional butcher to make the kill in their name. *Ramazan Bayramı* and *Kurban Bayramı* are national holidays, and schools and many businesses are closed for the duration; museums and other attractions generally close only for the first day of the holiday. Projected dates are as follows. In 2012: Ramadan, July 20 to August 18; Şeker Bayramı, August 19 to 21; Kurban Bayramı, October 24 to 28. In 2013: Ramadan, July 9 to August 7; Şeker Bayramı, August 8 to 10; Kurban Bayramı, October 14 to 18.

# FAQS

### Is Turkey cheap?

It depends on where you go. Istanbul, coastal towns in high season, and other tourist locations, like parts of Cappadocia, are quite a bit more expensive than elsewhere in Turkey. Hotels, especially in Istanbul can be expensive—even along the lines of Paris or New York—though there are budget options. Anything imported is also expensive, so a cup of coffee at Starbucks in Istanbul will cost about the equivalent of $3 and a burger meal at McDonald's can cost as much as $8. Anything you buy at the Grand Bazaar or on İstiklal Street, in Istanbul, will be much more expensive than the same wares purchased off the beaten track.

### How do I change money?
### Does Turkey use the euro?

The Turkish word for change office is *doviz*. In Istanbul and most other tourist hubs, they seem to be everywhere. The fees for changing money aren't usually too outrageous, even in tourist locales; however, your best option is to use your ATM card, with which you usually get that day's exchange rage. Turkey doesn't use the euro (and beware sellers who insist you pay in foreign currency, which is illegal). The currency in Turkey is the Turkish lira. At the time of printing $1 = 1.85 TL and €1 = 2.48 TL.

### Will it be hard to find an alcoholic beverage in a Muslim country?

The anise-flavored spirit rakı, Turkey's national drink, is the traditional accompaniment to a meal of mezes and fish. In large cities like Istanbul and İzmir, and in resort towns along the coast, rakı is consumed quite liberally, as is Efes, the national beer. However, in smaller towns and more conservative parts of the country (particularly central Anatolia), don't be surprised if alcohol is not for sale in restaurants or shops. Because of high taxes, alcoholic drinks, particularly those that are imported, are a fair bit more expensive in Turkey than they are in North America or Europe.

### Is Turkish food spicy?

Not really. Turkish cuisine is similar to Greek and Hungarian food. Many dishes consist of roasted meat and boiled or roasted vegetable and rice dishes. Turks often add red pepper on the side, but even heaped generously on your food, it generally won't set the mouth afire. The only thing that might take you by surprise is a roasted pepper, which often comes as a side with kebab dishes. Any food with too much heat is easily disarmed with a ubiquitous Turkish favorite—yogurt.

### Will Ramadan affect my visit?

Ramadan, the month of fasting between sunrise and sunset, is one of the most exciting times to be in Turkey because after sunset, most Turks party down. It's rumored that your average Istanbullu actually gains weight during the fast. Elsewhere in Turkey, the degree of adherence to the fast typically increases in proportion to how far east you venture. In Istanbul and other tourist destinations it's not a problem to find restaurants that are open during the day, although in smaller and more conservative towns the profusion of closed eateries and cafés might make it more difficult to get a bite to eat, but it's by no means impossible.

### Do I need to wear
### covered up clothes?

No man or woman on the street is ever forced to wear a headscarf, turban, or veil, though many Turkish women do. Due to Turkey's strict secularism, there are some government institutions where

the covering of women is banned. In mosques, however, all women—including tourists—are expected to wear headscarves and all visitors must remove their shoes. In Istanbul and in many coastal cities you will see women dressed provocatively and even wearing bikinis while in more conservative cities such behavior is frowned on. Female tourists anywhere who don't want to draw undue attention to themselves should err on the side of modesty.

## Are the people friendly?

Yes! Turks are renowned for their hospitality and any local will gladly tout this reputation. In Istanbul you might find some cosmopolitan snobbishness, depending on the neighborhood, but just about everywhere else throughout the country Turks are friendly, talkative, and passionate, and often sport large grins along with a hidden mischievous side. As long as you are polite and avoid insulting the nation, its symbols, or its politics, you'll do just fine and in all probability you'll be awed by how kind and friendly Turkish people are.

## What if I don't speak Turkish?

As in any European nation, it benefits salespeople and waiters in tourist hot spots to speak English, and many young professionals and students also make it a priority to learn English. Some schools even have their instruction entirely in English. There's a good chance that the proprietors of your hotel, and perhaps the restaurant servers that you meet will speak perfectly adequate English. Outside of these groups, and in more remote locations, your average Turk speaks little to no English but even still you probably won't have too big a problem. Turkish is not a complicated language, and learning a few key phrases is a good idea before traveling *(see the vocabulary lists at the back of this book)*. Turkish is also an easy language to read as it is written in the Latin alphabet and is entirely phonetic. For the most challenging of linguistic tangles, pointing in a dictionary or trying the same word in a few other languages will often suffice.

## Should I be afraid of terrorism?

Terrorism does, unfortunately, seem to be a part of the world we live in today and there is a certain amount of risk inherent in traveling anywhere. In Istanbul the risk of being the victim of a terrorist attack is not much higher than in any European capital: London and Madrid have both been host to terrorist attacks far greater in magnitude than anything in Istanbul. Elsewhere in Turkey the threat level depends on where you are. In the tourist-friendly cities of the Mediterranean and Aegean regions as well as Cappadocia the risk is negligible. In the east, where the government is still fighting Kurdish separatists, a bit more caution might be called for, though most of the violence takes place in remote areas where visitors are unlikely to venture. The key thing is to stay informed, keep a low profile, and bear in mind that while terrorist attacks are dramatic you still have better odds of being struck by lightning.

# GREAT ITINERARIES

## CROSSROADS OF FAITH, 9 DAYS

Once home to powerful Christian and Muslim empires, the area that makes up modern Turkey has played a crucial role in the development of both religions. This tour takes you to some of the most important religious sites in Turkey, places that still poignantly convey spirituality.

### Days 1 and 2: Istanbul

Arrive in Istanbul and check into a hotel in Sultanahmet. If you have time, visit two of the quintessential Istanbul sites: the Aya Sofya and the nearby Blue Mosque.

Start your second day with a visit to the Süleymaniye Mosque, one of the greatest achievements of Mimar Sinan, the Ottomans' favorite architect. Then head to the western edge of Istanbul's old city walls, where you'll find the Kariye Museum in what was the Byzantine Chora Church. It's filled with glittering mosaics and beautiful frescoes that are considered among the finest in the world. End your day in Eyüp Camii, a historic mosque complex on the Golden Horn that is one of the holiest areas in Istanbul.

### Day 3: Konya

Take a morning flight from Istanbul to Konya and pick up a rental car at the airport. In Konya you'll see the magnificent Mevlâna Museum and tomb, dedicated to the life and teachings of Rumi Celaleddin, the 13th-century mystic who founded the order of the whirling dervishes. The city's 13th-century Alaaddin Mosque is also worth a visit. In the evening, catch a live dervish performance at the cultural center behind the museum if they're performing.

### Days 4 and 5: Cappadocia

After Konya, head east toward the lunar landscape of Cappadocia, where the volcanic rock outcroppings and cliffs were used by local Christians centuries ago as churches, monasteries, and homes. One of the best places to see these unique structures is in the village of Göreme. Spend the night in one of the hotels built into the stone caves. Ürgüp has what is regarded by some as the best collection of boutique hotels in Turkey.

The attractions in Cappadocia are above ground and below it. Under siege from Arab invaders in the 7th through 10th centuries, local Christians built a series of underground cities—some going down 20 stories and capable of holding 20,000 people—where they sought refuge. The ruins in Kaymaklı and Derinkuyu are marvels of ancient engineering. Get an early start if you want to beat the summer crowds, and bring a flashlight.

If you have time, consider a visit to the Ihlara Valley, a deep gorge that has numerous monasteries and churches cut into its cliffs and a lovely green river running through it.

### Days 6 and 7: Cappadocia to Antakya

From landlocked Cappadocia, head south to the Mediterranean Sea and the city of Antakya, formerly known as Antioch, which played an important role in the early days of Christianity. It's a long drive of 482 km (300 mi), so plan on spending most of the day on the road. Fortunately, there's a highway for most of the way. If you get to Antakya early enough, head to the Church of St. Peter, in a cave on the outskirts of town. Blackened by 2,000 years' worth of candle smoke, this is per-

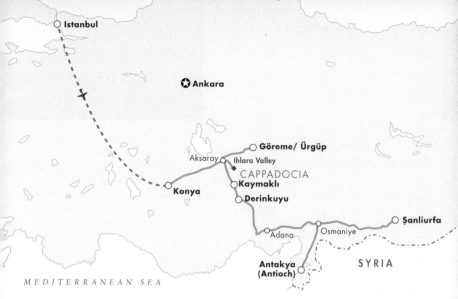

haps the oldest church in the world, where the apostle Paul preached to his converts.

The next day, spend the morning walking through the narrow lanes and the lively bazaar of Antakya's old town. Then visit the Archaeological Museum, which has an excellent collection of Roman and Byzantine mosaics and other artifacts. Antakya is famous for its Syrian-influenced cooking, so have lunch at one of the restaurants serving local dishes (Antik Han or Hatay Sultanı Sofrası are two good options). After lunch, begin your 351-km (218-mi) drive to Şanlıurfa, where you can stay in one of several grand old stone houses that have been converted into small hotels.

## Day 8: Şanlıurfa

Many Muslims believe the biblical patriarch Abraham was born in Şanlıurfa, and a fascinating and peaceful pilgrimage site has developed here, with mosques and a park with spring-fed pools filled with sacred carp. After lunch, make the quick drive to the small village of Harran, 45 km (28 mi) southeast of Şanlıurfa. Harran is mentioned in the Bible as a place where Abraham lived for a period, and the village, with its ancient stone walls and unique beehive-shape houses, has the look of a place that hasn't changed

much since biblical times. Another worthwhile side trip is the archaeological site of Göbekli Tepe, 15 km (9.3 mi) northeast of Şanlıurfa, and thought to be the world's first temple—6,000 years before Stonehenge.

## Day 9: Şanlıurfa and
## Return to Istanbul

You can fly back to Istanbul from Şanlıurfa, or from nearby Gaziantep (145 km [90 mi] away). If you have a flight from Şanlıurfa later in the day, take some time to explore Şanlıurfa's bustling and authentic bazaar, where coppersmiths hammer and tailors work on foot-powered sewing machines. If your flight is out of Gaziantep, consider driving there in the morning in order to have lunch at one of that city's famous restaurants. Imam Çağdaş, which has great kebabs and heavenly baklava, is your best bet.

## BEST BEACHES AND RUINS, 10 DAYS

It's fairly safe to say that the main features that attract visitors to Turkey are the beaches and the magnificent archaeological sites. This itinerary covers the best of both, along the two major coastlines. Adding a couple of days in Istanbul at the beginning or end makes a perfect trip.

### Days 1 and 2: Istanbul

Arrive in Istanbul and head to one of the charming small hotels in Sultanahmet (the Empress Zoe and the Sarı Konak Oteli are two good options). If you have time, go to see the awe-inspiring Aya Sofya and the nearby Blue Mosque.

The next day, visit Topkapı Sarayı to get a sense of how the Ottoman sultans lived (make sure to take a tour of the Harem). From there, go to the nearby Archaeological Museum, whose collection of Roman and Greek artifacts comes from many of the sites that you'll soon be visiting. In the evening, head by taxi to one of the little neighborhoods along the Bosphorus, such as Ortaköy or Arnavutköy, for a fish dinner by the waterside (if you time it right, you can take one of the limited Bosphorus commuter ferry services there, though none go back down to the Beyoğlu/Sultanahmet area at night).

### Day 3: Ephesus

On the morning of Day 3, take the roughly one-hour flight to İzmir and rent a car at the airport to make the quick 84-km (52-mi) drive down to the ancient Roman city of Ephesus. If you get an early flight out, you should be here by lunch. The site is one of the most popular tourist attractions in Turkey, and you'll see why: The buildings and monuments here are remarkably well preserved and easily give you the sense of what life must have been like in this important trading city 2,000 years ago. After Ephesus, visit the nearby Meryemana, a pilgrimage site for both Christians and Muslims where the Virgin Mary is believed to have spent her final years. You can spend the night in Selçuk, which is right on the doorstep of Ephesus, but better yet, head 10 km (6 mi) into the mountains above Selçuk and stay in the tranquil village of Şirince, surrounded by fruit orchards and vineyards.

### Day 4: Priene, Miletus, and Didyma

Start off your day with a visit to Priene, an ancient Greek city that sits on a steep hill looking out on a valley below—it's about 62 km (38½ mi) from Şirince. From there continue 16 km (10 mi) south to Miletus, another Greek city, where a spectacular theater is all that remains of its former glory. Twenty kilometers (12 mi) south of here is Didyma and its magnificent Temple of Apollo, its scale as grand as the Parthenon, with 124 well-preserved columns. To keep yourself from burning out on ruins, continue another 5 km (3 mi) to the white-sand beach of Altıkum (Note: This is not the same as the similarly named beach near Çeşme) and take a dip in the warm water, then have a meal at one of the numerous fish restaurants lining the shore. Drive back to the busy seaside resort town of Kuşadası, where there are several small *pansiyons* at which you can spend the night.

### Day 5: Aphrodisias

Get an early start for the drive to the ruins of Aphrodisias, a Roman city named in honor of the goddess of love, Aphrodite. High up on a plateau and ringed by mountains, Aphrodisias has a spectacular setting and as much to offer as Ephesus, although with significantly fewer crowds;

there are many ancient sites in Turkey, but Aphrodisias in quite evocative, especially after you've visited Ephesus. From here work your way down to the coast and the quiet town of Dalyan, where you can spend the next two nights in one of several riverside *pansiyons*.

### Day 6: Dalyan, İztuzu Beach, and the Rock Tombs of Kaunos

At Dalyan's riverside quay, you can hire a boat to take you on to the ruins of ancient Kaunos, a city dating back to the 9th century BC and famous for its collection of tombs cut into the surrounding cliffs. Watch for the herons and storks idling in the river's reeds when you stop to take a look at the ruins. Continue your day cruise to the famed İztuzu Beach, a 5-km (3-mi) stretch of undeveloped sand that's also a nesting ground for sea turtles. There are a few snack bars at the beach, but you might want to consider bringing a picnic lunch along.

### Day 7: Letoon, Patara, and Kaş

The mountainous coastal region south of Dalyan is the home of ancient Lycia. An independent and resourceful people, the Lycians built a series of impressive cities whose ruins are sprinkled throughout the area. To get a good glimpse of one of these Lycian cities, drive from Dalyan to Letoon, a UNESCO World Heritage Site with three fascinating temples dating back to the 2nd century BC. From here continue to Patara, another Lycian ruin that has the added bonus of being right next to one of Turkey's finest and longest beaches. You can spend the night in the relaxing little seaside town of Kaş, which has several good lodging and eating options. ■TIP→ **If you have an extra day, take the three-hour boat trip out of Kaş through the beautiful Kekova Sound and its fascinating underwater Greek and Roman ruins.**

### Day 8: Olympos

On your eighth day (ninth if you spend an extra day in Kaş), drive to the Lycian ruins of Olympos, which have running through them a small river that ends at a beautiful crescent beach backed by mountains. Stay in the little village of Çıralı, a good spot for an evening visit to the legendary Chimaera, small flames of ignited gas that shoot out of the rocks of a nearby mountain.

### Day 9: Antalya/Termessos (or Aspendos)

Spend your last night in the rapidly growing resort city of Antalya, but before going there head up into the rugged mountains above the city to visit the

dramatic site of Termessos, an impregnable city that both Alexander the Great and the Romans decided not to attack. (Alternatively, continue 48 km [30 mi] past Antalya to visit Aspendos, a spectacular Roman theater that is still in use today.) Return to Antalya in the afternoon and stay in one of the renovated old Ottoman houses in the Kaleiçi, the city's charming old town.

### Day 10: Return to Istanbul

If you have time before your flight back to Istanbul, use the morning to walk around the narrow streets of the Kaleiçi and then visit the city's large Archaeological Museum. If you need to stock up on souvenirs before your return, head to Antalya's bazaar before going to the airport.

### TIPS

Roads are mostly in good condition, though rarely wider than two lanes or lit at night, so we recommend not driving after sunset.

This trip takes you through some of the most popular spots in Turkey, so book lodgings in advance.

Consider doing this itinerary in the fall: prices will be lower, the crowds will be gone, it won't be baking hot, and the ocean will still be warm enough for swimming.

Many towns on this itinerary have fabulous weekly markets, when farmers and craftspeople from the area come to sell their goods; try to time some of your trip around one of them. Many markets are held on Saturday, but check locally.

# Istanbul

**WORD OF MOUTH**

"After dinner, we hopped on a one-hour boat cruise up the Bosphorus. Being on the water at dusk and seeing all the beautiful houses, hopping clubs, and candlelit restaurants definitely felt like a once-in-a lifetime experience. We hadn't planned on taking the cruise . . . but we were so happy we did!"

—dina4

# WELCOME TO ISTANBUL

Çiçek Pasajı

## TOP REASONS TO GO

★ **Change continents:**
Spend the morning in Europe and the afternoon in Asia, with just a ferry ride in between; how cosmopolitan is that?

★ **Cruise the Bosphorus:**
Taking a boat ride up the strait, past scenic waterfront neighborhoods and forested slopes topped with fortresses, is quintessentially Istanbul.

★ **Haggle in the bazaars:**
Bargain like the locals do as you make your way through the Grand Bazaar and Egyptian Bazaar—it may be a bit touristy, but it's fun.

★ **Marvel at ancient domes:** From the stunning Aya Sofya to the graceful Süleymaniye Mosque, the city's greatest works of imperial architecture never cease to impress, especially from the inside as you look up.

★ **Ogle at opulence:**
With their sumptuous decor and fascinating harem quarters, the Topkapı and Dolmabahçe palaces offer a glimpse of the splendor of the Ottoman Empire.

**1 Sultanahmet: The Historic Center.** The Blue Mosque, Topkapı Sarayı, Aya Sofya, and the Istanbul Archaeological Museums are just some of the impressive attractions in historic Istanbul. This is tourist central, so be prepared for crowds.

**2 The Bazaar Area and Environs.** Bargain your way through the Grand Bazaar, then follow narrow streets down to the Egyptian Bazaar and the docks on the Golden Horn. On your way, visit the Süleymaniye and other magnificent imperial mosques that rank among the most outstanding examples of Ottoman architecture.

Black Sea

Kilyos
Rumeli Feneri
Poyraz
Rumeli Kavağı
Anadolu Kavağı
Sarıyer
Akbaba
Tarabya
Beykoz
Yeniköy
Paşabahçe
Emiraan
Çubuklu
Rumelihisarı
Anadoluhisarı
Arnavutköy
Bebek **6**
Kandilli
Nişantaşı
Ortaköy
Taksim
Beşiktaş
Beylerbeyi
Atatürk Airport
Beyoğlu
Dolmabahçe Palace **5**
Çamlıca
Galata Bridge
Üsküdar
Ümraniye
Istanbul **1**
Yenikapı
Sultanahmet
Blue Mosque
**7**

Sea of Marmara

Bostancı
D100
KINALIADA
Burgaz
BURGAZADA
Heybeli
HEYBELIADA **8**
Büyük
BÜYÜKADA
PRINCES' ISLANDS

E80
E5
O1
O2
O4

Grand Bazaar

**2**

**3 The Western Districts.**
A gem of Byzantine art, the former Chora Church is the highlight of the western districts, which also include the historically Greek and Jewish neighborhoods of Fener and Balat. At the tip of the Golden Horn, Eyüp Sultan Camii is a place of pilgrimage for Muslims.

**4 Beyoğlu: Istanbul's "New Town."** With its elegant 19th- and early-20th-century apartment buildings, Beyoğlu is the place to see for yourself that new is a relative term in this city. The main pedestrian thoroughfare, İstiklal Caddesi, is lined with shops and cafés.

**5 Karaköy and Beşiktaş.**
The Istanbul Museum of Modern Art and Dolmabahçe Palace, the lavish home of the last Ottoman sultans, are among the attractions in these waterside quarters. A perfect pastime is sipping tea and watching the ships go by.

**6 The Bosphorus.** Hop on a ferry and zigzag back and forth between Asia and Europe, past grand palaces, ancient fortresses, fishing villages, and beautiful old wooden villas.

**7 The Asian Shore.** The pleasant neighborhoods on Istanbul's Asian side have fewer "sights" but there are interesting enclaves to explore, away from the throngs of tourists.

**8 Princes' Islands.** This nine-island archipelago in the Sea of Marmara has pine forests, gardens, beaches, and a welcome absence of motorized traffic—the perfect antidote to the noise and chaos of the big city.

## GETTING ORIENTED

Istanbul is a city divided. The Bosphorus—the 31-km-long (17-mi-long) waterway joining the Black Sea to the Sea of Marmara—separates the European side of the city from the Asian side. The European side is itself divided by the Golden Horn, an 8-km-long (5-mi-long) inlet that lies between historic Sultanahmet to the south and the New Town, known as Beyoğlu, to the north. In Beyoğlu, the 14th-century Galata Tower dominates the hillside that rises north of the Golden Horn; just beyond, high-rise hotels and other landmarks of the modern city radiate out from Taksim Meydanı (Taksim Square), not far above the Bosphorus-side neighborhood of Beşiktaş. To the north, the European suburbs line the western shore of the Bosphorus. The Asian suburbs are on the eastern shore.

Sabiha Gökçen Airport

Kartal

Pendik

0      4 mi

0      4 km

Ortaköy

Dolmabahçe Sarayı

# ISTANBUL STREET FOOD

As much as Turkish people love to sit down for a leisurely dinner, they're also serious snackers, day and night, so finding a quick bite to eat is never a problem. The only challenge is choosing among the numerous tempting options.

Street food is not an afterthought in Turkey. Turks are quite demanding when it comes to eating on the run, expecting what is served to be fresh and made with care. Although McDonald's and other chains have made inroads in Turkey, many people still prefer their country's original "fast food," which sometimes is not so fast at all. Rather, some of Turkey's most popular street food dishes require some tender loving care in preparation, and frequently will be cooked or assembled right before your eyes, though there are also simple things like roasted chestnuts available.

In Istanbul and other large cities, snack bars and food stalls are open from early morning until late into the night. Look for the crowded places: chances are they're the local favorite.

## FOR THE ADVENTUROUS

Fancy a grilled intestine sandwich or stomach soup? To make *kokoreç*, seasoned lamb intestines are wound up into a long, fat loaf, grilled over charcoal and then chopped up with tomatoes and served on a half loaf of crusty bread. *İşkembe* is a soup made out of tripe—cow stomach—and flavored with garlic and vinegar. It's usually sold in small eateries that serve nothing but this soup, said to be the ultimate way to prevent a hangover. For many late-night revelers in Turkey's big cities, a night out isn't complete without one of these pungent Turkish street food staples.

**2**

## BÖREK

This is the name given to a wide range of flaky filo dough pastries. The windows of *börek* shops usually display their freshly baked goods, long coils of rolled-up filo dough stuffed with either ground meat, potato, spinach, or cheese and baked until golden brown. *Su böreği* is a *börek* made of buttery egg noodles layered over crumbles of tangy white cheese and baked in a deep dish.

## DÖNER

This cheap and filling sandwich *(below)* is Turkey's most popular street food. Meat, usually lamb or chicken, is grilled on a rotating vertical spit, shaved off in paper-thin slices, and served in a pocket bread called *pide* or rolled up in a tortilla-like flatbread into a wrap called a *dürüm*. For many Turks, a *döner* sandwich, downed with a glass of refreshing *ayran* (a drink made of salted, watered-down yogurt), is a meal in itself.

## KUMPIR

Think of this as a baked potato on steroids. At *kumpir* stands, massive spuds are taken hot out of the oven, split open, and filled with an almost overwhelming assortment of toppings. Options include everything from grated cheese or yogurt to chopped up pickles and hot dog bits. It's not unusual for people to ask for six or more ingredients. The *kumpir*-maker then mixes it all up into a glorious mess and puts it back in the potato skin.

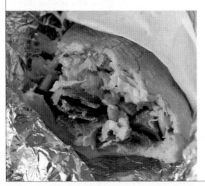

## MIDYE

In Turkey, mussels *(above)* truly deserve to be called street food. They're usually sold by roving vendors carrying big baskets filled with glistening black shells that have been stuffed with a combination of mussels, rice, and herbs and spices. Hungry pedestrians will flag down the seller and scarf down a few of the mollusks, which are served with a squeeze of lemon, before continuing on their way. As tempting as it may be to buy these delicacies on the street, however, the risk of food poisoning from shellfish means it's better to err on the safe side and eat *midye* only at snack bars or restaurants, where there are higher standards of hygiene. Some specialty snack bars serve mussels coated in batter and deep-fried, in addition to the stuffed form.

## SIMIT

Sort of the Turkish answer to the bagel, or a New York street pretzel, these humble ring-shape, sesame-coated breads are found all over Turkey. They're the ultimate street food: cheap, satisfying and—when fresh from the oven—delicious. And they're available all day long, from pushcarts found on almost every street corner. The *simit* has gone slightly upscale in recent years, with the appearance in Istanbul and other Turkish cities of several chains that serve *simits* and other baked goods.

Updated by
Vanessa H.
Larson

The only city in the world that can lay claim to straddling two continents, Istanbul—once known as Constantinople, capital of the Byzantine and then the Ottoman Empire—has for centuries been a bustling metropolis with one foot in Europe and the other in Asia. Istanbul embraces this enviable position with both a certain chaos and inventiveness, ever evolving as one of the world's most cosmopolitan crossroads.

It's often said that Istanbul is the meeting point of East and West, but visitors to this city built over the former capital of two great empires are likely to be just as impressed by the juxtaposition of old and new. Office towers creep up behind historic palaces, women in chic designer outfits pass others wearing long skirts and head coverings, peddlers' pushcarts vie with battered old Fiats and shiny BMWs for dominance of the noisy, narrow streets, and the Grand Bazaar competes with modern shopping malls. At dawn, when the muezzin's call to prayer resounds from ancient minarets, there are inevitably a few hearty revelers still making their way home from nightclubs and bars.

Most visitors to this sprawling city of more than 14 million will first set foot in the relatively compact Old City, where the legacy of the Byzantine and Ottoman empires can be seen in monumental works of architecture like the brilliant Hagia Sophia and the beautifully proportioned mosques built by the great architect Sinan. Though it would be easy to spend days, if not weeks, exploring the wealth of attractions in the historical peninsula, visitors should make sure also to venture elsewhere, in order to experience the vibrancy of contemporary Istanbul. With a lively nightlife propelled by its young population and an exciting arts scene that's increasingly on the international radar—thanks in part to its stint as the European Capital of Culture in 2010—Istanbul is truly a city that never sleeps. It's also a place where visitors will feel welcome: Istanbul may be on the Bosphorus, but at heart it's a Mediterranean city, whose friendly inhabitants are effusively social and eager to share what they love most about it.

# PLANNING

The **Museum Pass Istanbul** allows single entry into six of Istanbul's most popular state-run museums over a period of 72 hours: Aya Sofya, Topkapı Sarayı (excluding the Harem), the Istanbul Archaeological Museums, the Museum of Turkish and Islamic Arts, the Mosaic Museum, and Kariye Müzesi. At 72 TL, it's a savings of about 10 TL over the cost of paying for each museum individually, and it also confers discounts of between 10% and 30% off entrance fees at the private Rahmi M. Koç and Sabancı museums, and at all eight of these museums' gift shops. The other advantage of the museum pass is it allows you to bypass entrance lines, which will save time—a commodity you'll certainly need if you're going to pack in so many museums in just three days.

## FESTIVALS

The **Istanbul International Film Festival**, one of the city's most popular cultural events, takes place over two weeks in April, and screens come alive with a multinational array of images.

April also sees Istanbul's **Tulip Festival**, when parks all over the city become a riot of color.

The well-regarded **Istanbul International Music Festival**, held during several weeks in June, features mostly classical music performed by world-class musicians.

The **Istanbul Jazz Festival** is generally held in the first two weeks of July and brings in major names, new and old, from Turkey and around the world.

The **Istanbul Biennial** is held from mid-September to mid-November in odd years, and showcases cutting-edge work in venues around the city.

## GETTING HERE AND AROUND AND AWAY

### AIR TRAVEL

Most international and domestic flights arrive at Istanbul's Atatürk Airport, although an increasing number of both domestic and international flights on low-cost carriers fly into the newer Sabiha Gökçen Airport on the Asian side of the city.

Exits and taxi stands are well signposted as you emerge from customs. There is a slow metro directly from Atatürk Airport to the Aksaray neighborhood, where you can catch a tram to Sultanahmet, but it's much less of a hassle to take one of the regular shuttle buses operated by the Havaş company (10 TL to Taksim) or a taxi. Taxis and shuttle buses can be found at the main exit from the terminal building. There is no rail link to Sabiha Gökçen Airport, so you'll need to take a Havaş shuttle bus (12 TL to Taksim) or a taxi.

### BOAT TRAVEL

It's no surprise that Istanbul is well served by ferries. The main docks on the European side are at Eminönü and Karaköy (on either side of the Galata Bridge) and at Kabataş, while Üsküdar and Kadıköy are the most important docks on the Asian side. Traditional ferries operated by the Şehir Hatları, as well as faster-moving "sea bus" catamarans operated by two private companies (Turyol and Dentur), crisscross the Bosphorus day and night, and cost about the same as land-based public transport. With the exception of Bosphorus cruises, ferries are most useful for crossing the Bosphorus (rather than going up and down it) and for getting to the Princes' Islands.

## BUS TRAVEL

Bus service within the city is frequent, and drivers and riders tend to be helpful, so you should be able to navigate your way to major tourist stops like Sultanahmet, Eminönü, Taksim, and Beşiktaş. The fare is 1.75 TL and it is necessary to have an İstanbulkart to board.

Turkey has an extensive system of intercity buses for travel around the country, and Istanbul's large, chaotic Esenler Otogar is the heart of it. Esenler itself is a bit out of the way, though easily accessible by metro from Aksaray. Alternatively, many of the bus companies have offices around the city and operate shuttle buses, known as a *servis*, that collect passengers from downtown Istanbul and take them to their own ministations on the main freeway, allowing you to avoid the *otogar* completely.

A second, smaller bus station, at Harem on the waterfront on the Asian side of the Bosphorus, is easily accessible by ferry from Eminönü.

## CAR TRAVEL

If you're entering or leaving Istanbul by car, E80 runs from the Bulgarian border and through Turkish Thrace to Istanbul, continuing on to central Anatolia in the east; this toll road is the best of several alternatives. Getting out of the city by car can be challenging, as the signs aren't always clear. It's always useful to have a driving map.

Istanbul is notorious for congested traffic, a cavalier attitude to traffic regulations, poor signposting, and a shortage of parking spaces. In short, don't even think about renting a car for travel in the city.

## DOLMUŞ TRAVEL

A **dolmuş** is a cross between a taxi and a bus: they run set routes, leave when full, and make fewer stops than a bus, so they're faster. Most dolmuşes are bright yellow minibuses. Dolmuş stands are marked by signs but you can sometimes hail one on the street; the destination is shown on a roof sign or a card in the front window. Dolmuşes mostly head out to the suburbs, but visitors may find a few routes useful, including those that go from Taksim to Beşiktaş and from Taksim to the upscale shopping area of Nişantaşı/Teşvikiye (the fare on both routes is 2 TL). Dolmuşes also run from Taksim to the neighborhoods of Kadıköy (5 TL) and Bostancı (6.50 TL) on the Asian side, which is useful if you are coming back at night after the last boat.

## FERRY TRAVEL

One of the best ways to get in and out of Istanbul is by sea. A number of fast catamaran ferries leave from Yenikapı, which is south of Aksaray and a short taxi trip from Sultanahmet, to various ports on the southern side of the sea of Marmara. The most convenient are the ferries to Yalova for those heading to Bursa.

## FOOT TRAVEL

Istanbul is a walker's city, and the best way to experience it is to wander, inevitably getting lost—even with a good map, it's easy to lose your way in the winding streets and alleyways. When in doubt, just ask. Particularly in the old part of the city, most of the main sites are within a short distance of each other, and the easiest way to get to them is on foot. And when your feet get tired it's easy to use public transportation.

## FUNICULAR AND METRO TRAVEL

Istanbul's two short underground funiculars are convenient for avoiding the steep, uphill walk from the Bosphorus waterfront to Beyoğlu; each takes less than two minutes to ascend. The historic Tünel, in operation since 1875, connects Karaköy and Tünel Square. The ultramodern funicular from Kabataş (the end of the tram line) to Taksim is also convenient. The city has two underground metro lines: one starts in Şişhane (near Tünel), passes through Taksim, and continues north to the business districts, while the other connects Aksaray, west of Sultanahmet, with the airport and Esenler Otogar.

## TAXI TRAVEL

Taxis are metered and relatively cheap—a ride from Sultanahmet to Taksim is about 10 TL. Many drivers don't speak English, so it may be helpful to write your destination on a piece of paper, and to bring the business card of your hotel with you so you don't have problems getting back later. Ask your hotel to call a taxi or find a stand in front of a hotel—you'll be more likely to get a driver who won't take you the long way around.

## TRAIN TRAVEL

Istanbul has two main train stations: Sirkeci, on the Eminönü waterfront in Old Istanbul, and Haydarpaşa, on the Asian side of the Bosphorus. Trains in Turkey are known for being slow, though high-speed train routes to Ankara and Konya are in the works. The opening of a rail line under the Bosphorus will also change things dramatically; the much-delayed project is targeted to be completed by October 2013, in time for the 90th anniversary of the Turkish Republic.

## TRAM TRAVEL

There are several tram lines in Istanbul, but the one most useful to visitors runs from Kabataş (below Taksim) along the Bosphorus to Karaköy, across the Galata Bridge to Eminönü, and then to Sultanahmet and Beyazıt/the Grand Bazaar before heading out to the western part of the city. The fare is 2 TL for a token, or 1.75 TL if you have an İstanbulkart, and trams run from around 6 in the morning to just before midnight. There is also a slow but atmospheric historic tram that runs along İstiklal Caddesi between Tünel and Taksim; tokens have traditionally been sold onboard, but once the İstanbulkart comes into wider use that may no longer be possible.

## HOW MUCH TIME DO YOU NEED?

Istanbul is one of the most unique cities in the world and with two continents of treasures, three days will hardly do it justice. A week will give you time to enjoy the sights, sounds, and smells with a little leisure. Make sure to see the main sites like Topkapı, Aya Sofya, the Blue

Mosque, and the bazaars, then seek out more of what you like: there are plenty more Ottoman mosques and Byzantine monuments. Or you can just chill out, *çay* (tea) in hand, by the waters of the Bosphorus.

## IF YOU HAVE LIMITED TIME

Here's one way to plan your visit if time is limited: Start off as if riding a whirlwind, visiting the Blue Mosque and Aya Sofya to get a sense of the grandeur of the Byzantine and Ottoman empires. In the afternoon venture out of Sultanahmet to the Kariye Müzesi to see amazing frescoes and mosaics from the Byzantine era, then visit the beautiful Süleymaniye Mosque on your way back. Next, head to the Grand Bazaar, where you can wander until closing time at 7. If you're staying in Sultanahmet, take an evening stroll to see the floodlit domes and minarets of the Blue Mosque and Aya Sofya.

You could spend your second morning at Topkapı Sarayı, having lunch at one of the cafés in the compound or just outside the gates so that in the afternoon you can easily visit the Istanbul Archaeology Museums in the palace forecourt and/or the nearby Museum of Turkish and Islamic Arts. You'll have probably reached your quota of treasures-and-antiquities appreciation, so next immerse yourself in Istanbul street life. Head to Tünel Square in Beyoğlu, north of the Golden Horn, and follow İstiklal Caddesi through Galatasaray Meydanı, stopping at the Fish Market and Çiçek Pasajı (Flower Passage), to Taksim Meydanı, the center of the modern city.

With another day, you could see more of the Byzantine period, descending into the atmospheric underground cistern, Yerebatan Sarayı, then ogling the exquisite mosaics in the Mozaik Müzesi. For even more evidence of Ottoman power, head to the lower Bosphorus to see Dolmabahçe Sarayı, the naval and military museums, and Yıldız Parkı.

If you want to see the Bosphorus but don't have a whole day, either take a short, privately run cruise, or take an evening commuter ferry to relax after a hard day's sightseeing.

If you have more time, you can enjoy Istanbul with a little leisure. Think in terms of neighborhoods: you'll want to spend at least three days in the Old City, seeing the Byzantine and Ottoman monuments, and a day heading out to the less-visited western districts. Plan a full day around Karaköy, Beşiktaş, and Beyoğlu, and a day cruising up the Bosphorus. You won't have trouble filling additional time: maybe visit the Rüstem Paşa Camii in Eminönü to see its gorgeous tiles, then return to Sultanahmet to compare them to those in the Blue Mosque. Or another swing through the Grand Bazaar. Perhaps a trip to the Princes' Islands. Or just wander: few cities reward walkers more amply.

## MAGNIFICENT MOSQUES

There are many mosques in Istanbul. You won't have time to see them all, but you shouldn't leave the city without taking in the beauty and spirituality of at least several that rank as some of the most stunning architectural achievements in the world:

**2**

The **Blue Mosque**, for the sheer spectacle of domes, semidomes, minarets, and the 20,000 shimmering blue-green İznik tiles that lend the mosque its name.

**Rüstem Paşa Camii**, for İznik tiles in a magnificent array of colors and patterns.

**Süleymaniye Camii**, for its size, austere beauty, the enormous dome that seems to be held up principally by divine cooperation, and the tombs of the architect Sinan, his patron Süleyman the Magnificent, and the sultan's wife, Roxelana.

**Sokollu Mehmet Paşa Camii**, for elegance, harmony, and sumptuous tile work.

### SEE IT HERE

Many of the antiquities on view in Istanbul have been removed from the archaeological sites of Turkey's ancient cities. Seeing them here first will help you visualize what belongs in the empty niches you'll see elsewhere around the country.

### TOURS

Names of tour companies and their itineraries change frequently so it's best just to make arrangements through a travel agency or your hotel; the offerings are all pretty similar. If you join a group, a "classic tour" of the Aya Sofya, Blue Mosque, Hippodrome, and Grand Bazaar should cost about €35/$50/85 TL for a half day. For a full-day tour that also includes the Topkapı Palace and Süleymaniye Camii, as well as lunch, expect to pay about €65/$95/160 TL. Bosphorus tours include a cruise and excursions to sights like Rumeli Hisarı and the Dolmabahçe or Beylerbeyi palaces. Rates for private tours with a guide and driver are higher, and more cost-effective if you have a large party; for two people, expect to pay at least €100/$145/250 TL per person for a full day, and about a third less per person if you have four or more people. Keep in mind that admission fees and meals are generally not included in private tour rates, so this alternative ends up being considerably more costly.

### WHEN TO GO

Summer in Istanbul is hot and humid. Winter usually hits around October and lasts until April, and the months from November and February see a fair amount of rain. All the surrounding water generally keeps temps above freezing, but a cold wind blows off the frozen Balkans and there's an occasional dusting of snow. May and September are pleasant and the most comfortable times for exploring.

### VISITOR INFORMATION

There are several tourism information offices in Istanbul run by the Turkish Ministry of Culture and Tourism, including at both airports, in Sultanahmet (✉ *Divanyolu Cad. 3* ☎ *212/518–1802*), and just outside the entrance to the Sirkeci train station, near Eminönü (☎ *212/511–5888* ).

### THE İSTANBULKART

The Istanbul municipality recently introduced a "smart card," the İstanbulkart, designed to replace the older "smart ticket" known as the Akbil, but the process has not been without kinks. The card theoretically works on buses, trams, the metro, and most ferries, and there are plans for cardholders eventually to be able to pay for taxi rides and museum entrance fees with it. Aside from the convenience of not having to buy tokens for each ride, cardholders get a small discount on the first leg of a trip and a substantial discount on any transfers. However, there is a 6 TL nonrefundable fee for the card, so unless you plan to use public transportation extensively or are staying in Istanbul for a lengthy period, until the other functions of the card are rolled out it may be a better deal to just use tokens.

# EXPLORING

## SULTANAHMET: THE HISTORIC CENTER

Sultanahmet is the heart of Old Istanbul, where many of the city's must-see attractions are located: an incredible concentration of art and architecture spanning millennia is packed into its narrow, winding streets. At the eastern edge of the Old City, Topkapı Sarayı—the center of Ottoman power and the residence of the sultans for centuries—sits perched on the promontory overlooking the Bosphorus and the mouth of the Golden Horn. Behind the palace rise the imposing domes and soaring minarets of the Blue Mosque and Aya Sofya, two of Istanbul's most famous landmarks. As you walk through the Hippodrome, explore the underground Basilica Cistern, and view the Byzantine mosaics displayed in the Mozaik Müzesi, you'll also get a feel for what the city of Constantinople looked like more than a thousand years ago, well before the Turks conquered it in 1453. The three buildings that comprise the Istanbul Archaeological Museums showcase an incredible collection of artifacts going back even further in time, left by ancient civilizations that once thrived in Anatolia and around the region. When the call to prayer echoes from Sultanahmet's great mosques, pause for a moment to soak up the atmosphere here; nowhere else in Istanbul do you get such a rich feel for the magic of this ancient and mysterious city.

### TOP ATTRACTIONS

Ⓒ
Fodor's Choice
★

**Arkeoloji Müzeleri** (*Istanbul Archaeology Museums*). Step into this vast repository of spectacular finds, housed in a three-building complex in a forecourt of Topkapı Palace, to get a head-spinning look at the civilizations that have thrived for thousands of years in and around Turkey. The main museum was established in 1891, when forward-thinking archaeologist and painter Osman Hamdi Bey campaigned to keep native antiquities and some items from the former countries of the Ottoman Empire in Turkish hands. The most stunning pieces are tombs that include the so-called Alexander Sarcophagus, found in Lebanon, carved with scenes from Alexander the Great's battles, and once believed, wrongly, to be his final resting place. An excellent exhibit on Istanbul through the ages has artifacts from prehistory through the Byzantine and Ottoman periods and helps put the city's complex past into context. Exhibits on Anatolia include a section displaying some of the gold jewelry and other artifacts found in excavations at Troy. There is

**CLOSE UP**

# Istanbul: History in Architecture

Byzantium was already 1,000 years old when, in AD 326, Emperor Constantine the Great began to rebuild it as the new capital of the Roman Empire. On May 11, 330, the city was officially renamed "New Rome," though it soon became known as Constantinople, the city of Constantine. Constantine's successors expanded the city and gave it new walls, aqueducts, and churches.

Under the emperor Justinian (ruled 527–65) Constantine's capital reached its apogee, with the construction of the magnificent Hagia Sophia, or Church of the Holy Wisdom (known as Aya Sofya in Turkish) on the site of a church originally built for Constantine. This awe-inspiring architectural wonder still dominates Istanbul's skyline. Constantinople became the largest, wealthiest metropolis the Western world had ever seen.

The Byzantine Empire began to decline toward the end of the 11th century and a devastating blow came in 1204, when the Western Europeans of the Fourth Crusade, who were supposed to be on their way to recapture Jerusalem, decided that instead of going another thousand miles to fight a load of Muslims, they'd instead sack and occupy the Eastern Orthodox Christian city of Constantinople. The members of the Byzantine dynasty were forced to flee to Trabzon on the Black Sea coast, and although they eventually regained control of Constantinople, in 1261, neither the city nor the Byzantine Empire recovered.

Constantinople in the late Byzantine period was more a collection of villages set among ruins than a city. Byzantine artists set to work, however, to restore and redecorate the damaged churches, and in their work in the mosaics and frescoes of the Church of the Holy Savior in Chora, we can see the first breath of the Renaissance that would later be carried west to Italy by artists and intellectuals fleeing the arrival of the Turks.

The Ottoman sultan Mehmet II, known as Fatih (the Conqueror), conquered the much-diminished Constantinople in 1453, rebuilt it, and made the city once again the capital of an empire. The Turks named the new city as Konstantiniyye, but in time Constantinople seems to have been shortened to "Stanbul" by the Greeks and Westerners, and to "Istanbul" by the Turks. Another explanation says the name Istanbul is derived from the Greek *eis tin polin*, meaning "in the city" or "to the city"—for the Byzantines, "The City" was truly one and only.

In 1459 Mehmet II began building a palace on the hill at the tip of land where the Golden Horn meets the Bosphorus. Later sultans embellished and extended the complex until it grew into the fabulous Topkapı Sarayı. Most of the finest Ottoman buildings in Istanbul, however, date from the time of Süleyman the Magnificent (ruled 1520–66), who led the Ottoman Empire to its highest achievements in art and architecture, literature, and law. Süleyman and his court commissioned the architect Sinan (circa 1491–1588) to design buildings that are now recognized as some of the greatest examples of Islamic architecture in the world, including the magnificent Süleymaniye Mosque, the intimate Sokollu Mehmet Paşa Mosque, and the exquisitely tiled Rüstem Paşa Mosque.

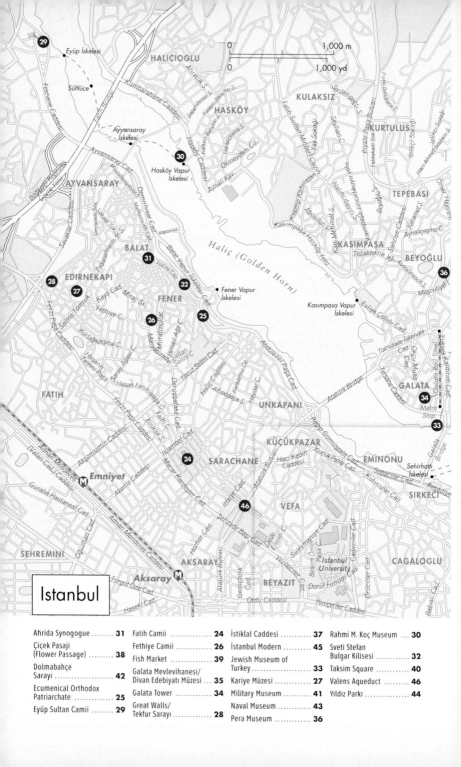

29

Eyüp İskelesi

HALICIOĞLU

0           1,000 m
0           1,000 yd

Sütlüce

KULAKSIZ

HASKÖY

KURTULUŞ

Ayvansaray
İskelesi

30

TEPEBAŞI

AYVANSARAY

Hasköy Vapur
İskelesi

KAŞIMPAŞA

BEYOĞLU

36

BALAT

31

Haliç (Golden Horn)

28

EDİRNEKAPI

27

32

FENER

Fener Vapur
İskelesi

Kasımpaşa Vapur
İskelesi

GALATA

26

25

34
Metro
Stop

33

FATİH

UNKAPANI

Atatürk Bridge

KÜÇÜKPAZAR

EMİNÖNÜ

SARACHANE

24

Sehirhattı
İskelesi

M  Emniyet

SİRKECİ

46

VEFA

SEHREMİNİ

İstanbul
University

CAGALOĞLU

Aksaray  M

AKSARAY

BEYAZIT

Ordu Caddesi

## Istanbul

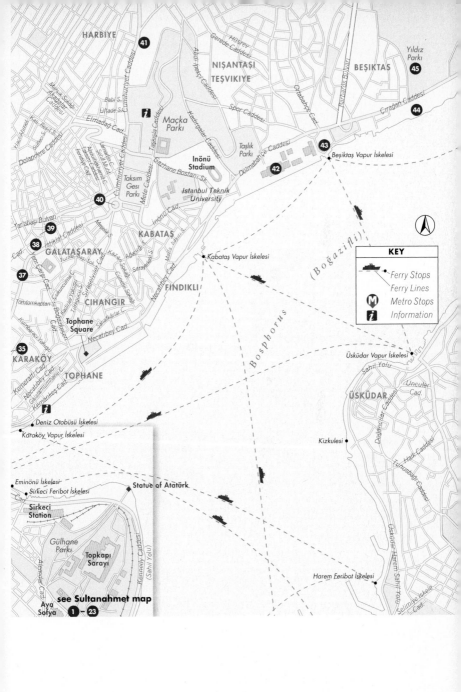

**UNKAPANI**

Atatürk Bridge

*Haliç (Golden Horn)*

Tersane Caddesi

Metro Stop

**KARAKÖY**

Ragıp Gümüşpala Caddesi

Atatürk Bulvarı

Hacı Kadın Caddesi

**KÜÇÜKPAZAR**

Küçük Pazar Cad.

Kıble Çeşme Cad.

**EMINÖNÜ**

Sobacılar Caddesi

Galata Bridge

Rıh Tım

Şehzadtı İskelesi

Eminönü İskelesi

Reşadiye Caddesi

Kutucular Caddesi

**20**

**23**

Eminönü

Sarı Beyazıt Cad.

Kâtip Çelebi Caddesi

Vefa Caddesi

Fetva Yokuşu Sokak

**Cafe Darüzziyafe** ✕

Şifahane Sokak

Kırazlı mescit Sokak

**Süleymaniye Camii**
**18**

Parçacı Sokak

Uzunçarşı Caddesi

Tahtakale Caddesi

**Yeni Cami**
**21**

**Mısır Çarşısı (Egyptian Bazaar)**
**22**

**SIRKECI**

Hamidiye Caddesi

Şah Pehlevi Caddesi

Aşir Efendi Caddesi

Himmet Sokak

**VEFA**

**Café Vefa Bazacısı** ✕

**19**

Süleymaniye Caddesi

Veznecıler

Cadırcılar Caddesi

Taşodaları Sokak

Orücüler Caddesi

Çakmakçılar Caddesi

Tarakçılar Caddesi

**17**

Tacırler Sokak

Mahmutpaşa Yok.

Taratcı Çafet. S.

Cemat Nadir Sokak

Eboussuud

İbanı

**CAGALOGLU**

Vidinli Tevfik Paşa Caddesi

**Istanbul University**

**BEYAZIT**

**16**

Darülfünun Caddesi

**Istanbul University**

**Beyazıt Cami**
**15**

University

Ordu Caddesi

Yeniçeriler Caddesi

Beyazit ✕

**13**

**Çorlulu Ali Paşa Medresesi**

**Kapalı Çarşı (Grand Bazaar)**
**14**

Nuruosmaniye Cad.

Turkocağı Cad.

Ankara Cad.

Mahmutpaşa S.

Kazım Gürkan Cadx

Yeniçeriler Cad.

Türbedal Sokak

Babıali Caddesi

Çatat Çeşme Sokak

Cemberlitaş

Divan Yolu Caddesi

**Museum of Turkish and Islamic Arts**
**12**

ℹ️

**7**

Atmeydanı

**KUMKAPI**

Turanlı Sokak

Mimar Paşa Cad.

Tiyatro Cad.

Gedikpaşa Camii Sokak

Piyerloti Cad.

Tavukhane Sokak

Atmeydanı

Asker Sokak

Türkeli Caddesi

Şakır Efendi

Bayrı Paşa Yokuşu

**11**

Kafesi Sokak

Mollataşı Caddesi

Kadırga Limanı Caddesi

Samsa S.

Piyerloti Cad.

Alışan Sokak

Taştaş Çeşme Sokak

Gedikpaşa Caddesi

Cinçi Meydanı Sokak

Nakilbent Sok.

Kumkapı İst. Caddesi

**Kumkapı Rail Station**

**10**

Aksaka Cad.

Ferferi

# Sultanahmet

0 ——— 500 m

0 ——— 500 yd

N

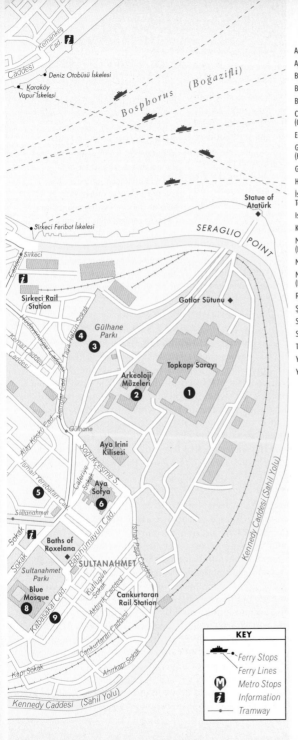

also an extensive collection of classical sculpture and even a model Trojan horse for the kids.

Don't miss a visit to the **Çinili Köşk** (Tiled Pavilion), one of the most visually pleasing sights in all of Istanbul—a bright profusion of colored tiles covers this one-time hunting lodge of Mehmet the Conqueror, built in 1472. Inside are ceramics from the early Seljuk and Ottoman empires, as well as brilliant tiles from İznik, the city that produced perhaps the finest ceramics in the world during the 16th and 17th centuries.

In summer, you can mull over these glimpses into the distant past as you sip coffee or tea at the café in the garden, surrounded by fragments of ancient sculptures.

## A COLUMN OF LUCKY CHARMS

The marble-and-brass **Sacred Column**, in the north aisle of Aya Sofya, to the left as you enter through the main door, is laden with legends. It's thought that the column weeps water that can work miracles, and over the centuries believers have worn a hole as they caress the column to come in contact with the miraculous moisture. It's also believed that if you place your thumb in the hole and turn your hand 360 degrees, any wish you make while doing so will come true.

The **Eski Şark Eserleri Müzesi** (Museum of the Ancient Orient) transports visitors to even earlier times: The vast majority of the panels, mosaics, obelisks, and other artifacts here, from Anatolia, Mesopotamia, and elsewhere in the Arab world, date from the pre-Christian centuries. One of the most significant pieces in the collection is a 13th-century BC tablet on which is recorded the Treaty of Kadesh, perhaps the world's earliest known peace treaty, an accord between the Hittite king Hattusili III and the Egyptian pharaoh Ramses II. Also noteworthy are reliefs from the ancient city of Babylon, dating to the era of the famous king Nebuchadnezzar II. ⊠ *Gülhane Park, next to Topkapı Sarayı* ☎ *212/520–7740* 🖅 *10 TL (total) for the 3 museums* ⊗ *Tues.– Sun. 9–7 in summer, 9–5 in winter; ticket sales until an hr before closing.*

**Fodor's** Choice ★    **Aya Sofya** (*Hagia Sophia, Church of the Holy Wisdom*). This soaring edifice is perhaps the greatest work of Byzantine architecture and for almost a thousand years, starting from its completion in 537, it was the world's largest and most important religious monument. As Justinian may well have intended, the impression that will stay with you longest, years after a visit, is the sight of the dome. As you enter, the half domes trick you before the great space opens up with the immense dome, almost 18 stories high and more than 30 meters (100 feet) across, towering above—look up into it and you'll see the spectacle of thousands of gold tiles glittering in the light of 40 windows. Only Saint Peter's in Rome, not completed until the 17th century, surpassed Aya Sofya in size and grandeur. It was the cathedral of Constantinople, the heart of the city's spiritual life, and the scene of imperial coronations. It was also the third church on this site: the second, the foundations of which you can see at the entrance, was burned down in the antigovernment Nika riots of 532. The emperor Justinian then commissioned a new church and, in response to his dictum that Aya Sofya be the grandest place of worship ever built—far greater than the temples whose columns were incorporated in the church—his master architects devised a magnificent dome. New architectural rules were made up as the builders went along, though not all were foolproof, since the dome collapsed during an earthquake just two years after the church was completed. The church stood a shell until a new architect built a steeper dome, and the aged Justinian finally reopened the church on Christmas Eve 563. Subsequent repairs and such structural innovations as flying buttresses ensured the dome remained firmly in place, making it the prominent fixture it is on the Istanbul skyline to this day. Over the centuries Aya Sofya has survived additional earthquakes, looting Crusaders, and the conquest of the city by Mehmet the Conqueror in 1453.

Mehmet II famously sprinkled dirt on his head before entering the church after the conquest as a sign of humility. His first order was for Aya Sofya to be turned into a mosque and, in keeping with the Islamic proscription against figural images, mosaics were plastered over. Successive sultans added the four minarets, *mihrab* (prayer niche), and *minbar* (pulpit for the imam) that visitors see today, as well as the large black medallions inscribed in Arabic with the names of Allah, Muhammad, and the early caliphs. In 1935, Atatürk turned Aya Sofya into a museum and a project of restoration, including the uncovering of mosaics, began.

Recent restoration efforts have, among other things, uncovered the large, beautifully preserved mosaic of a seraph, or six-winged angel, in the northeast pendentive of the dome, which had been plastered over 160 years earlier. The 9th-century mosaic of the Virgin and Child in the apse is also quite impressive: though it looks tiny, it is actually 16 feet high. To the right of the Virgin is the archangel Gabriel, while Michael, on the left, is almost totally lost.

The upstairs galleries are where the most intricate of the mosaics are to be found. At the far end of the south gallery are several imperial portraits, including, on the left, the Empress Zoë, whose husband's face and name were clearly changed as she went through three of them. On the right is Emperor John Comnenus II with his Hungarian wife Irene and their son, Alexius, on the perpendicular wall. Also in the upper level is the great 13th-century Deesis mosaic of Christ flanked by the Virgin and John the Baptist, breathing the life of the early Renaissance that Byzantine artists would carry west to Italy after the fall of the city to the Turks—note how the shadows match the true light source to the left. The central gallery was used by female worshippers. The north gallery is famous for its graffiti, ranging from Nordic runes to a complete Byzantine galley under sail. On your way out of the church, through the "vestibule of the warriors," a mirror reminds you to look back at the mosaic of Justinian and Constantine presenting Aya Sofya and Constantinople, respectively, to the Virgin Mary. ✉ *Aya Sofya Sq.* ☎ *212/522–1750* 🎟 *20 TL* ⏲ *Tues.–Sun. 9–7 in summer, 9–5 in winter (last entry 1 hr before closing time).*

Fodor's Choice ★ **Blue Mosque** (*Sultanahmet Camii*). Only after you enter the Blue Mosque do you understand the name: the inside is covered with 20,000

# Hammams

A favorite pastime in Istanbul is to spend time in a Turkish bath, or hammam, some of which are in exquisite buildings more than 500 years old. Hammams were born out of necessity—this was how people kept clean before there was home plumbing—but they also became an important part of Ottoman social life, particularly for women. Men had the coffeehouse and women the hammam, a place to gossip and relax. Now that people bathe at home, hammams are becoming less central in Turkish life. There are still bathhouses dotted throughout Istanbul, but many wouldn't survive without steady tourist traffic.

Most hammams have separate facilities for men and women. Each has a *camekan*, a large, domed room with small cubicles where you can undress, wrap yourself in a thin cloth called a *peştemal*, and put on slippers or wooden sandals—all provided. Then you'll continue through a pair of increasingly hotter rooms. The first, known as the *soğukluk*, has showers and toilets and is used for cooling down at the end of your session. Next is the *hararet*, a steamy and softly lit room with marble washbasins along the sides. You can douse yourself by scooping water up from one of the basins with a copper bowl. In the middle of the room is the *göbektaşı*, a marble platform heated by furnaces below and usually covered with reclining bodies. This is where, if you decide to take your chances, a traditional Turkish massage will be "administered."

The masseur or masseuse (who will always be of the same gender as the person receiving the massage) will first scrub you down with a rough, loofa-like sponge known as a *kese*. Be prepared to lose several layers of dead skin. Once you're scrubbed, the masseur will soap you up into a lather, rinse you off, and then conduct what will probably be the most vigorous massage you'll ever receive. Speak up if you want your masseuse to use a lighter hand.

After you've been worked over, you can relax (and recover) on the *göbektaşı* or head back to your changing cubicle, where you'll be wrapped in fresh towels and perhaps massaged a bit more, this time with soothing oils. Most cubicles have small beds where you can lie down and sip tea or juice brought by an attendant. Before you leave, it's good etiquette to tip your masseuse.

**Ayasofya Hürrem Sultan Hamamı.** This hammam, which reopened in 2011 following a several-year restoration process, is the ritziest—and most expensive—in the Old City. It has a prestigious history, having been built by Ottoman architect Sinan in 1556 on the order of Sultan Süleyman the Magnificent, in honor of his wife Roxelana (Hürrem). The setup here is more like that of a modern spa: there is no self-service option, reservations are strongly encouraged, and the cheapest treatment is a whopping 170 TL. In addition to traditional hammam services, modern treatments such as manicures, clay masks, and aromatherapy are offered. ⊠ *Babıhümayun Cad. 1* ☎ *212/517–3535* ⊕ *www.ayasofyahurremsultanhamami.com.*

**Cağaloğlu Hamamı.** Housed in a magnificent building dating from 1741, the Cağaloğlu Hamamı has long been considered one of the best in Istanbul. Florence Nightingale and Kaiser Wilhelm II once steamed here, and the clientele has remained generally upscale. Prices are steep, starting at about 75 TL for a self-service visit, 87 TL for the most basic type of scrub, and higher for massages. Unfortunately, the service at Cağaloğlu has gone noticeably downhill in recent years; guests complain of quick, perfunctory massages by attendants and persistent demands for tips. If you want to experience this famous hammam, consider going the self-service route, so you can relax at your own pace. ⊠ *Prof. Kazım Gürkan Cad. 24, Cağaloğlu* ☏ *212/522–2424* ⊕ *www. cagalogluhamami.com.tr.*

**Çemberlitaş Hamamı.** Built in 1584, the Çemberlitaş Hamamı is famous for its beautiful architectural design and has long been a favorite. However, service can be somewhat rushed and attendants are sometimes pushy in asking for tips. The self-service option is 45 TL. Fees for scrubbing by an attendant start at 69 TL. Avoid going between 4 and 8 pm, when it's busiest. ⊠ *Vezirhan Cad. 8, Çemberlitaş* ☏ *212/522–7974* ⊕ *www.cemberlitashamami.com.*

**Gedikpaşa Hamamı.** In operation since 1475, this hammam is unique in that both the men's and women's sections have small indoor plunge pools, added in modern times. Prices start at 35 TL for self-service and about 60 TL for a professional scrub. The atmosphere here is pleasantly less touristy than at other hammams, but standards of cleanliness are a little less stringent than they are at more expensive baths. ⊠ *Hamam Cad. 65–67, Beyazıt* ☏ *212/517–8956* ⊕ *www.gedikpasahamami.com.tr.*

**Süleymaniye Hamamı.** Part of the complex of buildings around the Süleymaniye Camii, and built, like the mosque, by Sinan in the 1550s, the Süleymaniye Hamamı is unique in being the only coed hammam in the Old City. The hammam caters specifically to couples and families—in fact, single travelers and single-sex groups cannot visit. It's no less touristy than the other hammams, but some may find the coed arrangement preferable to going to a sex-segregated hammam. Rates are 85 TL per person. ⊠ *Mimar Sinan Cad. 20, Süleymaniye* ☏ *212/519–5569* ⊕ *www. suleymaniyehamami.com.tr.*

2

Like the Cağaloğlu Hamamı, most Turkish hammams have separate facilities for men and women.

shimmering blue-green İznik tiles interspersed with 260 stained-glass windows; calligraphy and intricate floral patterns are painted on the ceiling. After the dark corners and stern faces of the Byzantine mosaics in Aya Sofya, this mosque feels gloriously airy and full of light. Indeed, this favorable comparison was the intention of architect Mehmet Ağa (a former student of the famous Ottoman architect Sinan), whose goal was to surpass Justinian's crowning achievement (Aya Sofya). At the behest of Sultan Ahmet I (ruled 1603–17), he created this masterpiece of Ottoman craftsmanship, starting in 1609 and completing it in just eight years, and many believe he indeed succeeded in outdoing the splendor of Aya Sofya.

Mehmet Ağa actually went a little too far though, when he surrounded the massive structure with six minarets: this number linked the Blue Mosque with the Masjid al-Haram in Mecca—and this could not be allowed. So Sultan Ahmet I was forced to send Mehmet Ağa down to the Holy City to build a seventh minaret for al-Haram and reestablish the eminence of that mosque. Sultan Ahmet and some of his family are interred in the stunningly tiled *türbe* (mausoleum) at a corner of the complex, which at one time also included such traditional Muslim institutions as an almshouse, an infirmary, and a school.

From outside the Blue Mosque you can see the genius of Mehmet Ağa, who didn't attempt to surpass the massive dome of Aya Sofya across the way, but instead created a secession of domes of varying sizes to cover the huge interior space, creating an effect that is both whimsical and uplifting. ⊠ *Sultanahmet Sq.* ☉ *Mosque: Daily 9–6:30 in sum-*

mer, 9–5 in winter; closed to tourists during prayer times. Mausoleum: Tues.–Sun. 9–4:30.

Fodor'sChoice  **Topkapı Sarayı** (Topkapı Palace). See the highlighted feature in this
★  chapter.

🔅  **Yerebatan Sarnıcı** (Basilica Cistern). The major problem with the site
Fodor'sChoice  of Byzantium was the lack of fresh water, and so for the city to grow,
★  a great system of aqueducts and cisterns was built, the most famous
of which is the Basilica Cistern, whose present form dates to the reign
of Justinian in the 6th century. A journey through this ancient underground waterway takes you along sparsely lit walkways that weave
around 336 marble columns that rise 26 feet to support Byzantine
arches and domes, from which water drips unceasingly. Classical music
plays softly in the background. The two most famous columns feature
upturned Medusa heads. The cistern was always kept full as a precau-
tion against long sieges, and fish, presumably descendants of those
that arrived in Byzantine times, still flit through the dark waters. A
hauntingly beautiful oasis of cool, shadowed, cathedral-like stillness,
the cistern is a particularly relaxing place to get away from the hubbub
of the Old City. Come early, though, to avoid the long lines and have a
more peaceful visit. ✉ Yerebatan Cad. at Divan Yolu ☎ 212/522–1259
⊕ www.yerebatan.com 💲 10 TL ⏱ Daily 9–6:30 in summer, 9–5:30
in winter.

## WORTH NOTING

🔅  **Gülhane Parkı.** Istanbul has precious few public green spaces, which
★  makes this park—once the private gardens of the adjacent Topkapı
Palace—particularly inviting. Shaded by tall plane trees, the paved
walkways, grassy areas, gazebos, and flower beds make this a relaxing
escape from the nearby bustle of Sultanahmet. Walk all the way to the
end of the park for excellent views of the Bosphorus and Sea of Marmara. There's a municipal-run café and a couple of places serving tea
and snacks inside the park. ✉ Alemdar Cad., Sultanahmet.

**Hippodrome.** It takes a bit of imagination to appreciate the Hippodrome,
once a Byzantine stadium for chariot racing with seating for 100,000,
since there isn't much here anymore, though the peddlars selling postcards, nuts, and souvenirs create a hint of the festive atmosphere that
must have prevailed during chariot races and circuses. Notably absent
are the rows and rows of seats that once surrounded the track and
the life-size bronze sculpture of four horses that once adorned the stadium—the Venetians looted the statue during the Fourth Crusade, and
it is now at St. Mark's Basilica in Venice. You can, however, see several
other monuments that once decorated the central podium. The **Dikilitaş**
(Egyptian Obelisk), from the 15th century BC, probably marked the
finish line. Theodosius I had it shipped over from Egypt in the 4th
century AD and commissioned the reliefs on the base, which show
the emperor in his royal box, which stood opposite, under what is
now the Blue Mosque. The **Yılanlı Sütun** (Serpentine Column) was
taken from the Temple of Apollo at Delphi in Greece, where it was
dedicated after the Greek victory over the invading Persians in the 5th
century BC. The **Örme Sütun** (Column of Constantine Porphyrogenitus)

Continued on page 62

# TOPKAPI

## SHOWPLACE OF THE SULTANS

——◆◈◆——

Like Russia's Kremlin, France's Versailles, and China's Forbidden City, Istanbul's Topkapı Sarayı is not simply a spectacular palace but an entire universe unto itself. Treasure house of Islamic art, power hub of the Ottoman Empire, home to more than twenty sultans, and site of the sultry Seraglio, the legendary Topkapı remains a world of wonders.

Astride the promontory of Saray-burnu ("Seraglio Point")—"the very tip of Europe"—Topkapı Sarayı has lorded over Istanbul for more than 5 centuries. As much a self-contained town-within-a-town as a gigantic palace, this sprawling complex perches over the Bosphorus and was the residence and center of bloodshed and drama for the Ottoman rulers from the 1460s to the 1850s. At one time home to some 5,000 residents—including a veritable army of slaves and concubines—Topkapı was also the treasure house to which marauding sultans brought back marvels from centuries of conquest, ranging from the world's seventh-largest diamond to the greatly revered Mantle of the Prophet Muhammad.

Today's visitors are captivated by the beauty of Topkapı's setting but are even more bewitched by visions of the days of ruby wine and roses, when long-ago sultans walked hand-in-hand with courtesans amid gardens lit by lanterns fastened to the backs of wandering giant tortoises.

As privileged as it was, however, Topkapı was rarely peaceful. Historians now recount horrifying tales of strangled princes, enslaved harem women, and power-mad eunuchs. Just in front of the main Gate of Salutation (from which decapitated heads were displayed centuries ago) stands the Fountain of the Executioner—a finely carved bit of onyx stonework where mighty vassals once washed the blood of victims from their hands in rose-petaled water. It is history as much as beauty that rivets the attention of thousands of sightseers who stream through Topkapı.

When you've had your fill of the palace's bloody yet beautiful past, venture to one of its marble-paved terraces overlooking the Bosphorus. Islands, mosques, domes, crescents shining in the sun, boats sailing near the strand: here shimmer the waters of the strait, a wonderland as seen by a thousand romantic 19th-century travelers—the Constantinople, at last, of our dreams.

Left: Imperial Hall in Harem

# FOUR CENTURIES OF BLOOD & POWER

Stretching through times of tragedy and triumph, the story of Topkapı is a saga worthy of Scheherazade. Built between 1459 and 1465 by Sultan Mehmet II, the palace was envisioned as a vast array of satellite pavilions, many topped with cupolas and domes (Turkish architectural conservatism liked to perpetuate the tents of the nomadic past in stone). Over the centuries, sultan after sultan added ever more elaborate architectural frills, until the palace acquired a bewildering conglomeration of buildings extending over four successive courtyards, each more exclusionary than the last.

Sultan Mehmet II

## MANSION OR MAUSOLEUM?
While Topkapı became the power center of the Ottoman Empire—it grew to contain the **state mint, the arsenal**, and the *divan* (chamber of the judicial council)—its most fearsome aspect was the **sultan's court**. Many of its inhabitants lived their entire adult lives behind the palace walls, and it was often the scene of intrigue and treachery as members of the sultan's entourage plotted and schemed, sometimes even deposing and assassinating the sultan himself.

## A SURFEIT OF SULTANS
Set with stained-glass windows and mother-of-pearl decorations the **"Gilded Cage"** was where the crown prices lived in strict confinement—at least after the old custom of murdering all possible rivals was abandoned in the 17th century (the greatest number of victims—19 brothers—were strangled in 1595 by order of the mother of Mehmet III; seven of his father's pregnant concubines were drowned, to boot). House arrest in this golden suite kept the internal peace but deprived the heirs to the throne of interacting with the real world. After Süleyman II spent 39 years in the Gilded Cage he proved so fearful that, in 1687, he nearly refused the sultanate. Indeed, many sultans who ascended the throne were, in effect, ruled by their mothers, the all-powerful *Valide Sultans* (Queen Mothers). The most notorious was Kösem, whose rule over two sultan sons ended in 1651 when she was strangled upon orders of a vengeful daughter-in-law. As much to escape this blood-stained past as to please visiting European royalty, Topkapı was finally abandoned in 1856 when Abdülmecid I moved his court to Dolmabahçe Palace.

Procession of Constantinople in the Hippodrome (detail)

⊕ Babihümayun Caddesi, Gülhane Park, near Sultanahmet Sq.

☎ 212/512-0480

⊕ www.topkapisarayi. gov.tr

▧ Palace: 20TL; Harem: 15TL

☾ Palace: Wed.–Mon. 9–7 from April to Oct., 9–5 from Nov. to March (last entry one hour before closing time). Harem: Wed.–Mon. 9:30–5 from April to Oct., 9:30–4 from Nov. to March

# Topkapı Sarayı

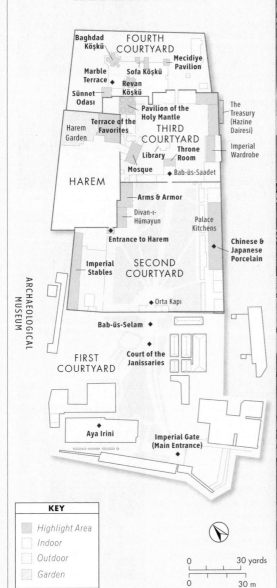

**Baghdad Köşkü**

**FOURTH COURTYARD**

**Mecidiye Pavilion**

**Marble Terrace**

**Sofa Köşkü**

**Revan Köşkü**

**Sünnet Odası**

**Pavilion of the Holy Mantle**

**Terrace of the Favorites**

**Harem Garden**

**THIRD COURTYARD**

The Treasury (Hazine Dairesi)

Imperial Wardrobe

**Library**

**Throne Room**

**Mosque**

Bab-üs-Saadet

**HAREM**

**Arms & Armor**

**Divan-ı-Hümayun**

Palace Kitchens

**Entrance to Harem**

**Chinese & Japanese Porcelain**

**Imperial Stables**

**SECOND COURTYARD**

Orta Kapı

**Bab-üs-Selam**

ARCHAEOLOGICAL MUSEUM

**FIRST COURTYARD**

**Court of the Janissaries**

**Aya Irini**

**Imperial Gate (Main Entrance)**

### KEY

| | |
|---|---|
| | *Highlight Area* |
| | *Indoor* |
| | *Outdoor* |
| | *Garden* |

0 —— 30 yards

0 —— 30 m

Imperial Gate

Harem garden

The Tiled Hall

# OF RICHES UNTOLD: TOPKAPI HIGHLIGHTS

### THE FIRST COURTYARD
Upon arriving from Istanbul's noisy streets, the magic city of an Oriental tale stretches before you. Also known as the First Courtyard, the **Court of the Janissaries** has always been freely accessible to the public. In the shade of its plane trees, the turbulent Janissaries—the sultan's armed guard—prepared their meals and famously indicated their discontent by overturning their soup kettles: a dreaded protest followed, several times, by the murder of the reigning sultan. Looming over all is the **Aya Irini** church, dating from the time of Justinian; it's believed to stand on the site of the first church of Byzantium but, uniquely for Istanbul, has never been converted to a mosque. To the left is the imposing **Archaeological Museum,** housing treasures from Ephesus, Troy, and other ancient sites.

Archaeological Museum

Gate of Salutation

### GATE OF SALUTATION
You begin to experience the grandeur of Topkapı when you pass through **Bab-üs-Selam** (Gate of Salutation). Süleyman the Magnificent built the gate in 1524; only a sultan was allowed to pass through it on horseback. Prisoners were kept in the gate's two towers before they were executed next to the nearby Executioner's Fountain. The palace's ticket office is on the walkway leading to this gate.

### THE SECOND COURTYARD
A vast rose garden shaded by cypress trees, the second, or **Divan**, courtyard was once the veritable administrative hub of the Ottoman empire, often the scene of great pageantry when thousands of court officials would gather before the sultan's throne. On the far left is the entrance to the Harem. Also on the left is the **Divan-ı-Hümayun,** the strikingly ornate open-air Assembly Room of the Council of State. Occasionally the sultan would sit behind a latticed window, hidden by a curtain, so no one would know when he was listening. On the right of the yard are the **Palace Kitchens**, where more than 1,000 cooks once toiled at immense ovens. The cavernous space now displays one of the world's best collections of porcelain, amassed over the centuries by Ottoman rulers. The Yuan and Ming celadon pottery were especially prized for their alleged ability to change color if the dish held poisonous foods.

Gate to the Divan

Kitchen area of the palace

## THE THIRD COURTYARD

As you walk through the **Bab-üs-Saadet, or Gate of Felicity**, consider yourself privileged, because only the sultan and grand vizier were allowed to pass through this gate. It leads to the palace's inner sanctum, the Third Courtyard, site of some of the most ornate of the palace pavilions. Most visitors here only got as far as the **Arz Odası**, the Audience Hall, or Throne Room, where foreign ambassadors once groveled before the sultan. Here, too, is the fabled **Treasury (Hazine Dairesi)**.

## CHAMBER OF SACRED RELICS

On the courtyard's left side is the Hasoda Koğuşu, housing the Chamber of Sacred Relics (1578), which comprises five domed rooms containing some of the holiest relics of Islam. Pride of place goes to the Mantle of the Prophet Muhammad, kept in a gold casket (exhibited behind shatter-proof glass). Nearby are the Prophet's Standard, or flag; hairs from his beard; his sword; a cast of his footprint; and teeth. Other relics, including the "staff of Moses" and the "cooking pot of Abraham," are also on view.

## THE IMPERIAL WARDROBE

An impressive collection of imperial robes, spanning many generations of the Ottoman dynasty, is displayed in a hall on the right side of the Third Courtyard. The sultans' oversized caftans and other garments, and the tiny costumes worn by the crown princes, are made of splendid silks and brocades and are stiff with gold and silver thread, tooled leather, and even jewels.

## THE FOURTH COURTYARD

More of an open terrace, this courtyard was the private realm of the sultan, and small, elegant pavilions are scattered amid tulip gardens overlooking the Bosphorus and Golden Horn. The loveliest of the pavilions, the **Baghdad Kiosk** (covered with İznik tiles), was built by Murat IV in 1638 after his conquest of Baghdad. Off the wishing-well terrace is the **Circumcision Room** (**Sünnet Odası**), also famed for its lavish tiling.

On the right side of the courtyard are steps leading to the 19th-century rococo-style Mecidiye Pavilion, now **Konyalı Restaurant** (open Wed.—Mon., lunch only), which serves excellent Turkish food and has a magnificent vista of the Sea of Marmara. On a terrace below is an outdoor café with an even better view. Go early or reserve a table to beat the tour-group crush.

İznik tiles

Dome atop Gate of Felicity

Interior Baghdad Kiosk

Circumcision Room colonnade

# PLEASURE DOMES:
# THE HAREM

Evoking the exoticism and mystery of the Ottoman Empire, the Harem is a maze of 400 terraces, wings, and apartments. These were the quarters of the sultan's courtesans, mostly Circassian women from the Caucasus (Muslim women were forbidden to be concubines).

Seeing the forty rooms that have been opened to the public reminds us that the Harem (the term means "forbidden" in Arabic) was as much about confinement as it was about luxury. Of the 1,000 women housed in the harem, many finished their days here as servants to other concubines.

Imperial Hall

Built around grand reception salons—including the Imperial Hall, the Crown Prince's Pavilions, and the Dining Room of Ahmet III—the Harem was studded with fountains, whose splashes made it hard to eavesdrop on royal conversations.

### WOMEN'S QUARTERS
Adjacent to the Courtyard of the Black Eunuchs (most of whom hailed from Africa's Sudan), the first Harem compound housed about 200 lesser concubines in tiny cubicles, like those in a monastery. As you move deeper into the Harem, the rooms become larger and more opulent; the four chief wives lived in grand suites around a shared courtyard.

Ornate ceiling in Harem

Most concubines were trained in music and poetry, but only those who achieved the highest status were given access to the sultan.

### APARTMENTS OF THE SULTANS
The sultan's own apartments are, not surprisingly, a riot of brocades, murals, colored marble, wildly ornate furniture, gold leaf, fine carvings, and, of course, the most perfect znik tiles. Nearby is the Gilded Cage, wher ethe crown princes wer kept under lock and key until they were needed.

Dining Room of Ahmet III

### APARTMENTS OF THE VALIDE SULTAN

The true ruler of the Harem was the *Valide Sultan*, the sultan's mother, and her lavish apartments lay at the heart of the Harem complex. For the young women of the Harem, the road to the sultan, quite literally (using a hallway known as the "Golden Way") ran through his mother.

Tickets for the Harem can be purchased at the separate Harem entrance (located near the Divan-ı-Hümayun in the Second Courtyard) and are allotted on a first-come, first-serve basis. Book early, after you buy your general admission ticket to the palace.

# DO YOU LOVE EMERALDS? DON'T MISS TOPKAPI'S TREASURY

If you love jewels, you're in luck—at the **Topkapı Treasury (Hazine Dairesi)** you can admire three of the world's most wondrous emeralds, which are embedded in the hilt of the fabulous Topkapı Dagger. Crafted in 1747, it was meant as a gift for the Shah of Persia; he could well have used it but it arrived too late—he was assassinated as the dagger was en route to him. Here also are two of the world's largest extant emeralds: uncut, they each weigh about eight pounds. Now displayed behind glass, they were originally hung from the ceiling as spectacular "lamps." Amazingly, even these mammoth gems were outshone by the 86-carat Spoonmaker's Diamond which, according to legend, was found by an Istanbul pauper glad to trade it for three wooden spoons. These are but six of the many jewels found here.

Sultan headgear

Spoonmaker's Diamond

A true cave of Aladdin spilling over four rooms, the treasury is filled with a hoard of opulent objects and possessions, either lavish gifts bestowed upon generations of sultans, or spoils garnered from centuries of war. The largest objects are four imperial thrones, including the gold-plated Bayram throne given to Sultan Murat III by the Khedive of Egypt in 1574. Also on display is the throne sent to Istanbul by the same unfortunate shah for whom the Topkapı Dagger was intended. All is enhanced by the beautiful display of turban crests and jewel-studded armor, with every possible weapon encrusted with diamonds and pearls—all giving testimony to the fact that, before the 18th century, it was the man, not the woman, who glittered like a peacock.

There are trinkets, chalices, reliquaries, and jewels, jewels, jewels. Ladies, be sure to hide your engagement rings—they will be overwhelmed in comparison!

Topkapı dagger

## ROCK STARS

The most glamorous jewel heist film ever, *Topkapi* (1964) is director Jules Dassin's dazzling homage to Istanbul, diamonds, and his famous *Never on Sunday* blonde (and wife), Melina Mercouri. Playing jet-set mastermind Elizabeth Lipp, she seduces a troupe of thieves into attempting to steal the Topkapı Dagger. Rooftop high jinks, a script scintillating with wit, the Oscar-winning performance by Peter Ustinov, and an eye-popping credit sequence make for a film almost as intoxicating as a visit to the Treasury itself.

was once entirely covered with gilt bronze, which was stripped off by vandals during the Fourth Crusade. Down the hill to the southeast, along Nakılbent Sokak, you can see the giant southern foundations of the Hippodrome. ✉ *Atmeydanı, Sultanahmet* 🎫 *Free.*

**İslam Bilim ve Teknoloji Tarihi Müzesi** (*Museum of the History of Science and Technology in Islam*). On the western side of Gülhane Parkı, this museum, opened in 2008 in the former stables of Topkapı Palace, chronicles the significant role

played by medieval Muslim scientists, inventors, and physicians—including such names as Avicenna and Averroes—in advancing scientific knowledge and technology while Europe was still in the Dark Ages. Exhibits cover subjects such as astronomy, navigation, mathematics, physics, warfare, and medical expertise. Unfortunately, almost none of the items on display are actual historical artifacts, but the models and reproductions built especially for the museum are quite interesting nevertheless. ✉ *Gülhane Parkı, Sultanahmet* ☎ *212/528–8065* 💰 *5 TL* ⊙ *Wed.–Mon. 9–4:30.*

**Küçük Aya Sofya** (*Little Aya Sofya*). Built by Justinian as the Church of Sergius and Bacchus (patron saints of the Roman army), this church is more commonly known as Küçük Aya Sofya, or "Little Aya Sofya," due to its resemblance to the great church up the hill. In fact, it was built just before Aya Sofya, in the 530s, and the architects explored here many of the same ideas of the larger church but on a smaller scale. The church was converted to a mosque around the year 1500 by Hüseyin Ağa, Beyazıt II's chief eunuch. Though the mosaics are long gone, a Greek inscription dedicated to Justinian, his wife Theodora, and the saints can still be seen running along the cornice of the colonnade. The marble and verd antique columns with their delicate, ornate capitals are also quite impressive, and you can climb the stairway to the upper-level gallery for a closer look. ✉ *Küçük Aya Sofya Cad.* ⊙ *Daily, sunrise–sunset except during prayer times.*

**Mozaik Müzesi** (*Mosaic Museum*). One of Istanbul's more fascinating sights, the small but well-done Mosaic Museum houses an excellent display of early Byzantine mosaics—some presented in situ—from the Great Palace of Byzantium, the imperial residence of Constantine, and other Byzantine emperors from when they ruled lands stretching from Iran to Italy and from the Caucasus to North Africa. This enormous residence reached from here all the way down to the sea and consisted of several terraces, with various palaces, churches, and parks, almost all of which are now gone. Only scant ruins remained by 1935, when archaeologists began uncovering what is thought to have been the floor of a palace courtyard, covered with some of the most elaborate and delightful mosaics to survive from the era. They include images of

# Safety Concerns?

2

Istanbul is, for a city of close to 14 million, very safe, especially in the areas frequented by tourists. Still, like any other big city that attracts hordes of travelers, Istanbul also has its share of unscrupulous touts and shills. The busy and crowded areas around Aya Sofya and Taksim Square seem to especially attract these types. Shoeshine boys sometimes drop their brushes when walking past helpful tourists, then try to massively over-charge for a quick clean. In Sultanah-met, most of the touts who approach you want no more than to steer you toward a harmless carpet shop where they will earn a commission, but the odd few might be less well inten-tioned. The nightclub ruse—in which a small group of friends offer to show a single tourist a night on the town then disappear, sticking their guest with a huge bill—tends to happen most often in the nightlife area of Beyoğlu. It can be hard to see through this scam because Turks are by nature exceedingly friendly and will go out of their way to help you—once you approach them. *The key is to watch out for those who approach you first and seem a little too eager to help, and whose English is just a little too polished.* Use your judgment, but don't be embarrassed to say no politely and move on if you feel accosted. You will certainly make many new friends dur-ing a visit to Turkey—just make sure you do it on your terms.

---

animals, flowers, hunting scenes, and mythological characters—idylls far removed from the pomp and elaborate ritual of the imperial court.

As you walk the streets of Sultanahmet you'll see many fragments of masonry and brickwork that were once part of the palace, and sev-eral cisterns have been found under hotels and carpet shops, some of which are open to visitors. New excavations on property owned by the Four Seasons Hotel are supposed to open as an archaeological park. Down by the water, there are extensive, very overgrown remains of the facade of the **Bucoleon Palace,** the private quarters of the emperors from the 6th to 11th centuries, which are gradually being shaken apart by the passing train line. ⊠ *Arasta Çarşısı, Kabasakal Cad., Sultanahmet* ☎ *212/518–1205* 💲 *8 TL* ☉ *Apr.–Oct., Tues.–Sun.; Nov.–Mar., 9–4:30.*

★ **Museum of Turkish and Islamic Arts** (*Türk ve İslam Eserleri Müzesi*). Süley-man the Magnificent commissioned Sinan to build this grandiose stone palace overlooking the Hippodrome in about 1520, for his brother-in-law, the grand vizier, Ibrahim Pasha, and today it is one of the most important surviving examples of secular Ottoman architecture from its time. The palace now houses the Museum of Turkish and Islamic Arts, which has an exceptional collection of Islamic art and artifacts dating from the 7th through 20th centuries, including Korans and other calligraphic manuscripts, metalwork, and wood and stone carvings. Among the highlights is a pair of 13th-century wooden doors—dec-orated with finely wrought brass plates and a bronze door knocker sporting dragon and lion figures—from the Great Mosque in Cizre, an ancient city on the Tigris River. The museum also has one of the world's most highly regarded collections of antique carpets (dating back to the

## SINAN THE ARCHITECT

The master architect Mimar Sinan, the greatest of the Ottoman builders, is said to have designed more than 350 buildings and monuments throughout Turkey. His genius as an architect lay in his use of proportion, and as an engineer he mastered the use of buttresses and other elements to create vast, open spaces. He was born in a Greek or Armenian village near Cappadocia and at about the age of 22 he was recruited through the *devşirme* (conscription) system to serve the sultan; these Christian conscripts were raised Muslim and trained to become the army and bureaucracy that formed the backbone of the empire. Sinan spent the next several decades of his life as a military engineer, before being appointed chief imperial architect at the age of 50. He then worked into his nineties building more than 80 mosques—some 50 in Istanbul alone—as well as religious schools, palaces, bridges, and caravansaries. Among the works attributed to Sinan are the Sokollu Mehmet Paşa, Süleymaniye, and Rüstem Paşa mosques, parts of the kitchens at Topkapı, two of the minarets at Aya Sofya, and the Selimiye Camii in Edirne. His tomb is beside his most important Istanbul mosque, the Süleymaniye.

13th century), examples of which are displayed floor to ceiling in the palace's enormous ceremonial hall. The lower level contains an ethnographic section with very informative, albeit slightly dated, exhibits on traditional life among nomadic Turkish tribes. After you've visited, take a coffee break in the museum's leafy courtyard and terrace overlooking the Hippodrome. ⊠ *Atmeydanı 46, Sultanahmet* ☎ *212/518-1805* 💷 *10 TL* ⊙ *Apr.–Oct., Tues.–Sun. 9–6:30; Nov.–Mar., 9–4:30.*

★ **Sokollu Mehmet Paşa Camii** (*Mosque of Sokollu Mehmet Pasha*). Built in 1571 for Sokollu Mehmet Pasha, a grand vizier to three successive sultans, this small mosque is not as grand as the Süleymaniye Camii, but many consider it to be the most beautiful of the mosques built by master Ottoman architect Sinan. Here, Sinan chose not to dazzle with size but to create a graceful, harmonious whole, from the courtyard and porticoes outside to the interior, where floral-motif stained-glass windows and gorgeous, well-preserved İznik tiles with both floral patterns and calligraphic inscriptions are set off by white stone walls. Inside, the *minbar* (pulpit), delicately carved in white marble and crowned with a tiled conical cap, is particularly noteworthy. ⊠ *Şehit Mehmet Paşa Yokuşu, Kadırga* ☎ *No phone* ⊙ *Daily sunrise–sunset except during prayer times.*

## THE BAZAAR AREA AND ENVIRONS

The area between the Grand Bazaar and the Egyptian Bazaar was historically the city's center of business and trade, and the streets here still teem with trades people and shoppers. You could easily spend hours exploring the Grand Bazaar, and the Egyptian Bazaar also has its charms. But take time to wander outside them, too, whether along Nuruosmaniye Caddesi with its upmarket jewelry, antiques, and carpet boutiques, or through the narrow, somewhat rundown streets—lined with stores and stalls selling all manner of everyday items at bargain prices, primarily to locals—that lead from the Grand Bazaar down toward the Golden Horn. Even though most of the old Byzantine and Ottoman buildings have long disappeared, the area gives an impression of what the city must have been like when it was the bustling capital of a vast empire. The beautiful Süleymaniye Mosque, one of the architect Sinan's master-

pieces, is grandly situated on a hilltop just a stone's throw from the Grand Bazaar and is worth a detour. The Rüstem Paşa Camii and Yeni Cami, both located near Eminönü on the waterfront, are also particularly striking. When exploring this area, it's a good idea to start at the Grand Bazaar and work your way downhill to Eminönü—it's a rather stiff climb the other way.

## TOP ATTRACTIONS

★ **Egyptian Bazaar** (Mısır Çarşısı). *See the highlighted Bazaars feature in this chapter.*

★ **Grand Bazaar** (*Kapalı Çarşı*). See the highlighted Bazaars feature in this chapter. ⊠ *Yeniçeriler Cad. and Çadırcılar Cad.* ☎ *212/519–1248* ⊘ *Mon.–Sat. 8:30–7.*

**NEED A BREAK?**

**Çorlulu Ali Paşa Medresesi.** The courtyard of the Çorlulu Ali Paşa Medresesi, not far from the Grand Bazaar, has a tea and water pipe garden that's popular with tourists as well as students from nearby Istanbul University. It may have sprouted a few too many souvenir shops, but it's still quite a pleasant place to take a break. The complex was built by Grand Vizier Çorlulu Ali Pasha, whose head was buried in the graveyard next door in 1711 after Ahmet III had it chopped off. ⊠ *Yeniçeriler Cad. 36/5* ⊘ *Open 24 hrs.*

**Rüstem Paşa Camii** (*Rüstem Pasha Mosque*). Tucked away in the back-streets just west of the Egyptian Bazaar, this Sinan masterpiece was built in the early 1560s for Rüstem Pasha, a grand vizier and son-in-law of Süleyman the Magnificent. Though it's unassuming from the outside, this is one of the most highly ornamented of the Ottoman mosques, and you're in for a treat when you step into the interior, which is decorated throughout with İznik tiles in a magnificent array of colors and patterns. The mosque—raised on a high terrace that's surrounded at street level by a warren of small shops—is reached via flights of interior stairs in the corners that lead up to a courtyard and portico, the facade of which is also lined with beautiful tiles. ⊠ *Hasırcılar Cad., south of Sobacılar Cad.* ⊘ *Daily sunrise–sunset except during prayer times.*

**Fodor'sChoice**
★ **Süleymaniye Camii** (*Mosque of Süleyman*). Perched on a hilltop opposite Istanbul University, Süleymaniye Camii is perhaps the most magnificent mosque in Istanbul and is considered one of the architect Sinan's

masterpieces. The architectural thrill of the mosque, which was built between 1550 and 1557, is the enormous dome, the highest of any Ottoman mosque. Supported by four square columns and arches, as well as exterior walls with smaller domes on either side, the soaring space gives the impression that it's held up principally by divine cooperation. Sinan was guided by a philosophy of simplicity in designing this mosque and, except for around the *mihrab* (prayer niche), there is little in the way of tile work—though the extremely intricate stained-glass windows and baroque decorations painted on the domes (added later) more than make up for that. Thanks to a three-year, multimillion-dollar restoration project completed in late 2010, the Süleymaniye can now be seen in its full glory. The tomb of Sinan is just outside the walls, on the northern corner, while those of his patron, Süleyman the Magnificent, and the sultan's wife, Roxelana, are housed in the cemetary adjacent to the mosque. The *külliye*, or mosque complex, still includes a hospital, library, hammam, several schools, and other charitable institutions that mosques traditionally operate, so take a stroll around the beautiful grounds—and don't miss the wonderful views of the Golden Horn. ⊠ *Süleymaniye Cad., near Istanbul University's north gate* ⊙ *Daily sunrise–sunset except during prayer times.*

**NEED A BREAK?**

**Darüzziyafe Restaurant.** The old soup kitchen of the Süleymaniye Camii has been returned to its traditional use as the Darüzziyafe Restaurant, serving a typical Turkish range of mezes and grilled meats in the leafy courtyard and cool, stone halls. ⊠ *Şifahane Cad. 6* ☎ *212/511–8415* ⊕ *www. daruzziyafe.com.tr.*

**Yeni Cami** (*New Mosque*). A dominant feature of the Istanbul skyline, thanks to its prime spot on the Eminönü waterfront, the "new mosque" is known as much for its history as its architecture. Its location, rising out of the Golden Horn, presented formidable engineering challenges to the former apprentice to Sinan who laid the waterlogged foundations in 1597. Due to sultans' deaths and complicated harem politics, it was not until 1663 that the project was finally completed, by the queen mother at the time: Turhan Hatice (who is buried in a mausoleum behind the mosque with her son, Mehmet IV, and several succeeding sultans). The entrance to the courtyard from the main square offers a marvelous view of the small domes and semidomes—66 in all—that appear to cascade down around the main dome, flanked by two minarets. Inside, almost every square inch of the interior is decorated—from the elaborate, multicolored İznik tiles to the intricately painted domes—while numerous windows, including in the wall of the *mihrab* (prayer niche), fill the mosque with light. ⊠ *Eminönü waterfront* ⊙ *Daily sunrise–sunset except during prayer times.*

## WORTH NOTING

**Beyazıt Camii.** Inspired by Aya Sofya and completed in 1506, this domed mosque holds the distinction of being the oldest of the Ottoman imperial mosques still standing in the city. Though the inside is somewhat dark, it has an impressively carved *mihrab* (prayer niche), and the large courtyard has 20 columns made of verd antique, red granite, and porphyry that were taken from ancient buildings. ⊠ *Beyazıt Meyd., Beyazıt ☉ Daily sunrise to sunset; usually closed during prayer times.*

**The Column of Constantine** (*Çemberlitaş*). This column stood at the center of what was a large circular marketplace or forum where Constantine formally rededicated the city on May 11, 330. Carved out of blocks of a reddish-purple stone called porphyry, which was especially prized by the ancient Romans, the column is 35 meters (115 feet) high and was once topped by a golden statue of Apollo, to which Constantine added his own head. Constantine was said to have placed various relics under the column, including an ax used by Noah to make the ark, a piece of the True Cross, and some of the leftover bread from the miracle of the loaves and fishes. ⊠ *Yeniçeriler Cad. and Vezirhan Cad.*

**Eminönü.** The transportation hub of Old Istanbul, Eminönü teems with activity. There are docks for both traditional ferry boats and faster "sea bus" catamarans that cross the Bosphorus (including the day-long Bosphorus cruises), as well as the Eminönü tram stop, the Sirkeci train station, and the departure area for buses headed to Istanbul's western districts. Thousands of people and vehicles rush through this bustling, frenetic neighborhood by the hour, and the many street traders here do a quick business selling everything from trinkets to designer knockoffs. From Eminönü, you can cross the Galata Bridge on foot or via the tramway to Karaköy, the gateway to the "New Town."

**Fatih Camii.** This complex consisting of a mosque, religious schools, and other buildings of a pious nature was the largest in the Ottoman Empire, and is still the heart of Fatih, Istanbul's most religiously conservative neighborhood. The original mosque, which was destroyed by an earthquake in 1766, was built from 1463 to 1470 by Mehmet the Conqueror on the site of the demolished Church of the Twelve Apostles, the burial church of Byzantine emperors from Constantine on. The 18th-century replacement is pleasant but unexceptional, though culturally it remains one of the most important mosques in the city. Behind the mosque is the reconstructed baroque-style tomb of the Conqueror himself, along with the far plainer tomb of his wife Gülbahar. On Wednesday, the area just north of Fatih Camii is taken over by one of the city's largest street markets, packed with locals buying everything from produce to clothing and housewares. It's best to avoid visiting the mosque at prayer times. ⊠ *Fevzi Paşa Cad., Fatih* 🕾 *No phone ☉ Daily sunrise–sunset.*

**Istanbul University.** The main campus of Turkey's oldest institution of higher learning originally served as the Ottoman war ministry—hence the magnificent gateway arch facing Beyazıt Square and the grandiose, martial style of the main buildings, which surround a long greensward filled with giant plane trees. The white marble 85-meter (279-foot) **Beyazıt Tower,** built in 1828 by Mahmud II as a fire-watch station, is the tallest structure in Old Istanbul and still one of the most recognizable landmarks in the area. Though it can no longer be climbed, it's worth seeing up close. ∎TIP➔ Because of its history as a nexus of political activism over the past several decades, the campus is largely closed to the public, though in theory tourists are allowed entrance from 9am to 3pm on weekdays. If you can get in, proceed through the main rectorate building

to the courtyard and garden behind it, from which there is a stunning view overlooking the Süleymaniye Camii. ⊠ *Fuat Paşa Cad., Beyazıt.*

**NEED A BREAK?**

**Vefa Bozacısı.** Popular in the Ottoman era, *boza* is a mildly alcoholic drink (about 1%) made from fermented millet. It's a thick beverage, served with a dusting of cinnamon on top, and it has a distinctive, slightly bitter taste; it's also said to be rich in vitamins B1, B2, C, and E. At the famous *boza* shop Vefa Bozacısı—which has been in business, little changed, since 1876—you can sample some boza for yourself in this living piece of 19th-century Istanbul. In summer they also serve lemonade, ice cream, and a drink called *şıra* (pronounced "shira") made from raisins. ⊠ *Katip Çelebi Cad. 104/1, Vefa* ☎ *212/519–4922* ⊕ *www.vefa.com.tr.*

> **TEA HOUSES**
>
> Istanbul is filled with teahouses—many with shady gardens—where people spend long hours quietly sipping glass after glass of tea. Sitting down at one of these teahouses—particularly if it has a nice view, like the one by the waterfront in Gülhane Park—is one of the simple pleasures of Turkish life.

**Şehzade Camii.** The medium-sized Şehzade Camii was built for Süleyman the Magnificent's eldest son, Prince Mehmet, who died of smallpox in 1543 at age 22. This was the great Ottoman architect Sinan's first imperial mosque and he called it his "apprentice work." The result is quite attractive, though it is plainer than the nearby Süleymaniye. The tranquil gardens contain several imperial tombs—including that of Prince Mehmet—decorated with some of the best İznik tiles in Istanbul. As of this writing the tombs were being restored, after which it is hoped they will be open to the public. ⊠ *Şehzadebaşı Cad., Fatih* ☉ *Daily sunrise to sunset; usually closed during prayer times.*

**Valens Aqueduct.** A Roman city needed its aqueduct, and Constantinople, which seriously lacked drinking water, finally got one in 375 under Emperor Valens. The aqueduct, which was just one element of a well-engineered water distribution system that extended for miles, was restored in the 16th century by the Ottoman architect Sinan and continued to function well into the Ottoman era. The best and most dramatic surviving section is that near Şehzade Mosque, where Atatürk Bulvarı, a major urban thoroughfare, passes through the great arches of the aqueduct—still one of Istanbul's most significant landmarks.

## WESTERN DISTRICTS

The historical peninsula's western districts are farther off the beaten path than the heavily tourist-trod Sultanahmet and bazaar areas, but the rewards of visiting are a number of interesting sights and a more authentic atmosphere. Just inside the ancient city walls, the former Chora Church, now Kariye Müzesi, contains a wealth of gorgeous Byzantine mosaics and frescoes whose splendor surpasses those in the Aya Sofya. The Great Walls themselves, sections of which have been restored, give an idea of the scale of the ancient city and of how Constantinople successfully resisted so many sieges before finally falling to the Ottomans in 1453. Along the water, Fener and Balat—once predominantly Greek and Jewish neighborhoods, respectively—are home to several historic churches, including the Greek Orthodox Patriarchate, as well as the city's oldest synagogue. Farther up the Golden Horn, the Eyüp Sultan Mosque complex is an important Muslim pilgrimage site.

## TOP ATTRACTIONS

**Eyüp Sultan Camii** (*Eyüp Sultan Mosque*). Muslim pilgrims from all over the world make their way to the brightly colored, tile-covered tomb of Eyüp Ensari (Ayyub al-Ansari)—a companion of the Prophet Muhammad who served as his standard-bearer—at this mosque complex on the Golden Horn. Ensari was killed during the first Arab siege of Constantinople (AD 674–78), and the eternal presence of a man so close to Muhammad makes this the holiest Islamic shrine in Turkey. His gravesite was visited by Muslim pilgrims in Byzantine times and "rediscovered" during Mehmet the Conqueror's siege of Constantinople. After the conquest, Mehmet monumentalized the tomb and built a mosque, where investiture ceremonies were held for successive sultans; the mosque currently on the site was built after the original edifice was ruined in the earthquake of 1766. The plane-tree-shaded courtyards and large numbers of visitors—particularly at midday Friday prayers—imbue Eyüp Sultan Camii with a sense of peace and religious devotion not found in many other parts of this often-frenetic city. A vast cemetery has grown up around the mosque, including the grand tombs of many other distinguished departed. It's best to avoid visiting at prayer times. ⊠ *Cami Kebir Cad., Eyüp* 🕾 *No phone* ⊙ *Daily.*

### VIEW FROM THE BRIDGE

The Galata Bridge, or Galata Köprüsü, connects Old Istanbul to the so-called New Town on the other side of the Golden Horn. The bridge was finished in 1994, replacing the old pontoon bridge that had been around since about 1910, when horse-, ox-, or mule-drawn carriages rattled across it for a fee. The bridge itself isn't much to look at, but it offers a postcard-worthy view of the main sights of the Old City, and is a particularly nice vantage point from which to watch the sunset.

**NEED A BREAK?**

**Pierre Loti Cafe.** The Pierre Loti Cafe, with its sublime view up the Golden Horn toward Aya Sofya and Topkapı, is a favorite with both visitors and locals. Bearing right as you leave Eyüp Sultan Camii, there's a steep walk that winds uphill through the cemetery, or you can take a pleasant cable car ride to the top (walk back toward the water and look for signs that say "Teleferik"; 2 TL each way). The café takes its name from the pen name of Julien Viaud, a French naval officer, author, and Turkophile who frequented the area in the late 19th century and wrote a famous autobiographical novel about his love affair with a harem girl. Though the historic coffeehouse itself serves only (nonalcoholic) beverages, there are some snack

Anastasis fresco, artist unknown, Kariye Müzesi

vendors and a restaurant nearby. **The main attraction here is the impressive view over the Golden Horn.** ☎ *212/616–2344.*

**The Great Walls.** The walls of Constantinople were the greatest fortifications of the medieval age and, although they were severely damaged by Sultan Mehmet II's cannon in the siege leading up to the Ottoman conquest of the city in 1453, large sections still stand more or less intact today. The walls were built in the 5th century after the city outgrew the walls built by Constantine, and they stretched 6.5 km (4 mi) from the Marmara Sea to the Golden Horn. The "wall" was actually made up of a large inner and smaller outer wall, with various towers and gates, as well as a moat. Parts have been restored and you can even climb around on top; the easiest section on which to do this is near Edirnekapı, a short walk uphill from Chora Church.

From Edirnekapı, if you walk along the inside of the walls for a few hundred yards north in the direction of the Golden Horn, you will come to what is known in Turkish as the **Tekfur Sarayı** (Hoca Şakir Cad.), a large three-story building that has an impressive facade and is built into the city walls. This 13th-century edifice represents the only significant remains of the multibuilding Palace of Blachernae, which served as the Byzantine emperors' primary residence after they recaptured Constantinople from the Latin Crusaders in 1261. Though the Tekfur Sarayı is supposedly being restored, little seems to have changed over the last several years, and entrance to the site is prohibited.

Fodor's Choice ★ **Kariye Müzesi** (*Kariye Museum or Church of the Holy Savior in Chora*). The dazzling mosaics and frescoes in the former Church of the Holy Savior in Chora are considered to be among the finest Byzantine artworks in the world. Most of the mosaics, in 50 panels, depict scenes from the New Testament and date from the 14th century. They are in splendid condition, having been plastered over when the church became a mosque in the 16th century and not uncovered until the 1940s. "Chora" comes from the Greek word for countryside; the original church here was outside the city walls that were built by Constantine the Great, but at the beginning of the 5th century AD Theodosius built new fortifications to expand the growing city, which brought the church inside the walls. The current edifice is believed to have been built in the 12th century.

The modern entrance is off to the side of the church but it's best to head straight to the original front doorway, in the outer narthex. Here, a large mosaic of Christ Pantocrator bears the phrase "I am the land (Chora) of the Living." This door leads to the inner narthex, where you can see the mosaic of Theodore Metochites, a kind of Byzantine prime minister, presenting the church to Christ. Metochites was responsible for the restoration and redecoration of the church after the damage wrought by the Fourth Crusade. To the left is a series of mosaics depicting the early life of the Virgin, based on the apocryphal gospel of St. James: moving clockwise, the series starts at the far end with her parents, Joachim and Anne, her first steps, her service in the temple, her marriage to Joseph, and, finally, the Annunciation. Above in the dome are the ancestors of the Virgin. The story continues in the outer narthex with the infancy of Christ, starting again at the far left end with the journey of Mary and Joseph to Bethlehem. It continues clockwise around the outer narthex, with the Nativity, the wise men before Herod, and the flight to Egypt. At the far right end is the massacre of the innocents, which continues gruesomely over several scenes, with the cycle ending with the return from Egypt and the presentation of the young Jesus in the temple. The ceiling vaults show various scenes from the ministry of Christ, including his temptation by the devil, the multiplication of loaves, and the transformation of water into wine. These continue in the south side of the inner narthex, with scenes of Christ healing the sick and a vast wall mosaic, known as the Deesis, which depicts Christ and the Virgin, along with two tiny imperial figures.

The nave itself is light and airy but has lost most of its decoration, though a mosaic of the Dormition of the Virgin survives over the door. The large side chapel was used for burials and contains several large tombs including, on the left, that of Theodore Metochites, which is surrounded by frescoes of saints and stories from the Old Testament. In the apse is an arresting image called the Anastasis, or "Resurrection"; it's one of the masterpieces of Byzantine art, with Christ raising up Adam and Eve from their tombs at the end of time. The fresco in the vault shows the Second Coming: Christ sits enthroned with the saved, while the damned are taken down to hell and an angel rolls up the heavens like a scroll.

The easiest way to reach Kariye Müzesi is by taxi, or you can take an Edirnekapı-bound bus from Eminönü or Taksim Square. The tree-shaded restaurant outside the church is a pleasant spot for lunch or a coffee before you trek back into town. ⊠ *Kariye Türbesi Sokak, (a*

*short walk north of Fevzi Paşa Cad., near Edirnekapı in Old City walls)*
☎ *212/631–9241* 💲 *15 TL* ⊙ *Apr.–Oct., Thurs.–Tues. 9–7 (ticket sales until 6); Nov.–Mar., 9–4:30.*

## WORTH NOTING

**Ahrida Synagogue.** Located in Balat, the city's historically Jewish district, Istanbul's oldest synagogue is believed to date back to the 1430s, when it was founded by Jews from the town of Ohrid in what is today Macedonia. The synagogue was extensively restored in 1992 to the Ottoman baroque style of its last major reconstruction in the 17th century. The most interesting feature of this Sephardic place of worship is the boat-shape wooden *bimah* (reading platform), whose form is thought to represent either Noah's Ark or the ships that brought the Jews from the Iberian Peninsula to the Ottoman Empire in 1492. To visit, you must apply by fax or email at least four days in advance to the Chief Rabbinate (follow the directions on their Web site). ⊠ *Kürkçü Çeşmesi Sok. 9, Balat* ☎ *212/293–8794* ⊕ *www.musevicemaati.com* ⊙ *Can be visited weekday mornings.*

**Ecumenical Orthodox Patriarchate** (*Church of St. George*). The Greek Orthodox Patriarchate, after being kicked out of Aya Sofya, wandered among several churches before settling here in the Church of St. George in 1601. Rebuilt after a fire in 1720, the church is a relatively simple basilica, though the interior has a refined atmosphere. Sarcophagi with the remains of some famous Byzantine saints, a Byzantine-era patriarchal throne, and two very old mosaic icons on the right side of the elaborate iconostasis are considered the most noteworthy features of the church. The main front gate of the compound has been welded shut ever since Sultan Mahmud II had Patriarch Gregory V hanged from it in 1821 as punishment for the Greek revolt. This small church is theoretically the center of the Orthodox world, though some Turks would like to claim that it serves only the dwindling community of Istanbul Greeks. ⊠ *Sadrazam Ali Paşa Cad., Fener* ☎ *212/531–9670* ⊕ *www. ec-patr.org* ⊙ *Daily 9–4.*

**Fethiye Camii** (*Church of Theotokos Pammakaristos*). This 12th-century church, originally part of a convent, served as the seat of the Orthodox Patriarchate from 1456 to 1587 and was then converted into a mosque, Fethiye Camii. While the main church building continues to function as a mosque, the beautiful side chapel has been turned into a small museum, with well-restored mosaics that are some of the best anywhere. The dome shows Christ Pantocrator ("ruler of all") surrounded by Old Testament prophets, while figures of Christ, saints, and patriarchs adorn the walls. In this chapel, Mehmet the Conqueror would talk religion and politics with his handpicked patriarch, Gennadius. ⊠ *Cami Avlusu Sokak off Fethiye Cad., Fatih* ☎ *212/635–1273* 💲 *5 TL* ⊙ *Apr.–Oct., Thurs.–Tues. 9–6; Nov.–Mar., 9–4:30.*

**Rahmi M. Koç Museum.** Housed on the grounds of an Ottoman-era shipyard on the shore of the Golden Horn, and in an adjacent foundry where anchors were cast for the Ottoman fleet, this museum complex is sponsored by one of Turkey's leading industrialists. The wonderful, eclectic collection includes planes, boats, a submarine, a tank, trucks,

trains, a horse-drawn tram, motorcycles, antique cars, medieval tele-
scopes, and every type of engine imaginable. Along with the many
vehicles and machines, interactive displays on science and technology,
as well as recreations of a sawmill and a 1920s olive oil factory, are of
special appeal to children. Located on the premises, the Café du Levant
is a Parisian-style bistro with art nouveau furnishings and a French
chef who turns out excellent classic French cuisine. Take a Golden
Horn ferry, a bus from Şişhane, or a taxi to get here. ⊠ *Hasköy Cad.
5, Hasköy* ☎ *212/369–6600* ⊕ *www.rmk-museum.org.tr* ⛁ *12.5 TL
⊙ Tues.–Fri. 10–5 year-round; Apr.–Sept., weekends 10–8, Oct.–Mar.,
weekends 10–6; Café du Levant: Tues.–Sun., lunch and dinner.*

**Sveti Stefan Bulgar Kilisesi** (*Bulgarian Church of St. Stefan*). One of the
most remarkable and oddest structures in Istanbul—and that's saying
a lot—this small neo-Gothic church looks like it's covered with elaborate stone carvings but when you get up close, you realize that it's all
cast iron. It was prefabricated in Vienna, shipped down the Danube
on barges, and erected on the western shore of the Golden Horn in
1898. The then-flourishing Bulgarian Orthodox community in Istanbul
was eager to have an impressive church of its own as a statement of
its independence from the Greek Orthodox Patriarchate; the Ottoman
Sultan had given the community permission to break away in 1870
but the first church built on the site had burned down. The Istanbul
municipality announced in mid-2011 that the church—one of the few
such surviving prefab cast-iron churches in the world—would undergo
restoration. Whether you can get in, the building, set in neatly tended
gardens by the waters of the Golden Horn, is an impressive structure
to look at. ⊠ *Mürsel Paşa Cad. 10, Balat ⊙ Daily 8–5.*

# BEYOĞLU: ISTANBUL'S NEW TOWN

Beyoğlu, the neighborhood on the hill above Galata, has traditionally
been thought of as the "New Town," and this is where you will feel
the beating pulse of the modern city: the district is a major destination
for eating and drinking, shopping, and arts and culture. "New" is of
course a relative term in Istanbul, and many of the grand, European-
style buildings you'll see here date from the late 19th century, when
Beyoğlu—then known as Pera—was one of the city's most fashionable
areas, home to large numbers of the city's non-Muslim minorities and
the foreign diplomatic community. After a period of decline in the latter decades of the 20th century, Beyoğlu was revived around the turn
of the millennium, as Istanbullus rediscovered the elegant old buildings
and incredible views.

The 14th-century Galata Tower, halfway up the hill from Karaköy,
dominates the skyline. Tünel Square, a short but steep uphill walk
from the tower, marks the start of İstiklal Caddesi (Independence
Avenue). Istanbul's main pedestrian street, İstiklal is lined with shops,
cafés, and nightlife venues; allow some time to stroll along this bustling thoroughfare and simply take in the scene. İstiklal climbs gently
uphill through Beyoğlu and across Galatasaray Meydanı (Galatasaray
Square) to Taksim Meydanı (Taksim Square), the center of modern

Istanbul. The Galata Mevlevihanesi (Galata dervish lodge), historic Fish Market, and private art museums and art galleries including the Pera are also in this area.

## TOP ATTRACTIONS

**Galata Mevlevihanesi** (*Galata Mevlevi Lodge Museum*). Istanbul's oldest Mevlevi dervish lodge, which served as a meeting place and residence for "whirling dervishes" (followers of the Sufi mystic Celaleddin Rumi) was founded on this site in 1491 and rebuilt after a fire in 1765. Recently restored, it now houses a small but interesting museum with displays of dervish garments, handicrafts, and other artifacts, along with background information about the Mevlevi order and Sufism more generally. The biggest draw is the *sema* dance ceremonies (popularly knowing as whirling dervish ceremonies) that are performed once each weekend in the lodge's ceremonial hall; check days/times in advance. ✉ *Galip Dede Cad. 15, southeast of Tünel Sq., off İstiklal Cad., Beyoğlu* ☎ *212/245–4141* 🖅 *5 TL; approx. 30 TL for sema ceremony* ⊗ *Tues.– Sun. 9–4:30.*

**Galata Kulesi** (*Galata Tower*). The Galata area was a thriving Italian settlement both before and after the fall of Constantinople, and the Genoese built this tower as part of their fortifications in 1349, when they controlled the northern shore of the Golden Horn. The hillside location provided good defense, as well as a perch from which to monitor the comings and goings of vessels in the sea-lanes below. The tower later served at times as a jail and at others as a fire tower and now houses a restaurant and nightclub at the top. The viewing gallery, which offers fabulous panoramic views of the city and across the Golden Horn and Sea of Marmara, is accessible by elevator and open during the day, for a fee—though it bears noting that similar views can be had at rooftop cafés and restaurants around the area. ✉ *Büyük Hendek Cad.* ☎ *212/293–8180* 🖅 *11 TL* ⊗ *Daily 9–8.*

**İstiklal Caddesi** (*Independence Avenue*). Lively İstiklal Caddesi is the heart of modern Istanbul. The street was once known as "La Grande Rue de Péra," for the Pera neighborhood—the name Pera means "across" in Greek, and it was used because the area was on the other side of the Golden Horn from the city proper. In the 19th century, palatial European embassies were built here, away from the dirt and chaos of the Old City. The wealthy cityfolk soon followed, particularly after the short funicular called the Tünel—the first underground urban rail line in continental Europe—was built in 1875 to carry them up the hill from their workplaces in the banks and trading houses of Karaköy. The area was traditionally non-Muslim, and the Greek, Armenian, Catholic, and Protestant churches here are more prominent than the mosques. Today İstiklal is a lively pedestrian area, full of shops (many of them international chains), restaurants, cafés, and cinemas. Turks love to promenade here, and at times it can turn into one great flow of humanity; even in the wee hours of the morning it's still alive with people. This is the Istanbul that never sleeps.

**WORTH NOTING**

★ **Fish Market** (*Balık Pazarı*). Next to the Çiçek Pasajı, the Balık Pazarı is a bustling labyrinth of streets filled with stands selling fish, fruits, vegetables, spices, and sweets—along with a couple of informal restaurants specializing in *kokoreç*, or grilled lamb intestines—all of which makes for great street theater. The fish market leads to **Nevizade Sokak**, a lively strip of bars and fish restaurants, all with outside tables packed with locals in summer.

**Üç Horan Armenian Church.** Hidden in plain view on the Nevizade side of the main street of the Fish Market is a pair of large black doors (usually open) leading through a courtyard to the Üç Horan Armenian Church. The first church was built on this site in 1807; after burning down in a fire, it was rebuilt in 1838 by Armenian Ottoman architect Garabet Amira Balyan, who also designed the Dolmabahçe Palace; finally, after another fire in 1870, it was rebuilt in stone, in its present form. The elegant old church is an unexpected sight amidst the bustle and chaos of the fish market. ⊠ *Balık Pazarı, Sahne Sok. 24* ☎ *212/244–1382* ☾ *Daily 8:30–5* .

**NEED A BREAK?**

**Tepebaşı Nargile Cafe.** Open 24 hours, this no-frills café—located on a large open terrace at the far end of the parking lot across from the Pera Museum—is a popular escape from the crowds of İstiklal Caddesi. It's primarily a tea place but also serves various other drinks and snacks, both sweet and savory. The main attraction is the view over the Golden Horn to the Old City.

**Çiçek Pasajı** (*Flower Passage*). One of Istanbul's grandest shopping venues when it was built in 1876, this Second Empire–style arcade was gradually taken over by Russian flower shops in the early 20th century—earning it the name "Flower Arcade." Later, the passage became dominated by famously boisterous *meyhanes*, or taverns. The arcade reopened in 1988 after a major restoration that rebuilt a section that had collapsed, and though it's still quite pretty, it feels more than a little like a reproduction. The venue now houses about a dozen rather pricey *meyhane*-style restaurants. For a more authentic local vibe, head over to nearby Nevizade Sokak. ⊠ *İstiklal Cad. 80, Beyoğlu.*

★ **Military Museum** (*Askeri Müze*). This large and fascinating museum boasts an extensive collection of swords, daggers, armor, and other weaponry, but it's not just for those interested in military history. Exhibits on the history of Turkic armies going back to the Huns, the Ottoman conquest of Istanbul, and more recent Turkish military engagements show the importance of military strength in shaping Ottoman history and modern Turkish society. Particularly imposing are the gorgeously embroidered silk tents used by the Ottoman sultans on campaigns. And don't miss the section of the great chain that the Byzantines stretched across the Golden Horn in 1453 during the Ottoman siege of the city. Atatürk was educated in this former military academy, and his personal effects from the 1915 Gallipoli campaign are touchingly humble. ■TIP→ The highlight is the Mehter, or Janissary military band, which performs 17th- and 18th-century Ottoman military music in full period costume in a special auditorium at 3 pm when they're in town (most days). Watching this 50-odd-member ensemble, with their thunderous kettledrums and cymbals, will certainly give you an idea of why the Ottoman army was so feared in its day. ⊠ *Valikonağı Cad., Harbiye* ☎ *212/233–2720* ⊠ *4 TL* ☉ *Wed.–Sun. 9–5.*

**Pera Museum.** A small private museum, housed in a grand, late 19th-century mansion, the Pera showcases a diverse range of exhibits. It's best known for its permanent collection of Orientalist paintings by both European and Ottoman artists, dating from the 17th to early 20th centuries and including panoramas of the city and scenes of daily life; *The Tortoise Trainer* by Osman Hamdi Bey—who also founded Istanbul's original Archaeological Museum—is particularly famous. Below that floor are two smaller permanent exhibits, one focusing on the history of Anatolian weights and measures from the Hittite period to the Turkish Republic, the other on Kütahya ceramics. The upper three levels house well-conceived temporary exhibits featuring local and international artists. ⊠ *Meşrutiyet Cad. 65, Tepebaşı* ☎ *212/334–9900* ⊕ *www. peramuzesi.org.tr* ⊠ *10 TL* ☉ *Tues.–Sat. 10–7, Sun. 10–6.*

**Taksim Square** (*Taksim Meydanı*). This square at the north end of İstiklal Caddesi is essentially a chaotic traffic circle and public transportation hub—though there is talk of pedestrianizing the area and making it into a true open plaza. The entrance to the Taksim Square station, from which both the subway and the funicular going down to Kabataş can be reached, is in the center of the square, so you'll probably end up here at one point or another. The open area at the top of İstiklal is dominated by the Monument of the Republic, built in 1928 and featuring Atatürk and his revolutionary cohorts. Around the square are Atatürk Cultural Center, the city's main concert hall; the high-rise Marmara Hotel; and, up the stairs, the small, grassy Taksim Gezi Parkı. Cumhuriyet Caddesi, the main street heading north from the square, is lined with travel agencies and airline ticket offices. Futher up Cumhuriyet, Vali Konağı Caddesi splits off from the avenue and veers right, taking you to Nişantaşı, the city's high-fashion district.

## KARAKÖY AND BEŞIKTAŞ

The lower-Bosphorus neighborhoods on the city's European side offer an eclectic mix of attractions, from symbols of late-Ottoman power to cutting-edge art spaces. Karaköy, located across the Galata Bridge from Eminönü, was formerly a major port, and its busy trading houses and banks made the neighborhood the economic hub of the late Ottoman Empire. Today the wealth is largely gone, and only ferry boats and cruise ships stop here, but the area still has a historic feel to it: Ottoman mosques line the waterfront area, and Istanbul's Jewish Museum is also here. The Istanbul Modern, nestled among the mosques in a former shipping warehouse near the Tophane tram stop, is the city's leading art museum. Tophane is also one of the most popular spots in Istanbul for *narghile* (water pipe) smoking, with a long row of cafés filled with customers puffing away. A short walk away, the stunning neoclassical Dolmabahçe Palace is one of Istanbul's most visited attractions outside of the Old City, each room more ornate and over-the-top than the last. Just beyond Dolmabahçe, the Naval Museum in Beşiktaş houses an impressive collection of Ottoman craft in a specially designed venue overlooking the water.

NEED A BREAK?

**Karaköy fish sandwiches.** Restaurants and cafés line the Karaköy waterfront by the passenger ferry landing, but for a truly delicious, cheap snack, the no-frills sandwich known as *balık ekmek*—literally "fish in bread"—may be one of your most memorable seafood meals in Turkey. The recipe is simple: take a freshly grilled fillet of fish and serve it in a half loaf of crusty white bread (adding onion and/or tomato slices is about as fancy as it gets). What makes *balık ekmek*, though, is the setting—in Istanbul, the best sandwiches are served alfresco from small boats that pull up to the atmospheric quays near the city's Galata Bridge, smoke billowing from their onboard grills.

## TOP ATTRACTIONS

Fodor's Choice ★

**Dolmabahçe Sarayı** (*Dolmabahçe Palace*). The name Dolmabahçe means "filled-in garden," from the fact that Sultan Ahmet I (ruled 1603–17) had an imperial garden planted here on land reclaimed from the sea. Abdülmecid I, whose free-spending lifestyle later bankrupted the empire, had this palace built from 1843 to 1856 as a symbol of Turkey's march toward European-style modernization. He gave father and son Garabet and Nikoğos Balyan—from a prominent Armenian family of late-Ottoman architects—complete freedom and an unlimited budget, the only demand being that the palace "surpass any other palace of any other potentate anywhere in the world." The result, an extraordinary mixture of Turkish and European architectural and decorative styles, is a riot of rococo: marble columns with gilt Corinthian capitals, huge mirrors, trompe l'oeil painted ceilings, inlaid parquet floors, rich brocade. Abdülmecid's bed is solid silver, the tub and basins in his marble-paved bathroom are translucent alabaster; more than 200 kilos (420 pounds) of gold were used throughout the palace. European royalty helped contribute to the splendor: Queen Victoria sent a Bohemian crystal chandelier weighing 4½ tons (still the largest in Europe) and Czar Nicholas I of Russia provided polar-bear rugs. The result is as over-the-top and showy as a palace should be, and every bit as garish as Versailles.

Dolmabahçe is divided into the public "Selamlık" and the private "Harem," which can only be seen on separate, oversized guided tours, which together take about 90 minutes. The Selamlık is far more opulent, befitting its ceremonial purpose, while the Harem shows how traditional social hierarchies and living arrangements continued despite the outwardly European decor. Atatürk, the founder of the Turkish Republic, spent his last days here, and visitors are shown his deathbed in the Harem; all the clocks in the palace remain permanently stopped at 9:05 am, the hour of his death on November 10, 1938.

After the tour(s), take time to stroll along the palace's nearly ½ km (¼ mi)-long waterfront facade and through the formal gardens. Two small buildings set back from the palace can be visited without a tour: the ornate Crystal Pavilion, which boasts a crystal piano and glass conservatory with a crystal fountain, and the Clock Museum, which has some of the most elaborate clocks you have ever seen. ■TIP→ The palace has a daily visitor quota, so call the reservation number, 212/327–2626, at least a day in advance to reserve tickets and to avoid lines of up to an hour long at the ticket booth. ⊠ *Dolmabahçe Cad., Beşiktaş* ☎ *212/236–9000* 🖅 *Selamlık 15 TL, Harem 10 TL, joint ticket 20 TL* ⊙ *Tues.–Wed. and Fri.–Sun. 8:30–4:30 in summer, 8:30–4 in winter. Last tickets sold at 3.*

**Fodor's Choice**
★
**Istanbul Modern.** A converted warehouse on the shores of the Bosphorus showcases modern painting, sculpture, photography, and works in other media from Turkey and around the world. The permanent collection tells the story of modern Turkish art from its late-19th-century Orientalist beginnings up through the present day, while a top-notch program of temporary exhibits features significant local and international contemporary artists. A guided tour (free on Thursday at 3 pm and 5 pm; call in advance to confirm availability and make a reservation; tours can be arranged on other days/times for 10 TL per person for groups of four or more) can give you a good introduction to the art scene in Turkey. The museum also has a gift shop, a small cinema, and a pleasant restaurant and café with beautiful views toward Topkapı Palace and the Sea of Marmara, along with good food that doesn't come cheap. ⊠ *Meclis-i Mebusan Cad. Liman İşletmeleri Sahası, Antrepo No. 4* ☎ *212/334–7300* ⊕ *www.istanbulmodern.org* 🖅 *14 TL* ⊙ *Tues., Wed., and Fri.–Sun. 10–6, Thurs. 10–8; closed Mon.*

## WORTH NOTING

**Jewish Museum of Turkey.** The history of the Jews in Turkey is much more extensive and colorful than the size of this small museum housed in the 19th-century Zulfaris Synagogue might suggest. Nevertheless, the museum provides a fascinating glimpse into the lives of Turkish Jews, whose presence in Anatolia is traced back to as early as the 4th century BC. In 1492, the Spanish Inquisition drove Sephardic Jews from Spain and Portugal, and Sultan Beyazıt II welcomed the refugees to the Ottoman Empire. A large Jewish population thrived here for centuries, and some older Turkish Jews still speak a dialect of medieval Spanish called Ladino, or Judeo-Spanish. Today, Turkey's Jewish community numbers about 23,000, most of whom live in Istanbul, which has 19 active synagogues (three of which are on the Princes' Islands). The museum exhibits, most of them based on items donated by local Jewish families, include photographs, documents, and an ethnographic section with changing exhibits on subjects such as marriage traditions. There are also religious items brought from some very old (no longer active) synagogues in other parts of Turkey. ⊠ *Karaköy Meydanı, Perçemli Sok. 1(off Tersane Cad. Perçemli is small street on your right as you come out of Tünel exit of underpass)* ☎ *212/292–6333* ⊕ *www.muze500.com* 🖅 *10 TL* ⊙ *Mon.–Thurs. 10–4, Fri. and Sun. 10–2.*

**NEED A BREAK?**
One of the great pleasures of Istanbul is to sit at one of the many nameless clusters of plastic seats and umbrellas that line the Bosphorus and watch the ships go by. A favorite is in Fındıklı behind the mosque, where, for the price of a tea, you can enjoy one of the best views in town, taking in everything from Dolmabahçe on the left, to Kız Kulesi just opposite and Aya Sofya on the right.

*Continued on page 90*

# Boom on the Bosphorus

Adjacent to the beautiful 19th-century Ortaköy mosque at Ortaköy Pier is the modern Bosphorus suspension bridge.

It's hard to talk about Istanbul without talking in riddles. Medieval yet modern, European yet Eastern, secular yet Islamic, Istanbul is—at one and the same time—one of the newest and oldest cities in the world.

In spite of recent instances of instability—1999 brought a major earthquake, 2001 saw the collapse of the Turkish Lira—Istanbul has been booming in terms of population (13 million at last count) and tourists in the past decade. Guardian of the Bosphorus waterway and Turkey's traditional gateway to the West, the city is busy polishing its image in hopes of becoming the easternmost anchor of the European Union. But as any Turk will tell you, Istanbul is not Turkey—it is a unique entity, and even that is an understatement.

City of 1,001 sights, Istanbul is packed with world-famous museums and monuments. Topkapı Palace, the Grand Bazaar, Aya Sofya (Hagia Sophia), and the Blue Mosque all render this a dream city, with a skyline of domes, minarets, and mosques that, at least on a misty morning, rise up like a vision from one of Scheherazade's tales. Thanks to its many startling juxtapositions, the texture of life in Istanbul is an attraction all by itself. To discover the Istanbul that exists underneath and between the famous landmarks, you need simply to venture outside, where you'll be immersed in the city's teeming streets, colorful *meyhanes* (taverns), and waterfront neighborhoods. To help visitors discover this elusive city, this 10-page "road map" attempts to chart Istanbul's psychological and cultural avenues.

# TWO WORLDS IN ONE

Part Europe and part Middle East, Istanbul can fascinate, frustrate, and enchant you all at once. Here old ways mix with modern in tight quarters, yielding out-of-sync images that make visitors pause and wonder.

Imagine an Armani-clad driver in a Lexus, shouting into a cell phone—and in the next lane, a vegetable cart pulled by a horse, taking the daily gridlock philosophically. Picture young women in designer jeans lined up for a new Western flick; passing by are matrons robed to the ankles, bound for evening prayer. This is a city where you can span five centuries simply by crossing the street, moving from the distant era of the sultans' seraglios to the ultra modernity of a sleek cocktail bar. Skyscrapers and mosques jostle for primacy, physically as well as sociologically.

Outside many houses of worship, rows of black shoes are often lined up. Wait

### BRIDGING THE OLD AND NEW TOWNS

There's a story that goes like this: Two families living on opposite shores used to meet in the evenings for a game of cards. Neither much liked crossing the Galata pontoon bridge after nightfall, so they took turns, saying "Tomorrow is your night to bridge." This became the name of the famous card game.

These days, traveling from the historic heart of Sultanahmet to the modern hub of "new" Istanbul—across the Galata Bridge—is only a trip of two miles, though it often seems like light-years. In some ways the timeless and the trendy parts of Istanbul rarely merge. In certain circles, it's a mark of distinction for cosmopolitans living in "new" Beyoğlu to never venture into old districts like Sultanahmet.

a few minutes and you might see their owners emerge in stocking feet, most wearing business suits. More than a few of these men have MBAs from universities in the United States. Watch how many whip out a cell phone as they ease back into their Prada loafers.

When the rattle of taxi traffic is dimmed by the voices of the *müezzins* calling the faithful to prayer, you remember that Istanbul is not just another metropolis; it's a city whose Islamic heritage is ever present. Such contrasts are part of the makeup of daily life for Istanbulites, many of whom juggle aspects of ancient and modern life just as they cross daily from one continent to the other. This is one of the most unique cities in the world; don't be surprised if you catch yourself wondering what continent you're on, or what century you're in.

Top left, Contemplation on the Bosphorus
Top right, Shopping on Istiklal Caddesi
Bottom left, View from Galata Tower
Bottom right, woman wearing headscarf

## ISTANBUL UNVEILED

In this city you can often tell what's on women's minds by looking at what's on their heads. Though the reasons why Turkish women wear different forms of clothing are complex, there are some general trends. Traditionally, most women wore a loosely tied headscarf called a *başörtüsü*. But in recent times, the influence of political Islam has led many religious urban women to adopt what some in secular circles rather disparagingly call the *türban*, a colorful headscarf, held in place by a clip under the chin and tightly tied so that no hair shows. Some of these women take the Islamic prescription towards modesty further and also wear a knee- or ankle-length overcoat called a *pardesü* A small minority of women in extremely religious circles wear the *çarşaf*, a floor-length black robe that veils their hair and envelops their entire body.

# WHERE PAST IS PROLOGUE:
## ISTANBUL'S GREAT ERAS

Thanks to the Greeks, Romans, Byzantines, Crusaders, Venetians, and Turks, Istanbul has been introducing new aspects of civilization for more than two thousand years. The comeback city, Istanbul has reinvented itself more times than Madonna. Here are the three main eras of its past.

### BYZANTIUM: THE "NEW ROME"

Originally settled by Megaran Greeks in the 7th century BC—it was said to be founded by a man called Byzas in 658 BC—Istanbul was first known as Byzantium until AD 330, when the Roman emperor Constantine moved the capital of his empire here; his minions, not surprisingly, began calling it Constantinople. Constantine converted to Christianity and ushered in a major building campaign for his *Nova Roma* (New Rome).

**Aya Sofya.** Completed in the year 537, the Hagia Sophia (Aya Sofya in Turkish) became the central church of Christendom and the major inspiration for the mosques of Islam. It was designed by the mathematician Anthemius and the scientist Isidorus. Using innovative architectural designs (that weren't always successful), they managed to create a massive dome that is 106 feet in diameter, which was unrivaled until St. Peter's Basilica was built in the 17th century. Mehmet the Conqueror converted the church into a mosque in 1453, and the four minarets were added by succeeding sultans. With the big middle dome resting on two half-domes, Aya Sofya has awed the faithful, and everyone else, too. It's still one of the most prominent buildings on the Istanbul skyline.

**Yerebatan Sarnıcı.** An almost churchlike peacefulness is found in this immense subterranean reservoir, first excavated by Constantine and then completed by Emperor Justinian during the 6th century. Built to keep a steady supply of fresh water for the city in case of a siege, it has more than 330 marble columns rising from the water. It's a wonderfully atmospheric place to visit, especially with the classical music playing in the background of the dimly lit caverns. On hot summer days, it's also a cool respite. See if you can spot the fish swimming below.

Mosaic, Aya Sofya

Aya Sofya

Medusa head pedestal, Yerebatan Sarnıcı

Right: Yerebatan Sarnıcı

**DID YOU KNOW?**

Before its 1987 restoration, the atmospheric Yerebatan Sarnıcı, also known as the Sunken Palace, could be explored only by boat. James Bond rowed through in *From Russia with Love.*

## OTTOMAN EMPIRE: TURKISH DELIGHT

As the seat of Christendom for the next millennium, Constantinople became the object of Ottoman conquest, which was finally achieved on May 29, 1453 by Sultan Mehmet II. Part of his "Islamization" of the city was transforming Aya Sofya into the Great Mosque. Succeeding sultans then lavished the city with mosques and palaces, many built by Sinan (c.1490–1588), architect to Süleyman the Magnificent.

**Topkapı Sarayı.** This sprawling complex was the main palace of the sultans. Both the nerve center of the Ottoman Empire and a fabulous treasure house, it still boasts riches encompassing the jewels of the Treasury and holy relics from the Prophet Muhammad. In a separate wing, visitors cannot help but imagine what pleasures were indulged in the secret world of the Harem.

Topkapı Sarayı

**Blue Mosque.** A stone mountain of domes, half-domes, and minarets, the Sultan Ahmet Camii was built during the early 17th century by Ottoman ruler Ahmet I, who wanted to prove that Islam could produce a building as impressive as Christendom's Aya Sofya. Inside, thousands of blue tiles create a dazzling symphony of arabesque patterns.

## BELLE EPOQUE: WESTERNIZATION

In the 18th century, military defeats led Ottoman rulers to look to Europe for ways to revitalize their society. Court officials returned from Paris raving about Versailles, and the ornate "Ottoman Baroque" style was born. Influenced by new commercial ties between France and Turkey in the 19th century, the Grand Rue de Péra (today's Istiklal Caddesi) was touted as the "Champs-Elysées of the Orient" and a flurry of Belle Epoque cafés set the city's sophisticated style.

Dolmabahçe Sarayı

**Dolmabahçe Sarayı.** Overlooking the Bosphorus, this 1856 palace was built in storybook Turkish-Indian Baroque style. A combination of a Moorish castle and an Italian Baroque palazzo, it flaunted more than 30,000 pounds of gold, an opulence that expressed the resolve of the sultans to sustain the grandeur of their declining empire in the heyday of European imperialism.

**Sirkeci Station.** With its pink marble façade, stained-glass windows, and exotic Seljuk-style archways, Istanbul's grand train station (1890) was the last stop of the Orient Express.

Sirkeci Station

Right: Blue Mosque

## DID YOU KNOW?

Sultan Ahmet commissioned this grand mosque, nicknamed the Blue Mosque. It's said that he was so enthusiastic about the project that, at times, he worked alongside the hired laborers.

# ISTANBUL NOW

Istanbul today is remaking itself—still—a process that has continued for several millennia. The city is constantly evolving, and three new landmarks prove it. They can be experienced in a day.

From the Four Seasons Hotel, take the tramway at the Sultanahmet stop towards Kabataş. Get off at the Tophane stop to find the Istanbul Modern on the Bosphorus shore.

From the museum, take a taxi or bus up the coastal road along the Bosphorus to Reina in Kuruçeşme.

**Four Seasons Hotel Sultanahmet.** Istanbulites rejoiced in 1996 when the infamous 19th-century Sultanahmet Prison—near the Topkapı Palace—was transformed into a luxurious Four Seasons Hotel. What a change from 1978, when Turkey's tourist industry virtually collapsed as Oliver Stone's *Midnight Express* premiered and revealed hell-on-earth to be a Turkish prison. Where criminals once did hard time, now off-duty screen stars chill out in suites decorated in opulent Ottoman style.

Four Seasons

**Istanbul Modern.** A symbol of the new Turkey, the country's first museum of modern art is housed in an old warehouse. Set next to the Karaköy maritime terminal, this museum has been extolled as a gateway between Turks and "the West." Part of a vast industrial space, à la London's Tate Modern, the museum's soaring halls house everything from 19th-century Orientalist masters to avant-garde videographers. But thanks to the nearby 16th-century Kılıç Ali Pasha Mosque and the views of the Old City across the water (best seen from the trendy café), historic Istanbul is never far away.

Istanbul Modern

**Reina.** Farther up the Bosphorus, the Kuruçeşme neighborhood is home to one of Istanbul's most famous nightclub venues: Reina, the see-and-be-seen hangout of the city's pretty people. Perched directly on the water's edge, the space has an open-air section that opens each summer with temporary outposts of the city's trendiest restaurants, while the nightclub part is open year round. Take the pulse of the fashionably dressed crowd while choosing from cuisines that range from Turkish to sushi, then stay to dance the night away under the stars.

# . . . . AND TOMORROW

"The hustle and bustle and energy of Istiklal as the trolley glides past."—photo by salexg, Fodors.com member

Istanbul has always been a city of startling juxtapositions. In the future, however, the constant pull between East and West, between modern and traditional, may create an underlying tension that will erupt to confound Turkish society and politics.

Long famed as the city of carpets, coffee, and Arabian Nights clichés, Istanbul is increasingly international in flavor. Dealers of rare kilims now compete with stores whose rugs are quite possibly milled in China, and the ever-burgeoning Starbucks is busy weaning customers away from traditional Turkish coffee.

With Ali Baba about to be elbowed out of the way by Burger King, it's little wonder that the Nobel Prize–winning Turkish novelist Orhan Pamuk has made the leitmotiv of *hüzün,* or melancholic nostalgia, the theme of his work. As Istanbul makes the leap into the 21st century, will the city of myth and legend be left behind?

## WHEN CULTURES COLLIDE

The onslaught of immigrants—some 50,000 people are said to relocate to Istanbul every month from the former Soviet Union and eastern Turkey—is changing the face, and psyche, of the city. While glossy photos focus on the skyscrapers being built in the business district, Anatolian immigrants erect *gecekondus*—homes "put up overnight"—in the outlying districts of the city. These working-class settlers have brought with them a wave of conservative Islam. For those who are intent on Turkey joining the EU, the rising conservatism means falling hopes.

Tolerance definitely has a place in current Turkish society, and most Istanbullus take pride in pluralism: they like to point to the famous mosaics commissioned by Emperor Justinian of Christ and the Virgin Mary that still glow on the walls of Aya Sofya, the church that was transformed into a mosque (today officially a museum)—truly a lesson in tolerance. On the other hand, this is the city where the crescent and the cross have battled many times.

**Naval Museum** (*Deniz Müzesi*). Founded in 1897 and located here since 1961, Istanbul's Naval Museum is set to open a huge, state-of-the-art, new building on the water's edge in mid-2012 that will enable it to fully showcase its vast collection of Ottoman-era vessels and maritime paraphernalia. The most impressive are the *kayıks* (caiques)—long, slim wooden boats rowed by dozens of oarsmen, which served as the primary mode of royal transportation for several hundred years. These graceful boats are decorated with intricate carvings covered with gold leaf and each has an equally ornate pavilion that was built for the sultan or his wife. Other highlights of the collection include a 17th-century Ottoman warship and a monstrous 23-ton cannon built for Sultan Selim the Grim. The museum's original building has remained open and will continue to house smaller artifacts—mostly ship models, paintings, and old maps—that give a good sense of the Ottoman Empire's onetime supremacy at sea. In the square just beside the museum are the tomb (usually locked) and a statue of Hayreddin Pasha, or "Barbarossa," the famous admiral of the empire's fleet in the Ottoman glory days of the early 16th century. ⊠ *Beşiktaş Cad., Beşiktaş* ☎ *212/327–4346* 🖾 *4 TL* ⏱ *Wed.–Fri. 9–5, weekend 9–7.*

**Yıldız Parkı.** The wooded slopes of Yıldız Parkı once formed part of the great forest that covered the European shore of the Bosphorus from the Golden Horn to the Black Sea. In the waning years of the Ottoman Empire, the park was the private garden of the Çırağan Sarayı, and the women of the harem would occasionally be allowed to visit. First the gardeners would be removed, then the eunuchs would lead the women across the footbridge from the palace and along the avenue to the upper gardens. Secluded from prying eyes, they would sit in the shade or wander beneath the acacias, maples, and cypresses, filling their baskets with flowers and figs. Today the park is still hauntingly beautiful, particularly in spring when the flowers bloom, and in fall when the leaves of the deciduous trees change color. At the top of the park is the relatively modest Swiss-style Yıldız Şale (Yıldız Chalet), where Sultan Abdülhamid II (ruled 1876–1909), who distinguished himself as the last despot of the Ottoman Empire, spent most of his time (he also lived in the Çırağan and Dolmabahçe palaces). Visiting dignitaries from Kaiser Wilhelm to Charles de Gaulle and Margaret Thatcher have stayed here as well. The chalet is often blissfully empty of other tourists, which makes a visit all the more pleasurable. Also in the park is the Malta Köşkü, a late 19th-century Ottoman pavilion that now houses a restaurant with period decor and views of the Bosphorus. ⊠ *Çırağan Cad.* ☎ *212/261–8460 for park, 212/259–4570 for chalet* 🖾 *Chalet: 4 TL* ⏱ *Park: daily 9–9; chalet: Tues. and Wed. and Fri.–Sun. 9–5 in summer, 9–4 in winter.*

# THE BOSPHORUS

Whether explored in person or seen from the vantage point of a boat on the water, the Bosphorus shores are home to some of the prettiest parts of the city. Both sides of the strait are dotted with palaces, fortresses, and waterfront neighborhoods and fishing villages lined with the old wooden summer homes, called *yalıs* (waterside mansions), which were built for the city's wealthier residents in the Ottoman era. As you cruise up the Bosphorus, you'll have the chance to disembark at some of these waterside enclaves for a stroll.

**Anadolu Kavağı.** Anadolu Kavağı, at the upper end of the Asian shore, is the final destination on the full Bosphorus cruises. A pretty little fishing village, it gets enough tourists to have a wide range of seafood restaurants, waffle stands, and ice-cream shops. The main attraction is the dramatically situated **Byzantine Castle**, a 15-minute walk uphill from the village past more restaurants and cafés. The hill was once the site of a temple to Zeus Ourios (god of the favoring winds), which dates back, legend has it, to the days when Jason passed by in search of the Golden Fleece. The castle, built by the Byzantines and expanded by their Genoese allies, is today in a fairly ruined state, but it's worth climbing up to it for the spectacular views over the upper Bosphorus to the blustery Black Sea.

**Arnavutköy.** This picturesque neighborhood just below Bebek is a pleasant place for a stroll. The waterfront is taken up by a row of beautiful 19th-century wooden *yalıs*, some of which now house fish restaurants. Up the hill from the water, narrow streets are lined with more old wooden houses, some with trailing vines.

**Bebek.** Bebek is one of Istanbul's most fashionable suburbs and is especially popular with the affluent expatriate boating set, thanks to the area's pretty, natural habor. The neighborhood has a number of upmarket cafés and restaurants and a few boutiques; there's also a small, shaded public park on the waterfront. The stretches of coastline both north and south of Bebek are perfect for a promenade. (Bebek is about 20–30 minutes by taxi from central Istanbul.)

**NEED A BREAK?**

**Mini Dondurma.** Mini Dondurma is a tiny ice-cream shop on Bebek's main street that has repeatedly been rated the best in town since it opened back in 1968. Their 22 flavors include the distinctive *güllü lokum* (rose-flavored Turkish delight) ice cream. The shop is open March through November. ✉ *Cevdet Paşa Cad. 38A, Bebek* ☎ *212/257–1070.*

**Beylerbeyi Sarayı** (*Beylerbeyi Palace*). Built as a summer residence for Sultan Abdülaziz in 1865, Beylerbeyi, on the Asian shore, is a bit like a mini-Dolmabahçe that incorporates a similarly eclectic mix of European and Turkish styles but is smaller, less grandiose, and has more of a personal feel. Beylerbeyi boasts ornately painted ceilings, Baccarat crystal chandeliers, gold-topped marble columns, and intricately carved wooden furniture; the central hall has a white-marble fountain and a stairway wide enough for a regiment. The magnolia-shaded palace grounds are also pleasant, while two waterfront bathing pavilions (one was for men, the other for women) stand out for their bizarrely fanciful architecture. You must join a tour to see the palace. ✉ *Çayırbaşı Durağı, Beylerbeyi* ☎ *216/321–9320* 💷 *10 TL* ☉ *Tues and Wed. and Fri.–Sun. 9:30–5 in summer, 9:30–4 in winter.*

**Emirgan.** The quiet suburb of Emirgan is best known for its large, attractive public park, **Emirgan Korusu**—formerly an estate owned by the

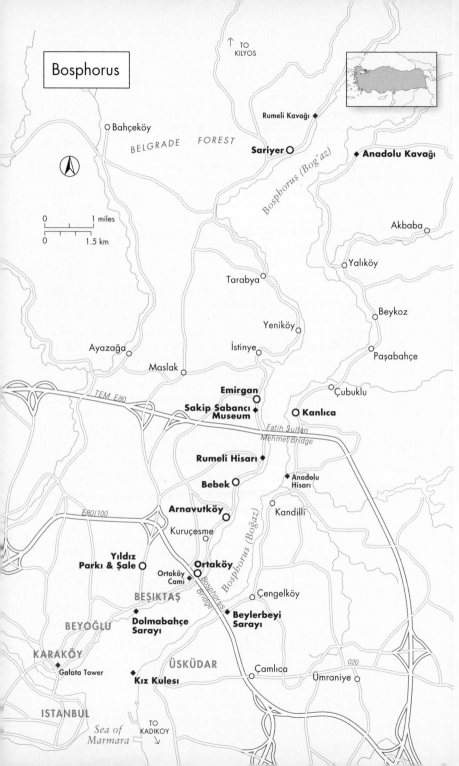

**CLOSE UP**

# Planning a Bosphorus Day Cruise

This ferry is leaving the Eminönü docks near Sultanahmet to cross the Bosphorus.

One of the most pleasant experiences in Istanbul—and an easy way to escape the chaos of the city—is a trip up the Bosphorus by ferry. There are several cruises that leave from the Eminönü docks in the Old City. If you want to go all the way to the mouth of the Black Sea, and have the time to make a day of it, you can take a "full Bosphorus cruise." These boats zigzag up the Bosphorus with set stops, arriving in the middle of the day for a three-hour break at either **Rumeli Kavağı** (European side) or **Anadolu Kavağı (Asian side),** two fishing villages with fortresses at the opening to the Black Sea. Then they zigzag back down to Eminönü. Operated by the Şehir Hatları, the ferries depart daily from the first quay on the right-hand side of the Galata Bridge (look for the sign that says "Boğaz İskelesi") at 10:35, noon, and 1:35 in the summer months (approximately mid-June to mid-September) and at 10:35 in the winter. A one-way ticket is 15 TL, while the round-trip costs 25 TL.

If your time is more limited, you can take a short cruise with no stops,

lasting two hours or less, which goes up approximately to the second Bosphorus bridge before turning around. Two private companies operate frequent daily trips: Turyol, on the left-hand side of Galata Bridge, has a set timetable (12 TL), while Boğaziçi Yol Tur, on the right-hand side, operates in a more ad hoc fashion (10 TL).

Alternatively, several commuter ferries leave from the Boğaz İskelesi between around 5 and 7 pm every day (more frequently on weekdays than weekends) and zigzag up the Bosphorus for a mere 2 TL. Note that taking one of these means catching a bus or taxi back later, as there are no return ferries until the morning. A number of buses run up and down both sides; most useful on the European side are the 25E (Kabataş to Sarıyer) and 25T (Taksim to Sarıyer). On the Asian side, several buses run from Üsküdar past Beylerbeyi, Anadolu Hisarı, and Kanlıca to Beykoz, from where the 15A continues up to Anadolu Kavağı.

Khedive of Egypt—which has flower gardens, a small pond, walking paths, and picnic areas. Three 19th-century wooden pavilions in the park have been restored and house restaurants and cafés. During Istanbul's annual Tulip Festival in April, visitors flock to Emirgan Korusu for its striking flower displays—in 2010, over a million tulips of dozens of different varieties were planted in this park alone. The flower, which take its name from the Turkish word *tülbend* (turban), was most likely introduced to Europe in the late 16th century via the Ottoman Empire, setting off the famous "tulip craze" in the Netherlands. Emirgan is also where the **Sakıp Sabancı Müzesi** is located—worth a visit if the temporary exhibit catches your fancy.

**Kanlıca.** Just north of the second Bosphorus bridge, the village-turned-suburb of Kanlıca has been famous for its delicious yogurt for at least 300 years, and small restaurants around the plane tree in the square by the quay serve this treat. Nearby, white 19th-century wooden villas line the waterfront. Kanlıca is the first stop on the Asian shore on the full Bosphorus cruise.

**Ortaköy.** The charming neighborhood of Ortaköy is popular with both locals and visitors, and a lovely spot to spend a summer afternoon or evening. Restaurants and cafés are clustered around the small square on the waterfront, which is dominated by the iconic silhouette of **Ortaköy Camii**, an elegant 19th-century Ottoman mosque designed by the same Armenian architects who built the Dolmabahçe Palace. The mosque is perched directly overlooking the water, with the imposing sight of the Bosphorus Bridge (built 1973) looming behind it. The narrow, cobblestoned surrounding streets are lined with stalls selling jewelry, scarves, trinkets, and small antique items, with a full-fledged crafts fair held on Sundays. Ortaköy is also considered the best place in Istanbul to try ⇨ *the street food called kumpir* (basically giant baked potatoes for which you can choose all sorts of fillings): look for the row of about a dozen food stands all competing for customers' attention.

☾ **Rumeli Hisarı** (*Castle of Europe*). Built on a hill overlooking the water, Rumeli Hisarı is the best preserved of all the fortresses on the Bosphorus and well worth a visit. Constructed in just four months in 1452, these eccentric-looking fortifications were ordered built by Mehmet the Conqueror directly across from Anadolu Hisarı, at the narrowest point of the strait. This allowed the Ottomans to take control of the waterway, and Mehmet and his troops conquered Constantinople the following year. The real fun here is in climbing on and around the towers and crenellated walls, which offer fabulous views of the Bosphorus and the nearby Fatih Sultan Mehmet Bridge. ✉ *Yahya Kemal Cad. 42, Rumelihisarı* ☎ *212/263–5305* 🎟 *3 TL* ⊙ *Thurs.–Tues. 9–4:30.*

**Sakıp Sabancı Museum** (*Sakıp Sabancı Museum*). The Sakıp Sabancı Museum opened in 2002 and quickly established itself as one of Istanbul's premier private museums, thanks to its world-class exhibits and stunning location in a historic villa overlooking the water in the leafy suburb of Emirgan. The permanent collection includes an excellent display of late-19th-century Orientalist and early Republican Turkish paintings, rare examples of Ottoman calligraphy, and antique furnishings such as exquisite Sevres vases, all from the private collection of the industrialist Sabancı family. The biggest draws, though, are the temporary installations—of a caliber equal to that seen at top museums around the world—which range from retrospectives on major artists like Rodin and Picasso to exhibits on Anatolian archaeology, Turkish painting, and masterpieces of Islamic art. Housed on the museum grounds, Müzedechanga Restaurant is a foodie destination in itself. Check the museum's Web site to see if the current temporary exhibit is of interest. ⊠ *Sakıp Sabancı Cad. 42, Emirgan* ☎ *212/277–2200* ⊕ *muze. sabanciuniv.edu* 🎫 *10 TL* ⊙ *Tues. and Thurs.-Sun. 10–6, Wed. 10–8.*

**Sarıyer.** One of the northernmost settlements on the European shore of the Bosphorus, Sarıyer, centered on a small harbor and backed by a row of seafood restaurants, still has the feel of a fishing village. As you stroll along the Bosphorus with the hustle of the big city at arm's length, you'll see majestic old *yalıs*—some of which are beautifully kept up, and others that have been abandoned and are in a sad state of deterioration. Sarıyer is one of the stops on the full Bosphorus cruises that leave from Eminönü and a nice place for a fish lunch.

# THE ASIAN SHORE

Spread out along the shoreline of the lower Bosphorus and the Sea of Marmara, the main residential districts on the Asian side have few "sights" as such but offer a pleasant change of pace from the faster tempo of the European side—as well as a welcome escape from the tourist crowds. Üsküdar has several Ottoman imperial mosques and presents a slice of Istanbul life that is more traditional than what visitors generally see on the European side. Farther down the coast, Kadıköy has a youthful, relaxed vibe; the pedestrian-only area off the waterfront and a lively nightlife are among its top draws. From Kadıköy, a short taxi or *dolmuş* ride takes you to the beginning of Bağdat Caddesi, or "Baghdad Avenue," a 6-km-long (3.7-mi-long) boulevard that is the Asian side's ritziest street, lined with elegant apartment buildings, upscale designer boutiques, and trendy restaurants. The avenue gets increasingly posh as you get farther away from Kadıköy and closer to Suadiye and Caddebostan. While this fashionable enclave is not that different from upscale districts in numerous other cosmopolitan cities, it's a nice venue for strolling and people-watching.

**Kadıköy.** Though there's no visible evidence of its beginnings as the ancient Greek colony of Chalcedon, the relaxed, suburban neighborhood of Kadıköy is a pleasant area to explore on foot. As you approach by ferry, look for the beautiful neoclassical-style Haydarpaşa train station, built out over the water on piles at the north end of the harbor. Built in 1908, the terminal is one of the most notable pieces of architecture on the Asian side and a classic Istanbul landmark. You can get off here, at the tiled Ottoman-era quay, or stay on the boat for a few more minutes until it reaches Kadıköy proper.

The area just up from the Kadıköy dock, to the right of busy Söğütlü Çeşme Caddesi, is known as the Çarşı, or "market"—a grid of narrow, pedestrian-only lanes filled with shops, cafés, nightlife venues, and a few modern churches. Güneşlibahçe Sokak, home to an assortment of fish restaurants and some bars, is particularly lively. Several streets up and farther to the right, Kadife Sokak, dubbed Barlar Sokağı, or "bars street," is the center of Kadıköy's nightlife, lined with small, wooden rowhouses occupied by bars with a casual, laid-back vibe. General Asım Gündüz Caddesi, two streets beyond, has branches of well-known Turkish and international clothing stores, movie theaters, and some eateries. If you come on Tuesday, head left down the street toward the bronze sculpture of a bull, where there begins a lively, open-air street market, mostly selling food and clothes. A tiny nostalgic tram runs in a clockwise direction up General Asım Gündüz, from where it loops down to the lovely waterfront neighborhood of Moda before stopping at the Kadıköy dock. If you've come this far on foot, it's nice to ride the tram back to the dock.

**Kız Kulesi** (*Maiden's Tower*). Fortified since Byzantine times, this little islet off the Asian shore guarded the busy shipping lanes and, now, restored and lit up, it's the star of the lower Bosphorus. The name Leander's Tower, as it was known in ancient times, associates the island with the legend of Leander, who was said to have swum the strait each night guided by the lamp of his lover, Hero—though this myth in fact took place in the Dardanelles to the south. The Turkish name "Maiden's Tower" comes from a legend associated with several offshore castles: as the story goes, a princess is placed on an island after a prophecy that she will die of a snakebite, but it happens anyway, when a snake comes ashore in a basket of fruit. The current tower, which dates to the 18th century, now houses an expensive but not all that impressive café and restaurant. Boats ferry visitors at regular intervals from Kabataş on the European side and Salacak (near Üsküdar) on the Asian shore. ☎ *216/342–4747* ⊕ *www.kizkulesi.com.tr* ✉ *No admission fee; round-trip boat fee 5 TL from Salacak, 7 TL from Kabataş for daytime visitors; boat transfers free in evening for restaurant and bar customers (reservations essential)* ⊙ *Daily 9 am–6:45 pm for visitors; 8 pm–midnight for dinner and bar.*

**Üsküdar.** One of the oldest inhabited areas on the Asian shore, Üsküdar takes its name from the 7th-century BC settlement of Scutari, though nothing now remains of that ancient town. Today, Üsküdar is a conservative residential neighborhood with a handful of noteworthy Ottoman mosques. The waterfront is set to change dramatically with the opening of the long-awaited Marmaray, a rail tunnel under the Bosphorus that will transport passengers from Üsküdar to Sirkeci in just four minutes (the expected completion date is late 2013). The ferry landing is dominated by Sinan's pretty, if somewhat dark, Mihrimah Sultan Camii, also known as the İskele Camii (built 1548). The large Yeni Valide Camii from 1710 and another Sinan mosque, the small, beautifully situated Şemsi Paşa Camii, are a short walk south. Sinan's Atık Valide Camii from 1583, the most architecturally significant mosque in the district, is a 15-minute mostly uphill walk from the waterfront on Hakimiyeti Milliye Caddesi and then on Dr. Fahri Atabey Caddesi. Another couple hundred yards up and to the left is the 17th-century Çinili Cami (Tiled

Mosque), which has splendid İznik tiles but is often kept locked for this reason.

# WHERE TO EAT

Istanbul is a food lover's town and restaurants abound, from humble kebab joints to fancy fish venues, with lots of excellent options in between. Istanbullus take their food seriously, holding establishments to a very high standard; the places that cater mostly to tourists are the ones that might let their standards slip.

Owing to its location on the Bosphorus, which connects the Black Sea to the Sea of Marmara, Istanbul is famous for seafood. A classic Istanbul meal, usually eaten at one of the city's rollicking *meyhanes* (literally "drinking places"), starts off with a wide selection of tapas-style small appetizers called *mezes* and then moves on to a main course of grilled fish, all of it accompanied by the anise-flavored spirit rakı, Turkey's national drink. The waiter will generally bring a tray over to your table to show off the day's *mezes* and you simply point to what you'd like. Note that the portions you get are usually larger than the samples shown on the tray, so don't over-order; you can always select a second—or third—round later. When it comes to the main course, fish can be expensive, so check prices and ask what's in season before ordering.

Although Istanbul's dining scene, though diverse, was once mostly limited to Turkish cooking, a new generation of chefs is successfully fusing local dishes with more international ingredients and flavors. Some, trained in the United States and Europe, are bringing home the contemporary cooking techniques they've learned abroad, and the result is a kind of nouvelle Turkish cuisine. Over the past few years, a handful of restaurants have opened at which the chef-owner entirely defines the vision and personality of the venue—though this may be old hat in Europe, it represents an exciting new trend in Istanbul.

The Sultanahmet area might have most of the city's major sights and many hotels, but it's lacking in good dining options, save for a few standouts. You'll have better luck if you head across the Golden Horn. The lively Beyoğlu district has everything from hole-in-the-walls serving delicious home cooking to some of Istanbul's sleekest restaurants. Or head to some of the small, charming neighborhoods along the Bosphorus, which are famous for their fish restaurants; with a few exceptions, these establishments tend to be more upscale and expensive.

Since Istanbullus love to go out, reservations are essential at most of the city's better restaurants. In summer, many establishments move their dining areas outdoors, and reservations become even more important if you want to snag a coveted outside table. For the most part, dining is casual, although locals enjoy dressing smartly when they're out. You may feel terribly underdressed if you show up in a restaurant dressed in shorts and a T-shirt, even in summer.

Despite Islamic proscriptions against alcohol, beer, wine, and the local spirit rakı are widely available, and at more upscale venues you can also find cocktails. Because of high taxes, however, alcoholic drinks—particularly anything imported—will usually be considerably more expensive than in North America or Europe. The national lager Efes is the most widely available beer; venues may carry two or three other domestic and international labels, but don't expect a wide selection. Yeni Rakı, a state-run monopoly until not long ago, has remained the most popular rakı brand despite a recent proliferation of new companies producing the spirit. Wine consumption in Turkey has traditionally lagged far behind that of beer and rakı, but in recent years that's been slowly changing as the quality of local wines has started to improve. The local wine industry is still in its fledgling stages compared to in other parts of the world, but there are some very drinkable domestic wines on the market, most priced at only a fraction of what you'd pay for an imported label. Turkish wines are made from foreign grapes as well as indigenous varietals, of which the most noteworthy are the reds Öküzgözü, Boğazkere, and Kalecik Karası and the whites Emir and Narince.

During the Islamic holy month of Ramadan—which falls in the summer through the year 2015—restaurants that cater primarily to tourists, and most venues in cosmopolitan parts of Istanbul like Beyoğlu, continue to operate normally. (In more traditional neighborhoods some restaurants close altogether or change their hours of operation.) In recent years, it has become increasingly popular to go to restaurants for *iftar*—the evening meal that breaks the daily fast—instead of having it in the home, as was traditionally done.

| WHAT IT COSTS IN U.S. DOLLARS | | | | | |
|---|---|---|---|---|---|
| | ¢ | $ | $$ | $$$ | $$$$ |
| Restaurants | under $10 | $10–$15 | $16–$22 | $23–$30 | over $30 |

Prices are per person for a main course at dinner or the equivalent for a meal of several small dishes.

## ASIAN SHORE

$$  
MIDDLE EASTERN  
✕ **Cercis Murat Konağı.** On the waterfront in posh Suadiye, the Istanbul outpost of the famous Cercis Murat Konağı restaurant in Mardin offers an equally remarkable culinary experience. Regularly changing menus draw from southeastern Turkey's rich, multiethnic heritage, featuring dishes from traditional Arab, Kurdish, and Assyrian cuisine that are rarely found in Istanbul restaurants. Come with a big appetite to taste everything from the authentic *mezes* and grilled meats to desserts like candied tomatoes with salep ice cream; there is also housemade red wine and signature Turkish coffee. Owner Ebru Baybara Demir, who hails from one of Mardin's Arab families, spent years researching her menu and employs an all-female kitchen staff from the region. ✉ *Yazmacı Tahir Sok. 22, Suadiye* ☎ *216/410–9222* ⊕ *www.cercismurat.com* ⌚ *Reservations essential* ✛ *1:6H.*

¢  
TURKISH  
Fodor's Choice  
★  
✕ **Çiya.** Three branches on the same street comprise one of Istanbul's most popular foodie destinations, and the reputation is well deserved. Chef-owner Musa Dağdeviren, who hails from the southeastern Turkish

# BEST BETS FOR
# FOR ISTANBUL DINING

With so many restaurants to choose from, how to decide? Fodor's writers and editors have chosen their favorites, by price, cuisine, and experience, in the lists below.

**Fodor's Choice★**

Çiya, ¢, p. 98
Giritli, $$$$, p. 110
Khorasani, $, p. 111
Lokanta Maya, $$, p. 106
Mikla, $$$$, p. 106
Münferit, $$, p. 106
Sofyalı 9, $$, p. 106

## By Price

**¢**

Antiochia, p. 103
Çiya, p. 98
Fıccın, p. 103

**$**

Adem Baba, p. 107
Karaköy Lokantası, p. 105
Khorasani, p. 111

**$$**

Cercis Murat Konağı, p. 98
Lokanta Maya, p. 106
Sofyalı 9, p. 106

**$$$**

Münferit, p. 106
Müzedechanga, p. 108

**$$$$**

Giritli, p. 110
Mikla, p. 106

## By Cuisine

**ECLECTIC**

The House Café, $$, p. 108
Istanbul Modern Cafe, $$, p. 105
Lokanta Maya, $$, p. 106
Mikla, $$$$, p. 106
Mimolett, $$$$, p. 113
Müzedechanga, $$$, p. 108

**KEBABS**

Antiochia, ¢, p. 103
Çiya, ¢, p. 98
Hamdi Et Lokantası, $, p. 109
Khorasani, $, p. 111
Zübeyir Ocakbaşı, $, p. 107

**MEZES**

Karaköy Lokantası, $, p. 105
Meze by Lemon Tree, $$, p. 106
Münferit, $$, p. 106
Sofyalı 9, $$, p. 106

**REGIONAL SPECIALTIES**

Cercis Murat Konağı, $$, p. 98
Çiya, ¢, p. 98
Fıccın, ¢, p. 103
Khorasani, $, p. 111
Rumeli Café Restaurant, $, p. 111

**SEAFOOD**

Adem Baba, $, p. 107
Giritli, $$$$, p. 110
Karaköy Lokantası, $, p. 105
Rumelihisarı İskele, $$$$, p. 109
Sofyalı 9, $$, p. 106
Sultanahmet Fish House, $$, p. 111

**TRADITIONAL OTTOMAN**

Asitane, $$, p. 110
Tuğra, $$$$, p. 109

## By Experience

**FINE DINING**

Asitane, $$, p. 110
Mikla, $$$$, p. 106
Mimolett, $$$$, p. 113
Seasons, $$$$, p. 111
Tuğra, $$$$, p. 109

**GREAT VIEW**

Banyan, $$$, p. 107
Hamdi Et Lokantası, $, p. 109
Istanbul Modern Cafe, $$, p. 105
Mikla, $$$$, p. 106
Müzedechanga, $$$, p. 108
Rumelihisarı İskele, $$$$, p. 109

**OUTDOOR DINING**

Asitane, $$, p. 110
Çınaraltı, $, p. 107
The House Café, $$, p. 108
Müzedechanga, $$$, p. 108

**ROMANTIC**

Banyan, $$$, p. 107
Mikla, $$$$, p. 106
Mimolett, $$$$, p. 113
Rumelihisarı İskele, $$$$, p. 109

**TRENDY VIBE**

Antiochia, ¢, p. 103
The House Café, $$, p. 108
Istanbul Modern Cafe, $$, p. 105
Kafe Ara, $, p. 105
Lokanta Maya, $$, p. 106
Meze by Lemon Tree, $$, p. 106
Münferit, $$, p. 106

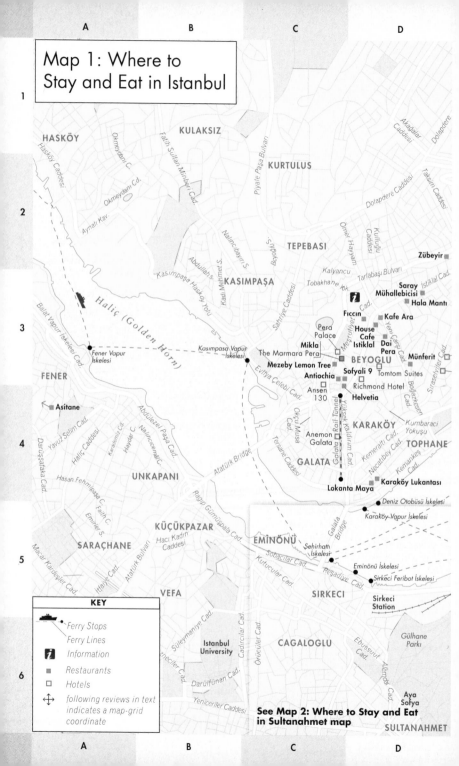

# Map 1: Where to Stay and Eat in Istanbul

HASKÖY

KULAKSIZ

KURTULUS

Hasköy Caddesi

Okmeydanı C.

Fatih Sultan Minberi Cad.

Piyale Paşa Bulvarı

Dolapdere Caddesi

Taksim Caddesi

Aynalı Kav.

Akadalar Caddesi

Dolapdere

Kasımpaşa Hasköy Yolu

Kad. Mehmet S.

Abdullah s.

Nalincibayırı S.

Beyoğlu

Kuluğlu Caddesi

Ömer Hayyam

TEPEBASI

KASIMPAŞA

Sahriye Caddesi

Kalyancu

Tobakhane Jok.

Tarlabaşı Bulvarı

İstiklal Cad.

Zübeyir

Saray
Mühallebicisi

Hala Mantı

Ficcin

Kafe Ara

Pera
Palace

House
Cafe
Istiklal

Dai
Pera

Mikla

BEYOGLU

Münferit

The Marmara Pera

Mezeby Lemon Tree

Sofyali 9

Tomtom Suites

Antiochia

Ansen
130

Richmond Hotel

Helvetia

Yüksek Kaldırım Cad.

KARAKÖY

Kumbaracı
Yokuşu

TOPHANE

Evliya Celebi Cad.

Okçu Musa Cad.

Boğazkesen Cad.

Sıraserviler Cad.

Kasımpaşa Vapur
İskelesi

Halıç (Golden Horn)

Fener Vapur
İskelesi

FENER

Asitane

Abdülezel paşa Cad.

Nalincemal C.

Yavuz Selim Caddesi

Haydar C.

Haliç Caddesi

Karaosmanız Cad.

Darüşşafaka Cad.

Hasan Fehmipaşa C. Fatih C.

Eminler C.

UNKAPANI

Atatürk Bridge

Tersane Caddesi

Anemon
Galata

GALATA

Lokanta Maya

Karaköy Lukantası

Necatibey Cad.

Kemankes
Cad.

Kemeraltı Cad.

Deniz Otobüsü İskelesi

Karaköy Vapur İskelesi

Ragıp Gümüşpala Cad.

KÜÇÜKPAZAR

Hacı Kadın
Caddesi

EMINÖNÜ

Şehirhattı
İskelesi

Galata
Bridge

Eminönü İskelesi

Sirkeci Feribot İskelesi

Macar Kardeşler Cad.

İtfaiye Cad.

Atatürk Bulvarı

SARAÇHANE

Sobacılar Cad.

Reşadiye Cad.

Kutucular Cad.

SIRKECI

Sirkeci
Station

VEFA

Süleymaniye Cad.

Cadırcılar Cad.

CAGALOGLU

Ebussuud Cad.

Gülhane
Parkı

Istanbul
University

Darülfünan Cad.

Oruçular Cad.

Alemdar Cad.

Aya
Sofya

Yeniçeriler Caddesi

## KEY

- Ferry Stops
- Ferry Lines
- 🛈 Information
- ■ Restaurants
- □ Hotels
- ⬦ following reviews in text indicates a map-grid coordinate

**See Map 2: Where to Stay and Eat in Sultanahmet map**

SULTANAHMET

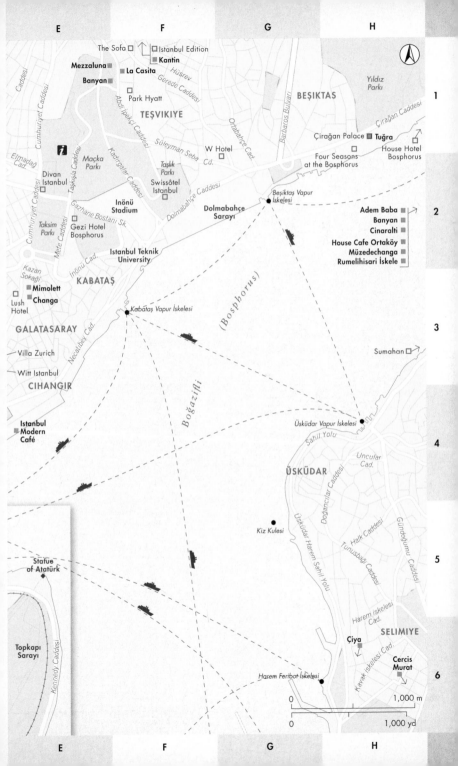

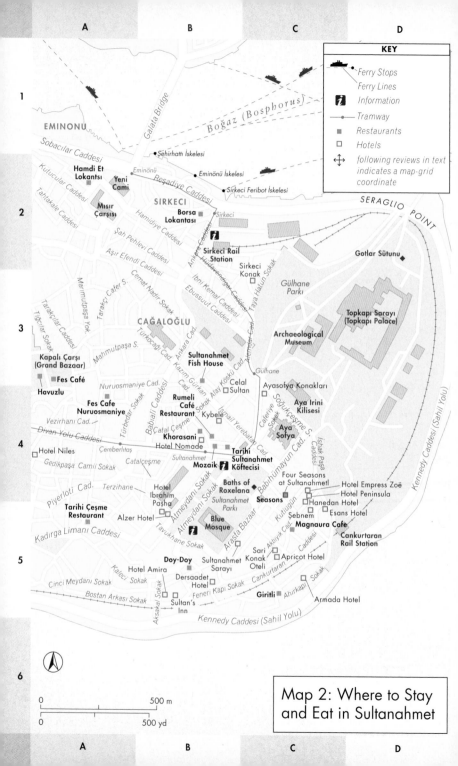

## KEY

- Ferry Stops
- Ferry Lines
- **i** Information
- Tramway
- Restaurants
- Hotels
- ⬌ following reviews in text indicates a map-grid coordinate

## Map 2: Where to Stay and Eat in Sultanahmet

EMINONU

Boğaz (Bosphorus)

Galata Bridge

SERAGLIO POINT

Sobacılar Caddesi

Hamdi Et Lokantası

Yeni Cami

Kulucular Caddesi

Tahtakale Caddesi

Mısır Çarşısı

Reşadiye Caddesi

Eminönü

Şehirhattı İskelesi

Eminönü İskelesi

Sirkeci Feribot İskelesi

SIRKECI

Hamidiye Caddesi

Borsa Lokantası

Sirkeci

Şah Pehlevi Caddesi

Aşır Efendi Caddesi

Sirkeci Rail Station

Ankara Caddesi

Sirkeci Konak

İbni Kemal Caddesi

Ebussuut Caddesi

Gotlar Sütunu

Gülhane Parkı

Topkapı Sarayı (Topkapı Palace)

Marmutpaşa Yok.

Tarakçı Cafer S.

Cemal Nadir Sokak

CAĞALOĞLU

Türkocağı Cad.

Ankara Cad.

Mahmutpaşa S.

Tığcılar Sokak

Archaeological Museum

Kapalı Çarşı (Grand Bazaar)

Fes Café

Havuzlu

Nuruosmaniye Cad.

Sultanahmet Fish House

Kazım Gürkan Cad.

Alay Köşkü Cad.

Aternan Cad.

Gülhane

Celal Sultan

Ayasofya Konakları

Aya Irini Kilisesi

Fes Cafe Nuruosmaniye

Vezirhanı Cad.

Türbedar Sokak

Babıali Caddesi

Çatal Çeşme

Rumeli Café Restaurant

Kybele

İsmail Yerebatan Cad.

Caferiye Sokak

Soğukçeşme Sokak

Aya Sofya

Divan Yolu Caddesi

Çemberlitaş

Khorasani

Çatalçeşme

Hotel Nomade

Sultanahmet

Tarihi Sultanahmet Köftecisi

İşhak Paşa Caddesi

Hotel Niles

Gedikpaşa Camii Sokak

Mozaik

Babıhumayun Cad.

Four Seasons at Sultanahmet

Hotel Empress Zoë

Hotel Peninsula

Piyerloti Cad.

Terzihane

Hotel İbrahim Paşa

Atmeydanı Sokak

Baths of Roxelana

Seasons

Hanedan Hotel

Esans Hotel

Tarihi Çeşme Restaurant

Alzer Hotel

Sultanahmet Parkı

Kutlugün Cad.

Şebnem

Magnaura Cafe

Kadırga Limanı Caddesi

Tavukhane Sokak

Atmeydanı Sokak

Blue Mosque

Arasta Bazaar

Akbıyık Cad.

Cankurtaran Caddesi

Cankurtaran Rail Station

Doy-Doy

Sultanahmet Sarayı

Sari Konak Oteli

Apricot Hotel

Hotel Amira

Kaleci Sokak

Dersaadet Hotel

Feneri Kapı Sokak

Cankurtaran

Aksakal Sokak

Ahırkapı Sokak

Cinci Meydanı Sokak

Bostan Arkası Sokak

Sultan's Inn

Giritli

Armada Hotel

Kennedy Caddesi (Sahil Yolu)

N

0 — 500 m

0 — 500 yd

city of Gaziantep, is something of a culinary anthropologist, serving recipes from around Turkey that you're unlikely to find elsewhere. His original venue, Çiya, makes a range of top-notch kebabs, but the biggest draw is the selection of seasonal and daily specials—both meat-based and vegetarian—featuring memorable flavor combinations. Desserts are equally remarkable and include candied olives, tomatoes, or eggplant, served with sweet clotted cream. Nearby Çiya Sofrası offers home-style dishes only, while Çiya Kebap 2 just does kebabs. No alcohol is served at the no-frills venues, but try the *şerbet*, a traditional drink made from various fruits. ⊠ *Güneşlibahçe Sok. 48B, Kadıköy* ☎ *216/336–3013* ⊕ *www.ciya.com.tr* ✦ *1:6A.*

## BEYOĞLU

¢  ✕**Antiochia.** Specialties of Turkey's southeastern Hatay province—an
TURKISH  area bordering Syria and influenced by Arab cuisine—are featured in a smart, bistrolike venue that's far more hip than the traditional grill houses that typically offer food from the region. The menu comprises fewer than 10 types of *mezes*, a couple of salads, and just three main dishes consisting of different preparations of lamb. But the lack of choice is more than made up for in the intense flavors of the dishes, which are served with the restaurant's uncommonly tasty flatbread. The small venue is cozy, with just a handful of tables inside. ⊠ *Asmalı Mescit Mah. Minare Sok. 21, Beyoğlu* ☎ *212/292–1100* ⊕ *www. antiochiaconcept.com* 🔔 *Reservations essential* ☉ *Closed Sat. lunch and Sun.* ✦ *1:3C*

$  ✕**Dai Pera.** Chef-owner Arzu Gürdamar likes experimenting with
ECLECTIC  food, and her menu includes traditional *mezes* as well as her own tasty creations, such as grilled cauliflower with tahini sauce or zucchini in strained yogurt with crushed almonds. Entrées tend to be simple home-style Turkish meat and chicken dishes, like grilled meatballs or lamb with eggplant puree, reinterpreted to please a contemporary palate. The laid-back atmosphere—plain wooden furniture, posters and artwork on the walls, funky jazz music playing—makes up for the slightly inexperienced service. ⊠ *Yeni Çarşı Cad. 54, Beyoğlu* ☎ *212/252–8099* ⊕ *www. dairestaurant.com* ✦ *1:3D.*

¢  ✕**Fıccın.** A number of homey rooms and storefronts on both sides of
TURKISH  narrow Kallavi Sokak are best known for specialties of the Circassian kitchen. These include the signature *fıccın*, a savory pastry filled with ground meat; a regional variation of *mantı* dumplings stuffed with meat or potatoes; and "Circassian chicken," a cold spread of shredded chicken in a creamy walnut sauce. The menu, which also includes traditional Turkish *mezes* and a few meat dishes, changes daily, and prices are extremely reasonable. ⊠ *Kallavi Sok. 13/1, Beyoğlu* ☎ *212/293–3786* ⊕ *www.ficcin.com* ✦ *1:3D.*

¢  ✕**Hala Mantı.** As its name suggests, this restaurant on busy İstiklal
TURKISH  Caddesi specializes in ravioli-like *mantı*, small pockets of pasta filled with ground meat; *hingal*, a variation eaten in the Caucasus with a cheese and potato filling, is also served. *Gözleme*, a type of very thin flatbread filled with ingredients such as cheese and spinach, then cooked on huge griddles as you watch, are very good; other options

## CLOSE UP

# Drinks with a View

Views of the city from the 360 Istanbul restaurant in the Beyoğlu neighborhood are stunning.

In recent years, Istanbul's newest venues have been aiming high, literally, as an increasing number of savvy entrepreneurs take advantage of the city's greatest natural asset—its spectacular views—and open rooftop dining and nightlife spots. The trend has been especially pronounced in the Beyoğlu neighborhood, which sits on a ridge overlooking the Bosphorus, the Golden Horn, and the sights of Sultanahmet.

With the notable exception of **Mikla**—an upscale restaurant at the top of the 18-story Marmara Pera Hotel that is one of the city's best—most of the venues offering panoramic views of the city tend to fall flat when it comes to the food. But they make great places for a pre- or postdinner drink—where

else in the world can you gaze at two continents with a martini in hand?

In Beyoğlu, the open-air (and therefore summer only) **NuTeras** is a chic lounge that serves finger food and looks out on the Golden Horn, while **Leb-i Derya** has two branches from which you can watch the sunset over the Bosphorus. The Leb-i Derya at the top of the Richmond is fully enclosed, while the one on Kumbaracı Yokuşu has a breezy, open-air terrace section. **360 Istanbul** also offers excellent views, though it's become a bit of a victim of its own success, and it's not always easy to get into. Finally, **5.Kat** in nearby Cihangir is a restaurant/lounge with a casual yet chic vibe, and excellent Bosphorus views as well.

include tasty home-style vegetable and meat dishes and kebabs. With bare wooden tables and paper napkins, the atmosphere is simple but homey. No alcohol is served. ✉ *İstiklal Cad. 137A* ☏ *212/292–7004* ✢ *1:3D.*

¢ ✕ **Helvetia.** The menu changes daily,
TURKISH but always features a variety of soups and side dishes, as well as more substantial fare such as meatballs in tomato sauce and curried chicken; vegetarian options, ranging from zucchini fritters to stewed vegetables, are also plentiful. The atmosphere is laid-back and the easiest way to order is to simply point at what you want from the day's specials, which are displayed in front of the open kitchen. No alcohol is served. ✉ *General Yazgan Sok. 8* ☏ *212/245–8780* ◷ *Closed Sun. lunch* ✢ *1:3C.*

$$ ✕ **Istanbul Modern Cafe.** The inventive menu, along with gorgeous water-
CONTEMPORARY front views and stylish industrial-chic decor—exposed air shafts and cement walls—warrant a visit whether you're interested in the art at the Istanbul Modern. A sleek, rectangular wooden bar dominates the dining room, which looks out onto Istanbul's Karaköy harbor (avoid visiting when there's a huge cruise ship obscuring the view); there is also seating on the waterfront deck. The menu includes lighter fare—including a variety of pastas, salads, and pizzas—and more substantial dishes like grilled steak with vegetable fettucine and pan-roasted salmon with fresh asparagus. ✉ *Meclis-i Mebusan Cad., Liman İşletmeleri Sahası, Antrepo 4, Karaköy* ☏ *212/292–2612* ⌕ *Reservations essential* ✢ *1:4E.*

$ ✕ **Kafe Ara.** This popular, wooden-floored hangout named after famous
INTERNATIONAL octogenarian Turkish photographer Ara Güler, whose black-and-white photographs of Istanbul line the walls (and who sometimes can be seen holding court here), is a nice place for a light meal or cup of coffee. The menu includes a handful of Turkish meat dishes along with more international fare, such as chicken tikka or tagliatelle with salmon. Salads, including one featuring grilled Cypriot halloumi cheese, are also good. No alcohol is served. ✉ *Tosbağı Sok. 2, Galatasaray, Beyoğlu* ☏ *212/245–4105* ✢ *1:3D.*

$ ✕ **Karaköy Lokantası.** This dual-format venue is a bustling daytime spot
TURKISH offering delicious, reasonably priced vegetable and meat dishes and a classy *meyhane* at night, serving an excellent variety of vegetable and seafood *mezes,* including octopus salad and salted, dried mackerel; fish and meat entrées are equally well-prepared. The gorgeous two-level dining room features blue and turquoise tiles, old-fashioned lamps, and long mirrors. Service is professional yet informal—during the midday peak, you may end up sharing a white-tablecloth-clad table with local

**BEER IN TURKEY**

For years, visitors to Turkey basically had one choice when ordering beer: Efes. These days, international brands like Miller, Tuborg, and Foster's are also brewed locally, and imports like Corona and Beck's are available, too. And in the world of microbrews, Taps, a brewpub in the Istanbul suburbs, has started to distribute its products to bars and grocery stores around the city. They also operate a restaurant on the Bosphorus just north of Bebek (✉ *Cevdetpaşa Cad. 119* ☏ *212/263–8700*).

businesspeople on their lunch break. ⊠ *Kemankeş Cad. 37A, Kara-köy* ☎ *212/292–4455* ⊕ *www.karakoylokantasi.com* ⊘ *Closed Sun.* ✛ *1:4D.*

**$$**
ECLECTIC
Fodor'sChoice
★

✕ **Lokanta Maya.** New York–trained female chef Didem Şenol offers what could be called "nouvelle Turkish" cuisine, based on seasonal, local, and primarily organic ingredients. A changing menu features tasty appetizers like grilled octopus with red onions and such main course options as caramelized sea bass with apricots and is served in warm, contemporary surroundings in a not-yet-gentrified area of Karaköy. ⊠ *Kemankeş Cad. 35A, Karaköy* ☎ *212/252–6884* ⊕ *www. lokantamaya.com* ⚱ *Reservations essential* ⊘ *Closed Sun. dinner, Mon. dinner* ✛ *1:4D.*

**$$**
TURKISH

✕ **Meze by Lemon Tree.** *Mezes* in this trendy and attractive spot put a clever international spin on traditional favorites—a gazpacho-like, basil-infused version of *acılı ezme* (red pepper spread) is served in a shot glass—while others, such as sea bream with chickpeas and mus-tard sauce, are friendly chef-owner Gençay Üçok's unique creations. Though slightly overshadowed by the inventive *mezes*, main dishes include standouts like lamb sirloin and a delicious variation on sea bass cooked in paper. ⊠ *Meşrutiyet Cad. 83B, Beyoğlu* ☎ *212/252–8302* ⊕ *www.mezze.com.tr* ⚱ *Reservations essential* ⊘ *Closed lunch* ✛ *1:3C.*

**$$$$**
ECLECTIC
Fodor'sChoice
★

✕ **Mikla.** The top floor of the 18-story ⇨ *Marmara Pera Hotel,* with sleek Scandinavian decor and a stunning 360-degree view of Istanbul, is a dramatic setting for the contemporary cuisine of American-trained Turkish-Finnish chef Mehmet Gürs. Turkish and Nordic influences appear in such dishes as smoked lamb loin with walnut pesto and white bean puree, and grilled grouper with sun-dried tomato, eggplant puree, and poached artichoke. A wide-ranging, though expensive, wine list features gems from Turkey and around the world. ⊠ *Meşrutiyet Cad. 15* ☎ *212/293–5656* ⊕ *www.miklarestaurant.com* ⚱ *Reservations essential* ⊘ *Closed lunch; Sun. in Nov.–Mar. and July and Aug.* ✛ *1:3C.*

**$$**
TURKISH
Fodor'sChoice
★

✕ **Münferit.** Owner Ferit Sarper's menu gives traditional *meyhane* fare a twist as contemporary as the surroundings: "Circassian chicken" is made with duck breast, while feta cheese is served baked in paper with porcini mushrooms and truffle oil. The wine list is extensive, and desserts are innovative, especially the house-made ice cream in flavors like tahini and sage. ⊠ *Yeni Çarşı Cad. 19, Beyoğlu* ☎ *212/252–5067* ⚱ *Reservations essential* ⊘ *Closed Sun.* ✛ *1:3D.*

**¢**
TURKISH

✕ **Saray Mühallebicisi.** This Istanbul institution, established in 1935, is best known for its desserts, which are temptingly displayed in the front window—from milk puddings to flaky baklava served with *kaymak* (clotted cream). Also on offer is the Turkish equivalent of American diner fare (eggs, chicken soup, and *döner*—meat carved off a spit), and the multistory premises are packed with customers at all hours. No alcohol is served. ⊠ *İstiklal Cad. 102* ☎ *212/292–3434* ⊕ *www. saraymuhallebicisi.com* ✛ *1:3D.*

**$$**
TURKISH
Fodor'sChoice
★

✕ **Sofyalı 9.** With Greek music playing in the background, photographs of Old Istanbul on the walls, and friendly, laid-back surroundings on a picturesque backstreet in Beyoğlu's Asmalımescit area, classic *mey-hane* food and atmosphere soar several levels above the norm. *Mezes,* whether from the regular menu or the daily specials, are all excellent; standouts include cubes of fried eggplant in a yogurt and tahini sauce and "Circassian chicken," a spread made with chicken and ground walnuts. Grilled fish and meat are also very good. A limited menu is served during lunch. ⊠ *Sofyalı Sok. 9* ☎ *212/245–0362* ⊕ *www.sofyali. com.tr* ⌁ *Reservations essential* ✛ *1:3D.*

$ ✕ **Zübeyir Ocakbaşı.** This *ocakbaşı*, or grill house, is popular for its deli-
TURKISH cious food, lively atmosphere, and authentic feel. Kebabs are cooked on a special grill over hardwood coals and the *mezes* are also particularly tasty; among them are such uncommon choices as *kabak ezmesi*, or pumpkin spread (available only in fall/winter), and Van-style *cacık*, a dip made from thick, strained yoghurt, cucumber, and herbs. ⊠ *Bekar Sok. 28, Beyoğlu* ☎ *212/293–3951* ⊕ *www.zubeyirocakbasi.com* ⌁ *Reservations essential* ✛ *1:2E..*

# BOSPHORUS

$ ✕ **Adem Baba.** Adem Baba is the Turkish version of a New England fish
SEAFOOD shack, with nets and crab traps hanging from the ceiling in two venues located across the street from one other. Families and groups come here to enjoy simple, fresh, and perfectly prepared fish, at much less than what they would pay at some of the fancier seafood restaurants along the Bosphorus (it's cheaper in part because no alcohol is served). A refrigerated display at the entrance holds the day's catch. To start, order the fried calamari and the tasty *balık köftesi* (fish cakes). Adem Baba is in Arnavutköy, a low-key Bosphorus neighborhood that's perfect for a stroll before or after dinner. ⊠ *Satış Meydanı Sok. 2, Arnavutköy* ☎ *212/263–2933* ⊕ *www.adembaba.com* ✛ *1:2H.*

$$$ ✕ **Banyan.** In a city where non-Turkish dining options are limited, Ban-
ASIAN yan stands out as one of Istanbul's most noteworthy Asian restaurants, thanks to its well-executed food and excellent location. Emphasizing organic ingredients, the menu spans a range of Asian cuisines and includes traditional dishes like dim sum, satays, and Thai curries. The kitchen also creates tantalizing modern dishes such as char-grilled filet mignon marinated in sake, and grouper in a white wine and coco-nut milk sauce. With an interior dominated by sleek woods and an outdoor terrace dotted with bonsai trees—to say nothing of the spec-tacular Bosphorus view—Banyan is one of Ortaköy's most popular ven-ues. ⊠ *Muallim Naci Cad. Salhane Sok. 3, Ortaköy* ☎ *212/259–9060* ⊕ *www.banyanrestaurant.com* ⌁ *Reservations essential* ✛ *1:2H..*

$ ✕ **Çınaraltı.** Named after the massive sycamore tree growing through
SEAFOOD the center of the restaurant and shading the upstairs terrace with its branches, Çınaraltı ("under the sycamore") has been in business for three decades in the same spot on Ortaköy's waterfront square. With its relaxed service, spacious feel, and simple but attractive decor, Çınaraltı has remained refreshingly unpretentious and reasonably priced in a neighborhood known increasingly for its trendiness. A refrigerated case inside holds the catch of the day—after sampling some of the *mezes*, go in and pick out your fish (make sure the price quoted is per fish or serving, not per kilo). ⊠ *İskele Meydanı 28, Ortaköy* ☎ *212/261–4616* ⊕ *www.cinaralti.com* ✛ *1:2H.*

This Istanbul street vendor is selling freshly roasted chestnuts.

**$$** ✕ **The House Café.** The largest and one of the most popular branches
ECLECTIC of this chain of upscale eateries, which first opened in Nişantaşı in
2002 and has successfully expanded to 10 locations, is directly on
the waterfront, with chic furnishings and two enormous open-air ter-
races. The international menu ranges from starters like Asian-style
crispy chicken fingers and halloumi cheese wrapped in vine leaves to
main-course salads, pastas, steaks, and the signature House Burger.
Two long wooden bars are perfect for enjoying a predinner drink from
the excellent cocktail list. A branch on İstiklal Caddesi in Beyoğlu is
lively and spacious, while a smaller one in nearby Tünel is quieter and
more intimate. The original venue, in chic Nişantaşı, has a laid-back
vibe and a shady garden. ⊠ *Salhane Sok. 1, Ortaköy* ⊠ *Atiye Sok. 10,
Nişantaşı* ☎ *212/227–2699 Ortaköy, 212/259–2377 Nişantaşı* ⊕ *www.
thehousecafe.com* ✢ *1:3D..*

**$$$** ✕ **Müzedechanga.** A beautiful, lush setting just a stone's throw from the
ECLECTIC Bosphorus, a Mediterranean-inspired menu, and sophisticated ambi-
ence makes this dining room in the Sakıp Sabancı Museum a draw in
its own right. Particularly recommendable are the small plates, which
include variations on traditional *mezes,* such as a pumpkin spread with
walnuts or fried zucchini flowers stuffed with lor cheese. Overseen by
award-winning London-based chef Peter Gordon, the menu also shows
international influences, as in the smoked salmon with mung beans or
catfish served with potato salad. The venue is especially relaxing in
summer, when the terrace is open. ⊠ *Sakıp Sabancı Cad. 42, Emirgan*
☎ *212/323–0901* ⊕ *www.changa-istanbul.com* ⌧ *Reservations essential* ⊗ *Closed Mon.* ✢ *1:2H.*

**$$$$** ✕ **Rumelihisarı İskele.** A romantic setting in a restored historic ferry ter-
SEAFOOD minal on the Bosphorus, just steps from the fortress for which the
neighborhood is named, is more than matched by a fine range of seafood. After ordering from the selection of mostly seafood-based *mezes*,
ask the waiter to recommend whatever fish is especially tasty that day.
Phone ahead for a table with a good view or, even better, outside
on the waterfront terrace in warm weather. ⊠ *Yahya Kemal Cad. 1,
Rumelihisarı* ☎ *212/263–2997* ⊕ *www.rumelihisariiskele.com* ⟡ *Reservations essential* ✛ *1:2H.*

**$$$$** ✕ **Tuğra.** Fitting for a restaurant housed in the Çırağan Palace, dinner
TURKISH here is a refined, luxurious affair, with formal service, rich Ottoman and
Turkish specialties, and one of the most high-end wine lists in Turkey
(Chateau Pétrus, anyone?). The menu features a variety of *mezes* and
pilafs, and entrées emphasize fish and meat, such as in the restaurant's
signature *külbastı*, lamb escalope served with pureed eggplant. Reserve
a table to dine alfresco in the small balcony, where marble columns
flank a beautiful Bosphorus view, or ensconce yourself in the elegant
interior, with its soaring ceilings, large mirrors and hanging oriental
lamps. ⊠ *Çırağan Cad. 32, Beşiktaş* ☎ *212/326–4646* ⟡ *Reservations
essential* ⓜ *Jacket required* ⊘ *Closed lunch* ✛ *1:1H.*

## EMİNÖNÜ AND THE GOLDEN HORN

**¢** ✕ **Borsa Lokantası.** This unpretentious spot, part of a small chain of self-
TURKISH service, cafeteria-style eateries that has been in business since 1927,
attracts a hungry crowd that comes to eat well-prepared, inexpensive
food. The baked lamb in eggplant puree and the stuffed artichokes
are especially good. There is also an appealing selection of desserts,
so you might want to leave room. Borsa is close to the ferry terminals
of Eminönü, making it convenient for a quick meal before or after
a boat ride on the Bosphorus or across to the Asian side of the city.
⊠ *Yalıköşkü Cad., Yalıköşkü Han 60–62, Eminönü* ☎ *212/511–8079*
⊕ *www.borsaselfservis.com* ✛ *2:2B.*

**$** ✕ **Hamdi Et Lokantası.** This Istanbul institution rates as one of the city's
TURKISH top restaurants for grilled meat. The delicious kebabs of minced lamb
mixed with pistachios or served on skewers with eggplant are among the
outstanding entrées, while the small *lahmacun* (Turkish pizza topped
with spiced ground meat) will make your mouth water. Hamdi's four
floors are generally packed with both tourists and locals, which makes
for a lively, even boisterous, atmosphere, but service can be a bit har-
ried; make sure that you get—and pay for—exactly what you order.
Reserve a table on the restaurant's terrace level, which has excellent
views of the Golden Horn and the Bosphorus. ⊠ *Kalçın Sok. 17,
Eminönü* ☎ *212/528–0390* ⊕ *www.hamdirestorant.com.tr* ⟡ *Reservations essential* ✛ *2:2A.*

## GRAND BAZAAR

**¢** ✕ **Fes Café.** Funky black-and-white Lucite chairs and fresh flowers on
CAFÉ the tables provide a shot of modern style in the heart of the Grand
Bazaar. Squeezed into a former market stall, the small kitchen turns

out simple sandwiches, salads, excellent fresh lemonade and fruit juices, homemade cakes, and other American-style fare. It's a great place to sit back and watch the comings and goings of the bazaar. A second, larger branch just outside the bazaar on Ali Baba Türbe Sokak offers a fuller menu that includes salads and other dishes. It also houses a small boutique selling products by sister company Abdulla, along with interesting housewares and jewelry from young Turkish designers. ⊠ *Halıcılar Cad. 58–62, Grand Bazaar* ☎ *212/528–1613, 212/526–3070* ⊕ *www. fescafe.com* ☾ *Closed Sun.* ✛ *2:3A.*

¢ ✕ **Havuzlu.** This lunch-only spot in a quiet corner of the sprawling Grand
TURKISH    Bazaar is a good place to refuel. Seating is in an atmospheric 500-year-old dining hall with large multicolored blown-glass chandeliers hanging from its vaulted ceilings. A large steam table at the front of the open kitchen holds a daily assortment of dishes, including a variety of stewed vegetables and meat. The food is good, but prices are rather high and aimed at the tourist market, so be sure to ask when making your selection (the printed menu doesn't list the daily specials). Havuzlu closes at 5 pm and does not serve alcohol. ⊠ *Gani Çelebi Sok. 3, Grand Bazaar* ☎ *212/527–3346* ⊕ *www.havuzlurestaurant.com* ☾ *No dinner, closed Sun.* ✛ *2:3A.*

## SULTANAHMET

$$ ✕ **Asitane.** One of Istanbul's most character-filled restaurants serves sea-
TURKISH    sonally changing menus based on the traditional cuisine of an Ottoman palace, which the restaurant's owners have carefully researched over the past two decades. Dishes feature unusual combinations of ingredients, such as eggplant stuffed with quail and baked melon with a pilaf and ground meat filling; the historical versions of more familiar contemporary Turkish dishes also make appearances. The atmosphere is elegant, service exceptional, and there's a pleasant, shaded courtyard open in summer. Asitane is conveniently located next to the Kariye Müzesi. ⊠ *Kariye Camii Sok. 6, Edirnekapı* ☎ *212/635–7997* ⊕ *www. asitanerestaurant.com* ⌕ *Reservations essential* ✛ *1:4A.*

¢ ✕ **Doy-Doy.** *Doy-doy* is a Turkish expression for "full" and, unlike many
TURKISH    other places in tourist-filled Sultanahmet, you can indeed fill up for a reasonable sum at this no-frills spot frequented by locals. A variety of kebabs and *pide*, a type of Turkish pizza baked in a wood-burning oven, with different toppings are served, and the lunchtime specials, including vegetable stew, meatballs, and eggplant and meat moussaka, are a particularly good deal. The two-level rooftop terrace, open in summer, has fine views of the Blue Mosque and Sea of Marmara—but don't expect to savor the view with a drink in hand, as no alcohol is served. ⊠ *Şifa Hamamı Sok. 13* ☎ *212/517–1588* ⊕ *www.doydoy-restaurant. com* ✛ *2:5B.*

$$$$ ✕ **Giritli.** A prix-fixe only menu of Cretan specialties includes a generous
SEAFOOD    multicourse meal and unlimited local alcoholic drinks (wine or rakı).
Fodor'sChoice    The food is outstanding, with an enormous selection of delicious *mezes*
★    like sea bass ceviche, herb-covered cubes of feta cheese with walnuts and green onion, and perfectly grilled calamari, followed by freshly caught fish. The restaurant garden, with its whitewashed walls and blue

trim, feels like a slice of the Greek islands in the middle of Istanbul. ✉ *Keresteci Hakkı Sok.* ☎ *212/458–2270* ⊕ *www.giritlirestoran.com* ⊛ *Reservations essential* ⊗ *Closed lunch* ✣ *2:5C.*

$ ✕ **Khorasani.** One of Sultanahmet's most popular restaurants emphasizes
TURKISH the Arab- and Kurdish-influenced cuisine of southeastern Turkey, from
Fodor'sChoice where the restaurant's owners hail. This translates to delicious *mezes*
★ like hummus, *muhammara* (hot pepper and walnut spread), and thyme salad, as well as unusual mains that include quail kebab and a pistachio kebab made with both lamb and beef. Diners can sit outdoors on the cobblestoned sidewalk or get a table inside to watch the chefs prepare kebabs over the large charcoal grill. ✉ *Ticarethane Sok. 39/41, Sultanahmet* ☎ *212/519–5959* ⊕ *www.khorasanirestaurant.com* ✣ *2:4B.*

$ ✕ **Magnaura Café Restaurant.** At this standout for high-quality food and
TURKISH pleasant ambience, the menu ranges from Turkish and Ottoman cuisine to international standards. Particularly notable are the steaks—the Marble Steak is grilled and served with flaming cognac, while the Boğaziçi Steak is marinated with vegetables in a terra-cotta pot. Greater attention is given to presentation than in most Sultanahmet restaurants. There's also a cozy rooftop terrace with a very partial view of the Marmara Sea. ✉ *Akbıyık Cad. 27* ☎ *212/518–7622* ✣ *2:5C.*

$ ✕ **Mozaik.** A restored old house with small, sun-dappled dining rooms,
ECLECTIC cozy furniture, and creaky wooden floors is a delightful refuge in the midst of busy Sultanahmet. Turkish specialties are served alongside salads, pastas, schnitzel, steak, and even a few Asian dishes, and in summer seating spills out into the alley beside the restaurant. ✉ *İncili Çavuş Sok. 1* ☎ *212/512–4177* ⊕ *www.mozaikrestaurant.com* ✣ *2:4B.*

$ ✕ **Rumeli Café Restaurant.** Particularly interesting at this charming spot
TURKISH on a quiet side street off Divanyolu are the specialties from Turkey's Kurdish and Armenian communities, such as *papaz yahnisi,* a Byzantine stew of lamb, potatoes, and pumpkin cooked in a terra-cotta dish. International dishes include a variety of salads, pastas, and steaks. The cozy interior, formerly the site of a book bindery, has Ottoman and Byzantine-style architectural details and hand-painted frescoes on the exposed brick walls. In summer you can sit outside at tables on the sidewalk or on the intimate roof terrace (with a partial view). ✉ *Ticarethane Sok. 8* ☎ *212/512–0008* ✣ *2:4B.*

$$$$ ✕ **Seasons.** A delightful gazebolike glass pavilion in the middle of the
TURKISH manicured garden courtyard of the Four Seasons is by far the ritziest restaurant in Sultanahmet (and one of the most expensive). The seasonal menu has Turkish and international specialties, with an emphasis on seafood and lamb at dinner; the lunch menu is lighter, featuring sandwiches, pizzas, and salads. For dessert, try one of the unique and decadent creations on the ice-cream menu, consisting of exotic flavors made in-house. On Sunday, the restaurant's brunch buffet (99 TL; no buffet during Ramadan) draws crowds from across Istanbul. ✉ *Tevkifhane Sok. 1* ☎ *212/402–3150* ⊛ *Reservations essential* ✣ *2:4C.*

$$ ✕ **Sultanahmet Fish House.** There are no obsequious waiters at Sultan-
SEAFOOD ahmet Fish House, no fancy dress code—just good, well-prepared, fairly priced seafood served in a friendly atmosphere. The mainly seafood *mezes* include sardines, octopus, and mackerel in olive oil, while

mains comprise a range of fish and a few kebabs; sea bass with saffron, cooked in a terra-cotta casserole, is a particular standout. Light blue and yellow walls, multicolored antique lamps hanging from the ceiling, and colorful nomad textiles make for an inviting atmosphere. ⊠ *Prof. İsmail Gürkan Cad. 14* ☎ *212/527–4441* ✛ *2:3B.*

¢ ✕ **Tarihi Çeşme Restaurant.** A rare find in Sultanahmet offers good food at reasonable prices, genuinely friendly service, and a congenial atmosphere that appeals to both visitors and local residents. The menu includes an excellent range of *mezes* and kebabs, as well as *pide*, or flatbread baked with different toppings—the Turkish version of pizza. There's a small, homey indoor seating area, but the biggest attraction is the lovely streetfront patio, shaded by vines and decorated with hanging lanterns. ⊠ *Kadırga Liman Cad., Küçük Ayasofya Camii Sok. 1, Sultanahmet* ☎ *212/516–3580* ⊕ *www.tarihicesmerestaurant.com* ✛ *2:5A.*

TURKISH

¢ ✕ **Tarihi Sultanahmet Köftecisi.** Like pizza for New Yorkers, humble *köfte* (grilled meatballs) inspire countless arguments among Istanbullus about who makes the best. Some of the most highly regarded are served on a simple menu—meatballs, lamb kebab, *piyaz* (boiled white beans in olive oil), and salad—that has remained virtually unchanged since 1920. Service is somewhat perfunctory, and this bustling place is not somewhere to linger, but the location just steps from the Blue Mosque and Aya Sofya makes it ideal for a quick and affordable lunch. ■ TIP➔ There are imitators with similar names on the same street, but Tarihi Sultanahmet Köftecisi ("Historic Sultanahmet Köftecisi") is considered the real deal. ⊠ *Divanyolu Cad. 12* ☎ *212/520–0566* ⊕ *www.sultanahmetkoftesi. com* ▭ *No credit cards* ✛ *2:4B.*

TURKISH

## TAKSIM AND NIŞANTAŞI

$$$ ✕ **Changa.** The innovative sister venue of ⇨ *Müzedechanga* occupies a three-story, early-20th-century townhouse near Taksim and is open only mid-October through May. Dishes combine flavors and ingredients from around the world, presented with aesthetic flair. A large circular "skylight" cut into the ground floor reveals the bustling basement-level kitchen below. ⊠ *Sıraselviler Cad. 47, Cihangir* ☎ *212/249–1348* ⌖ *Reservations essential* ⊗ *Closed lunch; Sun.; June–mid-Oct.* ✛ *1:3E.*

ECLECTIC

$ ✕ **Casita.** Turkish food with a twist includes *mantı*—a ravioli-like Turkish pasta traditionally stuffed with ground meat—and "Feraye" (a name the restaurant has even trademarked), which are *mantı* stuffed with cheese and spinach, potato and cheese, or chicken, and fried. The menu also features creative takes on other Turkish dishes, plus steaks and a variety of salads. The atmosphere is casual, and diners can either sit at

TURKISH

sidewalk tables in front of the restaurant or at tables looking onto a quiet garden. ⊠ *Abdi İpekçi Cad., Atiye Sok. 3, Nişantaşı* ☎ *212/327–8293* ⊕ *www.casita.com.tr* ✛ *1:1F.*

$ ✕**Kantin.** Şemza Denizsel finds the TURKISH freshest ingredients for her daily menus, written on chalkboards, that feature simply prepared but delicious Turkish dishes emphasizing meat and vegetables. Prices are somewhat high for the portion size, but you're paying for local, mostly organic foods, such as sourdough bread made with heirloom Anatolian wheat. The venue is especially popular at lunchtime with local professionals; if you can't land a seat in the upstairs dining rooms or pleasant backyard terrace, consider making a picnic from the side dishes and delectable baked goods sold at Kantin's street-level food shop. No alcohol is served. ⊠ *Akkavak Sok. 30, Nişantaşı* ☎ *212/219–3114* ⊕ *www.kantin.biz* ⌦ *Reservations not accepted* ⊘ *Closed Sun.* ✛ *1:1F.*

> ### TURKISH COFFEE
>
> Tea might be the beverage of choice in Turkey these days, but those in need of a coffee fix need not worry. Most teahouses serve Turkish coffee, although you may find a better cup by going to a more upscale café, which will probably use better coffee and take the time to prepare it properly. Well-made Turkish coffee should be thick and almost chocolaty, with espresso-like foam on top. Turks drink their coffee three ways: *sade* (plain), *orta* (medium sweet), and *şekerli* (extra sweet). It's usually served with a small glass of water and, frequently, a little piece of *lokum* (Turkish delight).

$$$$ ✕**Mimolett.** Murat Bozok trained abroad with top international chefs ECLECTIC including Joël Robuchon and returned to Istanbul to open what he hopes will become Turkey's first Michelin-starred restaurant. He offers a sophisticated, creatively presented menu that marries seasonal Mediterranean ingredients with French techniques—such as *foie gras* with pistachio sauce and apple-tomato jam, or tuna with olive and eggplant paste. Diners can order à la carte or have the tasting menu with or without pairings from the wine list, which is one of the most extensive in Turkey. Indoor dining areas are suitably elegant, while the quiet, foliage-lined back terrace, open in warm months, offers a lovely Bosphorus view. ⊠ *Sıraselviler Cad. 55A, Cihangir* ☎ *212/245–9858* ⊕ *www.mimolett. com.tr* ⌦ *Reservations essential* ⊘ *Closed lunch and Sun.* ✛ *1:3E.*

# WHERE TO STAY

*For expanded hotel reviews, visit Fodors.com.*

With the number of visitors to Turkey growing every year, Istanbul's hoteliers have been busy keeping up with the increasing demand. New lodgings, from full-service hotels to smaller boutique inns, are opening all the time, while older establishments are busy renovating and expanding. This means there are plenty more options than there were in the past, but because Istanbul is such a popular destination, it's not the travel bargain it used to be. It's also worth noting that hotels in Turkey tend to quote their rates in euros, which makes what might look like a good deal something less than that when paying in U.S. dollars. Most lodgings, save four- and five-star hotels, include a full Turkish breakfast with the room rate.

The majority of visitors to Istanbul stay in the Sultanahmet area—the Aya Sofya, Blue Mosque, Topkapı Palace, and most of Istanbul's major sites are in the neighborhood—which has the city's widest selection of hotels, smaller family-run *pansiyons* (guesthouses), and some charmingly stylish inns. Many of the rooms here tend to be on the small side, and bathrooms often only have showers, but what's lacking in space tends to be more than made up for in character and atmosphere. The downside to Sultanahmet is that at the height of the season, the area is overrun not only with tourists but touts who will try to steer you to their carpet shop. On the upside, stiff local competition means that Sultanahmet usually has the best deals in town; some hotels even offer a 5% to 10% discount for payment in cash.

For a less touristy taste of Istanbul, try the Beyoğlu area across the water, only a 10-minute cab ride or 20-minute tram ride from the sights of Sultanahmet. Beyoğlu has recently emerged as an attractive alternative to Sultanahmet, with many upscale hotels. Entrepreneurs have caught on to the tourism potential of the historic area, and are restoring elegant, century-old buildings and giving them new life as hotels. Staying in Beyoğlu puts you closer to Istanbul's best restaurants and nightspots and also gives you a chance to stroll through the area's lively backstreets.

For the most luxurious, indulgent accommodation options, stay in one of the large modern hotels that are mostly clustered around Taksim Square and up along the Bosphorus. Wherever you stay, you may notice that hoteliers are starting to embrace traditional Turkish design, and one new trend is to design hotel bathrooms inspired by hammams, or Turkish baths. Though the setup may be less familiar than a traditional shower or bath, these baths can be quite luxurious, with marble and heated floors.

| WHAT IT COSTS IN U.S. DOLLARS | | | | |
|---|---|---|---|---|
| ¢ | $ | $$ | $$$ | $$$$ |
| Hotels | under $100 | $100–$150 | $151–$225 | $226–$350 | over $350 |

Prices are for two in a standard double in high season, including 18% tax.

## ASIAN SHORE

**$$$$**
**Fodor's Choice**
**★**

**Sumahan.** What was once a derelict distillery on the Asian waterfront of the Bosphorus is now one of Istanbul's chicest and most original places to stay, with comfortable rooms and suites—all with incredible views of the water and decorated in a contemporary, minimalist style. **Pros:** waterfront location; stylish boutique hotel; intimate, secluded atmosphere. **Cons:** far from sights and commercial center; launch makes only a few trips a day. ⊠ *Kuleli Cad. 51, Çengelköy* ☎ *216/422–8000* ⊕ *www.sumahan.com* ⇆ *7 rooms, 13 suites* & *In-room: Wi-Fi. In-hotel: restaurant, tennis court, gym, parking* ⑩ *Breakfast* ⊕ *1:3H.*

# BEYOĞLU

**$$** 🏨 **Anemon Galata.** A meticulously renovated, century-old building in the heart of Galata, one of Istanbul's most picturesque neighborhoods, provides plenty of old-world atmosphere, and rooms are elegant and comfortable, if showing some wear. **Pros:** historic neighborhood; professional service. **Cons:** rooms facing street can be noisy at night; some rooms small; reached on steep, winding streets. ⊠ *Büyükhendek Cad. 5, Galata* ☎ *212/293–2343* ⊕ *www.anemonhotels.com* ⏎ *23 rooms, 7 suites* ⬥ *In-room: Wi-Fi. In-hotel: restaurant, business center, parking* ✛ *1:4C.*

**$$** 🏨 **Ansen 130 Suites.** The "suites" in this stylish and hip early-20th-century building are arranged with separate sleeping and living areas and decorated in a smart, minimalist style, with slightly retro touches; a few on the upper floors have excellent views of the Golden Horn. **Pros:** large, attractive suites; close to nightlife. **Cons:** though units are set up as studio apartments, they do not have kitchenettes; staff's English is a bit limited. ⊠ *Meşrutiyet Cad. 70, Tepebaşı* ☎ *212/245–8808* ⊕ *www.ansensuites.com* ⏎ *11 suites* ⬥ *In-room: Wi-Fi. In-hotel: restaurant, bar, some pets allowed* ⦿*| Breakfast* ✛ *1:3C.*

**$$$$** 🏨 **The Marmara Pera.** Though it doesn't look like much from the outside, trendy interior design, attentive service, and small-but-stylish rooms with retro-modern decor and large windows overlooking the city make this 18-story tower one of Istanbul's hippest places to stay. **Pros:** amazing views of city and Golden Horn; great location; excellent dining options. **Cons:** expensive for the size of the rooms; pool and fitness center are small. ⊠ *Meşrutiyet Cad., Derviş Sok. 1, Tepebaşı* ☎ *212/334–0300* ⊕ *www.themarmarahotels.com* ⏎ *200 rooms, 3 suites* ⬥ *In-room: Wi-Fi. In-hotel: restaurant, bar, pool, gym, some pets allowed* ✛ *1:3C.*

**$$$**
**Fodor's** Choice
★
🏨 **Pera Palace.** Extensive restoration has brought this Istanbul institution back to its former glory, with beautifully outfitted rooms and a small spa and indoor pool, yet plenty of period decorations and antique furniture retain a feeling of historical charm. **Pros:** beautifully restored historic venue; luxurious facilities. **Cons:** some rooms have small bathrooms; rooms on back side look onto street with lots of traffic. ⊠ *Meşrutiyet Cad. 52, Tepebaşı* ☎ *212/377–4000* ⊕ *www.perapalace.com* ⏎ *99 rooms, 16 suites* ⬥ *In-room: Wi-Fi. In-hotel: restaurant, bar, pool, spa, parking, some pets allowed* ✛ *1:3C.*

**$$$** 🏨 **Richmond Hotel.** Behind the facade of a turn-of-the-century building on lively pedestrian-only İstiklal Caddesi are comfortable rooms that feature decor and furnishings that are contemporary, if somewhat lacking in personality; about a dozen rooms have views of the Bosphorus, others of the busy street below, and some—to be avoided—of a dismal inner courtyard. **Pros:** located on main shopping and nightlife drag; efficient service. **Cons:** street-facing rooms can be noisy at night; some rooms are small; some rooms have dreary courtyard views. ⊠ *İstiklal Cad. 227, Beyoğlu* ☎ *212/252–5460* ⊕ *www.richmondhotels.com.tr* ⏎ *101 rooms, 2 suites* ⬥ *In-room: Wi-Fi. In-hotel: restaurant, bar, parking* ⦿*| Breakfast* ✛ *1:3D.*

# BEST BETS FOR
# FOR ISTANBUL LODGING

Fodor's writers and editors have chosen their favorite hotels, resorts, and B&Bs by price and experience. Fodor's Choice properties represent the very best, across price categories. You can also search by area for excellent places to stay; check out our reviews on the following pages.

## MOST ROMANTIC

Four Seasons Hotel Istanbul at the Bosphorus, $$$$, p. 117

Sumahan, $$$$, p. 114

Tomtom Suites, $$$, p. 117

W Hotel, $$$$, p. 118

## Fodor's Choice ★

Çırağan Palace Kempinski Istanbul, $$$$, p. 117

Dersaadet Hotel, $$, p. 120

Four Seasons Hotel Istanbul at Sultanahmet, $$$$, p. 120

Hotel Amira, $$, p. 121

Pera Palace, $$$, p. 115

Sumahan, $$$$, p. 114

Tomtom Suites, $$$, p. 117

## By Price

### ¢

Hotel Niles, p. 121

Hotel Peninsula, p. 122

### $

Esans Hotel, p. 120

Sarı Konak Oteli, p. 122

### $$

Dersaadet Hotel, p. 120

Hotel Amira, p. 121

### $$$

Pera Palace, p. 115

Tomtom Suites, p. 117

### $$$$

Çırağan Palace Kempinski Istanbul, p. 117

Four Seasons Hotel Sultanahmet, p. 120

Sumahan, p. 114

## By Experience

### BEST B&BS

Alzer Hotel, $$, p. 118

Esans Hotel, $, p. 120

Hotel Peninsula, ¢, p. 122

Sarı Konak Oteli, $, p. 122

Şebnem, $, p. 122

### GREAT VIEWS

Çırağan Palace Kempinski Istanbul, $$$$, p. 117

The Marmara Pera, $$$$, p. 115

Sumahan, $$$$, p. 114

Swissôtel Istanbul, $$$$, p. 118

## HISTORIC INTEREST

Çırağan Palace Kempinski Istanbul, $$$$, p. 117

Four Seasons Hotel Istanbul at Sultanahmet, $$$$, p. 120

Pera Palace, $$$, p. 115

## INTERIOR DESIGN

Divan Istanbul, $$$$, p. 123

The House Hotel Bosphorus, $$$$, p. 118

The Istanbul Edition, $$$$, p. 123

Witt Istanbul, $$$, p. 117

## LOCAL CHARACTER

Dersaadet Hotel, $$, p. 120

Hotel Empress Zoë, $$, p. 121

Hotel Ibrahim Pasha, $$$, p. 121

Kybele, $, p. 122

**$$$** **Tomtom Suites.** A restored 1901
FodorśChoice residence that once housed Francis-
★ can nuns offers superb accomoda-
tions and authentic character, with
guest rooms—some true "suites"
with separate sitting rooms, oth-
ers large open-plan spaces—fur-
nished with warm woods, textiles
in natural colors, high ceilings, and
original artwork. **Pros:** historic
building with romantic ambience;
on quiet street; helpful, welcom-
ing staff. **Cons:** only upper room
categories have sea views; reached
on steep streets. ⊠ *Boğazkesen
Cad., Tomtom Kaptan Sok. 18,
Beyoğlu* ☎ *212/292–4949* ⊕ *www.
tomtomsuites.com* ↝ *20 suites* ☖ *In-room: Wi-Fi. In-hotel: restaurant,
bar, business center* ⑂ *Breakfast* ✛ *1:3D..*

> ## CIHANGIR
>
> Istanbul's Cihangir neighborhood
> is not on most visitors' maps, but
> it deserves a look. Long known as
> a kind of bohemian quarter, it's
> filled with charming small cafés
> and restaurants—though not much
> in the way of historical or cultural
> sites, or much shopping—and it's
> far from the bustle of the city,
> though still walking distance from
> Beyoğlu's livelier areas. Witt Istan-
> bul and the Villa Zurich Hotelare
> both in Cihangir.

**$$$** **Witt Istanbul.** All accommodations here are suites—essentially very
large loft apartments with separate sleeping and living areas and (in
most) "kitchenettes" with marble countertops—and the design is contemporary and überchic: hardwood floors, exposed concrete ceilings,
neutral tones, and designer lamps and furniture. **Pros:** swanky, stylish design aesthetic; location in quiet residential neighborhood with
trendy café scene; personalized service. **Cons:** steep uphill walk from
nearby tram stop; venue is not that family-friendly; minimal public
spaces. ⊠ *Defterdar Yokuşu 26, Cihangir* ☎ *212/293–1500* ⊕ *www.
wittistanbul.com* ↝ *18 suites* ☖ *In-room: Wi-Fi. In-hotel: bar, business
center* ⑂ *Breakfast* ✛ *1:3D..*

## BOSPHORUS

**$$$$** **Çırağan Palace Kempinski Istanbul.** Once a residence for the Ottoman
FodorśChoice sultans, the late 19th-century Çırağan Palace (pronounced chi-rahn)
★ is Istanbul's most luxurious hotel, with ornate public spaces that feel
absolutely decadent and a breathtaking setting right on the Bosphorus—the outdoor infinity pool seems to hover on the water's edge and
most rooms, full of Ottoman-inspired wood furnishings and textiles
in warm colors, have balconies overlooking the Bosphorus as well. **Pros:**
grand setting in incredible location; over-the-top feeling of luxury. **Cons:**
exorbitant price of food and drinks; high rates, especially for rooms that
have no Bosphorus view. ⊠ *Çırağan Cad. 32, Beşiktaş* ☎ *212/326–4646*
⊕ *www.kempinski-istanbul.com* ↝ *282 rooms, 31 suites* ☖ *In-room:
Wi-Fi. In-hotel: restaurant, bar, pool, gym, spa, children's programs,
business center, parking* ✛ *1:1H.*

**$$$$** **Four Seasons Hotel Bosphorus.** A restored 19th-century Ottoman palace
with two modern wings exudes luxury; rooms and suites, a quarter of
which have Bosphorus views (others have garden and city views), are elegant yet understated, with soaring ceilings, muted tones, and Ottoman
touches such as handcrafted mirrors. **Pros:** luxurious accomodations

and service; beautiful views and location. **Cons:** expensive food, drinks, and Internet; underwhelming views from non-Bosphorus rooms, especially considering high rates. ⊠ *Çırağan Cad. 80, Beşiktaş, Istanbul* ☎ *212/381–4000* ⊕ *www. fourseasons.com/bosphorus* ↗ *145 rooms, 25 suites* ⟳ *In-room: Wi-Fi. In-hotel: restaurant, bar, pool, gym, spa, business center, parking, some pets allowed* ✛ *1:1H.*

**BREAKFAST IN ISTANBUL**

A Turkish breakfast of fresh bread, *beyaz peynir* (feta-like white cheese), tomatoes, cucumbers, and olives, and often jam or honey, is included at most hotels in Turkey, although not usually at the higher-end properties.

$$$$ 🖫 **The House Hotel Bosphorus.** Most of the stylish accommodations in a restored late-19th-century waterfront mansion have views of the Bosphorus, and some have private balconies; all are decorated in a chic, contemporary style—warm woods, neutral textiles, brass lamps, and engraved mirrors—with historical touches like high ceilings and floral moldings. **Pros:** hip hotel with intimate feel; waterfront location; attentive service. **Cons:** standard rooms and some bathrooms are small; located in popular nightlife area that can be loud at night. ⊠ *Muallim Naci Cad., Salhane Sok. 1, Ortaköy, Istanbul* ☎ *212/327–7787* ⊕ *www. thehousehotel.com* ↗ *8 rooms, 15 suites* ⟳ *In-room: Wi-Fi. In-hotel: restaurant, gym, business center* ⏷◎⏸ *Breakfast* ✛ *1:1H..*

$$$$ 🖫 **Swissôtel Istanbul.** In a superb spot just above Dolmabahçe Palace, the Swissôtel offers excellent facilities and—from most of the comfortable, businesslike guestrooms, currently being redone—magnificent views of the Bosphorus that extend all the way to Topkapı Palace across the Golden Horn. **Pros:** first-class service; extensive dining options; huge, top-notch gym. **Cons:** expensive food, drinks, and Internet; hotel can only be reached by taxi (or on foot); fairly impersonal atmosphere. ⊠ *Bayıldım Cad. 2, Maçka, Istanbul* ☎ *212/326–1100* ⊕ *www. swissotel.com* ↗ *514 rooms, 23 suites* ⟳ *In-room: Wi-Fi. In-hotel: restaurant, bar, pool, tennis court, gym, spa, parking* ✛ *1:2F.*

$$$$ 🖫 **W Istanbul.** An 1870s Ottoman residence is enhanced with posh ultramodernity—sexy lighting, chic East-meets-West decor, cool amenities like iPod docks, and attentive and personalized service. **Pros:** hip, cool atmosphere; ultracomfortable beds. **Cons:** some room features so high-tech they are not user-friendly; dim, nightclub-like lighting in public spaces may not suit all tastes; service is hit or miss. ⊠ *Süleyman Seba Cad. 22, Beşiktaş, Istanbul* ☎ *212/381–2121* ⊕ *www.whotels.com/ istanbul* ↗ *106 rooms, 28 suites* ⟳ *In-room: Wi-Fi. In-hotel: restaurant, bar, gym, spa, parking, some pets allowed* ✛ *1:2G.*

## SULTANAHMET

$$ 🖫 **Alzer Hotel.** Friendly service, attractive rooms, and a great location on the Hippodrome are complimented with wooden floors, old-fashioned furniture antique-style chandeliers, and textiles and wallpaper in pastel and cream colors, while flat-screen TVs bring the rooms up-to-date. **Pros:** central location; comfortable rooms. **Cons:** rooms facing Hippodrome can be noisy; high rates due to proximity to sights. ⊠ *Atmeydanı*

Sumahan

Four Seasons Hotel Sultanahmet

Hotel Empress Zoë

Pera Palace

72 ☎ 212/516–6262 ⊕ *www.alzerhotel.com* ⤙ *21 rooms, 1 suite* ⚲ *In-room: Wi-Fi. In-hotel: restaurant, business center* ⫶◎⫶ *Breakfast* ✛ *2:5B.*

$$ ⛫ **Armada Hotel.** Spacious, comfortable accommodations are a 10-minute walk from Istanbul's main tourist sites, and most rooms look out either to the sea or over the Old City—although one of the best views is at night from the hotel's rooftop Teras Restaurant, from where you can see Aya Sofya and the Blue Mosque. **Pros:** amazing views of the water; professional service; in quiet area. **Cons:** somewhat steep uphill walk from hotel to the sights of Sultanahmet. ⊠ *Ahırkapı Sok. 24* ☎ *212/455–4455* ⊕ *www.armadahotel.com.tr* ⤙ *110 rooms* ⚲ *In-room: Wi-Fi. In-hotel: restaurant, bar, parking* ⫶◎⫶ *Breakfast* ✛ *2:5C.*

$$$ ⛫ **Ayasofya Konakları.** Nine charming, pastel-color wooden mansions from the late 19th century have been restored by Turkey's Touring and Automobile Club and turned into a row of elegant guesthouses, where smallish rooms are furnished in period Ottoman style, with brass beds and chandeliers, wooden floors and furniture, and plush upholstery, and have either half-size tubs or showers. **Pros:** unique, historic buildings; location adjacent to Aya Sofya. **Cons:** high room rates because of location; some accommodations far from reception and dining area; most rooms lack TV and Wi-Fi. ⊠ *Soğukçeşme Sok.* ☎ *212/513–3660* ⊕ *www.ayasofyakonaklari.com* ⤙ *57 rooms, 10 suites* ⚲ *In-room: no TV, Wi-Fi. In-hotel: restaurant* ⫶◎⫶ *Breakfast* ✛ *2:4C.*

$$ ⛫ **Celal Sultan.** Three conjoined, restored town houses make up this compact, clean hotel that has new furnishings designed to look old-fashioned, and an inviting lobby with a delightful bar. **Pros:** hotel is on a quiet street; personable staff. **Cons:** some rooms and bathrooms are small; some guests report poor sound insulation in rooms; no safes in standard rooms. ⊠ *Salkımsöğüt Sok. 16, Yerebatan Cad.* ☎ *212/520–9323* ⊕ *www.celalsultan.com* ⤙ *53 rooms, 2 suites* ⚲ *In-room: Wi-Fi. In-hotel: restaurant, bar* ⫶◎⫶ *Breakfast* ✛ *2:4B.*

$$ ⛫ **Dersaadet Hotel.** Dersaadet means "place of happiness" in Ottoman Turkish and this small, cozy hotel lives up to its name—rooms have an elegant, even plush, feel, with colorful rugs on the floor, antique furniture, and ceilings hand-painted with Ottoman ornamental motifs. **Pros:** extraordinary level of service; lovely terrace; good value. **Cons:** some rooms modest in size; no view from rooms on lower floors. ⊠ *Küçükayasofya Cad. Kapıağası Sok. 5* ☎ *212/458–0760* ⊕ *www.dersaadethotel.com* ⤙ *14 rooms, 3 suites* ⚲ *In-room: Wi-Fi. In-hotel: restaurant* ⫶◎⫶ *Breakfast* ✛ *2:5B.*

Fodor'sChoice ★

$ ⛫ **Esans Hotel.** The emphasis at this restored wooden house is on guest satisfaction and the eight rooms are decorated with thoughtful attention to detail, with attractive wallpaper, upholstery, and linens in Ottoman motifs and shades of turquoise, champagne and dark brown; three have a sea view. **Pros:** located on quiet street; staff go out of their way to assist; good for families. **Cons:** no elevator; breakfast served in same area as reception. ⊠ *Yeni Saraçhane Sok. 4, Sultanahmet* ☎ *212/516–1902* ⊕ *www.esanshotel.com* ⤙ *8* ⚲ *In-room: Wi-Fi* ⫶◎⫶ *Breakfast* ✛ *2:5C..*

$$$$ ⛫ **Four Seasons Hotel Sultanahmet.** What a rehabilitation success story: a former prison steps from Topkapı Palace and Aya Sofya is now one

Fodor'sChoice ★

of Istanbul's premier accommodations, where rooms and suites are luxuriously outfitted with reading chairs, original works of art, and bathrooms with deep tubs and overlook the Sea of Marmara, the Old City, or a manicured interior courtyard. **Pros:** historic building surrounded by major tourist attractions; luxurious accommodations; exceptional service. **Cons:**

expensive Internet and food; limited fitness facilities; no view from rooms on lower floors. ⊠ *Tevkifhane Sok. 1* ☏ *212/402–3000* ⊕ *www. fourseasons.com/istanbul* ⟿ *54 rooms, 11 suites* ⌂ *In-room: Wi-Fi. In-hotel: restaurant, bar, gym, business center, parking, some pets allowed* ✛ *2:4C.*

**$$**
**Fodor'sChoice**
**★**
🛏 **Hotel Amira.** An attractive atrium between two wings houses the lobby, and well-appointed rooms are furnished in an eclectic mix of Turkish and contemporary styles, from ornate Ottoman ceiling patterns and metal lampshades evoking the Istanbul skyline to modern rugs and plush upholstery. **Pros:** extraordinary service; good value; guests feel pampered. **Cons:** some rooms not accessible by elevator; located on somewhat noisy corner; basement-level rooms can be dark. ⊠ *Mustafapaşa Sok. 79, Sultanahmet* ☏ *212/516–1640* ⊕ *www. hotelamira.com* ⟿ *31 rooms, 1 suite* ⌂ *In-room: Wi-Fi. In-hotel: bar, gym, business center* ⫶◯⫶ *Breakfast* ✛ *2:5B..*

**$**
🛏 **Hotel Empress Zoë.** At what is now a Sultanahmet institution, rooms and suites are varied and charming—standard rooms, with colorfully canopied four-posters, nomad textiles, and dark woods, have an almost rustic feel, while suites are more fully furnished, and some have marble-lined bathrooms done up to look like mini hammams. **Pros:** quirky, bohemian atmosphere; location just steps from major sights. **Cons:** no elevator; narrow staircases and labyrinthine layout require some climbing around; some rooms and bathrooms small and basic. ⊠ *Akbıyık Cad., 4/1* ☏ *212/518–2504* ⊕ *www.emzoe.com* ⟿ *14 rooms, 12 suites* ⌂ *In-room: no TV, Wi-Fi. In-hotel: bar* ⫶◯⫶ *Breakfast* ✛ *2:4C.*

**$$$**
🛏 **Hotel İbrahim Pasha.** What was once the home of an extended Armenian family offers small but attractively decorated rooms, some looking out toward the Sea of Marmara; deluxe rooms have separate sitting areas, and a handful have full bathtubs. **Pros:** location just off Hippodrome; cozy ambience and decor; excellent breakfast. **Cons:** standard rooms are small, with tiny bathrooms; most rooms don't have a view; rates for standard rooms are high for what is offered. ⊠ *Terzihane Sok. 9* ☏ *212/518–0394* ⊕ *www.ibrahimpasha.com* ⟿ *24 rooms* ⌂ *In-room: Wi-Fi. In-hotel: bar, business center* ⫶◯⫶ *Breakfast* ✛ *2:5B.*

**¢**
🛏 **Hotel Niles.** The elaborate lobby, with its carved wooden columns, plush antique furniture, chandeliers, and marble floors with oriental rugs, could well be a film set, as could the large "suite" rooms, with hammam-style bathrooms, divan sofas, and Ottoman-style woodwork; two bi-level suites are well suited for families. **Pros:** great value; close to

Grand Bazaar and tram stop. **Cons:** a little ways from the main sights; small bathrooms in standard rooms; somewhat unsightly nearby streets. ⊠ *Dibekli Cami Sok. 13, Beyazıt* ☎ *212/517–3239* ⊕ *www.hotelniles. com* ⤳ *29 rooms, 10 suites* ⚲ *In-room: Wi-Fi. In-hotel: bar, gym, business center* ✛ *2:4A..*

$   ⊞ **Hotel Nomade.** Twin sisters Esra and Hamra Teker opened their hotel in 1984, and they offer some of Sultanahmet's most appealing and reasonably priced lodgings, done in a stylish, minimalist design featuring wallpaper with pleasing modern patterns, attractive wooden floors, and a subtle use of color. **Pros:** gorgeous roof terrace; located right near tram stop; good value. **Cons:** small rooms and tiny bathrooms; no view from most rooms; very little storage space in rooms. ⊠ *Ticarethane Sok. 15* ☎ *212/513–8172* ⊕ *www.hotelnomade.com* ⤳ *16 rooms* ⚲ *In-room: Wi-Fi. In-hotel: bar* ⏐◎⏐ *Breakfast* ✛ *2:4B.*

¢   ⊞ **Hotel Peninsula.** One of the best values in Sultanahmet offers comfortable and clean rooms, with nice decorative touches that include mirrors, small artworks, and gauzy draped fabric; three rooms have a partial sea view. **Pros:** good value; convenient location near major sights. **Cons:** no elevator; loud call to prayer from mosque directly behind hotel. ⊠ *Adliye Sok. 6, Sultanahmet* ☎ *212/458–6850* ⊕ *www.hotelpeninsula. com* ⤳ *12 rooms* ⚲ *In-room: Wi-Fi* ⏐◎⏐ *Breakfast* ✛ *2:4C..*

$   ⊞ **Kybele.** Named after an ancient Anatolian fertility goddess, this charming little inn is lit by an incredible profusion of antique lamps—4,000 at last count—that hang from the ceilings in the overstuffed lobby and small but imaginatively decorated rooms. **Pros:** unique decor and atmosphere; warm, friendly staff. **Cons:** no roof terrace, elevator, or TVs in rooms; ornate, lamp-filled rooms may not appeal to everyone. ⊠ *Yerebatan Cad. 35* ☎ *212/511–7766* ⊕ *www.kybelehotel.com* ⤳ *16 rooms* ⚲ *In-room: no TV, Wi-Fi. In-hotel: restaurant, business center* ⏐◎⏐ *Breakfast* ✛ *2:4B.*

$   ⊞ **Sarı Konak Oteli.** The bright, clean rooms in an Ottoman-style building have modern furniture, though the decor also has Turkish and period accents like brass lamps, antique mirrors, and Ottoman-era etchings; some rooms have original tiled floors. **Pros:** hotel has cozy rooms and intimate feel; good value. **Cons:** standard rooms a bit small. ⊠ *Mimar Mehmet Ağa Cad. 42–46* ☎ *212/638–6258* ⊕ *www.sarikonak.com* ⤳ *18 rooms, 5 suites* ⚲ *In-room: Wi-Fi. In-hotel: bar* ⏐◎⏐ *Breakfast* ✛ *2:5C.*

$   ⊞ **Şebnem.** These clean, bright rooms with burgundy curtains and four-poster beds that have embroidered canopies are near the main sights of Sultanahmet and have a pleasantly laid-back vibe. **Pros:** extraordinarily friendly staff; excellent breakfast; lovely terrace. **Cons:** rooms on the small side; no elevator. ⊠ *Adliye Sok. 1* ☎ *212/517–6623* ⊕ *www. sebnemhotel.net* ⤳ *15 rooms* ⚲ *In-room: Wi-Fi. In-hotel: bar, business center* ⏐◎⏐ *Breakfast* ✛ *2:5C.*

$$$   ⊞ **Sirkeci Konak Hotel.** Smallish rooms emphasize local character, with wooden furnishings, hanging Ottoman-style brass lamps, traditional artwork, and kilims, while a full range of amenities and warm and helpful staff makes a stay especially rewarding. **Pros:** staff especially eager to please; excellent facilities; Gülhane tram station just steps away. **Cons:**

located amid drab car repair shops; lower-level rooms have lackluster views; poor soundproofing of rooms. ⊠ *Taya Hatun Sok. 5, Sirkeci* ☎ *212/528–4344* ⬚ *52 rooms* ⚬ *In-room: Wi-Fi. In-hotel: restaurant, bar, pool, gym, business center* ✛ *2:3C..*

**$$** ⬚ **Sultanahmet Sarayı.** The sultans meet Las Vegas in this glitzy recreation of an Ottoman palace, where marble stairways, columns, Greek statues, and fountains grace the public spaces, and opulent rooms are complete with cushioned divans for reclining and gazing out the windows and hammam-style bathrooms are lined with marble. **Pros:** prime location just behind Blue Mosque; elegant decor and feel. **Cons:** top-floor rooms small; hammam-style bathrooms not for everyone; rates a bit high. ⊠ *Torun Sok. 19* ☎ *212/458–0460* ⊕ *www. sultanahmetpalace.com* ⬚ *36 rooms, 9 suites* ⚬ *In-room: Wi-Fi. In-hotel: restaurant, parking* ⦿ *Breakfast* ✛ *2:5B.*

**¢** ⬚ **Sultan's Inn.** A good budget option on a quiet backstreet only a few minutes' walk from the major attractions of Sultanahmet has the ambience of a typical Turkish *pansiyon*, with small but clean and cozy rooms, some with tiny balconies; the rooftop terrace is green with abundant flower pots and curling vines and looks out on the Sea of Marmara and the Blue Mosque. **Pros:** warm, friendly atmosphere; pleasant terrace. **Cons:** small rooms; no elevator. ⊠ *Mustafapaşa Sok. 52* ☎ *212/638– 2562* ⊕ *www.sultansinn.com* ⬚ *17 rooms* ⚬ *In-room: Wi-Fi. In-hotel: business center* ⦿ *Breakfast* ✛ *2:5B.*

## TAKSIM AND NIŞANTAŞI

**$$$$** ⬚ **Divan Istanbul.** An Istanbul institution established in 1956 has been brought up to date to combine authentic Turkish and contemporary design elements—from the traditional Anatolian kilims in the rooms to the spectacular flower-like chandeliers by American glass artist Robert DuGrenier in the lobby—and the good-size rooms feel warm and inviting, with cozy sitting areas that have leather sofas and leather-topped desks; spacious bathrooms are done in a pleasing hue of travertine. **Pros:** first-class service; aesthetic design; high-quality dining options. **Cons:** fairly uninteresting views from most rooms; expensive food and beverages. ⊠ *Asker Ocağı Cad. 1, Taksim* ☎ *212/315–5500* ⊕ *www.divan. com.tr* ⬚ *149 rooms, 42 suites* ⚬ *In-room: Wi-Fi. In-hotel: restaurant, bar, pool, gym, spa, business center, parking* ✛ *1:2E.*

**$$$** ⬚ **Gezi Hotel Bosphorus.** Contemporary, minimalist decor infuses a bit more personality than you'll find in most business-caliber hotels, and rooms have views of the Bosphorus, the park, or the city; a particularly nice feature in the bathrooms is the full-length window in the shower— perfect for gazing out at the boats or the urban surroundings while you lather up under the rainshower. **Pros:** convenient location just across from Taksim's Gezi Parkı; classy atmosphere; helpful staff. **Cons:** some rooms and bathrooms are small; rooms on lower floors don't have much of a view. ⊠ *Mete Cad. 34, Taksim* ☎ *212/223–2700* ⊕ *www. gezibosphorus.com* ⬚ *60 rooms, 3 suites* ⚬ *In-room: Wi-Fi. In-hotel: restaurant, gym, spa* ⦿ *Breakfast* ✛ *1:2E..*

**$$$$** ⬚ **The Istanbul Edition.** A sophisticated oasis in one of the city's most bustling urban districts offers comfortable, spacious rooms that have a somewhat masculine feel—sleek woods, minimalist decor, textiles in champagne and cream tones—and offer the latest technology, with iPod docking stations and Bang & Olufsen flat-screen TVs. **Pros:** stylish, high-tech rooms; exceptionally attentive staff; luxurious spa and fitness facilities. **Cons:** hotel is far from sights and nightlife (though located next to a metro station); in-house Cipriani restaurant is expensive; dining and public areas overlook a busy expressway. ✉ *Büyükdere Cad. 136, Levent* ☎ *212/317–7700* ⊕ *www.editionhotels.com* ⟿ *77 rooms, 1 suite* ⚷ *In-room: Wi-Fi. In-hotel: restaurant, bar, pool, gym, spa, business center, parking* ⊹ *1:1F.*.

> **NARGHILES**
>
> *Narghiles* (also known as hookahs) and the billowy smoke they produce have been an integral part of Istanbul's coffeehouses for centuries. Once associated with older men who would spend their days smoking, sipping strong Turkish coffee, and playing backgammon, the *narghile* is having a renewed popularity with younger Istanbullus. They are often used with a variety of flavored tobaccos, such as apple or strawberry. Because the smoke is filtered through water, it's cool and smooth, though it can make you light-headed if you're not used to it.

$$ **Lush Hotel.** Quirky-chic and just a couple of blocks from Taksim Square nightlife, accommodations here vary widely in shape and design, with decorative touches ranging from exposed brick walls to furniture and interesting lamps in a mix of styles; fifth-floor rooms, done entirely in black, white, and gray, feel the most contemporary. **Pros:** central location; funky, hip atmosphere. **Cons:** some rooms and bathrooms are a bit cramped; location often noisy at night due to clubs and street traffic; not very family-oriented. E<STR>*Sıraselviler Cad. 12, Taksim* ☎ *212/243–9595* ⊕ *www.lushhotel.com* ⟿ *44 rooms* ⚷ *In-room: Wi-Fi. In-hotel: restaurant, parking* ⦿ *Breakfast* ⊹ *1:3E.*

$$$$ **Park Hyatt Istanbul–Maçka Palas.** A restored Italian-style art deco 1922 apartment building, in the high-end shopping district of Nişantaşı, offers spacious, elegant rooms decked out in sleek walnut with modern amenities alongside such old-fashioned touches as period chandeliers and black-and-white photographs of Istanbul. **Pros:** large rooms; located in trendy shopping and nightlife area; staff is friendly and efficient. **Cons:** most rooms have no view; spa rooms somewhat overwhelmed by their bathrooms. ✉ *Bronz Sok. 4, Nişantaşı* ☎ *212/315–1234* ⊕ *www.istanbul.park.hyatt.com* ⟿ *80 rooms, 10 suites* ⚷ *In-room: Wi-Fi. In-hotel: restaurant, bar, pool, gym, spa, parking* ⊹ *1:1F.*

$$$$ **The Sofa.** Design is the emphasis here, with large rooms that have attractive contemporary textiles and furniture, as well as the eponymous trademark sofa. **Pros:** luxurious rooms; original design and hip feel. **Cons:** rooms looking onto interior courtyard get little light; some guests complain of street noise and loud functions held on premises; staff could be more accomodating given high rates. ✉ *Teşvikiye Cad. 41–41/A, Nişantaşı* ☎ *212/368–1818* ⊕ *www.thesofahotel.com* ⟿ *65 rooms, 17 suites* ⚷ *In-room: Wi-Fi. In-hotel: restaurant, pool, gym, spa, some pets allowed* ⊹ *1:1F.*

# NIGHTLIFE AND THE ARTS

Istanbul's nightlife still revolves, in many ways, around its *meyhanes*, tavernlike restaurants where long nights are spent nibbling on mezes and sipping the anise-flavored spirit rakı. The atmosphere at these places—mostly found in the lively Beyoğlu area—is jovial, friendly, and worth experiencing. But there are lots of other options, too, again mostly in Beyoğlu, which has everything from smoky American-style dive bars to sophisticated lounges, performance spaces that host world-class live acts, and discos and dance clubs. In warm weather, much of the city's nightlife action shifts to the Bosphorus shore, where chic (and pricey) summer-only nightclubs play host to Istanbul's rich and famous, and those who want to rub shoulders with them.

For upcoming events, reviews, and other information about what to do in Istanbul, pick up a copy of the monthly *Time Out Istanbul* or bimonthly *The Guide,* both of which are English-language publications with listings of hotels, bars, restaurants, and events, as well as features about Istanbul. The English-language *Hürriyet Daily News* and *Today's Zaman* are also good resources for listings and for keeping abreast of what's happening in Turkish and international politics.

## NIGHTLIFE

### BARS AND LOUNGES

The side streets leading off from İstiklal Caddesi in Beyoğlu are full of small bars. Many cater to a student crowd, with cheap beer and loud music, but there are also comfortable and inviting lounges. In recent years, the trend in the neighborhood has been literally upward, with the opening of rooftop bars that usually have stunning views and fresh breezes. For more upscale bars, head to the neighborhoods and hotels along the Bosphorus.

BEYOĞLU

Fodor'sChoice

★

**5. Kat.** This rather pricey restaurant that turns into a trendy lounge/bar is on the fifth floor of an unassuming building in the quiet Cihangir neighborhood and offers wonderful views of the Bosphorus—along with fabulous cocktails. With its wooden furniture and potted plants, the upper-level terrace (open only in summer) makes you feel as if you're passing the time on somebody's roof deck. ⊠ *Soğancı Sok. 7, Cihangir* ☎ *212/293–3774* ⊕ *www.5kat.com.*

**Artiste Terasse.** Lined with mostly identical venues designed to evoke Parisian cafés, the alleyway known as "French Street" is undeniably touristy but has its charming side, too—especially at Artiste Terasse, a café and bar that has great views from its rooftop terrace. Live music is occasionally on offer. ⊠ *Cezayir Çıkmazı 4/9–10, Beyoğlu* ☎ *212/251–4425.*

**Balkon.** A sixth-floor bar and lounge, Balkon has excellent views of the Golden Horn and a laid-back outdoor deck. Despite the location in the increasingly trendy Asmalımescit area, drink prices are quite reasonable. ⊠ *Şehbender Sok. 5* ☎ *212/293–2052.*

**Cezayir.** Housed in an atmospheric century-old building, Cezayir is a trendy restaurant that also has a long bar and an attractive enclosed garden with a small lounge area. The venue gets crowded on weekends, when a DJ plays a mix of new and old dance music. ⊠ *Hayriye Cad. 12* ☎ *212/245–9980* ⊕ *www.cezayir-istanbul.com.*

**Indigo Pub.** A café that turns into a bar with a trendy yet low-key vibe, Indigo Pub has nicer than average wood-and-stone decor and a DJ who plays 1970s and '80s music in the late evenings. ⊠ *Tomtom Mah. Araca Sok. 5/A, Beyoğlu* ☎ *212/293–1174* ⊕ *www.indigopub.com.*

**K.V.** Tucked into a plant-filled, late 19th-century open-air arcade, K.V. has a brasserie kind of feel that's perfect for a quiet drink; a piano occasionally supplies live background music. ⊠ *Tünel Geçidi 10* ☎ *212/251–4338* ⊕ *www.kv.com.tr.*

Fodor'sChoice
★
**Leb-i Derya.** The reward for finding this seventh-floor rooftop restaurant and bar—in an apartment building with only a small sign out front—is a magnificent view overlooking the Bosphorus and the Old City. The small venue is popular with an almost-too-hip crowd of locals and expats who come for the cocktails and the views, so you may have to wait for a table if you show up without reservations. A second branch, at the top of the Richmond Hotel on İstiklal Caddesi, is calmer and a bit less "scene-y," catering to a slightly more mature crowd. ⊠ *Kumbaracı Yokuşu 57/6, Beyoğlu* ☎ *212/293–4989* ⊕ *www.lebiderya.com.*

**Şahika.** Nevizade Sokak is lined with *meyhanes* serving mostly identical menus, as well as lively bars like Şahika. The multistory venue has a different ambience on each floor, ranging from a pub atmosphere on the street level, to casual seating areas on the middle floors and a club-like vibe on the terrace, offering views of the Golden Horn. ⊠ *Nevizade Sok. 17, Beyoğlu* ☎ *212/249–6196* ⊕ *www.sahika.com.tr.*

BOSPHORUS
**Bebek Bar.** Bebek Bar, with its masculine interior decor that brings to mind a private club, and a breezy terrace directly overlooking the Bosphorus, attracts a dressed-up crowd. There is a particularly wide selection of liqueurs, scotch, and other spirits, as well as classic cocktails, making it a perfect spot for a before- or after-dinner drink. ⊠ *Bebek Hotel, Cevdet Paşa Cad. 34, Bebek* ☎ *212/358–2000.*

**The W Lounge.** The stylish yet comfortable lounge/bar in the W Hotel has leather divans, low tables, and signature cocktails—draws for a sophisticated, "scene-y" crowd. ⊠ *W Istanbul Hotel, Süleyman Seba Cad. 22, Beşiktaş* ☎ *212/381–2121.*

SULTANAHMET
**Hotel Nomade Bar.** The inviting and laid-back rooftop bar in the Hotel Nomade is one of the best options for a drink in the Sultanahmet area, which is not generally known for its nightlife. There are nice views of Aya Sofya and the sea beyond, and a relaxed vibe. ⊠ *Hotel Nomade, Ticarethane Sok. 15* ☎ *212/513–8172.*

ASIAN SHORE
**Karga Bar.** The longest established and most popular venue on Kadıköy's so-called "Barlar Sokağı" ("bars street"), Karga takes up several levels of an old wooden house, whose many small rooms and intimate niches provide a perfect laid-back hangout; there are also occasional live performances and art events. There's no sign out front but look for a building with a green facade and an emblem of a crow over the

doorway (karga means "crow" in Turkish). ⊠ *Kadife Sok. 16, Kadiköy* ☎ *216/449–1725* ⊕ *www.kargabar.org.*

## DANCE CLUBS

Istanbul has a vibrant dance club scene, though it's not for the faint of heart. Things typically get rolling at about midnight and go until 4 or 5 in the morning. The city's upscale clubs tend to be expensive—admission can be up to 40 TL or more—and there are no guarantees you'll get past the doorman, whose job it is to make sure only Istanbul's best dressed get in. Still, Istanbullus love to party and a good time is assured, if you get in.

**360 Istanbul.** One of the city's swankiest rooftop venues, 360 Istanbul runs a rather mediocre restaurant in the early evening, but becomes a fashionable club on Friday and Saturday after 11 pm, when a well-dressed crowd arrives to dance. In recent years the venue has become a bit too popular for its own good and has resorted to an increasingly exclusive door policy. If you can get in, the views are fabulous. ⊠ *İstiklal Cad. 163, Beyoğlu* ☎ *212/251–1042.*

**Anjelique.** Overlooking the waterfront in the popular neighborhood of Ortaköy, Anjelique has sleek decor, a classy atmosphere, and a more intimate feel than the larger nightclubs farther up the Bosphorus. Dinner is served to a well-heeled crowd before the venue turns into a dance club. ⊠ *Muallim Naci Cad., Salhane Sok. 5, Ortaköy* ☎ *212/327–2844* ⊕ *www.istanbuldoors.com.*

Fodor'sChoice **NuTeras.** The rooftop of a historic building looking out over the Golden
★ Horn is the venue for one of Istanbul's chicest nightclubs. There's a trendy bar and small dance floor, with sleek decor and a fashionable crowd to match the striking location. NuTeras is entirely open-air, so it's only open in summer, but in winter months the vibe continues indoors at sister venue NuPera (in the same building). ⊠ *Meşrutiyet Cad. 149* ☎ *212/245–6070* ⊕ *www.nupera.com.*

**Reina.** Directly on the Bosphorus, Reina is Istanbul's swankiest and most talked-about club, where the rich and famous come to be seen and the paparazzi await them—and it has all the pretension befitting such a venue. In summer, a half-dozen equally posh open-air restaurants, featuring different types of cuisines, open on the club's terrace. ⊠ *Muallim Naci Cad. 44, Ortaköy* ☎ *212/259–5919* ⊕ *www.reina.com.tr.*

**Sortie.** A short ways up the Bosphorus from ⇨ *Reina* and equally swanky, Sortie is nonetheless smaller and ever so slightly less pretentious. As at Reina, there are at least a half-dozen restaurants serving different cuisines. Entirely open-air, Sortie is only open in the summer. ⊠ *Muallim Naci Cad. 54, Ortaköy* ☎ *212/327–8585* ⊕ *www.sortie. com.tr* ۩ *Closed Oct.–Apr.*

## JAZZ CLUBS

Istanbul may not be a major spot on the world's jazz map, but this has been changing in recent years. Several top-notch jazz clubs have opened and, as a result, the number of well-known jazz musicians who come to perform in Istanbul is increasing.

Going out to hear Turkish music in Istanbul.

**JC's Istanbul Jazz Center.** JC's Istanbul Jazz Center would not seem out of place in New York or any other cosmopolitan city, with its sophisticated decor, top-quality instruments and acoustics, and a program that features well-known jazz musicians from the U.S. and Europe. The club's restaurant serves set menus and à la carte dishes. ⊠ *Muallim Naci Cad., Salhane Sok. 10, Ortaköy* ☎ *212/327–5050* ⊕ *www.istanbuljazz.com* ⊗ *Closed Sun. and Mon. and June–Aug.*

**Nardis Jazz Club.** A cozy, intimate space, Nardis Jazz Club is a well-regarded venue that hosts mostly Turkish jazz musicians and the occasional big name from abroad. The club only has room for 110, so reservations are strongly recommended. ⊠ *Kuledibi Sok. 14, Beyoğlu* ☎ *212/244–6327* ⊕ *www.nardisjazz.com.*

## LIVE MUSIC VENUES

As Istanbul's reputation as a hip city continues to grow, the quality of the live acts that come to town has been rising, too. Established and up-and-coming performers now frequently include Istanbul on their European tours, and the city has become a good place to catch a show—for a fraction of what you might pay for the same thing in Paris, London, or New York. Note that many live-performance venues close for part or all of the summer, when school is out and the city's elite departs for vacation.

Fodor'sChoice
★

**Babylon.** Babylon, in a converted warehouse, is Istanbul's top live music space, hosting world-famous jazz, rock, and world music performers. The sound system is excellent—the friendly crowds take their music seriously. It's closed in summer, when Babylon Aya Yorgi opens in the beach town of Çeşme, near Izmir. ⊠ *Şehbender Sok. 3, Beyoğlu* ☎ *212/292–7368* ⊕ *www.babylon.com.tr* ☉ *Closed June–Aug.*

Fodor'sChoice **Ghetto.** With an excellent sound system and attractively furnished prem-
★ ises, Ghetto brings in a diverse lineup of mainly international musical
acts performing jazz, pop, funk, world, and electronic music. In the
summer months, the interior venue closes and the rooftop hosts DJ parties with music in a variety of genres. ⊠ *Kamer Hatun Cad. 10, Beyoğlu*
☎ *212/251–7501* ⊕ *www.ghettoist.com* ☉ *Closed Sun.*

**Hayal Kahvesi.** A crowded, late-night hangout, Hayal Kahvesi draws a
mostly young crowd that likes live—and loud—rock and blues. Though
the ambience is little better than a dive bar, with scuffed wood floors
stained with beer, the music is generally good. ⊠ *Büyükparmakkapı
Sok. 19, Beyoğlu* ☎ *212/244–2558* ⊕ *www.hayalkahvesibeyoglu.com.*

**Salon.** Salon is a top-notch performance space housed in the headquat-
ters and cultural center of the Istanbul Foundation for Culture and
Arts (IKSV), one of the city's most important arts organizations. The
concert lineup includes both local and international acts spanning a
wide range of genres, including jazz, rock, alternative and world music.
⊠ *Sadi Konuralp Cad. 5, Şişhane* ☎ *212/334–0841* ⊕ *www.saloniksv.
com* ☉ *Closed mid-July–mid-Sept.*

## ARTS AND ENTERTAINMENT

Spring and summer are a lively time for the arts in Istanbul. The **Istanbul International Music Festival,** held for the duration of June, attracts
renowned artists from around the world performing classical music.
Shows take place throughout the city in historic buildings, such as Aya
Irini and Rumeli Hisar. The **International Theater Festival** takes place every
other year in May through early June, and attracts major stage talent
from across the globe. The **International Istanbul Jazz Festival** occurs every
July and has grown to include much more than just jazz. Recent head-
liners have included Herbie Hancock, Lenny Kravitz, and members of
the Buena Vista Social Club.

**Istanbul Foundation for Culture and Arts.** Tickets for all of these events can
be ordered online through Biletix (⊕ *www.biletix.com*) or by contact-
ing the Istanbul Foundation for Culture and Arts. ⊠ *Istanbul Kültür
Sanat Vakfı, Sadi Konuralp Cad. 5, Şişhane* ☎ *212/334–0700* ⊕ *www.
iksv.org.*

**Istanbul International Film Festival.** The annual Istanbul International Film
Festival, held over two weeks in April, presents films from around the
world. Check the Web site of the IKSV (⊕ *www.iksv.org*) for schedules,
and make sure to purchase tickets in advance, as the festival is extremely
popular. Seats are reserved.

### FILM

The strip of theaters along İstiklal Caddesi between Taksim and Galatasaray, a square at the midpoint of İstiklal Caddesi, shows the latest from Hollywood, with a few current European or Turkish movies
thrown in. There are also plush, modern theaters at the Cevahir mall
in Şişli, and at City's shopping mall in Nişantaşı. Most foreign films are

shown with their original sound track and Turkish subtitles, although many children's films are dubbed into Turkish. Look for the words *Ingilizce* (English) or *orijinal* (original language). Films in languages other than English will have subtitles in Turkish. When in doubt, ask at the ticket office whether the film is dubbed (*dublaj*) or subtitled (*altyazılı*).

## PERFORMANCE VENUES

**Akbank Sanat Cultural Center.** Sponsored by one of Turkey's largest private banks, Akbank Art Center hosts regular classical and jazz concerts. The center hosts the Akbank Jazz Festival, held annually over several weeks in late September and early October, as well as theater productions, films, and art exhibitions. ⊠ *İstiklal Cad. 8, Beyoğlu* ☏ *212/252–3500* ⊕ *www.akbanksanat.com.*

**Cemal Reşit Rey Concert Hall.** Near the Istanbul Hilton, Cemal Reşit Rey Concert Hall offers just about every kind of entertainment you could want: from chamber and symphonic music to modern dance, rock, folk, and jazz concerts. ⊠ *Gümüş Sok., Harbiye* ☏ *212/232–9830* ⊕ *www.crrks.org* ⊗ *Closed Jan. 1–15 and July–Sept.*

**Garajistanbul.** Opened in 2007 in the basement of a parking lot near Galatasaray Square, Garajistanbul is an experimental venue that hosts contemporary dance and theater, as well as musical, literary, and artistic events. ⊠ *Yeni Çarşı Cad., Kaymakam Reşit Bey Sok. 11A, Galatasaray* ☏ *212/244–4499* ⊕ *www.garajistanbul.org* ⊗ *Closed June–Sept.*

## WHIRLING DERVISHES

The Mevlevi, a Sufi brotherhood originally founded in Konya, are best known around the world as the whirling dervishes, mystics who believe ritual spinning will bring them closer to God. If you can't make it to Konya to see the *sema* ceremony in the place where it all began, there are a couple of venues at which to see them in Istanbul. It should be noted that these ceremonies—at least in Istanbul—have essentially turned into performances staged for tourists, lacking much religious context. Nonetheless, seeing the dervishes whirl tends to entrance even the least spiritual of people, and gives a window onto an interesting aspect of traditional Turkish culture.

**Hodjapasha Culture Center.** Housed in a nicely restored 15th-century hammam, the Hodjapasha Culture Center hosts whirling dervish ceremonies several nights a week. The hour-long event starts with a performance of classical Turkish music before the dervishes whirl. Though some are captivated by the whirling, others may find it excessively slow and hypnotic, so consider whether this sort of cultural experience is your cup of tea. Note that photography is not allowed during the ceremony. Hodjapasha also offers performances of traditional Turkish folk dancing, which are considerably more lively. Tickets are 50 TL for the dervishes and 60 TL for the folk dancing. ⊠ *Hocapaşa Hamamı Cad. 3/B, Sirkeci* ☏ *212/511–4686* ⊕ *www.hodjapasha.com.*

**Mevlana Education and Culture Society.** A local dervish group, the Mevlana Education and Culture Society (MEKDER) organizes *sema* ceremonies every Sunday evening that last about an hour and include traditional Mevlevi music and ritual whirling. Tickets cost 35 TL. ⊠ *Galata Mevlevihanesi, Galip Dede Cad. 15, Beyoğlu* ☎ *216/336–1662.*

# SHOPPING

Istanbul has been a shopper's town for, well, centuries—the sprawling Grand Bazaar, open since 1461, could easily be called the world's oldest shopping mall—but this not to say that the city is stuck in the past. Along with its colorful bazaars and outdoor markets, Istanbul also has a wide range of modern shopping options, from the enormous new malls that seem to be sprouting up everywhere to small independent boutiques. Either way, it's almost impossible to leave Istanbul without buying something. Whether you're looking for trinkets and souvenirs, kilims and carpets, brass and silverware, leather goods, old books, prints and maps, or furnishings and clothes (Turkish textiles are among the best in the world), you can find them here. Shopping in Istanbul also provides a snapshot of the city's contrasts and contradictions: from migrants from eastern Turkey selling their wares on the streets, to the leisurely, time-honored haggling over endless glasses of tea in the bazaars and back alleys, to the credit cards and bar codes of the plush, upscale Western-style department stores.

**İstiklal Caddesi** is a pedestrian-only boulevard with everything from global brands like Levi's and big-name Turkish companies such as Mavi to small shoe stores and bookstores. The high-fashion district is the upscale **Nişantaşı** neighborhood, 1 km (½ mi) north of İstiklal Caddesi—this is where you'll find the boutiques of established Turkish fashion designers, such as Özlem Süer, Arzu Kaprol, and Atıl Kutoğlu, as well as the flagship stores of high-end international brands such as Armani, DKNY, and Louis Vuitton. City's, a ritzy mall that opened in 2008, has designer shops like Class Roberto Cavalli—though because of the high import taxes, these name brands are usually more expensive in Turkey than they are in the United States. The **Cevahir** mall, in Şişli, has more than 300 stores selling foreign and local brand-name clothing and is a little easier on the wallet.

## MARKETS

In addition to the markets *listed below*, a flea market is held every Sunday along Çukurcuma Caddesi in the Beyoğlu area; along the Bosphorus in the Ortaköy neighborhood is a Sunday crafts market with street entertainment.

**The Arasta Bazaar.** Just behind the Blue Mosque, the Arasta Bazaar is a walkway lined with shops selling items similar to those you'll find at the Grand Bazaar (primarily carpets and ceramics), but often at lower prices. The atmosphere is also considerably calmer and, unlike the Grand Bazaar, the Arasta is open on Sunday. ⊠ *Sultanahmet.*

**Balık Pazarı** (*Fish Market*). The Balık Pazarı sells, of course, fish, as well as everything connected with food, from fresh produce to nuts and sweets. Though it's become rather touristy, you can still find all sorts of traditional delicacies here. ⊠ *Off İstiklal Cad., Beyoğlu.*

*Continued on page 142*

# SHOPPING IN ISTANBUL
## The Grand Bazaar & the Spice Market

Istanbul, historically one of the most important stops on the Silk Road, which linked the East and West through commerce, is today still a fabulous place to shop. You can find everything from the quintessential woven carpet to cheap trinkets, from antique copper trays to faux Prada bags. At the center of it all is the sometimes chaotic Grand Bazaar, also known as the Kapalı Çarşı or "Covered Bazar," which in many ways can be considered the great-grandmother of the modern shopping mall: it's been around since the 15th century, has more than 20 entrances, covers about 65 streets, and is said to have some 4,000 shops. It can be a bit intense, but it's a must-see. The following pages will help you get oriented so the experience will be less daunting. For comparison, check out the Spice Market in Eminönü; it's also several centuries old but specializes in spices and food items and is much calmer. It's great place to find picnic items and Turkish delicacies to take home (Turkish delight, anyone?).

# THE GRAND BAZAAR

This behemoth of a shopping complex was built by Mehmet II (the Conqueror) in 1461 over several of the main Byzantine shopping streets and expanded over the years. Today it's almost a town unto itself, with its own restaurants, tea houses, mosques, banks, exchange bureaus, post office, police station, health clinic, and several bathrooms nestled among the myriad shops.

Streets in the bazaar are named after the tradespeople who traditionally had businesses there, with colorful names in Turkish like "slipper-makers street," "fez-makers street," and "mirror-makers street." Today, although there's little correspondence between street names and the shops now found on them, the bazaar is still organized roughly by type of merchandise: gold and silver jewelry shops line the prestigious main street, most of the leather stores are in their own wing, carpet shops are clustered primarily in the center, and souvenirs are found throughout. The amazingly polylingual sellers are all anxious to reassure you that you do not have to buy . . . just drink a glass of tea while you browse through leather goods, carpets, fabric, clothing (including counterfeit brand names), brass candelabra, furniture, ceramics, and gold and silver jewelry.

✉ Yeniçeriler Cad. and Çadırcılar Cad.
🕗 Mon.–Sat. 8:30–7

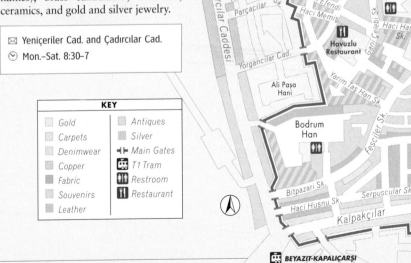

| KEY | |
|---|---|
| ☐ Gold | ☐ Antiques |
| ☐ Carpets | ☐ Silver |
| ☐ Denimwear | ⊷⊶ Main Gates |
| ☐ Copper | 🚋 T1 Tram |
| ☐ Fabric | 🚻 Restroom |
| ☐ Souvenirs | 🍴 Restaurant |
| ☐ Leather | |

Şeker

Mühürdar

Küçük Safran Hanı

Astarcı Han

İç Cebeci Han

Sarnıçlı Han

Cebeci Hanı

Lütfullah Efendi Sk.

Ağa Hanı Hatip Emin Hanı

Yorgancılar Cad.

Evliya Hanı

Çadırcılar Caddesi

Yuncu Hasan Sk.

Parçacılar

Lütfullah Efendi

Hacı Memiş

Gani Çelebi Sk.

Hacı Hasa Sk.

Havuzlu Restaurant

Yorgancılar Cad.

Ali Paşa Hanı

Yarım Taş Han Sk.

Bodrum Han

Fesciler Sk.

Bitpazarı Sk.

Hacı Husnu Sk.

Serpuscular Sk.

Kalpakçılar

🚋 BEYAZIT-KAPALIÇARŞI

Grand Bazaar Shops

## THE BEDESTEN

The domed *iç bedesten* (inner bazaar), aka the Cevahir Bedesteni, once a secure fortress in the heart of the bazaar, is the oldest part of the bazaar and historically where the most valuable goods were kept. Today the *bedesten* is the place to find unique items: it's filled with tiny shops selling an array of antiques that are of generally better quality than the souvenirs sold in the rest of the bazaar. Here you can find anything from pocket watches to vintage cigarette tins, from jewelry to Armenian and Greek religious items. Look for the double-headed Byzantine eagle over the door and you'll know you've found the heart of the bazaar.

# WHAT TO BUY

### JEWELRY

There are over 370 jewelry shops in the bazaar, and you'll find as many locals in them as tourists. Gold and silver jewelry are sold by weight, based on the going market price plus extra for labor, so there's room for bargaining. Sterling silver pieces should have a hallmark. In terms of semiprecious stones, amber and turquoise are especially popular.

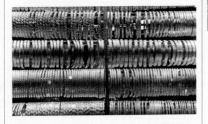

### CERAMICS

Turkey's ceramics tradition goes back to Ottoman times. Today, the most important distinction is between İznik and Kütahya designs; traditional İznik designs, recognizable by the blue, red, and green colors on a white background, are more intricate and more expensive. You'll see gorgeous bowls and plates in both styles, but note that many are coated with lead glazes and are not safe for use with metal utensils or hot food. Medium-size bowls and plates go for between 40-90 TL. Decorative tiles can be made of either ceramic or quartz, with quartz tiles selling for two to three times more than ceramic tiles.

### METALWARE (COPPER & BRASSWARE)

Turkey has a long tradition of metalworking, and you can find both new and antique copper and brass items engraved with elaborate designs. Round copper trays can run well into the hundreds of lira for large, intricately worked items if they're new, and into the thousands for antiques. Small serving trays can be acquired for around 100 TL. Most copper items are plated with tin to make them safe to eat from and therefore appear silver-gray in color. You can find pure copper items but these are suitable for decorative purposes only. Brass items like samovars and pitchers can be shiny if unoxidized or gray-black if oxidized. In general, brass costs more than copper because it's harder to work. Middle Eastern-style lanterns made of worked metal and glass are also neat to check out.

**INLAID-WOOD ITEMS**

You'll see a lot of wood items at the bazaar, beautifully inlaid with mother-of-pearl and different colored woods. Try to avoid imitation inlay: one clue that the inlay is fake is if the mother-of-pearl sections in the design are too uniform in color. You can also usually tell by weight and touch if a backgammon board is plastic. Price is also a dead giveaway: fake-inlay backgammon boards can be had for around 75 TL, whereas those made of walnut and real mother-of-pearl can go for 250-400 TL for a medium-size board. Prices vary based on the amount of inlay and intricacy.

**LEATHER**

Leather is a big industry in Turkey, and the Grand Bazaar has no shortage of stores selling leather jackets, bags, wallets, and shoes. When buying leather goods, look carefully at the quality of the workmanship, which can be assessed by examining seams, zippers, and linings. Imitation leather is, unfortunately, fairly widespread, and even dealers say they sometimes can't tell what's fake and what's not— one clue is that real leather is a bit softer than artificial leather. "Genuine fake" designer bags [i.e., imitation designer bags made with (supposedly) real leather] abound in the Bazaar and sell for around 250 TL.

**SOUVENIRS AND GIFTS**

The bazaar is chock-full of trinkets aimed at tourists—including ornaments featuring the ubiquitous evil-eye beads, Turkish tea sets, and fake designer clothing—but you can also find some nice souvenirs and gift items. Textiles like woven or embroidered pillow covers, and pashmina and silk scarves are inexpensive (12-25 TL apiece) and come in many designs and patterns. Tiny jewelry boxes made of camel bone and decorated with Persian-miniature-style paintings sell for about 30 TL. Turkey is also famous for its meerschaum, a mineral that is used primarily to make pipes; prices range from about 60-250 TL based on the quality of the meerschaum and the intricacy of the carving.

■TIP→ Exporting antiquities from Turkey is forbidden, and the ban is rigorously enforced. If you buy a carpet or other item that looks old, make sure you get certification from the seller that it's not an antiquity.

# BUYING A CARPET

Carpet salesmen in the Grand Bazaar, Kapalı Çarşı

It's almost impossible to visit Istanbul without making a detour into at least one rug shop, and you'll inevitably be poured a glass of tea (or several) while the salesman rolls out one carpet after another on the floor in front of you. Just remember, regardless of how many cups of tea you drink and how persistent the salesman, don't be pressured into making a purchase you don't want.

The vivid colors and patterns of Turkish carpets and kilims, which are flat-woven rugs (without a pile), are hard to resist. Patterns and colors vary by region of origin, and in the case of kilims they often have symbolic meanings.

The Grand Bazaar is, without a doubt, the most convenient place in Istanbul to buy a rug, since the sheer number of rug dealers means there is a wide selection. That said, don't go to the Grand Bazaar looking for bargains—there are enough tourists coming through every

day to keep prices on the high side.
■ TIP➔ **The Arasta Bazaar, near the Blue Mosque, also has a number of good rug shops in a more relaxed environment and at generally lower prices.**

When shopping for a carpet or kilim, the most important thing is to find a dealer you can trust. Avoid dealers who are pushy, and don't let anyone pressure into buying something. It's best to look at merchandise at several different shops before buying anything, in order to get an idea of prices and see what's out there. Ask lots of questions, such as what a carpet is made of (wool or silk), what kind of dyes were used, and where it was made (note that many so-called Turkish carpets are now made in countries like India and China). Note that silk carpets are considerably more expensive than wool ones, and kilims are generally less expensive than carpets because they involve less labor.

# GRAND BAZAAR TIPS

■ You may want to mentally prepare yourself for being aggressively pursued by merchants who are as shameless about making sales pitches as they are competitive over business; it can be overwhelming at first but underneath the hard sell most of the shop owners are quite friendly.

■ The Grand Bazaar is less crowded earlier on weekday mornings.

■ Once you're in the bazaar, spend some time getting your bearings and comparison shopping before you make any major purchases; this will help you get an idea of prices as well as narrow down what you'd like to buy.

■ Watch out for fakes, be they antique rugs, leather, or jewelry—if a dealer's price seems too good to be true, it probably is.

## CARPET AND KILIM TIPS

■ Ask for a Certificate of Authenticity for rugs that are handmade or antique.

■ A new (nonantique) rug should sit flat on the floor when it's laid out, and the edges should be straight.

■ Examine the back of a carpet to see how fine the knots are. The more knots per square inch, the finer the knotting will be and the more valuable the carpet.

■ The number of knots per square inch is not the only thing to go by when choosing a carpet. A lower-knot carpet made with high-quality wool and dyes is worth more than a higher-knot carpet made with poor materials.

■ Try to buy a carpet directly from the store owner, not a third party.

■ It's best to take your rug home with you. If you have it shipped, get a receipt describing exactly what you bought (not just a serial number), and take a picture of the item.

## BARGAINING AT THE BAZAAR

Prices at the Grand Bazaar are on the high side, due to high rents and the never-ending stream of tourists, but the convenience of the bazaar often makes it a good place to shop. Shop owners will expect you to bargain, so here are some tips.

■ Ask the price of several different items before focusing on the thing you really want, to get an idea of a store's prices and to make your intentions less obvious.

■ After the merchant quotes a price, make a counter-offer that's about half what they asked; then negotiate until you reach a price somewhere in the middle.

■ Do accept a shopkeeper's offer of tea. This gives you the chance to get familiar with the dealer. Accepting tea, however, does not obligate you to buy anything.

■ If you and the merchant can't reach a deal, starting to walk away often results in the merchant lowering the price.

■ The more items you buy from a merchant, the more you can bargain the price down.

## DID YOU KNOW?

The Grand Bazaar was ravaged twice by fire in relatively recent years—once in 1954, when it was almost destroyed, and once in 1974, in a smaller conflagration. In both cases, the bazaar was quickly rebuilt in something resembling the original style, with arched passageways and brass-and-tile fountains at regular intervals.

# THE SPICE MARKET

## MISIR ÇARŞISI, OR THE EGYPTIAN BAZAAR

The 17th-century Egyptian Bazaar, also known as the Spice Market, in Istanbul's Eminönü neighborhood, is a riot of colors and fragrances. Although some of the spice shops have recently given way to stalls selling tourist souvenirs like you'll find in the Grand Bazaar, the Spice Market, with its mounds of *lokum* (Turkish delight), bags of spices, and heaps of dried fruit and nuts, is still a wonderfully atmospheric place to shop for spices and other delicious edibles.

For the most part prices at the Spice Market are clearly marked. Unlike in the Grand Bazaar, bargaining is discouraged here—if you're buying a lot, you might get the seller to come down by 10%, but don't expect much more.

✉ Yeni Cami Meydanı, Eminönü
🕑 Mon.–Sat. 8:30–7, Sun. 9–6:30

## WHAT TO BUY

*Lokum*, or **Turkish delight**, in a wide variety of flavors, including rosewater and fruit-essenced, stuffed with pistachios or walnuts, or chocolate-covered. Merchants will enthusiastically ply you with free samples.

**Herbs and spices,** including cumin, sumac, turmeric, many varieties of pepper, and curry mixes. The best saffron (*safran*) found here comes from neighboring Iran, and although it's still not cheap it's less expensive than in the United States.

**Dried fruits,** particularly figs, dates, and apricots.

**Nuts,** including domestically harvested pistachios and hazelnuts.

Black and herbal **teas** and finely ground **Turkish coffee.**

**Caviar** is also sold here for less than in the U.S. or Europe due to Turkey's proximity to its source, the Caspian Sea. Considering the serious endangerment of sturgeon, however, you might think twice about buying it.

You'll also see a variety of rather questionable-looking concoctions being sold as natural aphrodisiacs or "Turkish Viagra." Draw your own conclusions about their reliability.

★ **The Egyptian Bazaar.** *See the highlighted feature in this chapter.* ⊠ *Near Yeni Cami Meydanı, Eminönü.*

Fodor'sChoice **The Grand Bazaar.** *See the highlighted feature in this chapter.*
★

Fodor'sChoice **Nuruosmaniye Caddesi.** One of the major streets leading to the Grand
★ Bazaar, Nuruosmaniye Caddesi has a pedestrian boulevard section lined with some of the Old City's most stylish (and high-end) shops, with an emphasis on fine carpets, jewelry, and antiques. ⊠ *Grand Bazaar.*

**Sahaflar Çarşısı.** The Sahaflar Çarşısı, reached through a doorway just outside the western end of the Grand Bazaar, is home to a bustling book market, with both old and new editions. Most are in Turkish, but English and other languages are also represented. The market is open daily, though Sunday has the most vendors. ⊠ *Grand Bazaar.*

## SPECIALTY STORES

### ANTIQUES

Antiques are a surprisingly rare commodity in this antique land, perhaps because the government, to ensure that Turkish culture is not sold off to richer nations, has made it illegal to export most kinds of antiques that are more than 100 years old. The Grand Bazaar, of course, is a good place to go antique hunting, but an even better option is the Çukurcuma area in Beyoğlu, which is filled with small shops carrying everything from small, Ottoman-era knickknacks to outsized antique marble tubs.

Fodor'sChoice **Alaturca.** Styled more like a grand private mansion than a store, Alaturca
★ has four floors that house a carefully selected—and very high-end—collection of antiques, including artwork, ceramics, metalwork, and Ottoman calligraphy. Just a small fraction of proprietor Erkal Aksoy's collection of antique carpets is on display here. ⊠ *Faik Paşa Yokuşu Sok. 4, Çukurcuma* ☎ *212/245–2933.*

**Artrium.** Artrium is a delightful shop located in a historic 19th-century passage just off Tünel Square. It has a range of antique items, including a fascinating collection of old prints and paintings, as well as some interesting ceramics, jewelry, and other handmade crafts. ⊠ *Tünel Geçidi 7, Beyoğlu* ☎ *212/251–4302.*

**Levant Koleksiyon.** The maps, engravings, calligraphic works, and charming old postcards with photographs of Ottoman-era Istanbul sold here are quite affordable. The shop sells both framed and unframed pieces, and they do professional framing on the premises. ⊠ *Meşrutiyet Cad. 64/B, Beyoğlu* ☎ *212/293–6333.*

Fodor'sChoice **Sofa.** Sofa is one of Istanbul's most highly regarded antiques stores,
★ located on pedestrian-only Nuruosmaniye Caddesi. Two-levels are filled with a fascinating collection of metalwork, original İznik and Kütahya ceramics, old maps and prints, textiles, vintage jewelry, artwork, and assorted other treasures. ⊠ *Nuruosmaniye Cad. 53A, Cağaloğlu* ☎ *212/ 520–2850.*

**Tombak.** In two shops around the corner from each other, Tombak stocks an eclectic collection of antique metal objects, tablewares, lamps, paintings, clocks, jewelry, and other interesting finds. ⊠ *Faik Paşa Yokuşu 22/A, Çukurcuma* ☎ *212/244–3681.*

**Ziya Aykaç Antikacı.** Ziya Aykaç Antikacı has a corner store in the Grand Bazaar filled floor to ceiling with antique fabrics, silverware, ceramics, and other treasures. ⊠ *Takkeciler Sok. 68–72, Grand Bazaar* ☎ *212/527–6082.*

## CARPETS

**Adnan & Hasan.** One of Istanbul's most reputable carpet dealers, Adnan & Hasan espouses a "hassle-free shopping" policy and is favored by the diplomatic community. The company offers a large selection of antique, semiantique, and new carpets and kilims, mostly from Anatolia, and the staff is friendly. ⊠ *Halıcılar Cad. 89–90–92, Grand Bazaar* ☎ *212/527–9887.*

**Dhoku.** Dhoku stands out among the traditional carpet merchants of the Grand Bazaar for its radically different, bold, contemporary styles, such as geometric designs and stylized floral patterns. Sister company Ethnicon (Takkeciler Caddesi 49–51) produces carpets using different-size squares of colorful fabric, reminiscent of American-style quilts. Both stores offer fixed prices. ⊠ *Takkeciler Sok. 58–60, Grand Bazaar* ☎ *212/527-6841.*

**Galeri Cengiz.** At the edge of the Arasta Bazaar, Galeri Cengiz sells boldly patterned rugs from throughout Turkey and Central Asia, as well as hand-woven bags, footwear, and accessories. ⊠ *Arasta Bazaar 155–157, Sultanahmet* ☎ *212/518–8882.*

**Odabaşı Halıcılık.** Odabaşi, in the Babıali Carpet and Kilim Bazaar, specializes in rugs and kilims, both antique and new, from Turkey and the surrounding region. Proprietor İsmet Odabasio is primarily a wholesaler of rugs with a busy export business to the United States, but he is happy to work directly with customers looking for special pieces at reasonable prices. ⊠ *Babıali Cad. Babıali Çarşısı 18/D 22–42, Cağaloğlu* ☎ *212/511–5983.*

**Şengör.** Established in 1918 and now run by the fourth generation of the Şengör family, Şengör has a large inventory of carpets from different regions of Anatolia. ⊠ *Takkeciler Sok. 65–83 and 98, Grand Bazaar* ☎ *212/527–2192.*

## CLOTHING

Istanbullus like to dress smartly and although the city might not be one of Europe's well-known fashion centers, it is certainly not lacking in places to buy clothes, from department stores selling famous international brands to the boutiques of Turkish designers. The charming Galata neighborhood is prime turf for up-and-coming fashion designers, where you can find unique designer clothes for a fraction of what they would cost in New York or Paris.

**Bahar Korçan.** One of Turkey's most innovative fashion designers, Bahar Korçan creates stylish women's clothes, often made using layers of gauzy fabric, with a sense of organic whimsy. Her decision to move her boutique to Serdar-ı Ekrem Caddesi several years ago started a trend, and the street is now home to a number of rising Turkish designers. ⊠ *Serdar-ı Ekrem Caddesi, Seraskerci Sok. 5, Galata* ☎ *212/243–7320.*

**Beymen.** Istanbul's version of Bloomingdale's, Beymen has suited door-men and sells expensive, up-to-date fashions from well-known international brands and designers. ⊠ *Abdi İpekçi Cad. 23, Nişantaşı* ☎ *212/373–4800.*

**Beymen Blender.** Just around the corner from Beymen, this concept store has a younger, hipper vibe, with clothing from trendy international designers and brands as well as jewelry collections by local Turkish designers. ⊠ *Bostan Sok. 10, Nişantaşı* ☎ *212/343–4800.*

Fodor'sChoice ★ **Gönül Paksoy.** Gönül Paksoy is known for her elegant and stunning collection of women's clothing that reinterprets Ottoman and tribal designs. The museumlike main store shows off some pieces created with vintage textiles, as well as new garments made using all-natural fabrics and dyes. A branch across the street at number 6/A focuses on jewelry, bags, shoes, and other accessories, all crafted in the designer's characteristic style. ⊠ *Atiye Sok. 1/3, Nişantaşı* ☎ *212/236–0209, 212/261–9081 branch.*

**İgüs.** With two shops in the Grand Bazaar, İgüs offers one of the widest selections of scarves and pashminas to be found anywhere. Prices are reasonable. ⊠ *Yağlıkçılar Cad. 29 and 80, Grand Bazaar* ☎ *212/512–3528.*

**Mavi.** Turkey's homegrown jean company, Mavi, has come a long way since its founding in 1991, with stores now in dozens of countries. The flagship Istanbul store near the top of İstiklal Caddesi (there are two other, smaller, branches further down the avenue) carries the brand's signature jeans, as well as a collection of hip Istanbul-themed T-shirts created by different guest designers. ⊠ *İstiklal Cad. 123/A, Beyoğlu* ☎ *212/244–6255.*

Fodor'sChoice ★ **Vakko.** One of Turkey's oldest and most elegant fashion houses, Vakko sells its own lines as well as clothing, shoes, and accessories from high-end international labels. The company is particularly well known for its collection of silk scarves and ties in a variety of traditional and modern designs, and a boutique in the Grand Bazaar focuses on these items, as well as accessories and chocolates. ⊠ *Abdi İpekçi Cad. 33, Nişantaşı* ☎ *212/248–5011* ⊠ *Akmerkez shopping mall, in Etiler* ☎ *212/282–0695* ⊠ *Bağdat Cad. 422, Suadiye (on the Asian side)* ☎ *216/463–2606.*

## ENGLISH-LANGUAGE BOOKSTORES

Many of the larger hotels and souvenir shops in Sultanahmet stock some English-language newspapers and books, mostly guides to the more famous sights. A more comprehensive range of reading material can be found at specialty bookstores in Beyoğlu and in the fashionable shopping district of Nişantaşı. Books originally published outside Turkey are marked up anywhere from 15% to 75%. Many newspaper stands throughout the city carry the *International Herald Tribune*. Some of the larger bookstores carrying English-language books include the following.

**Galeri Kayseri.** If you're looking for books about Turkey, this is the place to come. The two Galeri Kayseri shops are across the street from one another, and between them you'll find a thorough collection of nonfiction books about Turkey in a variety of subject areas, as well as a selection of Turkish and Turkey-related novels and elegant coffee table books on Islamic art, architecture, and culture. Number 58 is the main store, No. 11 is across the street. ⊠ *Divanyolu Cad. 58, Sultanahmet* ☎ *212/516–3366* ⊠ *Divanyolu Cad. 11, Sultanahmet* ☎ *212/511–7380.*

**Homer Kitabevi.** One of Istanbul's best bookstores, Homer carries an impeccable selection of English-language books, especially ones dealing with the politics and history of Turkey and the Middle East. ⊠ *Yeni Çarşı Cad. 12/A, Galatasaray, Beyoğlu* ☎ *212/249–5902.*

**Pandora.** One of Turkey's premier booksellers, Pandora has a dedicated English-language branch (located just across the street from its Turkish-language bookstore) and carries an impressive selection of books in all genres, with a particular emphasis on nonfiction. ⊠ *Büyükparmakkapı Sok. 8, Beyoğlu* ☎ *212/245–1667.*

**Robinson Crusoe.** About as appealing as a bookstore can get, Robinson Crusoe has two cozy levels lined floor to ceiling with a well-chosen selection of books, about a quarter of which are fiction and nonfiction in English. There is also a very good collection of magazines and journals. ⊠ *İstiklal Cad. 195/A, Beyoğlu* ☎ *212/293–6968.*

USED BOOKS    A number of stores, including the following, specialize in secondhand books, many in English, from dog-eared thrillers to rare old texts about the city. There is also a cluster of antiquarian booksellers in the Sahaflar Çarşısı, just outside the Grand Bazaar.

**Librairie de Pera.** A small shop filled with antiquarian books in English, French, German, and a smattering of other European languages, Librairie de Pera also sells old maps, prints, and other assorted treasures. ⊠ *Galip Dede Sokak 8, Beyoğlu* ☎ *212/243–3991.*

### HANDICRAFTS

Turkey is known for rugs, but there are plenty of other handicrafts to buy that will take up less space in your suitcase—and a smaller bite out of your spending budget.

Fodor'sChoice    **Abdulla.** Abdulla offers handmade fabrics, towels, tablecloths, and other
★    home textiles made of all-natural materials. The immensely appealing and stylish collection also includes luscious olive-oil soaps. ⊠ *Halıcılar Cad. 62, Grand Bazaar* ☎ *212/527–3684.*

Fodor'sChoice    **Armaggan.** A seven-story emporium with the cachet of a small bou-
★    tique, Armaggan offers an impressive and diverse high-end collection of homewares, accessories, design objects, jewelry, and all-natural textiles (including carpets and garments). The unique contemporary designs are inspired by traditional work, and the shop also shows work by contemporary Turkish artists. ⊠ *Nuruosmaniye Cad. 65, Nuruosmaniye* ☎ *212/522–4433.*

**Derviş.** At Derviş, the emphasis is on soaps and traditional Turkish bath accessories, as well as antique kaftans and robes from Anatolia. ⊠ *Keseciler Cad. 33–35, Grand Bazaar* ☎ *212/514–4525* ⊠ *Halıcılar Cad. 51, Grand Bazaar* ☎ *212/528–7883.*

Fodor'sChoice    **IKSV Design.** Run by the Istanbul Foundation for Culture and Arts in
★    the bottom level of the organization's headquarters, the IKSV Design

The centuries-old practice of smoking tobacco in a *narghile*, also known as a hookah or water pipe.

boutique focuses on local designers' work and has the sophistication of a museum shop. The varied collection includes jewelry, accessories, and decorative items by emerging designers, as well as reproductions of artwork by several 20th-century Turkish painters on ceramic items, pillowcases, and the like. ☒ *Sadi Konuralp Cad. 5, Şişhane* ☏ *212/334–0830.*

**İznik Foundation.** In the upscale suburb of Etiler, İznik Foundation is the flagship showroom of the commercial arm of a nonprofit group dedicated to reviving and preserving the classic art of İznik ceramic and tile work. Prices are high, but the quality is outstanding. ☒ *Cengiz Topel Cad., Tuğcular Sok. 1/A, Etiler* ☏ *212/287–3243.*

**Kaptan Bros.** Kaplan Bros. specializes in handworked copper and brass items, both old and new, and also sells stylish lanterns in traditional Middle Eastern and contemporary styles. ☒ *Terziler Sok. 30, Grand Bazaar* ☏ *212/526–3650.*

**Nick's Calligraphy Corner.** One of the most unusual stores in the Grand Bazaar—indeed, anywhere—is Nick Merdenyan's tiny shop in the İç Bedesten. The artist produces intricate calligraphic designs and miniature paintings, incorporating motifs from major world religions, on dried Dieffenbachia leaves; each unique piece is a small masterpiece. ☒ *İç Bedesten Şerif Ağa Sok. 24, Grand Bazaar* ☏ *212/513–5473.*

**Sır Çini.** In the gentrifying neighborhood of Galata, Sır Çini is the workshop and showroom of Sadullah Çekmece, a craftsman who makes both traditional and modern interpretations of İznik and Küthaya ceramics and sells them at reasonable rates. ☒ *Serdar-ı Ekrem Sok. 38, Galata, Beyoğlu* ☏ *212/293–3661.*

**2**

**Tulu.** At Tulu, Istanbul-based American textile collector and designer Elizabeth Hewitt carries her own designs as well as vintage pieces from Turkey, India, and around the world. Her beautiful collections of bed linens and other home textiles with brightly colored patterns are made using traditional hand-blocking techniques. ⊠ *Binbirdirek Mah. Üçler Sok. 7/A, Sultanahmet* ☎ *212/518–8710.*

## JEWELRY

Turkey has a long tradition of jewelry making, and many jewelers today are skilled at working with both gold and silver, designing beautiful pieces with a local flavor. Another trend is to take Ottoman-era charms and tile fragments and set them in silver or gold. You'll also see amber necklaces and ethnic Turkish silver jewelry threaded with coral and lapis lazuli.

**Aida Pekin.** At her tiny boutique in Galata, designer Bihter Ayda Pekin sells unique collections of whimsical jewelry under her label **Aida Pekin.** Many of the pieces incorporate motifs inspired by Istanbul, and prices are very affordable. ⊠ *Serdar-ı Ekrem 44/A, Galata* ☎ *212/243–1211.*

**Bagus.** In the Grand Bazaar's Bedestan area, Bagus has a large collection of silver handmade jewelry as well as intriguing items imported from around the world. ⊠ *Cevahir Bedestan 42–43, Grand Bazaar* ☎ *212/528–2519.*

**Horasan.** There are piles and piles of antique rings, bracelets, and necklaces from Central Asia at Horasan, as well as walls covered in strands of colorful beads made out of precious and semiprecious stones from which the staff will help you create your own jewelry. Prices are fair. ⊠ *Terlikçiler Sok. 37, Grand Bazaar* ☎ *212/519–3654.*

**Mor.** Mor, on a side street off İstiklal Caddesi, displays the work of a pair of designers who make funky, bold jewelry that incorporates antique and ethnic elements into modern design. The chunky pieces, mostly made using gold and stones, are affordably priced. ⊠ *Turnacıbaşı Sok., Sarayhan 10/B, Beyoğlu* ☎ *212/292–8817.*

Fodor'sChoice
★ **Özlem Tuna & Zerre Design Store.** At her boutique in the historic Büyük Yeni Han, designer Özlem Tuna carries her delightful collections of jewelry and delicate ceramic and metal tablewares that put a contemporary twist on traditional Turkish motifs. ⊠ *Büyük Yeni Han, Çakmakçılar Yokuşu, Tarakçılar Cad., Eminönü* ☎ *212/513–1361.*

**Urart.** One of Turkey's most established jewelry companies, Urart makes re-creations, and also chic interpretations, of ancient Anatolian designs and motifs; there are additional sales points in the Çırağan Palace and Hilton. ⊠ *Abdi İpekçi Cad. 18, Nişantaşı* ☎ *212/246–7194.*

## SPECIALTY FOODS

**Hacı Bekir.** Ali Muhiddin Hacı Bekir, who founded his sweets business back in 1777, is considered the inventor of Turkish delight. Today, the Hacı Bekir stores run by his descendents are still considered to be among the best places to buy the delicacy, which comes in a variety of different flavors and is sold fresh by the kilo or prepackaged. There are locations in Eminönü and on İstiklal Caddesi. ⊠ *İstiklal Cad. 83, Beyoğlu* ☎ *212/245–1375* ⊠ *Hamidiye Cad. 83, Eminönü* ☎ *212/522–0666.*

**Kurukahveci Mehmet Efendi.** On a backstreet just outside the western entrance to the Egyptian Bazaar is the tiny art deco–era flagship store of Kurukahveci Mehmet Efendi, Turkey's oldest coffee producer (founded 1871), whose finely ground coffee is legendary. Customers can purchase either beans or ground coffee, which makes a good souvenir of a trip to Turkey. ✉ *Tahmis Sok. 66, Eminönü* ☎ *212/511–4262.*

# SIDE TRIP: PRINCES' ISLANDS

*20 km (12 mi) off the coast of Istanbul from Sultanahmet.*

## GETTING HERE AND AROUND

Ferries (3 TL) and faster Seabuses (8 TL) depart from Katabaş, and take 90 minutes and 45 minutes, respectively. Schedules change with the seasons, so check beforehand for departure times (⊕ *www.ido.com. tr/en*). In summer the early evening ferries returning to the mainland are often very crowded, particularly on weekends.

No cars are allowed on the islands, so you'll do most of your exploring on foot. The cost of horse-drawn carriage tours varies by distance: it's about 20 TL to go to the Monastery of St. George, and 60 or 70 TL for a full-island circle tour. You can rent bicycles (10 TL per hour) from one of the shops near the clock tower on Büyükada: definitely a more fun (and more strenuous) way to get around. To get from one of the Princes' Islands to the other, hop aboard any of several daily ferries.

## EXPLORING

The Princes' Islands, known simply as Adalar in Turkish, are everything that Istanbul isn't: quiet, green, and car-less. They are primarily a relaxing getaway from the noise and traffic of the big city, though can be quite crowded on sunny weekends. Restrictions on development and a ban on automobiles help maintain the old-fashioned peace and quiet—transportation here is only by horse-drawn carriage or bicycle. There are no real "sights," per se; the attraction is the relaxed peaceful atmosphere. Of the nine islands, four have regular ferry service, but only the two largest, Büyükada and Heybeliada, are of real interest to the general traveler. Both are hilly and wooded, and the fresh breeze is gently pine-scented. They make fun day trips from Istanbul thanks to frequent ferries—both the atmospheric old boats and the faster, less atmospheric catamarans known as sea buses—from Katabaş, near Taksim at the end of the tram line.

The nine islands of the Sea of Marmara have provided various uses for the people of Istanbul over the years. Back in the days when the city was known as Constantinople, religious undesirables sought refuge here, while in the time of the sultans, the islands provided a convenient place to exile untrustworthy hangers-on. By the turn of the 18th century, well-heeled businessmen had staked their claim and built many of the Victorian gingerbread–style houses that lend the islands their charm. For several years in the 1930s, Büyükada, the largest of the islands, was the home of the exiled Leon Trotsky: the islands were considered to be safer than Istanbul, with its 35,000 hostile White Russian refugees.

From the ferry you can see the two smallest, uninhabited, islands, known in Greek and Turkish as the "pointy" Oxya/Sivri and the "flat" Plate/Yassı. Sivri's main claim to fame was that in the 19th- and early 20th centuries Istanbul's stray dogs would be occasionally rounded up

and dumped there, while Yassı was the site of the trial and execution of Prime Minister Adnan Menderes after the 1960 military coup. Two of the other inhabited islands are Kınalıada, popular with the city's Armenians, and Burgaz Ada, known to be more Greek, though neither have any significant sights.

### BÜYÜKADA

Büyükada is the largest of the Princes' Islands and generally the one with the most to offer. To the left as you leave the ferry, you'll see a handful of restaurants. **Yörük Ali Plaj,** the public beach on the west side of the island, is an easy walk from the harbor and also has a little restaurant.

To see the island's splendid old Victorian houses, walk to the clock tower and bear right. The most famous of these is the İzzet Paşa Köşkü, at 55 Çankaya Caddesi, where Trotsky lived while exiled here. To explore the island, carriages are available at the clock tower square or there are many places to rent bikes. The carriage tour winds up hilly lanes lined with gardens filled with jasmine, mimosa, and imported palm trees. After all of Istanbul's mosques and palaces, the frilly pastel houses come as something of a surprise. You can have your buggy driver wait while you make the 20- to 30-minute hike up Yücetepe Hill to the **Greek Monastery of St. George (Aya Yorgi),** a 19th-century church built on Byzantine foundations and with a view that goes on and on. As you walk up the path, notice the pieces of cloth, string, and paper that visitors have tied to the bushes and trees in hope of a wish coming true. This is a popular Orthodox Christian pilgrimage site. The outdoor restaurant next to the monastery, Yücetepe Kir Gazinosu, is known for its homemade wine, once made by the monks themselves, but now made by a family on the Aegean island of Bozcaada.

WHERE TO EAT
AND STAY
There is little difference from one spot on Büyükada's restaurant row to the next. Generally, the prices are more expensive the closer to the docks. The best bet is to look at a menu and ask to see the dishes on display. İskele Caddesi, one street behind the shore road, has some cheaper cafés.

### HEYBELIADA

Heybeliada, the closest island to Büyükada, is similar in appeal, and the quiet, lovely surroundings attract similar boatloads of day-trippers in summer, some hoping to avoid the crowds on the "big island."

The big building to the left of the dock is the **Deniz Kuvvetler** (Turkish Naval Academy). To the right of the dock are teahouses and cafés stretching along the waterfront. You can take a leisurely carriage ride, stopping, if the mood strikes, at one of the island's several small, sandy, and rarely crowded beaches—the best are on the north shore at the foot of **Değirmen Burnu** (Windmill Point) and **Değirmen Tepesi** (Windmill Hill).

Carriages on Heybeliada do not climb the hills above the harbor, where the old mansions and gardens are, but the walk is not that strenuous.

# The Sea of Marmara and the North Aegean

**WORD OF MOUTH**

"Pergamum [not pictured above] was wonderful and we had the ruins all to ourselves . . ."

—dgunbug

# WELCOME TO THE SEA OF MARMARA AND THE NORTH AEGEAN

## TOP REASONS TO GO

★ **Explore "Green Bursa":** Visit the Yeşil Cami (Green Mosque), stroll the covered bazaar, and make sure to try the local kebab specialty, *İskender kebap.*

★ **Go back in time at Troy:** Visit the ruins of this 5,000-year-old city of Homer's *Iliad,* where more than nine layers of civilization have been uncovered.

★ **Pay respects at Gallipoli:** Tour the battlefields and memorials where one of the key campaigns of World War I was fought.

★ **Ramble through ancient Pergamum:** Explore this spectacular showcase of the classical period, second in Turkey only to Ephesus.

★ **Relax in Assos:** Enjoy the quiet of Behramkale village; enjoy the Greek ruins; soak up the sun on nearby beaches.

★ **Shop for İznik tiles:** Watch craftswomen engrave ceramics; buy some to take home.

Ruins of the Temple of Trajan Acropolis of Pergamum

A Canakkale war monument at Gallipoli

## GETTING ORIENTED

**1** **Sea of Marmara.** You can still feel the Ottoman spirit in this part of Turkey, where you'll find some of the best examples of early Ottoman architecture, faithfully restored old thermal baths, the surviving arts of tile making and silk weaving, and wonderful old bazaars.

**2** **The Dardanelles.** The Gallipoli Peninsula, to the north of the straits connecting the Aegean and Marmara seas, is full of moving historical sites marking one of the bloodiest campaigns of World War I. Beautifully tended cemeteries stretch along the 35-km (22-mi) peninsula where

so many soldiers are buried. Çanakkale is south of Gallipoli.

**3** **North Aegean.** The combination of Greek heritage and Turkish rural life, set in an unspoiled natural setting of azure sea, curving coastline, and pine-clad hills, is perfect for unwinding. If you want to peek into the past, the ruins of Troy, Pergamum, and Behramkale (Assos) are within easy reach.

A ferry ride across the Sea of Marmara from Istanbul will take you close to İznik, famed for its beautiful tiles, and the old Ottoman capital of Bursa. The historic World War I battlefields of the Gallipoli Peninsula are best visited from Çanakkale or Eceabat, on either side of the Dardanelle straits; Çanakkale is also the jumping-off point for visits to the fabled ancient city of Troy. Farther down the Aegean coast you'll find a scenic hilltop village and ruins at Assos (Behramkale), the laid-back harbor town of Ayvalık and its nearby sandy beaches, and (a bit inland) the ancient ruins of Bergama (Pergamum).

Updated by Jennifer Hattam

The ruins of Bergama, Troy, and Assos, along with the Gallipoli battlefields, are the main draws of the region, but leisurely exploration is also rewarded with fresh air, a cool sea, great food, and havens in the wilderness.

The North Aegean and the Sea of Marmara area are rich in history, spanning many centuries and empires. Civilizations rose and fell at Troy for 5,000 years, and the ruins of Pergamum date from the time of Alexander the Great. The bustling city of Bursa was the first capital of the Ottoman Empire, before Istanbul. The battlefields of Gallipoli bear testament to the more recent past, World War I, while the backstreets of Ayvalık still echo with the footsteps of the Greeks who lived there until early in the 20th century.

The beaches in this region tend to be more pebbly (and the water a touch colder) than they are in other parts of Turkey, but they're also frequently less crowded. You can see the whole of the region in a week or, if you're based in Istanbul, on separate, shorter journeys. Spend at least one evening watching the sun go down over Homer's wine-dark sea, and you'll agree that the North Aegean has a little bit of everything—and a lot you won't find anywhere else.

# PLANNING

## GETTING HERE AND AROUND

### AIR TRAVEL

There are several small airports in the area. Turkish Airlines/Anadolu Jet and Bora Jet operate daily flights between Istanbul's Sabiha Gökçen airport and Çanakkale airport. There is also an airport in Edremit, 50 km (31 mi) north of Ayvalık, on the tip of the Gulf of Edremit, with daily flights on Bora Jet from Sabiha Gökçen; this is convenient if your destination is Ayvalık or Assos. Bursa, the largest city in the region, has an airport, but it is not served by direct flights from Istanbul.

**BOAT AND FERRY TRAVEL**

Fast ferries operate daily between Istanbul's Yenikapı terminal and ports in Yalova and Bursa and provide the quickest, most pleasant way to get to Bursa or İznik. The Yalova ferries run more frequently, approximately every two hours between 8 am and 7:30 pm, with a midday break. The journey takes just over an hour and costs about 15 TL to 20 TL each way for walk-on passengers and between 35 TL and 80 TL for a car including driver and one passenger (check the latest times and fares at ⊕ *www.ido.com.tr/en*). Boats also operate daily between Yenikapı and Bandırma, a good point from which to make your way to Assos or Ayvalık.

Since the Bandırma–Çanakkale road is normally less crowded than the Istanbul–Çanakkale road, when traveling to Gallipoli, you may want to take the boat to Bandırma and continue from there by car. Ferries to/from Bandırma/Istanbul run three times daily (five times daily on weekends), take two hours, and cost about 35 TL each way per passenger and 85 TL to 125 TL for a car including driver and one passenger. Reservations are essential during religious holidays and summer weekends, and advisable generally for weekends and anytime between June and August.

**BUS TRAVEL**

Buses are a good form of transport in this region, though the frequent stops on some routes, such as between Çanakkale and Edremit, can be frustrating. Most bus companies have branches both in the terminals and in the town centers. Several buses make the trip from Istanbul's Esenler terminal to Yalova (about four hours) and from there you can travel on to İznik or Bursa. The trip from Istanbul to Çanakkale is about six hours and costs about 40 TL. The trip from Bursa to Çanakkale is five hours and costs about 30 TL. From Çanakkale buses run almost every hour to İzmir, passing Ezine, Ayvacık, Edremit, Ayvalık, and Bergama on the way. The fare is about 35 TL.

**CAR TRAVEL**

The best way to explore this area is by car, especially if you wish to forego organized tours of Gallipoli, which is quite spread out, and will be visiting Alexandria Troas and some of the other lesser-known sights. Roads are quite good and well marked. There are several options for getting to the region Istanbul: one is to take the E80 headed for Ankara. At İzmit take Route 130 to Yalova; Route 575 connects Yalova and Bursa.

**TRAIN TRAVEL**

Train journey in this region is not advisable: Trains (and tracks) are old and painfully slow.

**GALLIPOLI TOURS**

If you have a car, you can tour the battlefields and memorials on your own, though a good guide can help bring the area's history to life. Hotels that offer tours will also often screen the feature film *Gallipoli* or the documentary *The Fatal Shore* before the trip to set the mood for the visit. Tours are conducted year-round out of Çanakkale and Eceabat, and typically run about 5½ hours, starting around noon in summer,

10:30 am in winter. (Tour companies operating out of Çanakkale will allow time to make the ferry trip to Eceabat before heading out on the peninsula.) Good walking shoes are advised and, in summer, a hat and water.

**Hassle Free Travel Agency.** This should be your first choice for a tour if you're staying in Çanakkale. Hassle Free also runs the Anzac House, a hotel/hostel in town, which is very practical if you're signed up for the tour. From Çanakkale tours to Gallipoli are about 80 TL per person including lunch, ferry crossing, entrance fees, and transport. ⊠ *Cumhuriyet Meydanı 61, Çanakkale* ☎ *286/213–5969* ⊕ *www.anzachouse.com.*

**TJ's Tours.** Standard tours to the battlefields cost about 60 TL, including lunch, transport, and admission fees. TJ's also offers private tours to the southern part of the peninsula (Cape Helles), daily tours to Troy, and snorkeling/diving excursions to shipwrecks around the Gallipoli Peninsula. They own a hostel in Eceabat that is slated to be remodeled into a boutique hotel by spring 2012. ⊠ *Kemalpaşa Mahallesi, Cumhuriyet Caddesi 5/A, Eceabat* ☎ *0286/814–3121* ⊕ *www. anzacgallipolitours.com.*

## LOCAL FLAVOR

Aegean cuisine is in many ways different from Turkish food elsewhere. The shared Turkish and Greek culture of the region's past, the climate and soil suitable for growing a wide range of vegetables, including tasty local greens and herbs, and the prevalence of olive trees and olive-oil production have helped the region develop a much more varied way of eating that is healthier than in other Turkish regions. Olive oil replaces butter, and fish, rather than meat, is the star on most menus. The class of dishes generally called *zeytinyağlı* (literally "with olive oil") mostly comes from this region; these are usually comprised of tomatoes, onions, and other vegetables cooked in olive oil and served cold. Vegetarians will be in heaven.

### LOCAL SPECIALTIES

Most cities in Turkey claim some kind of fame for their *köfte* (meatballs), but *İnegöl köfte*—traditionally cooked over charcoal—are especially delicious and said to have been invented in Bursa, as was *İskender kebap*, tender beef on *pide* (soft flatbread), soaked in tomato sauce, drizzled with hot melted butter, and served with yogurt on the side. Even if you haven't liked *İskender* elsewhere in Turkey, try it in Bursa, where it's far superior.

The Aegean region is known for mezes made with wild herbs collected in the area and cooked or dressed in olive oil. Cunda Island in Ayvalık is particularly famous for its amazing range of seafood and fish mezes and main dishes, enriched by lesser-known Greek specialties and the restaurants' own creations.

### PLANNING YOUR TIME

You can see a bit of the Sea of Marmara on a quick one- or two-day trip from Istanbul: you could do just a day in İznik (make sure you leave Istanbul early), but you'll want to spend a night, at least, in Bursa. The ferry from Istanbul's Yenikapı terminal to Yalova takes about an hour; from there, you can catch a bus to İznik or Bursa. There are also direct ferries to Bursa (Güzelyalı) from Yenikapı, though you should allow an hour to get between the ferry terminal and the city center by public transportation.

An optimal way to spend two days around the Sea of Marmara is to leave Istanbul by ferry early enough to be in Yalova by midmorning, then catch a bus or drive to İznik and have lunch by the lake. Next head into the center of town to visit the İznik Museum, Saint Sophia, and some of the famous tile workshops. If you leave İznik by late afternoon, you'll be in Bursa in the early evening. Spend the second day sightseeing in Bursa—don't miss Yeşil Cami, the covered bazaar, Ulu Cami, and the Muradiye Tombs. For lunch, make sure to try the *İskender kebap*. If you have time, you can take the gondola lift up Uludağ and enjoy the view from the mountain's pine-covered slopes. Head down to the Bursa ferry station in the early evening and catch the last boat back to Yenikapı terminal in Istanbul.

You can visit Gallipoli in a long, rushed day trip from Istanbul (as many tour operators do) but you're better off spending the night in Çanakkale and seeing the ruins of Troy as well. If you have five or six days, you can pretty much see everything in the vicinity, visiting İznik, Bursa, and Çanakkale then continuing on to Behramkale (Assos) and Ayvalık, with a visit to Cunda, Ayvalık's main island, and the ruins of Pergamum. Be warned, though: Once you get a taste of the area's natural beauty and relaxing vibe, you might want to stay longer.

## WHAT IT COSTS

| DINING AND LODGING PRICE CATEGORIES IN U.S. DOLLARS | | | | |
|---|---|---|---|---|
| | ¢ | $ | $$ | $$$ | $$$$ |
| Restaurants | under $5 | $5–$10 | $11–$15 | $16–$25 | over $25 |
| Hotels | under $50 | $50–$75 | $76–$150 | $151–$250 | over $250 |

Restaurant prices are for one main course at dinner or for two *mezes* (small dishes). Hotel prices are for two people in a standard double room in high season, including taxes.

## WHEN TO GO

The Southern Marmara and the North Aegean region are considerably cooler than the South Aegean and Mediterranean coast, but summer is still very hot. In July and August, the national park at Uludağ, in Bursa, remains refreshingly cool, and, with its skiing opportunities, is also an attraction in winter. If you're here in colder months, soaking in Bursa's thermal baths is a good antidote to the winter blues.

Travelers from New Zealand and Australia throng the Gallipoli Peninsula and nearby towns for the April 25 Anzac Day commemorations; other visitors may want to avoid the area at this busy time. Çanakkale, Gallipoli, and Troy—which Homer referred to as a windy city—can all be gusty in late summer and fall.

The Sea of Marmara

## SEA OF MARMARA

Although quite close to Istanbul, the area around the Sea of Marmara is sometimes overlooked, but there is much here to attract visitors interested in history and beautiful landscapes.

İznik, a center of early Christianity and an important city for the Ottomans, contains historical sights from the Roman, Byzantine, Seljuk, and Ottoman periods; the town's beautiful tiles are another reason to visit. Bursa, the first capital of the Ottoman Empire, boasts some of the finest examples of Ottoman architecture in its mosques and bazaars. You can visit either city as a day trip from Istanbul, though Bursa deserves at least an overnight stay. Both cities are, more or less, on the way to the Mediterranean, Central Anatolia, or even the North Aegean if you're traveling by ferry across the Marmara Sea.

## İZNIK

*190 km (118 mi) from Istanbul.*

Nature has been generous to İznik, which is beautifully situated around the east end of İznik Lake. You can swim (though the water can be chilly), picnic, or rent a kayak or paddleboat, and you can also soak in centuries of history and witness the city's legendary tile-making tradition, in full revival today.

An important city in early Christian history, İznik (known in ancient times as Nicaea) was the site of the First and Second Councils of Nicaea, which drew up the Nicene Creed that outlines the basic principles of Christianity and set the church's stance on iconography. The city was put on the map in 316 BC when one of Alexander the Great's generals claimed it. The Seljuks made the city their capital for a brief period in the 11th century, and Byzantine emperors-in-exile did the same in the 13th century, when Constantinople was in the hands of Crusaders. The production of famous İznik tiles, unequaled even today, was launched not long after the Ottomans captured the city in 1331.

### GETTING HERE AND AROUND

If you're driving, İznik is 190 km (118 mi) from Istanbul via Route 100 or E80 to İzmit and Route 130 to Yalova; it's 60 km (37 mi) east from Yalova via Route 595. Or take the ferry from Istanbul's Yenikapı terminal to Yalova (1 hour). The ferry trip lops 140 km (87 mi) off the journey.

In Istanbul, several buses (the 69A, 70KY, and 70FY are the most frequent) run from Cumhuriyet Caddesi (Republic Street) near Taksim Square to the Yenikapı terminal.

Once you arrive in Yalova by boat, if you don't have your own car, exit the ferry port, turn right and walk about 50 meters past the police station to the minibus station. Destinations are clearly displayed in the bus windows, and you'll find the one to İznik near a series of buildings on your right. The trip from Yalova to İznik costs about 9 TL.

İznik is easy to navigate and the town's sights are all easily within reach on foot. You'll almost certainly come across the city's walls as you explore. The four main gates date back to Roman times, and the city's two main streets intersect each other and end at these gates. Running east–west is Kılıçaslan Caddesi; north–south is Atatürk Caddesi. Saint Sophia church is at the intersection of these streets.

### ESSENTIALS

**Visitor Information.** This small booth downtown offers maps and brochures of the İznik area. If there's no one working inside, check at Saint Sophia next door. ⊠ *Atatürk Caddesi and Kılıçaslan Caddesi, next to Saint Sophia* ☎ *0532/665-0370.*

## EXPLORING

**İznik Müzesi.** A high-domed white room, constructed in 1388 as a soup kitchen to serve free food to the poor, houses such artifacts as Greek tombstones, Ottoman jewelry, pieces of Byzantine floor mosaics, and original İznik tiles. In the same complex are two mosques, the smaller Şeyh Kutbuddin Camii and the larger Yeşil Cami, notable for its colorfully tiled minaret and intricate stone-cutting work. ⊠ *Eşrefzade Mahallesi, Müze Sokak 11* ☎ *0224/757–1027* ⊆ *3 TL* ⊙ *Daily 8–noon and 1–5.*

**Lefke Kapısı** (*Lefke Gate*). The eastern gate to the ancient city was built in honor of a visit by the Roman emperor Hadrian in AD 120 and is

# İznik's Tiled Beauty

İznik tile makers believe that their tiles have magical properties. There is one sound explanation for this (alongside any number of unsound ones): İznik tiles, made from soil that's found only in the area, have a high level of quartz, an element believed to have soothing effects. It's not just the level of quartz that makes İznik tiles unique, though. The original tiles also have distinctive patterns and colors: predominantly blue, then green and red, reflecting the colors of precious stones. The patterns are inspired by local flora—flowering trees or tulips. These days artists use different colors and designs as well as the traditional ones.

İznik became a center for the ceramics industry after the 15th-century Ottoman conquest of Istanbul. To upgrade the quality of native work, Sultan Selim I (ruled 1512–15) imported 500 potters from Tabriz in Persia. The government-owned kilns were soon turning out exquisite tiles with intricate motifs of circles, stars, and floral and geometric patterns, in lush turquoise, green, blue, red, and white. Despite the costliness of the tiles, their popularity spread through the Islamic world, until the industry went into decline in the 18th century.

İznik tiles are expensive—more so than those produced in the rival ceramics center of Kütahya, 120 km (72 mi) farther south. A single tile costs about 40 TL; a small plate starts at the same price, but prices can run into the hundreds of dollars. İznik tiles are made of better-quality stone, with a higher quartz content, than those made elsewhere, so they're heavier and more durable, making them ideal for decorating high-traffic spaces, from airports to mosques. They're all handmade, with no artificial colors, and the designs tend to be more intricate and elegant than their rivals. The tile-makers' street (Salim Demircan Sokak), near the city center, is lined with small shops and workshops where you can see the tiles being made and buy the famous wares.

**The İznik Training and Education Foundation.** The İznik Training and Education Foundation, founded in the 1990s to revive the art of tile making, fashions large orders, often for overseas delivery. Even if you are not commissioning a job, you can see the beautiful craftsmanship and wander in the gardens. ⊠ *Sahil Yolu, Vakıf Sokak 13* ☎ *0224/757–6025* ⊕ *www.iznik. com* ☾ *Weekdays 8–6.*

**Süleyman Paşa Medresesi.** The Süleyman Paşa Medresesi, an early Ottoman theology school, is now a tile and ceramic bazaar with 10 workshops. They're grouped around a peaceful courtyard where you can enjoy a cup of tea. ⊠ *Maltepe Caddesi 27* ☾ *Apr.–Oct., daily 10–6:30; Nov.– Mar., daily 11–4 or 5.*

among the best-preserved remnants of the thick, sturdy fortifications that once encircled İznik. Some of the old inscriptions, marble reliefs, and friezes remain intact. Outside the gray stone and faded brick gate are the leafy city graveyard and Muslim tombs, some as old as 600 years, belonging to noblemen and lesser luminaries.

**Roman Theater.** The Roman Emperor Trajan asked the governor Plinius to construct this theater in the early 2nd century. Today the theater is little more than a pile of rubble but, wandering over the rocks, it's easy to imagine the former grandeur of the place. ⊠ *West of bus station near lake.*

**Aya Sofya** (*Saint Sophia*). A primitive mosaic floor is believed to date from the church's construction in the 6th century, during the reign of Justinian. Wall mosaics were added as part of a reconstruction in the 11th century, after an earthquake toppled the original church, and some fine fragments of frescoes date from the Byzantine era. ⊠ *Atatürk Caddesi and Kılıçaslan Caddesi* ⚏ *7 TL* ☉ *May–Sept., daily 9–6, Oct.–Apr., daily 8–5.*

**OFF THE BEATEN PATH**

**Termal.** A popular spa since Roman times, Termal is a good stop if you're en route between Yalova and either İznik or Bursa. The springs were used by the Ottomans, refurbished in 1900 by Sultan Abdül Hamid II, and regularly visited by Atatürk in the 1920s and 1930s. Termal is a self-contained resort with three hotels (Çamlık, Çınar, and Thermal), exotic gardens, a huge swimming pool, and four historic bath houses offer many options for soaking in the mineral-rich waters. The hotels also have private baths for guests only. Avoid summer weekends, when the place is absolutely packed and the crowds will probably outweigh the baths' relaxing properties—anyway, the hot baths are more appealing, and the rates cheaper, in other seasons. Also consider a walk in the pine forests, where you can enjoy a packed lunch. ⊠ *About 70 km (42 mi) west of İznik; 12 km (8 mi) southwest of Yalova on the way to Çınarcık* ☎ *226/675–7400* ⊕ *www.yalovatermal.com.*

**Tomb and Mosque of Abdülvahap.** If you're looking for a good spot to watch the sunset over İznik Lake, the tomb of Abdülvahap Sultan Sancaktarı, a hero of the battle in which the Ottomans captured the city in 1331, is well worth the trip for its sweeping view. From these monuments, on a clear evening the orange glow of sunset makes the surrounding mountains look like the backs of gigantic serpents sleeping in the lake. The spot—a short drive or a 30-minute walk (some of it uphill) from the city center—attracts couples young and old as well as extended families, many of whom bring dinner along to accentuate the experience. Take Kılıçaslan Caddesi east through the Lefke Gate and then follow the ruins of the Roman aqueduct along the road on your right until you can see the large Turkish flag on the hilltop near the tomb.

## WHERE TO EAT AND STAY

*For expanded hotel reviews, visit Fodors.com.*

¢ ╳ **Kenan Çorba & Izgara.** This popular spot just opposite the Saint

TURKISH Sophia museum specializes in soups and beans. İşkembe (tripe soup) is probably best for those who are into experimenting—you'll either hate it or love it—but the beans with sliced Turkish pastrami and rice, accompanied by tiny pickled peppers, is an all-around favorite. The restaurant opens early, at 5 am. ✉ *Atatürk Caddesi 93/B, opposite Saint Sophia* ☎ *0224/757–0235* ⊙ *5 am–8 pm.*

¢   ✕ **Köfteci Yusuf.** Turks love their
TURKISH   *köfte* (meatballs), and almost every city in the country makes a claim to fame based on its own way of preparing them. Locals fill the large, canteen-type tables of this casual bi-level eatery at almost all times of the day to enjoy *İznik köfte,* served with tomatoes, peppers, and onions. Other types of grilled meats are also on offer, with yogurt and salads as optional sides. ✉ *Atatürk Caddesi 73, opposite İznik Lycee* ☎ *0224/757–3597* ⊕ *www. kofteciyusuf.com.tr* ⊙ *Daily 11–11.*

$   ⊞ **Çamlık Motel.** On the quiet end of the lakefront, this plain but well-established hotel is one of the best places to stay in İznik, with simply furnished rooms—a choice few overlooking the lake—a large, charming garden, and a nice and reasonably priced lakefront restaurant. **Pros:** nice location near the quietest part of the lake; good restaurant. **Cons:** fairly basic accommodations; only four rooms face the lake; no elevator. ✉ *Göl Sahil Yolu* ☎ *0224/757–1362* ⊕ *www.iznik-camlikmotel. com* ⇆ *24 rooms* ⊘ *In-room: a/c, Wi-Fi. In-hotel: restaurant, parking* ¶⊙¶ *Breakfast.*

¢   ⊞ **Hotel Aydın.** This clean and simple spot near the lake in the center of town is run by friendly cousins Barbaros and Sertaç, whose grandfather opened the on-premises Aydo Patisserie, a café that serves justly famous homemade ice cream. **Pros:** in the center of town near Saint Sophia. **Cons:** lakefront prices without lakefront access; street noise in some rooms. ✉ *Kılıçaslan Caddesi 64* ☎ *0224/757–7650* ⊕ *www. iznikhotelaydin.com* ⇆ *18 rooms* ⊘ *In-room: a/c, Wi-Fi* ¶⊙¶ *Breakfast.*

¢   ⊞ **Kaynarca Hotel and Pansiyon.** The clean, well-maintained rooms make this a top budget choice, off the lakefront but near sights and inexpensive restaurants and with a kitchen for guest use and a large rooftop balcony. **Pros:** free maps and travel advice; good place to meet other travelers. **Cons:** no a/c in rooms; basic accommodations; breakfast not included in room price; lake is 10-minute walk away. ✉ *M. Gündem Sokak 1* ☎ *0224/757–1753* ⊕ *www.kaynarca.net* ⇆ *13 rooms* ⊘ *In-room: no a/c, Wi-Fi* ¶⊙¶ *No meals.*

---

## DINING IN İZNİK

The restaurants of the lakefront hotels are your best bet for drinks and dinner. While touring the sights, though, eat in the town center at any of the various establishments along or around Kılıçaslan Caddesi, where good *pide* (pizza-like flatbread), *lahmacun* (flatbread with ground meat on top, literally "meat with dough"), kebabs, and *esnaf* (home cooking) are easy-to-find and are low-cost options for a quick lunch. The many *çay bahçe* (tea gardens) along the lake offer cheap eats as well.

# BURSA

*240 km (150 mi) from Istanbul.*
An important center since early Ottoman times, Bursa is today one of Turkey's more prosperous cities (due to its large automobile and textile industries) and is also a pleasing mix of bustling modernity, old stone buildings, mosques, thermal spas, and wealthy suburbs with vintage wood-frame Ottoman villas. Residents proudly call their city Yeşil Bursa (Green Bursa)—for the green İznik tiles decorating some of its most famous monuments, and also for its parks and gardens and the national forest surrounding nearby Uludağ, Turkey's most popular ski mountain. The city can also lay claim to inventing two culinary staples: *İskender kebap* and *İnegöl köfte.*

> ### TAKE THE WATERS
>
> Bursa has been a spa town since Roman times. Rich in minerals, the waters are said to cure a variety of ills, from rheumatism to nervous complaints. The thermal springs run along the slopes of the Çekirge neighborhood, and mineral baths are an amenity at many hotels in this area. The historical Eski Kaplıca Hamamı is now affiliated with the Kervansaray Termal Hotel, but open to the public at reasonable rates for a soak, a scrub, or a massage.

Bursa became the first capital of the nascent Ottoman Empire after the city was captured in 1326 by Orhan Gazi, and the first five sultans of the Ottoman Empire lived here until Mehmet the Conqueror took Istanbul and moved the capital there. Each of the sultans built his own complex on five different hilltops, and each included a mosque, a *medrese* (theological school), a hammam, a kitchen house, caravansary, and tombs. It was in Bursa that Ottoman architecture blossomed, and where the foundations were laid for the more elaborate works to be found in the later capitals, Edirne and Istanbul. More than 125 mosques here are on the list kept by the Turkish Historical Monuments Commission, and their minarets make for a grand skyline.

### GETTING HERE AND AROUND
If you're driving, Bursa is 240 km (150 mi) from Istanbul via Route 100 or E80 to İzmit, Route 130 to Yalova, and Route 575 south from Yalova to Bursa; the Yalova–Bursa part of the trip is 72 km (45 mi). Bursa is 80 km (50 mi) from İznik.

From Istanbul, through Yalova, it's a four-hour bus trip to Bursa, including the ferry ride from Darıca to Yalova, and costs about 20 TL. A better option is to take the sea bus to Yalova or Bursa (Güzelyalı); near the quay in Yalova are buses to Bursa that cost about 9 TL and take one hour. From the Bursa ferry terminal, take the yellow bus to metro stop Organize Sanayý then the metro to the Demirtaş paşa İstasyon stop near the bazaar area downtown. The journey takes about an hour and costs 4 TL.

Bursa is a large city, stretching out along an east–west axis. The town square, at the intersection of Atatürk Caddesi and İnönü Caddesi, is officially named Cumhuriyet Alanı (Republic Square), but is popularly called **Heykel** (Statue), after its imposing equestrian statue of Atatürk.

East of Heykel is the Yeşil neighborhood, with Yeşil Cami and Yeşil Türbe. To the northwest is Çekirge, the thermal spa district, with the city's fanciest lodging options.

Buses from outside the city center converge on Heykel, from where you can reach most sites. Shared taxis with white destination signs on top regularly ply the route between Heykel and Çekirge; hop in or out at signs marked with a "D" (for *dolmuş*). The main bus routes run about every 15 minutes during the day and roughly every 30 minutes at night. There are signs and posted schedules at most major stops.

### ESSENTIALS
**Visitor Information** ✉ *Orhan Gazi Çarşısı 1, Heykel* ☎ *0224/220-1848.*

## EXPLORING
**Bursa Kent Müzesi** (*Bursa City Museum*). The Bursa Kent Müzesi at Heykel, in the city center right behind the statue, is a showcase for local history and handicrafts. Among the exhibits are impressive recreations of sections in a traditional bazaar, such as those for silk weavers and knife makers; artifacts relating to the history of Bursa and its first five sultans and to Atatürk during the independence war; and clothing, household items, and dioramas of life at home, school, and in the hammam. The exhibits are in Turkish, so get one of the English-language headsets at the entrance, though the audio does not provide full narration. ✉ *Atatürk Caddesi 8* ☎ *0224/220–2626* ⊕ *www.bursakentmuzesi. com* 🖃 *1.5 TL* ⊙ *Tues.–Sun. 9:30–5:30.*

**Emir Sultan Camii** (*Emir Sultan Mosque*). The daughter of Sultan Yıldırım Beyazıt built the Emir Sultan Camii in 1429 for her husband, Emir Sultan, amid cypresses and plane trees on a quiet hilltop overlooking the city. The single-domed mosque was badly damaged in the 1855 earthquake and was almost totally rebuilt by Sultan Abdülaziz. The two cut-stone minarets are considered great examples of rococo, and the assemblage faces an attractive courtyard that houses the tombs of Emir Sultan, his wife, and children. ✉ *Doyuran Caddesi* ☎ *No phone* 🖃 *Free* ⊙ *Daily sunrise–sunset.*

**Fodor's Choice** ★ **Kapalı Çarşı** (*covered bazaar*). The vast Kapalı Çarşı comprises many adjoining *hans* (caravansaries, inns for merchants) surrounding a *bedestan* (the central part of a covered bazaar, which is vaulted and fireproofed). Bursa sultans began building bazaars in the 14th century to finance the construction or maintenance of their schools, mosques, or kitchen houses. The precinct was soon topped with roofs, creating the earliest form of covered bazaar, and late in the century Yıldırım Beyazıt perfected the concept by building a *bedesten* with six woven parts connected by arches and topped by 14 domes. The complex was flattened by a massive earthquake in 1855, and parts were badly burned by fire in the 1950s, but Kapalı Çarşı has been lovingly restored to provide a wonderful flavor of the past. ■TIP→ Best buys here include silver and gold jewelry, thick Turkish cotton towels (for which Bursa is famous), and silk goods. ✉ *Behind Ulu Cami, Between Atatürk Caddesi and Cumhuriyet Caddesi* ⊙ *Mon.–Sat. 8–8.*

**Kültür Parkı** (*Culture Park*). The refreshingly green Kültür Parkı is laced with restaurants, tea gardens, a pond with paddleboats, and an amusement park. The park is always crowded and pleasantly animated, though it seems more like a busy public gathering spot than a place of refuge. Amid the lawns and boulevards is Bursa's **Arkeoloji Müzesi** (Archaeology Museum), though it's being renovated with no set completion date. The **Atatürk Müzesi** (Atatürk Museum), just opposite, is housed in a 19th-century French-style mansion containing old-fashioned furniture and displays a few exhibits on the great leader's life. ⊠ *Çekirge Caddesi and Stadyum Caddesi* ☎ *0224/234–4918 Archaeology Museum, 0224/234–7716 Atatürk Museum* ⊙ *Museums open Tues.–Sun. 8-5.*

★ **Muradiye Tombs.** The complex around the Sultan Murat II Camii (built 1425–26) is probably the city's most serene resting place, with 12 tombs tucked amid a leafy park. Among those buried here are Murat (1404–51), the father of Mehmet the Conqueror, and Mustafa (1515–53), the eldest son of Süleyman the Magnificent, who was strangled in his father's tent. Murat's plain tomb was built in accordance with his will, with an open hole in the roof right above the tomb to let the rain in. The most decorated tombs are those of two grandsons of Murat, Çelebi Mehmet and Cem Sultan, which are kept locked most of the time—ask the caretaker to open them for you. The historical complex also included a nearby hammam, *medrese* (now the ⇨ *Uluumay Museum*), and a kitchen house for the poor (now the restaurant ⇨ *Darüzziyafe*). ⊠ *Muradiye Mahallesi, Muradiye Caddesi* ☎ *0224/222–0868* 🏷 *Free* ⊙ *Daily 8–8.*

**Türk İslam Eserleri Müzesi** (*Turkish Islamic Arts Museum*). The Turkish Islamic Arts Musuem is housed in an attractive *medrese* (theological school), part of a complex that includes ⇨ *Yeşil Cami* and ⇨ *Yeşil Türbe*. Displayed in small rooms around a cool courtyard are inlaid wood, jewelry, calligraphy work, manuscripts, Turkish shadow puppets, carpets, coins, musical instruments, pottery, and traditional clothes embellished with colorful embroidery. ⊠ *Yeşil Caddesi, on west side of Yeşil Cami* ☎ *0224/327–7679* 🏷 *free* ⊙ *Tues.-Sun. 8–12 and 1–5.*

**Ulu Cami** (*Great Mosque*). The striking Ulu Cami dates from 1399, when Sultan Beyazıt had it constructed after vowing to build 20 mosques if he was victorious in the battle of Nicopolis in Macedonia; he settled for a compromise, this one mosque with 20 domes. The interior is decorated with an elegantly understated display of quotations from the Koran in fine calligraphy. The fountain, with taps on the sides for ritual washing before prayer, is inside the mosque rather than outside the entrance—an unusual feature. ■TIP➔ **Ulu Cami draws huge crowds during prayer times, which you'll probably want to avoid.** ⊠ *Atatürk Caddesi, across from Maksem Caddesi.*

**Uludağ Milli Parkı.** To fully appreciate why Bursa is called Green Bursa, take the 30-minute trip up the *teleferik* (gondola lift), a 15-minute bus or *dolmuş* ride from Heykel, to **Sarıalan point** in lush Uludağ Milli Parkı (Uludağ National Park). This terminus has panoramic views and is lively in summer, with restaurants and picnic areas. In winter it serves as a staging point for skiers and night-clubbers heading to the mountain's hotel area 7 km farther up (see ⊕ *www.uludaghotels.com* for information). ■TIP➔ **Take a sweater or jacket, as temperatures fall dramatically as you climb, even when it's warm downtown.** There are also various walking paths up the mountain between Bursa and Uludağ; the hike takes about three hours each way. ⊠ *Piremir Mahallesi, Teleferik Teferrüç İstasyonu Yıldırım* 🕾 *0224/327–7400* 🖭 *Roundtrip teleferik ride: weekdays 10 TL, weekends 15 TL* 🕙 *8:30–8.*

**Uluumay Müzesi** (*Uluumay Ottoman Folk Costume and Jewelry Museum*). The Uluumay Müzesi, opposite the Murat II Mosque and the ⇨ *Muradiye Tombs*, has a fine, though small, collection of traditional Ottoman costumes, some dating back to the 15th century, along with gorgeous silver jewelry. Mannequins displaying the costumes revolve to afford a thorough study of the colorful embroidery. The building is a *medrese*, a theological school, built in 1475 by Şair Ahmet Pasha, whose tomb is in its garden. A teahouse opposite the tomb in the garden overlooks the city. ⊠ *Muradiye Mahallesi, Murat Caddesi* 🕾 *0224/222–7575* 🖭 *5 TL* 🕙 *May–Oct., Tues.–Sun. 8:30–7; Nov.–Apr., Tues.–Sun. 9–5.*

Fodor'sChoice ★ **Yeşil Cami** (*Green Mosque*). A juxtaposition of simple form, inspired stone carving, and spectacular tile work, the Yeşil Cami is among the finest mosques in Turkey. Work on the building was completed in 1419, during the reign of Mehmet I Çelebi (ruled 1413–21). Its beauty begins in the marble entryway, where complex feathery patterns and calligraphy are carved in the stone; inside is a sea of blue-and-green İznik tiles. The central hall rests under two shallow domes; in the one near the entrance an oculus sends down a beam of sunlight at midday, illuminating a fountain delicately carved from a single piece of marble. The *mihrab* (prayer niche) towers almost 50 feet, and there are intricate carvings near the top. On a level above the main doorway is the sultan's loge, lavishly decorated and tiled; a caretaker will sometimes take visitors up to see it. ⊠ *Yeşil Caddesi* 🖭 *Free* 🕙 *Daily sunrise–sunset.*

**Yeşil Türbe** (*Green Tomb*). The "Green Tomb" is the resting place of Mehmet I Çelebi, built in 1421. The tomb is actually covered in blue tiles, added after an earthquake damaged the originals in the 1800s. Inside, however, are incredible original İznik tiles, including those sheathing Mehmet's immense sarcophagus—and these are indeed green. The surrounding tombs belong to Mehmet's children. ⊠ *Yeşil Caddesi* 🕙 *Daily sunrise–sunset.*

**NEED A BREAK?**

**Tea Gardens.** Several tea gardens behind the Yeşil Cami and Yeşil Türbe are pleasant places to have a sandwich or a pastry while taking in views of the city. On the street leading up to the mosque complex from Heykel you'll find some colorful, restored Bursa houses whose ground floors have been turned into gift shops.

## WHERE TO EAT AND STAY

The main decision for travelers staying in Bursa overnight is whether to lay their heads in Çekirge or downtown (Heykel). Accommodations in Çekirge are typically more upscale (and expensive) but most have thermal baths. Hotels downtown are closer to the sights but tend to be unremarkable.

*For expanded hotel reviews, visit Fodors.com.*

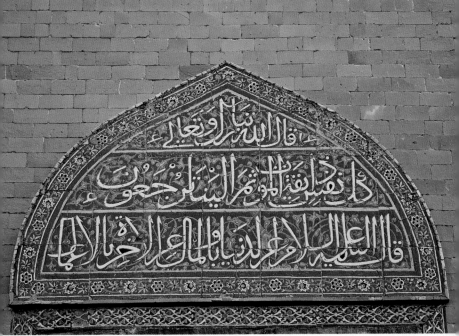

Inside Bursa's Yeşil Cami (Green Mosque), the array of green and blue tiles is mesmerizing.

**$$** ✕ **Arap Şükrü Çetin.** It's said that an Arab named Şükrü once opened a fish
**TURKISH** restaurant on Sakarya Caddesi, a narrow side street between Heykel and
★ Çekirge. Now the whole area carries his name, and his sons have filled the
street with similar restaurants, sometimes adding their own names to their
father's—in this case Çetin. The entire street is a lively and popular dining
spot, with outdoor tables and musicians wandering through. ⊠ *Sakarya
Caddesi 6, Arap Şükrü* ☎ *0224/221–1453* ☉ *Dinner only.*

**$** ✕ **Darüzziyafe.** The kitchen house built by Sultan Murat II in the 15th
**TURKISH** century to help feed the poor now serves Ottoman and Turkish cui-
★ sine in wonderfully atmospheric surroundings. *Hünkar beğendi* (tender
lamb on a bed of grilled-eggplant puree) literally means "the Sultan
liked it," and it's hard not to. The place is also known for its *köfte*
(meatballs), made with lamb, beef, chicken, and pistachios, and for
its Ottoman desserts. The terrace is pleasant, but dine indoors and
you'll feel like you're eating in the sultan's quarters. No alcohol is
served. ⊠ *Murad Caddesi 36 (across from Muradiye Tombs), Muradiye*
☎ *0224/224–6439* ⊕ *www.daruzziyafe.com.tr* ⌘ *Reservations essential.*

**$$** ✕ **Kebapçı İskender (Oğlu Cevat).** Eager patrons line up outside this little
**TURKISH** white-and-blue house near the bazaar to enjoy heaping servings of meat,
★ dished up by a grandson of the inventor of *İskender kebap,* Mehmet
İskenderoğlu. (He's pictured on the wall opposite Atatürk.) The kebab is
tender, the portions large, and the photograph-lined dining rooms quaint.
The kitchen closes by 6:30 during the week and 8 on weekends, so go
early. ⊠ *Atatürk Caddesi 60, at Orhan Sokak, Heykel* ☎ *0224/221–1076*
⊕ *www.iskender.com.tr* ☉ *Weekdays noon–6:30, weekends noon–8.*

**$** ✕ **Konak 18.** This old house in the Çekirge section of town, opposite
**TURKISH** the ⇨ *Çelik Palas Hotel,* is a local favorite, with a ground-floor terrace

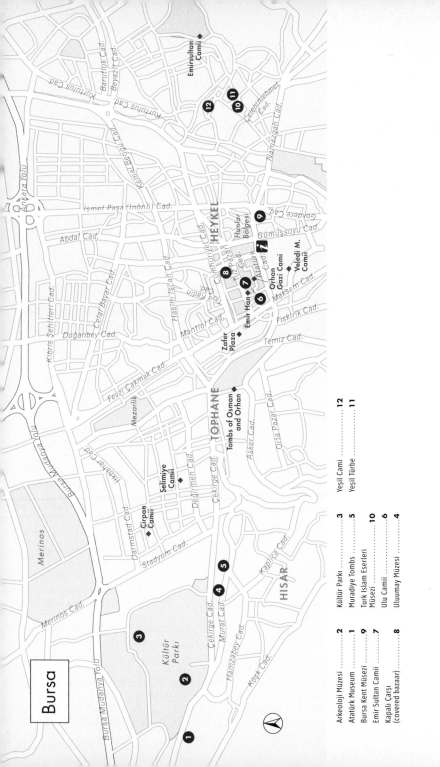

Bursa

overlooking ⇨ *Kültür Parkı*, live Turkish music on Saturday nights, and attentively prepared cuisine. Topping the menu are the grilled meats and fish and a tasty *avcı böreği* (hunter's pie), pastry filled with meat or cheese that's served as a starter. ⊠ *Çekirge Caddesi 18, Çelik Palas Oteli Karşısı* ☎ *0224/235–3707* ⊕ *www.konak18.com.tr.*

¢ ✕**Ömür Köftecisi.** *Köfte* (meatballs) is the thing to order here, served
TURKISH with grilled peppers and tomatoes. Among the salad options, *piyaz*
★ (bean salad with vinegar) accompanies *köfte* best. In the mornings, the soup is delicious, too. The location is charming, in the covered market by the Ulu Cami—the restaurant has the same architectural features as the *hans*, with brick and stone walls, and two domes in the ceilings painted in floral patterns. ⊠ *Ulu Cami Caddesi 7* ☎ *0224/221–4524* ⊙ *Tues.–Sun. 8:30–8.*

$$ ⌂**Hotel Çelik Palas.** The most venerable of the Çekirge spa hotels has
Fodor'sChoice gone glam with contemporary-style rooms, Las Vegas–worthy lounge
★ areas, and an outdoor pool deck with a stunning view of the city. **Pros:** excellent service; big rooms; luxurious spa area. **Cons:** pricey; not easy walking distance to most sights. ⊠ *Çekirge Caddesi 79* ☎ *0224/233–3800* ⊕ *www.celikpalasotel.com* ⤻ *164 rooms* ⚹ *In-room: a/c, Wi-Fi. In-hotel: restaurant, bar, pool, gym, spa, parking* ⎮⊙⎮ *Breakfast.*

$$$ ⌂**Hotel Gönlüferah.** Ottoman-style—high beds, velvet curtains, and
Fodor'sChoice ornamental hanging lamps—blend nicely with flat-screen TVs and high-
★ pressure showers, plus the hotel claims to have the city's best thermal baths. **Pros:** big, well-decorated, light-filled rooms; attentive service. **Cons:** pricey; extra charge for the thermal baths; far from sights; some bathrooms fairly small. ⊠ *1 Murat Caddesi 22, Çekirge* ☎ *0224/233–9210* ⊕ *www.gonluferah.com* ⤻ *70 rooms* ⚹ *In-room: a/c, Wi-Fi. In-hotel: restaurant, bar, spa* ⎮⊙⎮ *Breakfast.*

$$ ⌂**Safran Otel.** The comfortable accommodations, decorated partly in Ottoman tradition, are within walking distance of the center and most sights, but on a quiet hilltop opposite the tombs of Sultans Osman and Orhan. **Pros:** peaceful, close to the city center. **Cons:** no restaurant. ⊠ *Osmangazi Mahallesi, Ortapazar Caddesi, Kale Sokak 4* ☎ *224/224–7216* ⎙ *224/224–7219* ⊕ *www.safranotel.com* ⤻ *10 rooms* ⚹ *In-room: Wi-Fi. In-hotel: parking* ⎮⊙⎮ *Breakfast.*

## NIGHTLIFE

Nightlife in Bursa is liveliest in winter, and the best place is out of town in Uludağ, where Istanbul's elite fill the hotels of this ski resort on weekends and on holidays. There's popular Turkish and Western music, and lots of dancing. The rest of the year, nightlife in Bursa either imitates the Uludağ scene or sticks to Ottoman tradition with Turkish *fasıl* music, which can be found in restaurants such as Konak 18 or Darüzziyafe during weekend dinners. For nightclubs, try one of the places at the Kültür Parkı such as **Altın Ceylan.**

**Club Chyna (formerly Vici),** 7 km (4 mi) out of town on the way to Mudanya, or **Jazz Bar,** on the way to Uludağ, are other clubbing options; both are liveliest in winter. Near the center, Sakarya Caddesi (aka Arap Şükrü) is a popular spot year-round for *meyhane*-style dining accompanied by roaming musicians; past the restaurants is **M Pub (Kafe Müsadenizle).** It doesn't look much like a pub, but its shiny lounge and large terrace are among the nicer places in town to have a few drinks, if you're not averse to Turkish pop music.

## SHOPPING

Bursa's **Kapalı Çarşı** is the place to go if you want to shop in the traditional way but the city also has many modern stores. The Zafer Plaza mall at the east end of Atatürk Caddesi has many international brands, and instead of the tea gardens of the old bazaars you'll find a large Starbucks housed underneath a glass pyramid and a food court offering American and Turkish fast food.

**Kapalı Çarşı** (*covered bazaar*). As is traditional, each section of the Kapalı Çarşı, behind the ⇨ *Ulu Cami*, is dominated by a particular trade: jewelers, silk weavers, antique dealers. The Koza Han (Cocoon Caravansary) section next to the Orhan Gazi Mosque by the east entrance is the center of the silk trade. It has a lovely courtyard with a tiny *mescit* (prayer room) and a 150-year-old linden tree under which you can sip your tea. The Emir Han, behind the Ulu Cami, in the southwest section, is an interesting combination of jewelers and a religious books market, and also has a fountain and a courtyard tea garden. Antiques and souvenirs can be found in the small Eski Aynalı Çarşı section of the bazaar, between Koza Han and Emir Han. ⊙ *Mon.–Sat. 8–8.*

> ### SHOPPING IN BURSA
>
> Bursa has been a center of the silk industry since the coming of the Ottoman sultans and remains a good place to buy silk scarves, raw-silk fabric by the yard, and other silk products. The price of a silk scarf varies widely depending on design, brand, and quality, from as little as 5 TL to well over 100 TL; the same goes for the city's famed cotton towels, depending on their thickness and density. Bathrobes are a favorite souvenir, as they're high-quality and well-priced, but they might be a bit bulky to carry overseas.

# GALLIPOLI AND THE DARDANELLES

Most visitors come to this peaceful and scenic part of the country to pay their respects to the victims the crucial World War I battle, in which ANZAC (Australian and New Zealand Army Corps), British, and French troops clashed with Turkish forces, with massive losses on both sides. Battles have been fought over the Dardanelles, the commercially and militarily strategic strait separating Europe from Asia and connecting the Aegean Sea to the Marmara Sea, since the 13th-century BC war between the Achaeans and Trojans.

Today, you can visit the region year-round if your intent is sightseeing but spring may be the best time, when it's cool enough to walk comfortably around the sights, and when the area is at its most colorful, with wildflowers dotting the cemeteries and hillsides. Turks commemorate the World War I battle on March 18, and British, Australians, and New Zealanders on April 25. The second date, in particular, brings many travelers to the region for the emotional memorial services, but the mass influx requires that you make reservations for hotels and guided tours well in advance. It's probably best to avoid Gallipoli this time of year unless you wish to join the pilgrimage.

The battlefields are spread along a 35-km (22-mi) stretch of the Gallipoli Peninsula. Most visitors base themselves in Çanakkale, on the south side of the straits, rather than in Eceabat on the European side of the Dardanelles. Even though the latter is actually closer to the battlefields, Çanakkale is livelier, has more options for accommodation and dining, and is where most of the guided tours start. Regular ferries make the short crossing in both directions.

## GALLIPOLI

*310 km (192 mi) southwest of Istanbul.*

★ The Gallipoli Peninsula lies to the north of the Dardanelles. Turks call it Gelibolu—there's also a town of the same name about 40 km (25 mi) northeast of Eceabat. Thirty-one beautifully tended military cemeteries of the Allied dead from World War I line the Gallipoli battlefields. The major battles were in two main areas—along the coast between Kabatepe and Suvla Bay, and at Cape Helles, where the main Turkish memorial is located.

### GETTING HERE AND AROUND

From Çanakkale, take the car ferry to Eceabat and then head north along the coast from the ferry terminal, following Route D550/E87 as it turns westward to cut across the peninsula, where fruit stands and sunflower fields line the well-maintained road. It takes about 20–30 minutes to drive from Eceabat to the site entrance, where a well-signed loop road passes the main sights in the Kabatepe/Suvla Bay area, most of which have English-language explanatory texts. For a richer self-guided experience, the Australian Government Department of Veterans' Affairs (⊕ *www.anzacsite.gov.au*) offers detailed instructions for an "Anzac Walk" and other tours, including historical information and free audio commentaries to download. The Commonwealth War Graves Commission (⊕ *www.cwgc.org*) publishes a free pamphlet, "The Gallipoli Campaign, 1915," that can be picked up at hotels in Çanakkale or Eceabat or downloaded from the Web site. It contains a map of the battlefields, a basic history of the campaign, and short descriptions of key points of interest.

### EXPLORING

Fodor'sChoice **Lone Pine Cemetery.** The memorial at Lone Pine Cemetery bears the names
★ of some 5,000 Australian and New Zealand soldiers with unknown graves killed at Gallilopoli during a grueling eight-month World War I campaign to defeat the Ottoman forces. Savage hand-to-hand fighting took place on the battefield where the cemetery was established, and seven Victoria crosses, the highest award given by the British government for bravery and usually quite sparingly distributed, were awarded after the battle. This is the most affecting of all the ANZAC cemeteries, and the epitaphs on the tombstones are very moving.

**Cape Helles.** At Cape Helles, on the southernmost tip of the Gallipoli Peninsula, is a massive, four-pillared memorial to Turkey's World

# War and Peace

The Dardanelles have provided the world with many myths and heroes, romances and tragedies. The most recent, and the main reason that the region draws visitors today, was the Gallipoli campaign in World War I. In this offensive, Britain (with soldiers from Australia and New Zealand, then still British colonies) and France tried to breach Çanakkale's defenses in a campaign devised by the young Winston Churchill, at the time lord of the Admiralty. The goal was to capture Istanbul, control the entire waterway from the Aegean to the Black Sea, open up a supply channel to Russia, and pave the way for an attack on Germany from the south. After nine months of bloody fighting that left more than 50,000 Allied and perhaps twice as many Turks dead, the Allies admitted defeat and evacuated, beaten by the superior strategy of Lieutenant-Colonel Mustafa Kemal—later called Atatürk.

Churchill lost his job as a result of the failure in the Dardanelles, and his career suffered until the next world war, two decades later. Mustafa Kemal, on the other hand, became a national hero. He had been an insignificant lieutenant, unpopular among the ruling Committee of Union and Progress, but the fame he earned in this war helped him start and lead the war of independence against the occupying Allies. Soon his enemies were overthrown, and so were the Ottoman

sultanate and caliphate. A few years after the Gallipoli campaign, the modern, secular republic of Turkey emerged with Atatürk as president.

For the Australians and New Zealanders, WWI was their first real experience of war overseas, and the shocking losses they sustained left an indelible mark. For the Turks, it was an unexpected defensive victory. It was a war of pride, but also one that left behind many stories of kindness between soldiers on opposing sides. The Anzacs and the Turks came from opposite ends of the earth: there was no history of hostility, or even familiarity, between them, until they were told to kill one another, but in some ways the war marked the start of a friendship and thousands of Anzac pilgrims come to visit the battlefields every spring. Atatürk's speech, engraved on a Turkish monument in Anzac Cove, seemed to foresee this:

"Those heroes that shed their blood and lost their lives! You are now lying in the soil of a friendly country, therefore rest in peace. There is no difference between the Johnnies and the Mehmets to us, where they lie side by side here in this country of ours. You, the mothers who sent their sons from far-away countries, wipe away your tears. Your sons are now lying in our bosom, and are at peace. After having lost their lives on this land, they have become our sons as well."

War I dead. No one knows how many fell in battle; estimates vary from 60,000 to 250,000. If you take the ferry from Gallipoli to Çanakkale, look for the memorials to the campaign carved into the cliffs. The large one at Kilitbahir reads: "Stop, O passerby. This earth you tread unawares is where an age was lost. Bow and listen, for this quiet place is where the heart of a nation throbs."

LONE PINE

**Chunuk Bair** (*Çanak Bayırı*). The goal of the Allies was to occupy Chunuk Bair, occupying a strategic location overlooking the Gallipoli Peninsula. They failed, and Mustafa Kemal (Atatürk) became a hero and went on to establish the secular republic of Turkey. It was here that he told his soldiers, "I order you not just to fight, but to die." All the men of one of his regiments were wiped out, and he himself was saved miraculously when a bullet hit the pocket watch that was over his heart, but the line held. The hilltop holds Turkish trenches, a cemetery, and the New Zealand national memorial and offers good views of the peninsula and the Dardanelles strait.

**Kabatepe Museum and Information Center.** This small museum, with a poignant exhibit of photographs of soldiers, their uniforms, weapons, and other findings from the World War I battlefield, is undergoing a major renovation and is scheduled to reopen in 2012. ⊠ *Kabatepe Mevkii, Eceabat* ☎ *0286/862–0082.*

## ÇANAKKALE

*340 km (211 mi) southwest of Istanbul; 270 km (168 mi) from Bursa.*

West of Bursa, on the southern shore of the Dardanelles, Çanakkale is the largest city on the North Aegean coast and makes a good base for visiting the memorials and battlefields of Gallipoli, a half-hour ferry journey across the straits.

The heart of Çanakkale is in the docks area, and you really don't need to go inland. An Ottoman clock tower is between the two halves of the dock. Head toward the sea from this tower and you'll find the ferry that departs for historic Gallipoli. Hotels and restaurants are spread on either side of the docks, along the seafront. Most of the budget hotels, cheap dining options, and bars are in the streets behind the seafront to the left of the tower if you're facing the sea.

### GETTING HERE AND AROUND

By car from Bursa, Route 200 (which becomes E90) runs west toward Çanakkale; the trip is 270 km (168 mi) and takes about four hours. If you're heading for Çanakkale from Istanbul, take E80 west to Tekirdağ and then the E84, turning onto the E87 in Keşan to continue on to Eceabat's car ferry terminal. From Çanakkale, the E87 goes through Troy, Ezine, Ayvacık, Edremit, and Ayvalık. Ezine is 50 km from Çanakkale, and from there you can take the coast road west to Geyikli, where ferries run to Bozcaada, or to Alexandria Troas, Babakale, and Assos, all farther south. This is a coastal road that runs through small villages; it's a bit rough and winding, but quite scenic and enjoyable.

The bus trip from Istanbul to Çanakkale is about six hours and costs about 40 TL. From Bursa to Çanakkale is around five hours and costs about 30 TL. If the ride ends at the new bus terminal outside of town, you can take the city bus to the port area in about 20 minutes for a fare of 1.75 TL.

The Dardanelles
and the North
Aegean

GREECE
TURKEY

Kadıköy
Sea of Marmara
D550 Şarköy
Bolayır MARMARA
Gallipoli D550 Marmara Adası
Peninsula Gelibolu Marmara Adası
İmroz Turankoy
D550 Lapseki KAPIDAGI
Eceabat D200 Karabiga YARIMADASI
GÖKÇEADA Baliklicesme Bandırma
Çanakkale Gumuscay
The Dardanelles Kilitbahir Biga D200
Troy (Truva) (Ferry Crossing) Can D555 Sarikoy Bugdayli
Bozcaada Gonen Lake
BOZCAADA D550 Ahlatliburun Kus
Geyikli Ezine Sevketiye
Alexandria Troas Bayramic Findikli Manyas
Tavakli Bahceli Kalkim Susurluk
Apollo Smintheon Ayvacik Ida
(Kaz Daglari) Edremit D565
Babakale Küçükkuyu Balikesir Kepsut
Behramkale Edremit Körfezi D230
(Assos) Cunda Island Burhaniye Yaglilar
(Ali Bey Adası) Ayvalık D555
LÉSVOS Altinova Bigadic
Pergamum
Mitilini (Bergama) Turgutalp Sindirgi
Zeylindag Kinik Kirkagac D240
Candaru Körfezi Grynion
Myrina D550
Saricam Akhisar
Foça Yenibagarasi D565
CHÍOS Menemen
Chíos Manisa
Ildir D30
Balikliova İzmir D300

0 _____ 30 mi
0 _____ 30 km

AEGEAN SEA

## ESSENTIALS

**Visitor Information.** This small office by the ferry terminal provides maps, lists of local rent-a-car companies, and other useful information. ✉ *İskele Meydanı 65* ☎ *0286/217–1187* ⏲ *Weekdays 8:30–5:30, weekends 9:30–12:30 and 1:30–4:30.*

## EXPLORING

**Arkeoloji Müzesi** (*Archaeology Museum*). A number of finds from ⇨ *Troy*, including gravestones, jewelry, and kitchenware, have made their way to this quiet and somewhat cavernous museum on the southern end of town, along with artifacts from ⇨ *Assos*, ⇨ *Bozcaada*, ⇨ *Apollo Smintheon*, and other parts of the region. A massive sarcophagus is carved with funeral and sacrificial scenes, and another is painted with images of boar and stag hunts. Labels are in English and Turkish, and you'll probably have the entire place, along with its gazebo-filled garden, to yourself. ✉ *Barbaros Mahallesi, 100. Yıl Caddesi 49* ☎ *0286/217–6740* 💰*5 TL* ⏲ *Daily 8–5.*

**Çimenlik Fortress.** Built on the orders of Mehmet the Conqueror in 1462, after he successfully stormed Istanbul, the impressive waterfront Çimenlik Fortress now includes the **Deniz Müzesi** (Navy Museum). Inside and outside the high walls all kinds of weaponry are on display, including dozens of cannons, ancient and modern. There's also a replica of the World War I-era **minelayer ship Nusret** docked offshore. The real reason to come here, though, is for the sweeping view of the mouth of the Dardanelles and the Aegean. The fortress grounds are good for a nice stroll among the lawns and gardens. ⊠ *On waterfront, 3 blocks south of ferry dock, Fevzipaşa Mahallesi, Çimenlik Sokak* ☎ *0286/213–1730,* 🎫*4 TL* ☉ *Grounds: Daily 9–sunset; museum and ship: 9–5 (with break for lunch) Tues., Wed., Fri.–Sun.*

## WHERE TO EAT AND STAY

There are plenty of cheap places to grab a bite to eat in Çanakkale, with numerous bakeries and kebab shops clustered around Fetvane Street near the clock tower and the Yalı Cami.

*For expanded hotel reviews, visit Fodors.com.*

**$**
TURKISH
✕ **Gülen Pide & Kebap Salonu.** Cheery and bright, this casual two-floor eatery near the ferry dock serves delicious *pide* (Turkish pizza), topped with mincemeat, sausage, cheese, or any combination. There's also a wide variety of kebabs, *döner*, and other grilled meats, as well as the thin mincemeat-topped flatbread *lahmacun* and a small selection of traditional desserts. ⊠ *Cumhuriyet Meydanı 27/A* ☎ *0286/212–8800.*

**$$$**
TURKISH
★
✕ **Yalova Restaurant.** Take in views across the Dardanelles as you enjoy such seafood mezes as grilled octopus in vinegar and sardines wrapped in vine leaves, as well as grilled fish and meat. Fish prices are per kilogram and not listed on the menu, so be sure to ask before ordering, and the same goes for mezes, fruit plates, and other dishes that might show up on the table without your asking. ⊠ *Yalı Caddesi, Gümrük Sokak 7* ☎ *0286/217–1045.*

**¢**
🏨 **Anzac House.** This hotel/hostel near the clock tower is affiliated with the ⇨ *Hassle Free Travel Agency* and lures many backpackers with single, double, and triple/quad rooms as well as a large dorm, all clean and simply equipped, with shared baths on each floor. **Pros:** good value; nice terrace; convenient location. **Cons:** no private bathrooms; many rooms have no windows. ⊠ *Cumhuriyet Meydanı 61* ☎ *0286/213–5969* ⊕ *www.anzachouse.com* ⇨ *15 rooms* ⌂ *In-room: no a/c, Wi-Fi* ❄*No meals.*

**$**
🏨 **Hotel Helen.** Friendly, helpful service, good-size rooms and bathrooms, views of the Dardanelles, and a good location near the ferry terminal make this an excellent choice for touring the region. **Pros:** good service; pleasant decor; reasonable prices; central location. **Cons:** somewhat lacking in character. ⊠ *Kemalpaşa Mahallesi, Cumhuriyet Meydanı 57* ☎ *0286/212–1818* ⊕ *www.helenhotel.com* ⇨ *42 rooms* ⌂ *In-room: a/c, Wi-Fi. In-hotel: restaurant, bar, parking* ❄*Breakfast.*

**$**
★
🏨 **Kervansaray Hotel.** An old Ottoman house built in 1903 has large bay windows, a flower-filled courtyard, and small but elegantly furnished rooms. **Pros:** nice character; good location in the heart of the city; reasonable prices. **Cons:** small bathrooms; somewhat dated facilities. ⊠ *Kemalpaşa Mahallesi, Fetvane Sokak 13 (near clock tower)* ☎ *0286/217–8192* ⊕ *www.otelkervansaray.com* ⇨ *20 rooms* ⌂ *In-room: kitchen, Wi-Fi. In-hotel: restaurant, business center, parking* ❄*Breakfast.*

## NIGHTLIFE

Fetvane Sokak, on the left of the clock tower if you're facing the sea, is the main bar street: You can choose from spacious open-air bars dominated by pop music, or small, dark dives. Narrow Matbaa Sokak between Fetvane and Rıhtım Caddesi has been converted into a mini version of Istanbul's Nevizade, with bars and restaurants packed in side by side. **Tarihi Yalı Hanı,** the historic *han* near the end of Fetvane, has a coffeehouse in its ground-floor courtyard and places to drink beer and listen to music upstairs. On the other side of the ferry terminal, the **Telefone Café** (⊠ *Cevatpaşa Caddesi 24/A*) is popular with the locals for coffee or a drink. Some of the waterfront tea gardens north of the ferry terminal also serve beer.

## ECEABAT

*335 km (208 mi) southwest of Istanbul.*

Eceabat, on the Gallipoli Peninsula, is the closest town to the most-visited battlefields and cemeteries. The town is small and most of the restaurants and hotels are along the waterfront. So is the new Tarihe Saygı Parkı (Respect for History Park), which has maps, murals, and dioramas related to the Gallipoli battle, with text in both English and Turkish.

### GETTING HERE AND AROUND

The Eceabat ferry puts you right in the middle of town. Car ferries make the 30-minute crossing from Çanakkale to Eceabat every half hour from 7 am to midnight in both directions, and hourly late at night.

### WHERE TO EAT AND STAY

*For expanded hotel reviews, visit Fodors.com.*

**$$**
**TURKISH**
**★**
✕ **Liman Balık Restaurant.** Newer and shinier options on the peninsula have failed to tempt the Liman's loyal clientele away from this decades-old favorite, where large windows overlook a small park next to the sea. The fare is fish, meat, and meze, served as set menus or à la carte; all are fresh and tasty. The prawn casserole is especially good. Reservations are essential during war anniversaries. ⊠ *İsmet Paşa Mahallesi, İstiklal Caddesi 67* ☎ *0286/814–2755* ⊕ *www.limanrestaurant.net.*

**$$**
**SEAFOOD**
✕ **Maydos Restaurant.** A few minutes' walk from the ferry port, the Maydos specializes in seafood and meze—including a few unusual selections, such as anchovies with chopped olives. If the weather is good, ask for a table outside on the terrace, which has fine views across the Dardanelles. Connected with ⇨ *Hassle Free Travel Agency*, the restaurant offers a free boat transfer from Çanakkale. ⊠ *İsmetpaşa Mahallesi, İstiklal Caddesi (on shore road south of ferry port)* ☎ *0286/814–1454* ⊕ *www.maydos.com.tr/restaurant.*

**¢**
🛏 **Crowded House Hotel.** Don't let the grimy concrete exterior put you off; the interior is quite colorful and charming and offers bright, clean guest quarters and a nice restaurant. **Pros:** reasonable prices; pleasant common areas. **Cons:** rooms are basic. ⊠ *İsmetpaşa Mahallesi, Hüseyin Avni Sokak 5* ☎ *0286/814–1565* ⊕ *www.crowdedhousegallipoli.com* ⤵ *26 rooms* ⚘ *In-room: Wi-Fi. In-hotel: restaurant, bar, business center, parking* ⭕ *Breakfast.*

$$ ⊞ **The Gallipoli Houses.** Located in a small farming village between Eceabat and Kabatepe, Gallipoli Houses offers a relaxed, intimate getaway with large rooms that are rustic but comfortable, each with a terrace or balcony, and home cooking that includes a hearty breakfast and (for an extra charge) a delicious dinner. **Pros:** quiet, peaceful location; lots of atmosphere; close to battlefields; discounted prices are available for longer stays. **Cons:** getting around can be difficult without a car; closed in winter. ⊠ *Kocadere Village* ☎ *0286/814-2650* ⊕ *www.gallipoli.com.tr* ⤳ *10 rooms* ⚬ *In-room: Wi-Fi. In-hotel: some age restrictions* ⊗ *Open early Mar.–late Nov.*

$$ ⊞ **Grand Eceabat Hotel.** Soothing earth tones with green and blue accents predominate in the large, clean, well-equipped rooms—some have views of the Dardanelles, as does the rooftop bar-restaurant. **Pros:** modern hotel with nice views; central location; friendly staff. **Cons:** rooms facing ferry terminal can be noisy. ⊠ *Cumhuriyet Caddesi 2/D* ☎ *0286/814–2458* ⊕ *www.grandeceabathotel.com* ⤳ *33 rooms* ⚬ *In-room: Wi-Fi. In-hotel: restaurant, bar, parking* ⊙ *Breakfast.*

# NORTH AEGEAN

The ancient ruins at Bergama, Troy, and Assos draw most travelers to this relaxed, rural region, but those who linger will find the North Aegean to be one of the loveliest parts of the coastline, with unspoiled natural landscapes, sleepy fishing villages, and outdoor activities all year round. The whole area, so close to Greece, is also where you can see what life was like when the area was Greek, while experiencing its rural Turkish present. Ayvalık is the only large town in the region that can't fairly be called unspoiled, but even it has its own rewards.

## TROY (TRUVA)

*32 km (20 mi) south of Çanakkale on Rte. E87.*

Troy, known as Truva to the Turks and Ilion to the Greeks, is one of the most evocative place names in literature.

### GETTING HERE AND AROUND

Most tours to Troy operate out of Çanakkale, where independent travelers can also hop a minibus to the site, about a half-hour ride from town. If you're driving, the turnoff for Troy is about 30 km (19 mi) from the Çanakkale city center on Route E87 toward İzmir; the ruins are another 5 km (3 mi) farther south. Though it's easy enough to get to Troy on your own, with or without a car, a good guide will significantly enhance your visiting experience, as the ruins are, frankly, not much to look at without some knowledge of the city's history, both real and legendary.

In addition to the tours from Çanakkale or Istanbul, Mustafa Aşkin of the Hisarlık Hotel/Restaurant near the site gives one- to two-hour tours of Troy; he grew up in the area, speaks excellent English, and has written books about the fabled city. His narrative will illuminate easily overlooked features of the ruins (☎ *286/283–0026* ⊕ *www. thetroyguide.com*).

*Continued on page 186*

# TURKEY THROUGH THE AGES

According to an ancient saying, "Turkey is a man running West on a ship heading East." Today this adage is more apt than ever; amid the rumblings of a mildly Islamist government, the nation is also eager to join the EU. The ambivalence here underscores the country's age-old search for identity. Few can deny that Turkey—a country rich in history—is once again trying to remake itself.

Situated at the point where the continents of Europe and Asia come together, Turkey has served as the stomping ground for sundry migrations of mankind. Hittites, Persians, the armies of Alexander the Great, Romans, Byzantines, and Ottomans all have their place in the intriguing history of this land, whose early inhabitants, living on the vast Anatolian plain, created many of civilization's most enduring myths.

Ancient Troy, immortalized in Homer's *Iliad*, is located on Turkey's Aegean coast, while in Phrygia, it is said, Alexander the Great split the Gordian knot with his sword, fulfilling the prophecy that this feat would make him king of Asia. These colorful legends are no match for the plain facts of history, but together they make Turkey one of the most fascinating places on earth.

| TIMELINE | 25,000 BC Paleolithic humans inhabit Karain Cave in Anatolia | 7000 BC Anatolians begin to grow crops and raise livestock | 6500 BC Çatal Höyük thrives as the world's earliest urban settlement |

| Prehistory | 7000 BC | 6000 BC | 5000 BC |

Top: Archaeologist discovers obsidian objects in a Çatal Höyük house.
Right: Entrance to Karain Cave, Antalya.
Far right: Statues from Hacılar.

## 25,000 BC–3000 BC

### The Earliest Cultures

The history of the lands that comprise modern Turkey began to unfold as long as 25,000 years ago, on the plains of Anatolia (Asia Minor), where bones, teeth, and other evidence of early humans have been unearthed in the Karain Cave near Antalya. Some of the most fascinating finds include Göbekli Tepe (in southeast Turkey), the world's oldest known shrine, whose monolithic pillars and templelike structures were erected by hunter-gathers around 9500 BC. Then there are the first signs of agricultural life, from about 7000 BC, which have been found at Hacılar, near Bur-

dur. And by 6500 BC, Çatal Höyük, (near Konya)—often considered the world's first city—was at its height; evidence suggests that as many as 8,000 inhabitants lived in flat-roofed, one-story mud-brick houses, grew crops, and fashioned clay figurines representing a mother goddess. By 3000 BC the residents of many such Anatolian settlements were wielding tools and creating figurines hammered from gold, silver, and copper, and trading them with Mesopotamians to the east and Mediterranean cultures to the west.

■ Sights to see:
Karain Cave, Antalya
(⇨ Ch.5).
Çatal Höyük (⇨ Ch.6).

## 2000 BC–1200 BC

### The Hittites

Ushering in the Bronze Age, the Hittites arrived from lands north of the Black Sea around 2000 BC to establish a powerful empire that flourished for almost 800 years. They expanded their holdings as far east as Syria and, c.1258 BC, made an accord with Egypt's great Pharaoh Ramses II—the world's first recorded peace treaty. The Hittites adopted a form of hieroglyphics, developed a pantheon of deities, established a complex civil code, and built shrines and fortifications, many of which have been unearthed at such sites as Alacahöyük, Hattuşa and Kültepe.

c. 1258 BC Hittites make
the world's first peace accord,
with the Egyptians

Left: Lycian rock tombs, Right: Roman ruin,
Phaselis, Anatolia.

During this time, colonies were settled on the west coast of modern-day Turkey by Achaeans and Mycenaeans from Greece, who went on to wage a famous war against the Anatolians in Troy (c. 1200 BC), later immortalized by Homer in *The Iliad*. After their victory, not all Achaeans rushed back home.

■ Sights to see:
Troy (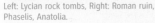 Ch. 3).
Museum of Anatolian Civilizations, Ankara (⇨ Ch. 6).

## 1200 BC–600 BC

## Invaders & Home-grown Kingdoms

With the passage of time, the Hittite society began to fall to encroaching civilizations. Lycians, Mycenaens, and other early Greeks sailed across the Aegean to establish Ephesus, Smyrna, and other so-called Ionian cities on the shores of Anatolia. The Phrygians also migrated to Anatolia from Thrace, flourishing for a mere century or so, until 690 BC—though long enough to leave the legends of kings Gordias and Midas: Gordias, of the intricate knot that could not be unraveled until Alexander the Great slashed through it with a bold stroke of his sword,

and Midas, of the touch that turned everything to gold. The Lydians emerged as a power in the 7th century BC by introducing the world's first coinage. With their vast gold deposits, they became so wealthy that the last of the Lydian kings has forever since been evoked with the term "rich as Croesus."

■ Sights to see: Lycian tombs at Fethiye and Carian tombs at Dalyan (⇨ Ch. 5). Greek ruins at Phaselis (⇨ Ch. 5).

Far left: Alexander the Great, King of Macedon, fighting, at Battle of Issus, mosaic, circa 100 BC.
Top: Arch at Ephesus.
Left: Temple of Trajan, built to honor Trajan, the Roman Emperor (98-117).

## 550 BC–50 BC

### Persians & Alexander the Great

The Persians invaded Anatolia in 546 BC and controlled the area for two centuries, until Alexander the Great swept across Asia. The young warrior's kingdom died with him in 323 BC, and Anatolia entered the Hellenistic Age. Greek and Anatolian cultures mixed liberally amid far-flung trading empires. None of these kingdoms were more powerful than Pergamum (present-day Bergama). Adorned with great sculptures such as the Laocoön and an acropolis modeled after that of Athens, it was one of the most beautiful cities of the ancient world.

■ Sights to see: Pergamum (⇨ Ch. 3).

## 100 BC–AD 100

### Romans & Early Christians

By the middle of the 1st century BC, Roman legions had conquered Anatolia, and Ephesus had become the capital of the Roman province of Asia Minor. As Christianity spread through the empire, it was especially well received in Anatolia. Saint John is said to have come to Ephesus, bringing Mary with him, and both are allegedly buried nearby. Saint Paul, a Jew from Tarsus (on Turkey's coast), traveled through Anatolia and the rest of the empire spreading the Christian word for 30 years, until his martyrdom in Rome in AD 67.

■ Sights to see: Ephesus (⇨ Ch. 4).

## 306–563

### The Rise of Constantinople

Constantine the Great became Roman emperor in 306 and made two momentous moves: he embraced Christianity and re-established ancient Byzantium as the capital of the increasingly unwieldy Roman empire. With the fall of Rome in AD 476, the Byzantine Empire ruled much of the Western world from its newly named capital Constantinople. The Byzantines reached their height under Justinian I (527–563), whose accomplishments include the Justinian Code (a compilation of Roman law), and such architectural monuments as the Aya Sofya.

■ Sights to see: Aya Sofya, Istanbul (⇨ Ch. 2).

527 Byzantine Empire
flourishes under Emperor
Justinian

1071 Seljuks defeat
the Byzantines

1300 Ottoman Empire
established

1520 Ottoman Empire
enters Golden Age

650 AD        950 AD        1250 AD        1550 AD

Top left: Map of
Constantinople.
Above: Wall tiles,
Topkapı Palace, Istanbul.
Bottom left: Byzantine
mosaic of Jesus, Aya
Sophia, Istanbul.
Left: Süleyman the
Magnificent.

**3**

**IN FOCUS TURKEY THROUGH THE AGES**

## 1071–1300 The First Turks

Around the 8th century, the nomadic Turkish Seljuks rose to power in Persia and began making inroads into Byzantine lands. The defeat of the Byzantine army in 1071 ushered in the Great Seljuk Empire and Seljuks converted their new subjects to Islam. In turn, Pope Urban II launched the First Crusade to reclaim Byzantium in 1097. Armies from Western Europe clashed with Seljuk forces for the next two centuries. The Mongols, under Genghis Khan, swept down from the north and put an end to the weakening Seljuks.

■ Sights to see:
Mevlana Museum, Konya
(⇨ Ch. 6).

## 1300–1500 The Rise of the Ottomans

By 1300, the Seljuk lands had been divided into independent states, known as the ghazi emirates. Osman I was one of the leaders, and began to expand what would come to be known as the Ottoman Empire, establishing a capital at Bursa. By the 14th century the Ottomans had extended their rule over most of the eastern Mediterranean. Constantinople, the last Byzantine holdout, fell in 1453 and became the new Ottoman capital, which it would remain until the founding of modern Turkey.

■ Sights to See
Topkapı Palace, Istanbul
(⇨ Ch. 2).

## 1520–1566 The Golden Age of the Ottomans

By the time of the reign of Süleyman the Magnificent, the Ottomans controlled lands stretching east into Persia, through Mecca and Medina (Islam's holiest cities), south into Egypt and west into central Europe. The empire entered its Golden Age under Süleyman, himself a poet and author of civil laws. Literature, music, and craftsmanship thrived, while Süleyman's architect, Sinan, built beautiful shrines such as the Süleymaniye Mosque in Istanbul.

■ Sights to see:
Süleymaniye Mosque, Istanbul (⇨ Ch. 2). Blue Mosque, Istanbul (⇨ Ch. 2).

TIMELINE

| 1876 Abdülhamid II becomes Sultan | Late 19th c. Ottoman Empire begins massacre of Armenian populations | 1915 Gallipoli campaign | 1923 Turkish Republic is established |

1875      1900      1925

**1571–early 1900s**

## The Long Decline

The defeat of the Ottoman navy in 1571 by a coalition of European forces at the Battle of Lepanto, off the western coast of Greece, heralded the end of Ottoman supremacy in the Mediterranean. Incompetent leadership plagued the empire almost continually over the next several centuries, and the empire shrank. Abdülhamid II supported liberal reforms when he became Sultan in 1876, and effectively Westernized many aspects of public works, education, and the economy. He also turned his energies to reinvigorating Islamic identity, aiming to unite the increasingly restive ethnic groups of the empire. Most infamously, he suppressed Armenian revolutionary groups and an estimated 300,000 Armenians were killed under his regime. A movement of revolutionary societies grew throughout the country and one in particular, the so-called Young Turks, rose up in revolution in 1908, deposing the Sultan. By the early 20th century, the days of the once great empire—now known as the "Sick Man of Europe"—were clearly numbered.

■ Sights to see:
Dolmabahçe Palace, Istanbul (⇨ Ch. 2)

**WWI–1938**

## The Birth of the Republic

World War I, during which the Ottomans sided with the Axis powers, put an end to what was left of the Ottoman Empire. In a key battle in 1915, the Allies landed at Gallipoli but were eventually repulsed with heavy losses. In 1920, the Treaty of Sèvres turned Ottoman lands over to France, Italy, Greece, and other victors, but a nationalist hero had come onto the scene: Mustafa Kemal formed the first Turkish Grand National Assembly in Ankara and led the forces that routed Greek armies, pushing across Anatolia to reclaim lands once part of the Byzantine

Top left, opposite: Battle of Lepanto. Bottom left, opposite: Süleymaniye Mosque. Bottom right, opposite: Sultan Abdülhamid II. Left: Mustafa Kemal Atatürk Above: Pera Palas Hotel, Istanbul, Turkey: Atatürk's bedroom preserved as a museum.

Empire. In 1923 the Treaty of Lausanne banished foreign powers and established the boundaries of a Turkish state with its capital in Ankara. Kemal—who took the name Atatürk (literally "Father of the Turks")—reinvented Turkey as a modern nation. Turkey embraced secularism and instituted widespread reforms that replaced religious law with secular jurisprudence, advanced education, implemented universal suffrage, and introduced a Western style of dress, abolishing the fez as a symbol of Ottoman backwardness.

■ Sights to see:
Gallipoli ( ⇨ Ch. 3).

## 1938–Present

## After Atatürk

Turkey has largely allied itself with the West since Atatürk's death in 1938, though the balance between secularization and the religious right has at times been precarious, with the military often stepping in to ensure the country's Western leanings. A military coup in 1960 removed a Democratic Party government that had reinstituted the call for prayer in Arabic and instituted other right-wing reforms. The military seized control in two other coups, in 1971 and 1980, while the government of Turgut Özal from 1983 to 1993 ushered in widespread legal and economic reforms. First

elected in 2002, the mildly Islamist AKP party has deftly led the country through the first years of the new millennium, steering Turkey through its candidacy for European Union membership, diplomatically denying U.S. requests to launch attacks on Iraq from Turkish airbases, and tentatively expanding the rights of the country's sizable Kurdish minority.

■ Sights to see:
The Anıtkabir (Atatürk's Mausoleum), Ankara ( ⇨ Ch. 6).

★ **Troy (Truva).** The wooden horse that stands outside the site is a modern addition, there to remind us of Homer's epics, but the city walls, layer upon layer of them, date back several millennia. Long thought to be a figment of the Greek poet Homer's imagination and written about in his epic *The Iliad*, the site was excavated in the 1870s by Heinrich Schliemann, a German businessman who had struck it rich in California's gold rush. While scholars scoffed, he poured his wealth into the excavations and had the last laugh: He found the remains not only of fabled Troy but of nine successive civilizations, one on top of the other, dating back 5,000 years (and now known among archaeologists as Troy I–IX). Subsequent excavations during the 1930s revealed 38 additional layers of settlements.

Schliemann found a hoard of jewels that he believed were those of King Priam, but have more recently been dated to a much earlier era. Adding to the controversy that surrounded his discoveries, Schliemann smuggled the jewels out of the country, and his wife was seen wearing them at fashionable social events. Schliemann later donated them to Berlin's Pergamon Museum, but they disappeared during the Red Army's sack of Berlin in World War II. They reappeared in 1993, when Moscow announced that its State Pushkin Museum of Fine Arts housed what they called the lost "Treasure of Priam." Though Germany, Greece, and Turkey have all claimed the treasures, recent custom dictates that archaeological finds belong to the country in which they were originally found; unfortunately, these have yet to make their way back to Turkey.

What you see of Troy today depends on your imagination or the knowledge and linguistic abilities of your guide. You may find the site highly suggestive, with its remnants of massive, rough-hewn walls, a paved **chariot ramp**, and strategic views over the coastal plains to the sea. Or you may consider it an unimpressive row of trenches with piles of earth and stone. Considering Troy's fame (and the difficulties involved in conquering it), the city is surprisingly small. The best-preserved features are from the Roman city, with its **bouleuterion** (council chamber), the site's most complete structure, and small theater. A site plan shows the general layout and marks the beginning of a sign-posted path leading to key features from several historical civilizations. ⊠ *Follow signs from Rte. E87, Tevfikiye Köyü* ☎ *0286/283–0536* ◁ *15 TL; parking: 3 TL* ⊙ *Apr.–Oct., daily 8–7; Nov.–Mar., daily 8–4:30.*

**WHERE TO EAT AND STAY**
*For expanded hotel reviews, visit Fodors.com.*

¢ ⌂ **Hisarlık Otel/Restaurant.** The only lodging in the immediate vicinity of the Troy ruins, run by three brothers, is very basic—expect not much more than a clean bed and a small but private bathroom—though the large shared balcony is pleasant, and the in-house restaurant serves typical yet good buffet-style Turkish fare. **Pros:** great location for touring Troy. **Cons:** basic rooms; prices somewhat high for what you get. ⊠ *Tevfikiye Köyü* ☎ *0286/283–0026* ▤ ◁ *11 rooms* ⌂ *In-room: Wi-Fi* ⊙ *Breakfast.*

OFF THE
BEATEN
PATH
**Bozcaada.** If you're heading south from Troy toward Alexandria Troas, you'll pass through Geyikli, where you'll see a signpost for Bozcaada, one of the two Aegean islands that belong to Turkey. If you have time,

spare a day for this island (though you'll probably then want to spare another) with its unspoiled harbor town, beautiful old houses, pristine sandy beaches, and lovely countryside covered with vineyards. The local wine may be the best you'll taste in Turkey without having to spend a fortune.

**Rengigül Konukevi.** The Rengigül Konukevi, a small B&B in a Greek-style 19th-century house, is a bit cluttered but has a lot of character. It has a large, lovely garden, and serves delicious breakfasts. ☎ *0286/697–8171* ⊕ *www.rengigul.net*

**Otel Kaikias.** Otel Kaikias, also a B&B, has elegantly furnished large rooms, a collection of old Greek books and Troy ornaments, and a basement full of wine made by the owners. ☎ *0286/697–0250* ⊕ *www.kaikias.com*

**Ferries.** The ferries run at least six or seven times a day in summer but much less frequently in winter. ☎ *444–0752* ⊕ *www.gestasdenizulasim.com.tr*

## BEHRAMKALE (ASSOS)

*25 km (16 mi) southeast of Gülpınar on coast road; 65 km (40 mi) south of Troy; 17 km (11 mi) south of Ayvacık.*

★  The port is a marvel, pressed against the sheer cliff walls. It's crammed with small hotels that were built of volcanic rock, a fleet of fishing boats, and a small rocky beach at each end. Behramkale village is home to the ruins of Assos: the acropolis. It has blossomed in recent years and now surpasses the port area in terms of prices—and perhaps in charm as well.

Outside June, July, August, and weekends the rest of the year, the area is less crowded and prices are likely to come down a bit, especially in the port. For more spacious and sandier beaches try Kadırga, on the way to Küçükkuyu.

### GETTING HERE AND AROUND

Buses from Çanakkale in the north and Ayvalık or İzmir in the south stop at Ayvacık, which is the closest (17 km) town to Behramkale. From there, minibuses make the 20- to 30-minute trip to Behramkale about every hour for 3.5 TL, though less frequently out of high season. Make sure you get one that also goes down to the port, if that's your final destination.

To take the minibus between the port and the village is a five-minute ride, costing 2 TL. The minibus also goes to Kadırga beach, a 15-minute ride. The lofty ruins of Behramkale, known in ancient times as Assos, provide a panoramic view over the Aegean. As you approach, the road forks, one route leading to the ancient, pretty village atop the hill and the other twisting precariously down to the tiny, charming harbor. Nowadays the name "Behramkale" is used for the village at the top and "Assos" for the port area.

## HOMER'S STORY

Because *The Iliad* was written 500 years after the war—traditionally believed to have taken place around 1184 BC—it's hard to say how much of it is history and how much is invention. Nonetheless, it makes for a romantic tale: Paris, the son of King Priam, abducted the beautiful Helen, wife of King Menelaus of Sparta, and fled with her to Troy. Menelaus enlisted the aid of his brother, King Agamemnon, and launched a thousand ships to get her back. His siege lasted 10 years and involved such ancient notables as Achilles, Hector, and the crafty

Odysseus, king of Ithaca. It was Odysseus who ended the war, after ordering a huge wooden horse to be built and left outside Troy's gates. Then the Greeks retreated to their ships and pretended to sail away. The Trojans hauled the trophy into their walled city and celebrated their victory. Under cover of darkness, the Greek ships returned, the soldiers hidden inside the horse crept out and opened the city's gates, and the attackers at last gained entry to Troy. Hence the saying: "Beware of Greeks bearing gifts."

### EXPLORING

**Acropolis.** The hilltop acropolis measures about five square city blocks. Founded about 1000 BC by Aeolian Greeks, the city was successively ruled by Lydians, Persians, Pergamenes, Romans, and Byzantines, until Sultan Orhan Gazi (ruled 1324–62) took it over for the Ottomans in 1330. Aristotle is said to have spent time here in the 4th century BC, and St. Paul stopped en route to Miletus in about AD 55. The textile and trinket sellers along both sides of the road will show you the way from the village. You're best off leaving your car on one of the wider streets and making your way on foot up the steep, cobbled lanes to the top of the summit, where you'll be rewarded with a sensational view of the coastline and, in the distance, the Greek island of Lesbos, whose citizens were the original settlers of Assos.

At the summit is the site of the **Temple of Athena** (circa 530 BC), which has splendid sea views but has been somewhat clumsily restored. A more modern addition, right before the entrance to the ruins, is the **Murad Hüdavendigâr Camii,** a mosque built in the late 14th century. The mosque is simple—a dome atop a square, with little decoration. The Greek crosses carved into the lintel over the door indicate the Ottomans used building material from an earlier church, possibly one on the same site. Back down the slope, on the road to the port, is a parking area for the **necropolis** and city walls stretching 3 km (2 mi), as well as the ruins of a gymnasium, **theater,** and *agora* (marketplace). Assos was known for its sarcophagi, made of local limestone, which were shipped throughout the Greek world. Unfortunately, most of the tombs are in pieces. ☎ 0286/721–7218 ◰ 5 TL ☯ Apr.–Oct., daily 8–7; Nov.–Mar., daily 8–5.

The ruins at Troy are not as well preserved as others in Turkey, but are still atmospheric.

## WHERE TO EAT AND STAY

Most hotels in Assos port include breakfast and dinner, though some will agree on deals for breakfast only. The fish restaurants are not cheap, but the fish will be fresh, the *mezes* are tasty, and it's all in a beautiful setting. Evening dining options in Behramkale are fairly slim, but many *pansiyons* serve good homemade local dishes to guests for an additional charge.

*For expanded hotel reviews, visit Fodors.com.*

$ ✕ **Assos Köyüm Restaurant.** There's no menu at this friendly, family-run spot in Behramkale's tiny main square: Just pick from the selection of *mezes* on display (don't miss the crunchy, garlicky greens called *deniz borülcesi*) and let one of the young waiters tell you what meat dishes are on offer that day, perhaps *köfte* (meatballs), chicken *şiş*, or *saç kavurma*, a sizzling plate of diced lamb and vegetables. The covered terrace looks over the village and down to the sea while a few seats out front allow diners to watch the comings and goings on the square. Alcohol is served. ✉ *Behramkale village square, by çay bahçesi, Behramkale* ☎ *0286/721–7424* ⊙ *Daily 8 am–10 pm.*

¢ ✕ **Kale Restaurant.** A few minutes' walk from the ⇨ *Acropolis*, this casual
TURKISH  eatery with stone tables and colorful flowerpots is a welcome stop on the way back from a visit to the ruins, especially on a hot day. The *ayran* (a salty yogurt drink) is thirst quenching and a great restorative. Try the *mantı* (Turkish ravioli in garlicky yogurt sauce), the *tavuk şiş* (chicken kebab), or the *gözleme*, thin Turkish pastry filled with minced meat, mashed potato, or cheese and cooked on a flat stone. ✉ *Acropolis road, Behramkale* ☎ *0543/317–4969* ▭ *No credit cards* ⊙ *Daily, noon–10 pm.*

**$$**    ⊡ **Assos Alarga.** With just three large, nicely decorated rooms in a gor-
Fodor'sChoice    geous old stone house centered on a shady courtyard, the Assos Alarga
★    offers a serene and intimate stay on the quiet end of Behramkale vil-
lage—and the pool and garden ensure the getaway atmosphere. **Pros:**
beautiful house and rooms; serene location; friendly owner and staff.
**Cons:** bathrooms on the small side. ⊠ *Behramkale 88, Behramkale*
☏ *0286/721–7260* ⊕ *www.assosalarga.com* ⤳ *3 rooms* ⌂ *In-room: no*
*TV, Wi-Fi. In-hotel: pool, parking* ⫯⊘| *Breakfast.*

**$$**    ⊡ **Assos Kervansaray Otel.** The best-located of the Behramkale hotels, at
the far end of the harbor, offers rooms in a variety of sizes and styles—
some are small and functional, some are large and equipped with Jacuzzis,
many have terrific views of the Aegean, and all take advantage of indoor
and outdoor pools, as well as a swimming pier and rocky beach. **Pros:**
romantic setting near the Aegean; swimming in pools and sea. **Cons:**
size and style of rooms varies, so ask to see several if the hotel is not full.
⊠ *Assos Liman (Assos Harbor), Behramkale* ☏ *286/721–7093, 286/721–*
*7198* ⊕ *www.assoskervansaray.com* ⤳ *80 rooms* ⌂ *In-room: Wi-Fi. In-*
*hotel: restaurant, pool, beach, water sports* ⫯⊘| *Some meals.*

**$$$**    ⊡ **Biber Evi.** Each of the cozy rooms in the lovely 150-year-old "Chili
Fodor'sChoice    House" is named after a variety of pepper grown in the garden (and
★    used in delicious meals served in the in-house restaurant) and each is
unique, with wood paneling, Ottoman decoration, old wood furni-
ture, and walls tiled with pepper designs. **Pros:** great atmosphere and
location; good breakfast; attractively decorated rooms. **Cons:** bath-
rooms are basic and showers are not enclosed. ⊠ *Behramkale Köyü*
*46, Behramkale* ☏ *0286/721–7410* ⊕ *www.biberevi.com* ⤳ *6 rooms*
⌂ *In-room: Wi-Fi. In-hotel: restaurant, bar.*

**$**    ⊡ **Eris Pansiyon.** You'll feel more like a friend than a paying guest in
the 250-year-old stone house that American retirees Emily and Clin-
ton Vickers operate as a *pansiyon,* offering comfortable rooms and no
end of hospitable touches: bookshelves full of English-language books,
homemade cake and tea in the afternoons, and delicious breakfasts
served on the terrace in nice weather. **Pros:** quiet and intimate; nice
garden; good food; on the edge of Behramkale, about 10 minutes' walk
from the acropolis. **Cons:** rooms are a bit basic. ⊠ *Behramkale Köyü*
*6, Kadirga Çıkışı, Behramkale* ☏ *0286/721–7080* ⊕ *www.assos.de/eris*
⤳ *3 rooms* ⌂ *In-room: no a/c, Wi-Fi* ⊟ *No credit cards.*

### NIGHTLIFE

**Uzun Ev Bar** (*Long House Bar*). You can have drinks at any of the hotel
bar-restaurants or check out the only actual bar in the Assos Harbor,
the Uzun Ev, which also serves a full menu of fish and *meze,* including
a variety of Aegean greens. The whitewashed stone walls with antique
bread-making equipment hanging from them give the interior some
character and there are eight tables outside by the harbor. The music is
good, too: soft jazz during the day, a live guitarist playing Turkish and
foreign music on weekend nights during the summer and holidays. It's
open until 2 or 3 am on summer weekends if there are still customers.
⊠ *Behramkale Köyü Sahili, Behramkale* ☏ *0286/721–7007.*

# AYVALIK

*48 km (30 mi) from Edremit, south on Rte. E87; or 117 km (73 mi) from Çanakkale on E87.*

★ Ayvalık is beautiful, stretching onto a peninsula and surrounded by islands, with many bays swirling in and out of its coastline. The bustling harbor town and Cunda Island across the way retain strong evidence of the Greek community that flourished here and prospered in the olive-oil trade until being deported in the population exchange of 1923. Atmospheric backstreets are full of colorful old Greek houses. A long, sandy beach is just a short minibus ride away and various pleasure boats stand ready to take visitors on swimming and snorkeling excursions.

Ayvalık has some of the finest 19th-century Greek-style architecture in Turkey, and recent restoration has begun to reverse decades of neglect. Unlike typical Ottoman houses (tall, narrow, and built of wood, with an overhanging bay window), Greek buildings are stone, with classic triangular pediments above a square box. The best way to explore is to turn your back to the Aegean and wander the tiny side streets leading up the hill into the heart of the old residential quarter (try Talat Paşa Caddesi or Gümrük Caddesi).

Several historic churches in town have been converted into mosques. St. John's is now the **Saatli Cami** (Clock Mosque). St. George's is now the **Çınarlı Cami** (Plane Tree Mosque). There are many mosques converted from churches in Turkey, but these are among the most striking—the elaborate style of Orthodox churches does not suit the plain minimalist style of mosques, and the unimpressive minaret erected later at the Çınarlı Mosque looks almost absurd. The pictures of the saints inside are painted over but can still be seen if you look carefully. The now-shuttered **Taxiarchis Church** holds a remarkable series of paintings done on fish skin depicting the life of Christ. Barbaros Caddesi on the south end of the pier will take you to the **Phaneromeni Church** (Ayazma Kilisesi), displaying beautiful stone craftwork, and to the **Hayrettin Paşa Camii,** also converted from a church.

In summer, Sarımsaklı Plajı, the 10-km (6-mi) stretch of sandy beach 7 km (4½ mi) from the center of town, is popular, and easily and cheaply reached by minibuses that stop near the harbor. It's a crowded resort with a mess of concrete hotels right behind the seafront, and traffic and parking can be a problem, but the beach and sea are lovely.

Day or evening cruises to the bays and islands of Ayvalık are enjoyable, and range from party-boat trips to lower-key swimming excursions to the Patriça Nature Reserve on the far side of Cunda Island. Hucksters on the docks will try and sell you a trip as you walk by the boats, and competition makes prices very reasonable—about 25 TL for a day trip including a fish meal. Diving trips are also available at a higher cost. The tours are offered from May until the end of October.

Şeytan Sofrası ("the devil's dinner table"), a hilltop 9 km (5½ mi) from town, on a right turn on the road from Ayvalık to Sarımsaklı, is the place to get a panoramic view of the islands and the bays and enjoy a cup of tea or a snack at one of the cafés. It's particularly lovely at sunset, when minibuses make the return trip from town for 5 TL.

### ESSENTIALS

**Car Rental** Avis Rent a Car
✉ *Talatpaşa Caddesi 67/B*
☎ *0266/312–2456* ⊘ *Daily 8:30–8:30.*

**Visitor Information** ✉ *In front of Tansaş supermarket, opposite harbor* ☎ *0266/312–4494* ⊘ *May–Sept., daily 8–7; Oct.–Apr., daily 8–5.*

### WHERE TO EAT AND STAY

Waterfront restaurants tend to be expensive, but the two *çay bahçe* (tea gardens) at the south end of the harbor are pleasant spots to enjoy a cheap plate of fried fish, mussels, or calamari (7 to 12 TL) along with a beer.

*For expanded hotel reviews, visit Fodors.com.*

A QUICK TRIP TO GREECE

A trip to the Greek island of Lesbos will allow you to see another country and culture with a sea journey of little more than an hour, though the timing of trips can be a challenge. Ferries depart from Ayvalık pier for Lesbos daily, but only the Wednesday, Friday, Saturday, and Sunday sailings at 9 am allow for a same-day return. The other days the boats don't sail from Ayvalık until early evening, with a morning return from Lesbos, so a tourist from Ayvalık would need to stay at least two nights. Fares are about 70 TL return.

¢ ╳ **Fırat Lokantası.** In the heart of Ayvalık, just north of Saatli Cami, this eatery serves up hearty lunches to hardworking street traders; it's tiny but almost always full, so you may need to share one of the dozen or so tables. The decor could not be plainer, but the Turkish home cooking is delicious: rice, beans, eggplant with minced meat, and lamb stew. This is the perfect place for lunch when wandering the historic part of the town. ✉ *Cumhuriyet Caddesi 25/A* ☎ *0266/312–1380* ▭ *No credit cards* ⊘ *Open Mon.–Sat. 7:30–4.*
TURKISH

¢ ╳ **Girit Mutfağı.** This tiny, women-run restaurant offers a daily selection of home-cooked dishes along the lines of sautéed chard, oven-cooked chicken, *köfte* (meatballs), soup, and chickpeas. If visiting in summer, don't miss the stuffed squash blossoms (*kabak çiçeği*). The *lor tatlısı* (ricotta cheese dessert) is delicious. Beer is available. ✉ *Talatpaşa Caddesi 15/A* ☎ *0266/312–2128* ▭ *No credit cards* ⊘ *Daily 9–9:30.*
TURKISH

$ ╳ **Hüsnü Baba'nın Yeri.** Tucked away from the water on a vine-covered cobblestone backstreet in Ayvalık's market area, "Father Hüsnü's Place" has friendly service, cheap prices, and tasty food. The rice-stuffed mussels, zucchini fritters, lightly fried *papalina* (a small local fish), potatoes croquette, calamari, and *deniz börülcesi* (samphire) in olive oil all go well with a glass of rakı or beer. Get a seat outside for the best atmosphere. ✉ *Tenekeciler Sokak 16* ☎ *0266/312–8714* ⊘ *9–midnight.*

$$ ⌷ **Butik Sızma Han.** What was once a century-old olive-oil factory on Ayvalık's harbor now offers comfortable and modern guest quarters, a pleasant, stone-walled lounge, and a sunny waterside deck. **Pros:** good location; full amenities; easy access to sea. **Cons:** downstairs rooms by lobby can be noisy; some interior areas a bit musty. ✉ *Gümrük Caddesi, 2. Sokak 49* ☎ *0266/312–7700* ⊕ *www.butiksizmahan.com* ⇏ *10 rooms* ⌂ *In-room: Wi-Fi. In-hotel: restaurant, bar, water sports* ⦿ *Breakfast.*

**$** ⛰ **Günebakan Taliani Hotel.** Perched on a hillside above Ayvalık's harbor, the 17 bright and airy rooms at the "Sunflower" are set throughout a rambling old house belonging to the family of the charming owner, Meliha. **Pros:** relaxed atmosphere; good hospitality; comfortable rooms; individually made breakfasts, served until late, and afternoon tea and fresh-baked snacks add to the homey vibe. **Cons:** a bit of a hike from town; facilities are a bit outdated. ✉ *13 Nisan Caddesi 163, just below main road out of town toward İzmir* ☎ *0266/312–8484* ⊕ *www. talianihotel.com* ⛴ *17 rooms* ⚄ *In-room: no a/c, kitchen, Wi-Fi. In-hotel: parking, some pets allowed* ⧓ *Breakfast.*

## CUNDA ISLAND (ALI BEY ADASI)

*Just off the coast of Ayvalık (connected by a causeway to mainland).*

Like Ayvalık, Cunda Island was once predominantly Greek, and some Greek is still spoken here. The island has a mix of the two cultures in its food, music, and nightlife, and lately has been deliberately cultivating this, having realized the tourism potential. There's a growing number of cafés, bars, bakeries, and small restaurants in the charming cobbled backstreets away from the water, which are full of old Greek buildings in various states of repair. At the top of the hill, the "Nostaljik Café" at the small Sevim and Necdet Kent Library (look for the stone windmill) is open 9:30 to 9:30 daily and has great views.

### GETTING HERE

There are regular buses to Cunda from Ayvalık, but the best way to travel is by boat (2.5 TL one way); they run every hour each way from 10 am to midnight in summer (June 15–September 15), and dock at the quay right in the middle of the restaurants in Cunda. In winter, buses are the only option.

### EXPLORING

**St. Nicholas Church.** Many of the island's varied Greek houses are well-preserved, and the 19th-century Greek church of St. Nicholas (better known as Taksiyarhis, or Taxiarchis, to the locals) in the middle of town is a landmark. With large cracks in the facade, caused by an earthquake in 1944, and the presence of birds flying around the airy domes, the place has a ghostly air. You can't go inside because of the danger of a collapse, but peer through the glassless windows to see some of the frescoes, several of which have been defaced—the eyes of the apostles have been gouged out. On the left side of the church's quiet courtyard is a small café and *pansiyon*, ⇨ *Zehra Teyze'nin Evi*, where you can sit and have a refreshment and enjoy the view of the church.

### WHERE TO EAT AND STAY

Cunda has become a popular place for accommodation and nightlife as well as dining. Unlike mainland Ayvalık, Cunda is purely a tourist resort and also attracts weekend escapers all year around, though it doesn't (not yet, at least) attract big tour groups. Most of the hotels on Cunda are quite expensive for what they offer, but the restaurants lining the waterfront, although also expensive, are among the best in Turkey. They're noted for their grilled *çipura* (a local fish) and for an amazing variety of other Turkish and Greek seafood dishes served grilled, fried, baked, or in cold salads. For casual eats, try Pizza Uno (not the American chain) in the center of town, a popular spot for kebabs, pasta, and *pide* as well as pizza.

*For expanded hotel reviews, visit Fodors.com.*

**$$$**
SEAFOOD
★
✕ **Bay Nihat.** The most popular and probably most expensive of the waterfront restaurants on Cunda offers a *meze* selection that is a feast for the eyes and stomach, and many options are original creations based on Greek and Turkish cuisine—cockles, octopus in mastic sauce, calamari in saffron sauce, and cured fish *pastırma* are among the unusual specialties. ⊠ *Sahil Boyu 21, Cunda Adası, Ayvalık* ☎ *0266/327–1777* ⊕ *www.baynihat.com.tr* ⚑ *Reservations essential* ⊗ *1–11.*

**$$**
⌂ **Zehra Teyze'nin Evi.** This small *pansiyon* with cozy, traditionally furnished rooms and a small garden is hidden among the trees in the courtyard of the ⇨ *St. Nicholas Church.* **Pros:** wonderful location; casual and warm atmosphere. **Cons:** standard rooms are quite small; pricey for what you get. ⊠ *Namik Kemal Mah. No. 7, next to Taksiyarhis Church, Alibey Adası, Ayvalık* ☎ *0266/327–2285* ⊕ *www.cundaevi.com* ⊷ *8 rooms* ⚷ *In-room: a/c, Wi-Fi. In-hotel: restaurant* ⊠ *Breakfast.*

## NIGHTLIFE

In Sarımsaklı, the beach area in Ayvalık, you'll find discos and clubs that play pop and electronic techno; Cunda has bars that play Turkish and Greek pop music. The island also hosts a short series of outdoor concerts in July; look for posters reading "Cunda Müzik Günleri" (Cunda Music Days) for dates and times.

# PERGAMUM (BERGAMA)

*62 km (39 mi) from Ayvalık; take Rte. E87 south approximately 44 km (27 mi), then follow signs to Bergama on Rte. 240.*

Fodor'sChoice
★
The windswept ruins of Pergamum, which surround the modern town of Bergama, are among the most spectacular in Turkey. Pergamum was one of the world's major powers, though it had only a relatively brief moment of glory, especially under the rule of Eumenes II (197 BC–159 BC), who built the city's famous library. Of more lasting influence perhaps was the city's Asklepion, an ancient medical center that had its heyday under the renowned early physician, writer, and philosopher Galen (131 AD–210 AD). By then Pergamum was capital of the Roman province of Asia, which for centuries supplied the empire with great wealth. Bergama has not been heavily influenced by tourism, except perhaps for the carpet shops at the base of the acropolis road. People still ride tractors, lead donkeys, and drive vegetable trucks through town, and a bus inching along behind a herd of sheep is not an uncommon sight.

## GETTING HERE AND AROUND

If you're coming from Ayvalık, drive 51 km (32 mi) south on the E87, then turn off following the signs to Bergama, another 11 km (7 mi). The bus from Ayvalık takes about an hour and a half and costs 8 TL. Frequent buses travel onward from Bergama to İzmir.

The Bergama bus terminal is 8 km (5 mi) out of the city center, but there's a free municipal shuttle service at least once an hour that stops near the post office and Red Basilica in the center of the old town. There's also minibus service for 1.5 TL. If a taxi driver tells you there's no bus service and tries to charge you 25 TL for the short trip, know that there are other options—or bargain with him.

There's no useful minibus service to the area's attractions, but in part thanks to the *teleferik* (gondola lift) to the acropolis, the town's three main sights are reachable by foot. If you want to hire a taxi to take you around, expect to pay 50 TL to 60 TL for the driver to shuttle you from site to site for a few hours. Some hotels have bicycles for guest use but local roads can be narrow and rocky and both the acropolis and the Asklepion are uphill from town.

### ESSENTIALS

**Visitor Information** ⊠ *Hükümet Konağı, B Blok, Ground Floor* ☎ *0232/631–2852* ⊙ *Daily 8:30–noon and 1–5:30.*

### EXPLORING

**Acropolis.** The most dramatic of the remains of Pergamum are at the acropolis. Take a smooth, 15-minute ride on the shiny new *teleferik* (gondola lift), which offers sweeping views on its way up the hill, or follow signs pointing the way to the 6-km (4-mi) road to the top, where you can park. The car park is across from the row of souvenir stands, which sell drinks, film, and reasonably good picture books containing site maps. Buy your ticket at the gate. Broken but still mighty triple ramparts enclose the **upper town,** with its temples, palaces, private houses, and gymnasia (schools). In later Roman times, the town spread out and down to the plain, where the Byzantines subsequently settled for good.

After entering the site through the Royal Gate, there are several different paths. To start at the top, pick the path to the far right, which takes you past the partially restored **Temple of Trajan,** at the summit. This is the very picture of an ancient ruin, with burnished white-marble pillars high above the valley of the Bergama Çayı (Selinus River). The vaulted foundations of the temple, later used as cisterns, are also impressive. On the terraces just below, you can see the scant remains of the **Temple of Athena** and the **Altar of Zeus.** Once among the grandest monuments in the Greek world, the Altar of Zeus was excavated by German archaeologists who sent Berlin's Pergamon Museum every stone they found, including the frieze, 400 feet long, that vividly depicts the battle of the gods against the giants. Now all that's left is the altar's flat stone foundation. There's much more to see of the **Great Theater,** carved into the steep slope west of the terrace that holds the Temple of Athena: It could seat some 10,000 spectators and retains its astounding acoustics.

Nearby are the ruins of the famous library, built by Eumenes II (197 BC–159 BC) and containing 200,000 scrolls. As the Pergamum library came to rival the great library in Alexandria, Egypt, the Egyptians banned the sale of papyrus to Pergamum, which responded by developing a new paper—parchment, made from animal skins instead of reeds. This *charta pergamena* was more expensive but could be used on both sides; because it was difficult to roll, it was cut into pieces and sewn

together, much like today's books. The library of Pergamum was transported in 41 BC to Alexandria by Mark Antony as a gift for Cleopatra. It survived there until the 7th century AD, when it was destroyed by the fanatical Caliph Omar, who considered the books un-Islamic.

Farther down the hill, following signs to the lower agora, the excavated living quarters of **Building Z** hold well-restored 2nd-century AD mosaics. ☎ *0232/631–0778* ✇ *TL 20; TL 8 for round-trip teleferik ride; TL 3 for parking* ☉ *Apr.–Oct., daily 8:30–7; Nov.–Mar., daily 9–5.*

**Arkeoloji Müzesi** (*Archaeology Museum*). Bergama's small Arkeoloji Müzesi, though not terribly well-lighted or inviting, houses a substantial collection of statues, coins, and other artifacts excavated from the ancient city as well as an ethnography section. A relief from the ⇨ *Kızıl Avlu (Red Basilica)* showing gladiators fighting bulls and bears and some elaborate sarcophagi and gravestones from the region are particularly noteworthy. The well-preserved statue of Nymphe comes from the site of Allianoi, a Roman spa town now submerged under the waters of a dam completed in 2010. ✉ *Cumhuriyet Caddesi 10* ☎ *0232/631–2884* ✇ *TL 5* ☉ *Apr.–Oct., Tues.–Sun. 8:30–6:30; Nov.–Mar., Tues.–Sun. 8:30–5:30.*

**Asklepion.** The Asklepion is believed to have been one of the world's first full-service health clinics. The name is a reference to Asklepios, god of medicine and recovery, whose snake and staff are now the symbol of modern medicine. In the center's heyday in the 2nd century AD, patients were prescribed such treatments as fasting, colonic irrigation, and running barefoot in cold weather. Roman emperors Hadrian, Marcus Aurelius, and Caracalla sought treatments at the Asklepion, and Galen, the physician and philosopher who was more or less a resident medic for the Roman Empire's star gladiators, was born in Pergamum and trained here.

The entrance to the complex is at the column-lined **Sacred Way,** once the main street connecting the Asklepion to Pergamum's acropolis. Follow it for about a city block into a small square and through what was once the main gate to the temple precinct. Immediately to the right is the **library,** a branch of the one at the acropolis. Patients also received therapy accompanied by music during rites held in the intimate theater, which is now used each May for performances of the Bergama Arts Festival. Nearby are pools that were used for mud and sacred water baths. A subterranean passageway leads down to the sacred cellar of the **Temple of Telesphorus,** where the devout would pray themselves into a trance and record their dreams upon waking; later, a resident priest would interpret the dreams to determine the nature of the treatment the patient required. ✉ *Follow Cumhuriyet Cad. west to Rte. E87; near tourist information office, follow sign pointing off to right 1½ km (1 mi)* ☎ *0232/631–2886* ✇ *TL 15; parking TL 3* ☉ *Apr.–Oct., daily 8:30–7; Nov.–Mar., daily 9–5.*

**Kızıl Avlu** (*Red Basilica*). The Red Basilica in Bergama is named for the red bricks from which it's constructed. You'll pass it on the road to and from the ⇨ *Acropolis*—it's right at the bottom of the hill, in the old part of the city. This was the last pagan temple constructed in Pergamum before Christianity was declared the state religion in the 4th century, when it was converted into a basilica dedicated to St. John. The walls remain, but not the roof. Most interesting are the underground passages, where it is easy to imagine how concealed pagan priests supplied the voices of "spirits" in mystic ceremonies. The main building is fenced off for ongoing restoration, but one of the two towers has been restored and has some displays inside; the other tower is used as a mosque. ☎ 0232/631–2885 ⬜ 5 TL ☉ Apr.–Oct., daily 8:30–7; Nov.–Mar., daily 8–5.

## WHERE TO EAT AND STAY

The run-down but charming old quarter, on the way to the acropolis, is the best place to stay, with several clean, inexpensive hotels.

*For expanded hotel reviews, visit Fodors.com.*

¢ ✗ **Arzu Pide and Çorba Salon.** In the heart of town, Arzu has inexpensive, simple, and satisfying Turkish fare and is popular with the locals, especially at lunchtime. The *pide*, *lahmacun*, and lentil soup are particularly tasty and the staff is friendly. The restaurant's interior is a bit cramped, but there are more tables on the sidewalk outside. ✉ Istiklal Meydanı 35 ☎ 0232/631–1187 ☉ 11–10.

TURKISH

$ ✗ **Bergama Sofrası.** Tucked alongside a 16th-century hammam in downtown Bergama, this casual room offers around 20 dishes—stews, casseroles, grilled meats, and soups (fewer options are available at dinnertime). Try the *kadın budu köfte* (ground meat mixed with rice and parsley and lightly fried in egg batter) and the *kemalpaşa*, a traditional sweet served with *kaymak* (clotted cream) and tahini, for dessert. No alcohol is served. ✉ Bankalar Caddesi 44 ☎ 0232/631–5131 ☉ May–Sept., daily 5 am–8 pm (sometimes later in summer).

¢ ▦ **Akropolis Guest House.** Rooms in this quiet hotel at the edge of town near the Kızıl Avlu (Red Basilica) vary in size and are clean and comfortable, with sturdy wood furniture and colorful fabrics, and a summer stay is enhanced by the small pool. **Pros:** near Red Basilica and the acropolis; good value and atmosphere. **Cons:** downstairs rooms may get noise from pool and common areas. ✉ Kurtuluş Mahallesi, Kayalık Sokak 3 ☎ 0232/631–2621 ⊕ www.akropolisguesthouse.com ⇲ 12 rooms ⌂ In-room: Wi-Fi. In-hotel: bar, pool ⦿ Breakfast.

$$ ▦ **Hera Hotel.** At one of Bergama's most attractive lodgings, set amid cobbled, winding lanes, the well-appointed rooms are each named after a Greek god or goddess and surround the courtyard of a beautifully maintained 200-year-old stone house. **Pros:** serene location; beautiful rooms; good hospitality. **Cons:** no restaurant, but there is a pleasant wine bar. ✉ Talatpaşa Mahallesi, Tabak Köprü Caddesi 21 ☎ 0232/631–0634 ⊕ www.hotelhera.com ⇲ 10 rooms ⌂ In-room: Wi-Fi. In-hotel: bar ⦿ Breakfast.

¢ ▦ **Odyssey Guest House.** The best budget deal in Bergama occupies two restored 19th-century Greek houses in the heart of the old town and offers clean, wood-floored rooms (some with private sitting areas and balconies), a generous breakfast buffet, do-it-yourself laundry facilities, and a book exchange. **Pros:** excellent value; friendly owners; central location. **Cons:** breakfast extra; cash only; some rooms have shared bathrooms. ✉ Talatpaşa Mahallesi, Abacıhan Sokak 13 ☎ 0232/631–3501 ⊕ www.odysseyguesthouse.com ⇲ 10 rooms; 1 4-bed dorm ⌂ In-room: no TV, Wi-Fi. In-hotel: laundry facilities ▭ No credit cards.

# The Central & Southern Aegean Coast

**WORD OF MOUTH**

"Of course Ephesus is a must site . . . I may have enjoyed the other sites less traveled as we were alone with many of the ruins (or at least there were far fewer people). But Ephesus is spectacular."

—dgunbug d

# WELCOME TO THE CENTRAL AND SOUTHERN AEGEAN COAST

## TOP REASONS TO GO

★ **Feast on seafood:** Enjoy a relaxing meal at one of the many seafood restaurants.

★ **Swim, windsurf, and scuba dive:** Some of the brightest and bluest waters in the Aegean region surround the coastal towns of Çeşme and Bodrum.

★ **Take a Blue Cruise:** A *gulet,* or wooden boat, is the perfect vehicle for exploring the Aegean coast, visiting secluded coves sprinkled along the pristine clear waters.

★ **Visit Ephesus:** For a glimpse into the Hellenistic, Roman, and Byzantine periods, take a walk through the ruins of Ephesus, lined with the remains of temples, houses, shops, and the famed Library of Celsus.

★ **Wander through Şirince:** This picturesque wine-making village is surrounded with lovely restored houses; the hills are great for hiking.

Bodrum

Ephesus

**1** İzmir and Çeşme. The port city of İzmir is the third largest city in Turkey, with enough sights and glimpses into everyday Turkish life to keep you well occupied for a day or two. Nearby Çeşme, a peninsula at the western tip of the region, has some of the region's most pristine waters. Some of the best beaches are located in Altınkum,

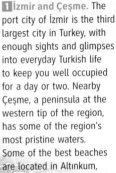

southwest of Çeşme. For the trendy beach clubs, head to Ayayorgi Bay and for nightlife, head to Alaçatı.

**2** Selçuk, Ephesus, and Şirince. Selçuk is the town nearest to the archaeological ruins at Ephesus and a charmer; it's also well worth the extra 10-minute drive to see the hill village of Şirince.

**3** Kuşadası and Environs. These days, Kuşadası's claim to fame is as a cruise port, with passengers disembarking for day trips to Ephesus; unless you like bland and overdeveloped ports, give it a miss. Nearby, however, are several sites worth visiting: The ancient Roman city of Aphrodisias, the layered limestone-travertine terraces and hot springs of Pamukkale, and the ruins of Didyma, Miletus, and Priene are worthwhile stops as you work your way south toward Bodrum.

**4** Bodrum Peninsula. Throbbing resort life has descended upon the coves and bays of this peninsula on the southern Aegean coast over the years but each town still has its own charms: some have excellent water sports, some are great for relaxation, and others are all about the nightlife.

## GETTING ORIENTED

In addition to gorgeous white-sand beaches, the crystal clear waters, and the variety of water sports and nightlife, the central and southeast Aegean regions of Turkey have some of the most captivating historical sites, including the ruins of Ephesus, Aphrodisias, and the travertine cliffs of Pamukkale.

**4**

Fishing boat on the Aegean Sea

St. John's Basillica, Selçuk

Updated by
Vildan Yahni

The Aegean is one of Turkey's most visited and most developed regions, for good reason: the area is home to some of Turkey's most captivating treasures, from gorgeous white-sand beaches to ancient ruins of Ephesus.

The Roman city of Ephesus is the big draw for sightseers, and rightfully so. Bodrum and its surrounding beach towns attract sunseekers from around the world and spoil them with sophisticated hotels and a buzzing nightlife scene. İzmir, Turkey's third-largest city, will surprise travelers with a nice collection of museums, markets, and lively seaside promenades. Then there are the many places in between these major stops—charming hill towns like Şirince; the otherworldly white cliffs and thermal springs at Pamukkale; ancient cities of Priene, Miletus, and Didyma; and long, sandy beaches at Altinkum and elsewhere along the coast.

# PLANNING

## BLUE CRUISES

Blue Cruises started in the 1970s as inexpensive boat tours catering to Turkish intellectuals, and they're still an enjoyable and relaxing way to explore the secluded coves of the Aegean coastline. Of course, nothing is inexpensive anymore, and there are plenty of luxury options. A typical Blue Voyage cruise lasts about seven days, but can be shorter or longer—there's not much to do other than reading, swimming, and relaxing, so many find that three or four days is optimal. April through October is the best time for a cruise; prices vary according to the month, the type of boat, and whether you opt for full board. You can arrange your trip before you leave home, or when you get to the docks. On the Aegean coast, Bodrum is the best place to hire a boat, with the most options. *See the "Blue Cruising" box in Chapter 5 for more information.*

For more information try these contacts:

**Aegean Yacht Services.** This respected blue cruise company arranges voyages and also builds boats. ☎ *252/313-8631* ⊕ *www.aegeanyacht.com.*

**Cano Yachting** ☎ *0532/481–6244* ⊕ *www.canoyachting.com.*
**Era Tourism** ☎ *252/316–2310* ⊕ *www.erayachting.com.*
**Motif Yachting** ☎ *252/316–2309* ⊕ *www.motifyachting.com.*
**Neyzen Tours** ☎ *252/316–7204* ⊕ *www.neyzen.com.tr.*

## GETTING HERE AND AROUND

### AIR TRAVEL

The quickest way to get to the Central and Southern Aegean coast is by plane. Daily flights connect Istanbul with airports in İzmir and Bodrum. Depending on the season, there are direct flights to İzmir and Bodrum from Ankara, Adana, and Antalya as well.

**Contacts Bodrum Airport Taksi (Bodrum/Milas Airport)** ✉ *Bodrum* ☎ *0252/523-0024* ⊕ *www.bodrumairporttaxi.com.* **Bodrum Tour** ☎ *252/524-5050* ⊕ *www.bodrumtour.com.* **Havalimanı Taksi (İzmir airport taxi)** ☎ *232/274-2075* ⊕ *www.izmirhavalimanitaksi.com.* **Havaş** ☎ *252/523-0040 Bodrum, 232/274-2276 İzmir, 212/444-0487 toll free* ⊕ *www.havas.net.* **Proper Car Rental & Airport Transfers** ☎ *252/316-9540* ⊕ *www.propercar.com/bodrum-airport-transfer.htm.*

### BUS TRAVEL

A number of bus lines serve the Aegean coast—Varan, Ulusoy, and Kamil Koç are the bigger ones, with luxury buses—but bus travel is not time efficient. The ride from Istanbul to İzmir takes around 9 hours, and from Istanbul to Bodrum about 12. There are bus lines linking İzmir, Selçuk, Kuşadası, Didyma, and Bodrum, too: typical travel times are: İzmir to Bodrum, 3½ hours; İzmir to Çeşme, 1 hour; İzmir to Selçuk, 1½ hours; İzmir to Kuşadası, 1¼ hours; and Çeşme to Bodrum, 4½ hours.

**Contacts Kamil Koç** ☎ *0212/444-0562 toll-free reservations* ⊕ *www.kamilkoc. com.tr.* **Ulusoy** ☎ *212/444-1888 toll-free reservations* ⊕ *www.ulusoy.com.tr.* **Varan** ☎ *212/444-8999 toll-free reservations,* ⊕ *www.varan.com.tr.*

### CAR TRAVEL

A car is a plus for exploring this region. Major roads and modern highways are in good condition and clearly marked, so driving from İzmir to Ephesus (in Selçuk) is quite easy; navigating some around the small winding roads around the towns of the Bodrum Peninsula can be tricky, so make sure to have a good map. Portions of the highway that runs along the Aegean coast are quite beautiful, especially as you approach Çeşme and Bodrum. For an idea of distances: İzmir to Ephesus, 79 km (49 mi); İzmir to Çeşme, 85 km (53 mi); İzmir to Selçuk, 46 km (29 mi); İzmir to Kuşadası, 100 km (62 mi); İzmir to Bodrum 243 km (155 mi), and Ephesus to Bodrum, 172 km (107 mi).

### FERRY OR HYDROFOIL TRAVEL

The Bodrum Ferryboat Association has ferry service from Bodrum to Kos, in Greece, and to Datça, between the Mediterranean and Aegean seas in Turkey. The Bodrum Express Lines Hydrofoil and Ferryboat Services has ferry and hydrofoil service from Bodrum to Sedir (Cleopatra Island) in Bodrum and Datça, Marmaris, Dalyan, and Didyma in Turkey, as well as to Kos, Kalymnos, and Rhodes in Greece. Make sure you bring your passport if traveling to Greece.

Contacts **Bodrum Express Lines** ☎ *252/316-1087* ⊕ *www.*
*bodrumexpresslines.com.* **Bodrum Ferryboat Association** ☎ *252/316–0882*
⊕ *www.bodrumferryboat.com.*

## TAXI AND DOLMUŞ TRAVEL

In resort towns like Çeşme, Bodrum, and Kuşadası, taxis have day and
night rates: from midnight till 6 am, prices are 50% higher, but there is
no charge for luggage. You can hail a cab on the street, or go to a taxi
stand. There are flat rates for traveling between towns, but bargaining
is appropriate. Traveling by *dolmuş* (shared minibuses) is a more economical way to travel in and around the resort towns. To get dropped
off along the driver's route, use the phrase *"inecek var,"* which means
"I want to get off."

Contacts **Alsancak Iskele Taksi** ⊠ *Alsancak, İzmir* ☎ *252/422-6754.* **Konak
Iskele Taksi** ⊠ *Konak, İzmir* ☎ *252/445–6618.*

## HOW MUCH TIME DO YOU NEED?

If you have extremely limited time, you could fly to İzmir and overnight
in Şirince or Selçuk, then visit Ephesus, the Ephesus Museum, and other
nearby attractions in one day, leaving again the next morning. With a
little more time, you could spend several hours visiting Aphrodisias on
the way to Pamukkale, make a relatively quick visit there, overnight in
Pamukkale town, then fly out early the next morning from Denizli. To
explore the region in depth, allow about 10 days, working your way
south from İzmir to Bodrum, stopping at sights along the way.

## LOCAL FLAVORS

Dining out along the Aegean coast is a pleasure, especially if you enjoy
seafood. There are countless seafood restaurants at all price ranges. A
typical meal includes an assortment of hot and cold mezes (appetizers), a mixed salad, and the catch of the day, capped off with a Turkish
dessert. To make it authentic, accompany your meal with rakı (similar
in taste to ouzo). Some of the more common fish you'll find along the
Aegean coast are *levrek* (sea bass), *çipura* (sea bream), *barbunya* (red
mullet), and *lahos* (grouper). Of course, there are plenty of meat and
kebab restaurants around, too, if that's what you're craving. *For more
about the fish you'll find on the menu in Turkey, see the "Seafood on
the Turkish Coast" food spotlight in Chapter 5.*

## VISITOR INFORMATION

Visitor Information offices are generally open daily between 8:30 am
and 2:30 pm and from 1:30 pm to 5 pm. See city listings below for
contact information.

## WHAT IT COSTS

| | | | | |
|---|---|---|---|---|
| **WHAT IT COSTS IN U.S. DOLLARS** | | | | |
| ¢ | $ | $$ | $$$ | $$$$ |
| Restaurants under $5 | $5–$10 | $11–$15 | $16–$25 | over $25 |
| Hotels under $50 | $51–$75 | $76–$150 | $151–$250 | over $250 |

Restaurant prices are for one main course at dinner or for two *mezes* (small dishes). Hotel prices are for two people in a standard double room in high season, including taxes.

### WHEN TO GO

July and August are the high season, and Ephesus gets lots of tourists, especially those coming in from the cruise ship port at Kusadasi. In June and September you'll have the beaches pretty much to yourself, though the water is cooler. If you want to visit the historical sights in mild weather, plan your trip between October and May—plus, crowds are fewer and accommodations more affordable. The winter months, however, can be a bit rainy.

# İZMIR AND ÇEŞME

İzmir, with its large, modern airport and national and international flight connections, is a major jumping-off point for visits to the South Aegean, and many make it a base for visits to Ephesus. Don't rush through İzmir, though; the city has some fascinating sights and a vibrant cosmopolitan edge.

Çeşme, at the westernmost end of the peninsula, is a coastal resort town with a shoreline of sandy beaches, crystal clear waters, several state-of-the-art marinas, and a dining and nightlife scene that competes with the major metropolitan cities in Turkey. Çeşme has long been popular with Turkish vacationers but somewhat off the foreign travel route, though this might change with a new six-lane highway that connects Çeşme with İzmir in only about 45 minutes.

## İZMIR

*565 km (351 mi) south of Istanbul.*

At first glance, Turkey's third-largest city (formerly known as Smyrna) may seem modern and harsh—even the beautiful setting, between the Gulf of İzmir and the mountains, doesn't soften some of the harshness of industrial districts and sprawling suburbs. Spend a few days here, though, either on your way to other parts of the South Aegean, or as a base for visiting Ephesus and the surrounding area, and you'll find an extremely pleasant city with 7,000 years of history, and much to occupy the modern traveler. An attractively refurbished promenade known as the Kordon follows the waterfront for almost 3 km (2 mi), chockablock with cafés and restaurants its entire length, and a refreshing wealth of landmarks include the ancient Kadifekale fortress, the Kemeraltı outdoor bazaar, and a collection of fine museums.

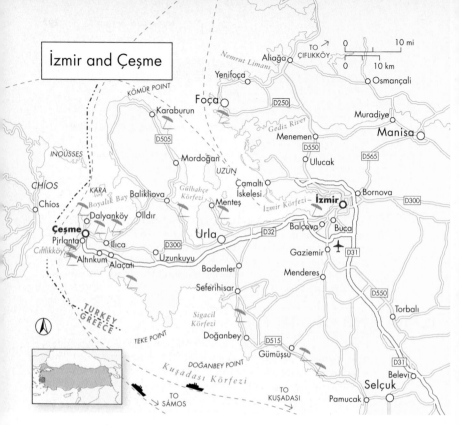

The waterside Konak district is at the heart of İzmir life, with shops, restaurants, and clubs that are continually moving farther afield along the waterfront into the narrow lanes of the old restored customs house originally built by Gustave Eiffel or on the Asansör (elevator), an early 20th-century relic that connects the slopes of Karataş, a Jewish enclave that is one more piece of this cosmopolitan city that will delight you with its richness.

### GETTING AROUND

While in İzmir, you can travel around by bus, the expanding metro system (one-way fare is 1.75 TL), *dolmuş*, or taxi. From the İzmir airport, the most comfortable and economical way to get downtown is via Havaş shuttle bus. One-way is about 10 TL.

### ESSENTIALS

**Taxi Information 26 Ağustos Taksi** ✉ *İzmir* ☎ *232/422–1958.*

**Üçkuyular Terminal Taksi** ✉ *İzmir* ☎ *232/278–1538.*

**Tour Information Ephesus Tours.** This tour company is based in Kuşadası but also offers tours of Ephesus starting from İzmir. ✉ *İzmir* ☎ *0256/613–0500* ⊕ *www.ephesustours.com.* **Vespera Travel.** This İzmir-based tour company offers tours to Ephesus and Pamukkale, as well as other destinations. ✉ *1721*

# History of İzmir

Turkey's third-largest city, with a population of approximately 3.3 million, was called Smyrna until the founding of the Republic of Turkey in 1923. A vital trading port, though often ravaged by wars and earthquakes, the city had its share of glory, too. Homer, the legendary Greek poet, is said by some to have been born in Old Smyrna sometime around 850 BC. Alexander the Great ousted the Persians and rebuilt the city at the foothills of what is today called Kadifekale in 333 BC.

İzmir fell into assorted hands after the Romans. It was an important religious center during the Byzantine Empire and was a battlefield during the Crusades, passing back and forth between the Muslims and Christians. Destroyed and restored successively by Byzantines and the Seljuks, Smyrna was held by the Knights of Rhodes in 1402 when the Mongol raider Tamerlane came along, sacked the city yet again, and slaughtered the inhabitants. The city came under the Ottoman Empire during the reign of Sultan Mehmet I Çelebi in 1426. Toward the end of the 15th century, Jews driven from Spain settled in Smyrna, creating a lasting Sephardic community. By the 18th and 19th centuries, Smyrna had become a successful, sophisticated commercial port with an international flavor and a sizable number of Italians, Greeks, Armenians, British, and French. This era came to an end with World War I, when Ottoman Turkey allied itself with Germany. In 1918 the Greek army, encouraged by the British and French, landed at the harbor and claimed the city. The occupation lasted until 1922, when Turkish troops under Mustafa Kemal Atatürk (the founder of the Turkish Republic) defeated the Greek forces and forced them to evacuate the city. On September 9, 1922, Atatürk made a triumphant entry into the port. The joy was short-lived—shortly thereafter a fire destroyed three-fourths of the city. Fanned by the wind, it burned wooden houses like matches and hidden stores of munitions exploded.

The city was quickly rebuilt according to a modern urban plan prepared by brothers Rene and Raymond Danger, French urban designers—and renamed İzmir. Like its name, much of the city dates from the 1920s, with wide boulevards, office buildings, and apartment houses painted in bright white or soft pastels.

*Sokak, Melek İş Hanı 4/D 312, Karşıyaka, İzmir* ☎ *0232/364–2705* ⊕ *www.vesperatravel.com.*

**Visitor Information** ✉ *Akdeniz Mahallesi, 1344 Sokak 2* ☎ *232/483–8086.*

## EXPLORING

**Kadifekale** (*Velvet Fortress*). Climb the windy, restored ramparts of the Kadifekale, built by Alexander the Great, for sweeping views of the city and its harbor, and use the castle to orient yourself when you're walking around the city. The name, which translates as "velvet castle," supposedly alludes to the resemblance of the present-day citadel's walls to rubbed velvet. Rebuilt after various mishaps, and enlarged and strengthened by successive conquerors, the structure looks like a childhood fantasy of a medieval castle, with solid stone blocks (some dating from Alexander's day), Byzantine cisterns, and Ottoman buttresses jutting out to support the walls. Locals will warn solo visitors (especially women) not to visit the Kadifekale alone for fear of being hassled or harassed.

**The Agora.** The agora at the foot of Kadifekale Hill, just off 816 Sokak (816 Street), was the Roman city's market. The present site is a large, dusty, open space surrounded by ancient columns and foundations. Part has been closed off for excavations, but there's still much to see, including the well-preserved Roman statues of Poseidon, Artemis, and Demeter at the northwest corner. To get here from Kadifekale, exit from the fortress's main gate and take the road that descends to the left; when you see steps built into the sidewalk, turn right and go down. ✉ *Namazgah Mahallesi, Anafartalar Cad., Konak* 📷 *3 TL* ☾ *Daily 8:30–noon and 1–5.*

**Alsancak.** North of the Archaeology and Ethnography museums is the Alsancak neighborhood, which attracts İzmir's trendy crowd. During the Ottoman period, the neighborhood was predominantly Jewish and Christian, and there are still a number of synagogues and churches in the area. The pretty two- and three-story Levantine houses with bay windows are tucked away along some of the backstreets, which perk up at night with the influx of young İzmirians drawn to the quaint cafés, bars, and restaurants. There are a number of boutique hotels in this neighborhood, so it's a good place to base yourself if you're staying in town for a few days.

**Arkeoloji Müzesi** (*Archaeology Museum*). Among the interesting artifacts at İzmir's archaeology museum are the 2nd-century statues of Demeter and Poseidon found when the agora was excavated. There is also an impressive collection of tombs and friezes, and a memorable, colossal statue of the Roman emperor Domitian (AD 51–96, ruled 81–96). ✉ *Cumhuriyet Bul., Bahribaba Parkı* 📷 *232/489–0796* 📷 *8TL (inlcudes admission to Etnoğrafya Müzesi)* ☾ *Tues.–Sun. 8:30–5:30.*

**Etnoğrafya Müzesi** (*Ethnography Museum*). The Etnoğrafya Müzesi, across the street from the Archaeology Museum, focuses on folk art and daily life. The collection includes everything from period bedrooms to a reconstruction of İzmir's first pharmacy. ✉ *Cumhuriyet Bul., Bahribaba Parkı, Konak* 📷 *232/489–0796* 📷 *8TL (inlcudes admission to Arkeoloji Müzesi)* ☾ *Tues.–Sun. 8:30–5:30.*

**Ahmet Piristina City Archive and Museum.** Just south of the Kültür Parkı (Culture Park) is the İzmir Ahmet Piristina City Archive and Museum, which chronicles 7,000 years of the city's history through colorful posters with informative descriptions in English and Turkish. The museum, in İzmir's old fire station, has a special section dedicated to the history of İzmir's multiple fires and its fire brigade. ✉ *Şair Eşref Bulvarı, 1/A* 📷 *232/441–6178* 📷 *Free* ☾ *Daily 9–6.*

**Karşıyaka.** Karşıyaka, which means the "opposite side/shore" in Turkish, is one of several purported birthplaces of the poet Homer, and was the residence of one of Turkey's most famous contemporary poets, Attila Ilhan. For years, it was a tranquil summer resort for İzmir's upperclass, but the area has been expanded and developed to accommodate İzmir's

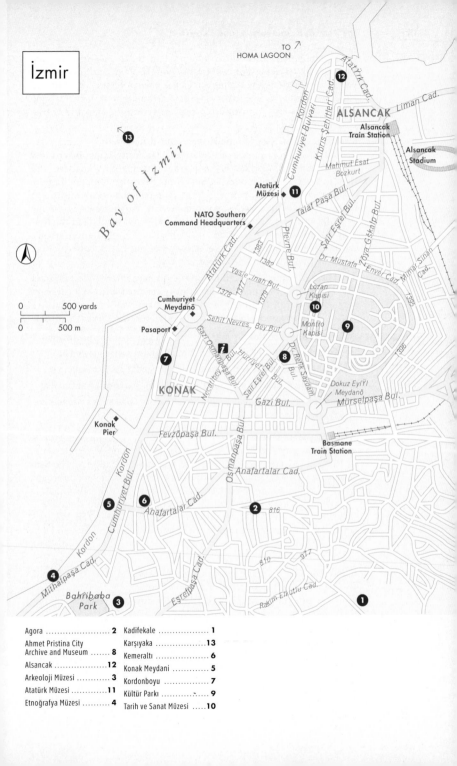

# İzmir

TO
HOMA LAGOON

Bay of İzmir

ALSANCAK

Alsancak
Train Station

Alsancak
Stadium

0     500 yards

0     500 m

Atatürk
Müzesi ◆ **11**

NATO Southern
Command Headquarters ◆

Atatürk Cad.

Talat Paşa Bul.

Kıbrıs Şehitleri Cad.

Cumhuriyet Bulvarı

Kordon

Atatürk Cad.

Liman Cad.

**12**

**13**

Mahmut Esat
Bozkurt

Şair Eşref Bul.

Dr. Mustafa Toya Göktalp Bul.

Enver Cad.

Mimar Sinan Cad.

Plevne Bul.

1383

1382

Vasıf İnah Bul.

1378   1377

1379

Cumhuriyet
Meydanö ◆

Pasaport ◆

**7**

KONAK

Konak
Pier ◆

Şehit Nevres   Bey Bul.

Gazi Osmanpaşa Bul.

Necatibey Bul.

Hürriyet Bul.

Şair Eşref Bul.

Dr. Refik Saydam Bul.

Lozan
Kapısı

**10**

Montro
Kapısı

**8**

**9**

1395

1396

Dokuz Eylül
Meydanö

Mürselpaşa Bul.

Gazi Bul.

Fevzöpaşa Bul.

Osmanpaşa Bul.

Anafartalar Cad.

Basmane
Train Station

Kordon

Cumhuriyet Bul.

Anafartalar Cad.

**5**

**6**

**2**   816

810   817

Kordon

Mithatpaşa Cad.

**4**

Bahribaba
Park

**3**

Eşrefpaşa Cad.

Rakım Elkutlu Cad.

**1**

growing population. On a hot summer day, the 20-minute ferry ride from Konak to Karşıyaka is a great way to cool off, and on arriving, you can walk along the commercial strip, İzmir's version of Istanbul's İstiklal Street. Try some *lokma* (sweet doughnut holes), for which the district is famous. You can catch the ferry from the Konak Pier; the cost is about 4 TL.

**Kemeraltı.** Konak Meydanı marks the start of Kemeraltı, a modern-day marketplace that is a maze of tiny streets filled with shops and covered stalls. Anafartalar Caddesi is the bazaar's principal thoroughfare, and there are lots of cafés and restaurants along Fevzipaşa Caddesi. Explore the smaller side streets, too, where you'll find minimarkets dedicated to musical instruments, leather, costume jewelry, and accessories, among other things. Go farther into Kemeraltı and you'll wind up at the **Kestane Pazarı** (Chestnut Bazaar), a smaller version of Istanbul's Spice Bazaar, where you'll find a good selection of spices, tea, coffee, fabric, and a vast number of confectioners.

The **Hisar Mosque**, beyond the bazaar, is the largest and oldest in İzmir. The **Kızlarağası Hanı** is an 18th-century restored Ottoman caravansary (*kervansaray* in Turkish) that houses many vaulted shops that sell quality Turkish goods, such as jewelry, miniatures, and rugs. ⊠ *Konak*.

**NEED A BREAK?**

**Ömer Usta Kahveci.** Making your way through Kemeraltı can be exhausting. Stop by Ömer Usta Kahveci for a shot of Turkish coffee brewed in the cup. The atmosphere is pleasant and lively, and if you're traveling in summer, there are plenty of shaded areas to keep you cool. Be aware that the cups can be scalding hot. ⊠ *905 Sok. 15, Hisar Cami back entrance* ☎ *232/425–4706*.

**Konak Meydanı** (*Konak Square*). At the water's edge, Konak Meydanı, is one of the city's two main squares (the other, Cumhuriyet Meydanı, or Republic Square; is to the north along Atatürk Caddesi). The **Saat Kulesi** (clock tower) stands out at the center of the plaza, with its ornate, late-Ottoman design. The tower was built in 1901, in honor of Sultan Abdulhamid, and the clock itself was sent as a gift from Kaiser Wilhelm II. The small, 18th-century single-domed **Konak Yalı Mosque**, set back from the clock tower, is decorated with colorful tiles and was built by Mehmet Paşa's daughter, Ayşe. Just north of Konak Meydani is Konak Pier.

**Konak Pier.** On the waterfront just north of Konak Meydani, Konak Pier was originally designed as a customs house by the famous architect Gustave Eiffel in the late 19th century. It's now an updated shopping mall with several restaurants and fabulous views. ⊠ *Waterfront*.

**Kordon.** The waterfront promenade is the most fashionable section of town. It starts at the museum complex in Bahribaba Parkı, in Alsancak, and stretches north along the busy harbor, past Konak Meydanı and NATO's Southern Command headquarters. Along the strip are several good seafood restaurants and cafés, all with outdoor seating overlooking the Aegean Sea. You can tour the area by *fayton* (horse-drawn carriages); carriages are stationed in the Cumhuriyet Meydanı, steps from the beginning of Kordon.

**Atatürk Müzesi** (*Atatürk Museum*). Along the Kordon is İzmir's small Atatürk Müzesi. The pale yellow Levantine house was presented to Atatürk as a gift and shows off photos and other mementoes of the founder of the Turkish Republic ⊠ *Atatürk Cad., 248* ☎ *232/464–8085* ☜ *3 TL* ⊘ *Tues.–Sun. 8:30–noon and 1–5.*

**Kültür Parkı.** İzmir's vast, central Kültür Park is home to approximately 8,000 trees as well as 14 exhibition halls, an open-air theater, a culture center, the History and Arts Museum, a paintings and sculpture museum, a sports arena, a swimming pool, tennis courts, and more.

**Tarih ve Sanat Müzesi** (*History and Art Museum*). On the grounds of the Kültür Parkı, this modern Tarih be Sanat Müzesi compound is made up of three buildings, which together showcase stone objects, ceramic objects, and precious artifacts. The jewelry in the precious artifacts exhibit dates from the Hellenistic, Roman, and Byzantine periods. ⊠ *East of Lozan and Montrö squares, in Kültür Parkı* ☎ *232/445–6818* ☜ *3TL* ⊘ *Tues.–Sun. 8:30–5:30.*

## WHERE TO EAT

**$$**
SEAFOOD
✕ **Balıkçı Hasan.** There are many popular seafood restaurants along the Kordonboyu waterfront in Alsancak but Balıkçı Hasan, with indoor and outdoor seating areas, is especially popular. They have an excellent selection of appetizers, as well as the usual seasonal seafood choices. ⊠ *Atatürk Cad. 186/A Kordon, Alsancak* ☎ *232/464–1354* ⊕ *www. balikcihasan.com.tr.*

**$$**
SEAFOOD
✕ **Balık Pişiricisi Veli Usta.** On the waterfront in the popular Kordonboyu area, this seafood restaurant has been open since 1970 and is especially popular with families. The specialty of the house is fillet of sole, and the atmosphere is friendly and fun. There is outside seating, as well as indoor tables. This is the most pleasant of several branches around the city. ⊠ *Atatürk Cad., 212A, Alsancak* ☎ *232/464–2705* ⊕ *www. izmirbalikpisirici.com.*

**$**
TURKISH
✕ **Bize Bize.** A long-standing family-style restaurant in the heart of Ilıca (with a branch in Çeşme) serves the best *köfte* (meatballs) in town, accompanied with a *piyaz* salad (navy beans, tomatoes, parsley, and onions). Make sure to leave room for the homemade *kunefe* (shredded wheat, cheese, syrup, and chestnuts). Wine and beer is served. ⊠ *5152 Sok. 81/C, Plaj Evleri, Ilıca, Çeşme* ☎ *232/723–1040 Ilıca, 232/712– 1746 Çeşme* ⊘ *Ilıca branch closed Nov.–Apr.*

**$**
TURKISH
★
✕ **Can Döner.** By the clock tower at the entrance of Kemeraltı, this small restaurant serves traditional *İskender döner* from the city of Bursa. The *döner* is sliced thin and topped with melted butter and tomato sauce. A glass of homemade *ayran* (plain yogurt drink) is the traditional accompaniment to the meal. Alcohol is not served. Come for lunch or an early dinner, as they're only open till 6:30 in the evening. ⊠ *Milli Kütüphane Cad. 9, Konak* ☎ *232/484–1313* ⊕ *www.candoner.com* ⊘ *Closed Sun.*

**$$**
SEAFOOD
✕ **Deniz.** Deniz means "sea" in Turkish, an appropriate name for this popular seafood eatery on the waterfront in Kordonboyu, on the ground floor of the İzmir Palas Hotel. The house specialty is *kılıç şiş*

Take a horse-drawn carriage ride along İzmir's Kordon, the waterfront promenade. —photo by eerkun, Fodors. com member.

(skewered grilled swordfish), and locals and tourists alike flock to the restaurant to try the *sütlü balık*, a hot appetizer prepared with sea bass, grouper, or a similar fish, and béchamel sauce—it's recommended that you order this dish when making a reservation or soon after arriving, as it takes about 45 minutes to prepare. ⊠ *Atatürk Cad. 188/B, Alsancak* ☎ *232/464–4499* ⊕ *www.denizrestaurant.com*.

$ ✕ **Kitchenette.** There are branches of this popular French-style bistro
BISTRO all over Istanbul—and now in İzmir, too. The menu includes brunch options as well as typical bistro salads, sandwiches, and French-inspired mains. It's fine if you're looking for a change from the Turkish food but don't expect anything fabulous. House-baked bread is a specialty. ⊠ *Forum İzmir shopping mall, Bornova* ☎ *232/339–4009* ⊕ *www. kitchenette.com.tr*.

$$ ✕ **Köşebaşı.** The İzmir outpost of this popular, upscale, and now interna-
TURKISH tional Istanbul-based meat and kebab restaurant has sprawling outdoor
★ seating overlooking the port city and the mountains. Specialties from the cities of Adana and Tarsus in the Southern Anatolian region include a tempting array of appetizers, such as mini *lahamcun* (Turkish-style pizza prepared with minced meat and spices), as well as excellent kebabs and meat dishes. It's a ways from downtown, and not a cheap taxi ride. ⊠ *Çeşme Çevreyolu, Limontepe Mevkii, Balçova* ☎ *232/278–2806* ⊕ *www.kosebasi.com*.

$ ✕ **Reyhan Patisserie.** With baked goods like chocolate cake, carrot cake,
TURKISH and local favorites prepared fresh daily this pastry shop has been popular for decades. This branch, in the heart of Alsancak, is also a

sit-down café serving Turkish-style breakfast. ⊠ *Mustafa Bey Cad. 24* ☎ *232/422–2802* ⊕ *www.reyhan.com.tr.*

¢ ✕ **Tarihi Kemeraltı Lokantası.** Established in 1939, this traditional Turkish
TURKISH restaurant near the Kemeraltı Bazaar is the place for typical home-style Turkish meals in modest surroundings. You can select your meal from the open display showcasing the specials of the day; prices are reasonable. It opens early for breakfast but closes at 8:30 in the evening. Alcohol is not served. ⊠ *Anafartalar Cad. 47/A, Veysel Çıkmaz Kemeraltı* ☎ *232/425–5393* ⊕ *www.tarihikemeraltilokantasi.com.*

$ ✕ **Yüzdeyüz Cafe & Restaurant.** The name means "one hundred percent,"
INTERNATIONAL and this popular spot on Konak Pier promises to deliver its customers with 100%—from the quality of the food, to the service, and the elegantly decorated indoor and outdoor dining areas. The international menu includes a bit of everything, from pizza to kebabs and even sushi. ⊠ *Konak Pier, Konak* ☎ *252/441–55963* ⊕ *www.yuzdeyuz.info.*

## WHERE TO STAY

*For expanded hotel reviews, visit Fodors.com.*

$$$ ⊟ **Crowne Plaza İzmir.** Off the beaten path in the neighborhood of Balçova, 23 km (14 mi) from the airport, this posh property overlooks İzmir Bay. **Pros:** free shuttle service to/from airport and the center of the city; state-of-the-art thermal spa and health center. **Cons:** far from the city center. ⊠ *Inciraltı Cad. 67, Balçova* ☎ *232/292–1300* ⊕ *www. cpizmir.com* ⇄ *219 rooms* ⌂ *In-room: Wi-Fi. In-hotel: restaurant, bar, pool, gym, spa, business center, parking, some pets allowed.*

$$ ⊟ **Hotel Kilim.** A central location on the fashionable Kordonboyu waterfront, bright decor, and bay and harbor views from most rooms compensate for the lack of character and local color. **Pros:** views; very good value. **Cons:** small rooms. ⊠ *Atatürk Bulvarı, Kazim Dirik Cad. 1* ☎ *232/484–5340* ⊕ *www.kilimotel.com.tr* ⇄ *75 rooms* ⌂ *In-hotel: restaurant, bar* ⫫ *No meals.*

$$ ⊟ **Karaca.** Attention to detail stands out here, with friendly and accommodating staff and spacious rooms, despite the dark, old-school furnishings. **Pros:** helpful staff; smaller and more intimate than many luxury hotels. **Cons:** rooms could use an update. ⊠ *Necatibey Bulvarı 1379 Sok. 55, Alsancak* ☎ *232/489–1940* ⊕ *www.otelkaraca.com.tr* ⇄ *73 rooms* ⌂ *In-room: Wi-Fi. In-hotel: restaurant, bar* ⫫ *Breakfast.*

$$ ⊟ **Mövenpick Hotel İzmir.** Steps from the Kordonboyu promenade, this posh outpost of the Swiss hotel chain is excellently located and some rooms have striking views of İzmir Bay. **Pros:** reasonably priced; fine-dining restaurant and location. **Cons:** small health and fitness center. ⊠ *Cumhuriyet Bulvarı 138, Pasaport, Alsancak* ☎ *232/488–1480* ⊕ *www.moevenpick-izmir.com* ⇄ *185 rooms* ⌂ *In-room: a/c, Wi-Fi. In-hotel: restaurant, pool, gym, laundry facilities, parking* ⫫ *Breakfast.*

$$$ ⊟ **Swissôtel Grand Efes İzmir.** Most of the elegantly decorated rooms have lovely views of the Aegean Sea and among the many amenities are indoor and outdoor swimming pools, a shopping arcade, and lush gardens for strolling. **Pros:** state-of-the-art spa and wellness center; centrally located; steps from the Kordonboyu waterfront promenade. **Cons:** feels like a large hotel and service can be a bit impersonal.

✉ *Gaziosmanpaşa Bulvarı 1* ☎ *232/414–0000* ⊕ *www.swissotel.com. tr/izmir/* ➪ *347 rooms, 55 suites* ☆ *In-room: a/c, Internet, Wi-Fi. In-hotel: restaurant, bar, pool, tennis court, spa, laundry facilities, business center, parking* ⦿ *No meals.*

## NIGHTLIFE AND THE ARTS

**Kültür Parkı.** For outdoor classical music concerts, check out the open-air theater in Kültür Parkı.

**Rain.** This is İzmir's seaside dining and entertainment complex—it has four restaurants (each with its own bar and cuisine), a coffeehouse, and a glamorous nightclub called **En Velo** with a dance floor and DJs that spin club music. ✉ *1649 Sokak 79, Karşıyaka* ☎ *232/372–2929.*

**State Opera and Ballet House.** The State Ballet and Opera House offers dance performances, chamber music, and pop and jazz concerts. Tickets can be purchased at the theater on the day of the performance. ✉ *Milli Kütüphane Caddesi* ☎ *232/484–6445* ⊕ *www.dobgm.gov.tr.*

The Alsancak neighborhood has a lively nightlife scene with an assortment of bars, especially along Gazi Kadýnlar Sokaði—a great street to check out in general, full of cafés and attractive Levantine homes.

**Eko Pub.** This pub is popular with expats and an over-twenty crowd. ✉ *Plevne Bulvarı No. 1, Alsancak* ☎ *232/421–4459.*

**Mavi Bar.** For rock music—sometimes live—Mavi Bar is your best bet. ✉ *Cumhuriyet Bulvarı 206* ☎ *232/463–0194.*

**Sardunya Bar.** A semialternative crowd hangs out at Sardunya Bar on one of Alsancak's popular streets, Kıbrıs Şehitleri. ✉ *1482 Sokak 11* ☎ *232/464–4665* ⊕ *www.sardunyabar.com.*

## SPORTS AND THE OUTDOORS

**Homa Lagoon (Homa Dalyani).** The Homa Lagoon (Homa Dalyanı), also called *kuş cenneti* (bird heaven), is a natural reserve on the Gediz Delta, on the north shore of İzmir Bay near Çamaltı. It's an excellent day trip out of the city. The delta's lagoons, mudflats, salt marshes, reed beds, and farmland provide diverse habitats to more than 230 species of birds, mammals, reptiles, and fish. Tours of the lagoon can be taken by car or on foot: all tours start at the visitor center and are free. Unfortunately, few of the staff members speak English. You'll need a car to get here, or you can hire a taxi for the trip. ✉ *İzmir* ☎ *232/482–1218.*

The most popular region for hiking and skiing near İzmir is the 120-km (75-mi) stretch between the Gediz and Küçük Menderes rivers.

HIKING    Trails on the slopes of **Mount Bozdağ**, 110 km (68 mi), from İzmir, are a welcome refuge from the city's suffocating heat. At Gölcük, trails climb gentle hills that cradle a lake that is ideal for a picnic. Several tour companies organize daily trips to the area from İzmir.

## SHOPPING

For high-end, brand-name, and designer clothing, the Alsancak neighborhood in Konak has it all.

**Bostanlı bazaar.** The open-air bazaar held on Wednesday, in the Bostanlı neighborhood of Karşıyaka, is known for its good-quality, inexpensive apparel: the earlier you go, the better the selection. ✉ *Karşıyaka.*

**Dösim.** Under the auspices of the Ministry of Culture and Tourism, the Dösim shops around the country sell top-quality Turkish handicrafts, books, and souvenirs. Prices are moderate to expensive. ✉ *Cumhuriyet Bulvarı No.115, Alsancak* ☎ *232/483–0789.*

## ÇEŞME

*85 km (53 mi) west of İzmir.*

Çeşme, known for its hot springs and beaches, has always been a summer resort for İzmirians, but in recent years the gorgeous sands have been luring Istanbullus and an international crowd, too. Despite rapid and often unsightly development, the town retains its provincial charm, and it's still more off the beaten path than the resorts of the Bodrum Peninsula. The real lures, understandably, are the beaches that span 29 km (18 mi) of coastline.

Çeşme has a large marina, but for sandy beaches and crystal clear waters, head to one of the nearby seaside villages. Ilıca, with its deluxe hotels, is closest and the most popular, with a long sandy beach. Dalyanköy is on the northern tip of the bay and is quite quiet and peaceful. The most beautiful beaches are in Çiftlikköy. Alaçatı, with its almost constant wind, is a windsurfer's paradise and is known for its restaurants and hotels. Boyalık Bay and Ayayorgi attract a hip crowd. The villages are close enough that you can move around by car or public transportation quite easily.

Public beaches are generally crowded and don't have amenities, so you'll do well to spend 20 TL or so to secure a spot with chaise lounges, umbrellas, towel service, and often a restaurant and bar. The swimming season starts in April and continues until mid-November—high season is July and August.

### GETTING HERE AND AROUND

The villages are quite close together so getting around by taxi, *dolmuş,* or rental car is quite easy. Bus service is limited. From Çeşme proper, Alaçatı is 12 km (7½ mi), Dalyanköy is 4 km (2½ mi), Ilıca is 6 km (about 3½ mi), and Çiftlikköy is 10 km (6 mi).

Çeşme Seyahat Bus Company provides the only bus service between İzmir and Çeşme. In summer, buses depart from Çeşme every 15 minutes, between 7 am and 8 pm. Reservations are highly recommended.

For a quick hop to a Greek Island, head to Chios (Sakız Adası in Turkish), about a 45-minute boat ride away. Several ferry companies at the Çeşme docks offer excursions; fares are about €15 to €25 (euro) per person.

### ESSENTIALS

**Bus Information Çeşme Seyahat Bus Company** ☎ *232/712–6499 Çeşme bus terminal, 232/716–8299 Alaçatı, 232/259–3415 İzmir/Üçkuyular bus station.*

### EXPLORING

**Alaçatı.** A pretty village 2 km (1 mi) south of Ilıca, Alaçatı bustles in the evening when the trendy cafés, restaurants, and boutiques fill with hip crowds. The main strip is always lively; to avoid the hubbub come in the afternoon when the crowd is mostly locals and storeowners, although it gets very hot. The beach at Alaçatı, about 2 km (1 mi) south of town, is ideal for windsurfing, with strong winds and few waves. Unfortunately, there is only a small, public beach here, but many of the private beach clubs and hotels with private beaches allow nonguests for a day rate. The water is cooler at Alaçatıt than it is at other beaches. Watersports like waterskiing, banana boat rides, and windsurfing are available here.

**Altınkum.** About 10 km (6 mi) from Çeşme, Altınkum has crystal clear and calm water. The area has yet to undergo a huge development boom and there are many private and public beaches to choose from. The best is Fun Beach Club (⊕ *www.funbeachclub.com*) with its expansive sandy beachfront, restaurant, and other beach amenities. There is a cover charge, but it's worth it.

**Ayios Haralambos.** Named after a patron saint, Ayios Haralambos is a large old Greek basilica. It's worth taking a look at the facade as you stroll down the main street of Çeşme's shopping district. The space is now used as a cultural center that hosts art exhibitions and chess tournaments. ⊠ *Inkilap Caddesi.*

**Boyalık Bay.** Just west of Ilıca, Boyalık Bay has a 5-km (3-mi) beachfront with many private and public beaches and hotels. The beach clubs and restaurants at Ayayorgi are popular with trendy İzmirians and Istanbullus.

**Dalyanköy.** About 5 km (3 mi) north of Çeşme, Dalyanköy is a small fishing village known for the excellent seafood restaurants that line the small harbor. The beaches are not that noteworthy, so save your trip out here for the evening, when you can wine and dine by the water.

**Genoese castle.** The 14th-century Genoese castle is very picturesque, with its stone walls lined with sun-basking lizards. The keep is often deep in wildflowers. The castle's museum displays weaponry from the glory days of the Ottoman Empire. ⊙ *Daily 8:30–11:45 and 1:00–5:15.*

**Ilıca.** Still a summer retreat for İzmir's wealthy, Ilıca fronts one of the peninsula's most popular beaches, with many hotels lined up along the crystal clear water and white sand. The public beach here is large but gets crowded on the weekends. There are lots of waves, but no amenities like bathrooms, lounge chairs, or umbrellas. The town has plenty of shops and eateries and is particularly known for its *kumru* (literally translated as "dove"), a Turkish-style panini sandwich prepared with *kaşar* (similar to mild cheddar cheese) cheese, *sucuk* (a spicy, Turkish beef sausage), salami, sliced tomatoes, and pickles stuffed inside a sesame-seed bread and served piping hot.

**Pırlantı Beach.** Pırlantı means "brilliant" or "diamond" and this beach outside Çiftlikköy (itself about 10 km [6 mi] from Çeşme) is indeed lovely, with a small section reserved for kiteboarding. There are many motels and *pansiyons* in this area as well as a camping ground.

### WHERE TO EAT

$$ ╳ **Beatrice.** A limited menu of delicious choices, prepared by Italian
ITALIAN owner and chef Beatrice, is served in a soothing atmosphere, accented with attentive service. Even the homemade bread is memorable.

Çeşme's beaches attract vacationers from all over the world.

⊠ *Kemal Paşa Caddesi, Barbaros Sok. 4, Alaçatı* ☎ *232/716–7040* ⌖ *Reservations essential* ⊙ *Daily 7 pm–midnight.*

**$**    ✕ **Cafe Agrilia.** This Italian restaurant in an old tobacco warehouse was
ITALIAN   around long before the rest of Alaçatı's trendy restaurants came on the
scene. The homemade tagliatelle with shrimp in a light, garlic sauce is
excellent. You can also get creative fresh fruit juice concoctions here
⊠ *Kemal Paşa Cad. 75, Alaçatı* ☎ *232/716–8594.*

**$$$**   ✕ **Dalyan Restaurant "Cevat'ın Yeri".** The outdoor terrace overlooking the
SEAFOOD   waterfront is the ideal spot in Dalyanköy for a seafood dinner. Every-
★    thing here is prepared with great attention to taste and presentation, and
the service is gracious. ⊠ *Liman Caddesi, Dalyanköy* ☎ *232/724–7045*
⊕ *www.dalyanrestaurant.com.*

**$**    ✕ **Dost Pide & Pizza.** Stopping here for *pide* (Turkish-style *calzones* stuffed
TURKISH   with a variety of ingredients that can include cheese, spinach, or meat)
is a highlight of a trip to Ilıca and a great choice for a quick lunch. The
menu also includes kebabs, *döner,* pizza, and desserts. ⊠ *5152 Sok. 27,
Ilıca* ☎ *232/723–2059* ⊕ *www.dostpidepizza.com* ⊙ *Open 24 hours a
day in season.*

**¢**    ✕ **Kumrucu Şevki.** Ilıca is known for *kumru*—Turkish-style panini pre-
TURKISH   pared with special homemade rolls and stuffed with salami, *sucuk*
(beef spicy sausage), cheese, and tomatoes and pickles—and Kum-
rucu Şevki serves the best in town. Pair your sandwich with a glass
of *ayran,* a refreshing yogurt drink. There are branches in Çeşme as
well. ⊠ *Yıldızburnu Mevki, 2, Ilıca* ☎ *232/723–2392 Ilıca* ⊙ *Open 24
hours a day.*

**$$** ✕**Kydonia.** In this spacious and
ECLECTIC casual waterfront dining room,
the emphasis is on hot and cold
mezes (appetizers)—more than 70
types are on offer and include tra-
ditional favorites from Çeşme and
the Greek island of Crete. Many are
made from seafood, and there are
many vegetarian choices as well.
You can accompany your meal with
a selection from the nice wine list.
✉ *Port Alaçatı Marina 63, Alaçatı*
☎ *232/716–0765* ⊕ *www.kydonia.com.tr* ⌕ *Reservations essential*
☾ *Daily 7 pm–midnight* ☾ *Closed Oct.–Apr.*

> **SWEET SPOT**
>
> **Imren.** For dessert, try local favor-
> ite Imren, where ice cream comes
> in many different flavors, and is
> served in a homemade waffle
> cone. *Sakız muhallebe* is a Turk-
> ish gumdrop pudding. ✉ *Tokoğlu*
> *Mah. Kemalpaşa Cad., Alaçatı*
> ☎ *232/716–8356.*

**$$$** ✕**Mi Casa Trattoria.** Although not far removed from the hub of the
INTERNATIONAL nightlife in Alaçatı, this comfortable bar and romantic dining room
is tucked away on a secluded side street. The excellent menu includes
Italian and international cuisine and is accompanied by a good wine
list. ✉ *1057 Sok., Alaçatı* ☎ *232/716-6075* ☾ *Daily 7 pm–midnight*
☾ *Closed Oct.–Apr.*

**$$** ✕**Tuval Cafe Restaurant & Bar.** Alaçatı's most popular restaurant is right
TURKISH in the heart of the action on Kemalpaşa Street, serving Turkish and
★ international dishes in indoor and outdoor dining rooms—outdoors
is the place to be on a warm summer night, when all the world seems
to stroll by. *Kemalpaşa Caddesi 83, Alaçatı* ☎ *232/716–9802 Alaçatı,*
*232/716–1444 Çeşme Marina* ⊕ *www.tuvalcafe.com* ☾ *9:30 am–1 am*
☾ *Closed Jan.–Mar 15, open weekends only* ☞ *Marina branch is open*
*year-round. Alaçatı is open only on the weekends from January 1 to*
*March 14 and then every day after March 15.*

## WHERE TO STAY

*For expanded hotel reviews, visit Fodors.com.*

### ALAÇATI

**$$$** ⊞ **Alaçatı Beach Resort.** Right on the beach and built of attractive Alaçatı
stone, this small, quiet resort is a fabulous getaway, with extremely
attractive rooms that open to sea-facing balconies. **Pros:** lots of nearby
water sports. **Cons:** you'll need your own transportation to visit
Alaçatı's center. ✉ *Çark Plajı, Liman Mevkii, Alaçatı* ☎ *232/716–6161*
⊕ *www.alacati.com* ⤴ *41 rooms* ⌂ *In-room: Wi-Fi. In-hotel: restau-*
*rant, bar, pool, tennis court, beach.*

**$$$** ⊞ **Alaçatı Marina Palace.** All 12 spacious and charmingly decorated
rooms and suites face a lawn, pool, and sea from their balconies and
terraces. **Pros:** close to the nightlife at Port Alaçatı Marina; just steps
from the beach; especially relaxing surroundings. **Cons:** need private
tranporation to reach downtown Alaçatı. ✉ *Liman Mevkii, Alaçatı*
☎ *252/716 0740* ⊕ *www.alacatimarina.com* ⤴ *12 rooms* ⌂ *In-room:*
*Wi-Fi. In-hotel: restaurant, pool.*

**$$$** ⊞ **TashMahal.** Stone floors, fireplaces, rich fabrics, and traditional fur-
nishings infuse a 150-year-old mansion on an atmospheric old back-
street with character. **Pros:** a short walk to resort center; lovely garden;
surrounding neighborhood is atmospheric; delicious breakfast. **Cons:**

not near the beach, but within walking distance. ✉ *Tokoğlu Mahallesi, 1005 Sok. 68, Alaçatı* ☎ *232/716–0122* ⊕ *www.tashmahalotel.com* ⤶ *8 rooms* ☖ *In-room: no TV, Wi-Fi. In-hotel: restaurant.*

### ÇEŞME

**$$** 🏨 **Kanuni Kervansaray Historical Hotel.** Built in 1528 during the reign of Süleyman the Magnificent, this old inn next to Çeşme's medieval castle is surrounded by stone walls and decorated in traditional Ottoman style, with kilims and low wooden furniture. **Pros:** historic setting; authentic look and feel; nice courtyard swimming pool and terrace; Turkish bath on premises. **Cons:** some distance from a beach. ✉ *Çarşı Mevkii Kale Yanı 5* ☎ *232/712–0630* ⤶ *29 rooms* ☖ *In-hotel: restaurant, bar, pool, business center, parking* ⊘ *Closed Nov.–Mar.*

**$** 🏨 **Pasifik.** The bright modern rooms of this pleasant hotel have sea views, and a setting about a 15-minute walk along the waterfront from Çeşme's main square ensures nighttime quiet. **Pros:** good value; nice quiet location. **Cons:** you'll need transportation to reach some of Çeşme's nicer beaches. ✉ *3264 Sok. Tekke Plajı Mevkii 16* ☎ *232/712–2700* ⊕ *www.pasifikotel.com* ⤶ *16 rooms* ☖ *In-room: no TV. In-hotel: restaurant* ⫯◯⫰ *No meals.*

### ILICA

**$$$** 🏨 **Ilıca Spa & Wellness Thermal Resort.** Elegant, attractive rooms and bungalows, many with sea views and some spreading over two levels, provide a perfect getaway and enjoy amenities that include a spa, several thermal pools, a private beach, and sunbathing platforms that extend out over the sea. **Pros:** great for families; self-contained with many amenities. **Cons:** long walk to Ilıca's nightlife and shopping area. ✉ *Boyalık Mevkii, Ilıca* ☎ *232/723–3131* ⊕ *www.ilicahotel.com* ⤶ *248 rooms, 12 suites, 3 bungalows* ☖ *In-room: Internet. In-hotel: restaurant, bar, pool, tennis court, gym, spa, beach, water sports, children's programs* ⫯◯⫰ *Some meals.*

**$$$$** 🏨 **Sheraton Çeşme Hotel, Resort & Spa.** Spacious, well-appointed rooms, a private beach, a sun deck extending into the sea, a spa, and no end of water sports are among the many amenities at this deluxe seaside resort in Ilıca. **Pros:** extremely comfortable accommodations; extensive resort amenities. **Cons:** expensive; half-board required in high season; need private transportation; international-style resort lacks local flavor. ✉ *Şifne Caddesi, 5152 Sok. 43, Ilıca* ☎ *232/723–1240* ⊕ *www.sheratoncesme.com* ⤶ *398 rooms* ☖ *In-room: Internet. In-hotel: restaurant, bar, pool, tennis court, gym, spa, beach, water sports, children's programs, business center, parking* ⫯◯⫰ *Some meals.*

### NIGHTLIFE

Çeşme has a happening nightlife scene, especially around the marinas. There are all sorts of restaurants, bars, and clubs with DJs or live music.

Outside Çeşme, the various beach towns have a more laid-back nightlife. **Yıldız Burnu,** the trendy waterfront in Ilıca, is lined with bars and lounges that cater to a young crowd. The beach clubs and bars in Ayayorgi Bay and Boyalık Bay are popular with the late-night crowd.

**Babylon Ayayorgi.** The popular Istanbul jazz club Babylon spends its summer seaside at the Ayayorgi Bay and doubles as a beach club and restaurant by day. Evenings bring live music—Turkiish and internationally recognized jazz, pop, and rock artists. ✉ *Ayayorgi Bay, Boyalık Bay* ☎ *232/712–6339* ⊕ *www.babylon.com.tr.*

★ **Monk by Babylon.** Çeşme's finest club, overlooking the marina, offers live music (Turkish, international, jazz) as well as an eclectic menu of excellent international cuisine. *Çeşme Marina* ☎ *232/712–9331* ⊕ *www.monk.com.tr* ☉ *Daily 5 pm– 2 am* ☉ *Closed Oct.–Apr.*

**Paparazzi.** The DJs at the popular Paparazzi spin music from the 1970s through the '90s, which is appropriate because the club has been around for almost 30 years. Partying goes till the wee hours of the morning. The food isn't bad, either. ✉ *Ayayorgi Bay, Boyalık Bay* ☎ *232/712–6767* ⊕ *www.paparazzi.com.tr.*

### SPORTS AND THE OUTDOORS

BOAT TOURS   During high season, daily boat tours to coves along the coastline leave from the main harbors in Çeşme and Ilıca. The cost varies, depending on whether lunch and beverages are served. One of the most popular stops is Donkey Island (Eşek Adası). Be warned that in high season the boats tend to be crowded and play loud music, so consider renting a boat privately.

KITESURFING   **Kitesurf Beach.** Pırlantı Beach (outside Çiftlikköy, about 10 km [6 mi] from Çesme) is also known as "Kitesurf Beach." If you have no experience and want to learn, you can enroll in one of several different courses available from the Kitesurf Beach School, from 300 TL and taught by IKO (International Kiteboarding Organization) qualified instructors. ☎ *533/270–8745* ⊕ *www.kitesurfbeach.com.*

### SHOPPING

The main street in Çeşme has many gift shops selling trinkets and souvenirs, beachwear, carpets, and leather items. There are also many jewelry stores selling silver and gold; bargaining is acceptable and expected. Çeşme Marina also has many high-end shops. Downtown Alaçatı is also great for shopping, and high-end retailers and jewelry stores occupy stone houses along the narrow lanes.

# SELÇUK, EPHESUS, AND ŞIRINCE

The ruins of Ephesus bring most visitors to Selçuk and the picturesque village of Şirince. You will need approximately a day to visit Ephesus and the Archaeology Museum in Selçuk and another day to visit some of the surrounding early Christian sites. Staying in Selçuk is convenient, while the hilltop village of Şirince offers a bucolic getaway that is within easy reach of what you will want to see.

# SELÇUK

*79 km (49 mi) south of İzmir on Rte. E87.*

Selçuk, the closest city to Ephesus, lies beneath an ancient fortress and is unfortunately often overlooked. The former farming village has interesting sights of its own to offer—St. John the Evangelist is said to be buried here and the city has one of the oldest mosques in Turkey, the İsa Bey Cami. The city is easy to navigate, and there are many casual restaurants along the main square and along the side streets where you can eat outside. The town hosts an annual camel-wrestling festival every January.

## GETTING HERE AND AROUND

By car, Selçuk is about 30 minutes from İsmir, following the well-marked Otoyol (toll highway) toward Aydın. The Selçuk exit is well marked.

Alternatively, if you do not want to rent a car, you can take a train or bus to Selçuk. Trains depart from the Basmane Station in İzmir and travel time is about two hours; for schedules and online tickets, visit ⊕ *www.tcdd.gov.tr*. Local bus companies also offer service to Selçuk, with departures from the bus terminal in İzmir.

## ESSENTIALS

**Bus Information Kamil Koç** ⊠ *İzmir Bus Terminal, İzmir* ☎ *232/444–0562, 0232/892–6263 Selçuk Bus Terminal* ⊕ *www.kamilkoc.com.tr.* **Metro Turizm** ⊠ *İzmir Bus Terminal, İzmir* ☎ *232/444–3455, 232/892–1859 Selçuk Bus Terminal* ⊕ *www.metroturizm.com.tr.*

**Visitor Information** ⊠ *Akdeniz Mahallesi, 1344 Sok. 2, İzmir* ☎ *232/483–5117.*

## EXPLORING

Fodor'sChoice
★ **Ephesus Archaeological Site.** *See the highlighted Ephesus feature in this chapter.*

★ **Ephesus Müzesi (Ephesus Museum).** *See the highlighted Ephesus feature in this chapter.*

**İsa Bey Cami** (*İsa Bey Mosque*). İsa Bey Cami is one of the oldest mosques in Turkey, dating from 1375. The jumble of architectural styles suggests a transition between Seljuk and Ottoman design: like later-day Ottoman mosques, this one has a courtyard, not found in Seljuk mosques. The structure is built out of "borrowed" stone: marble blocks with Latin inscriptions, Corinthian columns, black-granite columns from the baths at Ephesus, and pieces from the altar of the Temple of Artemis. ⊠ *St. John Sok.* ☉ *Daily 9–6.*

> **NEED A BREAK?**
>
> **Tadım.** Tea and a good selection of excellent *lokum* (Turkish delights) are sold at tiny Tadım. Hikmet Çeliker's family has been producing these delights for more than 250 years and ship their products worldwide. ⊠ *Emlak Bank arcade.*

**St. John Basilica.** The emperor Justinian built the St. John Basilica over a 2nd-century tomb on Ayasoluk Hill, believed by many to have once held the body of St. John the Evangelist. Eleven domes formerly topped the basilica, which rivaled Istanbul's Aya Sofya (Hagia Sophia) in scale. The barrel-vaulted roof collapsed after a long-ago earthquake, but the church is still an incredible sight, with its labyrinth of halls and marble

*Continued on page 232*

# EPHESUS
## CITY OF THE GODS

One would naturally think that the greatest Roman ruins are to be found in Italy. Not so fast! With an ancient arena that dwarfs the one in Pompeii, and a lofty library that rivals any structure in the Roman Forum, Ephesus—once the most important Greco-Roman city of the Eastern Mediterranean—is among the best-preserved ancient sites in the world. Set on a strategic trade route, it first won fame as a cultural and religious crossroads. Here, shrines honored the pagan goddess of fertility, St. Paul did some serious soul-searching, and—legend has it—the Virgin Mary lived out her last days. Today, modern travelers can trace the fault lines of ancient civilization in Ephesus's spectacular landscape of ruined temples, theaters, and colonnaded streets.

**THE AWESTRUCK ADMIRERS** who disembark from cruise ships and tour buses to wander through the largest Roman ruins of the Eastern Mediterranean are not really out of sync with ancient times, since Ephesus was a bustling port of call in the pre-Christian era. Home to upwards of 500,000 people at its height, Efes drew visitors from near and far with its promise of urbane and sybaritic pleasures, including baths, brothels, theaters, temples, public latrines, and one of the world's largest libraries. Even then, visitors approaching from the harbor (which has since silted up) could wander under the marble porticos of the Arcadian Way—the ancient world's Rodeo Drive—and visit shops laden with goods from throughout the Mediterranean world.

- ✉ Efes (Ephesus), 4 km (2.5 mi) west of Selçuk on Selçuk-Ephesus Rd.
- ☎ 0232/892-6010 (no official Web site)
- 💳 20TL; terraced houses, 15TL; parking: 7.50TL
- 🕐 Apr.—Oct., daily 8—7; Nov.—Mar., daily 8—5.

## SPIRIT & THE FLESH

Ephesus in pre-Hellenic times was the cult center of Cybele, the Anatolian goddess of fertility. When seafaring Ionians arrived in the 10th century BC they promptly recast her as Artemis, goddess of the hunt. With her three tiers of breasts, this symbol of mother nature was, in turn, both fruitful and barren, according to the season; as such, she was also worshipped by thousands as the goddess of chastity. The riches of her shrines, however, awoke greed; in the 6th century BC, Croesus, king of Lydia, captured Ephesus, but was himself defeated by Persia's Cyrus. The wily Ephesians managed to keep on good terms with everyone by playing up to both sides of any conflict but by the 2nd century BC, Ephesus had become capital of the Roman province of Asia and Artemis had been renamed Diana.

## THE GOSPEL TRUTH?

As with other Roman cities, Ephesus eventually became Christian, though not without a struggle. The Gospel of Luke recounts how the city's silversmiths drove St. Paul out of Ephesus for fear that his pronouncements—"there are no gods made with hands"—would lessen the sale of their silver statues. After Paul addressed a gathering of townsfolk in the amphitheater, the craftsmen rioted, but he succeeded in founding an early congregation here thanks to his celebrated "Epistle to the Ephesians." Another tourist to the city was St. John, who visited between 37 and 48 AD (he died here in AD 95 shortly after completing his Gospel); tradition has it he was accompanied by Mary, whom he brought to fulfill a pledge he had made to Jesus to protect her. Whether or not this is true, Ephesus's House of the Virgin Mary—where Mary is reputed to have breathed her last—soon became the earliest pilgrimage site in Christendom.

Top, Gateway to Odeon; Right, The Arcadian Way

## DID YOU KNOW?

When Ephesus became a Roman capital in the 2nd century BC, numerous shrines were erected to the ancient gods, including Hercules (figure at left). But by the 4th century, the early Christians had become mightier than the fabled hero and Ephesus's pagan temples were plundered for the building of numerous churches.

# PRECIOUS STONES: WHAT'S WHERE

"Is there a greater city than Ephesus?" asked St. Paul. "Is there a more beautiful city?" Those who dig ruins can only agree with the saint. Ephesus is the best preserved Greco–Roman city of the Eastern Mediterranean.

**1 Temple of Domitian.** One of the largest temples in the city was dedicated to the first-century Roman emperor.

**2 Odeon.** At this intimate theater, an audience of about 1,500 sat on a semicircle of stone seats to enjoy theatricals and music recitals.

**3 Prytaneion.** One of the most important buildings in town was dedicated to Hestia, goddess of hearth and home. Priests kept vigil to ensure her sacred flame was never extinguished.

**4 Curetes Street.** One of the main thoroughfares cuts a diagonal swath through the ancient city and was a processional route leading to the Temple of Artemis; "curetes" are priests of Artemis.

**5 Temple of Hadrian.** Elegant friezes and graceful columns surround the porch and main chamber of this monument to the 2nd-century Roman emperor. A frieze of Medusa guards the entrance to ward off evil spirits, and, in another, the

Christian Emperor Theodosius is surrounded by pagan gods—a sign that worldly Ephesus was a tolerant place.

**6 Slope Houses.** The luxurious homes of well-to-do Ephesians of the 1st to 7th centuries climb the slopes of Mount Koressos. Liberally decorated with frescoes and mosaics, this enclave is evocative of life in the ancient town.

**7 Library of Celsus.** One of the most spectacular extant ruins of antiquity, this remarkable two-storied building was commissioned in the 2nd century and was destined for double duty—as a mausoleum for Julius Celsus, Roman governor of the province of Asia minor and as a reading room stocked with more than 12,000 scrolls.

**8 Brothel.** Footsteps etched into the marble paving stones along Curetes Street led the way to one of the busiest businesses in town.

**9 Theater.** St. Paul preached to the Ephesians in this mag-

nificent space. The largest outdoor theater of the ancient world was carved out of the flanks of Mount Pion over the course of 60 years and seats as many as 40,000 spectators.

**10 Arcadian Way.** The grandest street in town, traversing the third of a mile between the harbor and the theater, was flanked by mosaic-floored porticos that were lined with elegant shops and—a luxury afforded by few ancient cities—torch-lit at night. This is where Cleopatra paraded in triumph.

**11 Stadium.** This 1st-century BC structure accommodated more than 70,000 spectators, who enjoyed such entertainments as chariot races and gladiatorial spectacles.

**12 Temple of Artemis.** A lone column rising from a swamp is all that remains of one of the Seven Wonders of the Ancient World. The largest building in the ancient Mediterranean, once surrounded by 127 columns, was a shrine to the goddess of fertility, abundance, and womanly concerns.

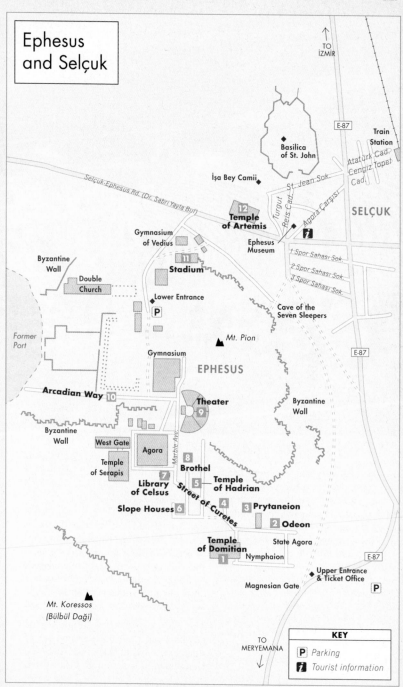

Ephesus and Selçuk

TO
İZMİR

Basilica
of St. John

E-87

Train
Station

İşa Bey Camii

St. Jean Sok.

Atatürk Cad.
Cengiz Topel
Cad.

Selçuk-Ephesus Rd. (Dr. Sabri Yayla But)

Turgut
Reis Cad.

Agora Çarşısı

SELÇUK

12
Temple
of Artemis

Ephesus
Museum

Gymnasium
of Vedius

7

1 Spor Sahası Sok.

2 Spor Sahası Sok.

3 Spor Sahası Sok.

Byzantine
Wall

11
Stadium

Double
Church

Lower Entrance

P

Cave of the
Seven Sleepers

Former
Port

Mt. Pion

E-87

Gymnasium

EPHESUS

Arcadian Way  10

Theater
9

Byzantine
Wall

Byzantine
Wall

West Gate

Agora

Marble Ave.

8
Brothel

Temple
of Serapis

7
Library
of Celsus

5

Temple
of Hadrian

Slope Houses  6

4

Street of Curetes

3  Prytaneion

2  Odeon

Temple
of Domitian
1

Nymphaion

State Agora

Upper Entrance
& Ticket Office

E-87

P

Magnesian Gate

Mt. Koressos
(Bülbül Dağı)

TO
MERYEMANA

| KEY | |
|---|---|
| P | Parking |
| i | Tourist information |

## PLANNING YOUR VISIT

Most people who tour Ephesus (Efes) base themselves in nearby Selçuk. If arriving by car, take the road from Selçuk to Kuşadası, turning left and following the signs to the archaeological site. There are two public parking lots, at the top and bottom of the site near the two main gates. Note that if you arrive by car you'll have to backtrack the hill one way or the other after walking the site (or opt for an inexpensive cab ride back). It may be best to forgo your car and take taxis to and from Selçuk. There is also a *dolmuş* (shared taxi) that connects with Selçuk.

### TIPS FOR TOURING

The main entrance (Lower Gate) is near the turnoff to Selçuk; for the upper Magnesian Gate, follow the signs for the Cave of the Seven Sleepers and House of the Virgin Mary (Meryemana). Since Ephesus is laid out on the slopes of Mounts Pion and Koressos, many opt to begin their tour at the upper Magnesian Gate, visiting the state and religious buildings on the higher reaches before descending to where most of the public arenas and agoras are located.

The main avenue runs about a mile downhill but there are any number of side streets with intriguing detours. Consequently, a minimum visit of two

## EPHESUS GUIDES

Perhaps the easiest way to see all the sights is to take a guided bus tour, which allows you to travel between the Ephesus site, the Ephesus Museum, the House of the Virgin Mary, and the Basilica of St. John stress-free. The day trip (lunch included) usually costs $75–$90. Tour agencies can be found in Izmir and Kuşadası, although the most convenient are located in Selçuk. Here are two recommended outfitters:

■ (✉ Atatürk Mah. 1019 Sok. 6, Selçuk ☎ 232/892-7364 ⊕ www. grandwonders.com).

■ (✉ Atatürk Mah. 1006 Sok. 4, Selçuk ☎ 232/892-9547 ⊕ www.perontour. com).

The guides who flock around the entrance gates to the main site, and are not particularly knowledgeable, and they usually charge around $50 for a two-hour tour. The best option—in addition to consulting one of the handy site guidebooks—is to rent the one-hour audio guides (10TL).

hours can easily stretch to four, not including an hour in the museum and an hour or two at nearby sites like the Cave of the Seven Sleepers and Meryemana.

You'll better appreciate the treasures of Ephesus Museum if you tour the ancient city first—knowing where the statuary, mosaics, and other artifacts were located raises them from the dust to life when you visit the museum. As for timing, a visit in early morning or late afternoon might help you skirt the heaviest of the cruise ship crowds from Kuşadası. In summer you'll want to avoid the midday heat and sun. Be sure to bring water.

Above, Library of Celsus

# WHO'S WHO IN ANCIENT EPHESUS

## ALEXANDER THE GREAT

Upon entering Ephesus in triumph after defeating the Persians in 333 BC, Alexander saw the reconstruction efforts of the temple to Artemis underway and offered to pay for the new edifice with the proviso that his name be inscribed over the entrance. The Ephesians, not wanting to offend their goddess, diplomatically informed the noble warrior and mighty king that it would not be right for one divine being to so honor another.

## ANDROKLOS

Banished from Athens upon the death of his father, King Kadros, in the 10th century BC, Androklos arrived at the shores of Asia Minor. The oracle at Delphi had told the prince that a fish and a boar would guide him on his way. A fish that Androklos was roasting on the beach leapt from the flames into the bush, and the commotion routed out a wild boar who led him to a fertile valley: the future Ephesus. Androklos went on to unite the twelve cities of Asia Minor as the Ionian League.

## HEROSTRATUS

Stories of all great cities include at least one villain, and in Ephesus the most infamous is Herostratus. One night in 356 BC, the deranged young man burned the most important building in town, the Temple to Artemis. As fate would have it, Alexander the Great was born the same night. The Roman historian Plutarch later observed that the goddess was "too busy taking care of the birth of Alexander to send help to her threatened temple." Ephesian authorities executed Herostratus and tried to condemn him to obscurity by forbidding the mention of his name, but this obviously didn't work.

## ST. PAUL

The well-traveled missionary stopped twice in Ephesus, of which he wrote in 1 Corinthians 16, "a great door and effectual is opened unto me, and there are many adversaries." Among them were local merchants, who were infuriated by Paul's proclamation that they should stop selling images of Artemis, lest the practice encourage the worship of pagan idols. Paul may have written his "Epistle to the Ephesians" while being held prisoner in Rome, before his execution in AD 67.

## ST. JOHN

Legend has it that the author of the Fourth Gospel arrived in Ephesus with the Virgin Mary and died at age 98. He had his followers dig a square grave, proclaimed "You have called me to your feast," and expired, or so people thought: dust could be seen moving above his grave as if he still drew breath. Emperor Justinian's cathedral—it would be the seventh-largest in the world if reconstructed—was built directly over St. John's grave.

Center, Silver tetradrachm issued by Erythrai ca. 200–180 BC, obverse: Alexander the Great as Herakles wearing the lion skin.
Above, Tomb of St John in Mezrai, St. John's basilica in Selçuk

# BEYOND THE RUINS: OTHER SIGHTS

House of the Virgin Mary

Cave of the Seven Sleepers

## THE HOUSE OF THE VIRGIN MARY (MERYEMANA)

Legend has it that the Virgin Mary traveled to Ephesus with St. John and spent her last days in this modest stone dwelling. Such claims were given a boost of credulity in the 19th century when a bedridden German nun had a vision that enabled her to describe the house in precise detail. A hallowed place of pilgrimage, the house has been visited by three popes. John is allegedly buried nearby beneath the now-ruined Basilica of St. John in Selçuk. Surrounded by a national park, Mary's house is 7 km (4 mi) southwest of Selçuk, near the entrance to ancient Ephesus. ⊠ *Off Rte. E87* ☎ *232/894–1012* 🕮 *12.50TL/ person, 7.50TL/car* 🕓 *Daily 7:30–sunset.*

## EPHESUS MUSEUM

While many of the finds from Ephesus were carted off to the British Museum in London and the Ephesus Museum in Vienna, some treasures remain in Selçuk. Among the mosaics, coins, and other artifacts are dozens of images of Artemis, including the famous statue of the fertility goddess with several rows of egg-shaped breasts. ⊠ *Agora Çarşısı opposite visitor center in Selçuk* ☎ *232/892–6010* 🕮 *5TL* 🕓 *Daily, Apr.–Oct., 8:30–7, Nov.–Mar., 8–5.*

## CAVE OF THE SEVEN SLEEPERS

Ephesus is awash in legend, but the story associated with this hillside cavern takes the prize. It's said that during persecutions ordered by the Roman Emperor Decius in the 2nd century, seven young Christian men were sealed into a cave and left to die. Two centuries later, in the 4th-century era of Christian tolerance, a farmer happened to unseal the cave and found the men, now aged, in deep slumber. On awakening, they wandered into Ephesus, as shocked at the affixed to churches as the townsfolk were confused by the sight of these archaically clothed characters who offered two-centuries-old coinage to buy food. After their deaths, a church was erected in their honor. The story has found its way into works as diverse as the Koran and the *Golden Legend*, the chronicle of the lives of the saints. ⊠ *South of Sor Sahası Sok. 3* 🕮 *Free.*

Fertility Goddess, Ephesus Museum

# Camel Wrestling

While Americans are busy stuffing turkeys and stocking up on Christmas trees, Turkish camels and their owners prepare for an intense season of travel, confrontation, and competition. Every year, around 100 male camels and their owners tour the Marmara, Mediterranean, and the Aegean regions to compete in more than 30 camel-wrestling festivals.

There are different theories about camel-wrestling's origins, although many argue it was a nomadic practice and part of the competition between caravan owners. Nomadic or not, these festivals have become a deep-rooted cultural pastime in Turkey. Their primary motivation: get the girl. Camels will wrestle only during their mating season, which lasts from November to March, and a female camel is paraded around to provoke them into these contests. The camels' mouths are tied during the match so that they can't do real harm to each other, and among the judges, separators (*urgancı*), and commentators (*cazgirs*), are 21 officials (not including the camel owners) moderating the events.

The camels begin their wrestling "career" at age four, when they are purchased from Iran. They train for the next four years and spend years 8 through 10 coming of age and developing their own strategies. Their rite of passage, much like that of Turkish boys occurs at this age, when the camels receive *havuts*, decorative cloths with their name and the word *maşallah* (may God protect him) sewn on the inside. According to camel owners and those familiar with the sport, wrestling is not a foreign, inhumane practice being imposed on the camels. On the contrary, these

*dayluk* (as they're called until age seven, when they become *tülü* or hairy) begin wrestling naturally in the wild during their first years out of the womb, and if trained, can continue until age 25.

Celebratory events actually begin the day before the match, during *halı gecesi*, or carpet night, when camels are flaunted around to percussive music, their bells jingling as they amble along. The camel owners, who often get to know one another during the prefestivities, are also dolled up in cornered caps, traditional neck scarves, and accordion-like boots.

To prevent wearing out the camels, the matches last no more than 10 minutes, and camels compete only once a day. The victor, the camel who gets the most points for outsmarting his rival by swiftly maneuvering and having the most control over the match (which might simply mean not running away), can win anywhere from $2,500 to $25,000, depending on the competition. There's usually a wrestling World Cup of sorts at the culmination of the festivals, in which the top camels compete.

The exact dates, times, and locations of the festivals change from year to year, but competitions are always held every Sunday between December and March. The central and southern Aegean cities of Selçuk, İzmir, Bodrum, and Kuşadası host camel-wrestling festivals. Local tourism offices will have specific information about that year's festivals. Tickets cost around 15 TL per match and can be purchased on-site.

—Evin Dogul

courtyards. It provides beautiful views both of Selçuk's castle and the Plain of Ephesus. ⊠ *Entrance off St. John Sok., just east of İsa Bey Cami* ☎ *No phone* ☉ *Daily 8–5.*

**Virgin Mary's House (Meryemana)** *See the highlighted Ephesus feature in this chapter.*

## WHERE TO EAT AND STAY
*For expanded hotel reviews, visit Fodors.com.*

¢    ✕ **Ejder Restaurant.** This popular spot overlooking the Selçuk aqueduct
TURKISH    is run by Mehmet and his wife, the sole cook. It may sometimes take a while to get your food, but the traditional kebabs and Turkish specialties are well worth the wait. Mehmet takes pride in his guestbook filled with customers' comments, so make sure to add a few lines. ⊠ *Cengiz Topel Cad. 9/E* ☎ *232/892–3296.*

$    ✕ **Eski Ev.** The Ottoman motifs seem a bit touristy, but the place is
TURKISH    done up nicely, with a peaceful, shaded courtyard for outdoor dining attached to an old house. A wide selection of Turkish mezes (appetizers) and main dishes (including lamb stew) are served on copper plates, and many choices for vegetarians are available, too. ⊠ *1005 Sok. 1/A* ☎ *232/892–9357.*

$$    ☥ **Hotel Akay.** Ottoman accents—floors covered with *kilim* (rugs), white-washed interior and exterior walls, latticed balconies, and arched windows and doors—abound, and some rooms surround a pool. **Pros:** comfortable, spacious rooms; one of the owners speaks very good English; prices include breakfast. **Cons:** small bathrooms. ⊠ *Atatürk Mahallesi, 1054 Sok. 3* ☎ *232/892–3172* ⊕ *www.hotelakay.com* ⚲ *25 rooms* ♿ *In-room: no TV, Wi-Fi. In-hotel: restaurant, bar, pool.*

$    ☥ **Hotel Bella.** A spacious terrace and a small library are among the
★    charming amenities at this small hotel near the St. John Basilica. **Pros:** large and inviting terrace; free shuttle service to/from Ephesus. **Cons:** some rooms are a bit small. ⊠ *Atatürk Mahallesi, St. John Sok. 7* ☎ *232/892–3944* ⊕ *www.hotelbella.com* ⚲ *12 rooms* ♿ *In-hotel: restaurant, bar, parking* ⦿ *No meals.*

$$    ☥ **Kalehan.** A century-old farmhouse is decorated in traditional Anatolian style, with antique furniture and dark timber beams, and is surrounded by a large landscaped garden with a pool that is most welcome after a day of sightseeing. **Pros:** refreshing pool and garden. **Cons:** some rooms can feel a bit stuffy. ⊠ *Atatürk Cad. 49* ☎ *232/892–6154* ⊕ *www.kalehan.com* ⚲ *56 rooms* ♿ *In-hotel: restaurant, bar, pool, parking, some pets allowed.*

¢    ☥ **Wallabies.** This tidy, cheerful place has a comfortable lobby and the smallish rooms, with whitewashed walls set off by honey-color wood trim, have delightful views of storks nesting on the ancient columns of an aqueduct. **Pros:** good value; many options for dining nearby; friendly and helpful staff. **Cons:** rooms are basic and a bit small. ⊠ *Cengiz Topel Cad. 4* ☎ *232/892–3204* ⊕ *www.wallabieshostel.com* ⚲ *24 rooms* ♿ *In-room: Wi-Fi* ⬛ *No credit cards* ⦿ *No meals.*

**4**

## SHOPPING

Selçuk's weekly bazaar is held on Wednesday and Saturday in the main square from 9 to 6. There's also a daily market by the İsa Bey Cami that sells souvenirs and Turkish-theme gifts.

# ŞIRINCE

*8 km (5 mi) east of Selçuk; 12 km (7½ mi) from Ephesus.*

Şirince (appropriately, the name means "cute" or "quaint") is a lovely little hilltop village. The picturesque cluster of shops, houses, and restaurants is set on a lush hill; the rows of houses create a long string of windows, which have decorative eaves with nature motifs. A former Greek enclave, Şirince has a 19th-century church and a stone basilica, also 19th-century, which has been restored and turned into an art gallery. In the past few years, the village has become popular with travelers visiting the nearby historical sites, and village shops cater to them with quality handicrafts and locally produced wine (the villagers also grow olives, peaches, figs, apples, and walnuts). Hiking around Şirence is quite pleasant, as the hills are much cooler than the lowlands.

### GETTING HERE AND AROUND

A narrow but well-marked road connects Selçuk and Şirince. The road is narrow and windy, so it is best to travel during daylight hours. You can also take the *dolmuş* (shared-ride minibuses) that depart periodically from Selçuk between 8:30 and 5. The last minibus usually leaves Şirince around 6.

### WHERE TO EAT AND STAY

*For expanded hotel reviews, visit Fodors.com.*

$   ✕ **Arşipel Restaurant.** The dining room at the Kırkınca Houses Pension is
TURKISH   the best in town, overlooking the lovely landscape and serving delicious
Fodor'sChoice   and authentic dishes prepared with oil produced from olives harvested
★   in the garden. Among the delicacies are creamy eggplant soup; *şevketi bostanı*, a root vegetable cooked with tender pieces of lamb; and homemade pasta, *erişte*, served in a light cream and almond sauce. You can accompany your meal with wines produced in Şirince. ✉ *Şirince Köyü* ☎ *232/898–3133* ⊕ *www.sirincearsipel.com.*

$   ✕ **Artemis Restaurant & Wine House.** The terrace and a dining room dec-
TURKISH   orated in traditional style afford a superb view of the valley. Baked lamb and other regional specialties are delicious, and a good selection of local wines is available. ✉ *Şirince Köyü* ☎ *232/898–3240* ⊕ *www. artemisrestaurant.com.*

$$   ⬚ **Kırkınca Houses Boutique Hotel.** Guest rooms are individually deco-
rated in rustic style with parquet floors and wooden furniture and a vine-shaded terrace is delightful; six restored Greek houses nearby are perfect for families and groups. **Pros:** helpful, attentive owners who were born and raised in the village; amenities include a Turkish bath (hammam) and free hiking tours. **Cons:** more expensive than other pensions in town. ✉ *Şirinçe Köyü* ☎ *232/898–3133* ⊕ *www.kirkinca.com* ⬚7 *rooms, 5 houses* ⬚ *In-room: no TV, Wi-Fi. In-hotel: restaurant, pool, some pets allowed* ⊙ *Breakfast.*

Dried peppers are strung together in an artful manner. —photo by sarabeth, Fodors.com member.

**$$** 🍽 **Markiz Konakları.** Rooms and suites in a Greek house and surrounding cottages are beautifully embellished with traditional furnishings, stone and whitewashed walls, rich textiles, and fireplaces and are set amid lush gardens. **Pros:** attractive and comfortable accommodations. **Cons:** more expensive than other Şirince lodgings but extremely good value. ✉ *6 Sokak 20/1* ☎ *232/898–3282* ⊕ *www.markizkonaklari.com* ⮎ *8 rooms* ⚘ *In-hotel: restaurant, spa.*

## KUŞADASI AND ENVIRONS

These days Kuşadası is primarily known as a cruise port. It's a brash, highly touristy place crammed with pubs, fish-and-chips restaurants, and tacky souvenir shops. On a positive note, Kuşadası is within easy reach of Ephesus and is also close to one of Turkey's most beautiful national parks, as well as Pamukkale and Aphrodisias.

### KUŞADASI

*15 km (9 mi) southwest of Selçuk on Rte. 515.*

Kuşadası long ago lost its local charm to invasive, sterile buildings and overpopulation, and these days it's overrun with cruise ship passengers disembarking to make a mad dash to Ephesus. So, what was a small fishing village up until the 1970s is now a sprawling, hyperactive town packed with curio shops and a year-round population of around 65,000, rising to about half a million in season with the influx of tourists and Turks with vacation homes.

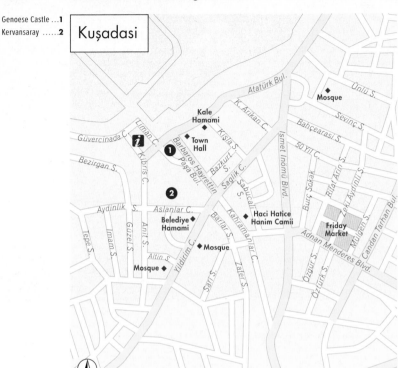

Kuşadası

GETTING HERE AND AROUND

Kuşadası is 85 km (53 mi) from the Adnan Menderes Airport in İzmir and 15 km (9 mi) from Selçuk. Several local bus companies provide service between İzmir and Kuşadası, while you can travel between Selçuk and Kuşadası by taxi or *dolmuş* (shared-ride minibuses).

ESSENTIALS

**Tour Operators Kuşadası Tours** ✉ *Candan Turhan Bulvarı, 104/1-2* ☎ *256/614–1282, 1-866/921-0299 toll-free from U.S.* ⊕ *www.kusadasitours.com.*

**Visitor Information** ✉ *Mahmut Esat Bozkurt Cad.* ☎ *256/614–1103.*

EXPLORING

**Genoese castle.** There aren't many sights in Kuşadası proper, but the causeway off Kadınlar Plajı (Women's Beach), just south of the harbor, connects the town to an old Genoese castle on Güvercin Adası (Pigeon Island). Today the site of a popular disco and several teahouses with gardens and sea views, the fortress was home to three Turkish brothers in the 16th century. These infamous pirates—Barbarossa, Oruc, and Hayrettin—pillaged the coasts of Spain and Italy and sold passengers and crews from captured ships into slavery in Algiers and Constantinople. Rather than fight them, Süleyman the Magnificent (ruled 1520–66) hired Hayrettin as his grand admiral and set him loose on enemies in the Mediterranean. The strategy worked: Hayrettin won victory after victory and was heaped with honors and riches.

**Kervansaray.** Kuşadası's 300-year-old *kervansaray*, now the Hotel Club Kervansaray, is loaded with Ottoman atmosphere. Its public areas are worth a look even if you're not staying here. ⊠ *Atatürk Bulvarı 1.*

**Samsundağ Milli Parkı** (*Dilek Peninsula National Park*). If you're looking for beaches, either head north from Kuşadası to Pamucak or travel 33 km (20 mi) south to the lovely Samsundağ Milli Parkı, which has good hiking trails and several quiet stretches of sandy beach. The Içmeler beach, closest to the entrance, is also the most crowded. Travel 15 minutes to Karaburun for a more low-key atmosphere. To get to the park, take the coast road, marked Güzelçamlı or Davutlar, for about 10 km (6 mi) south of Kuşadası. ⊙ *Open Apr.–Dec.*

## WHERE TO EAT AND STAY
*For expanded hotel reviews, visit Fodors.com.*

**$$**
SEAFOOD
✕ **Ali Baba Restaurant.** An appetizing and colorful display of the catch of the day greets you at the entrance to this waterside eatery, where the decor is simple, the view over the bay soothing, and the food good. Mezes (appetizers) include cold black-eyed pea salad, marinated octopus salad, and fried calamari, and several meat dishes are available for those not inclined toward seafood. ⊠ *Belediye Turistik Çarşısı 5* ☎ *256/614–1551* ⌳ *Reservations essential.*

**¢**
TURKISH
✕ **Nargileci Coşkun Abi.** An afternoon or evening in this casual café includes a snack of *gözleme,* a Turkish-style crepe, with fillings of cheese, spinach, or *ot* (Aegean wild herbs) and some time lingering with a *narghile* (water pipe). ⊠ *Belediye Düğün Salonu Karşışı* ☎ *256/612–8258* ⊟ *No credit cards.*

**$**
TURKISH
✕ **Öz Urfa.** The focus at this causal, 50-year-old spot is on kebabs and other Turkish fast food. The modest surroundings, including a pleasant terrace, are just off Barbaros Hayrettin Caddesi, the main thoroughfare. Alcohol is not served. ⊠ *Cephane Sokak 7/A* ☎ *256/612–9881* ⊕ *www. ozurfakebabs.com.*

**¢**
TURKISH
✕ **Yuvam.** "My Nest/Home" is truly that—it offers food you'd find in a Turkish home. At lunchtime, the food runs out quickly, so get there early to enjoy *mantı* (Turkish-style ravioli with plain yogurt and tomato/ butter sauce), okra *(bamya)* in a tomato-olive oil sauce, meat stew, and baked chicken with rice. Alcohol is not served. ⊠ *Kaleiçi Yedieylül Sok. 4* ☎ *256/614–9460.*

**$$**
🛏 **Hotel Carina.** Surrounded by beautifully landscaped gardens, all rooms are spacious and decorated with soft creamy tones and a smattering of reproduction-antique furnishings, and most have views of the pool and sea beyond. **Pros:** close to shops, restaurants, and nightlife. **Cons:** a good beach is not adjacent, but is only a short walk away. ⊠ *Yılancıburnu Bay 1* ☎ *256/612–4023* ⊕ *www.hotelcarina.com.tr* ⇴ *59 rooms* ⌂ *In-room: no TV, Wi-Fi. In-hotel: restaurant, bar, pool, parking.*

**$$**
🛏 **Hotel Club Kervansaray.** A refurbished 300-year-old inn that was once a way station for camel caravans is decorated in Ottoman style, and rooms are filled with kilims and Turkish folk art. **Pros:** historic Turkish decor; right across from the port. **Cons:** can be loud on live-music

nights. ⊠ *Atatürk Bulvarı 2* ☎ *256/614–4115* ☏ *26 rooms* ♿ *In-room: Wi-Fi. In-hotel: restaurant, bar* ⊚ *No meals.*

**$$** ⏲ **Kısmet.** Surrounded by beautifully maintained palm-shaded gardens,
★ this expanded Mediterranean villa is one of Turkey's classic getaways, set on a promontory overlooking the marina on one side and the Aegean on the other—and these sweeping sea views can be savored from terraces, the pool, and most of the guest rooms. **Pros:** nice view of the harbor and sea; central location near town and sights; gracious restaurants and bars; beautiful gardens. **Cons:** could use some updating. ⊠ *Türkmen Mahallesi, Akyar Mevkii* ☎ *256/618–1290* ⊕ *www.kismet. com.tr* ☏ *107 rooms* ♿ *In-hotel: restaurant, bar, pool, tennis court, beach, laundry facilities, parking.*

### NIGHTLIFE

**Barlar Sokak.** There are several Irish- and British-style pubs farther along Barlar Sokak.

**Club Kervansaray.** The Club Kervansaray has dining, dancing, and a show on most nights. ⊠ *Atatürk Bul. 2* ☎ *256/614–4115.*

# PAMUKKALE (HIERAPOLIS)

*170 km (105 mi) from Selçuk on Rte. E87 (follow road signs after Sarayköy); 191 km (119 mi) from Kuşadası.*

★ Pamukkale (pronounced pam-*uck*-al-lay), which means "cotton castle" in Turkish, first appears as an enormous, chalky white cliff rising 330 feet from the plains. Mineral-rich volcanic spring water cascades over basins and natural terraces, crystallizing into travertines—white curtains of solidified water seemingly suspended in air. The 17 hot springs at Pamukkale are believed to cure rheumatism and other ailments and have attracted visitors for millennia.

In the mid-1990s, the diversion of water from the springs to fill thermal pools in nearby luxury hotels reduced the volume of water reaching the site. This, combined with a huge increase in the number of visitors, discolored the water's once-pristine whiteness. As a result, wearing shoes in the water is prohibited to protect the deposits. Although Pamukkale is not as dramatic as it once was, for first-time visitors the white cliffs are still an impressive sight. Large sections of the site are now blocked off, as the authorities strive to conserve and restore a striking natural wonder to its former magnificence. However, you can still venture down the cliffs and soak in the water: the rock does get slippery so be careful.

If you have time, spend the night in Pamukkale, as the one-day bus tours from the coast are exhausting and limiting: you'll end up spending more time on the bus than you do at the actual site. A full day at Pamukkale will give you enough time to enjoy the water and the sites. There isn't much else to do in the area.

### GETTING HERE AND AROUND

Pamukkale is approximately a three- to four-hour drive from İzmir, Selçuk, Kuşadası, or Bodrum. There are daily bus tours from all of these towns to Pamukkale during the high season.

## EXPLORING

**Hierapolis.** Hierapolis is an example of how long the magical springs of Pamukkale have cast their spell on civilizations. The ruins that can be seen today date from the time of the Roman Empire, but there are references to a settlement here as far back as the 5th century BC. Because the sights are spread over about ½ km (¼ mi), prepare for some walking. Between the theater and the Pamukkale Motel are the ruins of a **Temple of Apollo** and

**WORD OF MOUTH**

"Pamukkale/Hierapolis is great, but try to go either in the early morning or late afternoon to miss the crowds. Also, at many of the ruins (Pergamum, Priene, Hierapolis), the signs have worn away so if you don't have a guide or guide book, it will be difficult to understand what was there)."
—heasereb

a bulky **Byzantine church.** The monumental fountain known as the **Nymphaion,** just north of the Apollo Temple, dates from the 4th century AD. Near the northern city gates is another indication of the town's former popularity, a vast **necropolis** (cemetery) with more than 1,000 cut-stone sarcophagi spilling all the way down to the base of the hill.

The stone building that enclosed Hierapolis's baths is now the **Pamukkale Müzesi,** a museum with a fine display of marble statues found at the site. ☎ *258/272–2077 for visitor center (for information), 258/272–2034 for museum* ☐ *20 TL* ☉ *Tues.–Sun. 8–noon and 12:30–6.*

Fodor's Choice ★ **Sacred Pool.** There are several reasons visitors flock to the thermal waters of the Sacred Pool at Hierapolis: the bathtub-warm water temps (a relatively constant 95 degrees Fahrenheit), the reputed therapeutic properties of the mineral-rich water, and the atmospheric marble columns and ancient stone carvings scattered about. The lushly landscaped complex has changing rooms, lock boxes (3TL) to store you stuff, and a snack bar. Entry to the pools is expensive (you need to pay to get into Hierapolis as well) but you can relax at the snack bar with a beverage if you don't want to spend the time/money. The pool gets crowded in the summer months so plan your visit for early morning or after the tour buses depart. The pool closes earlier in winter months but it's also much less crowded during the day. ⊠ *Inside Hierapolis* ☐ *25 TL* ☉ *8am–7pm.*

## WHERE TO EAT AND STAY

*For expanded hotel reviews, visit Fodors.com.*

$ TURKISH ✕ **Ünal Restaurant.** Good, simple village food and grills, including delicious skewered lamb *(kuzu şiş)*, at city prices: but that's to be expected in touristic Pamukkale. Meals are served on a patio during the summer months. ⊠ *Cumhuriyet Meydanı* ☎ *258/272-2451.*

$$$ 🏨 **Ayapam Boutique Hotel.** Spacious and airy rooms open to balconies overlooking the swimming pool and the travertines, and the many resortlike amenities include a hamman (Turkish bath), sauna, and Jacuzzi. **Pros:** sparkling new surroundings; lovely terrace; restaurant with panoramic view. **Cons:** a bit expensive for the area, but price includes a lavish buffet dinner. ⊠ *Kale Mahallesi, Bahçe Sokak 2/1* ☎ *258/272-2203* ⊕ *www.ayapamboutiquehotel.com* ⤺ *20 rooms*

## DID YOU KNOW?

The naturally heated water of the Sacred Pool at Hierapolis is believed to have healing properties; visitors have been coming here to be cured for centuries.

♿ *In-room: Wi-Fi. In-hotel: restaurant, bar, pool, gym, spa, parking* ◯ *Some meals.*

**$$** 🏨 **Hal-Tur Hotel.** All of the clean, fresh rooms at this distinctive white-stone hotel have balconies overlooking the travertines, and one large family room has its own large terrace with a Jacuzzi. **Pros:** staff is knowledgeable about Pamukkale and the surrounding area; rooms have a full view of the travertines in Pamukkale. **Cons:** a bit expensive given the fairly basic comforts. ✉ *Mehmet Akif Ersoy Blv. 45, Pamukkale, Denizli* ☎ *258/272–2723* ⊕ *www.haltur.net* ⏎ *11 rooms* ♿ *In-hotel: bar, pool, gym.*

## APHRODISIAS

4

*80 km (50 mi) from Pamukkale, west on E87 and south on Rte. 585 in the town of Geyre.*

Aphrodisias, the city of Aphrodite, goddess of love, is one of the largest and best-preserved archaeological sites in Turkey. It's interesting to compare this site to Ephesus, so although it's a bit of a detour, it's quite rewarding.

### GETTING HERE AND AROUND

You can reach Aphrodisias on the way to Pamukkale from Selçuk, İzmir, or Kuşadası. Most bus tours include Pamukkale on the tour as well, since these two sights are only 50 mi apart. You'll need a few hours to get a true taste of Aphrodisias. You will save much time and energy if you rent a car and visit Aphrodisias and the other nearby ancient sites on your own.

### EXPLORING

★ **Aphrodisias.** The city of Aphrodite, goddess of love, is one of the largest and best-preserved archaeological sites in Turkey. Though most of what you see today dates from the 1st and 2nd centuries AD, archaeological evidence indicates the local dedication to Aphrodite follows a long history of veneration of pre-Hellenic goddesses, such as the Anatolian mother goddess and the Babylonian god Ishtar. Only about half of the site has been excavated.

Aphrodisias, which was granted autonomy by the Roman Empire in the late 1st century BC, prospered as a significant center for religion, arts, and literature in the early 1st century AD. Imposing Christianity on the citizens later proved difficult, however, because of Aphrodite's large following. One method used to eradicate remnants of paganism was renaming the city, first Stavropolis (City of the Cross), then simply Caria, which archaeologists believe is the origin of the name of the present-day village of Geyre, which contains Aphrodisias in its borders.

The excavations here have led archaeologists to believe Aphrodisias was a thriving sculpture center, with patrons beyond the borders of the city—statues and fragments with signatures of Aphrodisian artists have shown up as far away as Greece and Italy. The towering Babadağ range of mountains, east of the city, offered ancient sculptors a copious supply of white and delicately veined blue-gray marble, which has been used to stunning effect in statuary, in spiral and fluted columns, and in the delicate reliefs of gods and men, vines, and acanthus leaves on decorative friezes.

The beauty of Aphrodisias rests in its details, and a good place to start absorbing them is the **site museum,** just past the ticket booth. The museum's collection includes several impressive statues from the site, including Aphrodite herself. ■TIP→ Pick up a guide and a map—you'll need them, as the signage is poor.

From the museum, follow the footpath to the right, which makes a circuit around the site and ends up back at the museum. The **Tetrapylon** is a monumental gateway with four rows of columns and some of the better remaining friezes. The **Temple of Aphrodite** was built in the 1st century BC on the model of the great temples at Ephesus. Its gate and many of its columns are still standing; some bear inscriptions naming the donor of the column. Next to the temple is the fine **Odeon,** an intimate, semicircular concert hall and public meeting room. Farther on is the **stadium,** which once was the scene of footraces, boxing and wrestling matches, and other competitions. One of the best preserved of its kind anywhere, the stadium could seat up to 30,000 spectators. The **theater,** built into the side of a small hill, is still being excavated. Its 5,000 white-marble seats are simply dazzling on a bright day. The adjacent **School of Philosophy** has a colonnaded courtyard with chambers lining both sides where teachers would work with small groups of students. ⊇ *Ruins 5 TL, museum 5 TL* ☉ *Daily 8:30–5.*

## PRIENE, MILETUS, AND DIDYMA

*Priene is 38 km (24 mi) from Kuşadası; from Priene it's 22 km (14 mi) to Miletus; from Miletus it's 22 km (14 mi) to Didyma; Didyma is 139 km (86 mi) from Bodrum.*

The three towns of Priene, Miletus, and Didyma make up part of Ancient Ionia. They're all within 40 km (25 mi) of each another, and if you get an early enough start, you can visit them all in one day. If you decide to spend a night in the area, you'll find the most hotels in and around Didyma, where the modern town has developed into a lively seaside resort.

### GETTING HERE AND AROUND

Tours to these towns can be arranged from İzmir, Kuşadası, and Bodrum. The Pamukkale Bus Company offers service from İzmir to Didyma, and minibuses departing Didyma stop at Priene and Miletus. You can also go to Didyma from Bodrum via the Bodrum Express Lines Hydrofoil and Ferryboat Services.

### ESSENTIALS

**Visitor Information Didyma** ⊠ *Eski Kaymakanlık Binası* ☎ *256/811–5707.*

## EXPLORING

**Didyma.** Didyma (*Didim* in Turkish), a resort town on the rise, was an important sacred site connected to Miletus by a road of statues. The temple of Apollo is here, as well as some beaches, which are increasingly frequented by Brits who have bought real estate in the area.

Didyma is famous for its magnificent **Temple of Apollo.** As grand in scale as the Parthenon—measuring 623 feet by 167 feet—the temple has 124 well-preserved columns, some still supporting their architraves. Started in 300 BC and under construction for nearly five centuries, the temple was never completed, and some of the columns remain unfluted. The oracle here rivaled the one at Delphi, and beneath the courtyard is a network of underground corridors used by temple priests for their oracular consultations. The corridor walls would throw the oracle's voice into deep and ghostly echoes, which the priests would interpret. The tradition of seeking advice from a sacred oracle here probably started long before the arrival of the Greeks, who in all likelihood converted an older Anatolian cult based at the site into their own religion. The Greek oracle had a good track record, and at the birth of Alexander the Great (356 BC) predicted that he would be victorious over the Persians, that his general Seleucus would later become king, and that Trajan would become an emperor.

Around AD 385, the popularity of the oracle dwindled with the rise of Christianity. The temple was later excavated by French and German archaeologists, and its statues are long gone, hauled back to England by Sir Charles Newton in 1858. Fragments of bas-reliefs on display by the entrance to the site include a gigantic head of Medusa and a small statue of Poseidon and his wife, Amphitrite. ⊠ *22 km (14 mi) south of Priene on Rte. 09–55* ☎ *No phone* ✆ *3 TL* ⊙ *Daily 8:30–6.*

**Miletus.** Before the harbor silted over, Miletus was one of the greatest commercial centers of the Greek world. The first settlers were Minoan Greeks from Crete who arrived between 1400 BC and 1200 BC. The Ionians, who arrived 200 years later, slaughtered the male population and married the widows. The philosopher Thales was born here in the early 6th century BC. He calculated the height of the pyramids at Giza, suggested that the universe was actually a rational place despite its apparent disorder, and coined the phrase *"Know thyself."* Miletus was also home to the mathematicians Anaximenes, who contended that air was the single element behind the diversity of nature; and Anaximander, whose ideas anticipated the theory of evolution and the concept of the indestructibility of matter. Like the other Ionian cities, Miletus was passed from one ruling empire to another and was successively governed by Alexander's generals Antigonus and Lysimachus and Pergamum's Attalids, among others. Under the Romans the town finally regained some control over its own affairs and shared in the prosperity of the region. St. Paul preached here at least twice in the 1st century.

The archaeological site is sprawled out along a desolate plain, and laced with well-marked trails. The parking lot is right outside the city's most magnificent building—the **Great Theater,** a remarkably intact 25,000-seat amphitheater built by the Ionians and maintained by the Romans.

Along the third to sixth rows some inscriptions reserving seats for notables are still visible, and the vaulted passages leading to the seats have the feel of a modern sporting arena. Climb to the top of the theater for a look at the defensive walls built by the Byzantines and a view across the ancient city.

To see the rest of the ruins, follow the dirt track to the right of the theater. A row of buildings marks what was once a broad processional avenue. The series begins with the **Delphinion,** a sanctuary of Apollo; a **Seljuk hammam** (bath) added to the site in the 15th century, with pipes for hot and cold water still visible; a **stoa** (colonnaded porch) with several re-erected Ionic columns; the foundations of a **Roman bath** and **gymnasium;** and the first story of the **Nymphaion,** is all that remains of the once highly ornate three-story structure, resembling the Library of Celsus at Ephesus, that once distributed water to the rest of the city.

To the south, the dirt track becomes a tree-lined lane that leads to the **Ilyas Bey Cami,** a mosque built in 1404 in celebration of its builder and namesake's escape from Tamerlane, the Mongol terror. The mosque is now a romantic ruin: the ceiling is cracked, dust covers the tiles, and birds roost inside. The path from the mosque back to the parking lot passes a small museum, the **Miletus Müzesi,** containing some artifacts from the site and the surrounding area. ⊠ *22 km (14 mi) south of Priene on Rte. 09–55* ☎ *No phone* 🖅 *Ruins 3 TL, museum 4 TL* ⊙ *Tues.–Sun. 8:30–6.*

★    **Priene.** Priene sits spectacularly atop a steep hill above the flat valley of the Büyük Menderes Nehir (Maeander River). Dating from about 350 BC, the present-day remains of the city were still under construction in 334, when Alexander the Great liberated the Ionian settlements from Persian rule. At that time, Priene was a thriving port, but as in Ephesus, the harbor silted over, so commerce moved to neighboring Miletus, and the city's prosperity waned. As a result, the Romans never rebuilt Priene and the simpler Greek style predominates as in few other ancient cities in Turkey. Excavated by British archaeologists in 1868–69, the site is smaller than Ephesus and far less grandiose.

From the parking area, the walk up to the Priene ruins is fairly steep. As the routes through the ruins are well marked, you won't need a map. After passing through the old city walls, follow the city's original main thoroughfare and notice the drainage gutters and the grooves worn into the marble paving stones by the wheels of 4th-century BC chariots. Continuing west, you come to the well-preserved *bouleterion* (council chamber) on the left. The 10 rows of seats flank an orchestra pit with a little altar, decorated with bulls' heads and laurel leaves at the center. Passing through the doors on the opposite side of the council chamber takes you to the **Sacred Stoa,** a colonnaded civic center, and the edge of the **agora,** the marketplace. Farther west along the broad promenade are the remains of a row of **private houses,** each of which typically has two or three rooms on two floors: of the upper floors, only traces of a few stairwells remain. In the largest house a statue of Alexander was found.

A block or so farther along the main street is the **Temple of Athena,** the work of Pytheos, architect of the Mausoleum of Halicarnassus (one of the Seven Wonders of the Ancient World) and the design was repeatedly copied at other sites in the Greek empire. Alexander apparently chipped in on construction costs for the temple, a dwelling for the goddess Athena rather than a place for worshippers to gather—only priests could enter. Walk north and then east along the track that leads to the well-preserved little **theater,** sheltered on all sides by pine trees. Enter through the stage door into the orchestra section and note the five front-row VIP seats, carved thrones with lions' feet. If you scramble up a huge rock known as Samsun Dağı (behind the theater and to your left as you face the seats), you will find the sparse remains of the **Sanctuary of Demeter,** goddess of the harvest; only a few remnants of the columns and walls remain, as well as a big hole through which blood of sacrificial victims was poured as a gift to the deities of the underworld. Since few people make it up here, it is an incredibly peaceful spot with a terrific view over Priene and the plains. Beyond are the remnants of a Hellenistic fortress. ⊠ *37 km (23 mi) from Kuşadası, southeast on Rte. 515, south on Rte. 525, west on Rte. 09–55 (follow signs)* ☏ *No phone* 🎫 *1.50 TL* ⊙ *Daily 8:30–6.*

OFF THE
BEATEN
PATH
**Altınkum.** For a break after all this history, continue another 5 km (3 mi) from Didyma south to Altınkum, popular for its white-sand beach. The sand stretches for a bit less than 1 km (½ mi) and is bordered by a row of decent seafood restaurants, all facing the water, and some small modest hotels.

## WHERE TO EAT AND STAY

*For expanded hotel reviews, visit Fodors.com.*

$ ✕ **Didim Şehir Lokantası.** The quality and price of the offerings make the
TURKISH trip—complimentary shuttle service is available—out to Yenihisar, a residential neighborhood, well worth the effort. The *İskender kebap,* thin strips of *döner* served on a bed of pita bread with tomato sauce and plain yogurt, is especially good. ⊠ *Çarşı İçi 822, Yenihisar, Didyma* ☏ *256/811–4488.*

$$$ ✕ **Kamacı 2.** One of the best restaurants in Altınkum is right on the water
SEAFOOD at the end of the pier. Prawns, seasoned and cooked to perfection, are a great appetizer to share. Evenings here can be romantic, especially when the moon is in view, and the seafood is fresh. ⊠ *Yali Caddesi Iskele Karşısı, Didyma* ☏ *256/813–2349.*

$$ ⛉ **Medusa House Pansiyon.** This small, unassuming restored stone house, one of the nicest accommodations Didyma has to offer, is designed for relaxation—the garden and the terrace have plenty of spots for quiet contemplation, and the traditionally furnished rooms are cozy. **Pros:** elegantly decorated; best value in the area. **Cons:** not much in the way of amenities. ⊠ *Next to Temple of Apollo, Didyma* ☏ *256/811–0063* 🛏 *7 rooms, 2 houses* ♿ *In-room: no a/c, no TV* ⦿| *Breakfast.*

$$ ⛉ **Orion Beach Hotel.** At this resortlike getaway on its own beach in Altınkum, sea views fill most of the bright and airy guest rooms, all with balconies. **Pros:** good value; pleasant decor; on the beach yet near to shops and restaurants. **Cons:** some distance to Miletus and other ancient sights. ⊠ *Yalı Caddesi 73, Altınkum, Didyma* ☏ *256/813–2041* ⊕ *www.orionhoteldidim.com* 🛏 *76 rooms* ♿ *In-room: Internet. In-hotel: restaurant, bar, beach, some pets allowed.*

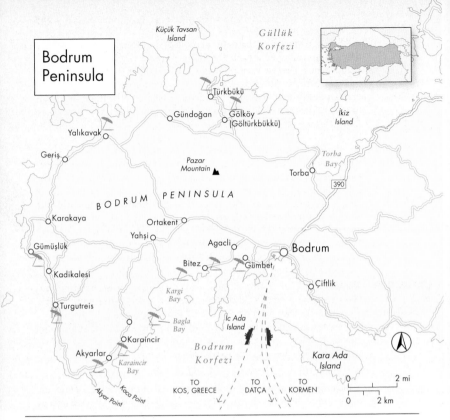

Bodrum
Peninsula

Küçük Tavşan
Island

*Güllük
Korfezi*

Türkbükü

Gündoğan    Gölköy
(Göltürkbükkü)

İkiz
Island

Yalıkavak

Geriş

*Torba
Bay*

Pazar
Mountain ▲

Torba

390

BODRUM    PENINSULA

Karakaya

Ortakent

Yahşi

Gümüşlük

Agacli

Bodrum

Bitez
Kadikalesi

Gümbet

Çiftlik

*Kargi
Bay*

Turgutreis

*Bagla
Bay*

İc Ada
Island

Karaincir

Akyarlar

*Bodrum
Korfezi*

*Kara Ada
Island*

*Karaincir
Bay*

Koca Point

Akyar Point

TO
KOS, GREECE

TO
DATÇA

TO
KORMEN

0          2 mi

0      2 km

## THE BODRUM PENINSULA

Until the mid-20th century, the Bodrum Peninsula was little known, and its gorgeous coastline was home to fishermen and sponge divers. Then a bohemian set (artists, writers, and painters) discovered Bodrum and put the place on the map. Today, Bodrum is booming, a year-round getaway for Turks and foreigners alike. You'll be in the center of the action in Bodrum town, the busiest spot on the peninsula, but a stay in one of the smaller villages nearby will reveal the region's quieter charms.

### BODRUM

*789 km (490 mi) from Istanbul; 242 km (150 mi) from İzmir; 161 km (100 mi) from Kuşadası; 125 km (78 mi) from Didyma.*

Bodrum is on the southern shores of a broad peninsula that stretches along two crescent-shape bays and has for years been the favorite haunt of the Turkish upper classes. Today thousands of foreign visitors come here, too. The town is throbbing with cafés, restaurants, and discos. Bodrum is decidedly not the quaint village it once was, but it's still beautiful, with gleaming whitewashed buildings covered in bougainvillea and unfettered vistas of the sparkling bays.

## GETTING HERE AND AROUND

The Bodrum Ferryboat Association has ferryboat service from Bodrum to the Greek island of Kos in Greece and Datça, across the bay on an adjacent peninsula. The Bodrum Express Lines Hydrofoil and Ferryboat Services also has ferryboat and hydrofoil services from Bodrum to Datça, Marmaris, Dalyan, and Didyma in Turkey and to Kos, Kalymnos, and Rhodes in Greece. Reservations are recommended; make sure to have your passport with you if traveling to Greece. You can also fly into the Bodrum Milas Airport from Istanbul and all major bus companies serve Bodrum, with direct service from Istanbul and İzmir.

> **GETTING AROUND BODRUM**
>
> Renting a car is a good idea if you wish to venture beyond Bodrum proper. Taxis are widely available, and *dolmuş* (shared ride minibuses) ply the route up and down the peninsula.

## ESSENTIALS

**Ferry Information Bodrum Express Lines** ✉ *Kale Cad. 18, Bodrum* ☎ *252/316–1087* ⊕ *www.bodrumexpresslines.com.* **Bodrum Ferryboat Association** ✉ *Kale Cad. 22, Bodrum* ☎ *252/316–0882* ⊕ *www.bodrumferryboat.com.*

**Travel Agencies/Tour Operators Neyzen Tours** ✉ *Kıbrıs Şehitleri Cad. 34, Bodrum* ☎ *252/316–7204* ⊕ *www.neyzen.com.tr.*

**Visitor Information Bodrum** ✉ *Barış Meydanı, Bodrum* ☎ *252/316–1091*✉ *Barış Meydanı 48, Bodrum* ☎ *252/316–1091.*

## EXPLORING

**Mausoleum.** Little remains of the extravagant white-marble tomb of Mausolus of Halicarnassus, one of the Seven Wonders of the Ancient World—and the source of the word *mausoleum.* During the 4th century, Bodrum (then called Halicarnassus of Caria) was governed by King Mausolos. Upon his death, Queen Artemisia, his wife and sister, ordered the construction of the great white-marble tomb, hence the word mausoleum was borne. The mausoleum must have been quite a sight—a solid rectangular base was topped by 36 Ionic columns, surmounted by a pyramid, and crowned with a massive statue of Mausolus and Artemisia (his wife and sister) riding a chariot. Many of the remains were used to build the Petronion and others were carried to the British Museum. There is really little left to see, and the site is not worth the price of admission. 🖼 *8 TL ☉ Tues.–Fri. 8–noon and 1:30–5:30.*

**Petronion.** The Petronion, also known as Bodrum Castle or the Castle of St. Peter, is one of the great showpieces of late-medieval architecture, built by the Knights Hospitaller (Knights of St. John) and completed in 1437. With German knight-architect Heinrich Schlegelholt at the helm, the builders incorporated green volcanic stone, marble columns, and reliefs from the remains of the mausoleum of Halicarnassus. The castle and its beautiful gardens, visible from every part of town, look as if they belong in a fairy tale. On the ramparts, you may recognize prominent coats of arms—those of the Plantagenets, d'Aubussons, and others. The five turrets are named after the homelands of the knights, who came from England, France, Germany, Italy, and Spain. The castle now houses the **Museum of Underwater Archaeology,** where displays include a 7th-century shipwreck as well as amphorae and other salvage excavated off the Aegean coast. ✉ *Kale Cad., Bodrum* ☎ *252/316–2516* ⊕ *www.bodrum-museum.com* ▣ *10 TL* ⊙ *Apr.–Oct., daily 10:30–7; Nov.–Mar., daily 10:30–5.*

**Bodrum Amphitheater.** Construction of the magnificent amphitheater began during the reign of King Mausolus, but the structure was finally completed during the Roman era and is one of the ancient city's best-preserved monuments and is still used for concerts and other performances. The view of Bodrum and the Aegean Sea is breathtaking from this vantage point. ✉ *Kıbrıs Şehitleri Cad., Bodrum* ▣ *Free.*

## WHERE TO EAT AND STAY

*For expanded hotel reviews, visit Fodors.com.*

**$$** ✗ **Denizhan Et Lokantası.** The best meats and kebabs in town in Bodrum
TURKISH are served in outlying Konacık, about 3 km (2 mi) from the center. Appetizers, including *lahmacun* (Turkish-style pizza topped with minced meat) and vegetable dishes prepared with just-picked produce from the garden are also very good. In warm weather, seating is on a terrace in front or a spacious back garden with views of the mountains and valley. The wine list is extensive. ✉ *Atatürk Bulvarı 277, Konacık, Bodrum* ☎ *252/363–7674* ⊕ *www.denizhan.com* ⚒ *Reservations essential* ⊙ *Daily noon–midnight.*

**$** ✗ **Gebora.** Casual seafood meals are served in modest surroundings on
SEAFOOD the waterfront in Yahşi-Ortakent, a quiet beach town 12 km (7½ mi) outside Bodrum. Gebora means "come here" in Bodrum dialect, and a loyal following heeds the call. Breakfast is also served. ✉ *Yalı Cad. 8, Yahşi, Ortakent* ☎ *252/348–3340.*

**$$$** ✗ **Gemibaşı.** This popular and long-standing presence near the marina
SEAFOOD serves the freshest seafood in town, in no-frills indoor and outdoor surroundings that are always packed during the season. House specialties include fish soup and octopus with pilaf. ✉ *Neyzen Teyvfik Cad. 176, Bodrum* ☎ *252/316–1220* ⊕ *www.gemibasi.com* ⚒ *Reservations essential* ⊙ *Daily noon–midnight.*

**$$$** ✗ **Kocadon.** A lovely palm-filled courtyard, soft jazz, and exquisite Medi-
MEDITERRANEAN terranean cuisine provide one of the loveliest dining experiences in Bodrum. À la carte and tasting menus are available. ✉ *Neyzen Tevfik Cad., Saray Sok. 1* ☎ *0252/316–3705* ⊕ *www.kocadon.com* ⚒ *Reservations essential* ⊙ *Daily 11:30–5 and 7–1.*

**$** ✗ **Köfteci Bilal'ın Yeri.** Turkish *shish*-style meatballs and Turkish home-
TURKISH style cuisine, served at just a few tables in a no-frills setting, have been a hit for more than half a century and are especially popular at lunch. Accompany any dish you order with homemade plain yogurt. Alcohol is not served. ✉ *Yeni Çarşı 2. Sok. 11* ☎ *252/316-3666.*

**$$** ✗ **Körfez.** This long-standing and modestly priced fish house overlooks
SEAFOOD the harbor and is especially noted for a wide selection of seafood appetizers that include delectable *deniz börülcesi*, shrimp cooked in butter and garlic and seaweed. Some meat dishes are also served, as is breakfast. ✉ *Neyzen Tevfik Cad.* ☎ *252/313–8248* ⊕ *www.korfezrestaurant. com.tr* ⊙ *Daily 10–midnight.*

Daily boat cruises from the marina in Bodrum's city center will take you to nearby coves and bays for a day of swimming and sunbathing.

$    ✕ **Liman Köftecisi.** *Köfte* (Turkish-style meatballs) are the specialty at this
TURKISH   casual and charming eatery in the heart of town, where the home-style cooking is excellent and the prices modest. Breakfast is also served. ✉ *Neyzen Tevfik Cad. 172* ☎ *252/316–5060* ⊘ *Daily 11 am–midnight.*

$    ✕ **Sünger Pizza.** Don't let the name fool you—in addition to excellent
ITALIAN   brick-oven pizza, pastas and Turkish dishes are also available. A house specialty is *Çökertme* kebab, thin slices of tenderloin of beef served over finely grated french fries, topped with plain yogurt and tomato sauce and garnished with lettuce and a few slices of tomato. Breakfast is also served. ✉ *Neyzen Tevfik Cad. 218* ☎ *252/316–0854* ⊕ *www. sungerpizza.com* ⊘ *Daily 8:30 am–11:30 pm.*

$$$   ▦ **Manastır Hotel & Suites.** A former monastery is a glorious perch overlooking the Bodrum Bay (*manastır* means monastery in Turkish). **Pros:** beautifully maintained; lovely surroundings; exquisite sea views. **Cons:** a bit of a trek from town. ✉ *Kumbahçe Mevkii Mustafa Kemal Cad. 37* ☎ *252/316–2854* ⊕ *www.manastirhotel.com* ⤴ *55 rooms, 18 suites* ⚘ *In-room: Wi-Fi. In-hotel: restaurant, bar, pool, spa* ❙◯❙ *Breakfast.*

$$   ▦ **Marina Vista.** A great location across from the marina, sea views from the nicely decorated rooms, and a pretty pool make this convenient in-town lodging seem like a resort. **Pros:** close to all restaurants and nightlife. **Cons:** have to travel to reach a beach. ✉ *Neyzen Tevfik Cad. 168* ☎ *252/313–0356* ⊕ *www.hotelmarinavista.com* ⤴ *87 rooms* ⚘ *In-room: Wi-Fi. In-hotel: restaurant, bar, pool.*

$$$   ▦ **The Marmara Bodrum.** Most of the elegantly decorated rooms at this hilltop aerie enjoy views of Bodrum and the sea from balconies and terraces, while a free shuttle service to a private beach club puts the seaside

within easy reach. **Pros:** nicely decorated and appointed rooms; beautiful surroundings; special promotional rates and packages offered from time to time. **Cons:** a bit of a distance from the city center. ✉ *Yokuşbaşı Mahallesi 18* ☎ *252/313–8130* ⊕ *www.themarmarahotels.com* ⤙ *96 rooms* ⚲ *In-room: Wi-Fi. In-hotel: restaurant, bar, pool, gym, spa, beach, business center, parking.*

## NIGHTLIFE

The nightlife scene in Bodrum is quite diverse. Bars and clubs with DJs or live music on Cumhuriyet (simply called "Barlar Sokağı," street with bars) attract the young and restless. Trendier and more chichi bars and clubs are on Neyzen Tevfik.

**Hadigari.** Hadigari is one of Bodrum's oldest and most popular live-music clubs and overlooks the Aegean and Bodrum Castle. On nights when live music is not on tap, DJs spin popular tunes. ✉ *Kaledibi* ☎ *252/316–0048* ⊕ *www.hadigari.com.tr* ☉ *7 pm–5 am.*

**Halikarnas "The Club".** Halikarnas bills itself as "probably the most amazing nightclub in the world." It is, in fact, rather like discos more commonly found in western Mediterranean resorts, complete with a huge dance floor, fog machines, laser lights, and theme nights. Reservations are recommended and there is an admission charge. ✉ *Cumhuriyet Cad. 178* ☎ *252/316–8000* ⊕ *www.halikarnas.com.tr.*

**Küba.** With topnotch food and music, Kuba is always crowded, especially on weekends. ✉ *Neyzen Tevfik Cad. 62* ☎ *252/313–4450* ⊕ *www.kubabar.com.*

**Marina Yacht Club.** The Marina Yacht Club is the first place both Bodrum locals and Turkish tourists will recommend for a night out for good live music (jazz, classical, etc.). The live music is as diverse as the age groups that come to listen. The dining area on the second floor has a long bar with a terrific view of the marina. ✉ *Milta Bodrum Marina* ☎ *252/316–1228.*

**Marine Club Catamaran.** Marine Club Catamaran is a full-fledged party at sea. The catamaran, a floating disco with a transparent dance floor and capacity for 1,500 clubbers, sails out to sea towards Karaada Island after midnight and returns to shore at around 4. Don't fret, there is a shuttle service that departs every half hour for those who want to return earlier. There is live and DJ music and six bars on board. Admission charge includes one drink. ✉ *1025 Sokak 10* ☎ *252/313–3600* ⊕ *www.clubcatamaran.com.*

**Mavi Bar.** A Bodrum institution, the small and quaint Mavi Bar (Blue Bar) occupies century-old premises and features live Turkish music—some of Turkey's most prominent rock stars have appeared here. ✉ *Cumhuriyet Cad. 175, Bodrum* ☎ *252/316–3932.*

**NewOld Club.** A two-story open-air space has elegantly decorated lounges in which to drink and socialize, and DJs spin dance, house, pop, and R&B tunes. ✉ *Kale Cad. 29, Bodrum* ☎ *252/316–9454* ☉ *Daily 7 pm–5 am.*

Each beach town around Bodrum has its own nightlife scene. Göltürkbükü's is the most renowned, frequented by the Turkish elite and international crowd; the waterfront is lined with bars and clubs.

**Ship Ahoy.** Ship Ahoy in outlying Göltürkbükü is usually packed to the hilt with clubbers tyring to squeeze into very small quarters well into the wee hours—no cover charge, but be prepared to pay a premium price for your drinks. ✉ *Yalı Mevkii, Göltürkbükü* ☎ *252/ 377–5070.*

> ### THE GREAT INDOORS
>
> If you'd rather just sit back and relax, or if you're recovering from an intensive workout, Bodrum's hammam is the place. There are separate facilities for men and women. ✉ *Opposite bus station on Cevat Şakir Rd.* ☎ *252/313-4129.*

## SPORTS AND THE OUTDOORS

The Bodrum Peninsula offers plenty of outdoor activities, including scuba diving, sponge diving, horseback riding, hiking, waterskiing, and windsurfing.

DIVING The sea around Bodrum provides some of the best diving in the Aegean. There are 16 dive spots. At least 10 schools are registered with PADI, the worldwide diving organization.

**Aegean Pro Dive Centre.** The Aegean Pro Dive Centre in Aktur/Bitez is one of the most reliable PADI-certified dive operators in Bodrum. ✉ *Kavaklısarnıç Sokak, Asarlık Sitesi 30, Bitez* ☎ *252/316–0737* ⊕ *www.aegeanprodive.com.*

**Erman Dive Center.** The Erman Dive Center has three locations in Bodrum: at the Bodrum Milta Marina; the Hapimag Resort Sea Garden; and the Kempinski Hotel Barbaros Bay in Yalıçiftlıkı. ☎ *252/368–9594* ⊕ *www. ermandive.com.*

**Motif Diving.** Also check out Motif Diving, with PADI-certified instructors. ☎ *252/316–6252* ⊕ *www.motifdiving.com.*

HORSEBACK RIDING Gündoğan is the best place for horseback riding, with nice forest trails; Ortakent and Turgutreis are good alternatives.

**Farilya Horse Ranch.** ✉ *Yukarı Göl Mevkii, Gündoğan* ☎ *252/357–7977.*

**Turgutreis Country Ranch.** ✉ *Pirenardi Mevkii Islamhaneleri, Turgutreis* ☎ *252/382–5654, 533/654–9586 for English* ⊕ *www.countryranch.net.*

**Yahşi Horseback Riding.** ✉ *Yeşil Vadi Yolu, Ortakent* ☎ *252/358–6382.*

WINDSURFING Bitez, Yalıkavak, and Fener, near Turgutreis, are ideal for for windsurfing.

**Kempinski Hotel.** Kempinski Hotel in Bodrum has windsurfing rentals and instruction. ☎ *252/311–0303.*

**Windsurfing Schools.** If you would like to try your hand at windsurfing or kiteboarding, try Fener Windsurf Club, on Fener Beach, about 20 km (12 mi) from the Bodrum city center. Instructors speak English. ☎ *252/393-8414* ⊕ *www.fenerwindsurf.com* ☾ *mid-Apr.–mid-Nov.*

## SHOPPING

There is an open-air bazaar every day of the week in Bodrum and in the surrounding towns. You will find fruits and vegetables and other foodstuffs; household goods; clothing, shoes, handbags; souvenirs; and at some, high-quality jewelry and rugs. The schedule of the bazaars is: Türkbükü on Monday; Bodrum (no food) and Gölköy on Tuesday; Ortakent, Gümüşlük, and Gündoğan on Wednesday; Yalıkavak on Thursday (probably the best of all of them for quality goods); Bodrum (fruits, vegetables, and other foodstuffs) on Friday; Turgutreis on Saturday; and Gümbet and Mumcular on Sunday.

**Ali Güven.** Bodrum's handmade sandals are renowned. The late Ali Güven, who once made sandals for Mick Jagger, was the most trusted and well established of the cobblers; his workshop continues to put out lightweight designs that are made from specially worked leather, very comfortable for the Mediterranean summer and aesthetically pleasing as well. ⊠ *Bodrum Sq..*

## THE BODRUM PENINSULA'S OTHER TOWNS

Visitors flock to the Bodrum Peninsula and its environs for its numerous coves, bays, and crystal clear waters, as well as its lively and active wining and dining and nightlife scenes. Each municipality and its surrounding villages have their own style, charm, and ambience, so where you decide to stay will be based on your personal preferences.

### AKYARLAR/KARAINCIR/TURGUTREIS

Akyarlar and Karaincir, on adjacent bays southwest of Bodrum, are ringed with some of the peninsula's most picture-postcard beaches. Turgutreis, due west on the opposite side of the peninsula, has a more developed coast, with a popular and lively bazaar. Its marina attracts the yachting crowd and is more touristy than the other bays. After swimming in the pristine sea at Akyarlar and Karaincir, the beaches of Turgutreis don't seem all that enticing.

#### WHERE TO EAT AND STAY

$    ✕ **EG Arşipel Cafe & Restaurant.** A clifftop retreat in Şevket Sabancı Park
TURKISH    (just outside Turgutreis) offers bird's-eye views and a nice selection of Turkish and international dishes. Alcohol is served, as is breakfast. ⊠ *Gazi Mustafa Kemal Bulvarı, Turgutreis* ☎ *252/382–2608* ☉ *Daily 8 am–2 am.*

$$    ⛨ **Castello di Akyarlar.** Plain but large and attractive rooms in this restored stone house with a view of the Greek island of Kos face a lovely garden and pretty little beach, and the laid-back ambience and beauty of the natural setting provide a restful retreat. **Pros:** beachfront; very attractive and restful surroundings. **Cons:** removed from the center of things in Bodrum. ⊠ *Akyarlar 45, Akyarlar* ☎ *252/393–6025* ⊕ *www.castellobodrum.com* ⊅ *20 rooms* ⌂ *In-hotel: restaurant, beach.*

$    ⛨ **Hotel Kortan.** Simple elegance is the motif in the tastefully decorated, contemporary-style rooms, all with sea views, and a private beach stretches in front of the hotel. **Pros:** nice seaside terrace with view for sunbathing. **Cons:** on the main stretch, so not very private. ⊠ *Atatürk Meydanı, Sabancı Cad. 5, Turgutreis* ☎ *252/382–2932* ⊕ *www.kortanotel.com* ⊅ *25 rooms* ⌂ *In-room: Wi-Fi. In-hotel: restaurant, bar.*

## BITEZ

The village of Bitez lies 8 km (5 mi) west of Bodrum, and its beach, the longest on the peninsula, is another 2 km (1 mi) to the south. The stone houses in the village were built right on the road to make room for mandarin trees in the backyard. Until several decades ago, residents picked and packed the mandarins onto camels, who then carried them to the nearby ports. Walk along the back roads of Bitez to take in the fresh, citric scent of the mandarins, intermingled with 500-year-old olive trees. The village also has a *kahve* (traditionally, a Turkish café where only men socialize and play backgammon) for women, opened up by the Bitez municipality. The *kahve* is on Atatürk Caddesi. Most of the sand in this semicircle cove is covered by chaises or plush pillows set up in little, enclosed enclaves. A pedestrian walkway leads through the 2-km (1-mi) stretch of beach, dividing the cafés and hotels from the shore.

> **SWEET SPOT**
>
> **Bitez Dondurması's.** People travel long distances for ice cream from Dondurması, which mixes fresh fruit—the mulberries are handpicked in the mountains—into the creamy concoction. A scoop may be overpriced, but delicious. ⊠ *Atatürk Cad., Bitez.*

### WHERE TO EAT AND STAY

**$**
MEDITERRANEAN
✕ **Bağarası.** Tables are tucked into a lovely hidden garden in summer and in cooler weather service is in a quaint, Bodrum-style one-story house. The Mediterranean cuisine includes some local favorites, such as *lokum pilav* (rice prepared with local herbs and spices) and *girit köfte* (Crete-style meatballs). Alcohol is served. ⊠ *Pınarlı Cad. 59* 🕾 *252/363 76 93* ⚲ *Reservations essential* ☉ *Daily noon–midnight; closed Mon. in winter.*

**¢**
TURKISH
✕ **Bitez Pidesi.** The *pide* (open- or close-faced pastry stuffed with meat, cheese, spinach, and other fillings) sold here is renowned locally, and little wonder. The crusts are crispy, the fillings delicious, and the prices at this no-frills eatery are unbeatable. ⊠ *Atatürk Cad. 98* 🕾 *252/363– 7925* ▭ *No credit cards.*

**$$**
TURKISH
✕ **Sarnıç Beach Club & Restaurant.** Though the beach scene and loud music make this spot a bit too much to handle during the day, things quiet down in the evening, when the seaside setting is serene and outstanding homemade *mantı* (Turkish-style ravioli, topped with a tomato and plain yogurt sauce), stuffed grape leaves, and other traditional favorites provide a casual meal. ⊠ *Aktur Sitesi-Çokertme Cad. 23* 🕾 *252/343–1433* ☉ *Closed Oct.–May.*

**$$$**
🕎 **Doria Hotel Bodrum.** A hilltop haven overlooking Bitez Bay is filled with artwork, and rooms and suites, decorated with breezy contemporary flair in soft hues, open to terraces and balconies and most have sea views. **Pros:** spacious rooms; glorious views; glamorous bars and restaurants. **Cons:** not on the beachfront, but the hotel has a private beach club nearby. ⊠ *Gündönümü Mevkii* 🕾 *252/311–1020* ⊕ *www. doriahotelbodrum.com* ⏎ *92 rooms, 11 suites* ఉ *In-room: Internet. In-hotel: restaurant, bar, pool, gym, spa, beach, business center, some pets allowed.*

## GÖLTÜRKBÜKÜ

The two coastal towns Gölköy and Türkbükkü, 20 km (12 mi) north of Bodrum, merged a decade ago to become Göltürkbükkü, the most glamorous part of the Bodrum Peninsula. Türkbükkü, which has been called the "St. Tropez of Turkey," is the summer playground of jet-setting, high-society Turks and foreigners, and its coastline is jam-packed with bars, cafés, restaurants, and boutiques. Gölköy is probably the better place to stay, as it has a slower pace and more stretches of undeveloped waterfront—and you can always head into Türkbükkü to socialize and party. Note that there's not much more to do in Gölköy besides sunbathe, as its layout makes it difficult to walk around. Neither beach has sand, but the water is accessible from wooden decks.

### WHERE TO EAT AND STAY

$  ✕ **Hoca'nın Yeri.** The specialty of the house at this modest eatery on the
TURKISH  boardwalk is *çiğ böreği*, a Crimean dish brought to Turkey that consists of flat, fried pastry stuffed with ground beef, onion, and spices. Turkish breakfast treats, such as *gözleme* (a crepe with different toppings), are on offer mornings. ⊠ *Yalı Mevkii 78, Göltürkbükkü* ☎ *252/377–5907* ⊙ *Closed Oct.–Apr.*

$$$  ✕ **Miam.** Wonderfully prepared seafood is served with polish, as are the
INTERNATIONAL  meat and pasta dishes; meals are accompanied by soothing sea views.
★  Breakfast is also served. ⊠ *Yalı Mevkii 51* ☎ *252/377–5612* ⌂ *Reservations essential* ⊙ *8 am–midnight.*

$$  ✕ **Sheanai.** While enjoying views of the tranquil Gölköy waterfront, you
TURKISH  can enjoy specialties that include especially tasty *börek* (pastries stuffed with meat, cheese, and spices), accompanied by delicious bread baked in the brick oven. Breakfast is available daily, and brunch is served on the weekends. The restaurant doubles as a beach club by day, so you may choose to linger in a lounge after lunch. ⊠ *Sahil Sok. 56, Gölköy* ☎ *252/357 76 35* ⊙ *Daily 8 am–11 pm.*

$$$  ▦ **Atami Hotel.** Tranquility on a secluded bay is the hallmark of this lovely retreat, where Japanese-accented rooms face the sea and private beach and yoga, massage, and meditation sessions enhance the relaxing atmosphere. **Pros:** yoga and meditation classes available; private beach; surrounding area is undeveloped, providing a sense of seclusion. **Cons:** need transportation to get to Gölköy, just 10 minutes away. ⊠ *Cennet Koyu Ilıca Bükü, Gölköy* ☎ *252/35-7-7416* ⟿ *31 rooms and suites* ⌂ *In-room: Internet. In-hotel: restaurant, bar, pool, spa, beach, parking.*

$$  ▦ **Karianda B&B.** A father-and-daughter team built and expanded this
Fodor's Choice  place with care, ensuring the modestly decorated rooms overlooking
★  lovely gardens and the sea are spic and span. **Pros:** cozy feel with everything at your fingertips; excellent food. **Cons:** the neighboring pension plays its music a bit loud sometimes but turns it down upon request. ⊠ *Cumhuriyet Cad. 104–106, Gölköy* ☎ *252/357–7303, 252/357–7819* ⊕ *www.karianda.com* ⟿ *25 rooms* ⌂ *In-room: no TV. In-hotel: restaurant, bar, beach.*

$$$$  ▦ **Maça Kızı Boutique Hotel & Restaurant.** The "Queen of Spades" is nestled on a hillside on a secluded bay at the tip of Göltürkbükkü, away from the crowds, and all the elegantly decorated rooms face the bay or gardens. **Pros:** private bay; sophisticated surroundings, with lots of wood and

stone; excellent restaurant. **Cons:** somewhat expensive. ✉ *Kesire Mevkii* ☎ *252/377–6272* ⊕ *www.macakizi.com* ↪ *81 rooms* ⚙ *In-room: Internet. In-hotel: restaurant, bar, pool, spa, beach, parking* †◎l *Breakfast.*

## GÜMÜŞLÜK

Gümüşlük, built on the ancient ruins of Myndos 23 km (14 mi) west of Bodrum, is one of the peninsula's more authentic, slower-paced, less-developed villages—no high-rises or large hotels are allowed. Much of the Myndos ruins are submerged underwater, but major land excavations are taking place to recover the ancient city, and a drainage system dating to Myndos's Roman civilization period has already been discovered. The town is popular for its fish restaurants on the water. One of the popular things to do is walk through the shallow water to Tavşan Adasıı, Rabbit Island. Glassmakers and other artists reside and keep shop here, and sometimes you can see them at work. The restored, hilltop Eklisia Church hosts many cultural and arts events, including a summertime classical music festival. If you have the time, and a car, you can make the trip up to Karakaya, a village of stone houses perched above Gümüşlük and surrounded with cactus and other foliage.

### WHERE TO EAT

**$$**
TURKISH
✕ **Aquarium.** At branches on the water in Gümüşlük and Yalıavak, begin a meal with stuffed zucchini flowers, roasted eggplant with *tulum* cheese, or rice with shrimp and octopus—you may want to just keep working your way through the starters, a meal in themselves. Whatever you choose, don't skip dessert—the *baklava* comes from the city of Gaziantep, known for having the best in Turkey. ✉ *Yalı Mevkii* ✉ *Çökertme Cad. 22, Yalıkavak* ☎ *252/385–4151 Gümüşlük, 252/394–3682 Yalıkavak, 0533/344–8943 Bodrum* ⊕ *www.aquariumgumusluk.com* ⚙ *Reservations essential* ☉ *Daily 8 am–2 am* ☞ *Open year-round.*

**$**
TURKISH
✕ **Limon Cafe.** Settle into a lovely, lemon-scented garden overlooking the ancient city of Myndos and enjoy the sunset and rural surroundings while savoring one of the house-specialty cocktails. Lunch or dinner should begin with the excellent fried calamari. Brunch is served on weekends. ✉ *Yalı Mevkii 1, about 2 km (1 mi) outside town* ☎ *252/394–4044* ⊕ *www.limongumusluk.com* ⚙ *Reservations essential* ☉ *Closed Oct.–Apr.*

## YALIKAVAK

This town on the northwestern tip of the Bodrum Peninsula is 20 km (12 mi) from Bodrum, surrounded by tangerine orchards and olive groves and easily identified by the beautiful windmills atop its hill. Once a tiny sponge-divers' village, Yalıkavak is still quiet, with some fine restaurants and a big marina, as well as many fine beaches ringing the surrounding coves. Strong wind makes Yalıkavak ideal for windsurfing.

### WHERE TO EAT AND STAY

**$**
TURKISH
✕ **Kavaklı Köfteci.** *Köfte* (Turkish-style meatballs) is the mainstay of this no-frills and popular eatery, and you can enjoy these delectable morsels with a side of *piyaz salad* (navy bean salad with or without onions), homemade bread, and *ayran* (plain yogurt drink). ✉ *Merkez Çarşı İçi* ☎ *252/385–4748* ⊕ *www.kavaklikofteci.com* ▭ *No credit cards* ☞ *cash only.*

$$$$ ⊡ **Kempinski Hotel Barbaros Bay.** This is by far one of the most beautiful deluxe hotel properties in all of Bodrum and located on a private bay in the secluded Yalıçiftlik. **Pros:** luxurious splendor; four fine-dining restaurants also open to nonguests. **Cons:** far from the Bodrum city center and nightlife. ⊠ *Kırağaç Koyu, Gerenkuyu Mevkii, Yalıçiftlik, Bodrum* ☎ *252/311 03 03* ⊕ *www.kempinski.com/bodrum* ⬏ *173 rooms and suites* � *In-room: a/c, Wi-Fi. In-hotel: restaurants, bar, pool, tennis court, gym, spa, beach, water sports, business center, parking* ☞ *Open year-round.*

$$$$ ⊡ **Palmalife Bodrum Resort & Spa.** Privacy is among the amenities at this lovely getaway, facing its own bay and offering sophisticated accommodations, some in villas set amid lush seaside gardens. **Pros:** beautiful and sophisticated contemporary surroundings; private beach, state-of-the-art spa and wellness center; welcoming bars and restaurants. **Cons:** expensive; need transportation to get around ⊠ *Gökçebel Mahallesi, Kızılburun Cad. 1* ☎ *252/396–6050* ⊕ *www.palmaliferesort.com* ⬏ *40 rooms and suites, 5 villas* ᗡ *In-room: Wi-Fi. In-hotel: restaurant, bar, pool, tennis court, gym, spa, beach, water sports, business center, parking.*

# The Turquoise Riviera

**WORD OF MOUTH**

"Kaş was my favorite. Small fishing village, hotel right on water, easy walk to center of town, boat cruises to Lycean ruins."

—Michel_Paris

# WELCOME TO THE TURQUOISE RIVIERA

## TOP REASONS TO GO

★ **Appreciate the land-scape:** Rugged pine-clad mountains plunge into a vibrant blue sea that's broken by remote peninsulas and distant Greek islands.

★ **Explore beaches:** Some of the Mediterranean's most perfect beaches are here; lie on your sun bed or plunge from a floating diving platform.

★ **Luxuriate in gorgeous lodgings:** Relax in a beautiful Ottoman nobleman's mansion-turned-hotel on the wild and rugged Datça Peninsula.

★ **See spectacular ruins:** Explore the ruins of spectacular ancient cities—from mountaintop Termessos to overgrown Olympos and the extraordinarily intact Roman theater at Aspendos.

★ **Take a Blue Cruise:** Sail into the turquoise waters of remote and pristine bays on your own chartered yacht.

★ **Trek the Lycian Way:** Choose a one-day or multiday hike along this trail that runs parallel to much of the Turquoise Coast.

View from the Acropolis of Simena

**1** **The Datça Peninsula.** A yacht chartered in Marmaris or Bodrum is the best way to visit the craggy hills and ancient coves of one of Turkey's most unspoiled stretches of coastline.

**2** **The Lycian Coast.** Rent a car from the Dalaman or Antalya airport and slowly explore the charming ports, boutique hotels, uncrowded beaches, and ancient ruins along the little-developed coastal circuit.

**3** **Antalya and Pamphylia.** Antalya is a vibrant city that has everything—an old city, beaches, good restaurants and nightlife—and it's a good place to base yourself for taking in the ancient sites of Aspendos, Perge, Termessos, and Phaselis. The area around Antalya, including Side and Alanya is considered historic Pamphylia.

Gulets harbored in Simena

Apollon Temple, Side

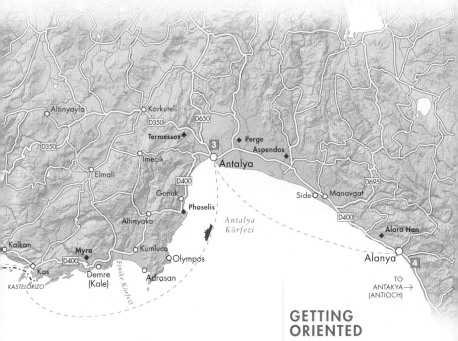

Altınyayla
Korkuteli
D350
D650
Termessos
D350
İmecik
3
Perge
Aspendos
Antalya
D695
Elmalı
D400
Gönük
Side
Manavgat
Phaselis
D400
Antalya
Körfezi
Altınyaka
Alara Han
Kalkan
Kumluca
Myra
Olympos
Alanya
D400
Kaş
4
KASTELÓRIZO
Demre
(Kale)
Adrasan
Finike Körfezi

TO
ANTAKYA →
(ANTIOCH)

## GETTING ORIENTED

The area known as the Turquoise Riviera stretches along the Mediterranean coast from the rugged and unspoiled Datça Peninsula on Turkey's southwestern tip to the resort hotels springing up along the Antalya-Alanya strip. The fir-clad mountains rising behind the coastline are punctuated by the ruins of splendid ancient Greek and Roman cities, through which passed the likes of Alexander the Great, Julius Caesar, and St. Paul.

Olüdeniz Beach

**4 East of Alanya.** The area east of Alanya is not much traveled but if you're heading to Antakya (Antioch) there are some interesting stops along the way and the drive is quite pretty.

# SEAFOOD ON THE TURKISH COAST

The kebab might be the first thing that comes to mind when you think about Turkish food, but in Istanbul and along Turkey's Aegean, Mediterranean, and Black Sea coasts, fresh fish is readily available.

With its miles and miles of coastline, it's not surprising seafood is an integral part of Turkish cuisine and Turks eat fish at lunch or dinner, usually either grilled or fried, and served with little more than a squeeze of lemon and a side of fresh arugula or slices of raw onion. Varieties might be a bit different from what you're used to, but these are some of the more common ones you'll find.

In winter, hearty fish soups—similar to chowder—are served in many restaurants.

Fresh fish served in restaurants is usually sold by weight, so be sure to ask the price before ordering.

## WILD VS. FARMED

Although many of the fish served in Turkey are seasonal, the growth of aquaculture in the country has led to a more dependable supply of certain types of fish, though many diners insist on eating the tastier (and more expensive) wild variety. If you want the open-sea version, ask for the *deniz* type, which is "from the sea."

### BARBUNYA

The tasty small red mullet is popular in Turkey. As the name implies, the *barbunya*'s skin is speckled with glistening reddish spots. The mild-tasting fish, usually only a few inches long, are typically panfried whole; an order of them can easily be shared. The prime season for *barbunya* is spring through early summer.

### ÇIPURA

Gilthead bream is the most popular fish caught in the Aegean area. Like *levrek,* it's a mild tasting fish with white, flaky meat, usually grilled whole and served unadorned. Fish farms now supply much of the *çipura* served in restaurants, but the wild variety, known as *deniz çipurasi* is also available.

### HAMSI

Size isn't everything. The finger-length anchovy is often referred to in Turkey as the "little prince" of fishes. In the Black Sea area, where *hamsi* are caught, the little fish is used in numerous dishes and forms an important part of the local economy. The most popular way *hamsi* is served is fried in a light coating of corn meal. Another popular recipe is *hamsi pilav*—a rice and anchovy dish infused with an aromatic mix of herbs and spices. *Hamsi* season is fall and winter.

### LEVREK

Sea bass is one of the most popular fish in Turkey, prized for its delicate, almost sweet taste and firm white meat. *Levrek* is usually charcoal grilled whole and served with a drizzle of oil and a squeeze of lemon. Or a whole *levrek* might be encased in sea salt and baked in the oven. Many restaurants serve the cheaper and smaller farmed variety of the fish. Wild *levrek* is known as *deniz levreği*. Both are available all year.

### LÜFER

This is the general name for bluefish, which are generally tastier than the U.S. varieties. Bluefish is popular enough that the different sizes have their own names: small bluefish are *çinekop*, large bluefish are *kofana,* and medium bluefish are *sarıkanat.*

### PALAMUT

Also known as bonito, *palamut* is related to tuna. Unlike *levrek* and *çipura,* it's a strong-tasting, oily fish, similar to mackerel. *Palamut* fillets are often grilled, but another popular—and perhaps tastier—way they are prepared is baked in the oven with an onion and tomato sauce. Palamut appears in Turkey's waters in fall through winter.

Updated by
Scott Newman

The Turquoise Riviera is just as stunning as the name suggests, with luminous blue-green ocean waves lapping at isolated coves and beaches that range from multicolor polished marble pebbles to miles of yellow sand. Spectacular archaeological ruins are never far away.

This part of Turkey's coast is home to some of the country's most iconic beaches—like Ölüdeniz, Patara, and İztuzu—it's also the place to find spectacular ruins from ancient cities of Greek, Roman, and Byzantine origin. Termessos, known as the Eagle's Nest, is said to have defied Alexander the Great because he was daunted by its height, and the Roman theater in Apsendos rivals the Colosseum in Rome.

In the west is the beautiful Datça Peninsula, a Mediterranean landscape of rolling hills and olive trees looking out on a sea dotted with Greek islands. East of Marmaris, a more-touristy town, lies the Lycian coast. Here you'll find a mix of ruins, rugged scenery, and beaches. Each Lycian coast destination has a distinct feel: Ölüdeniz, crowded but with a standout beach; laid-back, alternative Kabak; low-key Patara; upscale Kalkan; lively Kaş; and the green and relaxed Olympos area. Antalya is the biggest city and a tourist hub on this stretch of coast, with long beaches lined with resorts. The package tourists though often skip Old Antalya, which is filled with historic mansions, many of which are now boutique hotels, along a backdrop of sea and mountains. Antalya also has the coast's best museum and archaeological sites, including the Roman theater at Aspendos. East of the resort towns of Side and Alanya, the coast becomes rugged and you leave the tour buses far behind. There are still plenty of ruins, castles, and beaches but with more of the real Turkey.

## PLANNING

### BLUE CRUISING

A yacht charter in a *gulet,* a wooden motorboat or sailing boat, is the quintessential, relaxing way to explore Turkey's coast. For the full effect, plan at least four days and at best a week, perhaps from Antalya to Fethiye, or a tour of the Datça Peninsula from Marmaris. *For more information, see the Blue Cruising Close Up in this chapter.*

## FESTIVALS

For four days in the middle of September, the International Song Contest in Antalya brings open-air concerts to the area around the marina.

## GETTING HERE AND AROUND

### AIR TRAVEL

It makes the most sense to fly to the Turquoise Coast if you're coming from Istanbul or elsewhere in Turkey. The main airports here are in Dalaman and Antalya. Antalya is the busiest international airport in Turkey, serving the coast from Alanya to Kaş, including Side, Belek, Olympos, and Finike. Dalaman Airport serves the coast from Kaş to Datça, including Kalkan, Fethiye, Göcek, Dalyan, and Marmaris. There are also airports in Adana and Antakya.

A host of car rental concessions operate at all airports, including all international agencies. Havaş airport buses also link the two airports to major towns. Major hotels and travel agencies will arrange airport shuttles as well (usually for a fee). Yellow airport taxis are somewhat expensive for individuals but are usually well regulated with a clear legal pricing system prominently displayed and are a good option if you're sharing.

Taking a bus from Antalya airport into Antalya costs about $6; they're timed to meet all in-coming flights and leave the city center hourly. Buses to the airport leave the Turkish Airlines building on Cumhuriyet Caddesi (on the clifftop boulevard) once every hour or two. Another bus leaves from nearby **Wing Turizm** (☎ *242/244–2236*) at even more irregular times. Yet another option if you're leaving from Antalya main bus station is to take a bus down the highway east of Antalya, get out at the airport intersection, and take one of the taxis waiting there for the last 2 km (1 mi) into the airport itself, for which the taxi charges about $3—it's a bit of a hassle, but something to consider. A taxi to the airport from the center, by comparison, costs $20.

From Dalaman Airport, airport buses will take airline passengers east via Göcek to Fethiye harbor ($12) and west to Marmaris intercity bus terminal ($15). Theoretically, the buses will leave Marmaris three hours before any flight, and Fethiye 2½ hours before. For more precise information, call Havaş, the Dalaman operating representative.

**Contacts Havaş** ☎ *212/465–5656 central Turkey call center* ⊕ *www.havas.net/en/iletisim/.*

### BOAT AND FERRY TRAVEL

There are no longer any long-distance ferries serving the southwestern Turkish coast, though the ferry from Bodrum to Körmen, near Datça, can save a long road trip, and there are a number of ferries linking individual Turkish ports with Greek islands. In general, anyone with a U.S. or Western passport can visit Greece. Note that you need to be at the boats at least an hour before departure time to complete passport formalities. Be aware that shops and museums on Greek islands usually close during the midday heat and do not reopen until late afternoon, so it's sensible to stay a night or two if you are going to take the trouble of making the journey; however, day return tickets are usually significantly cheaper than open returns. There are frequent ferries from Marmaris and Fethiye to Rhodes, Datça to Symi, and Kaş to Kastellorizon.

**Contacts Yesil Marmaris** ☎ *252/412–2290* ⊕ *www.yesilmarmaris.com.*

### BUS AND DOLMUŞ TRAVEL

Inexpensive intercity buses travel between major towns all over Turkey—it's about $40 one way for the 12-hour journey from Istanbul to Antalya. These days, though, that's only about half the price of flying.

Buses and minibuses (*dolmuşes*) run regularly between the main Turquoise Riviera cities but rarely travel to remote archaeological sites such as Tlos and Pinara. Every city has an intercity bus terminal, and minibuses to smaller destinations usually set off from there, too. Major routes, such as Marmaris to Fethiye and Fethiye to Antalya, have hourly buses into the early evening; fares are typically about $7 per 100 km per person. Minibus schedules depend on the popularity of the route and these buses generally stop anywhere if asked to.

When the intercity bus terminal is outside the city center (as in Antalya), major companies usually provide minibus service from their city center locations to the station: ask for a *servis* (minibus transfer service) when you book your ticket, otherwise, finding your own way to the terminal can be difficult and time-consuming. The Varan Bus Company is more expensive than others, but has better service, a better safety record, and its own privately owned and spotlessly clean rest stops.

**Contacts Varan Bus Company** ☎ *212/467–7600 in Istanbul, 212/444–8999 national* ⊕ *www.varan.com.tr.*

### CAR TRAVEL

Once here, you'll find renting a car allows you to get around with the most ease; many of the sights you'll want to see are off the main road, and the area is filled with beautiful coastal drives.

Although the highways between towns are well maintained, smaller roads are usually unpaved and rough, and the twisty coastal roads require concentration. To estimate driving times, figure on about 70 km (43 mi) per hour. By car from Istanbul to Marmaris or Antalya is at least a 10-hour, 750-km (470-mi) trek. The speed limit is 90 kpm (56 mph) on most country roads—120 kpm (75 mph) on real highways—and for your own safety it's best to stick to it. The police have radars and they do use them.

All airports have several car rental associations to choose from, and many hotels can arrange car rentals. In general, the smaller and more remote the place, the cheaper the rental, but the more minimal the service.

### TAXI TRAVEL

Provincial taxis are somewhat expensive; fares generally work out somewhere near $2 per km traveled. It's best to take a taxi from an established taxi stand, where you see several lined up, since the drivers there will be regulars and if you should have a dispute or lose something, it is much easier to retrace the car that way. It's normal, however, to hail taxis in the street. For longer journeys, you may both wish to settle a price in advance, but within city limits, the taxi driver should automatically switch on the meter when you get in. As elsewhere, if he doesn't, insist upon it.

**TRAIN TRAVEL**

There is no train service on the Turquoise Riviera.

## HOW MUCH TIME DO YOU NEED?

If you just have a weekend or so on the Turquoise Riviera and want to see ancient sites, base yourself in Antalya and drive out to nearby Termessos, Olympos or Aspendos: they're some of the best preserved classical sites in the country.

A road trip around the Lycian coast is beautiful, and full of the ruins of ancient Lycian cities like Xanthos, Patara, and Olympos. Count on about 10 hours' total driving, starting in either Antalya or Dalaman. There are many unspoiled towns and lovely hotels en route. You could spend as few as three days, but five to seven would be more relaxing and allow for some beach time. A sample six-day tour would have you leave from Antalya and visit Termessos, then cross the mountains to Fethiye. Overnight in the mountains above Ölüdeniz. On Day 2, visit Ölüdeniz, the ghost town of Kaya or the pine-fringed beach at Kabak; overnight in the same hotel as the previous night. On Day 3, visit the ancient Lycian cities of Pinara, Xanthos, and Letoon, explore the Saklıkent canyon, and finish with a swim in Patara. Overnight in Patara, Kalkan, or Kaş. On Day 4, take a day-boat trip from Kaş to Kekova, and return to Kaş for the night. On Day 5, visit St. Nicholas's Basilica in Demre, have lunch in Finike, and visit Arycanda in the afternoon. Overnight in Çiralı and see the burning Chimera. On Day 6, visit Phaselis, then return to Antalya.

## LOCAL FLAVORS

Regional specialties along the coast include mussels stuffed with rice, pine nuts, and currants; *ahtopot salatası*, a cold octopus salad, tossed in olive oil, vinegar, and parsley; and grilled fish. Most of Turkey's tomatoes, cucumbers, eggplants, zucchinis, and peppers are grown along the coast, so fresh salads are delicious. In Lycia, a local home-cooking speciality is stewed eggplant with basil—wonderful if you're offered it. *Semiz otu* (cow parsley) is a refreshing appetizer in a garlic yogurt sauce.

*For more about great seafood see the "Seafood on the Turkish Coast" feature in this chapter.*

## TOURS

Trekking opportunities abound in this part of Turkey. For serious walkers, the 530-km (331-mi) Lycian Way is the standing challenge. If you prefer to have a guide, individually or as part of a group, contact Middle Earth Travel—they can also provide camping equipment.

The area is also great for rafting or trekking trips. The three main areas are around Fethiye and Ölüdeniz, in Köprülü National Park near Antalya, and along Alanya's Dimçay River. You'll pass through soaring canyons and under ancient Roman bridges. The Alraft Rafting and Riding Club, in Alanya, arranges rafting trips, as well as horseback riding treks.

Also in Antalya are Medraft and TransNature, both outdoor-sports specialists. In Fethiye, Aventura specializes in all kinds of activities, including paragliding. In Side, Get Wet can arrange all kinds of outdoor activities such as rafting, trekking, and mountaineering.

History- and religion-oriented tours are not uncommon around the south coast of Turkey area, particularly due to association with **St. Paul,** who evangelized the area. A 400-km (250-mi) trekking route known as the **St. Paul Trail** takes in some places he is known to have passed through. A guide isn't really necessary and the trekkers are usually independent—but Middle Earth Travel arranges tours. More traditional weeklong bus tours look at Christian sites in the Antalya area and then go on to Ephesus, where St. Paul preached in the theater. More information can be had from Paul's Place in Antalya.

### BOOKING A TOUR

If you want to book a local tour—anything from boat tours to trekking tours or local special-interest tours—you're best off wandering through the center of whatever town you're in. Choose a local travel agency that looks well kept, and chat with the owner. Don't hesitate to move politely on to another one if you feel hassled or inadequately served. You can also ask at your hotel: they're likely to recommend the agency that gives them the best commission, and they'll probably add a commission from you, too, but it can be worth the cost for convenience and reliability.

**Contacts Alraft Rafting and Riding Club** ☎ 242/513-9155. **Get Wet** ☎ 242/753-4071. **Medraft** ☎ 248/312-0083. **Middle Earth Travel** ☎ 384/271-2559 ⊕ www.middleearthtravel.com. **Paul's Place** ☎ 242/247-6857 ⊕ stpaulcc-turkey.com/pauls-place. **TransNature** ☎ 242/324-0011 ⊕ www.transnature.com.tr/eng/index.html.

| WHAT IT COSTS IN U.S. DOLLARS | | | | | |
|---|---|---|---|---|---|
| | ¢ | $ | $$ | $$$ | $$$$ |
| Restaurants | under $5 | $5–$10 | $11–$15 | $16–$25 | over $25 |
| Hotels | under $50 | $50–$75 | $76–$150 | $151–$250 | over $250 |

Restaurant prices are for one main course at dinner or for two mezes (small dishes). Hotel prices are for two people in a standard double room in high season, including taxes.

### WHEN TO GO

The ideal months on the Turquoise Riviera are May and June and September and October. Summers can be hot and humid, especially in July and August, and that's also when the beaches tend to be fuller and waterfront discos pump out their most egregious levels of noise.

Alanya and Side stay warmest longest. They're also best visited when charter tourists are least likely to be about, before or after the high season.

Along the Lycian coast, expect thunderstorms after late-October and an average 12 days of rain per month in December and January, otherwise, while not swimming weather, it can be sunshine and T-shirts. Snow graces mountain peaks well into May, a magnificent site across the ocean from Antalya and Fethiye. Although not a winter sun destination, it rarely drops below freezing on the coast. Some hotels stay open between mid-December and March, often with limited facilities.

# THE DATÇA PENINSULA AND MARMARIS

Modernity confronts antiquity in the westernmost portion of the Mediterranean coast. The beaches are gorgeous and the mood is laid back if you don't stay in the resort areas of Datça or Marmaris proper. Datça is quieter than Marmaris, but for even more charming and remote, Eski Datça and Reshadiye are lovely little villages where you can appreciate a calmer way of life.

## DATÇA PENINSULA

*Datça town is 76 km (47 mi) west of Marmaris and 167 km (104 mi) west of Dalaman on Rte. 400.*

If you make it all the way to the **Datça Peninsula,** you may never want to leave. It's a landscape of olives tree, pine forests in sheltered hollows, and stunning blue water. Until about 20 years ago, this was one of the most inaccessible parts of Turkey, and driving along the thin neck of land between the Aegean Sea to the north and the Mediterranean to the south feels like entering the gateway to another, older world. This is not somewhere to drop by for a day or two: you need at least three days to savor the uncluttered joys of this unique destination—far from the world of tour buses, it's a place with few pressures, but wide horizons and more than 50 little beaches for inner contemplation. The best time to visit is in spring, when the hills are carpeted in poppies, daisies, and wildflowers, and restaurants offer dishes concocted with wild thyme, rosemary, and other herbs that flourish in the hills and by the sea; in autumn, you can watch the locals harvest olives.

The timeless stone alleys of Eski Datça give a similar sense of being in another, less stressful world. The ancient ruins of Knidos are one of the loveliest and most evocative sites along the whole coast.

Datça is a small, little-developed port town with some characteristics of a resort. It's one of the most relaxed towns along the whole coast, but Eski Datça and Reşadiye are older and have more charm. Even if you don't stay here, spend an evening wandering around the harbor and sipping a drink at one of the quayside cafés. The weekly market is on Saturday, which is what attracts Greek islanders from nearby Symi. It's also the best place to arrange a boat trip to Knidos. A lovely day out and a meal at an unspoiled beach can also be had at Kargı Koyu, 3 km (2 mi) south of central Datça.

### GETTING HERE AND AROUND

There are two ways to get to Datça: either fly to Dalaman Airport and make the three-hour drive west to Datça or, more pleasantly, fly to Bodrum Airport and then take a two-hour car-ferry ride from Bodrum Port to Datça's Körmen Port. In the June–September season, these boats run from both ports at 9 am and 5 pm. In winter they run only on

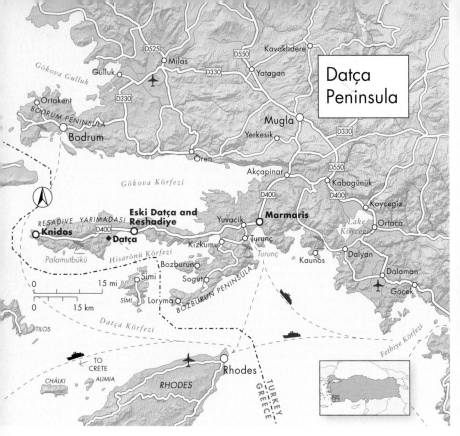

Monday, Wednesday, and Friday at 9 am from Datça to Bodrum and at 5 pm from Bodrum to Datça. Regular buses go to Marmaris from the Pamukkale office in town, and in summer *dolmuşes* to Yazıköy continue to Knidos.

## WHERE TO EAT AND STAY

*For expanded hotel reviews, visit Fodors.com.*

$ ✕ **Emek Restaurant.** Everything is made on the premises in the spotless
TURKISH kitchens of this excellent eatery, the best of the bunch overlooking Datça harbor. The owner and chief chef Seyyar Kantarlı says her secret is real olive oil and all fresh ingredients. Her son Uğur catches most of the fish—the fried squid and octopus are delicious—and wild Datça herbs make menus interesting in spring. The homemade bread is some of the best on the coast. The menu includes the usual range of seafood and Turkish grills, as well as various curries. Call in the morning to reserve a balcony table. ⊠ *Yat Limanı, Datça* ☎ *252/712–3375* ☉ *Closed Nov.–Feb.*

$ ✕ **Yeşim Bar Restaurant.** One of only three buildings on the pleasant beach
TURKISH at Kargı Koyu, Yeşim has sun beds, umbrellas, and showers available all day for customers. A lawn out back, with trees shading a bar, makes a cool respite from the sun. If you can, grab one of the prime tables under a tree on the beach itself. The menu includes pizzas, fish, and meat. The

bar is open late, so you can stay for a drink after dinner. ⊠ *Follow road south 3 km (2 mi) from Datça til you see beach; it's the first building past car park* ☎ *252/712–8399.*

$  🏨 **Bora Hotel.** If you want to stay in town, this simple hotel right behind Datça harbor has clean, bright rooms and new furnishings. **Pros:** central. **Cons:** unexceptional. ⊠ *Street behind the yacht harbor* ☎ *252/712–2040* ⊕ *www.borahotel.com.tr* ⇨ *18 rooms* ⚬ *In-room: a/c* ⊙ *Oct.–May.*

$  🏨 **Türk Evi.** Built in the style of an Ottoman mansion and set in a pretty garden just south of the yacht harbor, this small boutique hotel is a pleasant and relaxing place to stay. **Pros:** comfortable and unpretentious. **Cons:** no pool. ⊠ *Head west from harbor and look for signs* ☎ *252/712–4081* ⊕ *www.datcaturkevi.com* ⇨ *8 rooms* ⚬ *In-room: a/c, no TV, Wi-Fi. In-hotel: bar.*

$  🏨 **Villa Aşina.** All rooms have a sea view at this pretty little hotel that looks out over the Greek islands of Symi and Rhodes. **Pros:** simple but pretty rooms. **Cons:** a little out of town. ⊠ *From Datça harbor, head south along coast, following signs to Villa Aşina on left after large hill* ☎ *252/712–0443* ⊕ *www.villaasina.com* ⇨ *17 rooms* ⚬ *In-room: a/c, Wi-Fi. In-hotel: pool.*

### NIGHTLIFE
There are many bars along the yacht harbor.

**Club Gallus.** Club Gallus, just west of the port, serves as the main discotheque for Datça; doors don't open until after midnight.

## ESKI DATÇA AND RESHADIYE

*3 km (2 mi) inland from Datça harbor on the road to Reshadiye.*

★ Turkish satirical poet and polemical left-wing social critic Can Yücel retired to a modest old stone house in Eski Datça, setting an artistic tone for this pretty backwater spot, and for nearby Reshadiye. The formerly Greek-populated village is one of the few in Turkey that has survived intact. It's now experiencing fine restoration efforts that have produced several lovely small houses to rent. Nobody hurries through the stone-paved alleys.

### GETTING HERE AND AROUND
Eski Datça and Reshadiye are both just off the main Datça-Marmaris road, 3 km (2 mi) and 4 km (2½ mi) respectively. There is a regular bus service between Datça and both towns.

### WHERE TO EAT AND STAY
*For expanded hotel reviews, visit Fodors.com.*

¢  ✕ **Datça Sofrası.** This is an ideal lunch spot, with a vine-covered terrace
TURKISH  and traditional Turkish braised meats emerging from under a brasshooded charcoal brazier. The menu is also rich in vegetarian dishes and starters concocted from local wild herbs. The speciality is *bademli köfte* (meatballs with almonds). ⊠ *Hurma Sok. 16, Eski Datça* ☎ *252/712–4188* ▭ *No credit cards.*

$  ✕ **Elaki Restaurant.** Even if you don't stay at the Mehmet Ali Ağa Konağı
TURKISH  Hotel, consider soaking up its ambience for an evening at the hotel

restaurant. The seating is right beside the mansion, effectively the courtyard, and it's usually possible to have a look around. The food is more than a match for the location, eating here is a gourmet's delight, and the service five-star. The menu changes regularly, with a focus on Mediterranean and Ottoman dishes, making good use of the wild herbs of the area. The mezes are excellent, and the mixed platter recommended, as well as the smooth, light "fairy floss"-like desert laced with shredded chocolate and pistachios. There is an excellent wine cellar. ✉ *Kavak Meydan, Reshadiye* ☎ *252/712–9257.*

¢ **Dede Pansiyon.** This comfortable stone *pansiyon* is swathed in bougainvilleas and decorated with curiosities like concrete flagstones set with old bathroom fittings. **Pros:** spacious; with a maximum of 12 guests the place feels quiet and tranquil. **Cons:** difficult to find. ✉ *Can Yücel Cad., Eski Datça* ☎ *252/712–3951* 🌐 *www.dedepansiyon.com* *5 rooms, 1 suite* *In-room: kitchen. In-hotel: bar, pool, parking* *No credit cards.*

$$ **Eski Datça Evleri.** Eski Datça Evleri, or Old Datça Houses, is a collection of three traditional stone houses scattered through the village. **Pros:** beautiful; good if you want to be self-sufficient. **Cons:** walk to main house for breakfast; not all houses have Wi-Fi. ✉ *D1 Sokak 26, on right as you enter village, Eski Datça* ☎ *252/712-2129* 🌐 *www.eskidatcaevleri.com* *11* *In-room: kitchen, no TV, Wi-Fi.*

$$$$ Fodor's Choice ★ **Mehmet Ali Ağa Konağı.** A stay in this restored mansion offers the unique chance to experience the lifestyle and surroundings of a 19th-century Ottoman nobleman. **Pros:** absolutely beautiful; delicious food. **Cons:** small "cupboard" bathrooms in the mansion. ✉ *Kavak Meydan, Reshadiye, Datça* ☎ *252/712–9257* 🌐 *www.kocaev.com* *15 rooms, 2 suites* *In-room: Wi-Fi. In-hotel: bar, pool, business center* *Closed Nov.–mid-Apr.* *Breakfast.*

¢ **Yağhane Pansiyon.** If you're in search of help in channeling inner reflection, this comfortable stone-built hotel with a fine English lawn out front specializes in weeklong courses of yoga, meditation, Ayurvedic treatments, and "the search for your inner snake." **Pros:** ommmm. **Cons:** not for everyone. ✉ *Eski Datça* ☎ *252/712–2287* 🌐 *www.suryaturkey.com* *4 rooms* *In-hotel: restaurant* *No credit cards* *Breakfast.*

## KNIDOS

*38 km (24 mi) west of Datça.*

Windswept Knidos sits on a headland at the very end of the Datça Peninsula, at the point where the Aegean meets the Mediterranean. A primitive archaeological site, its ruins are scattered amid olive groves and a few hints of modern civilization. There is a small restaurant by the jetty where the tour boats arrive.

### GETTING HERE AND AROUND

Knidos is most romantic when reached by sea, as the ancients did, and in summer boats leave regularly from Datça, though the trip takes three hours each way, with swimming stops. By car, you can reach Knidos from Datça in 40 minutes over bumpy roads. *Dolmuşes* to Yazıköy go on to the ruins in season.

## EXPLORING

**Knidos.** Knidos was founded in the 7th century BC by Dorian Greeks and prospered because of its excellent location on shipping routes between Egypt, Rhodes, Ephesus, the Greek mainland, and other major ports. The center of the archaeological site is the large ancient agora or market place, down by the water and the ancient ports. If you continue up the hill on the ancient main street, with its views over the harbor and the modern lighthouse, you'll pass the temple of Apollo and then reach the circular temple of Aphrodite, which used to house a lifelike statue of Aphrodite, one of classical Greece's most famous statues.

### NAKED APHRODITE

In antiquity Knidos's main claim to fame was its 4th-century BC statue of Aphrodite. It was the first naked statue of a goddess, and when its commissioners, the people of Kos, saw it they were so shocked that they sent it back and asked for something a little more respectable. The citizens of Knidos were looking for a statue of Aphrodite at the time, and bought the rejected work, which rapidly became a hit, making Knidos an ancient tourist attraction, drawing travelers from afar, among them Cicero and Julius Caesar.

5

Around the back of the site is the Corinthian temple with its ancient sundial; back by the harbor is a small **odeon,** or concert hall. On the promontory with the lighthouse is the rectangular, stone **Lion Tomb.** The sad-eyed lion is in remembrance of a victory over Sparta. The original is now on display in the British Museum, along with another famous relic from Knidos, a statue of the goddess Demeter. Her **sanctuary,** however, is up the original stairway that leads to the upper portion of the town on the east side of the ruins. ⬛ $5.

**Palamutbükü Beach.** Just before Knidos a road heads south, past many fishing villages. The popular Palamutbükü Beach, in a long bay on the south side of the peninsula, is a nice place to stop after visiting the ruins. Behind the beach are a number of restaurants including the Aylin; each also serves on their own zone of sand.

★ Southwest of Marmaris is a second peninsula, the Bozburun Peninsula. Most visitors don't make it past the beach at Turunç, but if you do, the village of Bozburun still makes its living by fishing and boatbuilding. Beyond are other small coastal villages like Selimiye, Orhaniye, and Hisarönü.

## MARMARIS

*91 km (56 mi) west of the international airport at Dalaman.*

The big, brash resort city Marmaris has two faces, and they're hard to reconcile. From the sea, a thick line of resort hotels stretches around the northern edge of a great bay, the whole encircled by a magical necklace of pine-clad mountains. Behind those same hotels, however, the city has been overwhelmed by boxy concrete development and streets lined with a hundred generically named eateries. An annual horde of European tourists descends on these workaday establishments, but for the international traveler, there is little special about Marmaris that cannot be savored elsewhere in Turkey. It's a pretty spot, but there isn't much reason to linger unless you are meeting a yacht, traveling on to the Greek island of Rhodes, or perhaps taking up an unbeatable deal at one of the best resort hotels, some of which are spectacular worlds unto themselves (which is just fine given that you probably won't want to see much else here).

If you're in Marmaris, though, don't miss the city's best achievement, a 10-km (7-mi) **seafront promenade** that stretches all the way from the easternmost marina known as Netsal, past the old fortress, along the palm-lined main boulevard of town, and then out between the beach and the fancy hotels that line the coast, all the way west to the outlying resort of İçmeler. Along the way there are any number of cafés at which to pause for refreshment or to take in fine views of sea and mountains. For $5, the footsore can ride back on one of the shared water taxis that run up and down the coast in season (usually April–November).

There are few historic sites in what was until a few decades ago a small, sleepy fishing port. These include a modest 16th-century **citadel**, first built by Süleyman the Magnificent, shelled to bits by the French in the First World War and rebuilt in the 1980s. There is a small museum inside (both are closed on Monday).

Good day outings from Marmaris include a boat trip from the harbor to **Turunç** on a visit easily arranged by yourself, your hotel, or any of the many travel agencies. Another fine destination is **Sedir Island** (Cedar Island).

This will likely involve a bus ride north to the Gulf of Gökova and then a boat. Sedir harbors one of the most perfect beaches in the world—if only one could have it to oneself. The sand is made up of tiny egg-shape pearls of a luminous white marble, making the water brilliantly clear as you swim before the impressive escarpments of Mt. Kavak over the sea to the north. An hour's bus ride from Marmaris will also take you to the refreshing sulfurous mud baths near **Lake Köyeceğiz** or, on a long but doable day trip, to the town of **Dalyan** and the ruins of ancient Kaunos.

Marmaris Bay is also home to some of Turkey's biggest and busiest marinas, and is one of the main bases from which sailing yachts and wooden gulets can be chartered for Blue Cruises.

**GETTING HERE AND AROUND**

A series of color-coded minibuses run from the center of town for about $1; light green goes to the bus station, orange to İçmeler, and pink to the Pupa Hotel and the "yacht marina." A 60-minute catamaran service to the Greek island of **Rhodes** leaves Marmaris harbor every day at 9 am, returning at 4 pm, with a single or day return ticket costing $50. It's worth considering spending the night in Rhodes, since Greek island life typically grinds to a halt during the midday hours.

**ESSENTIALS**

**Marmaris Tourist office** ⊠ İskele Meyd. 2, by marina ☎ 252/412–1035 🖷 252/412–7277.

## WHERE TO EAT AND STAY

Some city blocks in Marmaris appear to be made up entirely of restaurants with a pavement-to-pavement profusion of tables and menus that seem like a catalog of world food. The most striking views can be had from café tables where the seafront promenade curves into the bay around the citadel, and these attract the tourists. The locals, however, prefer the slightly better-prepared food in restaurants that look out onto the Netsel yacht marina just to the east.

*For expanded hotel reviews, visit Fodors.com.*

$   ✕ **Pineapple.** This restaurant in the Netsel marina has a lot more style
ITALIAN   and dignity than you would guess from the name, and it's a great escape
★   from the mass tourism of Marmaris. The menu is eclectic but mainly Italian-theme. The house specialty is tender Anatolian oven-cooked lamb, but the chef also prepares pasta, pizza, steak, and Turkish grills. Their desserts are also famous. Above Pineapple is its sister restaurant, My Marina English Pub, which has quite nice views from its balcony. ⊠ *Netsel Marina* ☎ *252/412–0976.*

$   ✕ **Yat Marina Restaurant.** Far from Marmaris's madding crowds, this is
TURKISH   where to catch a flavor of the life of international yacht folk. The chefs don't go in for the omnibus menus common in town, preferring to concentrate their considerable talents on getting favorite Turkish dishes just right. There is also pasta, steak, and, not surprisingly, a lot of seafood. It's fun to walk around the busy marina where huge rigs pull millionaires' luxury motor cruisers from the water as European pensioners scrub the hulls of their much smaller "pocket" yachts. ⊠ *Follow coast road 8 km (5 mi) east out of Marmaris and park outside marina gate* ☎ *252/422–0022.*

$$$   ⊞ **Maritim Hotel Grand Azur.** This international resort is one of the few places with any real architectural style in Marmaris and its sleek, curving profile overlooks lush tropical gardens. **Pros:** nice private beach area. **Cons:** average rooms for the money. ⊠ *Kenan Evren Bulv. 13* ☎ *252/417–4050* ⊕ *www.hotelgrandazur.com* ⤳ *257 rooms, 30 suites* ⬦ *In-room: Internet, Wi-Fi. In-hotel: restaurant, bar, pool, tennis court, gym, beach, water sports* ⦿ *Some meals.*

$   ⊞ **Pupa Yacht Hotel.** This clean, simple hotel east of Marmaris is one of the rare establishments left in Turkey that is peaceful and right on its own little beach. **Pros:** room views any five-star hotel would kill for. **Cons:** rather basic rooms. ⊠ *Follow coast road east of Marmaris for 5 mi, and watch for PUPA YAT signs* ☎ *252/413–3566* ⊕ *www.pupa. com.tr* ⤳ *19 rooms* ⬦ *In-room: Wi-Fi. In-hotel: restaurant, bar, beach, business center* ⦿ *Breakfast.*

### NIGHTLIFE

Marmaris comes alive at night with a wide selection of bars and dance clubs. European charter tourists display the art of serious drinking on **Bar Street** in the old town and its four solid blocks of drinking establishments. The major clubs here offer seething dance floors, and it's generally an opportunity for excess.

**Back Street Garden Bar.** The largest open-air club on Bar Street is Back Street Garden Bar. ⊠ *Marmaris Bar Street, Old Town* ☎ *252/412–4048.*

CLOSE UP

# Blue Cruising

The most charming way to visit the Turquoise Riviera, or the Aegean coast, is on a Blue Cruise, on a *gulet*—a wooden motor yacht or sailboat. Time has done remarkably little to spoil the crystal clear waters, pine-clad inlets, and limpid lagoons. This will be one of the most unforgettable holidays you've ever had, but there is some organization necessary.

How much will it cost? *Gulets* come in all shapes and sizes, the majority with between 4 and 12 two-person cabins. To hire your own boat, prices work out to between $80 to $150 per person per day in July and August, about half that in April or October. Most charter on terms that cover all but food and drink. After a discussion with the boat's cook, you and a member of the crew go to the local supermarket and load up. Cabin charters—when you join a group of strangers—are generally on an all-inclusive basis, and start at about $300 per week.

When to go? May is pretty, uncrowded, and charters are cheap, but the water is cooler. June is warm and still not too busy. July and August are hotter, busier, and more expensive. September and early October are often perfect at sea, but the mountainsides are less green.

Other things to consider are how long you have and which port is closest to the sites you want to see. Fethiye is a major jumping-off point, as are Bodrum, Marmaris, and Göcek. Ideally, two weeks are needed to see the whole coast from Bodrum to Antalya, but most travelers only have a week.

Look for a boat with a large area for relaxing in the stern and a good flat space on the foredeck for sleeping outside in hot weather. Don't accept anything too squashed: eight cabins in a boat under 80 feet is too much. If you're out in July and August, look for air-conditioning—and enough power-generation capacity for it. Ask about extras like a windsurfer or kayaks.

The captain is important, too. Make sure you can communicate, and if you're arranging the cruise from abroad, insist on a telephone conversation before sending your deposit. Look for someone who listens to your wishes, and be wary if you are met with a patronizing "leave-it-all-to-me" attitude. If you want to sail rather than motor, you need to be doubly sure you have the right vessel. When you get to the boat, check the captain's license, insist on seeing life vests, and test emergency equipment like radios.

If you're hiring a boat after you've arrived in Turkey, you can walk down the quayside and haggle, but this can be risky in high season. Most people book months ahead. Look for operators registered with both the Turkish Association of Travel Agencies (TURSAB) and the Chamber of Shipping.

On the Internet there are sites for individual boats, and large agencies operating from major ports. For Marmaris, try ⊕ www.yesilmarmaris. com. Fethiye is popular, with ⊕ www. albatrosyachting.com, ⊕ www. bethereyachting.com, ⊕ www. compassyachting.com, ⊕ www. fethiyeyachting.com, or ⊕ www. alestayachting.com. Antalya is served by ⊕ www.olymposyachting.com.

**Malibu Beach.** The party goes on farther west, toward İçmeler, at the restaurant-bar Malibu Beach. ✉ *Uzunyalı 248 Sokak 9* ☎ *252/ 412–6778.*

At İçmeler Beach itself are dance clubs and karaoke bars with raucous crowds partying into the night.

**Marmaris Palace Beach Club.** For a more upmarket scene, try the Marmaris Palace Beach Club, out on a jetty between Marmaris and İçmeler. It has a restaurant and DJs offering a medley of house, chill-out, and trance music. ✉ *Marmaris Palace Hotel, Pamucak Mevkii, İçmeler* ☎ *252/455–5555.*

> ### FRANKINCENSE
>
> The area around Marmaris is known for its frankincense forests. On the water's edge, between the city and the Pupa Yacht Hotel, is a lovely national park. In Marmaris market you can buy the frankincense, which is the dried sap of the trees. As incense it's known to be quite soothing.

# THE LYCIAN COAST

Lycia is the heart of the Turquoise Coast. The rugged landscape dotted with pine forests and olive groves contrasts with stunning blue sea. While it's certainly not undiscovered territory, the lack of airports has limited development; you'll find charming port cities, unique hotels, and uncrowded beaches. The ancient Lycians had their own distinct culture and the coast holds some of Turkey's most fascinating ancient ruins: Xanthos, Pinara, Patara, Olympos, and Phaselis. This is also wonderful hiking terrain, and Lycia is the home to the 500-km (310-mi) Lycian Way, a trail that includes many good day hikes. There are many other adventures to be found in the region—paragliding from Ölüdeniz's 6,800-foot high Babadağ, kayaking around the sunken city of Kekova, and diving off Kaş. And seafood lovers will find plenty of fresh-off-the-boat treats.

## DALYAN

*25 km (16 mi) west of Dalaman Airport on Rte. 400 and local roads (follow signs).*

Dalyan is about 6 km (10 mi) southwest of the highway, and there are regular minibuses to the nearby town of Ortaca.

Dalyan is a lovely place for a three-day break, especially for those who prefer a quiet vacation in an environment that's been developed in a way that is sensitive to the natural surroundings and the native flora and fauna. The city is on the winding, reed-flanked banks of the Dalyan River, between the great expanse of Lake Köyeceğiz and the lovely beach of İstuzu. The town is known for its Carian tombs, which are carved into the cliff that rises behind the 15-foot high reeds fringing the undeveloped west bank of the river—an especially fine sight when floodlit at night. Boats lined up along the quayside in the center of town—they're all part of the Dalyan Kooperatifi and fares are regulated; there is no bargaining unless there are many idle boats—will take you on

The
Lycian Coast

Antalya
see detail
map

KEY

Beaches

Ferry Lines

expeditions to the beach, to sulfur baths, on explorations of the lake, to the ruins of the ancient city of Kaunos, and to the pretty bay of Ekincik. If your hotel is on the river, the boatmen will pick you up from there, too. Trekking and footpaths are developing fast, and include walks to Ekincik and elsewhere. Birdwatchers love the lake, where 180 species of bird have been logged. Local markets are also colorful: there's one in Dalyan on Saturday and one at the local center of Ortaca on Friday.

## EXPLORING

**İztuzu Beach.** The unspoiled sands of İztuzu Beach stretch for 8 km (5 mi), with the Mediterranean on one side and a freshwater lagoon on the other. In June and July *Caretta caretta* sea turtles lay their eggs here. This is a conservation area, and signs along the beach mark possible nesting places and warn you not to stick umbrellas in the sand or behave in other ways that could disturb the turtles. There are regular boats and minibuses from Dalyan for $5.

**Kaunos.** The ancient ruins at Kaunos can be reached in about 15 to 30 minutes by boat from Dalyan, or find the *geçit*, a rowboat crossing, then walk south for 30 minutes. Up from the port is the agora, or market place, with a restored fountain house and a ruined portico dotted with the foundation of statues. Up the hill, past the nice temple terrace, is a crumbling Byzantine basilica, a massive Roman bath restored as a site museum, and a well-preserved semicircular theater cut into the hillside in the Greek style. Most of the remains date from the 4th century BC, and reflect a blend of Carian and Lycian influences. From the ruins there is a pretty clifftop walk to Ekincik, which takes three to four hours with the possibility of returning by boat. ⌘ $5.

## WHERE TO EAT AND STAY

*For expanded hotel reviews, visit Fodors.com.*

$ ✕ **Dalyan La Vie.** This pleasant open-air restaurant, which occupies a
TURKISH prime spot on the river, opposite the tombs, is the most upmarket in
★ town. There's a wide selection of appetizers, then a fairly standard array of mains, with lots of seafood as well as steak, chicken, and pasta. Though not as gourmet as it aspires to be, the food is a definite step up from the kebab places that line the main street. ⊠ *Sağlık Cad., Maraş District. Follow Dalyan River bankside walkway 500 meters south from main square* ☏ *252/284–3166.*

$ ⊡ **Asur Hotel.** With a large swimming pool and gardens overlooking the Dalyan River, this one-story property is a good, less-expensive option. **Pros:** friendly service; good value. **Cons:** a bit far from town. ☏ *252/284–3232* ⊕ *www.asurotel.com* ⌁ *34 rooms, 10 suites* ⚲ *In-room: Wi-Fi. In-hotel: restaurant, bar, pool, gym* ⊘ *Closed Oct.–May* ⫿⊙⫿ *Breakfast.*

¢ ⊡ **Beyaz Gül.** This curious hotel is run by an old-fashioned Turkish
⟳ lady, and staying here is like living in a fairy-tale cottage. **Pros:** not your average hotel. **Cons:** the outdoor grounds are dominated by the restaurant. ⊠ *Balikhane Cad. 92/93, Maraş* ☏ *252/284–2304* ⊕ *www. beyazgul.info* ⌁ *4 rooms* ⚲ *In-room: Wi-Fi. In-hotel: restaurant, bar* ▭ *No credit cards.*

$$ ⊡ **Dalyan Resort.** This beautifully built hotel opened in 2005 on a bend
★ in the Dalyan River. **Pros:** nice pool area. **Cons:** upscale, but not a lot of character. ⊠ *Kaunos Cad. 50, Maraş, Dalyan—drive south along river from Dalyan town square and follow the many signs* ☏ *252/284–5499* ⊕ *www.dalyanresort.com* ⌁ *42 rooms, 2 suites* ⚲ *In-room: Wi-Fi. In-hotel: restaurant, bar, pool, spa* ⫿⊙⫿ *Breakfast.*

¢ ⊡ **Happy Caretta.** This small hotel is in a shady garden on the banks of
Fodor'sChoice the Dalyan River opposite the Kaunos tombs. **Pros:** beautiful riverside
★ gardens; friendly service; altogether lovely. **Cons:** a bit hard to find. ⊠ *Kaunos Cad. 26, Maraş District; drive south down Dalyan River and look for signs to right* ☏ *252/284–2109* ⊕ *www.happycaretta. com* ⌁ *10 rooms, 4 suites* ⚲ *In-room: Wi-Fi. In-hotel: restaurant, bar* ⫿⊙⫿ *Breakfast.*

# GÖCEK

*22 km (14 mi) east of Dalaman Airport on Rte. 400.*

For the visitor who wants a taste of the grandeur of the Turquoise Riviera, but has little time to spare, Göcek is perfect. The tranquil yachting resort town is a 20-minute drive over the mountains from Dalaman Airport, enjoys gorgeous vistas of sea and mountains, has easy access to the sea, and offers good, upmarket places to eat, sleep, and shop. It has avoided the excesses of package tourism and overdevelopment, and is focused on its pleasant, carless waterfront. Three marinas and an annual regatta make this a major center for Turkey's yachting world, and weekends see it awash with Istanbul *sosyete* (essentially the rich, frequently spoiled, and occasionally glamorous children of the upper classes) on parade. From Göcek, an hour's drive reaches the natural beauties of Dalyan, the sights around Fethiye/Ölüdeniz, or great Lycian sites like Tlos and Xanthos. There is only one private beach in Göcek itself, so hop on one of the several wooden tour boats that head out each morning to explore elsewhere.

The best swimming and snorkeling are around the beaches or in the coves of the **Twelve Islands,** strung out like a necklace across the mouth of the bay.

Göcek is in prime Blue Cruise territory, so you can join a day cruise or rent a yacht or a *gulet* for as much time and money as you have to spare. The most popular anchorages include Tersane, Kapı Creek, Cleopatra's Bay, the obscure ruins at Lydae, Tomb Bay, or the lovely island of Katrancı.

### GETTING HERE AND AROUND
The main highway passes immediately behind the town with exits to the east and west.

### EXPLORING
**Sundowner Beach.** The Sundowner Beach, run privately by Swissotel at the eastern end of Port Göcek marina, is one of the most spectacular—and expensive—on the Turquoise Riviera. It costs $20 for nonguests. For some this is a small price to pay for an excellently maintained beach and bar establishment, and a completely unspoiled, wraparound view of the bay and mountains. The beach is open 10 am to 6 pm, later if anyone wants to stay; the bar is open in the evening and dinner is served after 7 pm. ☎ *252/645–2760.*

### WHERE TO EAT AND STAY
*For expanded hotel reviews, visit Fodors.com.*

$     ✕ **Can.** This busy harborside fish restaurant is popular with Göcek
TURKISH  natives because the large interior space is open all year-round—and wireless Internet access is free. Though it moved into a new building in 2011, the restaurant has been around for more than 15 years and is a town institution. In summer, the seating extends out toward the waterfront, under broad tropical trees. Specialties are typical, like fish baked in salt, but the pride of the menu is its selection of 30 starters including tuna with onion sauce and cheese, served with arugula salad. The homemade bread is delicious, and wild mountain mushrooms are served as a side dish in spring and fall. ⊠ *Western edge of municipal harbor* ☎ *252/645–1507.*

$     ✕ **Özcan.** Cushioned bamboo chairs, attentive waitstaff, and possibly
SEAFOOD  the best grilled octopus you've ever tasted await you at Özcan, a fish
★    restaurant on the wide esplanade that makes up Göcek's main public harborside. The wide range of starters includes unusual mushrooms from the mountains out back, fresh seaweed dishes, and squid in garlic, oil, and lemon. The menu is predominately seafood but there are also

Sea kayaking around the Göcek Islands.

excellent kebabs and local lamb dishes. ⊠ *Middle of municipal yacht harbor.* ☎ *252/645–2593.*

$$$  🏨 **The Bay Beach Club.** This pretty hotel, made up of wooden cabins under the chestnut trees, opened in 2008. **Pros:** gorgeous waterfront family cabins. **Cons:** isolated. ⊠ *At Gunlüklü Beach, take the right-hand road* ☎ *252/633–6310* ⊕ *www.thebaybeachclub.com* 🛏 *47 cabins* ⌂ *In-room: Wi-Fi. In-hotel: restaurant, bar, pool, spa, beach, water sports* ⊘ *Closed Nov.–Mar.*

$  🏨 **Hotel Forest Gate.** This quiet cluster of white two-story villas sur-
★  rounded by pine trees has generous rooms organized around a pool shaded by a great carob tree, and a friendly atmosphere. **Pros:** nice pool area. **Cons:** out of the way; some rooms are just average. ⊠ *From main road, turn into Göcek at gas station at entrance of town and follow signs east* ☎ *252/645–2629* ⊕ *www.hotelforestgate.com* 🛏 *14 rooms, 9 suites* ⌂ *In-room: Wi-Fi. In-hotel: restaurant, bar, pool* ⧖ *Breakfast.*

$$$  🏨 **The Swissôtel Göcek Marina and Resort.** The Swissotel has all the lux-
ury and excellent service you'd expect from an international chain. **Pros:** professional and a stylish beach area. **Cons:** rooms are pleas-
ant but unexceptional with ordinary views. ⊠ *Cumhuriyet District, Göcek* ☎ *252/645–2760* ⊕ *www.gocek.swissotel.com* 🛏 *53 rooms* ⌂ *In-room: Wi-Fi. In-hotel: restaurant, pool, gym, spa* ⊘ *Nov.–mid-
Apr.* ⧖ *Breakfast.*

$  🏨 **Villa Danlin.** On Göcek's main shopping street, this is a good small hotel with rooms shielded from most noise. **Pros:** central. **Cons:** rooms nothing special, you're paying for location. ⊠ *Çarşı İçi* ☎ *252/645–
1521* ⊕ *www.villadanlin.com* 🛏 *13 rooms* ⌂ *In-room: a/c, Wi-Fi. In-
hotel: pool, laundry facilities* ⊘ *May–Oct.* ⧖ *Breakfast.*

$ 🏨 **Yonca Resort.** This small and friendly place is not really a resort—it's more like a family-run pension. **Pros:** friendly. **Cons:** tricky to find. ✉ *Gonca Sokak 7* ☎ *252/645–2255* 🔑 *6 rooms, 2 suites* ⚐ *In-room: Wi-Fi. In-hotel: restaurant, bar, pool.*

**EN ROUTE**

**Gunlüklü Beach.** If you get overheated on the main road between Göcek and Fethiye, and need an antidote to the relentless fashionability of Göcek, follow the brown sign south to Gunlüklü Beach. It's a good place to stop for a picnic in a forest of small chestnut trees or to take a swim from a dark-sand beach in the unspoiled bay. In season, a shop down by the beach sells basic food. Be forewarned, though: the beach tends to get crowded on weekends with Turkish day-trippers from Fethiye, and the facilities can be a bit rough and ready. The sand is darker than at other Turkish beaches. ✉ *About 10 km (6 mi) from Göcek, 17 km (11 mi) from Fethiye* 🚗 *$4 per car.*

## FETHIYE

*50 km (31 mi) east of Dalaman Airport on Rte. 400.*

This busy port town is a good base for exploring the ruins of ancient Lycia in the mountains that rise to the east. Fethiye was known in antiquity as Telmessus (not to be confused with Termessos, near Antalya), and was the principal port of Lycia from the Roman period onward. In front of the town hall is one of the finest of several tombs found throughout the city: this one represents a two-story Lycian house, with reliefs of warriors on both sides of its lid.

The small original town was once called Mekri and populated mainly by Greeks before the Greek-Turkish population exchange in 1924. It was renamed in 1934, after an Ottoman pilot called Fethi Bey. He was killed when he crashed in the mountains of Lebanon while attempting a historic flight that was to link all the Middle Eastern provinces of the Ottoman Empire on the eve of the First World War in 1914. Today's town is quite modern, having been substantially rebuilt after an earthquake in 1957. Strolling along the seafront promenade is a pleasant evening outing, and scuba-diving enthusiasts can choose between half a dozen dive boats that collect in the harbor. The town is most fun on Tuesday, when village folk flock into Fethiye for the weekly market. The harbor has many yachts available for Blue Cruising.

### GETTING HERE AND AROUND

Fethiye's modern bus station is 1 km (½ mi) east of the center. Buses running east and west along the coast depart regularly, and several a day cross the mountains for Denizli and Pamukkale. Minibuses to Ölüdeniz, Göcek and other nearby destinations leave from Akdeniz Caddesi, a few blocks west of the center.

### ESSENTIALS

**Official Tourist Office Fethiye** ✉ *İskele Karşısı 1* ☎ *252/614–1527.*

*Continued on page 285*

# MEZE: MOUTHWATERING MORSELS

Prepare your taste buds for a Turkish culinary experience: tangy yogurt, pungent garlic, fresh herbs, smoky eggplant, marinated salads, and roasted vegetables await.

Whether you're sitting down for dinner along Turkey's coast, in one of Istanbul's historic neighborhoods, or somewhere in the untouristed southeast, your meal will almost certainly begin with meze—the assortment of small dishes that are the heart and soul of Turkish cuisine. Similar to the idea of tapas, meze are more than just a quick snack or an appetizer. For Turks, eating meze is often a meal in itself—a languorous repast made up of countless small plates and an ample supply of rakı, the anise-flavored liquor that is Turkey's national drink and the preferred accompaniment to meze.

Dolma

Eating meze is a centuries-old national tradition, influenced by Persian, Arab, and Greek cooking, and you'll find regional differences in what's offered. Dishes in the country's southeast have more of a Middle Eastern influence, while those in Istanbul and the Aegean area have more of a Greek flavor. What they have in common, though, is the Turkish belief that the meze experience is about more than eating and drinking—freewheeling conversation is an essential component. As one famous Turkish saying goes: "The best meze is good table talk."

# WHAT'S ON THE MEZE MENU

A typical meze menu includes dozens of mostly meatless dishes, hot and cold, emphasizing freshness and seasonality. In Istanbul's *meyhanes*— rollicking, tavern-like restaurants that specialize in meze—servers arrive at your table with large trays piled high with small dishes. You choose whatever catches your eye.

Left: Octopus salad. Right: A variety of Turkish salads.

## TASTES TO EXPECT

When it comes to meze, Turks tend to have a conservative palate. Meze meals, for example, often start with the simplest but most traditional dish of all—a piece of tangy feta cheese accompanied by a slice of sweet honeydew melon and a glass of rakı. Meze restaurants (with some notable exceptions) are not trying to outdo one another by inventing ever more creative dishes. Rather, they stick with tried and true meze that have become the classics of Turkish cooking. Here are some of the traditional meze you should be on the lookout for:

## COLD (SOĞUK) MEZE

**BAKLA EZMES** —Dried fava beans that are cooked, mashed with garlic, olive oil, dill, and lemon juice, and turned into an earthy pâté.

**BARBUNYA PİLAKİ**—*Barbunya* beans (Roman or red beans), usually fresh from the pod, stewed in a garlicky tomato sauce.

**ÇERKEZ TAVUĞU**—A highlight of classical Turkish cooking, this dish consists of poached chicken that is ground with garlic and walnuts to make a deliciously enticing and flavorful dip.

**DENİZ BÖRÜLCESİ**—A wonderfully fresh-tasting dish made of samphire, a crunchy green that grows by the sea. It's cooked in olive oil and flavored with lemon juice.

**ENGİNAR**—Artichoke hearts stewed in olive oil with onion and carrot, served cold.

**EZME**—A salad of finely chopped tomatoes and onion, sometimes flavored with pleasantly astringent pomegranate molasses.

**HAYDARİ**—A dip made of thick and creamy strained yogurt, flavored with garlic and dill.

**İMAM BAYILDI**—Literally meaning "the imam swooned," this dish is one of Turkey's most famous: an eggplant is stuffed with onion, garlic, parsley, and tomato and stewed in olive oil.

**KISIR**—The Turkish version of tabbouleh, this is a tangy and somewhat spicy salad made out of bulgur wheat and red pepper paste.

**LAKERDA**—Turkey's take on lox, this is cured mackerel, sliced thick.

**MİDYE DOLMASI**—An Istanbul favorite sold by street vendors: mussels cooked with rice, pine nuts, currants, herbs, and spices and stuffed back into their shell.

**PATLICAN SALATASI**—An eggplant salad or dip, of which there are many variations (see the "Ubiquitous Eggplant" sidebar).

**SEMİZOTU**—When in season, purslane (a variety of green similar to watercress that's rich in vitamins and Omega-3 fatty acids) is mixed with yogurt to make a tangy salad.

**YAPRAK SARMA**—Grape leaves stuffed with rice, currants, and pine nuts.

**ZEYTİNYAĞLI**—Vegetables such as green beans and artichoke hearts that are stewed in olive oil and served cool or at room temperature. (*Zeytinyağı*, pronounced "zey-teen-yah," is the Turkish name for the oil.)

*Kabaklı börek* (filo pastries with zucchini).

## THE UBIQUITOUS EGGPLANT

According to Turkish culinary lore, there are more than a thousand ways to cook eggplant (*patlican* in Turkish, pronounced "patli-jahn"). That may be an exaggeration, but you could certainly lose count of how many dishes feature the humble nightshade—it's even made into a jam! The vegetable certainly plays a starring role on the meze tray: cubes of fried eggplant come covered in a yogurt and tomato sauce; charcoal-roasted eggplant is turned into a smoky puree; and sun-dried eggplants are served stuffed with rice and herbs.

### HOT (SICAK) MEZE

**ARNAVUT C ĞER**—Cubes of lamb's liver, fried with red pepper flakes.

**BÖREK**—Filo pastries, sometimes rolled up like cigars and stuffed with cheese, or layered over *pastırma*, which is spicy cured beef.

**DOLMA OR SARMA**—Stuffed grape leaves and other vegetables, such as peppers or cabbage, that are filled with a combination of rice, herbs, spices, and sometimes ground meat.

**KALAMAR**—Calamari rings batter-fried and served with an addictive sauce made of ground walnuts and garlic known as *tarator*.

**KARİDES**—Shrimp in a butter or tomato sauce, usually baked in a terra-cotta dish.

**MÜCVER**—Zucchini and herb fritters.

**PAZI SARMA**—Swiss chard stuffed with ground meat and rice, with yogurt on the side.

# HELPFUL WORDS TO KNOW

Eating out in Istanbul is often a festive experience.

Being confronted with a tray filled with dozens of little dishes can be daunting, but knowing a few key words will help you navigate the meze maze. Of course, there's nothing wrong with pointing at any mysterious meze and giving your waiter an inquisitive look—most will know a few words in English to help you along. Also remember, there is no need to order everything at once. You can order a few, then call your waiter back when you're ready for more.

**ACILI**—means "spicy."

**ACISIZ**–literally "not spicy."

**DOMATES**–tomato.

**ET**–meat: *kuzu* is lamb, *dana* is beef, *tavuk* is chicken; you'll rarely see pork, *domuz*, on menus.

**IZGARA**–grilled.

**KIZARTMA**–fried.

**PEYNİR**–cheese; *beyaz peynir* is feta cheese, *kaşar peynir* is a semi-soft yellow cheese.

**SALATALIK**–cucumber.

**SARIMSAK**–garlic; a dish with garlic in it is called *sarımsaklı*.

**SOĞAN**–onion; a dish with onions on top is called *soğanlı*.

Kısır

## AND TO DRINK?

Although wine and beer are gaining in popularity, anise-flavored rakı (similar to Greek ouzo or French pastis) is still the undisputed top choice for a drink to accompany meze. For years, the dependable Yeni Rakı brand was pretty much the only choice available, although new brands are now becoming popular. Rakı made by the brand Efe is worth seeking out.

Drinking rakı, like eating meze, has its own rituals. It's rarely drunk straight because it's so potent: 80 proof or higher. Typically, a shot of rakı is mixed with water, turning the drink a milky white. Most rakı drinkers also add ice. Even when diluted, rakı can be pretty strong, though fans say it goes down smooth with a slight sweetness. They also maintain that a good rakı buzz is conducive to entertaining conversation.

## EXPLORING

**Castle.** Along the crest of the hill overlooking the old town are the battlements of a castle, whose foundations date back to antiquity and were later built up by the 12th-century crusader Knights of St. John and the Ottoman Empire.

**Fethiye Museum** (*Fethiye Müzesi*). Fethiye has a relatively small but modern museum with an excellent collection of artifacts from nearby sites. There is some good scultpture, mostly from Tlos and the Fethiye theater. You'll also find the Letoon trilingual stela here—it's a stone slab with Greek, Lycian, and Aramaic inscriptions—and the mosaic from the Temple of Apollo. There are many finds from Caunus, Tlos, and Xanthos, and a series of altars and stelae dedicated to the gods in thanks. There's also some jewelry, an interesting golden bowl with figures of bulls, and a 19th-century Greek ship's figurehead. ⊠ *Off Atatürk Cad. (look for signs)* ⊠ *$3* ☉ *Tues.–Sun. 8:30–5.*

**Hammam.** The 16th-century hammam is still in use. Though it's a bit touristy, it's full of atmosphere, with 14 domes and 6 arches. It's a fine way to scrub off the barnacles after a long voyage. ⊠ *Hamam Cad., close to main harbor square* ☎ *252/614–9318* ⊕ *www.oldturkishbath.com.*

**Rock tombs.** Impressive ancient Lycian rock tombs are carved into the cliff that looms above town. The largest is the **Tomb of Amyntas,** presumably the burial place of a 4th-century-BC ruler or nobleman. Inside are the slabs where corpses were laid out. To reach the tombs, you'll have to climb many steps—the stairway starts at Kaya Caddesi, near the local bus station—but your effort will be well rewarded, particularly at dusk, when the cliffs take on a reddish glow. ⊠ *$2.*

**Theater.** The main road around the central harbor square of Fethiye also runs past the stage of the antique theater of Telmessus, a recent chance rediscovery that gives a sense of history to the modern buildings all around. The rest of the ancient town remains under its urban tomb.

**OFF THE BEATEN PATH**

**Kadyanda.** The ruins of ancient Kadyanda, on a remote shady ridgetop at more than 3,000 feet, a short drive north of Fethiye, are a pleasant trip in the heat of summer. You enter past some tombs to a large agora, or marketplace, behind which is the well-preserved running track and a collapsed temple. Heading back down the trail, you'll pass a large Roman theater. Watch out for the frequent large holes left by treasure hunters. The site is uphill from the mountain village of Üzümlü, which has some old houses. ⊠ *From Fethiye, take road north toward Göcek and look for turnoff for Üzümlü, continue through village looking for signs for Kadyanda* ⊠ *$5.*

### WHERE TO EAT AND STAY

*For expanded hotel reviews, visit Fodors.com.*

$

SEAFOOD

✕ **Fethiye Fish Market.** Fethiye's local market area includes several casual restaurants where you can buy your own fish and have it cooked for you, adding drinks, *mezes,* and salads. Inside the market are the lively **Recep's Place** and **Hilmi;** outside on 97 Sokak is the **Şamdan** restaurant, which has a wider menu. ⊠ *Just west of main market area, between Hükümet, Belediye, 96 and 97 streets.*

**$** ✕**Meğri Lokanta.** The Meğris pretty much rule the restaurant market
TURKISH  in Fethiye, but it's a well-deserved hierarchy, at least for now, as their
food is quite consistently the best in town. This excellent, straightforward Turkish meat restaurant is on the western edge of the bazaar
and much favored by local inhabitants. ⊠ *Western edge of the bazaar*
☎ *252/614–4047.*

**$$** ✕**Meğri Restaurant.** In the center of the bazaar the permanent part of this
ECLECTIC  restaurant has stone walls, high wood ceilings, and decorative kilims.
In summer, most of the large upscale restaurant spills out into a large
courtyard in the middle of the bazaar. A vast menu mixes dishes from
Asia, France, Turkey, and the Mediterranean. Portions are large and the
food is quite good. ⊠ *Eski Cami Geçidi Likya Sokak 8–9* ☎ *252/614–
4046* 🖷 *252/612–0446.*

**$$** ✕**MOD Yacht Lounge.** This glass-fronted, pleasingly modern café-restau-
INTERNATIONAL  rant on the harbor-front walkway has a chill-out nautical atmosphere
and the tables are moved out to the deck under the trees in summer. The
menu is modern and international, with pasta, seafood, and Turkish
grills. With an unimpeded view of the harbor and bay, it's also a great
place just to stop in for an evening drink. ⊠ *Ece Marina, Karagözler*
☎ *252/614–3970.*

**$$$** 🏨**Ece Saray.** Modeled on the grand hotels of the French Riviera, this is
an excellent luxury hotel in a lovely location on the harborfront. **Pros:**
quality accommodations, with lots of extras. **Cons:** sea but no beach.
⊠ *Ece Marina, Karagözler* ☎ *252/612–5005* ⊕ *www.ecesaray.net* ⤴ *34
rooms, 14 suites* ⚭ *In-room: Wi-Fi. In-hotel: restaurant, bar, pool, gym,
spa* ⦿| *Breakfast.*

**$$** 🏨**Yacht Plaza.** This fine medium-size hotel directly on the seafront has
its own yacht jetty, waterside bar, and pool. **Pros:** nice waterfront pool
area. **Cons:** back rooms have no view and traffic noise. ⊠ *Karagöller,
just east of Ece Marinapro* ☎ *252/612–5067* ⊕ *www.yachtplazahotel.
com* ⤴ *31 rooms* ⚭ *In-room: Wi-Fi. In-hotel: restaurant, bar, pool*
⊟ *No credit cards* ⦿| *Breakfast.*

## NIGHTLIFE

On weekends there are clubs off Hamam Caddesi in the center of
Fethiye. **Mango Bar,** a small indoor dance club with live Turkish music
some nights, is a reliable favorite.

Outside town there is a strip of cheaper, less appealing hotels along Çalış
Beach that stretches west of town—this is where the package tours from
northern Europe tend to stay and there are plenty of bars. It's a long
way to go for a drink if you're staying in town, but the scene has an
appeal for the younger crowd. During the week, nightclubs are busiest
in Hisarönü, between Fethiye and Ölüdeniz.

## SPORTS AND THE OUTDOORS

**Boat tours.** You can take one of the boats or water taxis in Fethiye's
harbors on a variety of boat tours, some including meals, to Göcek,
the Twelve Islands, or Ölüdeniz. Itineraries are posted, and there are
people on hand to answer questions. Be sure to shop around, as packages vary widely, and some tours are essentially booze cruises. Costs
range around $20 to $30 per person. If Ölüdeniz is your destination,

be aware that windy weather can make for heavy waves. Most tours leave about 10 am, returning about 6 pm.

# ÖLÜDENIZ

*60 km (38 mi) east of Dalaman Airport.*

Ölüdeniz (it means "dead sea") is one of Turkey's great natural wonders, an azure lagoon rimmed by beaches of white sand. The area, the picture-perfect scene most often featured in Turkish tourism promotion posters, can be reached by day cruise from Fethiye or other ports by car or dolmuş. One inland route is through Ovacýk (it's the shorter option if you're coming from outside Fethiye) but a prettier one leads past the ruined town of Kaya, climbing steeply from a point 1 km (½ mi) west of the harbor. The town itself is a bland package-tourist town, but the position and the natural park beach are stunning.

### GETTING HERE AND AROUND

Ölüdeniz is 8 km (5 mi) from Fethiye, via Hisarönü and Ovacýk. Head south from Fethiye's central bus station intersection onto Ölüdeniz Caddesi. Once you reach the shore, turn right for the National Park beach.

### EXPLORING

The water of Ölüdeniz is warm and the setting delightful, even with the crowds. The view is even more splendid from the air, and this is one of Turkey's premier locations for paragliding. Travel agencies in town will organize Jeep safaris into the high mountain pastures and villages in the mountains all around for about $40 for the day, with lunch.

**Ölüdeniz Natural Park.** If you want to bathe at the iconic sandbar that lies across the mouth of the lagoon, then you must enter Ölüdeniz Natural Park—go down to the seafront, turn west, then left at the fork where you can see the toll booth ($7 per car or $3 per person on foot). There's a capacious car park, but even from here, it can be a hot trek of several hundred yards. The crowds love it here, and the setting is absolutely beautiful, but the beach is still just a beach. Lounge chairs ($3) and umbrellas ($3) can be rented, and there are changing rooms, toilets, and a modest snack bar. Just around the corner a concession rents out paddleboats and kayaks for $11 to $13 per hour. The sea gets deep quickly and there several diving platforms anchored a short swim out.

Another sand beach can be found behind the park in the shallow, warm waters of the lagoon; this one is popular with families. Although theoretically public property, in practice this beach is run by the campsites and restaurants that line the shore. Use of their facilities, however, is unlikely to be much more expensive than those in the park itself.

The Lycian Way starts in the hills above Ölüdeniz, and one of its most pleasant sections is the three- to five-day walk to Patara.

### WHERE TO EAT AND STAY

*For expanded hotel reviews, visit Fodors.com.*

**$$**
**INTERNATIONAL**
✕ **Oyster Restaurant.** The Oyster Residence's restaurant, located at the western edge of the strip of bars and eateries along the beach, probably has the best food and the most style in town. The restaurant is set in

a small garden terrace, cozy, and tranquil despite its proximity to the busy waterfront area. The short menu includes lots of seafood, including swordfish kebabs, as well as steaks and baked lamb. There's lighter fare, like wraps and seafood salads, at lunch. Service can be slow. ⊠ *On water, one block east of main intersection, Ölüdeniz* ☎ *242/617–0765.*

¢ ⬚ **Sugar Beach.** The campsites by the lagoon, such as Sugar Beach, have also sprouted some decent air-conditioned bungalows and there's a nice beachfront bar and restaurant. **Pros:** on the beach; isolated from touristy Ölüdeniz. **Cons:** more focused on day-trippers. ⊠ *Past National Park Beach on left, Ölüdeniz* ☎ *534/414–0949* ⊕ *www. thesugarbeachclub.com* ⬚ *35 bungalows* ⚑ *In-room: Wi-Fi. In-hotel: restaurant, bar, beach.*

For a much more enjoyable experience, try one of the hotel/resorts off the beach, *listed below.*

$$ ⬚ **Meri Hotel.** Built in 1973, this hotel was the first—and last—to be allowed by the government to set up shop on the famed Ölüdeniz lagoon. **Pros:** location, location . . . location. **Cons:** average rooms; stairs. ⊠ *Ölüdeniz, well signposted* ☎ *252/617–0001* ⊕ *www.hotelmeri. com* ⬚ *70 standard rooms, 24 family rooms* ⚑ *In-hotel: restaurant, bar, pool, beach* ⍾ *All meals.*

$$ ⬚ **Montana Pine Resort.** It's not Montana, but it does have a splendid mountain setting, and the Sundowner Bar has a wonderful vista of the sea. **Pros:** professionally run; excellent rooms; many guests return every year. **Cons:** you'll have to walk the last 100 yards because outside vehicles aren't permitted. ⊠ *Ölüdeniz* ☎ *252/616–7108, 252/616–6366* ⊕ *www.montanapine.com* ⬚ *149 rooms, 5 suites* ⚑ *In-hotel: restaurant, bar, pool, gym* ☉ *Closed Nov.–May.*

¢ ⬚ **Ocakköy Holiday Village.** In an abandoned Greek village of stone
★ houses, this 6-acre spread is a delightful retreat. The predominantly English clientele keep coming back for the rural atmosphere and easy access to area sites. Many more of their compatriots, however, are buying apartments and villas that have disfigured the valley below; luckily, the hotel's trees and gardens keep the development at bay. Helpful staff make a stay here pleasurable, and suites have kitchenettes. There is a nice common central area with a pool, Jacuzzi, and restaurants, and a daily shuttle to Ölüdeniz. The hotel can arrange daylong boat excursions. **Pros:** good for families, relaxing, lots of extras. **Cons:** can seem overly resortish. ⊠ *4 km (3 mi) after the end of Fethiye on the Ölüdeniz road, a signpost shows the way at the first turning on the right. Keep right and head for the stone houses higher on the hill, Ocakköy, Fethiye* ☎ *252/616–6156, 252/616–6157* ⊕ *www.ocak-koy.com* ⬚ *8 rooms, 6 studios, 32 cottages* ⚑ *In-room: kitchen, Internet, Wi-Fi. In-hotel: restaurant, bar, pool.*

$$ ⬚ **Oyster Residence.** This elegant boutique hotel, nestled among olive
★ trees just off the beach, is a happy misfit in package-tourist dominated Ölüdeniz. **Pros:** oasis. **Cons:** some evening noise from nearby bars. ⊠ *Belcekiz Mevkii 1. sokak, Ölüdeniz* ☎ *252/617 0765* ⊕ *www. oysterresidences.com/Oyster.aspx* ⬚ *26 rooms* ⚑ *In-room: Wi-Fi. In-hotel: restaurant, bar, pool.*

The azure water of Ölüdeniz Bay is surrounded by white-sand beaches, attracting beachgoers from around the world.

## SPORTS AND THE OUTDOORS

**Ölüdeniz Kooperatif.** A good day out on a boat can be arranged by the skippers of Ölüdeniz Kooperatif, who work out of a kiosk halfway between the main body of hotels and the beach. Between May and November, their 15 boats will take groups out to coves with catchy names like Blue Cave, Butterfly Valley, Aquarium Bay, St. Nicholas Island, Cold Water Spring, Camel Beach, and Turquoise Bay. Trips usually run from 11 am to 6 pm, and cost about $12 per person with lunch (beer and cold drinks extra). It's a great way to see the area but you may find that your fellow passengers are more interested in beer than sightseeing.

PARAGLIDING   The first thing you'll notice in Ölüdeniz is people in the sky; paragliding is a busy industry here and a major spectator sport from the beaches. The launch point is about 1,700 yards up Mt. Baba, some 20 km (13 mi) by forest tracks from Ölüdeniz—the tour operators drive you up from town. Tourists flying tandem (it will cost around $100) with a pilot generally stay up for 30 to 40 minutes before landing gently on the beach. Full training to internationally recognized certificates in solo piloting is available. Most travel agencies can arrange a flight.

**Sky Sports** ✉ *Çarşı Cad.* ☎ *252/617–0511.*

## NIGHTLIFE

Most bars operate only in the season May to October; marquees to look for are **Grand Boozey Bar,** which specializes in satellite TV transmissions of British soccer matches, or **Fez.** On the waterfront you'll find the lively **Help Bar** and **Buzz bar**—these days, after a history of keeping the town awake, they are supposed to close at 1 am.

# KABAK

*15 km (9 mi) south of Ölüdeniz.*

If you like your beaches in deep coves, framed by towering cliffs and pine forests, without a deck chair or beach umbrella in sight, then you'll love Kabak. For years it was one of Turkey's best-kept secrets, attracting hippies and alternative types. These days, accommodations are multiplying, but it's still one of the quieter places along the coast.

## GETTING HERE AND AROUND

Just before the Fethiye road reaches Ölüdeniz, there's a turn to the left—from here it's 25 km (15 mi) to Kabak. There's regular *dolmuş* service from Fethiye via Ölüdeniz via the village of Faralya. The main road does not continue to the beach itself. A section of the Lycian Way starts behind Mama's Kitchen and drops to the beach in about 30 minutes—the less intrepid may find the path rough and steep in patches. Alternatively there is a Jeep *dolmuş* called "Last Stop" (☎ 531/345–7164) that takes passengers down a rough road to the beach. There are two three- to four-hour Lycian Way sections—Hisarönü–Faralya and on to Kabak—which you can do as one long day or two half days, staying in one of the cheap pensions in Faralya.

## WHERE TO EAT AND STAY

*For expanded hotel reviews, visit Fodors.com.*

$$ ⊤ **Olive Garden.** Perched on a terrace just down from the main road,
★ this friendly, family-run place has a million-dollar view. **Pros:** views; fresh and tasty food. **Cons:** no air-conditioning means cabins can get hot during day; walk to beach. ⊠ *Just down from Mamma's Restaurant, Kabak* ☎ *252/642–1083* ☞ *10 cabins* ⌂ *In-room: no a/c, Wi-Fi. In-hotel: restaurant, bar, pool.*

$ ⊤ **Turan Hill Lodge.** The Turan Hill Lodge is the oldest place to stay in Kabak, with a wide range of sleeping options surrounded by gardens. **Pros:** rooms with fans; lush garden. **Cons:** getting your luggage in; tiny pool. ⊠ *Take path down to beach, follow signs left/up as you reach bottom, Kabak* ☎ *252/642–1227* ☞ *17 rooms.*

# KAYA

*5 km (3 mi) east of Fethiye, either from the road west of the harbor or through Ovacık and Hisarönü.*

Atmospheric Kaya is a ruin of a different order from others along the Mediterranean coast. It was a thriving Greek community until 1923, when all the village's residents were sent "home" to Greece following a population-exchange agreement between the two countries. Nowadays it's pretty much a deserted ghost town, overgrown and slowly crumbling, with some Turkish village settlement on the edges.

## GETTING HERE AND AROUND

The easiest way to reach Kaya is to take the Ölüdeniz road as far as Hisarönü, then make a right turn marked 3 km (2mi) for Kaya. There is an alternate route signposted from Fethiye, which will take you directly over the hills, close to the Lycian tombs.

### WHERE TO EAT

$ ✕ **Levissi Garden Wine House and Restaurant.** This fine restaurant is in
ECLECTIC what was once the house of a prosperous Greek merchant. The spe-
★ cialties are steak and the ultratender Lamb Kleftiko, marinated in wine
and slowed cooked in a 400-year-old oven. There is a wine cellar with
more than 10,000 bottles, including a good selection of Turkish wines.
In the heat of summer, you can take refuge in the cool basement. The
restaurant floodlights the abandoned buildings all around at night,
making for a particularly evocative—or spooky, depending on your
take—atmosphere. They provided free transportation to hotels in the
Fethiye–Ölüdeniz area. ✉ *Kayaköy, Fethiye, near western ticket office*
☎ *252/618–0173.*

$ ✕ **Oba Kebab Evi.** In a pleasant, spacious garden a few hundred yards
TURKISH from the main slope of Kaya, this is a traditional Turkish meat restaurant where you order your meat, then cook it yourself on a charcoal
brazier supplied by the establishment. There are basic salads and appetizers to go with the mains. ✉ *Near the center of Kaya, look for the
signposted side street.* ☎ *252/618–0222.*

## GEMILER ISLAND

*8 km (5 mi) southwest of Kaya.*

**Gemiler Beach.** This pretty beach is a quieter option to busy Ölüdeniz.
An amphitheater of mountains encloses an offshore island scattered
with Byzantine remains dating from the 7th to the 9th centuries AD.
Although the island is close, there are no boats from the beach, only the
day cruises from Fethiye or Ölüdeniz. Many buses to Kaya continue on
to the beach in summer, or you can just drive down the road past Kaya
until the end. There is a small restaurant and café above the beach and
a variety of water sports are available.

## TLOS

*22 km (14 mi) east of Fethiye.*

A day expedition to Tlos, a spectacular ancient Lycian city high above
the valley of the Xanthos River, can be arranged from any town on the
coast from Göcek to Kaş.

### GETTING HERE AND AROUND

Head east from Fethiye on the D90/E400. After 20 km (12 mi), follow
signs for Antalya via Korkuteli. Drive another 1.2 km (0.75 mi), just
after the bridge, there is a right turn for Tlos and Saklıkent. After 8 km
(5 mi) there is a left turn for Tlos, 2.2 km (1½ mi).

### EXPLORING

**Tlos.** From the **acropolis** of Tlos a fine view can be had to the west of
the Xanthos Valley—then as now a rich agricultural area—and to the
east of the mountains that cradle Tlos's Roman theater. The fortress at
the summit is Turkish from the 18th century and was a popular haunt
of the pirate Kanlı ("Bloody") Ali Ağa. Below the fortress, off a narrow
path, is a cluster of rock tombs. Note the relief here of Bellerophon,
son of King Glaucus of Corinth, mounted on Pegasus, his winged steed.

The monster he faces is the dreaded Chimera—a fire-breathing creature witha lion's head, goat's body, and serpent's tail. (Famously, Bellerophon had been sent to the King of Lycia with a sealed message saying that he should be put to his death on arrival. Unwilling to kill this noble figure outright, the Lycians sent him on apparently fatal tasks like fighting the Chimera. He survived them all with the aid of Pegasus and won half a kingdom. The Chimera's fire can still be seen coming up from the ground near Çirali/Olimpo.) If you have time, hike over to the theater you saw from the fortress; among the ruins are carved blocks depicting actors' masks. Nearby, the old baths provide more good views of the Xanthos Valley. ⊠ *From Fethiye take exit to Rte. 400 and follow local road east to Antalya where a yellow sign marks right turn that leads southwest for 15 km (9 mi)* 🖾 *$5* ⊘ *Daily 8:30–sunset.*

**Yaka Park Restaurant.** Continue up the hill beyond Tlos to the nearby village of Yaka Köyü (it's signposted) and you'll reach the vast but peaceful Yaka Park Restaurant, which has become an attraction in its own right (avoid the imitations). On the site of a now-demolished windmill, it has its own trout farm, guaranteeing the fish will always be fresh. The chilly water is everywhere, gurgling around traditional Turkish wooden platforms where diners sit, and there is even a little channel in the bar where fish can swim around your chilled beer. 🖀 *252/634–0036.*

EN
ROUTE

🜄 **Saklıkent Gorge.** Continue south from Tlos, about 15 km, to reach this spectacular gorge, a popular spot for picnicking and a wonderful place to cool off on a hot summer's day. Children especially love wading up the walkway through the icy stream at the bottom of a deep rock crevasse. The first section is over a walkway above the torrent to a pleasant leafy tea garden, beyond which the adventurous can cross the glacial water and continue up the canyon. The determined with time to spare can reach a pretty waterfall at the end. The road here continues south to Çavdir, which is just across the highway from Xanthos, so you continue on. 🖾 *$3* ⊘ *Daily 8:30–sunset.*

## PINARA

*40 km (24 mi) southeast of Fethiye; 40 km (25 mi) north of Kalkan, look for sign on Rte. 400.*

Pınara (it means "something round" in Lycian) is a romantic ruin around a great circular outcrop backed by high cliffs, reachable from most holiday spots in western Lycia.

### GETTING HERE AND AROUND
From Fethiye take E90/D400 toward Kalkan 47 km (30 mi), and then take the right turn marked for Pınara. From there it's a further 6 km (4 mi) via the village of Minara.

### EXPLORING
**Pınara.** Pınara was probably founded as early as the 5th century BC, and it eventually became one of Lycia's most important cities. You need time and determination to explore, as it's widely scattered, largely unexcavated, and overgrown with plane, fig, and olive trees. You can park in the village of **Minare** and make the half-hour hike up the clearly

# Ancient Cultures of Lycia and Its Neighbors

Turkey's Mediterranean coast is steeped in 5,000 years of history—so much so that in Side, the hotels, restaurants, and nightclubs are literally built into the ruins of the Greco-Roman city.

Broadly speaking, the geographic divisions of the coastline of ancient times survive today. The westernmost area from Datça to Dalyan was part of Caria, an ancient Hellenistic kingdom based in nearby Bodrum/Halicarnassus. Caria reached the height of its power in the 4th century BC, and the tomb of its most famous ruler, Mausolus, was such a wonder of the world that it coined the word *mausoleum*. From Dalyan to Phaselis the coast is thought of as Lycia, after a people of very ancient but uncertain origin, some of whom possibly colonized this section of the Anatolian coast from Crete. It now hosts small-scale hotels and harmonious yachting ports. From Antalya to Alanya is the area called Pamphilia, thought to mean "the land of all the tribes," much of which is now quite built up and commercial.

Caria, Lycia, and Pamphilia share much the same rather obscure history, and museums (the best is in Antalya) exhibit relics from Bronze Age settlements that date back to 3000 BC. Our knowledge of indigenous cultures is patchy, but notable in many ways. In Homer's epic, Lycia's Sarpedon memorably declaims that the privileges of the elite must be earned by the elite's readiness to fight for their people. And although not a matriarchal society, Lycians are thought to have been matrilineal and gave women a more equal place than, say, ancient Greece. Some locals were fiercely independent and the people of Xanthos, for example, committed mass suicide rather than submit to the first Persian conquest, and later burned their city (again) rather than pay extra taxes to Rome's Brutus. In addition, the democratic, federal basis of the Lycian League is acknowledged as one source of the U.S. constitution.

Overall, the population of this whole area has long been a mixture of waves of new arrivals, from Greek colonists to Persian administrators, retired Roman legionaries and Turkic shepherds, to today's sunseekers. Despite wars, plagues, and population exchanges, however, there is some degree of continuity: genetic tests discovered that all two dozen of the local workers on a site north of Antalya were related to the bones that they had just dug out from 1,300-year-old graves.

marked trail. At the top of a steep dirt track, the site steward will collect your admission and point you in the right direction—there are no descriptive signs or good site maps.

The spectacular **Greek theater,** which has overlooked these peaceful hills and fields for thousands of years, is one of the finest in Turkey. It's perfectly proportioned, and unlike that of most other theaters in Turkey, its stage building is still standing. The site also contains groups of rock **tombs** with unusual reliefs, one showing a cityscape, and a cliff wall honeycombed with hundreds of crude rectangular "pigeonholes," which are believed to have been either tombs or food storage receptacles. Nearby villagers volunteer to show tourists this site; it's not a bad idea to accept the offer as they know the highlights. A tip is customary. ✉ $5 ⊙ *Daily 8:30–sunset.*

# LETOON

*63 km (39 mi) southeast of Fethiye; 17 km (11 mi) north of Kalkan on Rte. 400, just beyond the town of Kumluova.*

This site was not a city but a Lycian national religious center and political meeting point for the Lycian League, the world's first democratic federation. It's quite rural and the site can be reached on a day trip from western Lycia's main centers—Fethiye, Ölüdeniz, Kaş, or Kalkan. It's a magical site best visited in the late afternoon, perhaps after a visit to nearby Xanthos, which administered the temples in ancient times.

## GETTING HERE AND AROUND

There are several routes signposted including one from across the bridge from Xanthos, 5 km (3 mi). You can continue past Letoon to the western end of the Patara beach. There are occasional buses to Kumluova from Fethiye.

## EXPLORING

**Letoon.** Excavations have revealed three temples in Letoon. The first, closest to the parking area, dates from the 2nd century BC and was dedicated to Leto (hence the name, Letoon), the mother of Apollo and Artemis, who was believed to have given birth to the twins here, while hiding from Zeus' jealous wife, Hera. The middle temple, the oldest, is dedicated to Artemis and dates from the 5th or 4th century BC. The last, dating from the 1st century BC, belongs to Apollo and contains a copy of a mosaic depicting a bow and arrow (a symbol of Artemis) and a sun and lyre (Apollo's emblems). These are the three gods most closely associated with Lycia. Compare the first and last temples: The former is Ionic, topped by a simple, triangular pediment and columns with scroll-shape capitals. The latter is Doric, with an ornate pediment with scenic friezes and detailing, and its columns have undecorated capitals. Reerection of some columns of the Temple of Leto has made the site more photogenic. There is also a well-preserved Roman theater—look for the carvings of theatrical masks on the northern wall. The once-sacred pool, now filled with ducks and chirping frogs, lends atmosphere. About 10 km south of Letoon, the road continues to a beach. Across a rickety bridge at the river mouth are the ruins of an early Lycian fort called Pydnai. ✉ $3 ⊙ *Daily 8:30–sunset.*

# XANTHOS

*61 km (48 mi) southeast of Fethiye; 17 km (10 mi) north of Kalkan on Rte. 400.*

Xanthos, perhaps the greatest city of ancient Lycia, is famed for tombs rising on high, thick, rectangular pillars. Xanthos also earned the region its reputation for fierceness in battle. Determined not to be subjugated by superior forces, the men of Xanthos twice set fire to their own city, with their women and children inside, and fought to the death. The first occasion was against the Persians in 542 BC, the second against

Brutus and the Romans in the 1st century BC. Though the site was excavated and stripped by the British in 1838 and most finds are now in London's British Museum, the remains are worth inspecting. Allow at least three hours and expect some company: Unlike the other Lycian cities, Xanthos is on the main tour-bus route.

**GETTING HERE AND AROUND**

Xanthos is a short distance off Route 400. Buses along the highway will stop at the adjacent town of Kınık. And in summer there are frequent minibuses from Xanthos to Patara, Kalkan, and Kaş.

**EXPLORING**

★ **Xanthos.** You can start your exploration of Xanthos across from the parking area **theater,** built by Lycians in the Roman style. Inscriptions indicate that its restoration was a gift from a wealthy Lycian named Opromoas of Rhodiapolis, who helped restore many Lycian buildings after the great earthquake of 141 AD. Alongside the theater are two much-photographed pillar **tombs.** The more famous of the pair is called the Harpy Tomb—not after what's inside, but because of the half-bird, half-woman figures carved onto the north and south sides. Other reliefs show a seated figure receiving various gifts, including a bird, a pomegranate, and a helmet. This tomb has been dated to 470 BC; the reliefs are plaster casts of originals in the British Museum. The other tomb consists of a sarcophagus atop a pillar—a rather unusual arrangement. The pillar section is probably as old as the Harpy Tomb, the sarcophagus added later. On the side of the theater, opposite the Harpy Tomb and past the agora (the ancient meeting place), is the Inscribed Pillar of Xanthos, a tomb dating from about 400 BC and etched with a 250-line inscription in both Greek and Lycian, that recounts the heroic deeds of a champion wrestler and celebrated soldier named Kerei.

Across the road and past the parking area is the ancient agora, or market place, and a large Byzantine **basilica** with its abstract mosaics. Along a path up the hill are several sarcophagi and a good collection of rock-cut house tombs, as well as a welcome spot of shade. Xanthos's center was up on the acropolis behind the theater, accessible by a trail. 🎫 $2 ☉ Daily 9–sunset.

## PATARA

*70 km (44 mi) southeast of Fethiye; 20 km (13 mi) north of Kalkan, off Rte. 400.*

Patara was once Lycia's principal port. Cosmopolitan in its heyday—Hannibal, St. Paul, and the emperor Hadrian all visited, and St. Nicholas, the man who would be Santa Claus, is said to have been born here—the port eventually silted up. The dunes at the edge of the site are now part of one of Turkey's longest and completely unspoiled sand beaches. From here, too, runs one of the best sections of the Lycian Way, a three- to five-day walk to Ölüdeniz. Thanks to the ruins and the turtles that nest on the beach, new development was banned in the modern village, making it a quiet alternative to the style and bustle of nearby Kalkan.

# The Lycian Way

Until the 1950s, the only way to reach the Lycian coast was by boat or via bone-rattling trips through the mountains in antiquated motor vehicles. Even the main roads of today date only from the 1970s, which is why this was the perfect place to site Turkey's first and most famous long-distance trekking route, the Lycian Way.

The footpath runs for more than 480 km (300 mi), marked by red-and-white painted blazes every 45 to 90 meters (50 to 100 yards) along the sea, following ancient Roman roads, and sometimes clambering up barely visible goat tracks to peaks that rise to nearly 6,500 feet at Mt. Tahtalı, one of many high mountains known as Mt. Olympos in antiquity. The upsides include breathtaking views, innumerable ancient ruins, and a chance to accept hospitality in villages little touched by tourism or time. The downside is that backpacks can be heavy and hills steep, and while most of the path is well marked, finding the trail can occasionally be difficult and frustrating. If you lose the trail, go back to the last marker you saw and try again. Despite government support, the track has no legal status and is subject to adjustments due to road building, landslides, and fencing by landowners.

It would take a month to walk the Lycian Way from end to end, but there's a lot you can do without a tent. Because the trail crosses many towns and highways, it's easy to break up into day hikes, and you can cover about half the trail while staying in pensions that have sprung up along the way. Kate Clow, the Englishwoman who first designed and mapped the Lycian Way in 2000, recommends several popular day walks near Olympos; her book *The Lycian Way* is the only guide and source of good maps of the route, and the Web site ⊕ *www. lycianway.com* has updates and satellite grid references.

**Middle Earth Travel.** As a trekking agent and mule organizer, Clow recommends Middle Earth Travel. They operator treks on the Lycian Way, St. Paul Trail, Cappadocia, the Kaçkars and Mt. Ararat. ⊠ *Gaferli Mah., Cevizler Sokak 20, Göreme, Nevşehir* ☎ *384/271–2559,* ⊕ *www. middleearthtravel.com.*

The best times to walk are spring, when days are long and wildflowers are out, and autumn, when the seawater is warm and the weather cooler. Summer is too hot; in winter there may be some perfect days, but the weather is not reliable enough to make advanced plans.

**GETTING HERE AND AROUND**

The village is 3 km (2 mi) south of the highway, and the ruins and beach are a further 3 km (2 mi) along the same road. Main buses will drop you at the highway; frequent minibuses run between the beach, village, and Kınık (Xanthos), Kalkan, and Kaş, spring through fall.

**EXPLORING**

**Patara Beach.** Patara Beach, beyond the ruins, is a superb 11-km (7-mi) sweep of sand dunes popular with Turkish families and tourists from Kalkan yet never so crowded you need to walk far to find solitude. Umbrellas should only be planted within 20 yards of the sea to prevent disturbance to the nests of *Caretta caretta* turtles. There is a wooden café on the beach that has toilets, changing huts, umbrellas, loungers, drinks, and food.

**Ruins.** The ruins you'll find today are scattered among marshes and sand dunes. The city was famous for a time for its oracle and its still yet-to-be-found temple of Apollo. Herodotus wrote that the oracle worked only part-time, as Apollo spent summers away in Delos (probably to escape the heat!). The heavy stones that make up the front of the monumental **bathhouse** are impressive, and a **triple arch** built by a Roman governor in AD 100 seems a tenth of its age. Beyond are two theaters, several churches, and an impressive section of colonnaded street. Patara is now being excavated by Antalya's Akdeniz University and slowly emerging from the sands. ⌨ *$2*.

## WHERE TO EAT AND STAY

*For expanded hotel reviews, visit Fodors.com.*

¢ ✕ **Tlos Restaurant.** This simple little restaurant just off the main inter-
TURKISH section is keenly kept by a chef from the town of Bolu, legendarily the hometown of Turkey's best cooks. Individual attention is assured, and alcoholic drinks can be brought over from the Lumière Hotel opposite. There is an extensive menu with many hot and cold starters, seafood, and grilled meats. ⊠ *On the right just off the main street leading to the ruins through the village of Patara* ☎ *242/843–5135* ⊘ *Closed Nov.–Apr.*

¢ ▦ **Hotel Lumière.** Surrounded by trees, this is a pleasant place to rest after a day's sightseeing has gone on too long to reach the major centers on the coast. **Pros:** cool vibe; good value. **Cons:** rooms are okay, but nothing special. ⊠ *On left in village on way to Patara ruins. On the main street on the left as you come into town* ☎ *242/843–5091, 532/317–5399* ⊕ *www.hotellumiere.com* ⤵ *16 rooms* ⌂ *In-room: Wi-Fi. In-hotel: bar, pool, laundry facilities* ▯◎▯ *Breakfast.*

¢ ▦ **View Point.** One of the larger hotels in Patara, the View Point sits up on the hill west of town. **Pros:** friendly; well run. **Cons:** the walk up the hill. ⊠ *Up hill to left as you come into town* ☎ *242/843–5110* ⊕ *www.pataraviewpoint.com* ⤵ *27 rooms* ⌂ *In-hotel: restaurant, bar, pool* ⊘ *Closed Nov.–Apr.*

# KALKAN

*80 km (50 mi) southeast of Fethiye; 27 km (17 mi) west of Kaş, on Rte. 400.*

Kalkan has two distinct sides: on one hand it has fine restaurants and excellent hotels to match its superb, steep views of the Mediterranean Sea. But it's also a bit overpriced, and regulars complain that the recent explosion of foreign-owned villas has changed the town's character for the worse. The ranks of self-catering villas, often rented out on the Internet, are spreading up the mountainsides all around and ensure that tourism seasons are growing longer and more prosperous, though hotel and restaurants complain they are sending them out of business.

With only a small, rocky beach, a few narrow blocks of white-washed stone houses, and not much archaeology of its own, Kalkan is trying hard to develop its tourism offerings. It's an excellent base for touring the area and the surrounding sites.

### GETTING HERE AND AROUND

The highway is immediately behind town, so getting here is straightforward.

**Kalamus Travel.** Agencies in town like Kalamus Travel can arrange paragliding, diving, horseback riding, Jeep safaris, village visits, mountain walks, and guided trips to Lycian ruins. ✉ *Yalıboyu, also doing business as Mavi Real Estate* ☎ *242/844–2456* ⊕ *www.kalamustravel.com.*

### WHERE TO EAT AND STAY

*For expanded hotel reviews, visit Fodors.com.*

$ ✕ **Aubergine.** This restaurant is an exception to the general rule of avoiding harbor-front eateries. The menu is adventurous and well explained, and includes salmon *en croute,* stuffed sea bass with bacon, extra large steaks, ostrich fillet, and occasionally wild boar shot in the mountains. All the desserts are homemade. ✉ *On the harbor front* ☎ *242/844–3332.*

TURKISH

★

$ ✕ **Gironda.** This gourmet restaurant is designed like a rich villa with sumptuous sofas and plaster-of-paris statuary, and the excellent food alone merits a stay in Kalkan. The fare is outstandingly fresh and the dishes are well thought out: even a humble lamb pie topped with phyllo pastry pops with tastes of baby onion, sesame, and mushrooms. Other specialties are pan-seared sole in champagne sauce, eggplant with cheese, and fish baked in parchment, as well as a wide variety of pastas. Tables on the terrace upstairs enjoy great views of Kalkan Bay. ✉ *Two streets up from harbor in old town* ☎ *242/844–3136* ⌘ *Reservations essential* ⊘ *Closed Nov.–Apr.*

MEDITERRANEAN

Fodor's Choice

★

¢ ▦ **Happy Hotel.** Despite the unimaginative concrete block architecture, this is an attractive, well-run hotel overlooking Kalamar Bay and is good value. **Pros:** giant suites. **Cons:** limited service into town. ✉ *Head west of Kalkan to Kalamar Bay, follow road left as you come over ridge and follow signs down hill* ☎ *242/844–1133* ⊕ *www.happy.com. tr* ⤳ *32 standard rooms, 18 suites* ⌂ *In-room: Wi-Fi. In-hotel: restaurant, bar, gym.*

★

$ ▦ **Hotel Pirat.** This 1986 concrete hotel lacks personality and feels dated, but the location is great: right on the harbor, and the three pools have superb views over the bay. **Pros:** central location. **Cons:** not much in the way of looks, especially the ugly green carpet. ✉ *Kalkan harbor* ☎ *242/844–3178* ⊕ *www.hotelpirat.net* ⤳ *126 rooms, 10 suites* ⌂ *In-room: Wi-Fi. In-hotel: restaurant, bar, pool, beach, business center.*

**$$$**   ☷ **Hotel Villa Mahal.** Clinging to a cliff face with a wraparound view
Fodor's Choice   of Kalkan Bay, this immaculate establishment is one of Turkey's most
★   spectacular hotels. **Pros:** nice rooms; gorgeous location. **Cons:** isolated;
a long way down to the beach ⊠ *Patara Evler Yani, about 2 km (1 mi)*
*east of Kalkan. Down and around signposted road. Take care on pre-*
*cipitous last approach* ☎ *242/844–3268* ⊕ *www.villamahal.com* ⟿ *4*
*rooms, 2 suites* ♿ *In-room: no TV, Wi-Fi. In-hotel: restaurant, bar, busi-*
*ness center, some age restrictions* ☉ *Nov.–Apr.* ⏀ *Breakfast.*

⌐ EN
ROUTE
**Kapıtaş Beach.** Since neither Kaş nor Kalkan have proper beaches this
pretty spot between the two is a quite popular. Set in a narrow, steep-
sided inlet, a long metal stair takes you down and down to the beach
proper. The position between the dramatic cliffs is picturesque, though
the beach itself is small and can get crowded in summer.

## KAŞ

*107 km (67 mi) southeast of Fethiye via Rte 400; 180 km (112 mi) from*
*Antalya via Korkuteli mountain road.*

In the 1980s, Kaş, with its beautiful wide, island-filled bay, was the
main tourist destination on the Lycian coast, but it fell by the wayside
because it lacked a real beach and A-list attractions. This has, fortu-
nately, kept away the worst overdevelopment of the last few years, and
now Kaş is being rediscovered, with many restaurants and regular visi-
tors migrating from Kalkan. There are excellent hotels and restaurants,
the location is relatively central and the size is about right, making it
a good stop on your way along the coast. Like Kalkan, Kaş is also a
good base for sightseeing.

### GETTING HERE AND AROUND
Kaş is a scenic 27 km (17 mi) past Kalkan on Route 400. The road is
immediately above the town, and there are two turns with large—"Şehir
Merkezi" (city center)—and tiny signs for "Kaş." As you come into
town there are marked turns—right for the Çukurbağ Peninsula, and
left for the seafront hotels.

**Official Tourist Office Kaş** ⊠ *Cumhuriyet Meyd. 5* ☎🖷 *242/836–1238.*

### EXPLORING
**Kastellorizon.** The hour-long boat ride to the Greek Island of Kastellori-
zon (the name of the island is Meis in Turkey) gives you a taste both of
Greece and what Kaş must have been like before the 1924 population
exchange, when it was mostly populated by Greeks.

Isolated from the rest of Greece, Kastellorizon is one of the few islands
that have escaped major tourist development. All new houses on the
island must be built in the traditional manner. A day trip only allows
you to see the island during the hours most Greeks are having their
midday siesta, so it's worth trying to arrange to stay the night; there are
several hotels and a few *pansiyons*; try the Hotel Kastellorizo (⊕ *www.*
*kastellorizohotel.gr* ☎ *30 22460 49044*) on the harbor waterfront. The
island has an impressive 12th- to 16th-century crusader castle with
crenellated gray-stone walls, a large cave with fine stalactites, and the
1835 church of St. Konstantine and Eleni, which reused granite columns

The Lycian Coast Kaş > **301**

taken from the Temple of Apollo at Letoon in Lycia (usually locked) and a good small museum (free).

Meis Express (⊕ *www.meisexpress.com* ☎ *242 836–1725*) has an office on Kaş's waterfront. Boats leave at 10:20 am daily (20 euros for a day trip).

**Ruins.** Kaş was ancient Antiphellus, and has a few ruins, including a monumental **sarcophagus** under a massive plane tree, up the sloping street that rises behind the main square. The tomb has four regal lions' heads carved onto the lid. In 1842, a British naval officer counted more than 100 sarcophagi in Kaş—then called Antifili—but most have been destroyed over the years as locals nabbed the flat sidepieces to use in new construction.

A few hundred yards west of the main square, along Hastane Caddesi, is a small, well-preserved antique **theater,** amid the olive trees at the edge of town, with a superb ocean view. Next to the district prefect's office, east of the harbor, is an old wooden barn of the type once universally used as granaries in Lycian villages—and still clearly modeled on old Lycian architectural forms. Ask at Echo Bar to see their 3rd-century-BC cistern, carved from the solid rock. Kaş makes a good base for boat excursions, and a profusion of scuba-diving boats shows the growing demand for the area's rich underwater sights.

Other excursion options include Simena and Kekova Sound; Demre, site of the old church of St. Nicholas of Christmas fame; or Patara and Patara Beach. Be aware that high winds can make for a very rough ride, particularly round the cape to Kekova.

## WHERE TO EAT AND STAY
*For expanded hotel reviews, visit Fodors.com.*

$ ╳ **Bahçe & Bahçe Balik.** Bahçe is a courtyard restaurant serving delightful
TURKISH Turkish dishes in a quiet garden setting, just opposite Kaş's iconic 4th-century-BC King's Tomb. The waitstaff is one large family—each taking part in the preparation and serving of food. The starters are famous in Kaş. Especially tasty options are grated carrot with yogurt, mashed walnut, cold spinach, fish balls, and the *arnavut ciğeri* (fried liver prepared with chopped nuts). The same family has opened a fish restaurant opposite, Bahçe Balik. ⊠ *Anıt Mezar Karşisi 31* ☎ *242/836–2370.*

$$ ╳ **Chez Evy.** No place in Kaş has more character than this delightful
FRENCH restaurant. Prices might be high, but that's because Evy, who spent her
★ early life cooking on private yachts, has a tendency to serve portions that are double the size of anywhere else. The menu is short but varied, including wild boar from the mountains. Dining is in an intimate garden around the back in summer, where shared tables and Evy's big-hearted solicitousness create an atmosphere where everybody is soon talking to everybody else. A digestif is a special treat in the cozy bar with its eccentric decoration and Evy's dancing, cappucino-drinking red parrot. Rivals love to spread rumors that Evy's has closed, so check yourself (unfortunately, she is threatening to retire). In the November–April off-season, call for a reservation. ⊠ *Terzi Sokak 2, in small street behind Red Point bar* ☎ *242/836–1253* ⌑ *Reservations essential.*

$    ✕ **Ikbal.** This addition to the cluster of restaurants near the Lycian tomb
TURKISH    has earned a reputation for the quality of its food. Run by a German-
Fodor'sChoice    Turkish couple, it offers a mix of Turkish and Mediterranean dishes.
★    They take great pride in their warm starters, such as the delcicous
*paçanga börek,* a pastry filled with cheese and dried meat, and the
*emücver,* deep-fried eggplant—all of which are cooked fresh rather than
reheated as at most other restaurants. For main courses there are the
usual range of fish, *köfte,* lamb, chicken, and steak, and the dessert
menu is wide and tempting, including the popular apple pancakes.
⊠ *Süleyman Sandıkçı Sokak 6* ☎ *242/836–3193.*

$    ✕ **Mercan.** With a prime waterfront position, this is one of Kaş's old-
TURKISH    est establishments (in business since 1956), and it has a reputation for
quality of seafood and steepnees of prices. There is a wide choice of fish,
with the day's catch often displayed in a small water-filled boat at the
entrance, and a variety of over 30 starters and salads, plus kebabs for
those who aren't in the mood for fish. ⊠ *Waterfront* ☎ *242/836–1209.*

$$    ⊡ **Aquapark Hotel.** On the tip of the peninsula west of Kaş, the Aquapark
↻    is a resort with a long-standing reputation for excellent food. **Pros:** wow
views. **Cons:** the sloping site means lots of stairs. ⊠ *Take the road out
of Kaş to the Çukurbağ Peninsula, drive 2 km (1 mi) to the farthest
point on the road that does a circuit around the point* ☎ *242/836–
1902* ⊕ *www.aquapark.org* ↰ *81 rooms, 42 suites* ⟆ *In-room: no TV,
Wi-Fi. In-hotel: restaurant, bar, pool, tennis court* ⊙ *Closed Nov.–Apr.*
⊖ *Some meals.*

$$$    ⊡ **Gardenia.** The first thing you notice here is the art, aquired by the
★    owner on his off-season trips to Asia and South America; it fills the
lobby, expands up the stairs, and overflows into the rooms, setting
the tone for a boutique, design hotel. **Pros:** stylish. **Cons:** some rooms
small, no elevator and lots of stairs. ⊠ *Hükmet Cad. 41* ☎ *242/836–
2368* ⊕ *www.gardeniahotel-kas.com* ↰ *10 rooms, 1 suite* ⟆ *In-hotel:
restaurant, bar* ⊙ *Closed mid-Nov.–Apr.*

$$    ⊡ **Hadrian Hotel.** This is a beautifully designed and immaculately kept
Fodor'sChoice    waterfront hotel on the peninsula outside Kaş. **Pros:** gorgeous location;
★    romantic. **Cons:** hotel is 500 yards down a steep hill from the main
road, so a rental car is vital if you plan to do much sightseeing in the
area. ⊠ *Doğan Kaşaroğlu Cad. 10, south side of Çukurbağ Peninsula,
about 500 meters (1,640 feet) from tip. Well signposted once on pen-
insula* ☎ *242/836–2856* ⊕ *www.hotel-hadrian.de* ↰ *10 rooms, 4 suites*
⟆ *In-room: no TV, Wi-Fi. In-hotel: restaurant, bar, laundry facilities,
business center* ⊙ *Closed Nov. 15–Apr. 15* ⊖ *Some meals.*

$    ⊡ **Medusa Hotel.** This is probably the best run of the generally good
★    hotels that line the seafront road east of the harbor, particularly after
remodeling in 2009. **Pros:** friendly and helpful. **Cons:** small rooms; lots
of stairs. ⊠ *Küçük Çakül 62* ☎ *242/836–1440* ⊕ *www.medusahotels.
com* ↰ *36 rooms, 1 suite* ⟆ *In-room: Wi-Fi. In-hotel: restaurant, pool,
beach* ⊙ *Nov.–Apr.* ⊖ *Breakfast.*

## NIGHTLIFE

**Echo Cafe & Bar.** Echo Cafe & Bar is a well-run discotheque and is
often the venue for live-jazz performances. This is probably also the
only nightclub in the world to boast a 3rd-century-BC basement cistern

carved out of solid rock, now laid out with tables, and quieter than upstairs. The cistern was discovered by chance when the original building—a high-door former stable for camels, which were the main means of transport in Lycia until just a few decades ago—was being extended. ⊠ *On eastern edge of harbor.*

## SIMENA-KALEKÖY AND KEKOVA SOUND

*30 km (19 mi) east of Kaş.*

Simena (now known in Turkish as Kaleköy), Kekova Island, and its surrounding coastline are some of the most enchanting spots in Turkey, especially as the reflection of the full moon slowly traces its way across Kekova Sound. Kekova Island stands slightly off a shoreline notched with little bays, whose many inlets create a series of lagoons. One inlet features the disappearing apse of a Byzantine church behind one beach known as Tersane, whose bay is a favorite swimming spot. Climb up the hill behind and you'll see an even better preserved one on the far shore. The islands' coast is also famed for its "sunken city." Though swimming is now banned, it is still interesting to explore the fragments of the buildings partly submerged along the shore. Most of the day boats are large and reserved in advance for bus tour groups, but smaller boats can be hired by day-trippers; prices vary widely depending on the size of the boat and the mood of the captain. The village of Üçağız has small *pansiyons* and waterside restaurants, and is the base for boat trips across the bay to the island.

Simena-Kaleköy, a concrete-free village, has the look of the Greek islands before development. Reached by a 10-minute boat ride or half-hour walk from Üçağız, it's a pleasing jumble of boxy houses built up a steep rocky crag alongside layers of history: Lycian tombs, a tiny Greek theater, and the medieval ruins of Simena Castle atop the rocky hill. The best way to enjoy the place is to stay the night; you'll enjoy the place more once the day-trippers have departed, and there are now numerous basic *pansiyons* that, though rather expensive for the quality of the rooms, have balconies with sublime views. All offer boat pickups from Üçağız. Reserve well in advance, in season.

### GETTING HERE AND AROUND

Kevova Sound is a beautiful patch of water that needs to be explored by boat. Day trips leave from Kaş and Üçağız. Some boats come directly from Kaş while others bus their customers into Üçağız. Expect to pay around $40. If driving, look for a turnoff from Route 400 signposted "Üçağız," 14 km (9 mi) east of Kaş. After 16 km (10 mi) you'll reach Çevreli, where there is a turn to Üçağız, a further 3 km (2 mi).

### EXPLORING

**Aperlai & Apollonia.** West of Kekova are two small, infrequently visited ruins, linked together by a section of the Lycian Way; they make for a good day trip or overnight for those who want to get off the beaten track. Apollonia is on a small hill just southwest of the village of Sahil Kılınçlı on the Kaş–Üçağız road, 7 km (4½ mi) south of the highway. Take the branch road through the village then head west when you get to the top of the rise. First you'll see a good range of ancient Lycian tombs, scattered east and north of the walled acropolis hill. Continue west for the city proper; there's a small theater and a well-preserved church with views west over the coast toward Kaş. Back on the side road, look for the signed turnoff to the right then walk two hours down the hill to the ruins of Aperlae on a pretty little inlet. The city walls are impressively intact, and inside are a scatter of buildings including a well-preserved church, houses, and a bath building by the water, as well as the sunken remains of the ancient port, which you can explore with a mask and snorkel from the nearby **Purple House** *pansiyon* and restaurant, in nicely restored stone buildings. From Aperlai a 20-minute walk takes you to another restaurant on the Kekova inlets, and another three hours, first inland, and then along the water, will take you to Üçağız. Some boats drop you at the inlet and give you time to walk to Aperlai and back.

## WHERE TO STAY

*For expanded hotel reviews, visit Fodors.com.*

$$ ⌂ **Ankh Pansiyon.** This simple family establishment is the place to choose if you want to escape from the world and soak up the otherworldliness of Kekova Sound. **Pros:** more private than other places around. **Cons:** rooms lack character. ⊠ *Eastern side of village, follow signs through maze of streets* ☎ *242/874–2171* ⊕ *www.ankhpansion.com* ⇲ *8 rooms* ☖ *In-room: Wi-Fi. In-hotel: restaurant* ☼ *Closed Nov. 10– Apr.* ⚇ *Breakfast.*

$$ ⌂ **Kale Pension.** In a pretty stone building with lovely old wooden ceilings, this small lodging has a small courtyard on the eastern side of the waterfront. **Pros:** central yet separate; family-run; character. **Cons:** ground-floor rooms have less of a view. ⊠ *Just east of the Sahil Pension, follow the signs* ☎ *242/874–2111* ⊕ *www.kalepansiyon.com* ⇲ *11 rooms* ☖ *In-room: Wi-Fi. In-hotel: restaurant* ☼ *Closed Nov.–Apr.*

$$ ⌂ **Purple House.** This little *pansiyon* on an idyllic inlet is the ultimate escape from the mass tourisim of the Turkish coast. **Pros:** idylic escape. **Cons:** very basic. ⊠ *Aperlai* ☎ *0539/859–9196* ⇲ *6 rooms* ☖ *In-hotel: restaurant* ⊟ *No credit cards.*

$$ ⌂ **Sahil Pension.** This little *pansiyon* above a restaurant and general store is in the middle of things in the center of the Kaleköy waterfront. **Pros:** central location; great views. **Cons:** less private. ⊠ *Kaleköy waterfront, look for the shop* ☎ *242/874–2263* ⊕ *www.sahilpension.com* ⇲ *4 rooms* ☖ *In-hotel: restaurant.*

# DEMRE (KALE)

*37 km (23 mi) east of Kaş; 140 km (87 mi) southwest of Antalya on Rte. 400.*

Demre is where Saint Nicholas, who later became known as Father Christmas, made his reputation as bishop of the Greco-Roman diocese of Myra in the first half of the 4th century. Among his good deeds, St. Nicholas is said to have carried out nocturnal visits to the houses of local children to leave gifts, including gold coins as dowries for poor village girls; if a window was closed, said the storytellers, he would drop the gifts down the chimney.

Demre was one of the most important cities along the coast but its remains lie mostly under the concrete and large greenhouses of the modern city between the city center around the Church of St. Nicholas and the hillside to the north, where there is a theater and some rock-cut tombs. Demre is, however, primarily an agricultural region (it's known as the tomato capital of Turkey) and for most tourists a quick stopover on their trip along the coast.

**GETTING HERE AND AROUND**

Demre is right along Route 400. St. Nicholas Basilica is a few blocks off the highway, signposted "Noel Baba." The theater is about 1½ km (1 mi) further north.

**EXPLORING**

**Andriake.** Andriake was the port of ancient Myra and a major stopover on the Egypt-to-Rome route that supplied most of Rome's wheat. St. Paul changed ships here on his journey to Rome in 60 AD. Hadrian built a huge granary here—it's hidden in the bushes south of the road just before you get to the modern port of Demre, and is also clearly visible from the Kaş–Demre road, just west of Demre, as you come around the last bend. Recent excavations also found a synagogue in the same area. If you're willing to ford the waist-deep water of the creek, Üçağız is about a seven-hour walk on the Lycian Way with several pretty coastal sections.

**Myra.** The monuments of ancient Myra—a large, well-preserved Roman theater and a cliff face full of Lycian rock tombs—are about 2 km (1 mi) north of Kale, poorly marked by signs. The theater dates from the 2nd century AD and for a time was used for gladiator spectacles and wild animal hunts. In the cliffs above the theater there are some good reliefs (a stairway leads to a raised viewing platform so you can see them up close) and on the bits of pediments and statuary scattered about the grounds of the site. Just east of the theater, up a stone ramp, is a section of Lycian Way that leads to the acropolis, with nice views over the theater and town. There are also more tombs to the east. $7 ⊙ *Daily 8:30–5 or 5:30.*

**St. Nicholas Basilica.** A church was built around the tomb of St. Nicholas, aka Santa Claus, in the 6th century, but it was later destroyed in an Arab raid. In 1043 the St. Nicholas Basilica was rebuilt with the aid of the Byzantine emperor Constantine IX and the empress Zoë. It now stands near the center of Demre, a couple of blocks from the square. St. Nicholas's remains, however, were stolen and taken to Bari, Italy, in 1087, where the church of San Nicola di Bari was built to house them. A few bones remained, so the story goes, and these can be seen in the Antalya Museum. The church in Demre today is mainly the result of restoration work financed by 19th-century Russian noblemen. It's difficult to distinguish between the original church, parts of which may date back to the 5th century, and the restorations, although the bell tower and upper story are clearly late additions. A service is held in the church every year on December 6, the feast day of St. Nicholas, as part of the annual symposium and festival organized by the Father Christmas and Call to World Peace Foundation. $6 ⊙ *Daily 8:30–5:30.*

**DID YOU KNOW?**

The top of a submerged Lycian tomb juts out of the water near Kekova.

**Sura.** Sura was ancient Myra's most important pre-Christian holy site. Priests of Apollo would release holy fish into the sacred pool and then would "read" the future from the movements of the fish as they ate pieces of meat or bread thrown by worshipers. The site is just beside the turnoff to Kekova, a few hundred meters north of Andriake.

> **A NOTE ON NAMES**
>
> Demre is also known in Turkish as Kale, not to be confused with Kale, the Turkish name for Simena in nearby Kekova Sound, now usually Kaleköy to avoid the confusion. "Kale" is also Turkish for "castle."

There is a scatter of Lycian tombs and a small acropolis from where you can see the temple of Apollo in the overgrown valley below.

### WHERE TO EAT

$    ✕ **Ipek Restaurant.** One of the best of the group of traditional Turkish
TURKISH  *lokantas* around the church of St. Nicholas, Ipek doesn't look like much and the waiters can be surly, but the kitchen cooks excellent meat dishes that make this the restaurant of choice for many. ⊠ *As you exit the church, turn left along the pedestrian street. Ipek is 100 yards down, on the left* ☎ *242/871–5150.*

¢    ✕ **Nur Pastaneleri.** After paying your respects to St. Nick, repair here to
TURKISH  enjoy properly arctic air-conditioning and a cold drink or tea accompanied by some of Turkey's freshest *baklava*, the diamond-cut honeyed pastry with nuts. Until early afternoon the café also serves *su böreği*, a salty pastry flavored with feta cheese or mincemeat. ⊠ *As you exit the St. Nicholas Basilica, walk south to the square and on your right is a two-story modern shopping center with slim pillars down the facade; Nur Pastaneleri is on the corner* ☎ *242/871–6310.*

## FINIKE AND ARYCANDA

*111 km (70 mi) southwest of Antalya along Rte. 400.*

Finike is a good spot to stop for lunch or is a jumping-off point for Arycanda and a series of less glamorous Lycian sites that dot the citrus- and vegetable-growing coastal plain. The small port town is less touristy than other towns along the coast, and more friendly, helpful, and inexpensive. It's not the most exciting place to stay, but if you just want a decent bed for a night, it's the best option between Olympos and Kekova. A yacht marina harbors many European boats, but Finike, which makes most of its money from its acres of orange trees, seems to take their presence unfussily in its stride. A colorful town market is held every Sunday.

### GETTING HERE AND AROUND

Finike is right on the highway. The old road for Arycanda and Elmalı goes north from the major bend at the center of town, and soon crosses the river, where you can then join the new road. For Arycanda, drive 35 km (22 mi) north toward Elmalı, and then watch for the Arycanda sign to the right, at a popular roadside market.

These Lycian rock tombs have been carved into the cliffside of the ancient city of Myra.

## EXPLORING

**Arycanda.** The well-preserved walls and lovely location of Arycanda, high in a mountain valley above Finike, make this ancient Lycian town one of the most beautiful and least crowded archaeological sites on the Turquoise Riviera. A parking area and easy-to-follow trail lead up to the acropolis, first passing a church and the monumental **Roman baths**, perhaps Turkey's best-preserved bathhouse, with intact mosaic floors, standing walls, and windows framing the valley. The tombs, farther east along the trail, are more properly Roman rather than Lycian—it's worth the hike to see the carved gateway on the last one. At the top of the hills is a pretty ensemble of a sunken agora, or market, with arcades on three sides and an intimate odeon, or small concert hall, topped by a Greek-style theater with a breathtaking view of the valley and mountains often capped with snow. Even higher up is the town's stadium or running track. Farther north is a second, long thin agora, with a small temple above it. From here the official trail scrambles down to some Roman villas, but you may find it easier to backtrack. Back toward the car park is a temple of Trajan with an ancient Roman toilet underneath. ☎ *0535/856–6059* ✉ *$2* ⏲ *Daily 9–7:30.*

EN ROUTE **Elmali.** From Arykanda, you can continue north 60 km (37 miles) to the mountain town of Elmalı, the center of Turkey's apple (*elma*) industry. The main attractions are a glimpse of traditional Turkey and the cool mountain air, but Elmalı is also known for its traditional, half-timber houses and the Ömer Pasha Mosque (1602), which is one of the best Ottoman mosques in southern Turkey. Several important preclassical sites have been excavated in the area, and a hoard of nearly 2000 coins from the 5th century BC, called the "Treasure of the Century" was found near here. Most finds are now in the Antalya Museum, but a small museum, Elmalı Müzesi, opened here in 2011. ⊙ 9–2, *closed Monday.*

**WHERE TO EAT AND STAY**
*For expanded hotel reviews, visit Fodors.com.*

¢   ✕ **Altın Sofra.** This restaurant in the marina is famed for its lamb and
TURKISH   lambs' liver, but it serves a full menu including fish. There is a pleas-
★   ant garden shaded by plane trees and acacias. Everything here is so fresh the chef refuses to add anything but olive oil and salt to flavor his meats. ⊠ *Inside the yacht marina, 100 yards past the entrance* ☎ *242/855–1281.*

¢   ✕ **Anfora Balık Restaurant.** This unassuming-looking restaurant, in a cool
TURKISH   basement cavern set into the hillside by the main road above the yatch
★   marina, offers fine seafood and excellent value. Specialties include pots of cooked squid, octopus, and shrimp. The fried squid is famously fresh. ⊠ *Main road, just west of the center, 100 yards past the marina entrance on Kordon Cad. (Rte. 400)* ☎ *242/855–3888.*

¢   ⊞ **Hotel Grand Finike.** A large, bright, and well-furnished hotel just opposite the yacht harbor, the Grand Finike is an excellent and inexpensive place to stay, if somewhat unromantic. **Pros:** good value. **Cons:** there's little reason to stay in Finike. ⊠ *Center of town on main road, opposite yacht marina entrance* ☎ *242/855–5805* ⊕ *www.hotelgrandfinike. com.tr* ⊷ *52 rooms, 4 suites* △ *In-room: Wi-Fi. In-hotel: restaurant, bar, pool* ꞮⓄꞮ *Breakfast.*

## OLYMPOS AND ÇIRALI

*Olympos is 89 km (55 mi) southwest of Antalya from Rte. 400.*

★   Olympos and its "sister" towns, Çiralı and Adrasan, are places unique on the Turquoise Riviera for their natural beauty, ancient ruins, low-rise development, and easygoing culture that mixes international backpackers, Turkish students, and European families. All three towns are also next to some of the best day walks on the Lycian Way, though the Olympos ruins and beach are the main event in the area. All three are accessed via a secondary road, parallel to the highway. Olympos has the most character but can be noisy and crowded in summer and offers limited accommodations. The area above the valley is quieter, with better places to stay, but you'll have a short drive to the beach. Çiralı shares the beach with Olympos and is much quieter, with the best range of hotels. Little Adrasan feels like the beach town the world forgot—peaceful and a little scruffy.

**GETTING HERE AND AROUND**
Olympos is off Route 400, between Kumlucu and Tekirova. There are signposted turns to Adrasan (9 km/6 mi), Olmpos (12 km/7½ mi), and Çiralı (7 km/4½ mi). From Upper Olympos a second road connects to Adrasan. There is no direct road between Olympos and Çiralı, but it's a short walk along the beach.

## EXPLORING

The ancient city of Olympos is named after a nearby peak that towers above the mountain range behind the beach.

A lovely 500-yard walk through the overgrown site gives access to one end of the long sand-and-pebble beach, still unspoiled and backed by an amazing amphitheater of pine-clad mountains. The sights can be seen in a day, but the natural beauty and laid-back atmosphere can prove addictive. One of the hotels has a slogan: "Come for a day, stay for a week," and it's surprising how often that happens. Olympos is, perhaps, a little too beautiful for its own good: it's popular with backpackers and younger Turks, and in summer it can get crowded and noisy, with loud discos at night. Out of season, it returns to bucolic tranquillity. There is a no-concrete rule for development in the region, so accommodation is mostly in wooden cabins, as well as Olympos's famous "tree houses," best described as basic cabins on stilts. A few miles inland, out of the gorge, is a collection of other *pansiyons*, which can be quieter and more upmarket. The nearby town of Çıralı shares the long gorgeous beach and caters more to families and those looking for something quieter and more sophisticated; the *pansiyons* here are mostly wooden cabins among the fruit trees. There are few restaurants, and most lodgings include an evening meal.

**Olympos.** The ruins of the ancient city of Olympos, enshrouded in dense vegetation, have received little excavation and, as a result, are wonderfully atmospheric. Because the ruins are next to a river and shaded by tall firs, flowering oleander bushes, and a mountain gorge, they are also delightfully cool in summer, the perfect time to explore.

Olympos was once a top-voting member of the 2nd-century-BC Lycian League, but most of the buildings viewable today date from Roman times. Roman-era building started in earnest after officers—including the young Julius Ceasar—crushed a two-year-long occupation of the city by pirates in about 70 BC. Many tombs are scattered around the ancient city, which is reached by two parallel paths down to the beach. In the center of the northern half of the site is the large cathedral complex, once the main temple, which includes a much-photographed 18-foot-high gate, dedicated to Marcus Aurelius in AD 171 and mistakenly referred to by signs as a temple. Note how some walls around the site have clearly been rebuilt in later centuries with narrow arrow slits in the windows as if the city suddenly had to fortify itself. A second side path leads along a water channel to some interesting tombs and a large building, probably a grand mansion. At the beach exit is a poetic inscription on a sarcophagus in memory of an ancient ship's captain, along with a carving of his beached boat—not that different from today's *gulets*. From here you can also climb to a small acropolis and some medieval fortifications where ancients would keep a lookout for ships and pirates.

The southern side of the ancient city is best reached by crossing the riverbed (dry in summer) by the land-side ticket office and heading east toward the beach along a well-beaten path that starts with a remarkable row of tombs with their sliding-stone windows still in place. Farther along are shipping quays, warehouses, a gorgeously overgrown theater, a great bathhouse, and a church whose two great rows of granite columns have collapsed inward toward each other and now lie half-buried in what feels like the floor of a tropical jungle. Excavations by the river on what was probably the agora or marketplace began in 2011. Farther south along the beach are the walls of a medieval castle and church variously occupied and improved by Crusaders and also used as an outpost of Italian city-states. ⌨ *$2 or $4.50 for 10 visits.*

The long Olympos beach extends to Çıralı and is one of the wonders of Turkey—not least for how it has managed to escape the ravages of industrial tourism. The beach is mostly smooth white and multicolor marble pebbles mixed with some light gray sand. Float out on your back and marvel at the 5-km (3-mi) sweep of beach, the line of fir trees behind it, and the surrounding amphitheater of mountains that includes the 8,000-foot peak of Mt. Olympos. Several restaurants along the beachfront make great places to eat and while away an evening. Olympos and Çıralı are only separated by a short walk along the beach, but it's a long drive around the mountain.

**Chimaera.** At the far end of Çıralı, a half-hour evening scramble up a sometimes-steep path will bring you to the Chimaera, named after the ferocious fire-breathing beast of legend. Flames can still be seen rising from cracks in the rock, apparently also burning the gas deep below, since they reignite even if covered. In times past, the flames were apparently more vigorous, even visible by sailors offshore. The Chimaera is inland from the far southern end of Çıralı; take either of the main roads to the end then head inland. If you're staying in Olympos it's a 7-km (5-mi) 90-minute walk, so you may want to drive to the bottom of the hill, or take a tour. From the parking lot it's a half-hour walk up a lot of stairs. Most hotels in the area will arrange a tour. You can see the flames in the day, but they're best at night. ■ TIP→ **Bring a flashlight for all those stairs, since there's no lighting, and in peak season go as late as possible to avoid the crowds.** ⌨ *$3* ⊗ *24 hrs daily.*

About 10 mi from Olympos, between Kumluca and Olympos, **Adrasan** is a relaxed little town on a long beach that's a world away from the flashy resort towns. Don't expect five-star hotels, gourmet restaurants, tour buses or touts, just a great stretch of rarely crowded beach and some decent family *pansiyons*. Boat tours that take you to swim in local coves set off from the beach each morning at about 10 and cost about $25 including lunch. A long, wonderful, and mostly forest-shaded day's walk along the Lycian Way will take you through forests over Mt. Musa to Olympos; another walk will take you to the lighthouse at the point of the Tekke Peninsula; another more difficult route takes seven or eight hours and goes around the peninsula to the wonderful lighthouse at Cape Gelidonya and to the small beach town of Karaöz. Take the official Lycian Way guidebook (it comes with a map), adequate water, and preferably a guide for the often-lonely pathways. Note that there is limited public transport to Adrasan, so you're best off if you have a car.

The mythical chimera (for which the flame at Olympos is named) was a fire-breathing monster with the body of a goat, the head of a lion, and the tail of a serpent.

### SPORTS AND THE OUTDOORS

**Olympos.** Olympos is one of Turkey's premier **rock climbing** destinations. Kadir's, a few hundred yards up from the main cluster of buildings in the valley, has a climbing center that provides support for new and experienced climbers. ☎ 242/892–1316 ⊕ *www.olymposrockclimbing.com.*

### WHERE TO EAT AND STAY

*For expanded hotel reviews, visit Fodors.com.*

#### IN THE OLYMPOS VALLEY

¢ 🍴 **Şaban.** One of the older lodgings in the gorge, Şaban has become one of the most popular places for foreigners of all ages, and Olympos regulars say the food here is the best in the valley. **Pros:** friendly and comfortable. **Cons:** Olympos can be noisy and crowded in summer. ⊠ *Where the road crosses the dry stream, opposite the large, ugly "Turkomens" sign* ☎ *242/892–1265* 🛏 *50 bungalows, 10 treehouses, 1 dorm* 🕭 *In-room: Wi-Fi. In-hotel: restaurant, bar.*

#### ÇIRALI

$$ 🍴 **Arcadia.** Real care has been taken with the woodwork, including
★ the elaborate Ottoman-style wood ceilings, and these are the prettiest bungalows in the area. **Pros:** lovely cabins; friendly staff. **Cons:** less of an owner-run feel than other places. ⊠ *Far southern end of main beachfront road.* ☎ *242/825–7340* ⊕ *www.arcadiaholiday.com* 🛏 *10 cabins* 🕭 *In-room: no TV, Wi-Fi. In-hotel: restaurant, bar* 🍽 *No meals.*

¢ 🍴 **Canada Hotel.** Run by a Turkish-Candian couple, Şaban and Carrie, this hotel, a short distance out of Çıralı, is one of the friendliest and most popular in town. **Pros:** friendly; pool. **Cons:** distance from beach. ⊠ *On main road into Çıralı, on right before you cross bridge,*

*Çıralı* ☎ *242/825–7233* ⊕ *www.
canadahotel.net* ⤳ *26 rooms, 8
bungalows* ⚏ *In-hotel: pool.*

**BEYOND OLYMPOS**

Why go to Adrasan if you've seen
Olympos, you might ask. It's one
of Turkey's last quiet, basic, and
locally run beachfront holiday
spots. Hotels are also up to a third
cheaper than those in Çıralı.

**$   ⊤ Myland Nature Hotel.** Relaxed and
friendly, this *pansiyon* is across
from the beach, about halfway
along the beach road. **Pros:** friendly;
relaxed; close to the beach; good
food. **Cons:** cabins are nice, but not
exceptional. ✉ *Halfway along main
beachfront road, on left* ☎ *242/825–7044* ⊕ *www.mylandnature.com*
⤳ *13 cabins* ⚏ *In-room: no TV, Wi-Fi. In-hotel: restaurant.*

**ABOVE THE OLYMPOS VALLEY**

**¢   ⊤ Daphne House.** This pleasant stone hotel is on the edge of a pine forest. **Pros:** friendly vibe; tranquil environment. **Cons:** some rooms are
small and accessed by a spiral staircase. ✉ *50 yards after last turning
to Olympos, just past forest firefighters station with a very small sign*
☎ *242/892–1133* ⊕ *www.daphneevi.com* ⤳ *6 rooms* ⚏ *In-hotel: restau-
rant, bar, business center* ⊙ *Closed Nov.–Apr.* ⦿| *Breakfast.*

**¢   ⊤ Kekik Han.** This small, low-key stone hotel outside the gorge is in a
garden with a pool. **Pros:** very pretty; relaxing. **Cons:** out of the way;
smaller than Olympos Mitos. ✉ *As you descend from Rte. 400, look
for the sign down a dirt track about 500 yards before you reach a
river ford and the final turn for Olympos itself* ☎ *242/892–1158* ⤳ *7
rooms* ⚏ *In-room: Wi-Fi. In-hotel: restaurant, bar, pool* ⊙ *Closed Oct.
15–May 15* ⦿| *Some meals.*

**$$   ⊤ Olimpos Mitos.** This new hotel, just above the smaller Kekin Han, is
one of the nicest places to stay in the neighborhood. **Pros:** very pretty;
relaxing; even nicer than the Kekik Han. **Cons:** out of the way. ✉ *As
you descend from Rte. 400, look for sign down a dirt track about 500
yards before you reach a river ford and final turn for Olympos itself*
☎ *242/892–1158* ⊕ *www.olymposmitos.com* ⤳ *16 rooms, 6 suites*
⚏ *In-room: Wi-Fi. In-hotel: restaurant, bar* ⊙ *Closed Oct. 15–May 15*
⦿| *Some meals.*

**IN ADRASAN**

**¢   ✕ Chill House Lounge.** Chill is the perfect name for this relaxed spot,

MEDITERRANEAN   popular with locals taking a break from the beach or grabbing a bite.
Tables are mostly set out in the open area, in a prime spot toward the
southern end of the beach. The food ranges from snacks to grilled meat,
seafood, and pasta. In the evening, Chill evolves into a bar and the clos-
est thing Adrasan has to a disco. ✉ *Main beach road* ☎ *532/775–2626.*

**$$   ⊤ Ceneviz Hotel and Restaurant.** This hotel and restaurant set back
from the beach has modest, clean rooms, some with a sea view. **Pros:**
great budget option; good central location. **Cons:** rooms are quite
basic. ✉ *Deniz Mahallesi, Adrasan (halfway along Adrasan Beach)*
☎ *242/883–1030* ⊕ *www.cenevizhotel.com* ⤳ *18 rooms* ⚏ *In-hotel:
restaurant, bar* ⊙ *Closed Nov.–Apr.* ⦿| *Breakfast.*

**$$   ⊤ Ford Hotel.** This basic but small and comfortable hotel is between the
sea and a mountain on a prime spot at the southern end of the beach.
**Pros:** location near the beach. **Cons:** at the far end of town. ✉ *Sahil*

*Cad. 220, far end of the beach* ☎ *242/883–1044* ⊕ *www.fordhotel.net* ➷ *27 rooms, 2 suites* ⚲ *In-room: a/c, no TV. In-hotel: restaurant, bar, pool* ⚑ *Some meals.*

¢ ⛫ **Ottoman Palace.** This good hotel just inland from the beach is run by an English couple, John and Sue, and makes for a friendly base in Adrasan. **Pros:** friendly; nice building. **Cons:** not on the beach. ⊠ *A few hundred yards in from the beach, look for the yellow second floor* ☎ *242/883–1462* ⊕ *www.jonnyturk.com* ➷ *12* ⚲ *In-hotel: restaurant, bar, pool* ⚑ *Some meals.*

**NEED A BREAK?** **Tropik.** Not far from Olympos and Çirali, midway between Kumluca and Kemer, Rte. 400 passes by the great high spring of Ulupinar, which supplies water to much of this part of the Tekke Peninsula. This is a lovely spot to stop and eat in the heat of summer; there are wooden platforms under cool high trees, and water gurgles around you. The speciality is fish, which come from the fish farms at the bottom of the hill. One of the best restaurants here is the Tropik, where you can dine on a platform over the river or even at a table with your feet right in the cold spring water. Specialities include delicious oven-roasted lamb or, if you give some advance warning, an entire lamb roasted on a spit. A section of the Lycian Way goes from here across the valley to Çiralı, via the Chimaera; it's about a four- or five-hour trek. ☎ *242/825–0098.*

## PHASELIS

*60 km (37 mi) southwest of Antalya on Rte. 400.*

Majestically located at the edge of three small bays, the ruins of the ancient port city of Phaselis make an atmospheric stop along the Lycian coast.

★ **Phaselis.** The ruins of Phaselis, are as romantic as the reputation of its ancient inhabitants was appalling: Demosthenes the Greek called them unsavory, and Roman statesman Cicero called them rapacious pirates. Since the first Greek colonists from Rhodes bought the land from a local shepherd in the 7th century BC for a load of dried fish, classical literature is replete with the expression "a present from the Phaselians," meaning a cheap gift. Still, the setting is beautiful and Alexander the Great spent a whole winter here before marching on to conquer the east. A broad main street, flanked by some remarkably well-preserved buildings, cuts through the half-standing walls of the Roman **agora.** At each end of this main street is a different bay, both with translucent water ideal for swimming. A third bay, to the north, has great harbor stones carved by the ancients, and is less likely to be disturbed by tour boats.

A small **theater** with trees growing among the seats has a majestic view of Mt. Olympos, and fine **sarcophagi** are scattered throughout a necropolis in the pinewoods that surround the three bays. The ruins are poetic and impressive, ideal for a picnic or a day at the beach, but weekends and high-season days can be crowded and downright depressing when tour yachts from Antalya arrive with loudspeakers blaring. For some reason the refreshment stands at Phaselis are in a legal limbo, so today's pirates of Phaselis are the men selling overpriced drinks under the trees; bring your own. ▨ *$5 per person* ☉ *June–Sept., daily 8:30–7, Oct.–May, daily 8:30–5.*

**GETTING HERE AND AROUND**

The well-marked turnoff to Phaselis is a short distance north of Tekirova. From the turnoff to the ruins and beach is about 2 km (1.2 mi). A bus regularly runs from Tekirova as far as the ticket office, about halfway along this road.

**WHERE TO STAY**

*For expanded hotel reviews, visit Fodors.com.*

**$$** 🏨 **Sundance Natural Village.** This is a popular green-minded stopover for Lycian Way trekkers and arty types taking a break from Istanbul. **Pros:** no pool, TV, or disco. **Cons:** no pool, TV, or disco. ⊠ *Between Phaselis and Tekirova, follow the signs to the "ecopark" and keep going* ☎ *242/821–4165* ⊕ *www.sundance.web.tr* ⤙ *14 bungalows 3 lodges 10 treehouses* ⚒ *In-room: Wi-Fi. In-hotel: restaurant, bar.*

# ANTALYA AND PAMPHYLIA

When the Greeks migrated from central Turkey to the Mediterranean coast, around the 12th century BC, the area east of Antalya became known as Pamphylia, "the land of all the tribes," reflecting the mixed origins of the new inhabitants. The area was remote because the coast was cut off from the main trade routes by the mountains, which provide a spectacular backdrop. Mountain cities like Termessos and Selge were home to the Psidians.

Though it has preserved its old Ottoman center and Roman walls, today Antalya is easily the biggest city along the coast, with all the services and facilities you'd expect. It makes a good base for exploring the region's major archaeological sites: Termessos, Perge, Aspendos, Side, and even Olympos and Phasilis. East from Antalya, a long beach continues through Belek to Side and Alanya, with many (perhaps too many) resorts along the way. If an all-inclusive beach holiday isn't what you have in mind, consider staying in one of Old Antalya's wonderful pensions, which are in restored Ottoman houses.

## ANTALYA

*298 km (185 mi) northeast of Fethiye.*

Antalya is a definite tourist hub, and it's one of Turkey's fastest growing cities; these days the international terminals of Antalya airport are busier even than in Istanbul. Most visitors are on package tours, but Antalya is also a popular destination among Turks. The enormous hotels east of Antalya are themed on Ottoman palaces or the great sights of European capitals and attract increasing numbers of conferences, too.

Antalya has variety, sophistication, and the attraction of having one of Turkey's best museums. It is also quite large. You can happily stay

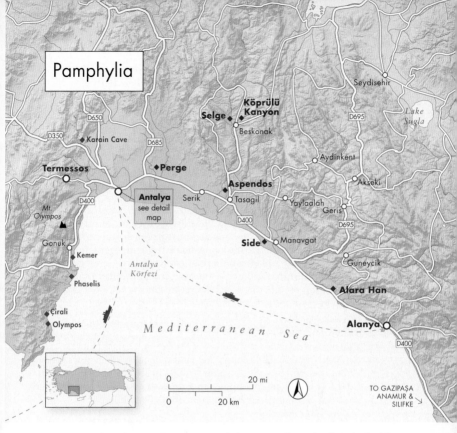

within the winding streets of the atmospheric harbor and old city, known as the Kaleiçi—where there are small houses, restaurants, *pansiyons,* and Mermerli Beach—hardly noticing the big urban conglomeration all around. On the hilltop above the harbor are tea gardens and bars with views that extend south to the Bey Mountains right and around to the Taurus Mountains to the north.

### GETTING HERE AND AROUND

The main bus station is north of the city, and there's a new tramline from here to the center ($2). Buses going to Phaselis, Olympos, and the Lycian Coast stop at a makeshift bus terminal opposite the Hillside Su Hotel, which is a much shorter taxi ride from the old city than the bus station.

A ring road bypasses the inner city and joins with the roads southwest to Olympos and the Lycian coast, and east to Side and Alanya. Another road heads north, signposted "Istanbul," and from this there is a left turn for Termessos and the mountain road to Fethiye. Signs and buses to the city center are marked "Kalekapısı." An older tram along the Antalya seafront, between Lara and the Antalya Museum, runs every half-hour ($1).

## ESSENTIALS

**Tourist Office** Antalya ⊠ *Anafartlar Cad. 31, head west from Saat Kulesi, and turn right onto Anafartlar Cad., the first major road* ☎ *242/241–1747.*

## EXPLORING

Fodor'sChoice
★
**Antalya Müzesi** (*Antalya Museum*). The province of Antalya has a rich collection of archaeological sites and their assembled finds mean a first-rate collection at the Antalya Müzesi. The star is Perge, statues from which fill gallery after gallery, including one just for the gods, from Aphrodite to Zeus. There are also Turkish crafts, costumes, prehistoric artifacts from the Karian Cave, and preclassical statues from Elmalı, with bits of Byzantine iconography and some prehistoric fossils thrown in. One gallery has several fine Roman sarcophagi from the 2nd century AD including a wonderful one illustrating the labors of a steadily aging Hercules. Upstairs are several coin hoards; the large one from Elmalı was recently returned to the museum after being smuggled to the United States. There is a reasonably priced good cafeteria and a gift shop. If you have the time, walk to the museum from the center of town along the clifftop promenade, which has a fine sea view. ⊠ *Konyaaltı Cad., heading west out of town* ☎ *242/241–4528* ☐ *$9* ☉ *Tues.–Sun. 9–6.*

**Karaalioğlan Parkı.** Shady Karaalioğlan Parkı is a traditional park with trees, grass, and benches, as well as a view of the Mediterranean. At the northwest end is a stone tower 49 feet tall, called Hıdırlık Kulesi. It dates from the 2nd century AD, and though no one knows for sure what it is, the best guess is that it was either a combined lighthouse and fort or a tomb. At sunset, sip a drink at the Castle Bar next door to enjoy an unforgettable panorama of the Bey Mountains. ⊠ *Agustos Cad. at Atatürk Cad.*

### INSIDE THE KALEIÇI (OLD TOWN)

The old town of Antalya lies within the fortified city wall; it's an excellent example of a traditional Ottoman neighborhood. A restoration project launched in the 1980s saved hundreds of houses, dating mostly from the 19th century. Most of these were converted into *pansiyons*, rug shops, restaurants, and art galleries.

★ **Hadrian's Gate.** One way to enter the old town is via Hadrian's Gate, a short walk from the main Saat Kulesi intersection, along the pleasant palm-lined Atatürk Caddesi outside the eastern edge of the old town walls. The gate was constructed in honor of a visit by the Roman emperor in AD 130 and has three arches, each with coffered ceilings decorated with rosettes. Ruts in the marble road show where carts once trundled through. From here a straight Roman road leads through town past Kesik Minare Camii to the Hıdırlık Kulesi and the sea.

**Kesik Minare Camii.** Kesik Minare Camii or the "Mosque of the Truncated Minaret" on Hıdarlık Sokak, was once the city's cathedral, and dedicated to the Virgin. It was probably built in the 5th century AD and later converted to a mosque. It's usually locked, but you can get a good look from the outside.

★ **Old Harbor.** Another way to enter the old city is via the old harbor, now filled with yachts, fishing vessels, and tourist-excursion boats. If you're in a car, follow the signs to the *yat limañ*, (harbor) and you'll find a

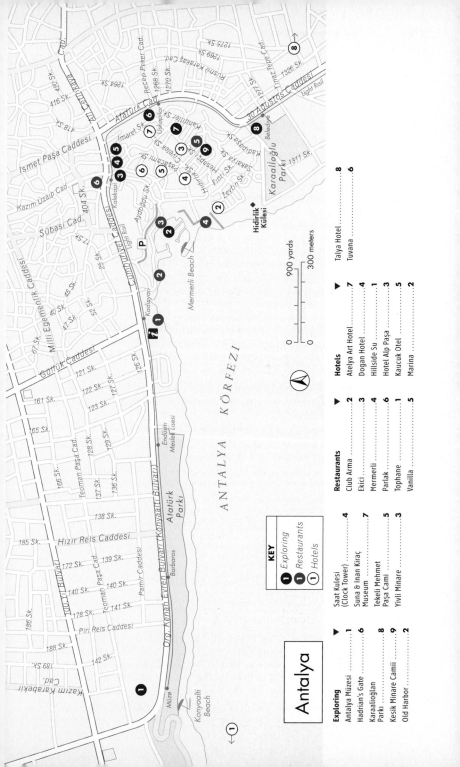

# Antalya

**KEY**
- ▶ Exploring
- ❶ Restaurants
- ① Hotels

**Exploring**

| | |
|---|---|
| ▶ | |
| Antalya Müzesi | 1 |
| Hadrian's Gate | 6 |
| Karaalioğlan Parkı | 8 |
| Kesik Minare Camii | 9 |
| Old Harbor | 2 |
| Saat Kulesi (Clock Tower) | 4 |
| Suna & İnan Kıraç Museum | 7 |
| Tekeli Mehmet Paşa Camii | 5 |
| Yivli Minare | 3 |

**Restaurants**

| | |
|---|---|
| Club Arma | 2 |
| Ekici | 3 |
| Mermerli | 4 |
| Parlak | 6 |
| Tophane | 1 |
| Vanilla | 5 |

**Hotels**

| | |
|---|---|
| ▶ | |
| Atelya Art Hotel | 7 |
| Dogan Hotel | 4 |
| Hillside Su | 1 |
| Hotel Alp Paşa | 3 |
| Kaucuk Otel | 5 |
| Marina | 2 |
| Talya Hotel | 8 |
| Tuvana | 6 |

ANTALYA KÖRFEZI

900 yards
300 meters

convenient, free parking lot behind the quaysides. From here you can head up any of the lanes leading north and east out of the harbor to get to the heart of the old town. Alternatively wander down from Saat Kulesi, forking to the right past the T-shirt and perfume shops, til you reach the bottom.

**Saat Kulesi** (*Clock Tower*). At some point one of the city's Roman towers gained a clock and is known as the Saat Kulesi (Clock Tower). Several of the old town's cobbled lanes pass through the wall here, and the area is also known as Kalekapısı (Castle Gate), which serves as one of the interfaces between the old town and the new. ☎ *242/242–4333.*

★ **Suna & Inan Kiraç Museum.** Fifty yards inside Hadrian's gate, turn left for the Suna & Inan Kiraç Museum (✉ *Hadrian's Gate*), a little oasis in a group of restored buildings decorated with an unlikely looking painted exterior that researchers say was the way most Antalya houses looked in Ottoman times. The museum is part of a privately funded research institute and has an excellent library of books on the region around Antalya—although these are accessible only with special permission— and a good range of guidebooks are on sale in the museum shop. The main display rooms have interesting pictures of Old Antalya and a couple of rooms with waxworks displaying a re-creation of Ottoman wedding scenes. The best part of the museum is the restored church in the garden, where there is a delightful display of historical kitsch from the potteries of the late Ottoman period. ✉ *Kocatepe Sokak 25* ☎ *242/243–4274* 💲 *$3* ⊙ *Thurs.–Tues. 9–noon and 1–6.*

**Tekeli Mehmet Paşa Cami.** Behind the clock tower, the Tekeli Mehmet Paşa Cami, a mosque believed to have been built around the end of the 16th century, is one of the finest surviving Ottoman mosques in the region.

**Yivli Minare** (*Fluted Minaret*). Dark blue and turquoise tiles decorate the Yivli Minare, a graceful 13th-century cylinder commissioned by the Seljuk sultan Alaaddin Keykubat I. The adjoining mosque, named for the sultan, was built on the site of a Byzantine church. Within the complex are two attractive *türbes* (tombs) and an 18th-century *tekke* (monastery), which once housed a community of whirling dervishes. The monastery is now used as an unremarkable art gallery. The Nigar Hatun Türbe (Tomb of Lady Nigar), next to the monastery, though built in Seljuk style, is a 15th-century copy. The *medrese* (theological school) adjacent to the Fluted Minaret has now been glassed in under a bus-station-style roof and is a tourist-oriented shopping center. On offer is the standard tourist fare throughout Turkey—pottery, copperwork, carpets, and tiles—but the prices are better than at most other resorts along the coast. ✉ *Cumhuriyet Cad., south side of Kalekapısı Mey.*

## WHERE TO EAT AND STAY
*For expanded hotel reviews, visit Fodors.com.*

$    ✕ **Club Arma.** You can't miss this restaurant—it has a spectacular loca-
TURKISH   tion halfway up the main road from the old harbor with a panoramic
★    view of the old city and the sea. Inside, airy stone arches give it elegant style despite the fact that this was once the port's petroleum depot. Club Arma is Antalya's most luxurious restaurant, serving octopus carpaccio, lobster, duck, chocolate soufflé, chestnut parfait, and fresh cheesecake,

along with a full range of foreign spirits and cigars from a humidor. At 11 pm, the dance club alongside swings into action. ✉ *Kaleiçi Yatlimanı 42* ☎ *242/244–9710.*

$ ✕**Ekici Restaurant.** This is the most reputable of the harbor-front restau-
TURKISH rants, with a spotless kitchen, good service, and excellent food. Typical
★ specialities are fish stew and fish baked in salt. Fish comes both from the sea and from fish farms (cheaper), and prices vary with the catch and the season. Even here, though, make sure you've agreed on the price of the fish before you order. They also have boats available as floating restaurants, where you can combine dinner with a short cruise. ✉ *Ka-leiçi Yatlimanı 38* ☎ *242/247–8190.*

$ ✕**Mermerli Restaurant.** This restaurant has an excellent view from the
TURKISH breezy terrace above the eastern end of the harbor, and prices are bet-ter than on the waterfront itself. The menu is wide-ranging, with fish, steak, Turkish grills, and all-day breakfast. It's a good spot for a meal if you want to relax at Mermerli Beach, down the steps from the res-taurant, which controls access to the bathing spot. ✉ *Banyo Cad. 25* ☎ *242/248–5484.*

$ ✕**Parlak Restaurant.** If shopping in the jewelry bazaar opposite the clock
TURKISH tower has tired you out, try this longtime Antalya favorite. The special-ity is chicken roasted over charcoal, but there's also a full range of fish, meat, and wide range of *mezes* to choose from as well. In summer, tables are spread out under the stars in front of the restaurant. ✉ *Zincirli Han, Kazım Özalp Cad. 7, just past the statue of Attalos* ☎ *242/241–9160.*

¢ ✕**Tophane.** Sitting in this tea garden, looking out to the harbor, sea, and
CAFÉ mountains beyond, is one of great pleasures of Antalya. The drinks and snacks are inexpensive, but the views are priceless. It's a good stop on the way to the museum—you can walk or catch the old tram, which leaves from here every half hour. ✉ *Cumhuriyet Alanı* ☎ *No phone* ▭ *No credit cards.*

$ ✕**Vanilla.** If you are kebabed out, this old city restaurant, owned by
INTERNATIONAL English chef Wayne and his Turkish wife Emel, does some of the best
★ modern international cuisine along the coast in a stylish contemporary setting. The menu includes an authentic Thai curry, foie gras, and an excellent wild mushroom risotto. The owners also operate a very cool lounge next door. ✉ *Hesapçı Sokak 33, main street in from Hadrian's Gate* ☎ *242/247 60 13* ⊕ *vanillaantalya.com.*

¢ ⌂ **Atelya Art Hotel.** Inexpensive and friendly, this hotel in an old man-sion has larger than usual rooms and a good location in the old town. **Pros:** good value. **Cons:** a little musty. ✉ *Kaleiçi Civelek Sokak 21, near Kesik Minare Mosque* ☎ *242/241–6416* ⊕ *www.atelyahotel.com* ⤴ *25 rooms, 2 suites* ⌂ *In-room: Wi-Fi. In-hotel: restaurant, bar* ▭ *No credit cards* ⍥ *No meals.*

$$ ⌂ **Doğan Hotel.** Every room is unique and tastefully done in this family-
★ run establishment, made up of three restored old houses. **Pros:** nice rooms and garden. **Cons:** some of the rooms are a little dark. ✉ *Mer-merli Banyo Sok. 5* ☎ *242/247–4654, 241–8842* ⊕ *www.doganhotel. com* ⤴ *41 rooms* ⌂ *In-room: Wi-Fi. In-hotel: restaurant, bar, pool.*

$$$$ ⌂ **Hillside Su.** This resort hotel is unforgettable for its all-white color scheme, from the room TVs to the floors, and it's popular with the

weekend crowd that comes in from Istanbul. **Pros:** funky, eclectic atmosphere. **Cons:** maybe too weird to be completely comfortable. ✉ *Dumlupınar Cad., Konyaaltı* ☎ *242/249–0700* ⊕ *www.hillside.com. tr* ↘ *294 rooms* ♿ *In-room: Wi-Fi. In-hotel: restaurant, pool, gym, beach* ⑂ *Some meals.*

$$  ⌗ **Hotel Alp Paşa.** This hotel, in a old mansion retored with a contem-
★  porary aesthetic, might be the most atmospheric place to stay in the old city. **Pros:** beautiful and stylish. **Cons:** small pool for a 60-room hotel; extras are expensive. ✉ *Hesapçi Sokak* ☎ *242/247–5676* ⊕ *www. alppasa.com* ↘ *60 rooms* ♿ *In-hotel: restaurant, bar.*

$$  ⌗ **Kauçuk Otel.** This small boutique hotel is made up of two small houses that have been authentically restored with an eye to contempo-rary design. **Pros:** pleasant oasis in bustling Kaleiçı. **Cons:** some street noise. ✉ *Paşa Camii Sokak 22* ☎ *242/244 23 77* ⊕ *www.kaucukotel. com* ↘ *8 rooms, 1 suite* ♿ *In-room: Wi-Fi. In-hotel: pool.*

$  ⌗ **Marina Hotel.** Three vintage Ottoman houses of white stucco with bay windows and dark-wood trim were restored and connected to make this attractive hotel in the historic heart of Antalya. **Pros:** nice pool area. **Cons:** rooms feel a little dated. ✉ *Mermeli Sokak 15* ☎ *242/247–5490* 🖷 *242/241–1765* ↘ *41 rooms* ♿ *In-hotel: restaurant, bar, pool* ⑂ *Breakfast.*

$$$  ⌗ **Talya Hotel.** This prime property rises over the cliffs just to the east of
★  Karaalioğlan Parkı, commanding spectacular views of the Bey Moun-tains (ask for a corner room; these have numbers that end in 17). **Pros:** modern, professional luxury hotel. **Cons:** rather characterless. ✉ *Fevzi Cakmak Cad. 30* ☎ *242/248–6800* ⊕ *www.divan.com* ↘ *204 rooms* ♿ *In-room: Wi-Fi. In-hotel: restaurants, bar, pool, gym.*

$$  ⌗ **Tuvana Hotel.** One of the classier options in Kaleici, this hotel is made up of four old houses. **Pros:** stylish. **Cons:** room sizes vary greatly. ✉ *Karanlık Sokak 18* ☎ *242/244 40 54* ⊕ *www.tuvanahotel.com* ↘ *45 rooms* ♿ *In-hotel: restaurant, bar, pool.*

## NIGHTLIFE AND THE ARTS

**Castle Café and Bar.** The perfect start to any evening out in Antalya starts by watching the sun set from the clifftop Castle Café and Bar, next to Hıdırlık Kulesi—you can accompany your drink with some of their sesame and garlic dip known as *hibeş*. ✉ *Hıdırlık Cad. 48/1* ☎ *242/242–3188.*

Other than the clifftop Castle Café and Bar, Antalya's bars are centered on three main areas: in Kaleiçi; in the new part of town, on Barlar Caddesi (Bar Street), running off Cumhuriyet Caddesi; and in Atatürk Park. Most visitors prefer Kaleiçi, where a profusion of bars competes for your attention.

**Club Arma.** For dancing, the smartest place in town is undoubtedly Club Arma, on the harbor road. ✉ *Kaleiçi Yatlimanı 42* ☎ *242/244–9710.*

The Atatürk Kulture Merkezi, also known as AKM, is a complex with an exhibition space and several theaters in a cliff-top park about 3 km (2 mi) west of the city center. There are concerts year-round—look for fliers posted around the city—and an annual film festival.

## SPORTS AND THE OUTDOORS

BEACHES **Konyaaltı Beach.** For many Turks, Antalya is synonymous with the thick crowds of holiday makers on Konyaaltı Beach, and in high season the pebble strand is a hot and somewhat off-putting sight. The city has worked hard to improve the quality of the beach experience, though, with especially impressive results on the 1-km (½-mi) section starting after the museum and ending under Su Hotel. The beach is largely divided up by concessions, each with its own restaurant, deck chairs, umbrellas, and showers.

**Mermerli Beach.** If you didn't know that Mermerli Beach was there, you'd never guess it. This small strip of sand and pebbles outside the harbor wall is reached from the Mermerli Restaurant halfway up the hill east of the harbor. The $6 price of admission to this quiet oasis in the heart of town includes loungers and umbrellas. ☎ 242/248–5484.

RAFTING Rafting has become a major activity from the big hotels, with several agencies offering trips up to various canyons. To avoid the crowds, it's best to get up to the water in the early morning before the package tourists are out of bed. Most companies will pick you up at your hotel. Alternative: You can drive out to Köprülü Canyon yourself, and visit the ruins of Selge, too.

**TransNature** ☎ 242/247–8688.

## SHOPPING

Thanks to its size—in 2006, about 800,000 people lived here—the shopping streets have more variety than anywhere else on the Turquoise Riviera, although the merchandise, in general, is the same sort of stuff you find all over Turkey. East and north of the old town walls are where the less expensive clothing shops are found, including some jewelry arcades. The old town is where to find more decorative souvenirs, travel agencies, boutique hotels, *pansiyons*, cheaper restaurants, and the nice little Mermerli Beach outside the harbor wall. The Kenan Evren Boulevard along the seafront cliffs toward the museum has the concentration of upmarket clothing shops, as well as the offices of airlines that run shuttle buses to the airport. A short taxi ride to the west of town is Antalya's fanciest mall, the Migros Shopping Center, on the main road to Kemer, behind Konyaalti and the Hillside Su Hotel: it has a large supermarket, eight cinemas, a large food court, and branches of almost all of Turkey's big clothing chains like Mavi Jeans, LCW for children's clothes, Derimod for upmarket leathers, Bisse and Abbate for shirts, Vakkorama and Boyner for general clothing, and all kinds of international brand-name shops like Swatch, Lacoste, and Tommy Hilfiger among its 100 shops.

NEED A BREAK? When driving east on Route 400 from Antalya toward Perge, Aspendos, Side, or Alanya, don't miss one of the region's great culinary experiences: a meal in the strip of restaurants by the highway in Aksu. Turks on business in Antalya will detour for miles just to eat here. Ease off the highway onto the feeder road when you see a pedestrian bridge about 6 km (4 mi) east of the Antalya airport intersection, then park where you can.

**Öz Şimşek.** *Turkish.* Try the superb kumin-flavored köfte meatballs with baked garlic and mild peppers along with a plate of mind-blowingly fresh *piyaz* (white beans in a sauce with sesame paste, tomato, parsley, egg, and olive oil). ⊠ *Berberoğlu Çarşıısı, Çalkaya* ☎ *242/426–3920* ⊙ *6am–11pm.*

**Ramazan'ın Yeri.** *Turkish.* At the southern foot of the pedestrian overpass, this restaurant was one of the first in the strip and offers a remarkable smorgasbord of all animal parts fit to eat. There is a full range of the normal kebabs and stews, but this is the place to experiment. The four daily soups include tripe and *paça*, normally boiled from the head of a calf. In the refrigerator you can select delicacies to follow: ribs, cutlets, liver, kidney, and heart. Calf's brain can be found among the cold appetizers. ☎ *242/426–3231* ⊙ *Open 24 hrs.*

## TERMESSOS

*37 km (23 mi) northwest of Antalya; take E87 north toward Burdur, bear left at fork onto Rte. 350 toward Korkuteli and follow signs to Termessos.*

★ Writers in antiquity referred to Termessos as the Eagle's Nest, and when you visit the site, 4,500 feet high in the mountains west of Antalya, you'll understand why. The city was impregnable and now offers stunning vistas over the beautiful scenery of Termessos National Park. The warlike and fiercely independent people who made their home here launched frequent raids on their coastal neighbors. They were not Greek but a native Asia Minor people who called themselves the Solymians, after ancient Mt. Solymus, which rises above the city. Termessos remained autonomous for much of its history and was quite wealthy by the 2nd century AD. Most of its remains date from this period.

A visit takes at least four hours, and there is no restaurant at the site, so pack water and lunch, and wear sturdy shoes.

### GETTING HERE AND AROUND

It's easiest to get to Termessos if you have a car, but tours can be arranged by agencies in Antalya, or you can catch any bus from the bus station to Korkuteli and get off at the Termessos intersection where taxis usually wait; one way is around $15.

### EXPLORING

**Karain Cave.** One kilometer (½ mi) north of the Termessos turnoff from E87 is the Karain Cave (follow the yellow signs for Karain). Archaeological digs since 1919 have already proved that it was inhabited as far back as the Paleolithic Age, making it one of the oldest settlements in Turkey. Later it seems to have become a religious center for primitive man. Many of the Karain finds—stone implements, bones of people and animals, and fossilized remains including those of hippopotamuses—are on display in Antalya Museum, but there is also a small museum on the edge of the high meadow where the cave is. Part of the cave itself is also electrically lighted and open to the public, but this is a small site and probably only worth stopping at if you have time after seeing Termessos. 🎫 *$3* ☉ *Tues.–Sun. 8–5.*

**Termessos.** The attractions in Termessos start right by the parking area, with a monumental **gate,** part of an ancient temple dedicated to Hadrian. The steepness of the path that leads up to the craggy remains of the city walls soon makes it clear just why Alexander the Great declined to attack. Next, on your left, are a **gymnasium,** a **colonnaded street** (half of whose many statue bases once supported likenesses of famed wrestlers), a **bath** complex built of dark gray stone blocks, and then, up and around, is a very ruined colonnaded street and the 5,000-seat **theater,** whose perch at the edge of a sheer cliff has one of the most spectacular settings in Turkey. From this staggering height you can see the sea, the Pamphylian plain, Mt. Solymus, and the occasional mountain goat or ibex. Farther around is the well-preserved *bouleterion* where the city council met, surrounded by several temples, the very overgrown market, and some huge underground cisterns. Termessos has one more wonder: several vast **necropolises,** with nearly 1,000 tombs scattered willy-nilly on a rocky hill. A signposted alternate route back to the car park takes you past several rock-cut tombs, and back at the car park another route from the ticket office takes you to another large collection of tombs. 🎫 *$6* ☉ *Daily 8:30–7.*

## PERGE

*22 km (14 mi) from Antalya, east on Rte. 400 to turnoff north at Aksu.*

Perge's biggest problem is that it suffers from comparison with its neighbors. It is, however, one of Turkey's best overall examples of a Roman city.

### GETTING HERE AND AROUND
The ruins are well signposted 2 km (1½ mi) north of the small town of Aksu, 22 km (14 mi) east of Antalya on Route 400. There are frequent buses from Antalya Otogar to Aksu.

### EXPLORING
**Perge.** Although Perge lacks the location of Termessos or an A-list attraction like Aspendos, it is one of the best places to get an overall impression of a classical Turkish city. The first thing you'll see is a splendid theater, which is unfortunately closed for repairs at this writing. The stadium next door is open and is one of the best preserved in the ancient world. The vaulted chambers under the stadium bleachers held shops; marble inscriptions record the proprietors' names and businesses.

The rest of the site is about 1 km (½ mi) north. After parking just outside the old city walls, you'll enter near the city's sturdy 3rd-century-BC garrison towers. Directly ahead is a fine, long-colonnaded avenue, unique for the water channel that ran down its center, starting at a fountain at the far end. This street was trodden by St. Paul as he passed by on his way to Psidian Antioch in the mountains. Beside the entrance is the old agora or marketplace; the slender, sun-bleached columns lining the street once supported a covered porch filled with shops. Look for a backgammon-like board game cut into a block of marble. Opposite is the well-preserved bathhouse. The rest of the site is rather overgrown, but the keen can hunt down churches and a gymnasium. 📷 *$9* 🕙 *Daily 8–7.*

## ASPENDOS

*49 km (31 mi) east of Antalya on Rte. 400 (follow yellow signs).*

Most experts agree that the theater in Aspendos is one of the best preserved in the world. A splendid Roman aqueduct that traverses the valley, another superior example of Roman engineering, utilized the pressure of the water flowing from the mountains to supply the summit of the acropolis. The water tower dates from the 2nd century AD, and its stairway is still intact.

### GETTING HERE AND AROUND

From Antalya, take Route 400 east and follow the yellow signs. There are frequent buses to the nearby town of Serik, but minibuses to Aspendos are rare.

### EXPLORING

Fodor's Choice
★

**Aspendos.** Pay your admission to the main site at what was once the actors' entrance to the theater. Built during the reign of Emperor Marcus Aurelius (ruled AD 161–180) by a local architect called Xenon, it is striking for the broad curve of seats, perfectly proportioned porticoes, and rich decoration. The Greeks liked open vistas behind their stages, but the Romans preferred enclosed spaces. The stage building you see today was once covered by an elaborate screen of marble columns, and its niches were filled with statues. The only extant relief on-site depicts Dionysus (Bacchus) watching over the theater. The acoustics are fine, and the theater is still in use—for concerts and for the Antalya International Opera and Ballet Festival, held every June and July, rather than for the wild-animal and gladiator spectacles as in Roman times. Aspendos is not just a Roman site—it was founded by the Hittites, and the Seljuk Turks used it as a royal palace in the 13th century. There are traces of the distinctive Seljuk red-and-yellow paintwork here and there.

Most visitors just see the theater, but the actual city is up a short zigzagging trail behind the theater. The rewards are a tall **Nymphaion**—a sanctuary to the nymphs built around a fountain decorated with a marble dolphin—and the remains of a Byzantine **basilica** and **market hall.** You can also see, below in the plain, the **stadium** and the **aqueduct** which used an ingenious syphon system. 📷 *$9* 🕙 *Daily 9–7.*

**Selge and Köprülü Kanyon.** Just east of Aspendos, a turnoff leads north to the ruins of Selge and Köprülü Kanyon, a popular spot for white-water rafting. Just before Beşkonak (30 km/18 mi) the road splits and one branch crosses the river, passing the pleasant riverside Selge and Perge restaurants. After 10 km (6 mi) the two roads meet again at the start of the canyon proper—you'll drive over a very well-preserved Roman bridge. There are dozens of raft operators on the river. One of the largest is **TransNature** (📷 *242/247–8688);* the Selge and Perge restaurants have local rafting guides as well. The rapids are rated fairly easy. From here you head another 15 km (9 mi) up a steep road through rock formations to the town of Zelve, the site of the Roman city of Selge. Just before you reach town, take the left turn and the impressive Roman theater will soon come into view. Most visitors are happy to clamber over the theater, but from the top you can see the ruins of the city itself on the hill opposite. The area is part of the St. Paul Trail hike. If you'd like to explore with a local guide, call Adem Bahar (☎ 535/762–8116).

## SIDE

*75 km (47 mi) east of Antalya on Rte. 400.*

Charter-tour hotels crowding along this stretch of coast threaten to overshadow Side, but at its heart this city's delightful mix of ancient ruins and modern amenities is an underestimated jewel. Sandy beaches run along each side of town, with the ruins in the middle, dotted with a few dozen T-shirt and jewelry shops. Side, like Antalya or Alanya, has all sorts of options, from late-night dancing, shopping to kayaking in mountain canyons. It's also close to the major sites of Aspendos and Perge, and less than an hour from Antalya airport. Like its bigger Pamphylian sisters, it's best visited out of the heat of the high season July and August, but weekends can be crowded, too. With the right hotel, it's still possible to experience how Side felt in the 1960s, when the city was off the beaten track, and the likes of dancer Rudolph Nureyev and French intellectual Simone de Beauvoir were visitors.

### GETTING HERE AND AROUND

Access to Side is via the town of Manavgat, 75 km (47 mi) east of Antalya on Route 400. There's a turnoff just west of Manavgat—it's another 11 km (7mi) to Side. There is a large parking lot just outside the walls of ancient Side. There are frequent buses from Antalya and Alanya to Manavgat, and minibuses from Manavgat Otogar to Side run every few minutes, stopping at the same parking lot.

**Official Tourist Office Side** ✉ *A mile north of the center on the main road* ☎ *242/753–1265* 🖶 *242/753–2657.*

### EXPLORING

Follow signs in from Route 400 for *Antik Side* and resist any sense of disappointment—it will dissipate when you suddenly find yourself driving onto the little peninsula through the delightful ruins of the Greco-Roman city. Through a last arch and past a colonnade behind the theater, park your car or, if staying in a hotel inside the town, ask to be let through the barricade that protects the harbor area from traffic. Ruins are all around: there's a lovely theater, with city and sea views from the top row, and 2nd-century AD temples to Apollo and Athena a few blocks south, on the tip of the peninsula. The town was founded by early Greeks, minting coins from 500 BC, but Side only began to expand when Pompey cleared out the slave-trading pirates in 67 BC. Most of the ruins, laid bare by one of the only systematic excavations of a whole city, date from the prosperous Roman period. One notable feature of the site is the well-preserved Roman communal public latrines.

**Side Müzesi** (*Side Museum*). The Side Müzesi is near the theater, in the restored Roman bath. The collection of Roman statues is small but one of the best in Asia Minor: it includes a gorgeous group of the marble torsos of the Three Graces, various cherubs, a brilliant satyr, and a bust of Emperor Hadrian. The sculpture garden behind the museum is larger than the museum itself and overlooks the Mediterranean. You may find the admission steep for the size of the museum. 🎟 *$6.*

★ **Temple of Apollo.** If you follow the main street full of shops selling jewelry and cheap clothes till you reach the water, and then turn left, you reach Side's picture-postcard Temple of Apollo, built of gleaming white marble that's set off beautifully by the blue ocean behind.

**Theater.** Opposite the Side museum is the city's large theater, rebuilt in the 2nd century, though the design is more Greek. There are views out over the agora, which is closed for excavations. 🎟 *$6.*

## WHERE TO EAT AND STAY
*For expanded hotel reviews, visit Fodors.com.*

$   ✕ **Orfoz.** If you want to eat in the harbor area, many would say this is
TURKISH   the best restaurant to choose: the bamboo chairs are comfortable, the tables well spaced, there are trees for shade, and the food is excellent. Fresh seafood is the speciality, including a melt-in-the-mouth octopus dish, but there's something for everyone on the international menu, including large, though expensive steaks. The view over the western beach is just right at sunset, the service is good, and if there's a chill in spring or autumn, attentive waiters bring blankets. ⊠ *Liman Cad. 58/C* ☏ *242/753–1362.*

$   ✕ **Paşaköy Bar and Restaurant.** Paşaköy's has reasonable food, but what
TURKISH   differentiates this pleasant restaurant from the rest is its weird and wonderfully kitsch garden, decked out with bizarre mock-classical statuary and stuffed animals. The grilled meat dishes are good, there's a kids' menu, the waitstaff is friendly and attentive, and the bartender can make a cocktail with a kick. ⊠ *Liman Cad. 98* ☏ *242/753–3622* 🕐 *Closed Dec.–May.*

$   ✕ **Soundwaves Restaurant.** This open-air restaurant on a pedestrian walk
MEDITERRANEAN   overlooking the sea is decked out like a pirate ship but, unlike its piratical neighbors in the harbor, has a long and reliable reputation; it's run by the same management as the nearby Beach House Hotel. If you're walking from the harbor, head 500 yards southeast through the temple and around the promontory. Specialities include fish baked in salt, garlic prawns, and thanks to an Australian half-owner, a deep-fried seafood dish called Tasmanian Squid. ⊠ *Barbaros Cad.* ☏ *242/753–1607* 🕐 *Closed Dec.–Apr.*

¢   🏨 **Beach House Hotel.** If you want a charmed few days on the Side sea-
🕐   front, this great-value hotel is the place to stay. **Pros:** friendly and help-
★   ful staff. **Cons:** opposite, rather than on, the beach. ⊠ *Barbaros Sokak* ☏ *242/753–1607* ⊕ *www.beachhouse-hotel.com* 🛏 *23 rooms* ⌂ *In-room: no a/c, Wi-Fi. In-hotel: restaurant, bar, pool* 🍽 *Breakfast.*

$$$   🏨 **Barut Hotel Acanthus.** This modest four-story hotel is done in Mediter-
ranean style, with whitewashed walls, dark-wood trim and terraces, a red-tile roof, and direct access to a fine sand beach. **Pros:** good beach location not too far from town. **Cons:** pretty average. ⊠ *Side Köyü,*

**DID YOU KNOW?**

The Roman theater of ancient Aspendos could seat an audience of about 7,000 people.

*Box 55* ☎ *242/753–3050* 🖷 *242/753–1913* 🛏 *104 rooms* ⛷ *In-hotel: restaurant, bar, pool, tennis court, beach, water sports* 🍴 *Some meals.*

¢ ☷ **Doğa.** This small and pleasant inn is in an old stone house a block from the beach. **Pros:** small size; character; organic food. **Cons:** not right on the beach. ⊠ *Lale Sokak 8, just in from Beach House Hotel* ☎ *242/753 6246* ⊕ *www.sidedoga.com/* 🛏 *7 rooms* ⛷ *In-room: Wi-Fi. In-hotel: restaurant, bar.*

¢ ☷ **Kamer Motel.** This modest, clean hotel in a quiet part of town has a great location on eastern shore, with views of the sea and a private though rocky beach area. **Pros:** nice views; good value. **Cons:** uninspired architecture and decor. ⊠ *Barabaros Cad. 47* ☎ *242/753–1007* 🖷 *242/753–2660* 🛏 *26 rooms* ⛷ *In-room: Wi-Fi. In-hotel: restaurant, bar, beach* 🍴 *Breakfast.*

### NIGHTLIFE

**Lighthouse.** Down by the harbor is the open-air Lighthouse discotheque and bar.

**Pegasus Bar.** On the shore west of the theater, almost behind the museum, this lounge is a good place to sit with a drink watching the sunset over the ocean; they have a vast range of cocktails, as well as 15 types of coffee, and live music at night.

**Royal Castle Bar.** The evening action begins after sunset as places like the Royal Castle Bar, just in from the water on the southwest corner—it keeps the Brits happy with its publike atmosphere and English football on the TV, and there is also live music most evening in season. ⊠ *Turgut Reis Cad. 62* ☎ *242/753–4373.*

### SPORTS AND THE OUTDOORS

BOAT TRIPS  Boat trips along the Manavgat River can be arranged either from the harbor at Side or from the town of Manavgat (on Route 400, 1 km [½ mi] east of the turnoff for Side). Prices vary widely according to the length of the trip and whether food is provided; you should definitely bargain. Times often change, but a boat also usually leaves each morning at 9 am for Alanya—check the evening before at the sales desk (☎ *No phone*) in the middle of the small Side harborfront. Boats stop to let you swim, and some arrange for activities such as jet skiing, waterskiing, or water parachuting; be warned, however, that not all the operators are properly licensed or insured, and serious accidents have occurred.

JEEP SAFARIS  Jeep safaris are also popular and can be arranged from one of several travel agencies in Side.

**Unser Tour.** One good option is Unser Tour. ☎ *532/413–8431 mobile, 242/453–5583 office* ⊕ *unserreisen.com.*

## ALARA HAN

*118 km (73 mi) east of Antalya or 43 km (26 mi) east of Side, turn north off Rte. 400 onto local road signposted Alara Han; the site is 9 km (6 mi) inland.*

The Seljuk Turks fostered the prosperity of their 11th- to 13th-century domains with trade protected by a network of *kervansarays*, or inns— also called *hans* in Turkish. One of the more romantic of these is Alara Han, built in the early 13th century and now beautifully restored with a fountain, prayer room, unusual lamp stands carved into the stone, and lions' heads on the base of the arches, and a majestic vaulted interior. In summer, the inland countryside location also provides welcome relief from the sweltering coast.

### THE SELJUK TURKS AND THE MEDITERRANEAN

The empire of the Roman Seljuks was the first Muslim empire to extend into Anatolia, long before the Ottomans arrived. It reached its height in the 13th century, when the Seljuks established full control of Turkey's Mediterranean and Black Sea coasts. Their capital was at Konya (Iconium), in central Anatolia, where winters were bitterly cold. As a consequence, the Seljuks established Alanya, the nearest point on the coast, as a secondary winter capital, and there are many Seljuk remains in the area, including the Alara Han.

For the energetic ready to scramble with hands and feet, an unusual hand-carved tunnel leads up to the Seljuk fortress built on the crags above the *han*. To get here, follow the road to the **Alara Cennet Piknik restaurant** (*544/260–5520*). A flashlight is essential to make the climb, but if you don't have one, ask at the Cennet Piknik to borrow one. Ask for directions across the vegetable fields to the tunnel entrance. Afterward you can eat freshly caught trout at the restaurant he'll cook you and relax with a cold drink on the riverbank, enjoying a cool breeze from the crystal clear snow-fed river.

### GETTING HERE AND AROUND

Turn north off Route 400 near the town of Okurcular, onto local road signposted "Alara Han"; the site is 9 km (6 mi) inland via the village of Uluguney. There is no public transport.

## ALANYA

*135 km (84 mi) east of Side on Rte. 400.*

Alanya is Turkey's hottest resort town—literally. Temperatures here are higher than almost anywhere else in Turkey, averaging 106°F (27°C) in July and August, and the waves lapping the long Mediterranean beaches that sweep toward Alanya's great rock citadel are only a degree or two cooler. This makes high summer in Alanya heaven for sun-starved, disco-loving, hard-drinking north Europeans but rather hellish for anyone seeking a quiet holiday surrounded by nature.

That said, Alanya is now home to one of Turkey's biggest year-round expatriate communities, and in spring and autumn it's a pleasantly warm and inexpensive choice for a few days of easily accessible swimming, historic sites, and good food. The city is cleaning up its act, so to speak: former wastelands of concrete-block apartments are now color-fully painted, Ottoman districts around the harbor are well on the way to being restored, and the new and old houses inside the magnificent red-walled citadel are an unspoiled, eclectic jumble. The best swimming place is known as Cleopatra's Beach—yet another accretion to the fables surrounding Mark Antony's courtship of the Egyptian queen—and its yellow sands extend northwest from the rock citadel. Foreign influence has led to improvements like automated touch-screen bike rentals around the center, hundreds of restaurants that can bill in multiple currencies, and a microbrewery called the Red Tower that serves what many to believe is the best beer in Turkey.

Alanya is famed for its sandy beaches, within walking distance of most hotels. Boats can be hired from the harbor for relaxing day tours to caves around the citadel rock and a view of the only surviving naval arsenal of the 12th and 13th century Seljuks. Alanya, called Kala-naoros by the Byzantines, was captured by the Seljuk sultan Alaaddin Keykubad in 1221 and became the Turkish Seljuks' first stronghold on the Mediterranean in their centuries-long migration westward. Several amusing stories explain the Seljuk sultan Alaaddin Keykubad's con-quest: one says he married the commander's daughter, another that he tied torches to the horns of thousands of goats and drove them up the hill in the dark of night, suggesting a great army was attacking. Most likely, he simply cut a deal; once settled, he modestly renamed the place Alaiya, after himself, and built defensive walls to ensure he would never be dislodged. The Ottomans arrived in 1471, and gave it its current name, Alanya.

**GETTING HERE AND AROUND**
The highway passes around the city's northern outskirts. The castle marks the center of town, and there are two distinct clusters of hotels, shops, and restaurants on either side of it. There are frequent buses from Antalya and Side, and less frequent ones to Anamur and Adana.

**Official Tourist Office Alanya** ⊠ *Damlataş Cad. 1* ☎ *242/513–1240* 🖷 *242/513–5436.*

**EXPLORING**
**Alanya Müzesi** (*Alanya Museum*). It's worth dropping by the small Alanya Müzesi, just to see the perfectly preserved Roman bronze statue of a gleaming, muscular Hercules from the 2nd century AD. Other bronze statues feature Hermes and a graceful woman. There is also a large collection of ancient ceramics and interesting limestone ossuaries and heads from the late Roman period, as well as pictures of some of the less famous sites in the area. Note the Ottoman Greek inscriptions in Karamanli—Turkish written with the Greek alphabet. ⊠ *Azaklar Sokak, south of Atatürk Cad., where the castle hill drops down to Cleopatra'sBbeach* ☎ *242/513–1228* 💰 *$2* ☉ *Tues.–Sun. 8:30–noon and 1:30–5:30.*

**Kale** (*citadel*). Views of the splendid castle or *kale*, on a mighty crag sur-rounded on three sides by the sea, dominate all roads into Alanya. The crenellated outer walls are 7 km (4 mi) long and include 146 towers. The road pierces these outer walls through a modern break, and heads up to the summit divided into two, one to the **İç Kale** (inner fortress) and one to the **Ehmediye;** both have places to park. Alternatively there is a regular city bus to the summit, which allows you to walk up or down through the old city's residential area, starting or ending at the Kızıl Kule; it's a hot walk in summer, though.

In the center of the castle are the remains of the original *bedestan* (bazaar), whose old shops are now rooms in a lackluster hotel, with the not very original name, the Bedestan Hotel. Along a road to the top of the promontory, a third wall and a ticket office defend the **İç Kale (Keep).** Inside are the ruins of a Byzantine church, with some 6th-century frescoes of the evangelists. Keykubad probably also had a palace here, although discoveries by the McGhee Center of George-town University—itself in a beautiful old Ottoman mansion perched on the cliff-face between the first and second ring of walls—indicates that in times of peace the Seljuk elite probably preferred their pleasure gardens and their hunting and equestrian sports on the well-watered plain below. Steps ascend to the battlement on the summit. A viewing platform is built on the spot where condemned prisoners and women convicted of adultery were once cast to their deaths. The ticket is also valid for the **Ehmediye** area, past the 17th-century Suleymaniye Camii, where a small citadel is built on the foundations of classical walls. ■TIP→ Admire the ruined monastery down below but do not attempt to descend toward it—the mountainside is very treacherous. ☎ *242/512–3304* ⊠ *$6 for İç Kale and Ehmediye* ⊘ *Tues.–Sun. 9–7.*

**Kızıl Kule** (*Red Tower*). A minor masterpiece of Mediterranean military architecture, the 100-foot-high Kızıl Kule, was built by the Seljuks in 1225 to defend Alanya harbor and the nearby shipyard known as the *tersane* (arsenal). Sophisticated technology for the time was imported in the form of an architect from Aleppo who was familiar with crusader castle building. The octagonal redbrick structure includes finely judged angles of fire for archers manning the loopholes, cleverly designed stairs to cut attackers off, and a series of troughs to convey boiling tar and melted lead onto besieging forces. Nowadays the Red Tower's cool passages house temporary exhibits, probably less captivating than the view from the roof. A short walk south along the water—or along the castle walls, if you prefer—is another defensive tower rising above the *tersane,* which is made up of five workshops all under an arched roof. Ships could be pulled up under the vaulted stone arches for build-ing or repairs, and the cover was likely also useful for storing war sup-plies. ⊠ *Eastern harbor at south end of İskele Cad.* ⊠ *$2.*

## WHERE TO EAT

$ ✕ **Filika Restaurant.** On a pretty terrace right on Cleopatra's Beach and MEDITERRANEAN looking up to the citadel towering overhead, this fine restaurant is where real-estate agents take new customers before hustling them off to the close-packed fields of villas and apartment blocks mushrooming on the flanks of the mountains north of town. The focus is on meat, steaks, kebabs, and lamb, including lamb with rosemary or, ironically, sprinkled with thyme like that which used to grow where the new devel-opments now stand. There is also a more basic snack menu for lunch. ⊠ *Güzelyalı Cad., diagonally opposite the museum* ☎ *242/519–3227.*

$$ ✕ **Güverte Restaurant.** Across from the Kaptan Hotel, this long-standing
TURKISH favorite has a delightful view of the harbor with excellent traditional
Turkish fare, focused on fresh seafood. If you're lucky, they'll have *grida*
(grouper) as a daily special; if not, try the fried squid with local "tara-
tor" sauce—a mixture of yogurt, garlic, lemon, walnuts, olive oil, and
bread. ⊠ *Çarşı Mahallesi, İskele Cad. 70* ☏ *242/513–4100.*

¢ ✕ **Özsüt Alanya.** This modern, air-conditioned cake shop is the best place
CAFÉ in town for restoring lagging caffeine or blood sugar levels—perhaps
before an assault on the citadel above. It's part of a modern chain that
has expanded rapidly through Turkish cities thanks to the excellent
cakes, pastries, and sweets. ⊠ *Çarşıı Mah., Iskele Cad., Kamburoğlu
Apt. 84, just before Red Tower* ☏ *242/512–2202.*

$$ ✕ **Red Tower Restaurant.** This is one of Turkey's first microbreweries, and
TURKISH the beer here is some of the best you'll find in the country. You have
★ the choice of a traditional pilsner, a light and sweeter Helles, a dark
Marzen ale, or a wheat beer. There's a different eatery on every floor,
including sushi and, of course, kebabs. All floors overlook the Alanya
harbor and the Red Tower fortifications. In summer you can eat on
the terrace across the road. On the roof is an open-air Skylounge Bar.
⊠ *Iskele Cad. 80* ☏ *242/513–6664.*

## WHERE TO STAY
*For expanded hotel reviews, visit Fodors.com.*

$ ⛫ **Elysée Beach Hotel.** This relatively quiet, clean, and modest hotel is
right on Alanya's Cleopatra's Beach, a short walk from the center of
town. **Pros:** central location and beach. **Cons:** few rooms have real
sea views. ⊠ *Saray Mah., Atatürk Cad. 145* ☏ *242/512–8791* ⊕ *www.
elyseehotels.com* ⟿ *60 rooms* ⛬ *In-hotel: pool, gym* ☾ *Closed Dec.
15–Mar. 1* ⦿*Some meals.*

$$ ⛫ **Grand Kaptan Hotel.** For dependable service and facilities, this seafront
hotel, 4 km (2 mi) east of town, is the grandest in Alanya. **Pros:** profes-
sional service; extensive facilities. **Cons:** not *right* on the beach; annex
rooms are not as good as the main building; some rooms lack private
bath. ⊠ *Oba Göl Mevkii* ☏ *242/514–0101* ⊕ *www.kaptanhotels.com*
⟿ *264 rooms, 8 suites* ⛬ *In-room: Wi-Fi. In-hotel: restaurant, bar, pool,
tennis court, gym* ⦿*All meals.*

$$ ⛫ **Grand Okan.** The four-star Grand Okan is the slickest hotel on
Cleopatra's Beach. **Pros:** fresh; some sea views; relatively central. **Cons:**
large, impersonal resort hotel. ⊠ *Atatürk Cad., west of center where
main road meets beach road* ☏ *242/519 1637* ⊕ *www.grandokan.com*
⛬ *In-hotel: restaurant, bar, pool.*

$ ⛫ **Kaptan Hotel.** This hotel near the Red Tower was the best in Alanya
before tourism development overwhelmed the town. **Pros:** central.
**Cons:** noisy. ⊠ *İskele Cad. 70* ☏ *242/513–4900* ⊕ *www.kaptanhotels.
com* ⟿ *76 rooms* ⛬ *In-hotel: restaurant, bar, pool.*

## NIGHTLIFE
Alanya's nightlife centers around its harbor and the explosive beat on
İskele Caddesi—although there are a few large dance clubs in Dimçay,
about 5 km (3mi) outside town. Bars often have extensive menus, and

restaurants frequently have live music or turn into impromptu discos after dinner.

**James Dean Bar.** The James Dean Bar is popular and less expensive than some of the other haunts on the strip. ⊠ *İskele Cad.* ☎ *242/512–3195.*

**Robin Hood Bar.** The Sherwood Forest–themed, three-floor Robin Hood Bar is the biggest on the block; it's open all year-round and tries to cater to all tastes. ⊠ *İskele Cad. 24* ☎ *242/511–7692.*

**Summer Garden.** Near the seafront on the road to Antalya, the Summer Garden offers free transport to five people or more from Alanya to it and its sister **Fresco** restaurant, both part of the same complex. The two large bars among the palm trees have a dance floor cooled with outdoor air-conditioning (really!). Open from 6 pm, the music doesn't stop until about 4 am. ⊠ *Konaklı Kasabasi* ☎ *242/565–0059, 535/768–1326* ⊙ *Open mid-May–mid-Nov.*

### SPORTS AND THE OUTDOORS

Alanya's main beach, known as Cleopatra's Beach, remains relatively uncrowded except in the height of summer. It's also easy to reach other nearby beaches, coves, and caves by boat. Legend has it that buccaneers kept their most fetching maidens at **Korsanlar Mağarası** (Pirates' Cave) and **Aşıklar Mağarası** (Lovers' Cave), two favorite destinations. Tour boats usually charge from $10 to $20 per person; hiring a private boat, which you can do at the dock near the Red Tower, should cost less than $30 an hour—don't be afraid to bargain.

**Alanya International Triathlon.** Organized sporting events are new for sweltering, nightlife-oriented Alanya, but the past few years have seen the advent of Alanya International Triathlon, in the cooler weather of late fall. There is also beach volleyball, basketball, handball, and other sporting events, especially in summer. ⊕ *www.alanya.bel.tr/Triathlon/index.htm.*

# EAST OF ALANYA

Few tourists continue east of Alanya, though it can be a scenic route to Cappadocia or onward to Antioch and eastern Turkey, and there are some interesting stops along the way. Mountains rise up from the sea and the road winds tortuously along the coast, which is pretty in spots, with a long stretch reminiscent of the Amalfi Coast or the French Riviera. Beyond the growing resort town of Gazipaşa the towns are mostly agricultural, with the occasional cluster of Turkish holiday houses, until the plain opens out again around the major cities of Mersin and Adana. As you head east, food and accommodation become cheaper, and you're more likely to have the sights to yourself.

## ANAMUR

*130 km (80 mi) southeast of Alanya on Rte. 400.*

Anamur is an uninspiring agricultural town, known throughout Turkey for its bananas. The roads both east and west of here are some of the windiest in Turkey. If you want to break up the journey, try one of the low-key resorts on the coast here. The main reasons to stop here, though, are the ruins of ancient Anemurium and the dramatic Marmure Castle.

**GETTING HERE AND AROUND**

There are regular buses to Anamur, but they are much less frequent than on other stretches of coast. The highway passes through the center of town, where there is a turn to Anamur's seaside suburb of İskele 2 km (12 mi) away. Anemurium and Marmure Kalesi, to the east and west respectively, are well signed.

**EXPLORING**

**Anamur Müzesi** (*Anamur Museum*). In the small Anamur Müzesi, in the waterfront district of İskele, there are finds from Anemurium and other sites in the area. The most interesting remains are some mosaics from the tombs, as well as a bronze head of Athena that was part of a set of scales. ⌧ *Free* ☉ *Daily 8–5*.

**Anemurium.** Five kilometers (3 mi) before Anamur is the marked turn-off to ancient Anemurium. The ruins here are extensive, mostly dating from the late Roman/early Byzantine period, and are built out of durable Roman concrete, which makes them better preserved but less picturesque than the average stone ruins. Beside the entrance is a **bath building**, once part of a gymnasium, with mosaics. Beyond this is a well-preserved small theater or **odeion**, opposite which is the scant remains of the large **theater**. Beyond, a second Roman **bath building** is easily the best preserved in the country, with even its great vaulted roof standing. Beside the road there are also numerous **tombs**, some with frescoes and mosaics. At the end of the road there's also a pebbly beach, where you can take a dip when you've finished, but no showers or other facilities. Beside the car park is the **Ören Antik Kent Restaurant**, with kebabs and fish, and a nice view over the ruins and the sea.

**Mamure Kalesi** (*Mamure Castle, also known as Mamuriye*). On the southeast edge of town, on the shore, the highway goes right past the Mamure Kalesi. Its precise date of construction is uncertain, but it was built in Roman times to protect the city, then known as Anemurium, from seaborne raiders. The castle was expanded and largely rebuilt by the Seljuks, who captured it in the 13th century, and again by the Karamanoğulları, who controlled this part of Anatolia after the Seljuk empire collapsed. Note the inscription to the Karamanoğulları prince, İbrahim Bey II, dating from 1450. The place is so impressively well preserved you'd think it was a modern reconstruction. ⌧ *$2*.

**WHERE TO STAY**

*For expanded hotel reviews, visit Fodors.com.*

$$ ⓣ **Ünlüselek Hotel.** In Anamur's beachfront suburb of İskele, this renovated waterfront hotel has spacious rooms with sea-view balconies. **Pros:** waterfront location. **Cons:** decor verging on kitsch; waterfront lounge/breakfast area a bit basic. ⊠ *Fahri Görgülü Cad., Hurma Sokak, İskele* ☎ *324/814–2121* ⚹ *In-room: Wi-Fi. In-hotel: restaurant, bar, beach, parking* ⍾ *Some meals.*

## SILIFKE

*Silifke is 120 km (74 mi) east of Anamur on Rte. 400.*

The small agricultural town of Silifke, beside the Göksu river, in which the German Emperor Barbarossa drowned in 1190, is dominated by its Byzantine castle.

### GETTING HERE AND AROUND

There are rare buses between Silifke and Anamur, and more frequent buses to and from Mersin.

### EXPLORING

**Seleuceia Trachea.** In the vicinity of the castle, remains have been found indicating there was a settlement here as far back as the Bronze Age, though most of what can be seen today is from the Roman city known as Seleuceia Trachea, or Calycadnos Seleuceia. The ruins include a theater, a stadium, and the Corinthian columns of the 2nd-century AD Temple of Zeus. Also left are a basilica and tomb dedicated to St. Thecla, St. Paul's first convert and the first female Christian martyr. Most interesting is the cave church where Thecla lived—the Patriarchate in Istanbul now organizes services here sometimes.

**Silifke Müzesi** (*Silifke Museum*). Local finds are displayed in this small museum, just out of the city center toward Anamur. 🖼 $2 ⊙ *Daily 8–5.*

**Uzuncaburç.** Up in the mountains 30 km (19 mi) north of Silifke is Uzuncaburç, a small village dotted with the ruins of Diocaesaria, a town run by the priests of Zeus Olbios. Most of the ruins are stretched along the ancient main street: a theater, a curious columned structure that once marked the main crossroads, a fountain, the temple of Zeus, one of the earliest surviving buildings in Corinthian style and later converted to a church, and a temple of Tyche. North of the temples is the impressive North Gate. To the northeast is a well-preserved five-story watchtower. The most straightforward road here is signposted north from Silifke; after 6 km (4 mi) you'll pass ancient Imbriogon (Demircili), where there are four well-preserved temple tombs.

## HEAVEN AND HELL

*17 km (10 mi) east of Silifke.*

Known as heaven and hell, these naturally occurring caves figure prominently in mythology.

### GETTING HERE AND AROUND

Turn north off Route 400 at Narlıkuyu onto local road signposted "Cennet ve Cehennem Derisi"; the site is 3 km (2 mi) inland.

### EXPLORING

**Heaven and Hell.** These two dramatic holes in the ground have been the local attraction since before Roman times. Once you pass through the village you'll see the wall of the Roman Temple of Zeus Corycus, later reused as a church, just past it is a small café and the ticket booth. Beyond you'll see a large completely enclosed valley, caused by an ancient subsidence, sort of a sinkhole. The valley is called the **Valley of Heaven,** "Cennet Deresi." A five-minute walk takes you down to the peaceful green floor and the well-preserved 5th-century AD Byzantine Church of the Virgin Mary, missing only its roof. The path then leads down into a huge aircraft-hanger-like natural cavern, which may have been the site of a spring known among the ancients as the Fountain of Knowledge.

Back up the stairs a short walk leads to the **Valley of Hell**, "Cehennem Derisi," which is narrower, with walls too steep to enter, and deep enough for little sunlight to reach the bottom. A dark and gloomy place, pagan, Christian, and Muslim sources all identify it as an entrance to hell. The road continues to a third cavern, the **Cave of Wishes**, "Dilek Mağarası," a peaceful place known to the Romans as an area to find the best crocuses, and you may be met by villagers selling bunches of the flowers.

Down the hill from the highway is the village of Narlikuyu, a picturesque inlet dotted with fish restaurants. This was the site of ancient Corycos, and now there's a small museum that houses an excellent mosaic of the "three Graces" part of the Roman bath building. 🖼 $2.

## KIZ KALESI

*22 km (14mi) east of Silifke on Rte. 400.*

This small town is easily the best place to stop on the long drive east of Alanya; it's a bit scruffy but there's a nice stretch of beach, but it's most famous for its picture-perfect castle sitting just off the shore.

### GETTING HERE AND AROUND

The town itself, between the highway and the sea, is small and most hotels have frequent signs.

### EXPLORING

**Kız Kalesi** (*Maiden's Castle*). On an island just off the coast is the Kız Kalesi. The island is known to have been a settlement as early as the 4th century BC, though the castle is nowhere near that old. Several offshore castles in Turkey bear the same name, which comes with a legend of a king, a princess, and a snake: the beautiful princess, apple of her father's eye, had her fortune read by a wandering soothsayer who declared she would die of a snakebite. The king therefore sent her to a castle on a snake-free island. Destiny, however, can never be avoided, and the offending serpent was accidently delivered in a basket of grapes sent as a gift from her father's palace. More prosaicly, the castle was an important part of the row of defenses along the coast that were built and rebuilt over the centuries to stop invaders from Syria entering Anatolia via the coast route to Antalya. What you see is mostly 11th-century Byzantine rebuilding to keep out the Crusaders based in Antioch. Boatmen will offer to take you out, but hiring a paddleboat is the most popular way to explore.

### WHERE TO STAY

*For expanded hotel reviews, visit Fodors.com.*

$$$ 🏨 **Club Barbarossa Hotel.** This modern hotel, right on the Kız Kalesi, has great views of the castle, its own section of beach, and air-conditioning. **Pros:** nice modern rooms; great location. **Cons:** hotel

The three Graces, or Charities, depicted in this mosaic are said to have linked arms to show that one kindness should lead to another.

building itself is rather dated and old. ⊠ *Head down the peninsula and look for signs on your left* ☎ *324/523–2364* ⊕ *www.barbarossahotel. com* ⤣ *79 rooms* ⚲ *In-room: Wi-Fi. In-hotel: restaurant, bar, pool, gym, beach* ⦿*Some meals.*

$ ⛾ **Yaka Hotel.** This is easily the most popular budget option in Kiz Kalesi and archaeologists working on nearby sites often stay here. **Pros:** popular; friendly. **Cons:** not right on the beach. ⊠ *On your left as you head down to the peninsula* ☎ *324/523–2444* ⊕ *www.yakahotel.com.tr* ⤣ *16 rooms* ⚲ *In-room: no TV, Wi-Fi.*

# MERSIN

*85 km (53 mi) east of Silifke.*

Mersin is a large port town, with a reputation as one of Turkey's most modern and secular cities. While archaeologists traced the city's origin back 8,000 years, for the modern visitor there is little appeal. If you're looking for a break in driving, though, the city's waterfront has a nice promenade, and the free museum inside the Mersin Cultural Center has a small but worthwhile collection. If you want to stop for lunch, the Ali Baba Gözen Restaurant, opposite the waterfront near the Hilton Hotel, 2 miles west of the city center, serves distinctive regional kebabs.

## GETTING HERE AND AROUND

Mersin is about 73 km (45 mi) east of Viranşehir, stretching for miles along the coast. There are frequent buses to and from Silifke, Adana, and many other Turkish cities.

## EXPLORING

**Viranşehir.** On the western outskirts of Mersin are the ruins of ancient Soli, or Viranşehir. Roman general Pompey the Great settled reformable pirates here. There is a long row of Corinthian columns, part of an ancient colonnaded street; look for the human and animal figures carved into the capitals. To find the ruins, look for a small sign marking the turnoff to the right as you're heading east to Mersin, just after the Soli Shopping Mall.

## TARSUS

*28 km (17 mi) east of Mersin on Route E90.*

The dusty, sleepy provincial town of Tarsus is known as the place where St. Paul was born some 2,000 years ago. There are a broad range of Roman, Byzantine, and Turkish remains, and effort is now being put into restoration. No individual site is exceptional, but all together, Tarsus makes for the most interesting stop between Kız Kalesi and Adana. Most sites are fairly close together—you might be better off driving to the Church of St. Paul.

Near the center of town, beside the tourist office where you can collect a map, is an excavated section of Roman Road. North of here is a well set in a small garden, traditionally identified as connected to the house of St. Paul, though the less pious may doubt it is worth the $2 entry. South of the well are some of Tarsus's best-preserved old houses, many of which are being restored. Head east on the main road and you'll find the Eski Cami, which is now a mosque, but which was built as a church by the Armenians in 1102. Opposite the Eski Cami is the 19th century Makam-ı Şerif, which is said to have been built over the grave of the Prophet Daniel. Nearby are the 16th century Ulu Cami, or Great Mosque, and a covered bazaar known as the **Kırkkaşık,** or "40 Spoons" from the same period. To the south is the Church of St. Paul, a Greek-style church from the 19th century, now a museum ($2). West of here in the Tarsus American College, established by Presbyterian missionaries in 1888 and still in operation. Back toward the main street, the only surviving piece of antiquity is the **Gate of Cleopatra.**

## GETTING HERE AND AROUND

Route E90 passes along the southern edge of the city, so you need to take the old Adana Bulavarı into the center. Most of the frequent buses between Mersin and Adana stop here, but there is no actual bus station or luggage storage; buses stop just east of the Makam-ı Şerif Mosque.

## WHERE TO STAY

*For expanded hotel reviews, visit Fodors.com.*

$$$   ⊤ **Konak Efsus.** This excellent boutique hotel, open since 2009, is as good a reason as any to stop in Tarsus. **Pros:** nice rooms. **Cons:** Do you want to stay in Tarsus? ⊠ *Tarihi Evler Sokak 31–33, Tarsus* ☎ *324/614–0807* ⊕ *www.konakefsus.com/* ↩ *9 rooms* ⚭ *In-room: Wi-Fi. In-hotel: restaurant.*

# ADANA

*69 km (43 mi) east of Mersin on Rte. E90.*

Adana is Turkey's fourth-largest city after Istanbul, Ankara, and İzmir, but it's the least known to tourists because it's a commercial and industrial center, though there are a few first-rate attractions. The Archaeology Museum, due to reopen in 2012 after renovations, has a good small collection; next door is Adana's most prominent building and the largest mosque in Turkey, the Sabancı Merkez Camii. Completed in 1998, it is largely a copy of 16th-century Selimiye Mosque of Edirne. Heading south along the river is another symbol of the city, the impressively long **Taş Köprü,** or "stone bridge," built by the Emperor Hadrian in 125 AD and restored by later rulers. Inland is the **Ulu Camii,** more Arabic in style than Turkish. One of the prettiest mosques in the country, its patterned stonework has been well restored. Behind the mosque is Adana's lively market area, with several old mosques, including the Yağ Camii (Oil Mosque) on Alimunif Caddesi, built in 1501 incorporating a Byzantine church.

East of Adana, across the Çukurova Plain, there are many ancient remains, including several castles, mostly dating back to the Armenian rulers of the 12th to 14th centuries AD. The easiest to reach, **Yılan Kalesi,** the "Castle of the Snake," sits unmissably beside the main highway, 40 km (25 mi) east of town: take the marked turn off and drive up to the parking lot, beside the small restaurant and ticket booth. There isn't a lot to see, but the walls are well preserved and the views of the fertile Çukurova Plain from the top are impressive. Farther east, just before Osmaniye and the turnoff to İskenderun, is a second Armenian Castle, Toprakkale; 70 km (45 mi) north of Yılan Kalesi via Ceyhan, is Kozan, another fine castle that was an important residence of the Armenian rulers of Cilicia; 28 km (17 mi), north of Ceyhan, you pass the small village of Ayşe Hoca, and just east of here are the extensive, but largely unexcavated remains of ancient Anazarbos. Don't miss the impromptu museum in the garden of the house of Mrs. Hatun Dilci, the former site guardian.

About 130 km (81 mi) northeast of Adana is **Karatepe,** an important late Hittite site that makes a (long) day trip from Adana or a worthwhile detour if you're heading to Antakya. Karatepe was a fortress founded in the 8th century by Asatiwatas, the ruler of the post-Hittite state of Adana. A short walk from the parking area are two ancient gateways where dozens of well-preserved carved stones, once the foundation of mudbrick walls, have been left in places as an open-air museum. There are lions guarding the entrance, mythological creatures and warriors, but also scenes of everyday life: a fishing boat, musicians and a woman feeding her baby. There is also a small indoor museum behind the ticket office. The area around the site is a beautiful national park, and you can picnic here or swim in the adjacent dam. Between Kozan and Karatepe is Kadirli, which has a well-preserved Byzantine church.

## GETTING HERE AND AROUND

The main east-west road in Adana, Turhan Cemal Beriker Boulevard, passes the museum and Sabancı Mosque and divides the old and new city. There are frequent buses to Mersin, Osmaniye and İskenderun.

Both Yılan Kalesi and Toprakkale are beside Route E90, but there is no exit from the newer O50 tollway. Toprakkale guards the route south to İskenderun and Antakya. Karatepe is 30 km (19 mi) north of Osmaniye, which is 94 km (58 mi) east of Adana on the E90. Pass through Osmaniye, following signs for Kadirli, then the large signs for Karatepe. Alternately, from Kozan, there is a road, via Kadirli, to Karatepe.

## WHERE TO EAT AND STAY

*For expanded hotel reviews, visit Fodors.com.*

$   ✕ **Yüzevler.** For most Turks Adana means Adana kebab, minced lamb
TURKISH   slow charcoal-grilled on a long wide metal skewer. Everyone in Adana has an opinion on where to find the best Adana kebab, but the traditional favorite is Yüzevler. Obviously, the kebabs are the star of the show, but the *pide* (Turkish pizza) is also good, and this is probably one of the safest places to try the famous raw ground meat *Çiğ Köfte*, literally "raw köfte"; it's "cooked" with spices. ⊠ *Ziyapaşa Bulvarı, 64018 Sokak, near Ziyapaşa 20* ☎ *322/454–7513.*

$   🏨 **Akkoc Butik Otel.** This new and well-run midsize hotel isn't quite boutique, but it does a nice job of filling the gap between the city's two- and five-star accomodations. **Pros:** in the cool part of town. **Cons:** more of a business hotel. ⊠ *Cemalpaşa Mah. 63005 Sokak 22* ☎ *322/459–1000* ⊕ *akkocotel.com.tr/* 🛏 *30 rooms* 🛎 *In-room: Wi-Fi. In-hotel: restaurant, bar, business center* ❑ *No meals.*

$   🏨 **Hotel Bosnali.** Adana finally has a true boutique hotel, in a restored 19th-century mansion in the heart of the old city. **Pros:** central; beautiful. **Cons:** often booked out by tour groups. ⊠ *Seyhan Cad. 29* ☎ *322/ 359–8000* ⊕ *www.hotelbosnali.com/* 🛏 *10 rooms, 2 suites* 🛎 *In-room: Internet, Wi-Fi. In-hotel: restaurant, parking.*

# ANTAKYA (ANTIOCH)

*191 km (118 mi) from Adana, east on Rte. E90, south on Rte. E91.*

Antakya is perhaps better known by its old name, Antioch. Founded in about 300 BC by Seleucus Nikator, one of Alexander's generals, the city grew quickly, thanks to its strategic location on the trade routes. After the Roman occupation began in AD 64, Antioch became the empire's third most important city, after Rome and Alexandria. Famed for its luxury and notorious for its depravity, it was chosen by St. Paul as the objective of his first mission to the gentiles. After enduring earthquakes and Byzantine and Arab raids, it fell to the crusaders in 1098; Egyptian raiders nearly leveled it in 1268. A late addition to the Turkish Republic, it was occupied by France after 1920 as part of its mandate over Syria, which still has an outstanding territorial claim on it. Though the city reverted to Turkey just before World War II, it still maintains a distinctive character. The people of Antioch are mostly bilingual, speaking both Turkish and a local dialect of Arabic. In the cobbled streets of the old quarter, on the east bank of the River Orontes, you can also hear Syriac (Aramaic), the language spoken by many of Turkey's Christians.

**GETTING HERE AND AROUND**

The old city, on the east bank of the river, is relatively compact; the museum is across the bridge on the west bank. Senpiyer Kilisesi, north of the old city, is far enough to drive. There are frequent buses to Adana, Osmaniye, and Gaziantep, though sometimes you need to change in İskenderun.

**EXPLORING**

**Habib Neccar Cami.** The River Orontes (*Asi* in Turkish) divides Antioch in two. In the old town you will find the Habib Neccar Cami, a mosque on Kurtuluş Caddesi, just south of St. Peter's. Parts of the building date from the 7th century, making it Turkey's oldest mosque (there was also a renovation in the 17th century). Just north is the bazaar quarter, a real change of pace: the feel here is more Syrian and Arab than Turkish.

**Harbiye.** Most mosaics at the Hatay Museum come from villas in Harbiye, originally called Daphne, a beautiful gorge of laurel trees and tumbling waterfalls that was said to have been chosen by the gods for the Judgment of Paris and that contained one of the ancient world's most important shrines to the god Apollo (7 km [4 mi] south of Antakya on Route E91). Mark Antony chose it as the venue for his ill-fated marriage to Cleopatra in 40 BC. Daphne was also a favorite resort for wealthy Antiochenes and developed such a reputation for licentiousness, it was put off-limits to the Roman army.

★ **Hatay Müzesi** (*Hatay Museum*). Although little survives of old Antioch, the large collection of mosaics in the city's museum hints at the city's glorious past. Experts consider the dozens of Roman mosaics of Hatay Müzesi—portraying scenes from mythology and figures such as Dionysus, Orpheus, Oceanus, and Thetis—among the highest achievements of Roman art. There is a beautiful marble sarcophagus and a giant statue of the Roman Emperor Lucius Verus. The area's preclassical past is also well represented—check out the 3,000-year-old, four-foot-tall lion, which entered the museum's garden by crane in 2011. ✉ *Gündüz Cad. 1, in central square on right bank of Orontes* ☎ *326/214–6167* 💰 *$5* 🕐 *Tues.–Sun. 9–6:30.*

**Latin monastery.** The Catholic Church maintains its presence with a small church on Kutlu Sokak, several winding blocks in from the Sermaye Mosque. Enter its small courtyard from the side street. You may recognize the image of the church bell, with the mosque minaret behind it—it's on tourist office brochures as a symbol of religious harmony.

**Senpiyer Kilisesi** (*Church of St. Peter*). On the northern edge of town is Senpiyer Kilisesi, or Saint Peter Church, a tiny cave high up on a cliff, blackened by centuries of candle smoke and dripping with water seeping out of the rock. It's here that the apostle secretly preached to his converts and where they first came to be called Christians, and it may well be the oldest of all churches. The church's facade was added by the Crusaders in the 11th and 12th centuries. Mass is celebrated here on the first Sunday of every month. The area was a cemetery in classical times, and there are numerous rock-cut tombs around. A path leads up to giant carved face of Charon, the legendary boatman who took the dead across the river Styx. ⊠ *Off Kurtuluş Cad., well signposted* ⌛ *$5* ⊙ *Daily 9–noon and 1–6.*

**Samandag and Seleuceia ad Pieria.** You'll find a beach at Samandag (also known as Çevlik Beach), as well as tasty but inexpensive fish, 28 km (17 mi) south of Antakya. You'll also find the scant remains of Antioch's old port, Seleuceia ad Pieria. The attraction here is a large underground water channel, 1,400 meters (1,526 yards) long, which was built entirely by hand in the 1st century AD to prevent flooding. Nearby there are some large rock tombs.

## WHERE TO EAT AND STAY
*For expanded hotel reviews, visit Fodors.com.*

¢    ✕ **Antik Han.** Welcome to the Hummus Zone. The *mezes* are particularly
TURKISH    good at this restaurant with a rooftop terrace, and there's a pleasant courtyard where you can relax and eat. There are a good range of local kebabs and other dishes. Alcohol is available. ⊠ *Hurriyet Cad.* ☎ *No phone.* ═ *No credit cards.*

¢    ✕ **Hatay Sultan Sofrası.** Tour groups often take up this restaurant, but
TURKISH    with good reason: the food is delicious and inexpensive. You'll find all the usual Turkish dishes with some local specialties including the Yogurt Asi soup and a range of *börek* pastries. ⊠ *İstiklal Cad. 20* ☎ *326/213–8759 No phone.*

$$    ⛢ **Arsuz Hotel.** On its own private beach in Arsuz (also called Uluçınar), just south of İskenderun, this clean, bright, and airy hotel has a lush garden leading down to a private beach. **Pros:** beach. **Cons:** rooms are small and basic. ⊠ *(Uluçınar), Arsuz* ☎ *326/643–2444* ⚲ *104 rooms, 3 suites* ⚶ *In-room: Wi-Fi. In-hotel: restaurant, bar, beach* ⊙ *Closed Nov.–Apr.*

$$    ⛢ **Büyük Antakya.** This giant white pyramid of a building may be unattractive on the outside, but looks can be decieving: inside you'll find a cool marble lobby and bright, well-maintained rooms with big windows. **Pros:** professional and helpful service; old-school ambience. **Cons:** decor is a bit out of date; a bit impersonal; pricey for where you are. ⊠ *Atatürk Cad. 8* ☎ *326/213–5860* ⊕ *www.buyukantakyaoteli.com* ⚲ *70 rooms, 2 suites* ⚶ *In-room: Wi-Fi. In-hotel: restaurant, bar.*

$    ⛢ **The Liwan Hotel.** This stylish hotel in a restored 1920s mansion is easily the best of the new crop of boutique hotels in town. **Pros:** excellent quality. **Cons:** some street noise echoed by the old floor tiles. ⊠ *Silahlı Kuvvetler Cad. 5* ☎ *326/215-7777* ⊕ *www.theliwanhotel.com* ⚲ *24 rooms* ⚶ *In-room: Wi-Fi. In-hotel: restaurant, bar.*

# Cappadocia and Central Turkey

## WITH ANKARA AND KONYA

**WORD OF MOUTH**

"We did a lot of hiking while in Cappadocia . . . Love Valley, Red Valley and Pigeon Valley. Red Valley at sunset is like a dream. Other attractions we saw were Kaymaklı, Göreme Open Air Museum, Göreme National Park, Zelve Open Air Museum (wow), and Uçhisar Castle. . . . We also enjoyed just driving the country-side and checking out the little villages."

—chickenlittle

# WELCOME TO CAPPADOCIA AND CENTRAL TURKEY

## TOP REASONS TO GO

★ **Balloon over Cappadocia:** Dangling high above the spectacular terrain in a basket, you'll sail past rock cones and fairy chimneys.

★ **Explore underground cities:** Kaymaklı, Derinkuyu, and the region's other vast, multistoried subterranean complexes were equipped with kitchens, sewage systems, and stables, and once housed tens of thousands of inhabitants.

★ **Hike the valleys of Cappadocia:** Trails lead past fantastic rock formations and to cave entrances that open on ornately decorated churches.

★ **Luxuriate in a cave:** Some of Cappadocia's finest hotels are tucked into elaborately appointed caves, where soft lighting, fireplaces, and even Jacuzzis are common amenities.

★ **Peer into the past:** Ankara's impressive Museum of Anatolian Civilizations showcases treasures dating back millennia, left by the numerous cultures that have occupied these lands.

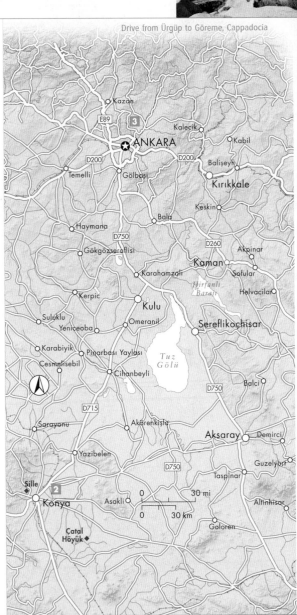

Drive from Ürgüp to Göreme, Cappadocia

**1** Cappadocia. The weirdest natural landscape you're ever likely to see is a giant outdoor sculpture garden of elaborate pillars, needles, and cones. As if these natural phenomena weren't enticing enough, hundreds of caves house elaborately frescoed churches from the early days of Christianity.

**2** Konya. One of Turkey's most popular pilgrimage sites—a shrine to the 13th-century philosopher Rumi—is in Konya, the spiritual home of the whirling dervishes. Elegant ancient mosques enhance the holy feel of the city. Not far away, the archaeological site of Çatal Höyük is one of the world's oldest known human settlements.

**3** Ankara. Turkey's capital is the best place to witness the enduring legacy of Atatürk, founding father of the secular Turkish Republic. Museums and historical sites are scattered a stone's throw from the ancient citadel, which offers panoramic views of the city.

# GETTING ORIENTED

Central Turkey stretches across a vast, arid plateau, littered with the ruins of ancient civilizations, slashed by ravines in places and rising to the peaks of extinct volcanoes in others. Think of the region as a triangle, with Ankara, Turkey's sprawling capital, to the northwest; Cappadocia, the land of surrealistic geological formations, to the east; and Konya, the city where the dervishes whirl, to the southwest, en route to Antalya and the Mediterranean coast.

6

Artisans at work, Avanos.

Updated by
Vanessa H.
Larson

Some of the oldest known human settlements were established in the hills and valleys of Central Anatolia, but today the main attraction here is the magical landscape of Cappadocia, where wind and rain have shaped the area's soft volcanic rock into a kind of fairy-tale landscape.

In Cappadocia you'll discover unimaginable rock formations, spectacular valleys, ancient cave churches, and underground cities that reach many stories beneath the surface and could house thousands of people. The small towns of Ürgüp, Göreme, Uçhisar, and Avanos are good spots to base yourself for exploring the region's otherworldly landscape. Whether hiking through the amazing terrain on foot, exploring underground passageways, or floating over the incredible scenery in a hot-air balloon, you'll find Cappadocia to be unlike anyplace you've ever been before.

Southwest of Cappadocia is Konya, home to the tomb of Rumi—the 13th-century founder of the whirling dervishes—and to a fascinating museum dedicated to him. Known as Turkey's most religiously conservative city, Konya is not a place for those looking for nightlife (alcohol can be difficult to find) or a dining-out scene. But centuries-old mosques and stately religious seminaries lend some historic character to Turkey's seventh-largest city.

The region's other major city is Ankara, Turkey's capital and second-largest metropolis. Though this modern city is somewhat lacking in character, it has one of the best archaeological museums in the country and a handful of historical sights of interest, including a citadel that encloses a character-filled neighborhood. Also in Ankara, the imposing mausoleum of Atatürk, founder of the Turkish Republic, offers visitors a great deal of insight into the modern Turkish psyche.

As you travel through the Turkish heartland, you'll see mostly agricultural regions—the province of Konya, with its vast plains where grains and other crops are grown, is known as the country's breadbasket—and encounter a slice of provincial life.

# PLANNING

### ANATOLIAN EATING

Central Anatolia is the one region in Turkey that does not touch water, so fish has to be trucked or flown in. Be prepared for a lot of meat; that means kebabs and lamb, often with yogurt and tomato sauce. In Konya you'll encounter *etli ekmek*—flatbread topped with ground lamb and spices—and you'll find *lahmacun,* a kind of flatbread Turkish pizza, throughout the region. Main courses are usually preceded by a delicious array of mezes, which here often include hot hummus and *pastırma* (Turkish pastrami).

Restaurants that cater to tourists serve beer, wine and liquor, including rakı. In Cappadocia, wine is produced locally, with varying results; local whites, like the Emir, tend to be better than the reds, which include the Kalecik Karası. In Konya and other conservative towns, it can be difficult to find alcohol. Whatever you eat and drink, you'll find it easy to dine in atmospheric surroundings—restored caravansaries, caves, Ottoman mansions, whitewashed courtyards. In some traditional restaurants you'll sit on cushions on the floor, and your meal might occasionally be accompanied by live music.

### BEST WALKS IN CAPPADOCIA

The most memorable experiences you're likely to have in Cappadocia are hikes through the valleys, clambering up tall, soft rock formations that rise in endlessly entertaining forms. You can do these with or without a guide, but a guide's expert knowledge is usually a bonus:

**Rose Valley (Güllüdere),** where cave entrances lead to beautiful, ornately decorated churches.

**Güvercinlik Vadisi (Pigeon Valley),** a scenic valley dotted with a myriad of dovecotes.

**Love Valley (Aşk Vadisi),** perhaps named for the preponderance of phallus-looking rock protrusions.

**Ihlara Valley,** where fresco-decorated churches are carved into cliffs above a river.

**The Soğanlı Valleys,** where you'll encounter few other travelers as you explore hundreds of dwellings and churches cut into the cliffs.

### GETTING HERE AND AROUND

#### AIR TRAVEL

Air travel isn't much more expensive than bus travel, and flying to Central Anatolia saves a lot of time. Ankara's Esenboğa Airport is served by direct flights from several European cities, as well as many domestic flights. There are direct flights from Istanbul and İzmir (and in the summer, also from Antalya) to the Kayseri airport —within an hour's drive of most of Cappadocia, and a shuttle will take you from the airport to any hotel in the main towns for 15TL–20 TL (hotels will also arrange pickups for guests). The Nevşehir airport is even closer to the towns of Cappadocia, though it is served by just two flights a day from Istanbul.

### BUS TRAVEL

Cappadocia and Central Anatolia are well served by intercity buses, but the distances from other places you are likely to be visiting are long. The 10- to 12-hour trip to Cappadocia from Istanbul costs about 70 TL. Buses link most towns and cities within the region, and fares are reasonable (about 30 TL or less from Ankara to most anywhere in Central Anatolia). In Cappadocia there are buses connecting the towns, making it easy to get around, at least in summer; bus service is much less frequent in winter.

### CAR TRAVEL

Once you're here, renting a car is a good idea because you'll probably be traveling around a lot. The highways in Central Anatolia are generally well maintained and lead to all the major sights. Minor roads, however, are rough and full of potholes. On narrow, winding roads, look out for oncoming trucks, whose drivers often don't stay on their side of the road, and be especially careful at night, when farm vehicles without proper running lights and animals are likely to be on rural roads.

There are good roads between Istanbul and the main cities of Anatolia: Ankara, Konya, and Kayseri. However, truck traffic on the main highway from Istanbul to Ankara, a distance of 454 km (281 mi), can be heavy. Two long stretches of toll road (*ücretli geçiş*) linking Istanbul and Ankara—E80 to beyond Düzce and E89 south from Gerede—provide some relief from the rigors of the other highways.

From Ankara, Konya is 261 km (162 mi) to the south, while Kayseri—the gateway to Cappadocia—is 312 km (194 mi) to the southeast.

You can also travel from Central Anatolia on major highways to the Mediterranean and Black Sea coasts: from Ankara, E90 (also known as Route 200) leads southwest toward Sivrihisar; continue southwest on E96 to Afyon, where you can pick up highways going south to Antalya or west to İzmir. Route E88/200 leads east out of Ankara and eventually connects with highways to the Black Sea coast.

### TRAIN TRAVEL

Regular rail service connects both Istanbul and İzmir to Ankara, and direct trains also run from Istanbul to Konya (*see specific cities for information*). Trains generally take longer than buses—often a lot longer—but most are equipped with sleeper cars, which can be quite comfortable. The Istanbul–Ankara corridor is, however, being outfitted with new rails to allow high-speed trains, so the trip will become faster in the coming years. A high-speed train runs from Ankara to Konya and the trip takes less than two hours (as opposed to three to four by bus or car). There is also a regular-speed Ankara–Kayseri train, but bus travel is generally much faster on that route. There is little train service between small towns in Central Anatolia.

### HOW MUCH TIME DO YOU NEED?

In Cappadocia, you can fit in the open-air museums, major valleys, and an underground city in two days, but you may want to spend several more days just soaking up the enchanting landscapes and enjoying the region's comfortable lodgings. We suggest flying to Nevşehir or Kayseri and picking up a car (the easiest way to see the region). Ürgüp, Göreme,

Avanos, and Uçhisar are all good places to base yourself, and offer a wide variety of hotels.

Though Ankara is not considered much of a vacation destination, it is home to some significant sights. You could spend a day seeing the highly regarded Museum of Anatolian Civilizations, repository of the best archaeological treasures found in Turkey, and the Anıtkabir, Atatürk's mausoleum, saving some time to explore the citadel area as well.

You can see Konya's famous museums and ancient mosques and seminaries in half a day, or a day if you include a side-trip to the archaeological site of Çatal Höyük. The city also makes a good stopping-off point if you're traveling between Cappadocia and Antalya or elsewhere on the Mediterranean coast.

## TOUR OPTIONS

In Cappadocia, consider joining a tour or hiring a private guide for at least one day. Guides know the terrain and can lead you to places you might not otherwise find, filling you in on fascinating details about the geology of the region, its early inhabitants, and other information. Expect to pay anywhere from 70 to 120 TL per person for a daylong group tour (prices vary based on the size of the group and prestige of the company). Prices for a private tour run from about 220 to 300 TL per person. Local tourist offices and hotels can make recommendations, or contact one of these companies directly.

**Argeus.** One of Cappadocia's best-regarded agencies, Argeus runs small group tours (maximum eight people) and also does private tours. ☎ *384/341–4688 in Ürgüp* ⊕ *www.argeus.com.tr.*

**Argonaut Escapades.** A small yet established agency, Argonaut Escapades specializes in individually tailored tours, particularly walking tours. ☎ *384/341–6255 in Ürgüp* ⊕ *www.argonautturkey.com.*

**Rock Valley Travel.** Family-run Rock Valley Travel organizes day tours of Cappadocia with a maximum of 12 per group, at reasonable prices; they can also arrange private tours. ☎ *384/341/8813 in Ürgüp* ⊕ *www. rockvalleytravel.com.*

**Turkish Heritage Travel.** This well-regarded company organizes cultural travel tours, cooking classes, and other programs aimed at introducing guests to authentic Turkish culture. Their knowledgeable, personal guides also lead more traditional group and private tours of Cappadocia. ☎ *384/271–2687 in Göreme* ⊕ *www.goreme.com.*

**Ürgüp Turizm.** The knowledgeable and professional team at Ürgüp Travel run top-notch tours around Cappadocia and beyond, and can also arrange private tours. They're especially good at leading hikes out into the funky Cappadocia landscape. ☎ *384/341-5015 in Ürgüp* ⊕ *wwww. urguptravel.com.*

**Kirkit Voyage.** Horseback riding, hiking, mountain biking, camping, and other outdoor activities are the specialty of this agency, which also organizes sightseeing tours in Cappadocia. ☎ *384/511–3259 in Avanos* ⊕ *www.kirkit.com.*

| WHAT IT COSTS IN U.S. DOLLARS | | | | |
|---|---|---|---|---|
| | ¢ | $ | $$ | $$$ | $$$$ |
| Restaurants | under $10 | $10–$15 | $16–$22 | $23–$30 | over $30 |
| Hotels | under $100 | $100–$150 | $151–$225 | $226–$350 | over $350 |

Restaurant prices are for one main course at dinner or for two mezes (small dishes). Hotel prices are for two people in a standard double room in high season, including taxes.

## WHEN TO GO

Much of Central Anatolia is blazing hot in summer and freezing cold in winter. The best time to visit is in the spring (May) before the crowds and heat arrive, or early fall (September), when the crowds are gone and winter hasn't yet arrived.

## WHERE TO BASE YOURSELF IN CAPPADOCIA

**Göreme** has lodging options ranging from backpacker digs to fancy rock-cut hotels, and it's the most convenient base if you don't have a car, close to the Göreme Open-Air Museum and many of the most scenic valleys. The town is quite busy and has a rather touristy feel to it.

**Ürgüp** is more tranquil than Göreme, and a bit farther from the main attractions. Although it doesn't have the delightful fairy chimneys of Göreme, it does have a growing cluster of hotels carved out of the rock; these are generally small lodgings that cater to a more upmarket clientele.

**Uçhisar**, between Nevşehir and Göreme, is central enough to be a good base and calmer than other nearby towns. High on a rock outcropping, Uçhisar has incredible views of the surrounding valleys. It's popular with French tourists and non-Turkish signs and information are as likely to be written in French as English.

**Avanos** is at the north end of Cappadocia, on the banks of the Kızılırmak; it's quiet but scenic, and is known for its handicrafts, particularly pottery.

# CAPPADOCIA

Cappadocia comprises the triangle of land formed by the towns of Nevşehir to the west, Ürgüp to the east, and Avanos in the north. Inside this triangle is one of the most unusual natural landscapes you're ever likely to see. More than 10 million years ago, three volcanoes in Cappadocia erupted, dropping lava, mud, and ash over the region. Over eons, the explosive products of Mt. Erciyes, Mt. Hasan, and Mt. Melendiz cooled and compressed to form tufa, a soft, porous rock easily worn by erosion. Water poured down, carving and separating giant ridges of rock into gorgeous valleys. Wind whipped around the formations, further shaping them into elaborate pinnacles, cones, pillars, and mounds. Harder layers of rocklike basalt resisted erosion longer, and often ended up perfectly balanced, like hats, on top of a tall cone. Oxidation gave the formations color, and then humans began to do their own carving and shaping.

Cappadocia

In effect, the region has become a giant outdoor sculpture garden and the valleys here are full of so-called "fairy chimneys"—rock formations in improbable shapes of cones and enormous spires. Walks through these valleys are unforgettable; you might feel like you're wandering around on another planet. One of the great pleasures of being in Cappadocia is that you still often feel like a lone explorer here. Mystical experiences are not uncommon among those hiking across these valleys of wild geological formations.

Indeed, Cappadocia has an undeniable spiritual side, and its natural endowment is only part of the attraction. The region is thought to have been first occupied by the Hatti and then by the Hittites, who ruled much of Anatolia between about 1800 and 1200 BC and worshipped a pantheon of anthropomorphic gods. The area was later occupied by a series of regional states before Tiberius claimed Cappadocia as a province of Rome in AD 17. Early Christians, who more than anyone else have left a human mark on Cappadocia, began settling in the region not long afterward.

The Christians who established secluded communities here apparently found the otherworldly landscape suitable both to their aesthetic tastes and to their need to hide from persecution. They sat on Cappadocia's rock pillars for years at a time in prayer and carved hundreds of churches into the soft rocks, decorating them with beautiful frescoes. You can still explore these churches, and by the end of a trip you won't be surprised when you duck into a nondescript cave entrance and find carved columns, a domed roof, and vivid frescoes.

Arab raiders also came into the region sporadically between the 7th and 10th centuries, forcing the inhabitants underground, where they renovated and expanded subterranean cities left by earlier peoples. It's believed that many sprawling underground complexes have yet to be discovered, and the true extent of some of the nearly 40 underground cities scattered throughout the area that have been found is still unknown.

Cappadocia remains an exotic place in other ways, too. You'll see local residents traveling between farms and shops in horse-drawn carts. Women drape their houses with strings of apricots and paprika for drying in the sun, and nomadic workers pitch their tents beside fields and cook on fires that send smoke billowing through the tent tops. In the distance, minarets pierce the sky, silhouetted against distant mountains. Even the hotels are exotic—many occupy caves, and are some of the most delightfully unusual lodgings in which you'll ever stay.

## NEVŞEHIR

The provincial capital, Nevşehir is not a particularly attractive town but it's an important transportation hub for the Cappadocia region. Though the Nevşehir airport is the closest to Cappadocia, it's small and served mostly by charter flights and two Turkish Airlines flights from Istanbul per day.

### GETTING HERE AND AROUND
The airport is 30 km (19 mi) northwest of the city, in the village of Tuzköy; public minibuses go from the airport to downtown Nevşehir, but you'll probably want to take a shuttle directly to whatever town you're staying in. Nevşehir is also the transfer point for local minibuses, so if you're not traveling around Cappadocia by car, you'll probably end up passing through the town a few times to change buses as you visit the sights (for example, if you are going to Derinkuyu or Kaymaklı from the Göreme area, you'll need to change buses in Nevşehir).

### ESSENTIALS
**Visitor Information** ⊠ *Atatürk Bul., next to hospital* ☎ *384/213–3659.*

## ÜRGÜP

*300 km (180 mi) south of Ankara; 80 km (48 mi) west of Kayseri airport; 23 km (14 mi) east of Nevşehir.*

Ürgüp is known these days for its excellent small hotels, many of which are restored cave houses in the picturesque Esbelli neighborhood and overlook the town and the nearby cliffs dotted with man-made caves. Some beautiful old homes that were formerly owned by Greeks, who were a significant presence in the town until the Greek-Turkish population exchange in 1923, have also been converted into hotels.

# Ballooning in Cappadocia

One of the best ways to appreciate the expansive, diverse landscape of Cappadocia's landscape is from above, in a hot-air balloon. The flights begin just after 5 am, the safest time to fly because of the calm air, and last about an hour or an hour and a half. A skilled pilot can take you right into a valley, sail through it so the rock cones loom on either side, then climb the edge of a tall fairy chimney. The trip usually ends with a champagne toast, a ballooning tradition. Cappadocia is an ideal place to experience ballooning not only because of its spectacular scenery, but also because the region's microclimate, with calm weather and a high number of flying days per year, makes it one of the best and safest places in the world for ballooning. Balloon trips are primarily offered from April through November.

Ballooning over Cappadocia at Sunrise."
—photo by rward, Fodors.com member

Ballooning prices tend to be inflated in Cappadocia because hotels and tour agencies make high commissions for booking flights, but a flight you book on your own will not necessarily be cheaper. Note that some companies give a small discount if you pay in cash. Transfers to and from your hotel are included in the price.

**Contacts Butterfly Balloons.** Owned by Turkish Heritage Travel, Butterfly Balloons keeps things personal by flying with fewer passengers than some of its competitors do. The friendly, well-qualified pilots have American and European commercial pilot's licenses. ☎ 384/271–3010 in Göreme ⊕ www.butterflyballoons.com.

**Cihangiroglu Balloons.** The folks at Cihangiroglu Balloons run a professional outfit with local staff and ground crew. The eponymous pilot, Cihangir Cihangiroglu, is a pro at navigating to the best spots. ☎ 384/219-2665 ⊕ www.cihangirogluballoons.com.

**Kapadokya Balloons.** The first balloon company to be established in Cappadocia, highly regarded Kapadokya Balloons has been in business since 1991 and prides itself on its experienced team and professionalism. ☎ 384/271–2442 in Göreme ⊕ www.kapadokyaballoons.com.

**Royal Balloon.** Though relatively new, Royal Balloon works with some of the most experienced Turkish and foreign pilots in Cappadocia. The company emphasizes boutique service and is the only outfit to offer passengers a hot buffet breakfast. ☎ 384/271–3300 in Göreme ⊕ www.royalballoon.com.

6

Downtown Ürgüp is a tacky jumble of buildings built up mostly for the tourism industry, but you'll find banks, money exchanges, travel agencies, trinket shops, and even a Turkish bath and a few bars. During the winter months, some of the hotels and restaurants in Ürgüp close, which means fewer options for travelers but a more tranquil atmosphere for those who are around.

### GETTING HERE AND AROUND

Ürgüp is not quite as close to the sights and scenic valleys as some other Cappadocian towns, so you may want to rent a car if you base yourself here. Minibuses travel regularly between Ürgüp and other Cappadocian towns in high season, less frequently in low season.

Ürgüp is larger than Göreme, Uçhisar, and other nearby towns and somewhat spread out. From the Esbelli neighborhood, where many nice hotels are located, it's a pleasant 10-minute downhill stroll to the town center—you may want to take a taxi when coming back to your hotel at night to avoid the steep climb.

### ESSENTIALS

**Visitor Information** ✉ *Kayseri Cad. 37, inside park* ☎ *384/341–4059.*

### EXPLORING

**Turasan Winery.** Ürgüp's Turasan Winery, established in 1943 and one of the region's largest producers, offers factory tours and wine tastings. Cappadocians have been making wine for thousands of years, though you'll have to judge for yourself how successful they are. (Note that when it comes to local varietals, whites are usually better than reds.) In recent years Cappadocian vintners like Turasan have expanded and improved their range of offerings, while keeping their wines generally quite affordable—and vineyards add even more to the scenery. ✉ *Çimenli Mevkii* ☎ *384/341–4961* ⊕ *www.turasan.com.tr* ⌨ *Free factory tours, 12 TL for cellar visit and 3 tastings* ⊙ *Daily 8:30–sunset.*

### WHERE TO EAT AND STAY

*For expanded hotel reviews, visit Fodors.com.*

**$$**   ✕ **Ehlikeyf.** On the second floor of a building in the center of town, this
TURKISH   restaurant has great views over the town square and the Seljuk tombs,
**Fodor's**Choice   and some of the best food you'll find in Cappadocia. The baked lamb
★   and chicken dishes are excellent and the shepherd's salad with pomegranate dressing is memorable if you're craving some greenery. On weekend nights after 9 pm there is often traditional Turkish music, too. ✉ *Cumhuriyet Meydani, Ust Kat* ☎ *384/341-7100* ⊕ *wwww.ehlikeyf.com.*

**$$**   ✕ **Old Greek House.** About 5 km (3 mi) from Ürgüp, in the sleepy village
TURKISH   of Mustafapaşa, the Old Greek House serves delicious home-cooked
**Fodor's**Choice   specialties, including a variety of mezes, meat dishes like *karnıyarık*
★   (eggplant stuffed with tomatoes and ground meat), and homemade baklava. Portions are generous, and the set menus are a genuine feast. Seating is on cushions on the floor around low, round tables or at regular-height tables in the central courtyard. The building, a 250-year-old Greek mansion, still has original frescoes on the stone walls and original painted wooden ceilings. The house is also an inn, with 13

simple but comfortable rooms. ⊠ *Mustafapaşa* ☏ *384/353–5306* ⊕ *www.oldgreekhouse.com.*

$$ TURKISH ✕ **Şömine.** Right on the main square, this welcoming lair takes its name from the fireplace in the center that warms guests in winter; in summer, you can dine outside on the rooftop terrace, where there is often live guitar music. Regional specialties include *testi kebabı,* a meat and vegetable dish cooked in a clay pot, which you break open yourself by whacking it with a large knife; and vegetable or meat stews baked on a clay tile, or *kiremit.* ⊠ *Cumhuriyet Meydanı 9, on main square* ☏ *384/341–8442* ⊕ *www.sominerestaurant.com.*

**WORD OF MOUTH**

"In Cappadocia we stayed at what was probably my favorite hotel of any I have ever been to—The Esbelli Evi. So many people on Fodors.com recommended this place—and we were not disappointed." —Ian

$$ TURKISH Fodor'sChoice ★ ✕ **Ziggy Cafe.** The ambience is especially inviting—attractive table arrangements, richly upholstered armchairs, wood trim, and wrought-iron lamps, and an upstairs terrace with sofalike seats and stone-topped tables—and the Mediterranean-inspired menu is refreshingly lighter than the heavy meat-based fare typical of Central Anatolia. Starters are particularly tasty; to sample a variety, try the tasting menu, of which 9 out of 12 items are mezes. In a space below the restaurant, owner Nuray Suzan Yüksel sells her handmade jewelry. ⊠ *Tevfik Fikret Cad. 24, Yunak Mah.* ☏ *384/341–7107* ⊕ *www.ziggycafe.com* ⚠ *Reservations essential.*

$$$ ⌂ **Elkep Evi.** Large rooms are comfortable and attractively furnished with wooden latticework cabinets and other old-fashioned pieces, and in the large garden, dotted with old wooden artifacts, guests can relax in hammocks or eat breakfast overlooking the town and surrounding valley. **Pros:** homey atmosphere; wonderful views; restaurant serving home-cooked food. **Cons:** a lot of stairs to reach some rooms. ⊠ *Esbelli Sok. 26* ☏ *384/341–6000* ⊕ *www.elkepevi.com.tr* ⇲ *18 rooms, 3 suites* ⚿ *In-room: no TV, Wi-Fi. In-hotel: restaurant, some pets allowed* ⊠ *Breakfast.*

$$ Fodor'sChoice ★ ⌂ **Esbelli Evi.** Large, comfortable, and spotlessly clean cave rooms, carved into a rocky hillside, have homey antique furniture, while suites also have gardens, sitting rooms, and giant bathrooms with double-headed showers and claw-foot tubs; all is overseen by the gracious host-owner, Süha Ersöz. **Pros:** extremely hospitable and attentive staff; good for families; excellent value. **Cons:** closed in winter. ⊠ *Esbelli Sok. 8* ☏ *384/341–3395* ⊕ *www.esbelli.com* ⇲ *4 rooms, 10 suites* ⚿ *In-room: kitchen, Wi-Fi. In-hotel: laundry facilities, business center, some pets allowed* ☉ *Closed Dec. 1–Mar. 1* ⊠ *Breakfast.*

$$$$ Fodor'sChoice ★ ⌂ **Sacred House.** Each room in this opulent 250-year-old Greek mansion is a veritable work of art and decorated with flair—ornate candelabras, statues of cupids, carved doors—but it still feels comfortable and even luxurious, and bathrooms, many with Jacuzzis, are similarly extravagant. **Pros:** unique, romantic ambience; close to town center; excellent food. **Cons:** no views from most rooms; not good for families with kids; room decor is intense and somewhat dark. ⊠ *Dutlucami Mah. Barbaros*

*Hayrettin Sok. 25* ☎*384/341–7102* ⊕*www.sacred-house.com* ⌁*12 rooms* ♿*In-room: no TV, Wi-Fi. In-hotel: restaurant, bar* ❡❍*Breakfast.*

$$ ⊡ **Serinn House.** Filled with contemporary flair—sleek wood, hip designer rugs and furniture, glass-enclosed showers with sand-color stone tiles that match the cave walls—these cave accommodations looking onto a courtyard are cozy and unpretentious, and a relaxed atmosphere prevails. **Pros:** sophisticated decor; highly personal service; outstanding breakfast. **Cons:** low lighting in bathrooms; closed in winter months. ⊠ *Esbelli Sok. 36* ☎*384/341–6076* ⊕ *www.serinnhouse. com* ⌁*6 rooms* ♿*In-room: no a/c, no TV, Wi-Fi* ☉ *Closed Nov. 1– Apr. 1* ❡❍*Breakfast.*

**Fodor's Choice** ★

$$ ⊡ **Ürgüp Evi.** These large, charming cave rooms with soft lighting, fireplaces, wooden floors, and big, comfortable beds have wonderful views over the town and countryside. **Pros:** relaxed atmosphere and hospitality; good for families. **Cons:** rather steep uphill walk to hotel. ⊠ *Esbelli Mah. 54* ☎*384/341–3173* ⊕ *www.urgupevi.com.tr* ⌁*10 rooms, 2 suites, 1 house* ♿*In-room: no TV. In-hotel: business center* ❡❍*Breakfast.*

$$$ ⊡ **Yunak Evleri.** Cave rooms cut into the cliff and stone-walled accommodations in an old Greek mansion are luxurious and stylish, with wood floors, wrought-iron beds, and Ottoman-theme decorative touches—and all have balconies or open to a shared terrace. **Pros:** stylish, luxurious atmosphere; inviting public spaces. **Cons:** views from rooms vary; some rooms rather dark. ⊠ *Yunak Mah.* ☎*384/341–6920* ⊕*www. yunak.com* ⌁*23 rooms, 7 suites* ♿*In-room: no TV, Wi-Fi. In-hotel: restaurant, business center* ❡❍*Breakfast.*

## GÖREME

*10 km (6 mi) northeast of Nevşehir; 7 km (4 mi) northwest of Ürgüp.*

Bustling Göreme offers the most options for hotels, dining, nightlife, and other commercial enterprises. Traditionally, the town has been more or less inundated with backpackers, who still find plenty of inexpensive lodgings, but recently some midrange and higher-end hotels have opened, too. There are Internet cafés in the main square, a couple of laid-back bars, and a used-book shop that stocks a surprisingly good collection of foreign titles. But the main reason to be here is to see some of the most spectacular fairy chimney valleys in the region and the nearby Göreme and Zelve open-air museums, both UNESCO World Heritage Sites and two must-sees in Cappadocia. The Göreme "museum," which tends to be packed with tourists, is a cluster of fairy chimneys famous for its spectacular cave churches. Somewhat less crowded Zelve is a valley filled with rock caves, which provides a glimpse into how people lived in the rock-cut communities.

### GETTING HERE AND AROUND

Small yet centrally located Göreme is the most convenient base for exploring Cappadocia if you don't have a car. The Göreme Open-Air Museum is a pleasant 1½ km (1 mi) walk from the town; to get to Zelve, another 6 km (4 mi) past the Göreme museum, take a taxi, rent a scooter, or join a day tour.

Some of the area's most beautiful valleys and hiking trails begin just at the outskirts of Göreme. Although the town itself is somewhat hilly (like most of Cappadocia), it's compact and easily navigated on foot.

## EXPLORING

Fodor'sChoice **Göreme Open-Air Museum.** *See the highlighted Cappadocia feature in*
★ *this chapter.*

**Zelve Open-Air Museum.** *See the highlighted Cappadocia feature in this chapter.*

## WHERE TO EAT AND STAY

*For expanded hotel reviews, visit Fodors.com.*

$$$ ✕**A'laturca.** One of the best restaurants in Göreme, A'laturca serves a
TURKISH delicious array of mezes, including hummus with *pastırma* (Turkish
★ pastrami) and grilled calamari. Main courses are stylishly presented renditions of such Turkish classics as *ali nazik* (grilled meat served over eggplant with yogurt), but variations on steak, chicken, and seafood are all excellent and portions are generous. The decor—terra-cotta-tile floors with kilims—is elegant but not overdone. For dessert, don't miss the walnut-stuffed dried apricots and figs, served warm with clotted cream. ⊠ *Gaferli Mah.* ☎ *384/271–2882* ⊕ *www.alaturca.com.tr* ⟃ *Reservations essential.*

$$ ✕**Orient Restaurant.** The menu is extensive and diverse—typical mezes
ECLECTIC and grills are served, as well as a range of steak and lamb options, chicken served with sauces of saffron or spinach, and even pasta. But what's most impressive is the four-course set menu, with several choices of appetizers, mains, and desserts that provide excellent food at an unbeatable value. The lanterns hanging from the traditional wooden ceilings and the carved stone walls decorated with copper trays create an ambience that's attractive and cozy. ⊠ *Adnan Menderes Cad. 3* ☎ *384/271–2346* ⊕ *www.orientrestaurant.net.*

$$$ ✕**Seten Restaurant.** A magnificent old mansion perched at the top of
TURKISH Göreme's hotel hill is the setting for great food and a beautiful view. Seating is outside in summer or inside in small rooms with just a few tables, an intimate setting in which to enjoy such delicious dishes as stuffed squash blossoms and a range of mezes. The restaurant's specialty, Tokat-style kebab—eggplant and meat cooked vertically so the juices of the two mix—is baked in the traditional oven on the terrace. ⊠ *Aydınlı Sok. 42* ☎ ⊕ *www.setenrestaurant.com* ⟃ *Reservations essential.*

$$$$ ⌂**Anatolian Houses.** At this romantic getaway, with a beautiful setting among the fairy chimneys, rooms combine plush, antique-accented decor with modern conveniences (including superb bathrooms, most with Jacuzzis), and pampering touches include a small but inviting indoor-outdoor pool, hammam, and sauna. **Pros:** feels extremely luxurious; unique and romantic atmosphere. **Cons:** given the high prices, service could be better; a bit over the top. ⊠ *Gaferli Mah.* ☎ *384/271–2463* ⊕ *www.anatolianhouses.com.tr* ⟿ *33 suites* ⌂ *In-hotel: pool, business center, parking* ⦿ *Breakfast.*

$$ ⌂**Aydınlı Cave House Hotel.** Mustafa Demirci converted his centuries-old family home into a beautiful guesthouse, and he has since taken

*Continued on page 370*

# ROCK OF AGES
## UNEARTHING HOLY CAPPADOCIA

A fantasy come true, Cappadocia's phantasmagorical landscape of rock pinnacles, or "fairy chimneys," is one of Turkey's most otherworldly sights. A natural hideout—thanks to Mother Nature's chiseling tools of wind and water—the region became a sort of promised land for Anatolia's earliest Christians. Over the course of the 6th to 12th centuries, these early Cappadocian dwellers incised the fantastic escarpments of Göreme and Zelve with a honeycomb of cave churches. Today you can trace the saga of the early Christians' religious faith by exploring this spectacular setting. As the first monks might have proclaimed: You have to believe it to see it!

Opposite: Cappadocia. Top: Göreme National Park

# AN EARLY CHRISTIAN WONDERLAND

Remote and inaccessible, Cappadocia seemed custom-made for early Christian communities, whose members erected their churches in hollowed-out caves and expanded vast underground cities to hide from enemies and live reclusive monastic lives.

The story of Cappadocia begins more than ten million years ago, when three volcanoes began a geological symphony that dropped lava, mud, and ash over the region. Over eons, frequent eruptions of Mt. Erciyes, Mt. Hasan, and Mt. Melendiz covered considerable parts of the land with tufa—a porous rock layer formed of volcanic ash—over which lava spread at various stages of hardening.

Erosion by rain, snow, and wind created soaring stone "fairy chimneys," surrealistic shapes of cones, needles, pillars, and pyramids, not unlike the looming pinnacles of Arizona's Monument Valley. As time went on, earthquakes added valleys and rivers (mostly long-vanished) and slashed rifts into the fragile tufa. Depending on the variable consistency of the rock, the changes occurred more or less violently, with utterly fantastic results.

## A REAL RUBBLE-ROUSER

Fast forward some millennia. Persecuted by authorities and often on the run from invading armies (Cappadocia was a frontier province), early Christians found the region's cliffs, rock pinnacles, and tufa caves ideal for the construction of their secluded colonies. Within 200 years of the death of Jesus, a regional bishopric had been established in nearby Kayseri.

By the 4th century the number-one industry of Cappadocia was prayer, and the early recluses carved dwellings into Cappodocia's malleable stone, their only tools sharpened sticks. The simplicity of construction set a fashion that quickly led to the formation of anchorite colonies. These early monastic communities deftly combined the individuality of meditation with the communal work favored by St. Basil.

Above,: Rock formations (chimneys) in the Göreme Valley

### THE WORD MADE ROCK

The worship of God remained of uppermost importance here, and cave chapels and churches proliferated, especially throughout the Göreme Valley. When Arab raiders swept throught the region in the 7th and 8th centuries, large numbers of Christians sought refuge in rocky hide-outs and underground cities like Derinkuyu and Kaymaklı, which grew sufficiently large to house populations of up to 20,000 people.

After the Isaurian dynasty of Byzantine emperors repulsed the Arabs in 740, hollowed-out churches began to appear above ground. Reflecting contemporary Byzantine architectural styles, they were decorated with geometrical paintings. Following Empress Theodora's restoration of the use of holy imagery in the 9th century, churches were given increasingly ambitious frescoes. Many of these were painted in color schemes that rivaled the yellow, pink, and russet hues of their rock surroundings.

### WHAT CREATED CAPPADOCIA'S "FAIRY CHIMNEYS"?

The volcanoes that formed Cappadocia are inactive now, but the most recent may have erupted just 8,000 years ago; Neolithic humans depicted the eruption in cave dwellings at Çatal Höyük (near present-day Konya). Nature continues to sculpt the landscape of Cappadocia. In the future, it is likely that some formations now visible will have turned to dust, and other forms will have been separated from the mountains, providing new experiences for tomorrow's travelers.

Top, Göreme Open-Air Museum.
Bottom: Rock homes, Göreme Valley

# GÖREME: A ROCKBOUND HEAVEN

A UNESCO World Heritage Site, the Göreme Açık Hava Müzesi (Göreme Open-Air Museum) is a must-see for its amazing landscape and churches. These rock-hewn holy sanctuaries may be *in* the earth but they are not *of* it.

While Cappadocia is sprinkled with hundreds of ancient churches—most built between the 10th and 12th centuries, though some as early as the 6th century—the best are found in the open-air museum at Göreme. Many Göreme churches are built in an inscribed Greek cross plan, a common Byzantine design, wherein all four arms of the church are equal in length.

The central dome almost always features a depiction of Christ Pantocrator ("Omnipotent"). Though dictated in part by Cappadocia's landscape, the small size and intimate feel of Göreme's rock-cut churches was also deliberate: the monastic community living here designed them not as houses of worship for the public but as chapels where members of the community could engage in solitary prayer and worship of specific saints.

## EARTH AS ART

Most churches were commissioned by local donors who hired teams of professional artists—some local and some brought from as far away as Constantinople—to paint elaborate frescoes of scenes from the Old and New Testaments and the lives of the saints.

Visible in places where frescoes have peeled off, underlying geometric designs, crosses, and other symbols were painted directly onto the rock walls in red ochre. It is thought that these decorations were made when a church was first carved out of the rock, in order to consecrate the space. Sometime later, professional artists then painted their detailed frescoes on top of these designs. Note that the eyes of some of the figures have been scratched out, probably much later by Muslims who believed that visually representing human beings was blasphemous.

Above: Göreme Valley. Photo by yversace, Fodors.com member. Opposite: Elmalı Kilise (Church with the Apple).

## TIPS FOR VISITING GÖREME

In summer, get an early start to beat the heat and the crowds, or go after 5 PM, when it's cooler and the crowds have thinned. The open-air museum covers a large area, with hundreds of caves and crannies to explore, almost all of which are easily reachable on paved paths. Allow a good two hours to get the most out of your visit. Note that no photography of any kind is allowed inside the churches. ⊠ About 1.5 km (1 mi) southeast of Göreme town center. ☎ 384/271-2167 ☜ 15TL ⏲ Daily Apr.-Oct. 8-7, Nov.-Mar. 8-5, last entry 45 min. before closing.

# WHAT TO SEE AT THE GÖREME OPEN-AIR MUSEUM

Fresco of St. George and St. Theodorus killing the dragon in Yılanlı Kilise.

**1 Convent & Monastery.** After you enter the site, you'll see a steep rock to your left: this housed a six-story convent, which had a kitchen and refectory on the lower levels and a chapel on the third; large millstones lay ready to block the narrow passages in times of danger. Opposite is a monastery with the same plan. Unfortunately, in 2007 these structures were deemed unsafe and are now closed to visitors.

**2 Elmalı Kilise (Church with the Apple).** Accessed through a tunnel, this 11th-century church has wonderfully preserved frescoes of biblical scenes and portraits of saints; red and gray tones predominate. There are an impressive nine domes: eight small and one large; the largest shows Christ Pantocrator "on His heavenly throne." You can see the red-ochre geometric designs and crosses where the frescoes have peeled off.

Elmalı Kilise (detail of fresco)

**3 Barbara Kilise** (Church of St. Barbara). Above the Elmalı Kilise, this chapel has only a few frescoes, including Christ Pantocrator and St. Barbara. Far more interestingly, most of the chapel is decorated with red ochre symbols painted on the rock, including geometric designs and some unusual, almost whimsical, creatures.

**4 Yılanlı Kilise** (Snake Church/Church of St. Onuphrius). Small but intriguing, this church takes its Turkish name from the scene on the left wall depicting St. George slaying the dragon, which here takes the form of a snake. More unusual is the story of St. Onuphrius, on the right wall of the church: the naked saint is depicted with both a beard and breasts. While the official story says that St. Onuphrius was a pious hermit who lived in Egypt, another version has it that the saint was a loose woman who repented, embraced Christianity, and was given a beard.

**5 Refectory/Kitchen.** You can still imagine the huge rock-carved dining table packed at mealtimes with priests. The table could seat 40 to 50 people; carved into the opposite wall is the place allotted for wine-making. There are several kitchens in Göreme, but this refectory (near the Yılanlı Kilise) is the largest.

**6 Karanlık Kilise** (Dark Church). Entrance to this church, which was extensively restored by UNESCO, costs an extra 8 YTL, because of the exceptional group of frescoes. Vibrant scenes, dominated by deep blue colors, decorate the walls and domed ceiling; the frescoes have retained their brilliant colors due to the structure of the church, which lets in little light (hence the name). The frescoes show scenes from the Old and New Testaments; the Crucifixion scene is particularly intense.

**7 Çarıklı Kilise** (Church of the Sandal). Climb up a metal ladder to reach this church, named after the footprints (some might say indentations) below the Ascension fresco; some believe these to be casts of Jesus' own footprints. The beautiful frescoes in this 11th-century church have been restored and portray a similar narrative cycle to those in the Karanlık Kilise. Note also the geometric and floral patterns between the frescoes. The church was closed to visitors after a 2011 cave in, but it is

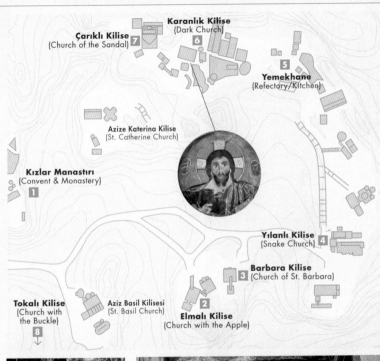

**Çarıklı Kilise**
(Church of the Sandal) **7**

**Karanlık Kilise**
(Dark Church) **6**

**5**

**Yemekhane**
(Refectory/Kitchen)

**Azize Katerina Kilise**
(St. Catherine Church)

**Kızlar Manastırı**
(Convent & Monastery) **1**

**Yılanlı Kilise**
(Snake Church) **4**

**Barbara Kilise**
(Church of St. Barbara) **3**

**Tokalı Kilise**
(Church with
the Buckle) **8**

**Aziz Basil Kilisesi**
(St. Basil Church)

**Elmalı Kilise**
(Church with the Apple) **2**

hoped that it will be repaired and reopened.

**8 Tokalı Kilise** (Church with the Buckle). Don't miss this church, across from the main museum area and a short way down the road toward Göreme (use the same entrance ticket). The oldest church in the open-air museum, and one of the

largest and most impressive, it has high ceilings and brilliant blue colors. It's made up of an "Old Church" and a "New Church." The former was built in the early 10th century, and less than a century later it became the vaulted atrium of the "New Church," which was dug deeper into the rock; both sections have

well-preserved frescoes depicting the life of Christ. This is the only church in Göreme in which the narrative scenes take place in chronological order. The church is to remain open while it undergoes restoration.

Left: Interior of Çarıklı Kilise, Christian murals dating from the 11th century AD.
Right: Murals from Tokalı Kilise

## GREAT HIKES

One of the most rewarding walks from Göreme is through the **Rose Valley** (Güllüdere), where cave entrances lead to multi-storey, ornately decorated churches with columns that are two or three stories high. Roman graves, now unreachable, are adorned with Christian crosses and sit high upon eroded fairy chimneys. A hike through the valley often ends up at **Paşabağı**, the great monastic settlement of fairy chimneys. There are also spectacular hikes through **Love Valley** (Aşk Vadisi), perhaps named for the preponderance of phallus-like rock protrusions.

Though farther afield, the lush **Ihlara Valley** (see the listing in this chapter) also hosts a wealth of rock-carved churches, which are an interesting contrast to those at Göreme because they were carved and decorated not by professional artists, as in Göreme, but by local monks living in the remote valley. The liturgical cycle depicted in the frescoes is somewhat abridged and the style more improvised. There are occasionally even spelling errors, such as in the Kokar Kilise, where the abbreviation of Jesus' name is misspelled with the Greek letters HC instead of IC.

# ZELVE'S CAVE DWELLINGS

In typical Cappadocian fashion, man once again combined with nature to create Zelve, a village of rock-hewn houses that even Fred Flintstone would have envied.

While the prizes at Göreme are the fresco-decorated churches, the outdoor museum at Zelve Açık Hava Müzesi (Zelve Open-Air Museum) provides a fascinating look at how people lived in fairy-chimney communities. Zelve was a center of Christian monastic life in the 9th through 13th centuries, and the town was inhabited until the early 1950s, when erosion and cracking began causing slabs of rock to fall and villagers were moved out of the hundreds of cave dwellings.

The site is only about 2,145 feet long, but there's plenty to explore. The valley is made up of several uneven, naturally carved rows of fairy chimneys. These and just about every spare rock-face shelter hundreds of dwellings that vary in size—some are just simple cavelike openings and others are multi-storey houses with rooms on several floors linked by stairs carved deep inside the rocks. There's also a rock-cut mosque and several small churches. Some of the structures have collapsed and giant pieces of carved ceiling lie upside down on the ground.

Be prepared to climb around, and definitely bring a flashlight or you won't be able to explore some of the most interesting and extensive dwellings. You can probably see the whole place in a little over an hour, but you could easily spend more time.

---

✉ 6 km (4 mi) northeast of the Göreme Open-Air Museum, 3 km (2 mi) off the road to Avanos.

☎ 384/271-3535 💳 8TL

⊙ Daily, Apr.-Oct. 8-7, Nov.-Mar. 8-5, last entry 45 min. before closing.

---

6

IN FOCUS ROCK OF AGES

over the place next door as well to offer large rooms decorated in a tasteful, restrained style with simple wood and metal furniture, and travertine-lined bathrooms with good-size showers. **Pros:** friendly, hospitable owner and staff; nice rooms; slightly less far up the hill than some other lodgings, if you wish to avoid the climb. **Cons:** lots of stairs to upper-level rooms and breakfast area. ⊠ *Aydınlı Sok. 12* ☎ *384/271–2263* ⊕ *www.thecavehotel.com* ☙ *8 rooms, 4 suites* ☖ *In-room: no a/c, no TV, Wi-Fi. In-hotel: business center* ⊺⊙⊦ *Breakfast.*

> **TAKE A FLASHLIGHT**
>
> Take a flashlight, or better yet, a headlamp, to explore many of the rock-cut churches, underground cities, and cave dwellings. Small hotels will often lend you a flashlight, or if you hire a guide, make sure to ask if they can supply equipment.

**$$$** 🛏 **Cappadocia Cave Suites.** Comfortable rooms, most of which are quirkily shaped and etched out of fairy chimneys, combine antiques, old-fashioned wrought-iron beds, and folk-art bedspreads, with such modern conveniences as satellite TVs, subtle lighting, and Jacuzzis in most bathrooms (a few have showers instead). **Pros:** luxurious feel; layout allows for privacy; attentive staff. **Cons:** service could be improved; lots of steps to reach some rooms and common areas. ⊠ *Gaferli Mah., Ünlü Sok. 19* ☎ *384/271–2800* ⊕ *www.cappadociacavesuites.com* ☙ *21 rooms, 13 suites* ☖ *In-room: Wi-Fi. In-hotel: restaurant, business center, parking* ⊺⊙⊦ *Breakfast.*

**$$** 🛏 **Kelebek Hotel.** A combined backpacker-type *pansiyon* and rather posh
**Fodor's Choice** hotel offers accommodations that range from small, basic cave rooms to
★ spacious, antiques-filled suites overlooking a tranquil garden courtyard. **Pros:** exceptionally helpful staff; good value; excellent breakfast. **Cons:** hotel is a longish uphill walk from town center; some *pansiyon* rooms noisy due to proximity to common areas. ⊠ *Aydınlı Mah.* ☎ *384/271– 2531* ⊕ *www.kelebekhotel.com* ☙ *21 rooms, 12 suites* ☖ *In-room: no TV, Wi-Fi. In-hotel: restaurant, pool, some pets allowed* ⊺⊙⊦ *Breakfast.*

**$$** 🛏 **Kısmet Cave House.** At this lovely, cozy retreat in a quiet part of Göreme, each of the carefully decorated rooms (three are cave rooms, the others are stone-walled) is named after a different flower, which features in colorful paintings on the walls and wooden furniture. **Pros:** extraordinary hospitality; beautiful, inspired decor; personal, intimate feel; dinner can be served in the dining area on request. **Cons:** rooms are not so large; ground-floor rooms can be a bit noisy. ⊠ *Kağnı Yolu 9* ☎ *384/271–2416* ⊕ *www.kismetcavehouse.com* ☙ *7 rooms, 1 suite* ☖ *In-room: no TV, Wi-Fi* ⊺⊙⊦ *Breakfast.*

## UÇHISAR

*7 km (4 mi) east of Nevşehir; 3 km (2 mi) southwest of Göreme.*

A beautiful village on a hill, built around a fairy chimney known as Uçhisar Castle, Uçhisar has some of the nicest places to stay in Cappadocia. There are some carpet and rug shops here, but most of the town is quiet and residential, with clustered stone houses overlooking the valleys. Chickens peck along backstreets and are tended to by women who live in nearby caves. From here, it's easy to take off for a walk through Pigeon Valley (Güvercinlik Vadisi), so named for the birds the villagers raise in distinctive-looking cotes lodged in the walls of the valley.

### GETTING HERE AND AROUND

Despite being fairly centrally located, Uçhisar is less frequently served by minibuses than other nearby towns are, and especially during the low season it can be difficult to get to and from the town without a car. Once you're in the town, however, restaurants, hotels, and shops are conveniently located within walking distance of one another; the main attraction, Uçhisar Castle, is no more than a stone's throw from any hotel; and some hiking trails can be accessed from the edge of town.

### EXPLORING

**Uçhisar Kalesi** (*Uçhisar Castle*). Uçhisar Kalesi is not so much a "castle," as its Turkish name implies, but the highest fairy chimney in Cappadocia. It was used as a fortress in the late Byzantine and early Ottoman periods, and later inhabited by the locals. The striking formation is riddled with rock-cut houses, giving it a Swiss-cheese look but it was evacuated in the 1960s when erosion put everything in danger of collapse and the structure was declared a disaster zone (residents were moved to safer dwellings in the shadow of the giant rock). There's a great view of the town and the valleys from the top (though you'll have to have to do a good bit of climbing to get there), and it's a beautiful spot from which to watch the sunset. ⊠ *Near center of town* ☏ *No phone* ⊇ *5 TL* ☉ *Daily 8–sundown.*

### WHERE TO EAT AND STAY

*For expanded hotel reviews, visit Fodors.com.*

$$
TURKISH
★

✕ **Center Restaurant.** It's the opposite of fancy, but locals say this friendly, unpretentious place on the village square is the best restaurant in Uçhisar. It's also reasonably priced. The specialty is a tagine of lamb and artichokes, but even mezes like *cacık* (yogurt with cucumber, herbs, and garlic) and salads like *çoban salatası* (shepherd's salad) are far above average. In warm weather, seating is in a shady garden. ⊠ *Belediye Meydanı* ☏ *384/219–3117.*

$$$
TURKISH

✕ **Elai Restaurant.** French flair, stone walls, an Ottoman-style fireplace, and stylish table settings all combine to create an elegant atmosphere that complements the menu of Turkish and international cuisine. A standout among the sophisticated offerings is the *şaşlık kebabı*, a delicately spiced skewer of lamb served over roasted tomatoes and a phyllo tart filled with pureed eggplant. A terrace on the lower slopes of Uçhisar Castle is a lovely spot for a meal in good weather. ⊠ *Eski Göreme Cad. 61* ☏ *384/219–3181* ⊕ *www.elairestaurant.com* ⋐ *Reservations essential.*

**$$**    ⛺ **Argos in Cappadocia.** Luxurious accommodations, a commitment to
Fodor'sChoice    excellent service, and environmentally friendly practices quickly made
★    the Argos in Cappadocia a top recommendation since opening in 2010.
**ros:** calm atmosphere, extremely comfortable rooms; friendly and help-
ful staff. **Cons:** it's very hard to leave. ⊠ *Asagi Mahalle Kayabasi Sok.
23* ☏ *384/219-3130* ⊕ *www.argosincappadocia.com* ⤴ *42 rooms* ⌂ *In-
room: a/c, no TV, Wi-Fi. In-hotel: restaurant, bar, laundry facilities,
parking* ⫶○⫶ *Breakfast.*

**$$$$**    ⛺ **Cappadocia Cave Resort.** With plush decor that veers to over-the-top
(some rooms have round beds next to Jacuzzis), the largest spa in the
region, and a sushi bar, this resort could almost make you forget you're
in Cappadocia—were it not for the excellent views of the valley below.
**Pros:** luxury; extensive spa and dining facilities. **Cons:** Vegas-like decor
and lighting in some public areas; room decor and size vary greatly.
⊠ *Tekelli Mah. Göreme Cad. 1* ☏ *384/219–3194* ⊕ *www.ccr-hotels.
com* ⤴ *57 rooms, 22 suites* ⌂ *In-room: Wi-Fi. In-hotel: restaurant, bar,
pool, gym, spa, business center, parking* ⫶○⫶ *Breakfast.*

**$$$**    ⛺ **Les Maisons de Cappadoce.** French architect Jacques Avizou has
Fodor'sChoice    restored more than a dozen old houses and turned them into some of
★    the most beautiful places to stay in Cappadocia, elegantly blending rus-
tic and modern decor and providing such amenities as kitchens—and in
one house, a beautiful heated swimming pool. **Pros:** lovely atmosphere
and magnificent views; houses provide privacy and a less touristy experience; great for families. **Cons:** some studios and their kitchenettes are
smallish; accommodations are far from reception. ⊠ *Belediye Meydanı
24* ☏ *384/219–2813* ⊕ *www.cappadoce.com* ⤴ *16 houses* ⌂ *In-room:
kitchen, no TV, Wi-Fi. In-hotel: some pets allowed* ⫶○⫶ *Breakfast.*

**$$$$**    ⛺ **Museum Hotel.** The Museum Hotel, a cluster of comfortable, attrac-
★    tively decorated rooms in caves and stone buildings connected by labyrinthine passages, is a work of art, filled with the owner's impressive
collection of antiques, from metalwork to Ottoman caftans to carpets.
**Pros:** unique decor and setting; romantic, luxurious feel; beautiful scenery. **Cons:** rooms vary in size and views; some guests say service could
be more attentive, given the price. ⊠ *Tekelli Mah. 1* ☏ *384/219–2220*
⊕ *www.museumhotel.com.tr* ⤴ *7 rooms, 23 suites* ⌂ *In-room: Wi-Fi.
In-hotel: restaurant, bar, pool, business center, parking, some pets
allowed* ⫶○⫶ *Breakfast.*

## AVANOS

*17 km (11 mi) northeast of Nevşehir; 10 km (6 mi) north of Göreme;
12 km (7 mi) northeast of Uçhisar.*

Avanos is a fun little town on the Kızılırmak (Red River), so named
for the red hue of the clay that lines its banks. A wobbly footbridge
crosses the river near the busy town square and a couple of cafés are
located along the waterfront (there are bridges for vehicles a short way
up- and downriver). Avanos is known for pottery made from the river's
clay, a craft that vies with tourism as the biggest industry; the local potters specialize in Hittite shapes and designs inspired by pieces found in
archaeological digs across Central Anatolia. Many potters also make

ornate pieces in unusual shapes, as well as functional painted items such as wine goblets and tea sets. Pottery is a family affair in Avanos, and as you walk around and check out the local shops selling decorated clay pots and vases, you'll notice family members painting the pieces their fathers and grandfathers make. Almost all the local potters will demonstrate for free how pottery was made in the old days—with a kick wheel and clay from the river.

Avanos is also famous for its underground tunnels, some of which may lead to as-yet-undiscovered underground cities or link up with larger ones in Kaymaklı and Derinkuyu. It seems there's a network of secret passages underneath just about every house, which the residents probably once dug in case there was an urgent need to hide or escape. Özkonak, discovered off a dirt road 15 km (9 mi) north of Avanos, is thought to be quite large, but has not been as extensively excavated as Derinkuyu and Kaymaklı, and only four levels are currently accessible to the public. Compared to those other underground cities, it's far less interesting.

### GETTING HERE AND AROUND

Though located slightly farther afield from Cappadocia's main sights, Avanos is connected to other towns and sights by direct roads and is easy to reach if you have a car; minibuses also connect Avanos with other Cappadocian towns. Most hotels, restaurants, shops, and businesses are along the northern bank of the river or just a short walk away.

### WHERE TO EAT AND STAY

*For expanded hotel reviews, visit Fodors.com.*

$$ ╳ **Bizim Ev Restaurant.** The fanciest restaurant in Avanos has a covered
TURKISH upstairs terrace and a tavernlike interior where local wines are displayed on huge racks. Kilims and pottery hang from the stone walls, and lanterns placed in niches add to the ambience. The delicious but heavy house specialty is *bostan kebabı*, chicken, turkey, or beef cooked with mushrooms, eggplant, onions, and peppers, topped with cheese, and served in a clay pot. Vegetable appetizers in olive oil and a variety of meat dishes dominate the rest of the menu. ⊠ *Orta Mah. Baklacı Sok. 1* ☎ *384/511–5525* ⊕ *www.bizim-ev.com.*

$ ▥ **Kirkit Pension.** In these five converted Ottoman stone houses, the clean rooms are decorated with carpets and Uzbek blankets, and some upper-level units have nice views of the river. **Pros:** friendly, relaxed atmosphere. **Cons:** bathrooms pretty basic; some small rooms. ⊠ *Atatürk Cad. 50* ☎ *384/511–3259* ⊕ *www.kirkit.com* ⇨ *17 rooms* ⌂ *In-room: no a/c, no TV, Wi-Fi. In-hotel: restaurant, laundry facilities, some pets allowed* ⵏⵓ*Breakfast.*

$ ▥ **Sofa Hotel.** At this charming complex of more than a dozen late-Ottoman houses, sitting areas, labyrinthine passages, and shady outdoor spaces with carpeted floors and long Ottoman-style benches abound, and rooms are decorated with wood furniture, carpets, and pretty linens. **Pros:** very good value; nice ambience and decor. **Cons:** rooms vary a lot in size, decor, and amenities. ⊠ *Orta Mah. Gedik Sok. 9* ☎ *384/511–5186* ⊕ *www.sofa-hotel.com* ⇨ *33 rooms* ⌂ *In-room: Wi-Fi. In-hotel: business center* ⵏⵓ*Breakfast.*

6

## SHOPPING

The shops are generally open seven days a week during tourist season, from 9 to around 6, depending on business.

**Avanos Çarşı Seramik** (*Chez Ferhat*). Avanos Çarşı Seramik has an excellent array of pieces and will usually give customers a pretty good deal. ⊠ *Near PTT (post office)* ☎ *384/511–4871.*

**Chez Ali Baba.** Friendly, family-run Chez Ali Baba gives up to 15 days of free pottery-making classes to anyone interested. ⊠ *Fırınbaşı Sok., up and to right from PTT* ☎ *384/511–3166.*

**Chez Galip.** Chez Galip, the oldest, most famous and by far the funkiest of the pottery shops, has two branches. The branch in the center of town is remarkable not just for its ceramics but also for being the home to what its owner says is the world's largest collection of human hair—more than 15,000 locks are on display. ☎ *384/511–4240.*

**Ömürlü Seramik.** You can browse the extensive inventory, see the artists at work, and try your hand at the wheel yourself at this friendly shop off the Ürgüp-Kayseri road. If you're really lucky, and the shop isn't too busy, you might find yourself in the midst of impromptu music and dance festivities. ⊠ *Yeni Mah. 3. Cad. 2. Sok. No. 26* ☎ *384/511–3231* ⊕ *www.omurlu.com.*

## HACIBEKTAŞ

*40 km (25 mi) northwest of Avanos on Rte. D765.*

The mystic and philosopher Hacı Bektaş Veli founded a Muslim sect here in the 13th century that was a synthesis of Sunni and Shiite thought, blended with a touch of Christianity. He gained a following of Sufi dervishes, the Bektashis, as well as some considerable political influence; the Janissary corps of warriors of the Ottoman Empire, established a century after Hacı Bektaş' death, made Bektashism their official order and revered him as their spiritual leader. A three-day festival celebrating Hacı Bektaş begins on August 16 each year and is a colorful, popular affair, with Sufi dancing and music in the streets, while souvenir shops sell trinkets with pictures of Atatürk, Hacı Bektaş, and the Imam Ali. Unless you're in town for the lively festival, or have a particular interest in Sufism or mystic beliefs, however, you're likely to find Hacıbektaş a bit uninteresting.

**Hacıbektaş Müzesi.** Hacı Bektaş is buried in a tomb inside the museum, the main attraction in town. ⊠ *In center of town, Hacıbektaş* ☎ *384/441–3022* ⊕ *www.hacibektas.com* ▣ *3TL* ☉ *Tues.–Sun. 8–5.*

## DERINKUYU AND KAYMAKLI

*Kaymaklı is 20 km (12 mi) south of Nevşehir on Rte. 765; Derinkuyu is 9 km (6 mi) south of Kaymaklı on Rte. 765.*

The underground cities of Cappadocia have excited the imaginations of travelers since the Greek mercenary leader/historian Xenophon wrote about them in the 5th century BC. No one really knows for sure who dug the cities, or when, or why. Hittite artifacts found in some of

The underground city of Derinkuyu is believed to have been home to thousands of people.

the cities point to their having been initially constructed during pre-Christian times, but the underground networks were certainly modified and probably also significantly expanded later by the early Christians who inhabited them. Some of the cities are merely passages between different belowground dwellings. Others really deserve the title of "city": The largest, including Kaymaklı and Derinkuyu, have multiple levels and were equipped to house thousands of people for up to a couple of months at a time. The impermeable tufa, or porous rock, of Cappadocia kept the insides of the cities dry, while ventilation shafts supplied air and interior wells provided water. Ground-level entrances were cleverly disguised, and in the event that invaders did make their way in, huge millstonelike stones were used to block off different passageways and secure the city.

### GETTING HERE AND AROUND

If you're traveling without a car, you can get to Kaymaklı and Derinkuyu using public minibuses; you'll need to take a bus from whichever town you're staying in to Nevşehir and change there to a Niğde-bound bus. From Nevşehir it's about a half hour to Kaymaklı and an additional 10 minutes or so to Derinkuyu.

An easier and probably more time-efficient option is to join a day tour of Cappadocia, leaving from Göreme or Ürgüp. Tours usually include a visit to one of the underground cities, where your guide will help you navigate the labyrinthine passageways and provide background that will bring the place to life.

If you visit the cities on your own it's a good idea to arrive as early in the day as possible, before the tour groups arrive. During peak season, it's easier to explore Kaymaklı because—unlike Derinkuyu—it has separate in and out tunnels, which means less congestion and shorter waiting times.

### EXPLORING

**Derinkuyu.** Derinkuyu, meaning "deep well," is the deepest of the known underground cities that have been explored. Eight floors, reaching to a depth of 55 meters (180 ft), in this subterranean labyrinth are open to the public, though there may be more floors that are unexplored. There are stables, wineries, a chapel, school, scores of other interconnected rooms, and as many as 600 entrances and air ducts. You'll also see ventilation shafts that plunge as deep as 55 meters (280 ft) from ground level. In parts, you'll have to walk doubled over almost in half for a hundred meters (about 330 feet) through a cave corridor. A visit here is an amazing, almost surreal, experience but you probably won't want to spend more than an hour inside. ■TIP➔ **Derinkuyu is on the way to the Ihlara Valley and many tour groups stop here, so it's often more crowded than Kaymaklı.** ☎ 384/381–3194 💌 15 TL ☯ Apr.–Oct., daily 8–7; Nov.–Mar., daily 8–5; last entry 45 min before closing.

**Kaymaklı.** About 9 km (6 mi) north of Derinkuyu, Kaymaklı was discovered in 1950 and is believed to be the largest of Cappadocia's underground cities in square area, though it's not as deep as Derinkuyu. It's believed that many of the current homes in the area are connected to the caves, and the story is told that before parts of the underground city were closed off to the public, unsuspecting home owners periodically found tourists popping up in their living rooms. The city extends below ground for eight levels, of which only four are currently open to the public. Sloping corridors and steps connect the floors, with cemeteries, and kitchens on every other level. The ceilings are low here and almost impossible for tall visitors to navigate. ☎ 384/218–2500 💌 15 TL ☯ Apr.–Oct., daily 8–7; Nov.–Mar., daily 8–5; last entry 45 min before closing.

**OFF THE BEATEN PATH**

**Soğanlı Kaya Kiliseleri** (*Soğanlı Rock Churches*). You'll need your own transportation and some time to get to the magnificent Soğanlı Valleys, about 80 km (48 mi) southwest of Kayseri on Route 805 toward Niğde; look for the sign off the highway just after Yeşilhisar. You'll likely be alone to explore hundreds of rock dwellings and churches cut into the cliffs on the sides of these two valleys that form a V shape. A path follows a little stream past enormous, house-size boulders and comes to churches with domed ceilings and hundreds of other dwellings and rooms that curve around a wooded canyon. It's completely quiet except for the birds chirping and the frogs croaking. Climb up the cliff face and look around from the top and you'll be rewarded with incredible views. ☎ No phone 💌 3 TL ☯ Daily 9–5.

6

# IHLARA VALLEY

*About 110 km (66 mi) southwest of Nevşehir; about 52 km (32 mi) west of Derinkuyu.*

## GETTING HERE AND AROUND

If you're coming from Nevşehir, take Route 300 west to Aksaray, then drive 42 km (25 mi) southeast past Selime. If coming from Derinkuyu, head west on the winding road called Gülağaç Yolu.

## EXPLORING

★ **Ihlara Valley.** The landscape changes dramatically when you head south through Cappadocia toward Ihlara: the dusty plains turn rich with vegetation, and the Melendiz River carves a rift into the sheer tufa cliffs, which rise up to 490 feet. If you have enough time to spend in Cappadocia, it can be refreshing to see green—and water—as you hike through the lush valley and explore some of the dozens of churches hidden in nooks above the river.

There are three entrances to the 14-km-long (8½-mi-long) valley: from Selime at the north end, from Belisırma in the middle, and from Ihlara at the south end. Walking the entire valley will take you the better part of a day, but if you just want to get a taste of it, the most interesting section is the Ihlara Vadi Turistik Tesisleri, where a cluster of fresco-decorated churches are within walking distance of one another. You have to walk down more than 400 steps to get there. Belisırma village, inside the valley roughly a three-hour walk from either end, has a handful of scenic restaurants. ⊠ *Ihlara Vadi Turistik Tesisleri, 2 km (1 mi) from Ilhara village* ☎ *No phone* 🖼 *5 TL* ☉ *Summer, daily 8–7; winter, daily 8–5.*

# NIĞDE

*126 km (78 mi) southwest of Kayseri on Rte. 805; 85 km (53 mi) south of Nevşehir on Rte. 765.*

Niğde has many new factories and old farms, a lot of dust, and not a whole lot that's worth seeing. In the 13th century, the city flourished under the Seljuks, who built the triple-domed Alaaddin Camii and the neighboring 11th-century fortress. The Ak Medrese, built in 1409, has stone carvings and a small museum and cultural center. A little outside of town is Eski Gümüşler Monastery, the only real reason to come to Niğde as a traveler.

## EXPLORING

**Eski Gümüşler Manastiri** (*Eski Gümüşler Monastery*). The ticket man here says the 11th-century Eski Gümüşler church inside the complex has the only picture of a smiling Virgin Mary in the world. Others say that this is due to an error made during the church's restoration. Whatever the case, the frescoes inside, though dark, are beautiful and amazingly well preserved. (The "smiling" Virgin is in a rock niche in the back left corner of the church.) Parts of the monastery were carved as early as the 7th century but most of the frescoes are from around the 11th century; they were painted over by local Turkish Muslims, for whom depicting humans was a sin (idolatry). The pictures were cleaned and carefully recovered in the 1960s. In a room above the church are frescoes of animals, thought to be depicting scenes from Aesop's fables—an unusual example of nonreligious art in this region. The monastery also contains a kitchen, rock-carved monks' chambers around the central courtyard, and two levels of underground rooms that may have been used in part as a water reservoir. The sign for the monastery will be one of the first things you'll see at the entrance to Niğde from Kayseri; it's about 3 km (2 mi) down the road from there. ⊠ *9 km (6 mi) northeast of Niğde, left off Rte. 805, in village of Gümüşler* ☎ *No phone* 🖃 *3 TL* ☉ *Summer, daily 8–6; winter, daily 9–5 in winter; guard will unlock bldg. for you.*

# KONYA

*258 km (160 mi) south of Ankara; 142 km (88 mi) southwest of Ihlara.*

Konya is famous for being the location of Rumi's tomb, and is also known throughout Turkey as a religious and rather conservative city. Its mainly religious sights attract Muslims on pilgrimages and Turkish schoolchildren on trips, as well as foreign and Turkish tourists. The Mevlâna Museum, which houses Rumi's tomb, is quite impressive, and the sense of religious devotion and reverence among visitors is immediately palpable. The city also has a long and interesting history, including its stint as the capital of the Seljuk Empire from the mid-12th through the 13th centuries, and some notable ancient mosques and theological seminary buildings showcase the characteristic architectural style of that period.

The city is experiencing a boom in popularity that coincides with the surging interest worldwide in the Sufi mystic poet Mevlâna Celaleddin Rumi and the rise to power of a moderate Islamist government in Turkey. During the annual Mevlâna Festival that takes place each December *(see the Mevlâna Celaleddin Rumi Close Up box)*, Konya is transformed by an influx of pilgrims—and other curious souls—who come from around the world to honor and observe the anniversary of the Mevlâna's death. At other times of the year, Konya is a quiet provincial city, and you can probably see most of the sights in about a day. Dervish ceremonies are only held once a week outside of festival time, which means it's about as easy to see them in Istanbul as in Konya. While you're in the city, make sure to try the local specialty, *etli ekmek*—flatbread topped with minced meat and spices.

## GETTING HERE AND AROUND

Konya is served by major bus companies Ulusoy and Kamil Koç, as well as local firms Metro, Kontur, and Özkaymak.

Traveling by train from Istanbul to Konya takes as long as, or longer than, going by bus. On the upside, the train is not much more expensive than the bus, and you can get a compartment in a sleeper car. The daily Meram Express costs 88 TL; it leaves Istanbul at 7:40 pm and arrives in Konya at 8:40 the next morning. From Konya, it departs at 5:05 pm and arrives in Istanbul at 6:35 the next morning. Alternatively, the Adana-bound İç Anadolu Mavi Tren leaves Istanbul at 11:50 pm daily, arriving in Konya at 12:29 the next day. From Konya, it departs

"The predominant practice with wish trees, as can be seen here, is to tie small pieces of fabric or plastic to the branches of the tree, and then to make a wish." —photo by txupham, Fodors.com member

at 8:44 pm and arrives in Istanbul at 8:58 in the morning. The cost is 85 TL for a sleeping compartment. Train travel between Ankara and Konya is less than two hours on a high-speed rail line; trains run four times daily in each direction and an economy class ticket costs 25 TL.

Modern Konya is extremely spread out, but its tourist attractions are all concentrated in the city center near Alaaddin Tepesi (Alaaddin Hill). Konya's bus terminal is about 15 km (9 mi) north of the city center; it's a 30-minute tram ride from the terminal to the Alaaddin tram stop downtown. The airport, 18 km (11 mi) to the northeast, and the train station, 3 km (2 mi) southwest of the city center, are both accessible only by city bus or taxi. Taxis are relatively inexpensive for short distances downtown but can add up if you are going to the bus terminal or airport.

### ESSENTIALS

**Bus Information Kontur** ☎ 332/265–0080 ⊕ www.kontur.com.tr. **Metro** ☎ 332/265–0040 ⊕ www.metroturizm.com.tr. **Özkaymak** ☎ 332/265–0160 ⊕ www.ozkaymak.com.tr.

**Tour Information Selene Tour.** Selene Tour organizes tours in Konya and to nearby destinations, such as Çatal Höyük, in addition to helping visitors make arrangements to attend the annual Mevlâna festival. Owner Mete Horzum is a dervish himself and is knowledgeable about Konya, Rumi, and Sufism. ✉ Aziziye Cad. Ayanbey Sok. 22/B ☎ 332/353–6745 ⊕ www.selene.com.tr.

**Visitor Information** ✉ Aslanlı Kışla Cad. 5, behind Mevlâna Museum ☎ 332/351–1074.

## EXPLORING

**Alaaddin Cami** (*Alaaddin Mosque*). Completed in 1220 and restored in the 1990s, this graceful mosque crowning Alaaddin Tepesi (Alaaddin Hill) is in the Syrian style—unusual for Anatolia; the architect was Syrian. The pulpit stands in a forest of marble columns taken from Roman temples. Most of the hill is devoted to a park, which contains a café. Below are the scanty remains of a Seljuk palace—two venerable stumps of walls. The city has for some reason deemed it expedient to throw an unsightly concrete shelter over them. ⊠ *Alaaddin Parkı* ✆ *8:30–5:30.*

**Arkeoloji Müzesi.** A magnificent portal marks the remains of the Sahip Ata complex, a group of structures dating from the late 13th century. Mosque buildings here have been converted into an **Arkeoloji Müzesi** (Archaeology Museum). The most significant room has recent findings from the 7000 BC Neolithic site of ⇨ *Çatal Höyük*, including pottery, jewelry, weapons and tools, and the remains of an infant burial; these are accompanied by quite informative explanations. There are also artifacts from the Bronze Age and Greek and Roman periods; the 3rd-century AD marble sarcophagus depicting the Twelve Labors of Hercules is outstanding. ⊠ *Larende Cad.* ☎ *332/351–3207* 💳 *3 TL* ✆ *Tues.–Sun. 9–12:30 and 1:30–5:30.*

**Çini Eserleri Müzesi** (*Ceramics Museum*). The Büyük Karatay Medresesi— a seminary founded in 1251 by Celaleddin Karatay, a Seljuk emir—is now home to Konya's Ceramics Museum. It's easy to understand why this particular building was selected for that purpose: the seminary (which also houses the emir's tomb, in a small room to the left of the main hall) is beautifully decorated, its dome lined with blue and white tiles that create a dazzling effect. A frieze beneath the dome is in excellent condition as well, and the hunting scenes on the rare figurative tiles from the Kubadabad Palace in Beyşehir show the influence of Persia on Seljuk art. Included in the spectacular collection are figurines of humans and animals, with vine leaves highlighting them with shades of cobalt blue and turquoise. ⊠ *Alaaddin Bul., at intersection with Ankara Cad.* ☎ *332/351-1914* 💳 *3 TL* ✆ *Tues.–Sun. 8–5.*

Fodor'sChoice
★ **Mevlâna Museum.** When the Sufi mystic poet Mevlâna Celaleddin Rumi died in 1273, he was buried in Konya beside his father and a great shrine was erected above them. As Rumi's mystic teachings of love and tolerance, ecstatic joy and unity with God spread and his poetry gathered a greater following, his mausoleum drew pilgrims from all parts of the Islamic world. In 1926, three years after the establishment of the Turkish Republic, his shrine was declared a museum, though the Sufi order he founded had been officially banned in 1925 as part of the drastic secularization of Turkish society under Atatürk. Today the museum is one of the most visited sites in Turkey, attracting more than 2 million people a year, the majority of them Turks. The Sufi dervishes have also been assigned a special status as "Turkish folk dancers," allowing them to perform their mystic whirling without the state overtly recognizing its undeniable religious basis.

The shrine is a holy site and, in line with Muslim traditions, women visiting it are required to cover their heads; scarves can be borrowed

*Continued on page 386*

# TURKEY'S
# WHIRLING DERVISHES

... ... has many expressions. The Mevlevi dervishes *sema* ritual may be the world's most mesmerizing.

As a means of attaining mystic union with God, the spinning "dance" of the Whirling Dervishes is considered one of the world's great spiritual rituals. A profound meditation in motion—this is no "Riverdance" theatrical spectacle—the *sema* ceremony of the Mevlevi dervishes is actually a form of worship. In breathtaking fashion, they whirl not to induce a trance but to symbolize how all things in the universe revolve, a belief expounded by the great 13th-century mystic Mevlâna Celaleddin Rumi, founder of the Mevlevi Order. Buried in Konya, this hallowed figure espoused the use of dance as a surrender to the divine; he described it as such: "Dancing is when you rise above both worlds, tearing your heart to pieces and giving up your soul." As you may learn, there's nothing like a Sema experience to add a spiritual spin to your visit to Turkey.

# AROUND THE WHIRL

Extremely detailed and specific directions govern even the slightest pattern and gesture in the ritual dance of the whirling dervishes.

**①** To help lift themselves into the spiritual realm, the *semazen* dancers are accompanied by musicians, who play the *ney* (reed flute) and the kettledrum, whose beating signals God's call to "be."

**②** First dropping their black cloaks—to signify the shedding of earthly ties—the dervishes stand with their arms crossed over their chests, a posture that represents the number one, a symbol of God's unity. Their costumes are full of symbolism: the conical hat, or *sikke*, represents a tombstone, the jacket is the tomb itself, and the floor-length skirt, or *tennure*, a funerary shroud. The latter is hemmed with chain to allow it to rise with dramatic effect.

**③** The dervishes' endless spinning—always to the left, counter-clockwise—symbolizes the rotation of the universe. To receive God's goodness, they keep their right hands extended to the sky; to channel God's beneficence to earth, their left hands point toward the ground.

**④** The dervishes usually perform for four *selams*, —or salutes—each to a separate musical movement. For the last, they are joined by their Sheikh Efendi—incarnating the figure of Rumi—who stands on a red sheepskin (oriented toward holy Mecca) to represent the channel of divine grace. At the climax, he and the *semazenbaşi* (dance master) join the others and whirl in their midst. At the finale, the dervishes put their cloaks back on—a symbol of return to the material world.

Above: The Sufi mystic, Mevlāna Celaleddin Rumi, inspired the whirl of the dervishes.

## WHERE THE DERVISHES WHIRL

Ever since the days of the Ottoman sultans, the the Mevlevi dervishes' *semas* have been wildly popular events. In Konya, dervishes present their spinning dances during the annual, mid-December Mevlâna festival, a week-long series of events dedicated to Rumi. **Konya's Tourism Information Office** (tel. 332/351–1074) can help you find tickets and make hotel reservations for the festival; it is wise to book tickets as far in advance as possible. The dervishes have been assigned a special status as "Turkish folk dancers," and their presentations are scheduled in many cities around Turkey (in fact, you stand a better chance of catching them in Istanbul than Konya) and, frequently, in cities around the world. Check with local tourist boards and hotel concierges to see if your itinerary might coincide with a whirling dervish ceremony.

# Mevlâna Celaleddin Rumi

The Mevlâna Museum in Konya calls Rumi (also known as Jalal al-Din Muhammed Rumi, or simply as "Mevlâna") a "Turkish theosophic philosopher," though in reality he was born in present-day Afghanistan and wrote his poetry in Persian. Born in the city of Balkh on September 30, 1207, he came to Konya in 1228, when it was a part of the Seljuk Empire. By that time the young Rumi had already been deeply influenced by mystic readings and had made the hajj to Mecca.

Rumi's transformative spiritual moment came in 1248, when his companion, Shams Tabrizi, a dervish who initiated Rumi into Islamic mysticism, mysteriously disappeared. Rumi's grief at his beloved friend's disappearance—suspected to be a murder—sparked a prodigious outpouring of searching verse, music, dance, and poetry. After years of searching for his friend and teacher, Rumi found himself in Damascus, where he had a revelation that the universe was one and each person could be his own holy universe. He exclaimed:

*"Why should I seek? I am the same as he.*

*His essence speaks through me.*

*I have been looking for myself!"*

For the rest of his life, Rumi attributed much of his own poetry to Shams, and in a way that would become characteristic and controversial, mixed his love with his fellow man with his love for God and God's love for man. Rumi became known for his tolerance, his espousal of love, and his use of dance and song to reach spiritual enlightenment. Toward the end of his life, he spent 12 years dictating his masterwork, the *Masnavi*, to a companion. He died in 1273, and the Mevlevi order of dervishes, famous for their *semas*, or whirling ceremonies, was founded after his death.

The central theme of Rumi's philosophy is a longing for unity—of men, of the universe, with God and with God's spirit. Rumi believed in the use of music, poetry, and dancing as facilitators for reaching God and for focusing on the divine. Through ecstatic dancing, singing, or chanting, Sufi worshippers believed they could negate their bodies and vain selves, becoming empty vessels to be filled with love, the essence of the divine. In Rumi's poetry, he talks of God as one might a lover, and the ecstatic states reached through dancing and singing sometimes border on the erotic. In recent years, Rumi's legacy has been revived, ensuring that his timeless teachings endure. His epitaph suggests he would have been happy with that:

"When we are dead, seek not our tomb in the earth, but find it in the hearts of men."

at the entrance to the museum. Visitors are also required to put plastic covers on over their shoes. You first pass through a courtyard with a large *şadırvan*, or ablutions fountain. At the entrance to the mausoleum are two gorgeous carpets, one from the 17th century and the other from the 18th. The interior of the mausoleum resembles the inside of a mosque, with its intricately painted domes, ornate chandeliers, and Islamic inscriptions on the walls. It is well lighted and there is music playing, unusual for a Muslim holy place and a further hint that

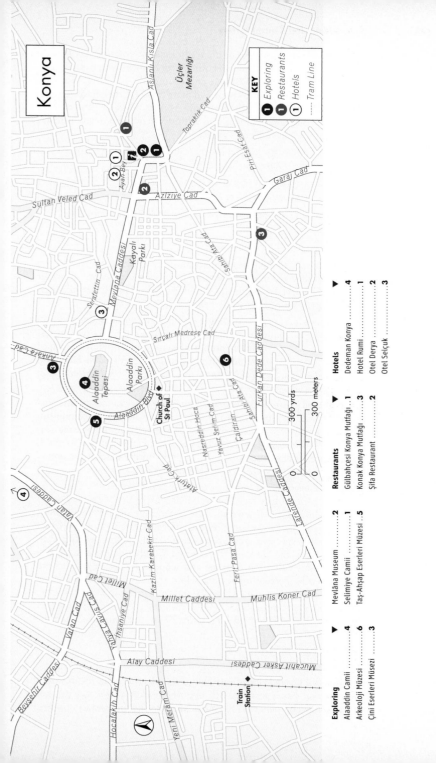

# Konya

**KEY**

- ➊ Exploring
- ➊ Restaurants
- ➀ Hotels
- ----- Tram Line

**Exploring** ▶

Alaaddin Camii ................4
Arkeoloji Müzesi .............6
Çini Eserleri Müzesi .........3
Mevlâna Museum .............2
Selimiye Camii ...............1
Taş-Ahşap Eserleri Müzesi ..5

**Restaurants** ▶

Gülbahçesi Konya Mutfağı ..1
Konak Konya Mutfağı ........3
Şifa Restaurant ..............2

**Hotels** ▶

Dedeman Konya ..............4
Hotel Rumi ...................1
Otel Derya ...................2
Otel Selçuk ..................3

0    300 yrds

0    300 meters

Rumi was not a proponent of the traditional interpretations of Islam. The room contains many dervish tombs, all of them with carved stone turbans that serve as headstones and beautifully decorated in ornate cloth. Rumi's tomb is the largest and at its head are two massive green turbans. The place is usually filled with Muslim pilgrims standing with their palms outward in prayer, and it is not uncommon to see men and women crying before Rumi's grave.

Rumi was famous for his inclusiveness and would have welcomed you here, no matter what your beliefs. He said:

*"Come, come, whoever you are.*

*Wanderer, idolator, worshipper of fire,*

*Come even though you have broken your vows a thousand times.*

*Come, and come yet again.*

*Ours is not a caravan of despair."*

The two rooms on the left contain beautifully preserved prayer books; dervish clothing and musical instruments; robes and a *seccade,* or prayer rug, that belonged to Rumi; and a mother-of-pearl box containing hair from the prophet Mohammed's beard.

The former kitchen of the complex (to the right of the main entrance) has a display of mannequins dressed as dervishes carrying out various activities in a kitchen, dining area, and living room, giving an idea of what life was like in the dervish brotherhood. ⊠ *Mevlâna Mahallesi* ☎ *332/351–1215* ✉ *3 TL* ☉ *May–Oct., Tues.–Sun. 9–7, Mon. 10–7; Nov.–Apr., Tues.–Sun. 9–5, Mon. 10–5.*

**Selimiye Camii** (*Mosque of Selim*). Sultan Selim II began this mosque just across from Rumi's tomb in 1558, when he was heir to the throne and governor of Konya; the structure was completed after he became Sultan Selim II. The style is reminiscent of that of Fatih Camii in Istanbul, with soaring arches and windows surrounding the base of the dome. ⊠ *Opposite Mevlâna Museum on Mevlâna Meyd.*

**Taş-Ahşap Eserleri Müzesi** (*Museum of Stone and Woodwork*). The minaret of the 13th-century İnce Minare Medresesi, or the "Seminary of the Slender Minaret," is bejeweled with glazed blue tiles. Unfortunately, it is now only half its original height, after a lightning strike in 1901. Note also the especially ornate decoration of the building's entry portal. Now serving as the Museum of Stone and Woodwork, the İnce Minare displays a fine collection of stone and wood carvings. Highlights are the fascinating Persian-influenced Seljuk stone reliefs, which include double-headed eagles, winged angels, and strange creatures that are part human and part bird or beast. ⊠ *Alaaddin Bul., west side of Alaaddin Tepesi* ☎ *332/351–3204* ✉ *3 TL* ☉ *Summer, Tues.–Sun. 8–7; winter, Tues.–Sun. 8–5.*

## WHERE TO EAT AND STAY

*For expanded hotel reviews, visit Fodors.com.*

$    ✕ **Gülbahçesi Konya Mutfağı.** Just behind Mevlâna's tomb, this restored
TURKISH   old mansion has a terrace with one of the best views you can get of the tomb complex and Selimiye Mosque. In the upstairs rooms,

guests sit in traditional Turkish style, crossed-legged on cushions around low, round tables. Specialties include the tasty but heavy *tirit,* a layered concoction of cubed flatbread, yogurt, onions, and chopped lamb, drizzled with melted butter and sprinkled with parsley and ground sumac. There are also variations on *etli ekmek,* such as the "Mevlâna," made with cheese in addition to ground meat. ⊠ *Aziziye Mah. Gülbahçe Sok. 3, Karatay* ☎ *332/353–0768* ⊕ *www. gulbahcesikonyamutfagi.com* ⚄ *Reservations essential.*

**$$** ✕ **Konak Konya Mutfağı.** An old mansion down the road from Mevlâna's tomb is a lovely setting in which to enjoy local specialties. The baby okra soup is said to be among the best in Konya, and meat dishes are

TURKISH
★

> ## THE SELJUKS
>
> Some of Konya's most important historical sites were built by the Seljuks, members of a nomadic Turkic tribe that probably originated in or around Mongolia. The Seljuk Turks converted to Islam in the 10th century and began to push westward. They ruled much of Anatolia from the late 11th through the beginning of the 14th centuries. Seljuk architecture is similar to the Gothic architecture that was flourishing in Europe when the Seljuks dominated the Middle East. Many of the mosques, castles, and caravansaries that brood over various Turkish villages were built in this style.

**6**

excellent—but make sure to save room for the *hoşmerim,* an intensely rich local dessert made of panfried clotted cream, flour, milk, and sugar, sprinkled with ground pistachio nuts. In winter, guests eat in small dining rooms with simple decor and in summer, seating is in the garden. ⊠ *Akçeşme Mah. Piriesat Cad. 5, Karatay* ☎ *332/352–8547* ⊕ *www. konakkonyamutfagi.com* ⚄ *Reservations essential.*

**$** ✕ **Şifa Restaurant.** Far from fancy, this long-standing but consistently popular Konya mainstay serves standard Turkish dishes, along the lines of kebabs and meatballs, plus local specialties—the *etli ekmek* (flatbread topped with ground meat and spices) and *fırın kebabı* (lamb roasted in the oven in a clay pot) are especially tasty. Service is speedy, and you can watch the activity on Mevlâna Caddesi from the floor-to-ceiling windows. ⊠ *Mevlâna Cad. 50/A* ☎ *332/352–0519.*

TURKISH

**$$$** ⬚ **Dedeman Konya.** The lobby of this 18-story tower in downtown Konya exudes opulence (though some may find it a bit overdone) and rooms are spacious and nicely furnished, with all the amenities of a first-rate business hotel. **Pros:** high-class service; multiple dining options; extensive fitness center. **Cons:** hotel is about 3 km (2 mi) from Konya's tourist attractions. ⊠ *Özalan Mahallesi, Sille Kavşağı, Selçuklu* ☎ *332/221–6600* ⊕ *www.dedeman.com* ⤳ *186 rooms, 20 suites* ⚄ *In-room: Wi-Fi. In-hotel: restaurant, bar, pool, gym, spa, business center, parking, some pets allowed* ⦿ *Breakfast.*

**$$** ⬚ **Hotel Rumi.** The fifth-floor roof terrace has excellent views overlooking Mevlâna's tomb—which is just around the corner, making these clean and comfortable rooms with modern bathrooms an excellent option for sightseers. **Pros:** location; professional service; good value. **Cons:** some rooms smell strongly of smoke. ⊠ *Durakfakih Mah. Durakfakih*

*Sok. 5* ☎ *332/353–1121* ⊕ *www.rumihotel.com* ➲ *30 rooms, 3 suites* ⚭ *In-room: Wi-Fi. In-hotel: restaurant, gym, parking* ⊙ *Breakfast.*

¢ ⛨ **Otel Derya.** These lean, well-maintained rooms on a quiet backstreet just steps from the Mevlâna Museum are outfitted with flat-screen TVs, but are otherwise somewhat basic—and priced accordingly. **Pros:** clean and good value. **Cons:** limited storage space in rooms; staff do not speak much English. ⊠ *Aziziye Mah., Ayan Bey Cad. 15, Karatay* ☎ *332/352–0154* 🖷 *332/352–0155* ⊕ *www.otelderya.net* ➲ *33 rooms* ⚭ *In-room: Wi-Fi. In-hotel: parking* ⊙ *Breakfast.*

$$ ⛨ **Otel Selçuk.** One of Konya's oldest hotels is not much to look at from the outside, but from the moment you step into the lobby you can feel its distinguished, slightly old-fashioned atmosphere. **Pros:** elegant atmosphere; Western-style service. **Cons:** cramped bathrooms. ⊠ *Mevlâna Cad., Mahzar Babalık Sok. 4* ☎ *332/353–2525* ⊕ *www.otelselcuk.com. tr* ➲ *77 rooms, 6 suites* ⚭ *In-room: Wi-Fi. In-hotel: restaurant, gym, business center, parking, some pets allowed* ⊙ *Breakfast.*

### SHOPPING

**Konya's Bazaar.** Konya's bazaar was once known for its rug shops, but these now are more likely to be found around Alaaddin Caddesi. The bazaar does have an amazing array of ordinary goods, and some interesting antiques and handicrafts can also occasionally be found. ⊠ *Market district, near intersection of Selimiye Cad. and Karaman Cad.* ⊙ *Mon.–Sat. during daylight hrs.*

**Karavan Kilim Shop.** At this treasure trove down the street from the Mevlâna Museum, thousands of carpets and kilims are piled up in a huge, dark-wood, old-fashioned showroom that feels like a rich man's bazaar. There are also copper items, handicrafts, and antiques, including an extensive collection of carved wooden doors. ⊠ *Aziziye Mah., Ayanbey Sok. 6/A* ☎ *332/351–0425.*

**OFF THE BEATEN PATH**

**Horozlu Han and Sille.** If you're heading out of Konya in the direction of Ankara, look for the fabulous Seljuk portal at the entrance to the ruined Horozlu Han, a former caravansary near the four-lane beginning of Route 715. At Sille, 8 km (5 mi) northwest, St. Helena, mother of Constantine the Great, built a small church in AD 327. Nearby, frescoed rock chapels overlook the shores of a tiny artificial lake.

## ÇATAL HÖYÜK

*48 km (30 mi) southeast of Konya on Rte. 715 to Çumra and then about 20 km (12 mi) north of Çumra to the site; follow the road signs.*

Çatal Höyük is the site of one of the oldest human settlements ever found, dating to about 7000 BC, during the Neolithic period.

### GETTING HERE AND AROUND

A round-trip taxi from Konya to Çatal Höyük will cost between 80 TL and 120 TL, depending on your bargaining skills. Alternatively, you can take a bus to the town of Çumra and then a taxi to the site, for around 30 TL altogether. There are also public minibuses labeled Küçükköy/Karkın that leave from Konya's downtown Eski Otogar and go to the village where the site is located. These are infrequent, however, so make sure you inquire before leaving Konya about the time of the last returning bus, so you don't get stranded in the village.

## EXPLORING

**Çatal Höyük.** It's believed that as many as 8,000 people lived here at a time, as far back as 7000 BC, in mud-brick houses that were adjacent to one another. The site was inhabited for some 1,400 years, with new houses being built over old ones, resulting in time with a buildup of mounds. The name Çatal Höyük means "forked mound," a reference to the two distinctive mounds separated by an indentation, which you can clearly see as you approach the site.

The British archaeologist James Mellaart discovered and initially excavated Çatal Höyük between 1961 and 1965. He found ancient wall murals, the earliest known pottery, human burials, and many domestic artifacts. Female figurines and other findings are believed to point to the worship of a mother goddess by the prehistoric inhabitants of Çatal Höyük. Other theories have been presented about goddess worship at the site, but the iconic figurines—many of which are on display in the Museum of Anatolian Civilizations in Ankara—remain symbolic of Çatal Höyük.

Summer is the most interesting time to visit the site, when you can watch dozens of archaeologists, comprising several international teams, at work on the excavations. The "Experimental House," near the entrance, is a re-creation of a prehistoric Çatal Höyük adobe home. It has been rendered to look as realistic as possible, with foodstuffs, animal pelts, reed mats on the floor, and murals on the walls. The museum, though small, is modern, attractive, and informative. However, almost all the artifacts in the museum are re-creations, the originals having been taken off to either the Ankara Museum of Anatolian Civilizations or the Konya Archaeology Museum.

The excavations are protected by two open-air hangarlike structures. The South Shelter covers the deepest excavations, begun by James Mellaart and restarted in 1993. Excavations here have uncovered 13 separate settlement layers, and you can get a good idea of the different layers from the visitor area at the top. Unfortunately, explanations are somewhat minimal. The North Shelter houses several excavation areas, and detailed illustrations and numbered photos explain what's what. ☎ 332/452-5217 ⊕ *www.catalhoyuk.com* ⚏ Free ☉ Daily 8–5.

# ANKARA

*258 km (160 mi) north of Konya; 454 km (281 mi) southeast of Istanbul.*

Right after the War of Independence, in 1923 Ankara was made the fledgling Turkish Republic's new capital—in part because it was a barren, dusty steppe city more or less in the middle of nowhere, and therefore considered to be secure. The city still feels that way somewhat, despite being the center of Turkish political activity and having a population of more than 4 million. Although the city doesn't come close to having the historical richness or vibrancy of Istanbul, Ankara offers visitors a sweeping overview of the history of this land, both ancient—at the highly regarded Museum of Anatolian Civilizations, repository of the best archaeological treasures found in Turkey—and modern, at the Anıtkabir, the colossal mausoleum to Mustafa Kemal Atatürk, founding father of the secular Turkish Republic. Atatürk's larger-than-life persona and impact on the country can be sensed more powerfully at the Anıtkabir than anywhere else in Turkey. Indeed, the capital city as a whole is permeated by the great man's fascinating and enduring legacy, and is nothing less than a monument to his overpowering will.

Despite its largely modern appearance, Ankara is in fact an ancient settlement that was occupied successively by the Hittites and other Anatolian kingdoms, the Greeks, Romans, Byzantines, Seljuks, and Ottomans. Glimpses of these layers of history can be seen in the Citadel and Ulus areas, where a few Roman ruins are haphazardly juxtaposed with Seljuk-era mosques, centuries-old Ottoman caravansaries, and nondescript modern buildings. The top of the ancient citadel offers excellent views of the city, and within the walls is a fascinating neighborhood.

Ankara is also a pleasantly green and easily navigable city, with restaurants, clubs, and hotels that are increasingly diverse and cosmopolitan. This is at heart a government and college town, so you'll also find more relaxed attitudes here than in many other parts of Anatolia.

### GETTING HERE AND AROUND

Staying at a hotel inside the citadel or in the surrounding neighborhood of Ulus gives you close proximity to almost all of Ankara's sights, and the citadel hotels, especially, are full of historic charm. Aside from a few restaurants, however, the old part of the city has little to nothing to offer in the way of nightlife and can feel somewhat deserted at night. The downtown neighborhoods of Kavaklıdere and Çankaya are bustling, with many fine restaurants, shops, and clubs—but you'll need to take a taxi or bus to reach the city's main attractions from these districts.

GETTING HERE    Flying from Istanbul to Ankara saves a lot of time and is not much more expensive than taking the bus. From the airport, a good option for getting downtown is the Havaş shuttle service, which costs 10 TL. Shuttles pick up passengers in front of the terminal near flight arrivals and make several stops, including the Havaş office in Ulus (19 Mayıs Stadium, B Gate) and, later, the bus station; passengers can board shuttles going to the airport at the same locations. Shuttles going in both directions generally leave every half hour between 4 am and 9 pm and less frequently at night.

Traveling between Istanbul and Ankara by train takes about the same as, or longer than, by car or bus. However, travel times are set to decrease with the completion of a (much-delayed) new high-speed rail line, one leg of which— Eskişehir to Ankara—has already been completed. Passengers can board a traditional train in Istanbul and transfer in Eskişehir to a high-speed train, with a total travel time of about 5½ hours. There are several connecting trains daily; the total fare is 50 TL for an economy-class ticket.

It is also possible to travel the whole way from Istanbul to Ankara in a traditional train, which gives you the option of traveling overnight in a sleeper car. The Ankara Express—which is by far the most comfortable overnight train in the country—travels daily between Ankara and Istanbul, leaving each city at 10:30 pm and arriving the next morning at 7. The price is 70 TL per person for two people sharing a sleeper compartment or 100 TL for one person in a single compartment. The Anadolu (Anatolia) Express also runs between Ankara and Istanbul, with simultaneous departures from both cities at 10 pm and arrivals at 7 am. Tickets are 30 TL each way, but there are no sleeper cars on this train, just regular seats.

If you're traveling from the Mediterranean coast to Ankara by train, the best option is the İzmir Mavi, or Blue Train, which departs İzmir at 7:40 pm, arriving in Ankara at 9:30 am; it departs Ankara at 7:50 pm and arrives in İzmir at 9:05 am. The cost is 70 TL per person in a double compartment or 92 TL for one person in a single compartment.

The trip from Konya to Ankara on a high-speed train takes under two hours; trains run four times daily and the cost is 25 TL for an economy class ticket.

GETTING AROUND
Ankara is a big city with chaotic traffic, and you'll save yourself a lot of grief if you park your car and use public transportation. The main neighborhood encompassing the old part of the city is called Ulus; this is where most of the tourist attractions are, and it's quite compact and walkable.

Taxis are more expensive in Ankara than in Istanbul—a taxi from the airport, approximately 35 km (20 mi) from the city center, can cost you about 60 TL, while a taxi from the Çankaya area to the citadel can cost up to 20 TL. Cabs can easily be hailed around the city, or ask your hotel to call one.

There are two subway lines in Ankara: the Metro, which runs north from Kızılay; and the Ankaray, which goes east–west from the AŞTI bus station in the western suburbs, through Kızılay and on to Dikimevi in the east. It's easy to get downtown from Ankara's *otogar* (AŞTI), which connects directly to the Ankaray. Take the Ankaray to the Kızılay stop and then transfer to the Metro (using the same ticket) if you want to continue north to Ulus. The fare is 1.75 TL and tickets can be purchased 2, 5, or 10 at a time; trains run between approximately 6 am and midnight.

### ESSENTIALS

**Bus Information Havaş.** ☎ 312/398–0376 for airport office, 312/310–3555 for downtown office ⊕ www.havas.com.tr. **Ulusoy.** ☎ 444-1888 toll-free ⊕ www.ulusoy.com.tr.

**Train Information Ankara train station.** ✉ Talatpaşa Bul. at Cumhuriyet Cad. ☎ 311–0620 for info and reservations, 312/311–6515 alternate number, 444–8233 national call center.

**Visitor Information** ✉ Main officeGençlik Parkı İçi 10, Ulus ☎ 312/324–0101 ✉ Esenboğa Airport ☎ 312/398–0348 ✉ Ankara train station, Ulus ☎ 312/309–0404.

# From Genghis Khan to Atatürk

Tamerlane, the fearsome descendent of Genghis Khan, laid siege to Ankara in 1402 and wrested control of the city away from Beyazıt, the Ottoman sultan. Then, perhaps bored with the landscape or seeking greater riches in the abundance of China, Tamerlane and his Mongol horde quickly gave the city back to the Ottomans and turned around and headed back east toward the Mongol plains. Tamerlane died just three years after the Battle of Ankara.

Tamerlane's brief victory in Ankara was but a later scene in the city's long history. Local legend attributes Ankara's foundation to the Amazons, the mythical female warriors, but many archaeologists have factually indentified it with Ankuwash, thought to have been founded around 1200 BC by the Hittites and then taken over by the Phrygians around 700 BC. The city was known to the Greeks and Romans as Ancyra or Ankyra, and later as Angora, famed for its wool. Alexander the Great conquered Ankara centuries before Augustus Caesar annexed the city to Rome in 25 BC.

Over the coming millennia Ankara was attacked and worn down by Persian, Arab, Seljuk, Mongol, and Ottoman invaders. By the early 20th century, it was little more than a provincial town with nice goats and an illustrious past. In 1919, as World War I and the Turkish War of Independence raged, Mustafa Kemal Atatürk made Ankara the headquarters of his secular resistance movement.

When Turkey was declared a republic four years later, Ankara was declared its capital. Atatürk mobilized the young nation's resources to make the city a symbol of a modern and secular Turkish city built on European lines. Tens of thousands of workers streamed in on foot to help build it, with designers intentionally abandoning Ottoman architecture in favor of a symbolic, stark modernism influenced by the Vienna cubist and German Bauhaus schools.

As with most planned cities, Ankara today is mostly convenient and pretty lacking in character. Despite Atatürk's dreams, it never made a serious bid to overtake Istanbul as the country's cultural capital.

## EXPLORING

Fodor's Choice ★ **Anadolu Medeniyetleri Müzesi** (*Museum of Anatolian Civilizations*). The Museum of Anatolian Civilizations is a real gem, one of the two places in Ankara that you should definitely not miss (the ⇨ *Anıtkabir* is the other). Many of Turkey's best ancient treasures are housed here, providing some insight into the incredible amount of history that has been played out in these lands. The museum covers every major civilization that has occupied this territory, going back nearly 10 millennia. Though the museum is relatively small and descriptions are in English, a guide may be helpful in directing your attention to the most important pieces. Agree on a price in advance.

The museum is housed in a restored 15th-century *bedestan* (similar to a caravansary), with exhibits arranged chronologically, starting to the right of the entrance and proceeding counterclockwise. One of

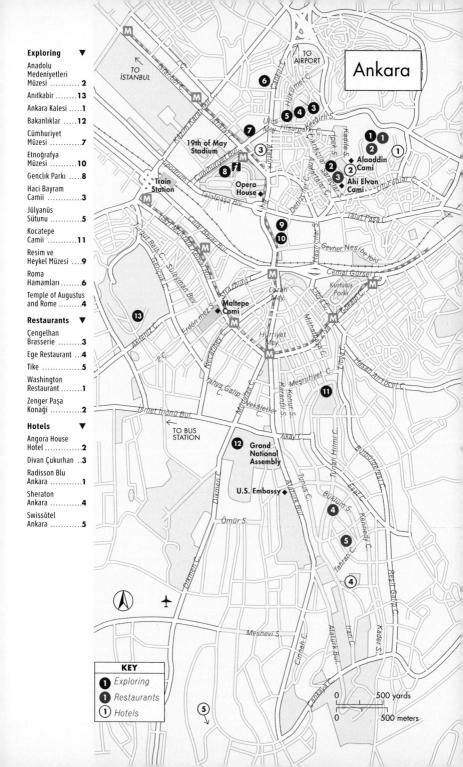

# Ankara

**KEY**

① Exploring

① Restaurants

① Hotels

the highlights is the section on the Neolithic site of Çatal Höyük (near Konya), one of the oldest human settlements ever discovered. The findings, which date to circa 7500 BC, include wall frescoes, bull heads, pottery, and the famous mother goddess figurines for which Çatal Höyük first became known.

Also particularly striking are the Hatti artifacts, with their stylized stag and bull sculptures and drawings. From the Assyrian trade colonies period (1950–1750 BC) come numerous clay cuneiform tablets, the earliest written records found in Anatolia. These palm-size tablets, some enclosed in their own clay "envelopes" and describing marriage contracts, debt notices, slave trading, and other everyday transactions in minuscule cuneiform script, are fascinating. These are followed by bronze sculptures, including more bull figures, from the Hittite period, and a copy of the 13th-century BC Treaty of Kadesh, the world's first known peace treaty. The clay tablet recording a copy of the treaty—the original of which was etched in silver—was found at the ancient Hittite capital Hattuşa, some 200 km (124 mi) east of Ankara. The museum's central hall displays monumental stonework from around Anatolia, including a series of well-preserved neo-Hittite reliefs depicting the epic of Gilgamesh, from the archaeological site of Karkamış in Gaziantep.

About a third of the museum—including the Urartian, Phrygian, and Roman sections—will be closed through 2012 for renovations. In the interim, highlights of those sections are displayed in temporary cases in the main hall. ⊠ *Gözcü Sokak 2* ☏ *312/324–3160* ⊕ *www.anadolumedeniyetlerimuzesi.gov.tr* ☏ *15 TL* ☉ *May–Sept., Tues.–Sun. 8:30–7; Oct.–Apr., Tues.–Sun. 8:30–5.*

Fodor'sChoice **Anıtkabir** (*Atatürk's Mausoleum*). Atatürk's picture is on every single
★ piece of Turkish currency, his visage hangs in just about every office and official building in the country, and his principles and ideas are the foundations of modern Turkish political thought. So his vast mausoleum, perched on a hilltop overlooking the capital city he built, is on a scale suitable to his stature in Turkey. A marble promenade flanked with Hittite-style lions leads to the imposing mausoleum, where a huge sarcophagus lies beyond a colonnade with inscriptions from his speeches and below a ceiling of brilliant gold mosaics. Soldiers march endlessly around the site, and nearly every important foreign dignitary who visits the capital goes to lay a wreath here in tribute to the man who, it is not an exaggeration to say, created modern Turkey. After Atatürk died in 1938, his body was laid to rest in the building that now houses ⇨ *Ankara's Ethnography Museum.* The construction of the Anıtkabir

**WORD OF MOUTH**

"We left the train station and went directly to the Anatolian Civilizations Museum. I'm not a huge museum fan, but this one was pretty good and not so big that it was overwhelming. After about two hours at the museum we then made our way to Ataturk's Mausoleum. Wow! What a place, it's gigantic! We were there just before noon and it was not very crowded. We did get to see a changing of the guard."
—LowCountryIslander

took nine years, from 1944 to 1953. Exactly 15 years after his death, Atatürk's remains were interred under the huge sarcophagus here.

An adjoining museum contains personal belongings from the revered man's life, including his clothes, automobiles, and personal library. The corridors underneath the tomb house an in-depth exhibit on the 1919–1922 War of Independence. The focal points are three enormous dioramas, each more than 35 meters (100 feet) in length, depicting the three major theaters of war: Çanakkale (1915), Sakarya (1921), and the Great Attack (1922). These are accompanied by rather intense sound effects—explosions, gunfire—to further dramatize the events. A map at the end of the Çanakkale hall shows Turkey and the territorial claims various other nations were making on it at the time, which gives some insight into why the Turks felt so besieged. Other exhibits explain major developments during the early Republican period, particularly Atatürk's reforms and legacy. There is also a gift shop with every kind of Atatürk souvenir imaginable.

To reach the mausoleum, you can take the metro to Tandoğan and walk up the long road that ascends from the main entrance at the northern end of the grounds. A quicker way is to take a taxi to the alternate entrance on Akdeniz Caddesi, on the southeast side. ⊠ *Anıt Cad. (main entrance) or Akdeniz Cad. (alternate entrance)* ☎ *312/231–7975* ⊕ *www.tsk.mil.tr/anitkabir/index.html* ⊠ *Free* ☉ *Nov. 1–Jan. 31, daily 9–4; Feb. 1–May 14, daily 9–4:30; May 15–Oct. 31, daily 9–5.*

★ **Ankara Kalesi** (*Ankara Citadel*). Ankara's main historic sites are clustered around its ancient citadel (known as the Hisar or Kale in Turkish), high on a hill overlooking the city. Though the citadel's precise origins are not known, the inner and outer walls standing today are thought to have been built between the 7th and 9th centuries, during the Byzantine period; look for the even older architectural fragments, including bits of stonework with Greek and Roman inscriptions, that were haphazardly incorporated into the fortifications. Although the modern city has grown up around the citadel, the area inside the walls has retained an almost villagelike atmosphere, an entire neighborhood with winding, cobblestoned streets and old houses built with timber and plaster.

The easiest place to enter the citadel is from Parmak Kapısı (Finger Gate), also known as Saat Kapısı (Clock Gate), across from the Divan Çukurhan. Head toward the center, where you'll see the recently restored Şark Kulesi (Eastern Tower). Climb up the stone steps to the tower's upper ramparts for excellent panoramic views of the city.

The citadel is also home to Ankara's oldest mosque, Alaaddin Camii, built in 1178 and located just opposite the Şark Kulesi. Unfortunately, it is rarely open and little can be seen from the outside. More interesting are the 13th-century Arslanhane Camii (or Ahi Şerafettin Camii) and 14th-century Ahi Elvan Camii, just outside the walls and tucked along the winding streets that slope down from the citadel to Ulucanlar Caddesi, the main street that forms the southern boundary of the citadel neighborhood. These mosques are remarkable for their original wooden ceilings, columns made from whole tree trunks, and Seljuk-style tiled prayer niches. ⊠ *Uphill from Museum of Anatolian Civilizations, Ulus.*

**Bakanlıklar.** Ankara's government district takes up the area west of Atatürk Bulvarı from Hürriyet Meydanı at the northern tip to the Türkiye Büyük Millet Meclisi (Grand National Assembly), the parliament building, at the intersection with İsmet İnönü Bulvarı on the southern end. Within walking distance, in the Kavaklıdere neighborhood, is Embassy Row, with its gardens, fine restaurants, and world-class hotels.

**Cumhuriyet Müzesi** (*Museum of the Republic*). In Turkey's first parliament building, which now houses the Museum of the Republic, politicians debated principles and policies that would shape the Turkish Republic as a modern secular nation. The great hall where parliament convened from 1924 to 1960 is decorated in Seljuk and Ottoman styles, with an ornately inlaid wooden ceiling, enormous crystal chandelier, and a loggia-like gallery from which dignitaries addressed the assembly. The museum comprises a small exhibit on the early years of the republic; although signs are only in Turkish, a free English audio guide is available. ⊠ *Cumhuriyet Cad. 22, off Ulus Meyd., Ulus* ☎ *312/310–5361* 🖅 *3 TL* ⊘ *Tues.–Sun. 8:45–5.*

**Etnoğrafya Müzesi** (*Ethnography Museum*). Atatürk used this Ottoman Revival–style building as an office, and his body lay here for 15 years after his death while his enormous mausoleum was being built. The small but interesting museum houses a rich collection of Turkish carpets, folk costumes, weapons, Islamic calligraphy, and ceramics. The display of woodwork, which includes intricately carved doors, portals, *mimbars* (mosque pulpits), and Seljuk thrones—some pieces dating as far back as the 13th century—is especially impressive. ⊠ *Talatpaşa Cad. and Türkocağı Sok., Ulus* ☎ *312/311–3007* 🖅 *3 TL* ⊘ *Tues.–Sun. 8:30–12:30 and 1:30–5:30.*

**Gençlik Parkı** (*Youth Park*). The pleasant Gençlik Parkı has been recently refurbished and, though not large enough to make you forget you're in the middle of the city, is a nice place for a stroll. Plantings are manicured and a small man-made lake is surrounded by a trellised walkway. Ankara's main tourist information office is also in the park. ⊠ *Cumhuriyet Cad. and İstiklal Cad., Ulus.*

**Hacı Bayram Camii** (*Hacı Bayram Mosque*). Dating to 1427, Hacı Bayram Camii is one of Ankara's most important sacred sites. Built of yellow stone and brick, the mosque is named after the revered founder of the Bayrami order of dervishes, Hacı Bayram, whose tomb is next to the minaret. The mosque reopened in 2011 after a major restoration and the construction of a showily decorated new wing that takes more than a little away from the site's historic character. ⊠ *Hacı Bayram Veli Cad., north of Hisarparkı Cad., Ulus* ⊘ *Daily sunrise to sunset, except during prayer times.*

**Jülyanüs Sütunu** (*Column of Julian*). A stone's throw from the Temple of Augustus, in a small traffic circle surrounded by government buildings, is the Column of Julian, erected in honor of Emperor Julian the Apostate (361–363), the last pagan Roman emperor. The column has 15 fluted drums and a Corinthian capital, and commemorates a visit by Julian in 362, as he passed through town on way to his death in battle with the Persians. ⊠ *off Hükümet Caddesi, Ulus.*

## MEET THE HITTITES

Around 1800 BC a people called the Hittites, who like the Persians spoke an Indo-European language (unlike the Turks, whose language is Ural-Altaic), apparently entered Anatolia after crossing the Caucasus steppes beyond the Black Sea. They claimed the city of Hattusa—with a fortress, temples, large administrative buildings, houses, cemeteries, and decorated gateways and courtyards—as their capital and soon began to build an empire. They worshipped a storm god and a sun goddess, and had a well-ordered society with written laws. At their height, they conquered Babylon and battled the Egyptian pharaohs. Their reign came to an end after some 600 years, when tribes from the north sacked and burned Hattuşa in 1200 BC. The Phrygians then became the dominant people in the region.

One of the most famous finds in Hattuşa is a copy of the Treaty of Kadesh, signed between the Hittite and Egyptian empires after what might have been the largest chariot battle ever fought, involving some 5,000 chariots. Boğazkale, a satellite settlement, is about 5 km (3 mi) north of Hattuşa. There's not a lot to see there, though Yazılıkaya, about 2 km (1 mi) east of Hattuşa, is far more interesting. Yazılıkaya is thought to have served as Hattuşa's religious sanctuary; its name simply means "rock with writing." The walls here are covered with drawings of Hittite gods, goddesses, and kings from about 1200 BC. On the main shrine, 42 gods march from the left to meet 21 goddesses coming from the right. In the middle is the weather god Teshub with horns in his cap, and the goddess Hepatu riding a leopard. It's thought that funeral rights for kings were performed here.

The Hittite cities are about 200 km (124 mi) northeast of Ankara, a two-hour drive. Guided trips, however, will shed a great deal of light on what are often otherwise unintelligible piles of rocks arranged in squares. The American Research Institute in Turkey, or ARIT (☎ *312/427–2222*), arranges periodic and highly praised guided excursions.

**Kocatepe Camii** (*Kocatepe Mosque*). It took 20 years to build this gigantic neo-Ottoman mosque in the center of Turkey's secular capital. Officially opened in 1987, the huge, illuminated edifice dominates the Ankara skyline at night and is one of the city's most prominent landmarks. The prestigious mosque is the site of most military and official funerals, and the Kocatepe complex also includes shopping venues on the lower floors. ⊠ *On Mithat Paşa Cad., Kızılay* ⊙ *Daily sunrise to sunset.*

**Resim ve Heykel Müzesi** (*Painting and Sculpture Museum*). These galleries, housed in an ornate marble building next door to the Ethnography Museum, display a vast collection of paintings and some sculptural works by late Ottoman, modern, and contemporary Turkish artists. With a few exceptions, most modern Turkish artists have not earned international recognition, but this collection provides an interesting glimpse at how Turkey's artists have been influenced by Western trends over the last century and a half. Schools of art such as Impressionism and Abstract Expressionism are represented among the portraits, landscapes paintings, and other works on display. ⊠ *Talatpaşa Cad. and Türkocağı Sok., Ulus* ☎ *312/310–2094* ⚑ *Free* ⊙ *Tues.–Sun. 9– noon and 1–5.*

**Roma Hamamları** (*Roman Baths*). You can't bathe at this 3rd-century complex just north of Ulus Square, but you can see how the Romans did. The large bath system includes a frigidarium, tepidarium, and caldarium (cold, warm, and hot rooms), as well as steam rooms that had raised floors. An illustration near the entrance shows the layout of the Roman city superimposed over a map of the modern area, indicating just how little of ancient Ancyra has been excavated. Scattered around the open-air site are various stone fragments, some of which appear to be ancient gravestones, with Latin and Hebrew inscriptions. ⊠ *Çankırı Cad. 54, Ulus* ☎ *312/310–7280* ⚑ *3 TL* ⊙ *Summer, daily 8:30–5:30; winter, daily 8:30–5.*

**Temple of Augustus and Rome.** Though it's in a rather sad state today, the Temple of Augustus and Rome, built 25–20 BC, is of great historical significance—inscribed in marble on the walls of the temple is the most complete Latin and Greek text of the *Res Gestae Divi Augusti*, in which the Emperor Augustus lists his deeds. The temple is now largely supported by metal scaffolding and the site can only be viewed from a walkway put up around it. ⊠ *Next to Hacı Bayram Camii, Ulus.*

## WHERE TO EAT AND STAY

*For expanded hotel reviews, visit Fodors.com.*

$$   ✕ **Çengelhan Brasserie.** The glass-roofed courtyard of the Rahmi M.
TURKISH   Koç Museum (the Ankara counterpart of the Istanbul museum, which
★   focuses on the history of transport, industry, and communications), next to the Divan Çukurhan hotel, provides a relaxed and stylish dining experience, accented with the soothing splashing of a fountain and classical music playing in the background. Service is excellent and the menu is Turkish and contemporary—shrimp casserole with porcini mushrooms, a starter, and grilled chicken with thyme and traditional *firik* pilaf are especially well done. The restaurant stays open in the evening after the museum closes. ⊠ *Necatibey Mah., Depo Sok. 1, Ulus* ☎ *312/309–6800* ⚑ *Reservations essential* ⊙ *Closed Mon.*

$$   ✕ **Ege Restaurant.** This charming spot just off fashionable Tunalı Hilmi
SEAFOOD   Caddesi specializes in Aegean-style fish dishes (*Ege* is the Turkish name for the Aegean Sea) and the decor—painted wood chairs with simple cushions, blue-and-white walls with a fish motif—transports you straight to the Aegean islands. To top it off, a map of the region is painted on the ceiling. The wide selection of fish comes from both the Aegean and Black seas, and the seafood-based mezes are also excellent. ⊠ *Büklüm Sok. 54/B, Kavaklıdere* ☎ *312/428–2717* ⊕ *www. egerestaurant.com* ⚑ *Reservations essential* ⊙ *Closed Sun.*

$$   ✕ **Tike.** At this Istanbul-based kebab chain, the excellent mezes include
TURKISH   *mütebbel*, chopped smoked eggplant and garlicky yogurt topped with
Fodor's Choice   ground pistachios. The "Tike kebab," a version of spicy Adana kebab
★   (skewers of spicy ground lamb), is delicious, and the *çöp şiş* (diced lamb shish kebab) melts in your mouth. The decor is contemporary, the vibe is trendy, and the glass-roofed back section opens onto an attractive

patio and garden. ■TIP→ The tiny appetizers brought over at the beginning are not complimentary, so send back what you do not want to eat and pay for. ⊠ *Billur Sok. 17/A, Kavaklıdere* ☎ *312/426–0141* ⊕ *www.tike. com.tr* ⌲ *Reservations essential.*

$$ ⤬ **Washington Restaurant.** Don't expect to be wowed by the food, as
TURKISH the menu is far from cutting-edge, but the draws are the city views and the old-school ambience of this classic Ankara institution just inside the citadel. The fare is international—particularly Russian, with specialties such as borscht, chicken Kiev, and beef Stroganoff— along with standard Turkish mezes and kebabs. ⊠ *Doyran Sok. 5/7, Kaleiçi, Ulus* ☎ *312/311–4344* ⊕ *www.washingtonrestaurant.com.tr* ⌲ *Reservations essential.*

$$ ⤬ **Zenger Paşa Konağı.** Several levels of a restored 18th-century Ottoman
TURKISH mansion in the citadel offer excellent panoramic views of the city. Decor is rustic-traditional, with wooden chairs and kilims. The good range of mezes and kebabs include *saç kavurma,* a meat dish cooked over an alcohol flame as you watch. The restaurant also makes *pides* (Turkish pizzas) and a tasty village-style flatbread called *bazlama.* There is live Turkish music every night but Sunday, and although the place has an undeniably touristy side, it's also popular with locals. ⊠ *Doyran Sok. 13, Kaleiçi, Ulus* ☎ *312/311–7070* ⊕ *www.zengerpasa.com* ⌲ *Reservations essential.*

$$ ⌷ **Angora House Hotel.** A beautifully restored 19th-century Ottoman
★ house inside the walls of Ankara's ancient citadel has the feel of a private home—six charming, good-size rooms have original wood floors and ceilings, antique chandeliers, and comfortable beds, and breakfast is served in the living-dining room in winter and in the courtyard in summer. **Pros:** located in historic area; property has lots of character; friendly staff. **Cons:** neighborhood can be noisy at night; somewhat difficult for vehicles to reach; no elevator. ⊠ *Kale Kapısı Sok. 16, Hisar, Ulus* ☎ *312/309–8380* ⊕ *www.angorahouse.com.tr* ⤶ *6 rooms* ⌂ *In-room: a/c, Wi-Fi. In-hotel: parking* ⦿❙ *Breakfast.*

$$$ ⌷ **Divan Çukurhan.** Elegant rooms in a restored 16th-century caravan-
Fodor's Choice sary at the edge of Ankara's citadel are each decorated in a different
★ style, such as Indochinese, Venetian, Tibetan, and Ottoman, and feature antique furniture, hardwood floors, and original works of art; some have views of the citadel or city. **Pros:** unique historical atmosphere; highly personalized service; quiet, oasislike rooms. **Cons:** poor Wi-Fi and cell phone reception in rooms; located at the top of a steep hill. ⊠ *Necatibey Mah., Depo Sok. 3, Ulus* ☎ *312/306–6400* ⊕ *www.divan. com.tr* ⤶ *16 rooms, 3 suites* ⌂ *In-room: a/c, Wi-Fi. In-hotel: restaurant, bar, gym, business center, parking, some age restrictions* ⦿❙ *Breakfast.*

$$$ ⌷ **Radisson Blu Hotel, Ankara.** The only international chain hotel in Ankara's historic Ulus district is somewhat lacking in flair but has comfortable rooms, with light-color woods and colorfully patterned, contemporary carpets and curtains. **Pros:** convenient location near major tourist attractions, next to metro station; predictable Radisson standard of service and amenities. **Cons:** hotel overlooks a loud, busy expressway (to avoid street noise, request a back-facing room); decor feels rather generic. ⊠ *İstiklal Cad. 20, Ulus* ☎ *312/310–4848* ⊕ *www.*

6

*radissonblu.com* 🖪 *183 rooms, 19 suites* ⟨ *In-room: Wi-Fi. In-hotel: restaurant, bar, gym, parking.*

$$$$ 🔲 **Sheraton Ankara.** Unlike many large international chain hotels, the Sheraton Ankara has personality: the tall, white, round tower is an Ankara landmark; the attractive lobby and chic bar have refreshingly bold textures and lighting; and the spacious rooms have contemporary decor, modern bathrooms, and good views of the city. **Pros:** located in bustling nightlife and shopping district; professional service; excellent fitness facilities. **Cons:** large complex can feel somewhat impersonal; expensive food, drinks, and Internet. ⊠ *Noktalı Sok., Kavaklıdere* ☎ *312/457–6000* ⊕ *www.sheratonankara.com* 🖪 *292 rooms, 19 suites* ⟨ *In-room: Wi-Fi. In-hotel: restaurant, bar, pool, tennis court, gym, parking, some pets allowed.*

$$$$ 🔲 **Swissôtel Ankara.** A setting in the posh Çankaya district is part of the allure here, as are style and sophistication—rooms have elegant decor in soothing colors; large bathrooms have deep tubs and separate rain showers; and an extensive wellness center includes a half-Olympic-size indoor pool, a beautiful hamam, sauna, full spa, and large fitness room. **Pros:** upscale yet relaxed ambience; excellent service, dining options, and fitness facilities. **Cons:** hotel is in a residential neighborhood far from major sights and a short drive from nightlife; expensive food, drinks, and Internet. ⊠ *Yıldızhevler Mah. Jose Marti Cad. 2, Çankaya* ☎ *312/409–3000* ⊕ *www.swissotel.com* 🖪 *141 rooms, 6 suites* ⟨ *In-room: Wi-Fi. In-hotel: restaurant, bar, pool, gym, spa, business center, parking, some pets allowed.*

## SHOPPING

**Kavaklıdere.** The upscale district of Kavaklıdere—and in particular the main drag, Tunalı Hilmi Caddesi—is home to a range of Turkish and international brands and designer labels. Karum shopping mall, next door to the Sheraton, has more of the same.

**Kızılay.** The pedestrian area of Kızılay, especially Konur Sokak, is a good place to find books and Turkish music.

**Samanpazarı.** The area from Atpazarı Sokak down the hill from the citadel toward Samanpazarı has narrow, winding streets with shops selling antiques, handicrafts, carpets, metalwork, and other items. There are also a few such shops inside the citadel, aimed mostly at tourists but with some interesting wares.

# Excursions to the Far East & Black Sea Coast

**WORD OF MOUTH**

"We took a boat ride on Lake Van in eastern Turkey to this tiny island [Akdamar], where there is a 10th century Armenian church decorated with marvelous reliefs. I found this ruin of a gravestone outside the church, looking toward the lake."

— photo by nddavidson, Fodors.com member

# WELCOME TO THE FAR EAST AND THE BLACK SEA COAST

## TOP REASONS TO GO

★ **Explore the ruins of Ani:** This ancient city was once the seat of a small Armenian kingdom.

★ **Float in Lake Van:** As in Israel's Dead Sea, the water is rich in minerals and very alkaline; you'll be remarkably buoyant in the startlingly blue water.

★ **Take the ferry to Akdamar:** The uninhabited island and its monastery are worth the trek.

★ **Journey up Mt.** Nemrut: The massive stone heads looking out over the horizon are an impressive sight to behold.

★ **Visit the cliffside monastery of Sümela:** The climb is fairly strenuous, but just seeing this remarkable sight is unforgettable.

★ **Wander through the bustling bazaars of Urfa and Gaziantep:** Craftsmen in these ancient cities still work the same way they have for centuries.

**1** The mountains of the Black Sea coast around Trabzon and the Sümela Monastery. This region is like no other part of Turkey. With lush green valleys, snow-capped peaks, and small villages with chaletlike homes, it looks like a little piece of Switzerland.

**2** The region between Kars and Van. This is Turkey's eastern frontier, filled with wide-open vistas, high mountain plateaus, and natural and man-made wonders, all offering a wonderful mix of adventure and history. Here you can see the haunting ancient city of Ani, the majestic Mt. Ararat, and the various sites around Lake Van, especially the island church of Akdamar.

**3** Around Diyarbakır and Mardin. This area, part of ancient Mesopotamia, is steeped in history. The old cities are filled with honey-color stone homes and small hillside villages surrounded by vineyards and look something like a Turkish Tuscany.

**4** Gaziantep and Urfa. Traveling around these cities will give you the flavor of the Middle East, from the bustling bazaars where coppersmiths bang away with hammers, to the spicy local cuisine. This is also the best spot to organize a visit to the huge stone heads atop Mt. Nemrut.

Mt. Nemrut

Climbing Mount Ararat, Doğubeyazit

## GETTING ORIENTED

For the visitor who makes it to Turkey's eastern regions, the rewards are plentiful: beautiful scenery, wild nature, countless historic sites, and ancient cities where life has not changed much over the centuries. Turkey's eastern half is so vast that it's possible to divide it into separate regions, each offering something different for travelers.

**7**

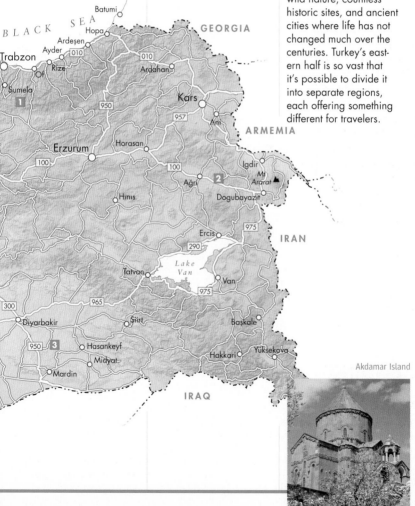

BLACK SEA

Batumi

Hopa

Ardeşen

GEORGIA

Ayder

Trabzon

Of    Rize    010

Ardahan

Sumela    **1**

950

Kars    **1**

957

Ani

ARMENIA

Erzurum    Horasan

100    100

Ağrı    **2**    Igdir

Mt Ararat

Hınıs    Doğubeyazit

Ercis    975

IRAN

290

Lake Van

Tatvan    Van

975

300    965

Diyarbakir    Siirt    Başkale

950    **3**

Hasankeyf

Midyat    Hakkari    Yüksekova

Mardin    Akdamar Island

IRAQ

Updated by
Scott Newman

Eastern Turkey may not have the resorts, luxury hotels, and chic restaurants found in the more-visited parts of the country, but the rewards of travel here—impressive sites, both natural and man-made—are many. The itineraries layed out in this chapter are suggestions for enjoying the region to the fullest, and you may want to combine them or otherwise alter them to suit your particular tastes.

However you decide to experience eastern Turkey, there is much to see and do. The Black Sea area has rocky beaches backed by the majestic Kaçkar Mountains—a slice of the Alps in Turkey—where you can hike, relax in picturesque mountain villages, or visit the historic city of Trabzon and the cliff-side monastery of Sümela. The remote area between the cities of Kars and Van, in Turkey's far east, has the ancient city of Ani and the towering Mt. Ararat, which some believe is the resting place of Noah's Ark. The walled city of Diyarbakır and beautiful nearby towns of Mardin and Midyat lie in the heart of the ancient region known as Mesopotamia, where you can wander historic neighborhoods and visit churches that date back to the 3rd and 4th centuries. The area around the ancient cities of Gaziantep and Urfa, Turkey's southeast, is especially steeped in biblical history, though bustling local bazaars and scrumptious local cuisine will fortify you before a sunrise visit to the mountaintop temple of Nemrut Dağı.

# PLANNING

### BEING CAREFUL

During the 1980s and '90s, large parts of Turkey's east and southeast (but not the Black Sea area) were the scene of bitter fighting between the separatists of the Kurdistan Workers' Party (PKK) and Turkish security forces. The fighting has largely stopped, which has allowed tourism in the region to get off the ground again. Cities you're likely to visit are now safe and have been for 10 years. There are still incidents, particularly near the Turkey–Iraq border and in such places as Hakkari and Şirnak. But these are remote areas where few tourists, let alone Turks, go, and the Turkish army will actively stop you from visiting any troubled areas.

## DINING

Food in the Black Sea area relies on dishes made with dairy, corn flour, and seafood, especially *hamsi,* which is locally caught anchovy. Although meat kebabs rule the rest of the east, most restaurants will also offer a variety of delicious vegetable dishes cooked in olive oil, along with stews and other ready-made hot dishes, which are usually meat-based.

## DO YOU SPEAK TURKISH?

These areas are less touristy and finding English speakers can sometimes be a challenge, though most hotels will usually have someone on staff who speaks at least some basic English. In a pinch, try a combination of hand gestures and key English words that nonspeakers are likely to know.

## GETTING HERE AND AROUND

Getting to eastern Turkey once meant grueling bus rides that sometimes took more than a day. The arrival of budget air travel has changed this dramatically, and several domestic airlines now crisscross Turkey. Feeling the competition, Turkey's national carrier, Turkish Airlines, has started slashing fares on domestic routes. Best of all, Turkey's airlines don't penalize you for buying a one-way ticket, so it's possible to fly into one city and depart from another, which can save a lot of time and money.

You'll probably find that a rental car is the easiest way to take in the sights of eastern Turkey, allowing you to reach some of the more remote spots and explore at your leisure. Cars are readily available in most larger towns. You can also travel between major cities by bus—this transport is usually by minibus.

## HOTELS

With some notable exceptions, the hotels in the east are basic, with little in the way of the luxuries you might find along Turkey's coastline.

## TIPS FOR EXCURSIONS

### TRABZON AND BLACK SEA

**Getting here:** Fly to Trabzon from Istanbul.

**How much time?** Two days let you see Trabzon and Sümela; with another one or two days, you can also go to Çamlıhemşin.

**Getting around:** We recommend flying in. If you just want to see Sümela you can take a tour from Trabzon; it's possible to get around with regional buses, but you'll save time and see more if you rent a car

**When to go:** May–September is the best season. There is less rain, and the area, particularly the Kaçkar Mountains, is blissfully cooler than the rest of Turkey. Fall in the mountain forests can be especially beautiful.

**Top sights:** The Aya Sofya in Trabzon, the Sümela Monastery complex, mountain summer villages around Ayder.

**By yourself or with a guide?** It's easy to see most of the area by yourself, though touring the Kaçkar Mountains is best done with a guide.

### KARS, MT. ARARAT, AND LAKE VAN

**Getting here:** To save time, fly to Kars from Istanbul and then fly back from Van (or the other way around).

**How much time?** Four or five days are enough. If you have more time, stay an extra night in Van and do one of the side trips along the lake.

**Getting around:** Intercity buses are an option, though you might want to rent a car for more comfort and the freedom to explore at your leisure.

**When to go:** Because of their altitude, Kars and Van are usually pleasant in summer, though the sun can still be quite strong. May and June, when the area is especially green and covered with wild flowers, are good months to visit. Winter is cold and dreary in Turkey's east, and from late October to early April many sites are inaccessible because of snow.

**Top sights:** The ruins of Ani, Doğubeyazıt's fantastic Ishak Paş Sarayı, the island church of Akdamar in Lake Van.

**By yourself or with a guide?** You may want a guide for a visit to Ani, the area around Mt. Ararat, and for some of the sites around Lake Van.

### DIYARBAKIR, MARDIN, MIDYAT, AND HASANKEYF

**Getting here:** Fly in and out of Mardin or Diyarbakir from Istanbul or other Turkish cities.

**How much time?** Three to four days will give you enough time to see this area. With extra time, spend another night in Mardin or Midyat.

**Getting around:** You can reach the major towns by minibus, but to get to the remote monasteries and churches you will need to rent a car.

**When to go:** Summer can be oppressively hot, with temperatures over 100°F, and winter is cold and damp, so the best time to visit is in spring (late April through early June) or fall (September to early November).

**Top sights:** The bazaar and side streets of Mardin, the exquisite stone homes of Midyat, and the monasteries of Deyr al Zaferan and Mor Gabriel. The walls of Diyarbakir and ruins at Hasankeyf, beside the Tigris, are also memorable.

**By yourself or with a guide?** Touring by yourself is a good option, since distances are short and much of the excursion is really about walking around old towns and soaking up the atmosphere.

### GAZIANTEP, MT. NEMRUT, AND URFA (ŞANLIURFA)

**Getting here:** Fly in and out of Gaziantep or Urfa from Istanbul or other Turkish cities.

**How much time?** Three or four days are enough time to see this area; with extra time, spend another night in Gaziantep to try another of the city's great restaurants.

**Getting around:** We recommend flying, then renting a car, although it's possible to get around on intercity buses.

**When to go:** Summer can be oppressively hot, with temperatures over 100°F, and winter is cold and damp and Mt. Nemrut is inaccessible because of snow. The best time to visit is in spring (late April through early June) and fall (September–early November).

**Top sights:** Mt. Nemrut, the Gaziantep Museum, the bazaar in Gaziantep, the carp pools in Urfa.

**By yourself or with a guide?** It's easy to see this area by yourself, though you might want to take a guided tour of Mt. Nemrut from Gaziantep.

| WHAT IT COSTS IN U.S. DOLLARS | | | | | |
| --- | --- | --- | --- | --- | --- |
| | ¢ | $ | $$ | $$$ | $$$$ |
| Restaurants | under $5 | $5–$10 | $11–$15 | $16–$25 | over $25 |
| Hotels | under $50 | $50–$75 | $76–$150 | $151–$250 | over $250 |

Restaurant prices are for one main course at dinner or for two mezes (small dishes). Hotel prices are for two people in a standard double room in high season, including taxes.

### WHEN TO GO

Spring and fall are generally the best times to visit these areas, with the exception of the Black Sea coast, which is usually less rainy in summer but still quite cool compared to the rest of Turkey, which can be sweltering.

# TRABZON AND THE BLACK SEA COAST

Updated by
Scott Newman

Of all of Turkey's regions, the Black Sea coast least fits the bill of what most visitors imagine to be "Turkish." Instead of long, sandy beaches lined with resorts, the Black Sea's shores are rocky and backed by steep, lush mountains. And instead of sunny days, the area is often shrouded in mist. Culturally, the area has had as much Greek, Georgian, and Armenian influences as it has Ottoman and Turkish. Although less visited than other parts of Turkey, the region is also one of the most rewarding. This excursion will take you to the Black Sea coast's most interesting destinations, from the historic seaside town of Trabzon and the nearby monastery complex of Sümela, clinging dramatically to the side of a cliff in a deep valley, to the Kaçkar Mountains, whose 15,000-foot peaks tower over the area.

Trabzon, wedged between the Black Sea and the green mountains that rise behind it, is a city with a long historic pedigree that stretches back to Byzantine times, though today it's quite modern and, like many other cities in the region, is cursed with an overabundance of ugly concrete buildings. A little exploring, though, reveals the city's past, perhaps best represented by the magnificent Byzantine-era Aya Sofya church. Trabzon is also a good base for visiting the fascinating (though defunct) Orthodox monastery complex of Sümela, breathtakingly hidden in a narrow valley and clinging to the side of a steep cliff. Although the monastery, which was functioning until the 1920s, and its beautiful frescoes have over the years been victims to vandalism, an extensive restoration project is under way.

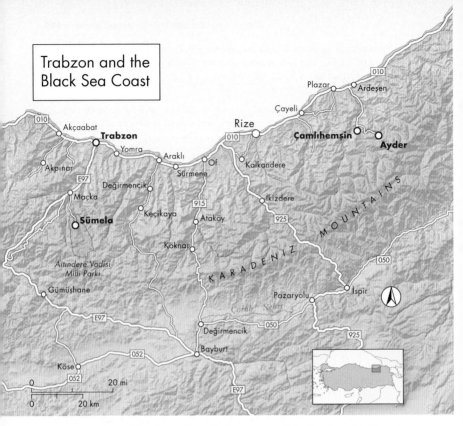

As you head east from Trabzon, toward the border with Georgia, you will pass through Rize, Turkey's tea-growing capital, where hills are carpeted with carefully laid-out rows of dark green tea plants. From there you'll soon approach several valleys that lead up into the majestic Kaçkar Mountains, dotted with small villages with wooden homes that evoke the Alps. Up in the Fırtına valley is Ayder, a mountain village that serves as a wonderful base for hiking and exploring the area's mountain trails and *yaylas,* the high-pasture summer villages where the rhythms of life seem to have changed little over the centuries.

## TRABZON

Trabzon has a dramatic location, perched on a hill overlooking the sea, with lush green mountains behind. Once the capital of the empire founded in 1204 by Alexius Comnenus, grandson of a Byzantine emperor, the city was famed for its golden towers and glittering mosaics. Today's Trabzon seems far removed from that imperial past: the city is bustling and modern, with a busy port, crowded streets, and seemingly little to distinguish it from many other provincial Turkish towns. It only takes a little digging, though, to get under the modern surface. Byzantine-era churches, such as the lovely Aya Sofya, a smaller version of the similarly named church in Istanbul, can be found not far from modern apartment buildings. The city's old town, meanwhile, with its Ottoman-era houses, pedestrian-only streets, and lively bazaar are a nice break from the concrete and crowds.

You can spend a day exploring the city, which is also a good base for a visit to the Sümela Monastery. At night, have a fish dinner by the Black Sea or up in the hills overlooking the city.

### GETTING HERE AND AROUND

There are several daily flights to Trabzon from Istanbul, Ankara, İzmir, and Antalya. Fares are competitive, so check with the different airlines to see who has the best.

Trabzon is a long way from other Turkish cities you may be visiting—1,071 km (665 mi) from Istanbul, 744 km (462 mi) from

> ### TURKISH NUTS AND TEA
>
> Economic life on the Black Sea is dominated by two crops: hazelnuts and tea. Near Rize, the hills are covered in row after row of tea plants, tended to by villagers who harvest the leaves in late spring. Every year, more than 200,000 tons of tea are harvested in the area, most of it for domestic consumption. Turkey is also the globe's leading producer of hazelnuts, responsible for more than 80% of the world's supply. Hazelnuts, often fresh off the tree and still in their shell, are easy to find in shops and on the street throughout Turkey, especially in late summer and early fall.

Ankara, and 591 km (367 mi) from Kayseri; rather than making the long drive or taking a bus you're better off flying to Trabazon and renting a car there. The bus ride from Istanbul to Trabzon takes almost 20 hours, but at around 70 TL, it can be half as expensive as flying. There is frequent daily service from Istanbul's Esenler bus terminal and Ankara's AŞTİ bus terminal. Be sure to choose a company with comfortable seats.

Bus service between towns runs frequently and is inexpensive. The company with the most reliable and frequent service is Ulusoy, which has an office just off Trabzon's main square, Atatürk Alanı.

Renting a car, though, is the most convenient way of getting around the Black Sea region, and allows you to explore the mountains more easily. Avis has an office in downtown Trabzon, as well as one at the airport. There are also several local companies around Trabzon's Atatürk Alanı.

### ESSENTIALS

**Guided Tours** Eyce Tours in Trabzon can help with arranging tours to Sümela and the region around Trabzon.

**Tour Information Eyce** ☎ 462/326–7174 ⊕ www.eycetours.com.

**Visitor Information** ✉ Cami Sok., behind mosque near Meydan, near Atatürk Alanı ☎ 462/326–4760.

### EXPLORING

**Atatürk Alanı** (*also called Taksim Meydanı*). The heart of Trabzon's social activity is its pleasing central square, Atatürk Alanı, also known simply as Meydan, up İskele Caddesi from the port. In Byzantine and Ottoman time the camel caravans assembled here before heading across the mountains. Today the square is full of shady tea gardens and surrounded by most of the city's hotels and restaurants.

**Atatürk Köşkü.** Trabzon's weathy citizens once retreated to villas in the hills above town. Greek banker Konstantin Kabayanidis built this attractive white gingerbread house, set in a small forest with nice views of the city below, and Atatürk stayed here in 1924, 1930, and 1937. Much of the original furniture remains in place. ⊠ *Soğuksu Cad., 7 km (4 mi) southwest of Trabzon's central square* ☎ *462/231–0028* ☙ *$1.50* ☉ *May–Sept., daily 8–7; Oct.–Apr., daily 9–5.*

★ **Aya Sofya** (*Church of the Holy Wisdom, or St. Sophia*). Trabzon's best-known Byzantine monument sits on a bluff overlooking the Black Sea. The ruined 13th-century church, converted into a mosque in Ottoman times, has some wonderful Byzantine frescoes. The west porch houses the real masterpieces: technicolor angels on the ceiling, Christ preaching in the temple, the Annunciation, and the wedding at Cana, all executed in a style that shows strong Italian influence. Often overlooked are the graffitti of ships, carved into the outside of the apse by sailors for good luck. A shaded tea garden near the entrance is a popular place for breakfast. ⊠ *Kayakmeydan Cad.* ☎ *462/223–3043* ☙ *$2* ☉ *May–Sept., daily 9–6; Oct.–Apr., Tues.–Sun. 8–5.*

**Çarşi Cami.** The city's largest mosque, the Çarşi Cami, was built in 1839 and is joined to the market by an archway.

**Citadel.** Trabzon's Byzantine-era citadel, set between two ravines, is still an imposing event though it's pretty much a ruin. The remains of the Byzantine palace are insignificant, though the ramparts were restored after the Ottoman conquest in 1461 and are a testament to the fact that no army ever took Trabzon by force, though many tried. Inside the citadel walls is the 10th-century church of **Panaghia Chrysokephalos** (the Virgin of the Golden Head), which was the city's cathedral, where many of it rulers were married, crowned, and buried. The Ottomans converted it into a mosque, the **Ortahisar Cami,** in the 15th century. Not much is left of the building's Byzantine glory, although the soaring walls and massive columns are still impressive. ⊠ *Kale Cad.; from Hükümet Cad. (off Maraş Cad.), follow Tabakhane Bridge over gorge, turn left.*

**Bazaar.** The pedestrian-only Kunduracılar Caddesi leads into the maze of the covered bazaar, which includes a 16th-century *bedestan*, or market, that has been restored and now houses several cafés and some gift shops selling unremarkable trinkets. The bazaar largely sells cheap clothes to locals, but does have a small but appealing section of coppersmiths, who make a variety of bowls, trays, and pots. ⊠ *Just past Cumhuriyet Cad.*

**Trabzon Museum.** The Trabzon Museum is housed in a 1910 mansion built for a local banker. The ornate rooms of the main floor have been restored and filled with period furniture. The basement holds a variety of archaeological finds from the Trabzon region, while upstairs is the collection devoted to local people and their culture. ⊠ *Zeytinlik Cad. 10* ☎ *462/322–3822* ☙ *3 TL* ☉ *Tues.–Sun. 9–5.*

**Sekiz Direk Hamam.** Turkey's oldest, still-functioning hammam is thought to be Byzantine, from the 12th or 13th centuries. The name comes from the 8 (*sekiz*) columns (*direk*) that support the dome of the hot room in the men's section. ⊠ *Sok. 1* ☎ *462/322–1012* ☜ *15 TL.*

## WHERE TO EAT AND STAY

*For expanded hotel reviews, visit Fodors.com.*

$  ✕ **Boztepe Aile Gazinosu.** Grilled meat
TURKISH  and fish are the specialties at this retreat above the city in Boztepe Park and in good weather are served in a shady garden or on an outdoor terrace. The views of the Black Sea and Trabzon's harbor are lovely. Finish your meal with tea served in an old-fashioned samovar. ⊠ *Boztepe Mahalesi* ☎ *462/321–4536.*

$$  ✕ **Fevzi Hoca.** Fevzi Hoca is Trab-
SEAFOOD  zon's most serious seafood restaurant. There's no menu, and you'll be shown the fish available—this usually includes Trabzon's local obsession, *hamsi* (anchovies). The restaurant's status is noted by photos of famous Turks dining on the premises. ⊠ *Maraş Cad. İpekyolu İş Merkezi* ☎ *462/326–5444.*

$  ✕ **Kebabci Ahmet Usta.** This sleek modern dining room on lively pedes-
TURKISH  trian Uzun Sokak offers all the standard kebabs and *pides,* plus a few rarer dishes such as *talaş kebabı* (sawdust kebab), lamb wrapped in pastry, and *orman kebabı* (forest kebab), lamb on the bone with vegetables. There are also local specialties such as *kuymak,* a thick syrup of cornmeal, and several dishes with *lahana,* the local cabbage. ⊠ *Uzun Sok. 56* ☎ *462/326–5666.*

$  ✕ **Murat Balık Salonu.** This small, no-nonsense restaurant on the north
TURKISH  side of Atatürk Alanı serves perfectly grilled Black Sea fish. A glass case in the front holds the day's catch: red mullet, mackerel, anchovies, bass, trout, or whatever else is in season. The small dining room, painted an electric green, is usually filled with local men who come in for a quick and unceremonious meal. ⊠ *Park Karşısı* ☎ *462/322–3100* ➟ *No credit cards.*

$$  ▦ **Horon Hotel.** The best things about these spacious rooms one block
★  off the main square is the helpful service and rooftop restaurant, with a good-value prix-fixe menu and views over the sea. **Pros:** central; helpful English-speaking staff; parking and valet service are a blessing. **Cons:** some noise from bar, especially on weekends. ⊠ *Sıramağazalar Cad. 125* ☎ *462/326–6455* ⊕ *www.otelhoron.com* ➟ *44 rooms* ♨ *In-room: Wi-Fi. In-hotel: restaurant, bar* ❡*Breakfast.*

¢  ▦ **Hotel Nur.** At Trabzon's best budget option, rooms are spotless (though small and painted bright green), some overlook the main square, and those in front on the higher floors even have a sea view. **Pros:** overlooks the town square; helpful English-speaking staff. **Cons:** call to prayer

> **BLACK SEA SPECIALTIES**
>
> Size isn't everything, as the miniscule *hamsi* (Black Sea anchovy) proves. Though usually not much longer than your finger, the *hamsi* is often called the prince of the Black Sea fish, and it's found in an almost endless variety of dishes: fried in a coating of cornmeal, served in a fragrant pilaf, baked into bread, or thrown into an omelet (there have even been some attempts at making *hamsi* ice cream). Also try *muhallema* (a type of Black Sea cheese fondue) and honey made in the high mountain villages of the Kaçkars.

7

from the mosque next door may disturb you in the morning. ⊠ *Cami Sok. 15* ☎ *462/323–0445* ₤ *462/323–0447* ⇨ *20 rooms* ⏀*l Breakfast.*

$$$ ⊞ **Novotel Trabzon.** Half of the large, modern rooms face the sea, and
★ all are just footsteps from the beach. **Pros:** beach; quality rooms and service. **Cons:** out of town; somewhat generic. ⊠ >*Cumhuriyet Mah Kasutsu Beldesi, Yumra; turn toward sea from lights opposite Dunya Ticaret Merkezi (World Trade Center) and Cevahir Mall* ☎ *462/455– 9000* ⇨ *204 rooms, 4 suites* ⅄ *In-room: Wi-Fi. In-hotel: pool, room service, restaurant, bar.*

$$ ⊞ **Usta Park Hotel.** Comfortable-though-sparse rooms off Atatürk Alanı are complimented by a rooftop restaurant with nice sea views and a welcoming lobby. **Pros:** Turkish bath and sauna; within walking distance to city's main attractions; juice bar and patisserie. **Cons:** some rooms face another building across an alley; sauna and fitness rooms are small. ⊠ *Iskenderpaşa Mah. 3* ☎ *462/326–5700* ⊕ *www.ustaparkhotel. com* ⇨ *114 rooms, 6 suites* ⅄ *In-room: Wi-Fi. In-hotel: restaurant, bar, gym* ⏀*l Breakfast.*

$$$ ⊞ **Zorlu Grand Hotel.** Trabzon's fanciest hotel offers large, elegant, and comfortably furnished rooms; a marble-lined, atriumlike lobby topped by a stained-glass dome and done up in an art deco–meets-Moorish style; and a courteous and professional staff. **Pros:** central location; extensive facilities; helpful staff. **Cons:** expensive spa services; some rooms overlook busy streets. ⊠ *Maraş Cad. 9* ☎ *462/326–8400* ⊕ *www. zorlugrand.com* ⇨ *143 rooms, 14 suites* ⅄ *In-room: Wi-Fi. In-hotel: restaurant, bar, pool, gym, laundry facilities, parking* ⏀*l Breakfast.*

## SÜMELA/MEREYEMANA

*47 km (29 mi) south of Trabzon.*

The Sümela Monastery (also known as the Monastery of the Virgin, and *Mereyemana* in Turkish) is a spectacular and unforgettable sight, perched some 820 feet above the valley floor and often lost in the clouds.

**GETTING HERE AND AROUND**

Many companies in Trabazon offer day trips to Sümela, usually for about 30 TL; one reliable choice is Ulusoy, on Taksin Caddesi. If you are driving, take Route 885 to Maçka, then head east on the road to Altındere National Park.

**Ulusoy** ⊠ *Taksim Cad., Trabzon* ☎ *462/321–1281.*

**EXPLORING**

**Monastery of the Virgin.** Set in a dramatic valley and clinging to the side of a sheer cliff, the Sümela Monastery is stunning to behold. Orthodox monks founded the retreat in the 5th century, living in cliff-top caves surrounding a shrine housing a miraculous icon of the Virgin painted by St. Luke. The labyrinth of courtyards, corridors, and chapels date from the time of Emperor Alexius III of Trebizond, who was crowned here in 1340—the monastery continued under the sultans and the monks remained until the Greeks were expelled from Turkey in 1922. Although the icon and other treasures have been removed, extensive frescoes

It's worth the hike to get to the Sümela Monastery. —photo by Brenda Easton, Fodors.com member

done between the 14th and 18th centuries remain. They are not as well preserved as those at Trabzon's ⇨ *Aya Sofya*, and sections have been chipped away or scribbled over by graffiti artists, but they are impressive nonetheless in their depictions of Old and New Testament images—look for an Arab-looking Jesus, an almost African Virgin, and a scene of Adam and Eve, expelled from Eden, taking up a plough. The first, lower parking lot is beside the river and Sümela Restaurant. From here a well-worn trail to the monastery is a rigorous 40-minute hike. Further on is a second, upper parking lot, at the level of the monastery, a 15-minute walk away on a level path. Most organized day excursions from Trabzon drop you at the upper lot and collect you from the lower one. ⊠ *Altındere National Park* ☎ *No phone* 🖃 *9TL, 12 TL for parking* ⊙ *Apr.–Oct., daily 9–6; Nov.–Mar., daily 9–4.*

### WHERE TO EAT

$ ✕ **Sümela Sosyal Tesisleri.** Just below the Sümela Monastery, a series of
TURKISH  open-air wood patios spread out along a thunderous rushing stream making wonderful use of the stunning location. You can order fresh trout or choose from a few regional dishes, such as *kuymak*, the Black Sea version of cheese fondue. Alcohol is available. ⊠ *Sümela Manastiri* ☎ *462/531–1207.*

$ ✕ **Sümer Restaurant.** These wooden gazebos set on the edge of a small
TURKISH  river are a fine spot to have lunch or dinner after visiting Sümela, a 15-minute drive away. There is a wide selection of mezes, along with regional specialties such as *canlı alabalık*, trout baked in butter, and *kaygana*, an omelet made with Black Sea anchovies. On the week-

ends, the place is filled with families from Trabzon on country outings. ✉ *Maçka Sümela Manastırı Yolu Km 2* ☎ *462/512–1581.*

Northeast of Rize, several forested valleys lead from the Black Sea into the towering and beautiful Kaçkar Mountains. Dotted with small villages, the cool mountains are a great place for hiking or just kicking back and checking out the alpine views. The mountains are also home to several *yaylas*, high-pasture villages that are inhabited only during the summer and are accessible only by footpath.

**Morina Balık Lokantası.** This unassuming restaurant on the coastal road halfway between Trabzon and Rize serves some of the best fish in the area. There's always a varied selection of freshly caught options—including meaty salmon steaks—cooked over hot coals or fried in a dusting of corn flour. The tomato-based fish chowder is also tasty. A pleasant garden is shaded by creeping vines. This is definitely worth a stop. ✉ *35 km (22 mi) out of Trabzon in direction of Rize, Çamburn/ Sürmene* ☎ *462/752–2023.*

**Zıraat Parkı.** Rize, 75 km (47 mi) east of Trabzon and the capital of the Black Sea's tea-growing region, sits above a small bay but below the foothills of the lush Pontic Mountains. There's not much to do here, though you can stop for a glass of the local brew in the hilltop Zıraat Parkı, a botanical garden near the town's western entrance. There's a small kiosk in the parking lot that sells gift packs of tea.

## ÇAMLIHEMŞIN

*124 km (77 mi) northeast of Trabzon; 22 km (14 mi) south of Ardeşen.*

The small village of Çamlıhemşin, at the junction of two rushing rivers, serves mainly as a gateway to mountain valleys above, particularly to the village of Ayder. Yet this is a pleasant and quiet overnight stop before heading up into the Kaçkars. There's not much to do here other than look out on the green mountains and listen to the river flowing by.

### GETTING HERE AND AROUND
You will probably want to make the excursion to Çamlıhemşin by car, the only real way to explore the villages and valleys. Follow the coast east from Trabzon to Ardeşen, then drop down to Çamlıhemşin on a well-marked road.

### WHERE TO EAT AND STAY
*For expanded hotel reviews, visit Fodors.com.*

$ ✕ **Moyy Restaurant.** The dining room of the Moyy Miniotel shares the
TURKISH same historic chestnut building and cool vibe. A range of local foods
★ includes *muhlama*, the local version of cheese fondue, and excellent coffee and cakes are served. Background music is accompanied by the gushing of a river out back, which you can enjoy from a balcony. ✉ *İnönü Cad. 35* ☎ *464/651–7487.*

$$ ⌂ **Fırtına Pansiyon.** This *pansiyon* in a converted schoolhouse, wth six rooms and three bungalows, is set amid green mountains in a completely solitary spot and is the most inviting of the few places to stay in Firtina Valley. **Pros:** beautiful environs and a quirky style. **Cons:** quite remote; intermittent hot water; shared bathrooms. ✉ *Şenyuva Köyü*

☎ 464/653–3111 ⊕ *www.firtinavadisi.com* ➳ *6 rooms, 3 cabins* ⚬ *In-room: no TV* ▭ *No credit cards* ⊘ *Closed Oct.–Mar.* ⫶⧊ *Some meals.*

$$
**$$** ⧊ **Moyy Minotel.** Earthy and arty, traditional and modern, with lots of
Fodor'sChoice exposed timber, this beautiful 80-year-old chestnut building beside the
★ river brings a different experience to the area, with six surprisingly styl-
ish rooms with such touches as cute wooden bathroom cabinets and
funky stone bowl basins; try to get one of the three river-view rooms.
**Pros:** cool and intimate; good for visiting both the Fırtına valley and
Ayder. **Cons:** traffic noise in some rooms; small bathrooms. ⊠ İnönü
Cad. 35 ☎ 877/662–6988 ⊕ *No web* ➳ *6 rooms.*

**OFF THE
BEATEN
PATH**

Most people take a left out of Çamlıhemşin and continue up to the
mountain village of Ayder, but continuing straight on the road takes you
into the Fırtına Valley, an often mist-shrouded place that sees few visitors and seems forgotten by time. Waterfalls and streams tumble out of
the mountains, which are covered by thick stands of green pines. Small
villages with peak-roofed two-story wooden houses cling to the mountainsides. As you drive along the road, you'll pass several examples of
the elegant Ottoman-era humpback bridges spanning the rivers. Zil
Kalesi is a small but spectacular castle along the road some 20 km (12
mi) outside Çamlıhemşin.

## AYDER

*90 km (56 mi) northeast of Rize; 17 km (11 mi) southeast of
Çamlıhemşin on well-marked road.*

At 4,000 feet and surrounded by snowcapped mountains and tumbling
waterfalls, the mountain village of Ayder, with its wooden chalets and
wandering cows, can seem like a piece of Switzerland transported to
Turkey. Once a sleepy *yayla*, a high-pasture village where locals would
live in the summer, Ayder has become a popular destination for Turkish tourists and, increasingly, foreign ones. Although a few years ago
the village's bucolic nature was threatened by overdevelopment, local
laws have now ordered all building to be done in the local style, with
wooden exteriors and peaked roofs. Summer weekend crowds can fill
the small village to capacity, but the setting remains magnificent and
the nights, when the stars put on a glorious show in the sky above,
are still marvelously quiet. The village is also an excellent base for day
hikes or extended treks in the Kaçkars and for visiting some of the less
accessible *yaylas* in the region to see a way of life that has changed little
over the centuries.

The easiest *yayla* to visit from Ayder is Yukarı Kavron, about 10 km
(6 mi) from the village along a dirt road. A collection of squat stone
houses, it's set on a high plateau surrounded by gorgeous mountains.
There are several nice hikes leading out of the village. There is regular
minivan service in the morning out of Ayder to the *yayla*, although it's
best to check with your hotel or *pansiyon* about the exact schedule.

Ayder has a grassy main square that during the summer frequently plays
host to festivals celebrating local Hemşin culture, with music played
on a local version of the bagpipe (known as the *bağlama*) and *horon*
dancing, which has men and women dancing together in a big circle.

## EXPLORING

**Hot Springs.** Ayder is also known for its hot springs, reputed to cure all types of ailments. True or not, the springs, housed in a modern, marble-lined building near the village's mosque, are good for a relaxing soak after a day of hiking. There are separate facilities for men and women, as well as private rooms for couples that want to bathe together. ☎ 464/657–2100 💷 9 TL ⊙ Mar.–Nov., daily 7–7; Dec.–Feb., daily 10–6.

## OUTDOORS

There are lots of hiking opportunities in the area, but most involve serious uphill sections. Well signposted from Ayder is the route to Hazindak, a collection of pretty wooden chalets on a ridge, which is a strenuous climb of around three hours. Much easier is the walk from Yukarı Kavron, a village just south of Ayder, up a valley to a series of lakes. The hike to the first, Adsız Göl (Nameless Lake), should take 1–2 hours. You can continue up the ridge to see a second lake down below.

## WHERE TO EAT AND STAY

*For expanded hotel reviews, visit Fodors.com.*

$    ✕ **Ayder Sofrası.** In good weather, the place to sit is the nice stone-lined
TURKISH    terrace with wooden picnic tables that look over the mountains and the waterfall. The kitchen turns out trout and local dishes such as stuffed cabbage and *muhallama,* the local cheese fondue, as well as meat options, and serves an open buffet breakfast every day. ⊠ *Ayder Kapalıcaları* ☎ 464/657–2037.

¢    ✕ **Nazlı Cicek.** In a shaded ravine near the entrance to town, this family-
TURKISH    run and popular spot serves tasty, extremely fresh trout that is taken fresh from one of the cement pools on the premises. They also serve the usual assortment of grilled meats. You can eat inside the cozy dining room, which has colorful Hemşin fabrics on the walls, or outside on the relaxing terrace, near a running stream. ⊠ *Ayder Merkez* ☎ 464/657–2008.

$    ⌂ **Kuşpuni Dinlenme Evi.** Set on the edge of a green field, this wooden chalet has large, comfortable rooms, and colorful rugs and kilims in the hallways add a homey feel. **Pros:** beautiful terrace with wonderful views; owners are helpful in arranging excursions; more peaceful than other *pansiyons.* **Cons:** small shower cabinets. ⊠ *Yukarı Ambarlik* ☎ 464/657–2052 ➷ *15 rooms* ⌂ *In-hotel: restaurant* ⊙ *Closed Oct.–Apr.* ⦿ *Breakfast.*

$$    ⌂ **Natura Lodge.** Some of the front rooms at this basic inn have wonderful views, and the staff is extremely knowledgeable about the outdoor activities in the area; an on-premises agency arranges water rafting and guided hikes. **Pros:** beautiful views from some rooms; trekking advice available; alcohol served. **Cons:** not much character, showers are not enclosed. ⊠ *On left, just past springs* ☎ 464/657–2035 ⊕ *www. naturaotel.com* ➷ *21.*

$    ⌂ **Serender Pansiyon.** Some of the simple rooms are quite small, but they have wonderful views of the mountains and waterfalls, and a lovely terrace where breakfast is served looks out on pastures and the mountains; there's the occasional sound of a cowbell in the distance. **Pros:**

peaceful surroundings. **Cons:** some rooms are small; showers are not enclosed. ✉ *Yukarı Ambarlik; on your right, at end of second cluster* ☎ *464/657–2201* *19 rooms* *Breakfast.*

# KARS, MT. ARARAT, AND LAKE VAN

Turkey's east is a region filled with stark contrasts: dusty plains and soaring mountains, simple villages, and bustling cities. Near Turkey's border with Armenia and Iran, this remote region is also filled with natural and man-made wonders and, for the visitor, offers the chance to see a part of Turkey that has yet to be invaded by the tourist hordes. Although this means that you may not find all the amenities and services available in western Turkey, the friendliness and hospitality of the area's predominantly Kurdish locals will very likely make up for it.

This excursion starts in Kars, which spent the early part of the 20th century under Russian occupation and still looks in places like a small Russian town. More than anything else, though, Kars serves as the base for exploring the haunting Ani, one of Turkey's most important historical sites. Once the capital of an Armenian kingdom that ruled the area more than a thousand years ago and that filled the city with stunning churches, Ani is today more like a ghost town, filled with ruins that still manage to evoke the city's former glory. Its location, at the edge of a windswept gorge with snowcapped mountains in the background and grassy fields stretching out to the horizon, only adds to Ani's mystique.

From Kars continue to Doğubeyazıt, a dusty town not far from the Iranian border. Although the town isn't much to look at, it's blessed with being almost at the foot of the mythical Mt. Ararat, the 16,850-foot peak that some believe is the resting place of Noah's ark. A perfect cone rising to the sky from the flat plains around it, Ararat is quite a sight to behold. Also in Doğubeyazıt is the Ishak Paşa Saray, an 18th-century palace in the hills above town that seems as if it was transported straight out of a fairy tale.

The next stop is Van, a modern and bustling city that is the economic capital of Turkey's east. Use this city as a base for exploring the area around the nearby Lake Van, one of Turkey's most fascinating natural wonders. Surrounded by mountains, the lake's blue-green waters are rich in minerals and very alkaline, meaning that even the poorest swimmer will float with ease. The region around the lake is home to several intriguing historical sites, most important the magical island of Akdamar and its 10th-century Armenian church. It's an area that you could easily spend several days exploring.



## KARS

The setting for Turkish novelist Orhan Pamuk's somber novel *Snow*, Kars, not far from Turkey's border with Armenia and Georgia, looks like the frontier town it is: forbidding and grayish, set on a 5,740-foot plateau and forever at the mercy of the winds. Yet, with its low buildings and compact town center, Kars has a relaxed, small-town feeling to it. The city has a reputation as being a liberal and secular-minded

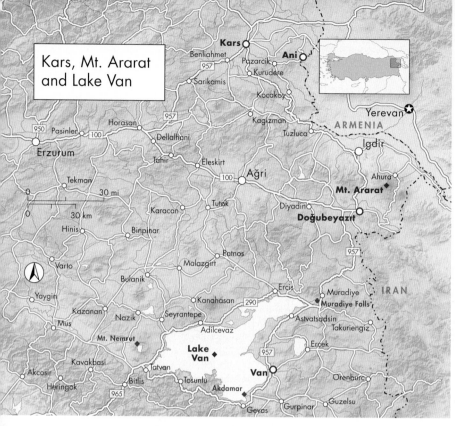

**Kars, Mt. Ararat and Lake Van**

outpost, and it certainly has more bars and licensed restaurants than other towns in the conservative east. The lifting of restrictions on visiting the ancient city of Ani—previously a closed military zone—has meant more tourists are coming through the area, giving locals the incentive to upgrade what Kars has to offer and there are signs of a new breath of life all over town. Some of Kars's Ottoman-era historic buildings are being beautifully restored as part of an ambitious project sponsored by the California-based Global Heritage Fund. Kars makes for a nice side dish to the main course that is the nearby mesmerizing site of Ani.

This minirevival is only the latest twist of history in a city that has had at least its own share of ups and downs. Since 1064, Kars has been besieged over and over, by various and sundry invaders: from the Akkoyunlu to the Mongol warriors of Tamerlane. In the 19th century alone, it was attacked three times by czarist armies from Russia. The Turks retook the city in 1920, and Kars was formally ceded to Turkey after the war of independence in 1921. The Russian influence is still obvious in many buildings.

## Spotlight on the Armenians

Armenians were once an integral part of the ethnic mix in Turkey's east, although today none remain in the region. What happened to them is a topic of sensitive debate in Turkey.

There were various Armenian kingdoms in the region starting in the 3rd century BC and lasting until almost the 11th century AD. After that, the Armenians—who adopted Christianity in AD 301—became the subjects of a succession of rulers, from the Byzantines, to the Persians, and finally the Ottomans. Armenians became the bankers and traders of the Ottoman Empire and ended up living throughout the Ottoman world, with Istanbul eventually becoming one of their main cultural centers. There are many examples of Armenian buildings, and many that still stand across Turkey were hugely influential on Seljuk architecture. The Armenian Balyan family were the sultan's official architects, designing Istanbul's Dolmabahçe Palace among many other important buildings.

During World War I, when the Ottomans came under attack by Russia and the other Allied powers, some Armenians in the east saw this as a chance for independence and rose up in revolt. The Ottomans deported the entire Armenian population of Anatolia to Syria and Iraq, a process that led to significant deaths and suffering. Many did not arrive, and Armenian survivors and U.S. consular staff reported massacres. The Armenians claim that hundreds of thousands (some claim even 1.5 million) perished and have been trying to have the events of the time recognized as genocide. The Turks, while admitting that large numbers of Armenians died at the time, say this was the result of war and disease, which also cost the lives of many others living in the region, and they point to the deaths of Turkish and Kurdish villagers in revenge attacks. Some 70,000 Armenians still live in Turkey, mostly in Istanbul.

### GETTING HERE AND AROUND

The Kars airport is 6 km (4 mi) outside of town. Turkish Airlines, Atlas Jet, and Pegasus have regular flights from Istanbul to Kars and SunExpress flies from İzmir to Kars.

There are daily buses from Istanbul and Ankara to cities in the east, but it's a long trip (22 hours from Istanbul, 18 from Ankara) and not much cheaper than flying. The train is not the best option: the trip from Istanbul to Kars (38 hours or more) is brutally slow, though it's cheap and the trip through Erzurum and Sivas is scenic. If you are planning on limiting your explorations outside Kars to Ani, you can arrange a tour. Otherwise, you will want to rent a car to visit other outlying sights.

### ESSENTIALS

**Guided Tours** The English-speaking guide Celil Ersözoğlu is a good option in Kars. He can arrange for trips to Ani and to some of the Armenian and Georgian monuments in the area.

**Tour Contacts Celil Ersözoğlu** ☏ 532/226–3966 ✎ celilani@hotmail.com.

A typical traffic jam in eastern Turkey. —photo by BrendaE, Fodors.com member

**Visitor Information** ✉ *Hakim Ali Riza Aslan Cad. 15, one block south of the Grand Hotel Ani* ☏ *474/223–6817* 🖷 *474/223–4623.*

## EXPLORING

**İç Kale** (*Kars Castle*). İç Kale overhangs the town from a high, rocky vantage point. Though it dates from the 10th century, in 1386 Tamerlane swept violently through the region and razed the original structure, and most surviving fortifications were commissioned by Lala Mustafa Paşa in 1579. The castle has gone through some restoration in recent years and the panoramic views of Kars merit the 10-minute walk uphill. ✉ *Kale Cad.* ☏ *No phone* 🎟 *2 TL* ⊙ *Daily 9–sunset.*

**Kars Museum** (*Kars Müzesi*). Kars Museum, near the train station on the eastern edge of town, is signposted, but a long walk from the center and a little difficult to find—you may want to taxi. There's a lot of pre-classical pottery, as well as the beautiful doors of an Armenian church. Easily missed outside is the railway carriage where Ottoman General Kazım Karabekir signed the treaty of Kars with the Soviet Union, settling today's border. ✉ *485 Cumhuriyet Cad.* ☏ *474/212–2387* 🎟 *Free* ⊙ *Daily 8:30–5:30.*

**Kümbet Cami** (*Drum-Dome Mosque*). The Kümbet Cami, at the foot of the hill by Kars River, was originally the Armenian Church of the Twelve Apostles, built in the 10th century. You can still make out the apostles on the exterior of the drum-shape cupola. The mosque is often locked, in which case the only view is through a rusty gate, but the exterior is architecturally interesting. ✉ *Kale Cad., at foot of İç Kale.*

**Taşköprü.** Just northwest of Kümbet Cami is the **Taşköprü,** known as "the Stone Bridge," of Seljuk origin dating from the 1400s and built of volcanic rock. On either side of the bridge you will be able to see some of the restoration projects being undertaken by the Global Heritage Fund. On the south side is the 300-year-old home of famed poet Nemik Kemal, which is being turned into a cultural center, while on the north side a row of Ottoman-era riverside timber and stone homes has been restored and painted. There are also plans to restore two ancient hammams near the bridge. ⊠ *Kars.*

> ### LOCAL FOOD
>
> Along Halitpaşa Caddesi are a number of inviting shops that sell Kars' specialty, an aged *kaşar* cheese that tastes much like an Italian pecorino. Many shops also sell local honey, and you can also do as the locals and stop by in the morning for a takeout breakfast of delicious *"bal* and *kaymak"*—honey with clotted cream.

### WHERE TO EAT AND STAY

*For expanded hotel reviews, visit Fodors.com.*

$ ✕ **Ani Ocakbaşı.** As the name implies—Ocakbaşı means "hearth"—the
TURKISH emphasis on grilled meats, the usual kebabs plus the Black Sea meatball specialty, *Akçaabat köfte.* The kitchen also prepares some local stews, but usually only at lunchtime. ⊠ *Kazım Paşa Cad. 28* ☎ *474/212–0423.*

¢ ✕ **Kadın eli yöresel yemekleri.** "Women's hands local home cooking" is
TURKISH a rough translation of the name, and it pretty well sums up the way things work in this old Russian building, where old tile blends with modern fittings, and an open kitchen fills one end. The menu changes regularly, and dishes are posted in Turkish and English on a chalkboard. Try *karnayarık,* eggplant stuffed with meat, or *mantı,* Turkish ravioli. Alcohol is served. ⊠ *Halitpaşa Cad. 41* ☎ *543/617–6611.*

$ ✕ **Ocakbaşı Restoran.** The kebabs are simple and tasty, and embroidered
TURKISH curtains, rust-color tablecloths, and waiters in shiny vests add a bit of atmosphere—though the cave effect is a bit weird. Try the *Ali Nazik kebab* or the *Eyder kababi,* pieces of grilled meat, cheese, parsley, sesame and egg yoke in a calzonelike wrapping. Kars goose, a local specialty, is also served. ⊠ *Atatürk Cad. 276* ☎ *474/212–0056.*

$$ 🛏 **Grand Hotel Ani.** Some of the large, modern rooms enjoy views of the mountains, and amenities abound—from "foot" spas in the bathrooms to a gym and a large indoor pool. **Pros:** among the better lodgings in town; central location; pleasant restaurant and bar. **Cons:** mountain views, but only from upper floors; decor is somewhat cold. ⊠ *Ordu Cad. 15* ☎ *474/223–7500* ⊕ *www.grandani.com* ↘ *68 rooms, 4 suites* ⌂ *In-room: Wi-Fi. In-hotel: restaurant, bar, pool, gym, spa.*

$ 🛏 **Hotel Karabağ.** Once one of Kars's top hotels is a little frayed at the edges these days, with faded carpets and plastic plants in the lobby, but the rooms are good-sized and the staff is friendly. **Pros:** good value, spacious rooms; the helpful staff can advise on excursions; comfortable lounge and bar. **Cons:** a little dated; irritatingly fast auto-switch off lights in halls. ⊠ *Faik Bey Cad. 184, at Atatürk Cad.* ☎ *474/212–3480* 📠 *474/223–3089* ↘ *45 rooms, 5 suites* ⌂ *In-room: no a/c, Wi-Fi. In-hotel: restaurant* ⑩ *Breakfast.*

7

$$$   ⚏ **Kar's Otel.** A wonderfully restored late 19th-century Russian-built mansion is extremely stylish, with a cool, minimalist white-and-gray color scheme, original art on the walls depicting monuments in Kars, and comfortable rooms furnished with contemporary flair. **Pros:** plush and modern rooms; a warm welcome after a day of skiing or sightseeing. **Cons:** rooms starting to show wear; top-floor rooms can get hot; limited facilities. ⊠ *Halitpaşa Cad. 79* ☎ *474/212–1616* ⊕ *www. karsotel.com* ⤳ *5 rooms, 3 suites* ⚙ *In-room: Wi-Fi. In-hotel: restaurant, bar* ▮⊙▮ *Breakfast.*

### NIGHTLIFE

**Barış Club.** Kars is not a party town, and there's not much alcohol to be had. If you want a drink, Barış Club is one of your better options, and there's often live music. The place is popular with students, so it's busy during term and dead in summer. ⊠ *Kale Yolu Atatürk Cad. 33* ☎ *473/233–0702.*

# ANI

*42 km (26 mi) east of Kars.*

The ruins at Ani are what draw most people to this remote area of Turkey. Until the Mongol invasion of 1236, Ani (also called Ocaklı) was the chief town of a medieval Armenian kingdom, with 100,000 inhabitants and "a thousand and one churches," according to historical sources. Although it was occupied by the Mongols, Ani still had a large Armenian population well into the 14th century. In 1319 the city was struck by a terrible earthquake, after which the townspeople began to leave.

### GETTING HERE AND AROUND
Take Route 36–07 from Kars.

### EXPLORING

Fodor's Choice ★   **Ruins of Ani.** Scarcely a half-dozen churches remain at Ani, all in various states of disrepair, but even so, the sprawling site is breathtaking—crumbling majesty amid stark, sweeping countryside, tiny Kurdish settlements, and fields of wildflowers. There is a haunted, yet strangely meditative, feeling at the site, an open-air museum holding what are considered some of the finest examples of religious architecture of its period.

Ani has little shade and can get quite hot in summer, so be sure to bring a hat and water. You should plan on spending two or three hours at the site if you want to see the highlights, although you could spend an entire day exploring the ruins. The city was built on an easily fortified triangular promontory bounded on two sides by steep river gorges; the third side is closed by the mighty walls, which stretch for more than 8,200 feet and are 32-feet tall, raised in AD 972 by the Armenian king.

Enter through the Aslan Kapısı (Lion's Gate), one of three principal portals. Take the path on the left to the Church of the Redeemer. This circular church was built in 1035 but hit by lightning in the 1950s, slicing it neatly in half, leaving a surrealistic representation of an Armenian church with the rubble of its former half in the foreground. Next to it is the *bezirhane,* a former oil press. Beside the walls is the best preserved of three churches in Ani dedicated to St. Gregory, the Armenian prince who converted his people to Christianity. Built in 1215 by a wealthy Armenian merchant, Tigran Honentz, it is the most impressive ruin in Ani, not least because it's at the foot of a ravine with a view over the Arpaçay River. Inside, note the remarkable cycle of murals depicting the lives of Christ and St. Gregory. If you follow the path into the gorge, you will come to the striking Kusanatz (Convent of the Three Virgins), on a rocky outcrop.

At the center of the site is the former cathedral, built in 1001 by the architect Trdat. It was once topped by a large dome that fell in an earthquake in 1319. During periods of Muslim rule the structure served as the Fethiye (Victory) mosque. A short distance away is the Menüçehir Cami, which clings to the heights overlooking the Arpaçay River and was originally an Armenian building, perhaps a palace; the minaret, added in 1072, is thought to be the first Turkish building within the country's modern borders.

Return to the walls along the excavated main street, past the shattered ruins of another minaret. Soon you will reach the Church of the Holy Apostles. The church itself is in ruins, but its large Narthex, erroneously called a Seljuk caravansary, is well preserved with impressive stonework. From here head west toward the second gorge, and find a path backtracking to another small but well-preserved church dedicated to St. Gregory. Continuing back beside the gorge to the walls, you will pass the foundations of the massive round Church of King Gagik. 🖂 *No phone* 📧 *5 TL* 🕙 *Daily 9–6.*

## DOĞUBEYAZIT AND MT. ARARAT

*Doğubeyazıt is 192 km (119 mi) southeast of Kars.*

The scrappy frontier town of Doğubeyazıt (doh-*oo*-bay-yah-zuht) is a good base from which to enjoy views of Turkey's highest and most famous mountain, the majestic Mt. Ararat (Ağrı Dağı). Not far from the Iranian border, the place seems neglected, if not downright forgotten, with dusty streets and crumbling buildings. But the pace here is laid-back and the locals are friendly. You'll share the town with sheep and travelers bringing in contraband cigarettes and other cheap goods from Iran. There aren't many carpet and kilim shops here compared to tourist spots in western Turkey, so you can wander the main street, Çarşı Caddesi, without being bothered too much. A day is probably enough time to spend here, catching an early visit to the sites around Mt. Ararat and then the İshak Paşa Saray at sunset.

### ESSENTIALS

**Guided Tours** Tour offices in Doğubeyazıt tend to go in and out of business every week, so if you need a guide, you're best off asking at your hotel and/or getting recommendations from other travelers.

### EXPLORING

★ **İshak Paşa Saray** (*İshak Paşa Palace*). Doğubeyazıt's only sight, the enchanting İshak Paşa Saray, is in the mountains southeast of town. The fortified palace was built in the late 18th century by local potentate Çolak Abdi Paşa and his son İshak. The interior of the building features ornate stonework, a fantastic mixture of Georgian, Persian, and classical Ottoman styles, but the gold-plated doors were carted off by Russian troops in 1917 and are in St. Petersburg's Hermitage Museum. Like Istanbul's Topkapı, the palace is divided into three areas: the first courtyard, open to all; the second courtyard, which holds the mosque and meeting rooms once used by the Paşa and other important personages; and the third courtyard, an inner sanctum housing the massive kitchen and the harem. Note how most rooms are small and equipped with their own hearths for the long cold winters.

Visit in the morning or late afternoon, when the sun casts a deep orange glow over the palace. Across the valley are an early Ottoman mosque and the ruins of an older and more traditional fortress—whose foundations are Urartian but which was rebuilt several times through the centuries. (You can clamber up to the fortress on a rough trail that starts next to the mosque; look for the two Uratian figures carved in the rock.) There is a restaurant and teahouse above the palace, as well as a few Kurdish mud-brick houses. ⊠ *6 km (4 mi) southeast of town on road to Göller* ☎ *No phone* ⛃*3 TL* ☉ *Daily 9–5.*

**Mt. Ararat** (*Ağrı Dağı*). Mt. Ararat, an extinct volcano covered with snow even in summer, soars dramatically 16,850 feet above the arid plateau, dominating the landscape. According to Genesis, after the Great Flood, "the waters were dried up from off the earth; and Noah removed the covering of the ark, and looked, and behold, the face of the ground was dry." The survivors, as the story goes, had just landed on top of Mt. Ararat. Many other ancient sources—Chaldean, Babylonian, Chinese, Assyrian—also tell of an all-destroying flood and of one man who heroically escaped its consequences. The mountain can be easily viewed from Doğubeyazıt, although actually climbing it requires a permit that can only be obtained several months in advance, and the trek must be done with a licensed agency. Be prepared for a lot of walking on gravel, and be forewarned that the summit is often shrouded in clouds. Local tour offices will take you on a day trip that includes a visit to a village at the base of the mountain, which is the closest you can get to Ararat without a permit.

## WHERE TO EAT AND STAY

*For expanded hotel reviews, visit Fodors.com.*

$ ✕**Murat Camping.** Despite the rustic name (there is a small campground
TURKISH on the premises), this large space with an outdoor terrace on a hillside just below the Ishakpaşa Sarayı, is Doğubeyazıt's only option for a big night out. The furniture is a bit dated, but the views of Doğubeyazıt and the surrounding mountains are commanding. You'll find the usual selection of mezes and kebabs, live Turkish music in the evenings, and wine, beer, and rakı. ⊠ *Ishakpaşa Sarayı; on road up to palace, and just before it* ☎ *472/312–0367* ▭ *No credit cards.*

¢ ✕**Öz Urfa Kebap.** Looking something like a hunting lodge, with walls
TURKISH of rough wood boards, this kebab house has more atmosphere than most other places in town and works a bit harder at providing good service. On offer are several kinds of well-made kebabs, as well as an

## HARK! THE ARK!

Mt. Ararat is where, according to biblical accounts, Noah's Ark may have come to rest during the great flood. Locals around Mt. Ararat have been selling Christian pilgrims old planks reputedly from Noah's Ark since medieval times, and fragments of ancient timber embedded in the ice have been brought back by various ark-hunting expeditions over the years—though radiocarbon-dating tests have been inconclusive.

Satellite photos showed something embedded in a glacier at 12,500 feet, but further examination proved it to be nothing more than a freak formation in the strata.

Nevertheless, expeditions by Christian groups constantly make new claims, and a second Noah's Ark was "discovered" in the 1980s on a hillside 20 km (12 mi) southeast of Ararat—though to most eyes, this "ark" is nothing more than a pile of rocks.

assortment of *pides* cooked the traditional way in the wood-burning oven. ⊠ *Ismail Beşikçi Cad. 34* ☎ *544/218–0418.*

$    ☂ **Grand Derya Hotel.** The exterior qualifies this modest choice for "an ugliest hotel in Turkey" award, but inside are large and well-maintained rooms, all with balconies, and those in front with views of Mt. Ararat. ⊠ *İsmail Beşikci Cad. 157* ☎ *472/312–7531* ☞ *40 rooms, 20 suites* ⌂ *In-hotel: restaurant, parking.*

$    ☂ **Hotel Nuh.** The relatively large rooms are on the basic side, though the hotel's greatest asset is the view of Mt. Ararat—enjoyed from most rooms and the large rooftop restaurant. **Pros:** great views of Mt. Ararat; good English is spoken; within walking distance of city center and markets. **Cons:** decor leans toward drab. ⊠ *Büyük Ağrı Cad. 65* ☎ *472/312–7232* ☞ *65 rooms* ⌂ *In-room: no a/c, Wi-Fi. In-hotel: restaurant, bar* ⧉ *Breakfast.*

**NEED A BREAK?**

If you're driving from Doğubeyazıt to Van, there's not much to see along the way. So the lovely Muradiye waterfalls, some 83 km (51 mi) southwest of Doğubeyazıt, come as a welcome relief. From a small parking lot, a bouncy suspension bridge crosses a swiftly flowing stream and gives you a good view of the 20-foot falls. The area is filled with green poplar trees and local families who come here to picnic. A simple teahouse has a lovely view of the tumbling falls and is the perfect spot for taking a rest.

## VAN, LAKE VAN, AND ENVIRONS

*Lake Van is 171 km (106 mi) from Doğubeyazıt, continuing past Muradiye to the town of Van.*

Van is the commercial center of eastern Anatolia, and modern streets are lined with shops both modern and traditional and choked with traffic. There's a definite sense of bustle to the town, with restaurants and cafés filled with young people, many of them students from the local university. With its collection of rather uniform-looking and ugly cement buildings, what Van really lacks is a sense of history, which should not be surprising. The Van of today dates back to the early 20th century, when it was rebuilt some 5 km (3 mi) farther inland from Lake Van after being destroyed in battles with the Armenians and Russians during World War I. Old Van first appears in history 3,000 years ago, when it was the site of the Urartian capital of Tushpa, whose formidable fortress—built on a steep cliff rising from the lakeshore—dominated the countryside. What remains of Old Van, in a grassy area near the lake, is a melancholy jumble of foundations that cannot be sorted out; only two vaguely restored mosques, one 13th-century, the other 16th-century, rise from the marshland.

### GETTING HERE AND AROUND

Turkish Airlines, Pegasus, and Atlas Jet have regular flights from Istanbul and SunExpress flies to Van from İzmir and Antalya. The airport is on the south of the city, on the road toAkdamar and Tatvan. The airport and city center are just off the main highway that skirts the southern portion of Lake Van. If you're traveling by car, Van is 176 km (110 mi) south of Doğubeyazıt on D975.

### ESSENTIALS

**Guided Tours** The Ayanis travel agency in Van can help with travel arrangements and with organizing tours in the Lake Van area.

**Tour Contacts Ayanis** ☎ *432/210–1515.*

**Visitor Information** ✉ *Cumhuriyet Cad 223, just south of Fevzi Çakmak Cad.* ☎ *432/216–2018* 🖷 *432/216–3675.*

### EXPLORING

Fodor'sChoice
★

**Akdamar.** On the tranquil, uninhabited islet of Akdamar, among the wild olive and almond trees, stand the scant remains of a monastery that include the truly splendid **Church of the Holy Cross.** Built in AD 921 by an Armenian king, Gagik Artzruni of Vaspurakan, the compound was originally part of a palace, but was later converted to a monastery. Incredible high-relief carvings on the exterior make the church one of the most enchanting spots in Turkey. Much of the Old Testament is told here: Look for Adam and Eve, David and Goliath, and Jonah and the whale. Along the top is a frieze of running animals; another frieze shows a vineyard where laborers work the fields and women dance with bears; and, of course, King Gagik, almost hidden above the entrance, is depicted, offering his church to Christ. The wall paintings in the interior of the church underwent an extensive restoration in 2006 and after much controversy a cross was placed on the dome in 2010. The monastery operated until World War I, and since 2010 annual religious services have been allowed. To reach Akdamar from Van, follow Route 300 to Gevaş, which is about 20 mi away. Just past Gevaş, you'll see ferries waiting at the well-marked landing to collect the required number of passengers—between 10 and 15—for the 20-minute ride. Normally it costs 7 TL per person, but if there aren't enough passengers, the round-trip is 100 TL. ✉ *Rte. 300, 56 km (35 mi) west of Van* ☎ *No phone* 🖂 *3 TL* ☼ *Daily sunrise–sunset.*

The Armenian Church of Holy Cross, on the uninhabited islet of Akdamar, is a work of art, inside and out.

★ **Lake Van** (*Van Gölü*). Lake Van is Turkey's largest and most unusual lake: 3,738 square km (1,443 square mi) of eerily blue water surrounded by mighty volcanic cones, at an elevation of 1,725 meters (5,659 feet). The lake was formed when a volcano blew its top and blocked the course of a river, leaving the water with no natural outlet; as a result the lake is highly alkaline and full of sulfides and mineral salts, six times saltier than the sea. Lake Van's only marine life is a small member of the carp family, the *darekh,* which has somehow adapted to the saline environment. Recreational water sports are limited, and beaches along the rocky shores are few and far between. Swimming in the soft water is pleasant, but try not to swallow any—it tastes terrible.

The towns of Adilcevaz and Ahlat, on Lake Van's north shore, are worth visiting only if you're in the area; you'll probably want to head instead to Van and the nearby island of Akdamar, along the lake's south shore.

**Van Kalesi** (*Van Castle*). Steps—considerably fewer than the 1,000 claimed in local tourist handouts—ascend to Van Kalesi, the sprawling Urartian fortress on the outskirts of town. A path branches right to Urartian tombs in the sheer south rock face; a cuneiform inscription here honors King Xerxes, whose Persian troops occupied the fortress early in the 5th century BC (look for the red metal fence on the southeast side). The crumbling ramparts are still impressive, but as is often true in these parts, it's the view—sweeping across the lake and mountains— that makes the steep climb worthwhile. A taxi from the new town should cost no more than 10 TL one-way. Cheaper *dolmuşes* (shared taxis) depart regularly from the north end of Cumhuriyet Cadessi and are marked "Kale." 🖼 *Free ☯ dawn–dusk.*

**Van Müzesi** (*Van Museum*). The new city's main attraction is the small but well-arranged archaeological and ethnographical collections, which display many Urartian artifacts, particularly metalwork: rich gold jewelry; belts and plates engraved with lions, bulls, and sphinxes; and a carved relief of the god Teshup, for whom their capital was named. An inner courtyard has some intriguing humanoid stelae found in Hakkâri, in the mountains to the south. The small garden has a varied collection ranging from Urartian sculptures to Turkish tombstones. ⊠ *Cengiz Cad., 1 block east of Cumhuriyet Cad., behind Belediye (Municipality)* ☎ *432/216–1139* ⊞ *Free* ☉ *Daily 9–5.*

> **DID YOU KNOW?**
>
> The kingdom of Urartu (known as Ararat in the Bible) first appeared in this region in the 13th century BC and by the mid–8th century BC ruled an empire extending from the Black Sea to the Caspian Sea. Known as expert builders, stonemasons, and jewelry makers, the Urartians created gold necklaces and bracelets, often incorporating a distinctive lion's head motif, that are some of the most prized holdings in Turkish museums.

**OFF THE BEATEN PATH**

**Çavuştepe and Hoşap Kalesi.** From Van, drive 35 km (22 mi) south on the Hakkari road, where the side road to Çavuştepe is signposted on your right. Here you can clamber around the stone foundations of the ruined 8th-century BC Urartian fortress-city Sardurihinli. Nearby are temple ruins of perfectly cut basalt and the remains of a palace with great underground chambers. If you continue 15 km (9 mi) southeast on the same road, you'll reach Hoşap Kalesi (Castle), a dramatic fortress looming over a river chasm. The complex, built in 1643 by the local tribal lord Sari Süleyman Bey, was used as a base to "protect" (i.e., ransack) caravans and included a palace, mosques, baths, and a dungeon. The great gate, with its carved lions and an inscription in Farsi, is quite a show of strength; a passage, partly carved through bedrock, leads into the complex from here. ☉ *Hoşap Kalesi: Daily 9–5.*

**Mount Nemrut.** Across the lake from Van is one of Turkey's loveliest natural wonders, the beautiful and rarely visited crater lakes of Mount Nemrut (Nemrut Dağı, which should not be confused with the more famous Mt. Nemrut farther west). From Tatvan, 146 km (91 mi) west of Van, a rutted road leads up the mountain to the 10,000-foot-high rim of what was once a mighty volcano. From the rim of the crater, you can see down to the two lakes below—a smaller one fed by hot springs and larger "cold" one. A loose dirt road leads down to the lakes, where very simple tea stands have been set up. The inside of the crater has an otherworldly feel to it, with its own ecosystem: stands of short, stunted trees and scrubby bushes, birds and turtles, and cool breezes. Few tourists make it to the lakes, and chances are your only company will be local shepherds and their flocks.

**WHERE TO EAT AND STAY**

*For expanded hotel reviews, visit Fodors.com.*

$    ✕ **Grand Deniz Turizm.** A pebbly lakeside beach set with plastic tables is a

TURKISH    good spot for lunch or dinner after a visit to Akdamar. The food, which includes local dishes such as kebabs and trout baked in a terra-cotta dish, is delicious. You can swim off the rocks here and use one of the showers afterward, and if you're lucky the restaurant's Van cat, with one yellow eye and one blue, will be around. ⊠ *Van-Tatvan Karayolu Km 40, Gevaş* ☎ *432/612–4038.*

$ ✕**Kervansaray.** Hidden up some stairs on the west side of Cumhuriyet Cadessi, this basic kebab place is little bit more refined than the competition around town. There's a broad range of the typical kebabs, plus a few more unusual choices, such as *Beyti kebab*, meat in pastry, here with cheese. ⊠ *Cumhuriyet Cad.* ☎ *432/215–9482.*

¢ ✕**Kebabistan.** Filled with musta-
TURKISH chioed men sipping tea, this basic eatery serves the usual kebabs and hot prepared dishes, as well as good

**BREAKFAST IN VAN**

Breakfast is special in Van: it's served meze-style, with an array of small dishes best shared among several people. There's a variety of locally made cheeses, eggs (fried, alone or with salami, or hard-boiled), and, most important, *kaymak*, a delicious clotted cream that's eaten on bread with honey. The city has many small restaurants that serve breakfast all day, but the best ones are along Kahvaltı Sokak, parallel to Cumhuriyet Caddesi; *Kahvaltı* is the Turkish word for breakfast. The street is filled with many competing restaurants but Sütçü Fevzi, at No. 9, 432/216–6618, is especially good.

*pide* and *lahmacun*, flatbread topped with ground meat and baked. The main dining room is a hive of activity, but upstairs is a comfortable, quieter room. ⊠ *Sinemalar Sok.* ☎ *432/214–2273.*

$ ✕**Tamara Ocakbaşı.** Each table at this popular eatery in the Tamara
TURKISH Hotel is equipped with its own *ocak*, or hearth, and you cook your meat yourself. You can also choose a table on the terrace, where your kebab arrives cooked. There's also a decent range of mezes. ⊠ *Yüzbaşıoğlu Sok. 1* ☎ *432/214–3296.*

$$ ▥ **Büyük Urartu.** One of the town's best lodging options makes an
★ attempt at character with reproductions of Urartian art on the walls throughout and gold-embroidered bedspreads and floral wallpaper in the small but pleasant guest rooms; some of these face the noisy street—so ask for one in back, though some may overlook a brick wall. **Pros:** 24-hour room service and information desk; live music three nights a week; pool and sauna. **Cons:** hotel books up quickly; popular with tour groups. ⊠ *Cumhuriyet Cad. 60* ☎ *432/212–0660* ⊕ *www. buyukurartuotel.com* ⤳ *72 rooms, 3 suites* ⌂ *In-room: Wi-Fi. In-hotel: restaurant, bar, pool* ⦿ *Breakfast.*

$$ ▥ **Merit Şahmaran.** At this comfortable, well-run hotel 12 km (7½ mi) west of town on Lake Van, ask for one of the lakeside rooms, which have views of the lake and mountains—all rooms are large, with good beds, nice decor, and modern bathrooms with big cabinet showers. **Pros:** great location; full bar and decent restaurants. **Cons:** well out of town; waterfront disco could be noisy. ⊠ *Edremit Yolu Km 12, Edremit* ☎ *432/312–3060* ⊕ *www.merithotels.com* ⤳ *90 rooms* ⌂ *In-room: Wi-Fi. In-hotel: restaurant, bar, pool, beach, parking* ⦿ *Breakfast.*

7

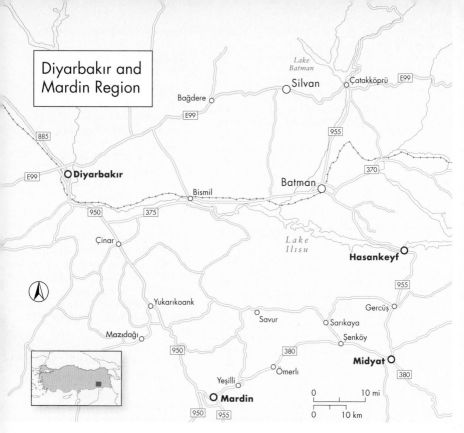

Map: Diyarbakır and Mardin Region

Lake Batman • Silvan • Çatakköprü [E99]
Bağdere
[E99]
[885]
[E99] O **Diyarbakır**
[955]
Bismil • Batman [370]
[950] [375]
Çınar
Lake Ilısu
**Hasankeyf** O
[955]
Yukarıkoank
Savur • Sarıkaya • Gercüş
Mazıdağı • Şenköy
[950] [380] **Midyat** O
Yeşilli • Ömerlı [380]
**O Mardin**
[950] [955]

0        10 mi
0        10 km

**$$** :::Tamara Hotel. A good range of facilities, large rooms, and a central location compensate for the rather bland decor; all rooms are nicely furnished with modern pieces, and the choicest are those facing the street in the new wing. ⊠ *Yuzbasioglu Sok. 1* ☎ *432/214–3296* ☎ *69 rooms* ♿ *In-hotel: restaurant, bar.*

## DIYARBAKIR, MARDIN, MIDYAT, AND HASANKEYF

Saying that Turkey's southeast region has a rich history is an understatement. This is, after all, part of the ancient area known as Mesopotamia: the land between the Tigris and the Euphrates rivers, where modern civilization got its start. This excursion takes you into the heart of this historic region, to cities that trace their past not over centuries, but over millennia, and through landscapes that seem unchanged with time. The area is also the historic home of the Assyrian Christians, one of Christianity's oldest sects, and several fascinating Assyrian churches and monasteries can be visited.

The excursion begins in Diyarbakır, which has long been the region's commercial, cultural, and political center. Surrounded by a thick basalt wall that dates back to Roman times, Diyarbakır's old city has

CLOSE UP

# Spotlight on the Kurds

An estimated 20 million Kurds live in the mountainous region that covers parts of Iran, Iraq, Syria, and Turkey. Separated by ethnicity and language from their neighbors, the Kurds have for centuries found themselves the subjects of the area's various rulers.

Turkey has the region's largest Kurdish population, with an estimated 12 million, most of them living in the country's southeast region. When the new Turkish Republic was founded in 1923, severe restrictions on Kurdish language and culture were put in place, part of a larger effort to unite the country's various ethnic groups under one national identity. During the 1980s, the Kurdistan Workers' Party (PKK), a militant Marxist group, began a bloody separatist war against the Turkish state that ended up

costing the lives of more than 30,000 and caused great damage to social and economic life in the southeast. The PKK called for a ceasefire in 1999, after its leader was captured by Turkey, and its fighters retreated to the mountains of northern Iraq. Attacks have continued on a reduced scale since then and wax and wane with the political climate, but violence is usually confined to small area along the Iraqi border and is nowhere near the level of the 1980s and '90s. At the same time, as part of its efforts to join the European Union, Turkey has over the past few years passed legislation aimed at easing the cultural and political restrictions on the Kurds and has promised to revitalize the local economy, bringing a guarded sense of hope to the battle-scarred region.

7

cobblestone lanes that lead to grand old homes hidden behind high stone walls (some of these homes are now open to visitors), intriguing old churches and mosques, and a lively bazaar spread through a maze of narrow lanes.

From here you continue to Mardin, one of the most magical cities in Turkey. Sitting like a crown that looks down on a wide plain below, Mardin is a wonderful place to wander. The narrow streets are lined with old stone homes, gorgeous mosques, and a bazaar where donkeys still carry most of the goods. Spend the day walking around, then relax in the evening at the terrace of one of the local restaurants and look out at the view of the plains below and the stars above. Make sure to visit Dayrul Zafran, an ancient Assyrian Christian monastery in the hills just outside Mardin.

Midyat is one of the best-preserved small towns in Turkey. Once home to a sizable Assyrian Christian community, its old city is today mostly a ghost town, with many of its former residents now living in Europe. What they left behind is an incredible collection of honey-color stone homes with exquisite carvings on their exteriors and several historic churches. As in Mardin, this is a wonderful place to spend a few hours walking around and soaking up the atmosphere. Mor Gabriel, another isolated Assyrian monastery, is a fascinating place to visit.

From Midyat, you can make the quick trip to Hasankeyf, a small town that sits in an enchanting spot on the banks of the Tigris River. Spend a few hours exploring Hasankeyf's cliff-top citadel, which dates back to Roman times, and a series of ancient cliff dwellings nearby, and then head down to the river, where you can eat lunch on a veranda that sits on stilts right over the Tigris's gently flowing waters.

## DIYARBAKIR

Called Amida by the Romans and Amid by most locals, the ancient city of Diyarbakır commands a bluff above the Tigris River and is encircled by a 5½-km (3-mi) stretch of thick, impregnable black-basalt walls, built at the orders of Constantine the Great. Inside these walls lie twisting alleyways, old stone homes, mosques, and a lively bazaar. The city's long history has meant it's seen quite a succession of rulers, from the Assyrians to the Urartians and Romans, and finally the Ottomans, who took control of the city in 1515. Diyarbakır, today the cultural capital of Turkey's Kurdish southeast, has been an important regional commercial and cultural center for centuries, and there are some wonderful old houses, mosques, and churches in the cobblestone lanes of the old town.

In the 1980s and '90s, Diyarbakır was forced to absorb a large number of villagers fleeing the fighting in the countryside between Kurdish militants and Turkish security forces. Many villages were compulsorily evacuated, and this huge influx of mostly poor villagers taxed the already poor city's infrastructure and social services and has left lasting social problems. In more recent years, though, the local municipality has embarked on several restoration and beautification projects, such as renovating historic homes in the old city and opening them up to visitors, which is helping bring the city's charm closer to the surface. Locals are generally welcoming to visitors, but you may feel uncomfortable walking the dirt-poor backstreets of old Diyarbakır, where aggressive children will pester you for money. It's one of the few places you may feel uncomfortable on your own. You may want to stick to the main streets and hire a guide to explore the old city in depth.

### GETTING HERE AND AROUND

Turkish Airlines, Onur, and Pegasus Airlines have flights from Istanbul to Diyarbakır. SunExpress operates flights from İzmir and Antalya. There are daily buses from Istanbul to Diyarbakır; the ride takes close to 20 hours and costs about $45. From Diyarbakır, minivans leave the local bus-station for the one-hour trip to Mardin.

The train ride from Istanbul to Diyarbakır is long—more than 35 hours—but scenic, and inexpensive: about $35 TL (first class) to 70 TL (sleeper bunk).

### ESSENTIALS

**Visitor Information** ✉ *İçkale, northeast corner of old city* ☎ *412/221–2173* 🖷 *412/221–1189.*

### EXPLORING

**Bazaar.** Diyarbakır's bazaar encompasses the half-dozen streets surrounding Ulu Cami; most stalls are shrines to wrought metal—gates, picks, shovels, plumbing fixtures, plastic shoes, and other things you probably would not want to carry home in your luggage. Across the street from the mosque is the grand 16th-century **Hasan Paşa Hanı,** a photogenic *kervansaray,* housing a few carpet and souvenir dealers and a tranquil place to stop for a tea.

**Cahit Sıtkı Tarancı Müzesi.** Down a narrow alleyway near the Ulu Cami in the old city, the Cahit Sıtkı Tarancı Müzesi is a historic home dating back to 1734 that has been renovated and turned into an ethnographic museum, with rooms displaying scenes of life as it once was in Diyarbakır. The museum, which has a pleasant courtyard with a fountain, offers probably the best opportunity of seeing what an old Diybarbakır house looked like. Opening hours can be erratic. ⊠ *Ziya Gökalp Sok. 3* ☎ *412/223–8958* 💲 *Free* ☉ *Daily 9–5.*

**City walls.** The Romans left a strong mark on Diyarbakır—not only did they lay the foundations for its famous city walls, but they created the basic layout of the old town: a rough rectangle with two main streets that cross and connect the four gates that are found at each compass point. The walls were reconstructed by the Byzantine Emperor Constantius in AD 349 and further restored by the Seljuks in 1088 and again 120 years later by Artakid Turcoman emir al Malik al-Salih Mahmud. On the whole, the walls remain in good shape along their entire length; indeed, if you feel like a bit of an adventure, the best way to appreciate these great walls is to wander along the top. Of the original 72 towers, 67 are still standing, decorated with myriad inscriptions in the language of every conqueror and with Seljuk reliefs of animals and men; you can also explore their inner chambers and corridors. The easiest and safest section to explore is around **Dağ Kapısı** (Mountain Gate). Alternatively, to make a circuit of the city walls on foot, start at the **Mardin Kapısı** (Mardin Gate), on the south side near the Otel Büyük Kervansaray, and take the wall-top path west toward the **Urfa Kapısı** (Urfa Gate), also called the Bab er-Rum. About halfway you will come to the twin bastions **Evli Beden Burcu** and **Yedi Kardeş Burcu**—the latter is also known as the Tower of Seven Brothers and was added to the fortifications in 1209. From here you can see the old Ottoman bridge over the Tigris, called **Dicle Köprüsü** (Tigris Bridge). Continue clockwise along the city wall, and you'll eventually reach another gate, the **Dağ Kapısı** (Mountain Gate), which divides Diyarbakır's old and new towns. Farther east, inside the ramparts, are the sad remains of the **Artakid Saray** (Artasid Palace), surrounded by a dry, octagonal pool known as the **Lion's Fountain.** Not long ago there were two carved lions here, now there's only one; what happened to the other is a mystery.

**İç Kale** (*Inner Fortress*). The İç Kale, or inner castle of Diyarbakır's old town, is a circular fortress that once held the city's palace and other important buildings. Today the most notable landmark is the 16th-century **Hazreti Süleymaniye Cami** (Prophet Süleyman Mosque), also known as the Citadel Mosque. It has a tall, graceful minaret and is striped with black basalt and pale sandstone, a favorite design of this city's medieval architects. Its courtyard fountain is fed by an underground spring that has probably supplied cold, clear water to the city for 5,000 years. The area is the focus of a major restoration and rejunvination project. ⊠ *İzzet Paşa Cad.* ☎ *No phone* ☉ *Daily dawn–sunset.*

**Kasım Padişah Cami.** The old town's most recognizable monument is the Dört Ayaklı Minare (Four-Legged Minaret) of the Şeyh Mutahhar Mosque. The minaret balances on four basalt columns, a marvel of medieval engineering. Legend has it that your wish will come true if you pass under the minaret seven times. ⊠ *Yenikapı Cad.* ☏ *No phone.*

**Meryem Ana Kilisesi.** Diyarbakır was once home to a large Christian population—Armenians, Chaldeans, and Assyrians—and several churches remain in the city, although the only one that still holds regular services is the Assyrian Orthodox Meryem Ana Kilisesi, on the western end of the old city. A peaceful oasis in the midst of the bustling city, the church, said to be built on the site of what was a temple used by sun worshippers, has a large courtyard lined with basalt stones. Parts of the church date back to the fourth century—look for the remains of the Roman arch beside the altar—but most of the structure is medieval. Services are held every Sunday at 8 am, although only a few people usually show up. ⊠ *Ana Sok. 26* ✚ *Near city gate off Melik Ahmet Cadessi* ☏ *No phone* ◷ *Daily 9–5.*

**Ulu Cami** (*Great Mosque*). In the center of the old city is the Ulu Cami, one of the oldest mosques in Anatolia. Though the present form dates from the 12th century, in an older form the structure served as the Byzantine basilica of St Thomas; its colonnades and columns are made from bits and pieces of earlier Roman and Byzantine buildings. Note the Arabic-style flat-roofed and rectangular plan, closely resembling the great Ummayid Mosque of Damascus and unlike the square-shape and domed mosques common in Turkey. ⊠ *Gazi Cad., opposite Yapı Kredi Bank* ☏ *No phone* ◷ *Daily 10–sunset.*

## WHERE TO EAT AND STAY

*For expanded hotel reviews, visit Fodors.com.*

**$**
TURKISH

✕ **Çarşı Konağı.** You have to pass through a small door off one of Diyarbakır's narrow old city lanes to get to this simple restaurant, in a restored historic stone home with a shaded courtyard—ask for directions. The small menu is made up of kebabs and delicious *sac tava,* chunks of beef sautéed in a woklike pan with tomatoes and green peppers; it's served in the pan, with a mound of flatbread to soak up the tasty juices. This is also a pleasant spot to cool off with a cup of coffee or tea. ⊠ *Telegrafhane Sok., off Gazi Cad. Çarşı* ☏ *412/228–4673* ▭ *No credit cards.*

**$**
TURKISH

✕ **Çemçe Diyarbakır Mutfağı.** Head here if you want to sample authentic local dishes, such as *perde pilaf* (chicken and rice baked inside a pastry shell) or for the more adventurous, *mumbar* (lamb intestines stuffed with rice and ground meat). The food, served buffet style, is well made and the setting—an old stone house with several small dining rooms decked out with rugs and antiques—is charming. ⊠ *In Greenpark Hotel, Gazi Cad. 101* ☏ *412/229–4345.*

**$**
TURKISH

✕ **Haşim Usta.** Diyarbakır's best-regarded choice for fine dining is slick and modern, in the new part of town, and offers good food and a diverse menu. Among the regular kebabs the *kuşbaşı* (small pieces of loin of lamb with cinnamon, dried mint, cumin, and black pepper) is a standout, as are some more unusual variations, such as a peach kebab.

They also serve the local specialty *kaburga*, a sheep's ribcage, cooked with rice inside, that the waiter dissects for you. Alcohol is available. ✉ *Cahit Sıtkı Tarancı Sok., Aslan Apt. 3* ☎ *412/229–2624* ⊕ *www. hasimusta21.com.*

$$$ 🏨 **Greenpark Hotel.** Although the lobby and rooms are somewhat characterless, this is certainly Diyarbakır's fanciest place to stay, with large and comfortable guest quarters, all with desks and some with small couches. **Pros:** quality service; wide range of facilities. **Cons:** for the price, rooms are a bit lacking. ✉ *Gazi Cad. 101* ☎ *412/229–5000* ⊕ *www. thegreenparkdiyarbakir.com* ⟿ *107 rooms, 7 suites* ⌂ *In-room: Wi-Fi. In-hotel: restaurant, bar, pool, gym, spa, business center* ¶◎¶ *Breakfast.*

$$ 🏨 **Otel Büyük Kervansaray.** At this attractive 16th-century *kervansaray*
★ with sandstone walls and vaulted ceilings, rooms are on the small side, but you're really paying for the atmosphere and the location—and there is a lovely courtyard with a fountain where you can eat dinner or have a drink, and the hotel pool is a welcome sight in Diyarbakır's heat. **Pros:** wonderful character and atmosphere; pool and lovely courtyard. **Cons:** rooms and bathrooms are quite small; some furniture is a little dated. ✉ *Gazi Cad.* ☎ *412/228–9606* 📠 *412/228–9606* ⟿ *31 rooms, 14 suites* ⌂ *In-hotel: restaurant, bar, pool* ¶◎¶ *Breakfast.*

$$ 🏨 **SV Business Hotel.** As the name implies, these bright, decent-size rooms just inside Dağ Kapısı, Diyarbakır's main city gate, offer comfort and modern amenities rather than character. **Pros:** good location; modern facilities; good value. **Cons:** could be anywhere. ✉ *İnönü Cad. 4 Dağkapı* ☎ *412/228–1295* ⌂ *In-room: Wi-Fi. In-hotel: restaurant, bar, gym, business center.*

## MARDIN

*96 km (60 mi) southeast of Diyarbakır.*

★ With historic stone houses clinging to a citadel-topped mountain that overlooks a vast plain below, Mardin has a magical setting. The city was hit hard by the violence of the 1980s and '90s, and populated largely by Arabs, but on the edge of the Kurdish zone, slid off Turkey's tourist map. The return of calm to the region has meant that travelers are rediscovering this enchanting city's mazelike old town, intricately decorated homes, and lively bazaars. Mardin has been featured in several popular Turkish TV drama series, and has become popular with tourists from Istanbul and other western Turkish cities. Some nice hotels and restaurants have opened up to serve them—there's even a film festival.

One of the big pleasures in Mardin is simply walking the old town's narrow cobblestone lanes and seeing what you come across. Although there are many ugly cement homes that have been built in recent years, the remaining historic homes give the city a great deal of charm. The stone used to build the old homes is the color of golden sand and looks especially beautiful at sunset. A short distance outside the city is the still active Syriac Monastery of Deyrul Zaferan, parts of which date back to the 5th century.

## GETTING HERE AND AROUND

Turkish Airlines, SunExpress, Onur, and Pegasus Airlines have flights from Istanbul to Mardin. There are frequent minivans to Urfa, Diyarbakir, and Midyat. If you are traveling through the region by car, Mardin is 105 km (65 mi) south of Diyarbakır on D950.

## EXPLORING

**Bazaar.** Mardin's lively bazaar runs parallel to the old town's main street, Birinci Caddesi, and is refreshingly free of the stalls selling the usual tourist gifts. This is the place to come if you're looking to buy a new saddle for your donkey or a copper urn—or as is more likely, if you just want to get the feel of an authentic town bazaar. There are also spice shops, fresh fruit and vegetable stands with the produce of the season piled high, and assorted other shops catering to local needs. In the center of the bazaar is the 12th-century Ulu Camii, with its beautifully carved minaret.

**Kasimiye Madrasa.** The Kasimiye Madrasa, signposted a short distance west of the city center, was completed around 1459 by Sultan Kasim of the Akkoyunlu dynasty. The building has two clear halves: To the right is the mosque and to the left, through a beautiful doorway, are cells for the theological students, surrounding a pretty courtyard. ⊠ *Near city center* 🔳 *Free* ☉ *Dawn–dusk.*

**Kirklar Kilisesi** (*Church of the 40s*). Mardin was once home to a large Christian community and several churches still remain in the city, although only a few are functioning. The most likely to be open is the Kirklar Kilisesi, an Assyrian Orthodox church. It's on a narrow lane a hundred yards or so west of the Mardin Museum. Parts of the church date back to the year 569, though most of what you see is medieval. There are some beautiful stone carvings and a shady courtyard. Neighborhood children will offer to take you there, which is probably a good idea, since it can be hard to find. ⊠ *217 Sağlik Sok. 8* 🕾 *No phone* 🔳 *Free* ☉ *Daily 8–5.*

**Mardin Museum.** The small Mardin Museum is on the city's main square, in a grand old stone house that used to be the home of an Assyrian Catholic patriarch. The stone relief carvings on the exterior are quite exquisite, and the small collection includes displays from archaeological digs around Mardin, with pieces from the Roman, Byzantine, Seljuk, and other periods. One floor has an ethnographic exhibit showing life in old Mardin. ⊠ *Cümhurriyet Meydanı* 🕾 *482/212–1664* 🔳 *3 TL* ☉ *Mon.–Sat. 8–5:30.*

**Post office.** One of the best examples of an old Mardin home is the current post office. ⊠ *On Birinci Cad., across street from an open-air teahouse, in center of town.*

**Zinciriye Medrese.** Built in 1385 by Artukid Sultan İsa, this *medrese* sits up just above the rest of the city, and its crenulated dome forms a Mardin landmark. The compound includes a courtyard, now a tea garden; a mosque; and a tomb intended for the sultan. Head up to the upper terrace for one of the best views of the city. ⊠ *Near city center* 🔳 *Free* ☉ *Dawn–dusk.*

**OFF THE BEATEN PATH**

**Orthodox Dayrul Zafran** (*Saffron Monastery*). Just 10 km (6 mi) southeast of Mardin is the Syrian Orthodox Dayrul Zafran. Begun in the 5th century and partially restored in the 19th century, the monastery is still in use and sits like a golden jewel in the scrubby hills of a hidden side valley. Highlights include the main church and the burial chapel, which date from the 5th century and are filled with Roman detailing, and an underground chamber, said to be a former sun temple—the heavy stone ceiling is a miracle of Roman engineering. You may catch sight of one of the *rahip* (priests) who still speak and teach Aramaic, the language of Christ. ⊠ *Off road from Mardin to Nusaybin* ☎ *No phone* ⌨ *3 TL* ⊙ *Daily 9–11:30 and 1–4:30 (5:30 in summer).*

## WHERE TO EAT AND STAY
*For expanded hotel reviews, visit Fodors.com.*

**$**
TURKISH

✕ **Antik Sur.** A restored old vaulted *han*, on the city's main road, is a good place to escape the midday heat. Aside from the range of kebabs typically found in southeastern Turkey, the menu includes a few local dishes, including *kaburga*, rice-stuffed lamb's rib cage. ⊠ *1 Cad. 8/34* ☎ *482/212-2425.*

**$$**
TURKISH
Fodor'sChoice
★

✕ **Cercis Murat Konağı.** Mardin's best restaurant, and one of the finest in Turkey, occupies a restored stone house with several terraces that provide spectacular views of the plain that unfolds below the town. Dishes served are authentic local ones, such as lamb braised in a tangy green plum sauce and *kitel raha*, layers of mince and chickpea dough. There is also a full spread of tantalizing cold and hot mezes, including tasty chickpea fritters and, owing to the Arab influence on Mardin, hummus and falafel. A locally made red wine is served traditionally, in metal bowls. ⊠ *Birinci Cad. 517* ☎ *482/213–6841.*

**$**
TURKISH

✕ **Kebabçi Yusuf Ustanın Yeri.** This outdoor eatery in the heart of town (across the street from the post office, one of the loveliest old buildings in Mardin) serves tasty kebabs and frothy village *ayran*, a salted yogurt drink you can find bottled around the country but here is drunk the traditional way: with a ladle from metal bowls. The kebabs are served with fresh flatbread, so you can make your own wrap. ⊠ *Birinci Cad. Üçyol Mevkii* ☎ *482/212–7985* ▭ *No credit cards.*

**$$**

▦ **Artuklu Kervansarayi.** Entering this *kervansaray* that dates back to 1275 will make you feel as if you're taking a trip back in time: The walls are thick stone; the narrow, mazelike corridors seem like something out of a medieval castle; and colorful rugs and antiques accent the decor. **Pros:** wonderful atmosphere; nice public areas. **Cons:** rooms are small with no view; alcohol is not served. ⊠ *Birinci Cad. 70* ☎ *482/213–7353* ⊕ *www.artuklu.com* ⇆ *40 rooms, 3 suites* ⌂ *In-room: Wi-Fi. In-hotel: restaurant, parking* ❙⚬❙ *Breakfast.*

**$**

▦ **Baday Butik Hotel.** These three rooms near the bazaar provide Mardin's only really good budget option, with two standard units that share a nice terrace with a view and a large attic suite with its own terrace. **Pros:** affordable; run by personable family; nice surroundings. **Cons:** limited services and amenities. ⊠ *Kültür Sok. 3* ☎ *482/212–8586* ⇆ *3* ⌂ *In-room: a/c.*

**$$**

▦ **Büyük Mardin Oteli.** This modern hotel is on the edge of Mardin and has good views of the old city and the plain below. **Pros:** elevator—one of the few hotels in town without lots of stairs; nice views. **Cons:** out of center; lacks character of other places in town. ⊠ *Yeniyol Cad.* ☎ *482/213–1047* ⊕ *www.buyukmardinoteli.com* ↝ *43 rooms, 11 suites* ⚘ *In-room: Wi-Fi. In-hotel: restaurant, bar, gym, parking* †○† *Breakfast.*

$$ ⊞ **Erdoba Konakları.** These rooms in a series of historic homes, with
★ modern additions, have stone walls and nice but smallish bathrooms, while suites are especially atmospheric and commodious and well worth the extra price. **Pros:** quality rooms and service; good food. **Cons:** standard rooms are small and have no views; the hotel books quickly and is often full. ⊠ *Birinci Cad. 135* ☎ *482/212–7677* ⊕ *www. erdoba.com.tr* ↝ *45 rooms, 10 suites* ⚘ *In-room: Internet. In-hotel: restaurant* †○† *Breakfast.*

$$ ⊞ **Zinciriye Hotel.** Two adjacent old houses just below Mardin's landmark Zinciriye Medrese are simple, elegant, and filled with character, with magnificent views from rooms that are comfortable and pleasantly atmospheric but vary greatly in size. **Pros:** central location; nice views; excellent public spaces. **Cons:** some rooms are small. ⊠ *1 Cad.* ☎ *482/212–3322* ⊕ *www.zinciriye.com* ↝ *15 rooms* ⚘ *In-room: Wi-Fi.*

# DARA

*36 km (22 mi) southeast of Mardin off Route D955.*

Dara was one of the most important fortress towns on the Romano-Byzantine eastern frontier, built by the Emperors Anastasius and Justinian in the 5th and 6th centuries. So important was Dara that when the Persians captured the town in 573/4, the Emperor Justin went mad, and was wheeled around in a cart for the rest of his life, biting those who came too close. As you arrive you will see a series of huge quarries that were later reused for tombs. The last in the row is the most interesting, with an elaborately carved facade. Among the ruins are an enormous cistern, the excavated main street (labelled "agora," a Roman bridge, and what's left of the city's massive walls.

## GETTING HERE AND AROUND

Head east from Mardin on the D955 toward Nusaybin, passing the turnoff for Deyrul Zaferan. After 20km (12mi), just past Akıncı there is a signposted turn left for Dara, a further 9.4 km (6 mi). There is no public transport on this side road.

# MIDYAT

*67 km (42 mi) east of Mardin.*

★ Not far from Mardin, the lovely old town of Midyat is an architectural gem that has remained largely untouched by the blight of concrete—although the new part of the city is dismal. Formerly almost an exclusively Assyrian Christian town, old Midyat is filled with an astonishing number of beautiful homes built of stone the color of honey or golden sand. Walking through Midyat's narrow streets reveals house after beautiful house, many of them with gorgeous ornamental carving work on their exteriors. Many of Midyat's Christians left during the violence of the 1980s and '90s, and Kurdish has become the dominant language of the old town. The homes and churches remain, and now that a relative calm has returned to the region, some of them are even being renovated for use as summer homes by Assyrians who used to reside here but currently have their primary residences in Western Europe. Midyat now has some excellent hotels, and you can spend a quiet day or two exploring the city and visiting some of the nearby Assyrian churches and monasteries; this is also a good base for visiting the historical monuments at the nearby riverside town of Hasankeyf.

**GETTING HERE AND AROUND**

Midyat is 67 km (41mi) east of Mardin on D380. Regular minibuses make the trip between the two towns.

**EXPLORING**

**Mor Barsaumo Church.** With their numbers dwindling, Midyat's Assyrian community rotates services throughout the old town's churches, so it's hard to know which one will be open. Your best bet is the Mor Barsaumo Church, open most afternoons. It has a beautiful chapel with distinctive locally made artwork and lovely stonework. ⊠ *Şen Cad. 21, southern end of the old city* ☏ *No phone* ☞ *Free.*

**Monastery of the Mother of God.** In the villages around Midyat are dozens of churches, many still in use and dating back to the 5th through 8th centuries. The area suffered considerably during the Kurdish uprising, and many Christians moved to Germany, Sweden, and Australia, though a small number are beginning to return and many visit in summer. The most extraordinary religious site is the Monastery of the Mother of God at Hah (Anıtlı), probably from the 6th century, which has an elaborately carved classical interior and exterior, and is the only Byzantine church, other than the Aya Sofya in Istanbul, to use a dome and two half-domes to create a rectangular space. The monastery is 3 miles off the Dargeçit road, which is off the Hasankeyf road. Closest to the Hasankeyf road, though, off a short but rather rough road that leads to the village of Barıştepe, is the similarly ancient Mor Yakup Church. ⊠ *Anıtlı* ☞ *Free* ☉ *Dawn–dusk.*

**Shiluh.** The Syriac Christians have a long tradition of wine making, but Shiluh is the region's first professional winery. Shiluh has a shop in the center of Midyat, but the winery is 7 km (4 mi) from Midyat on the road to Mor Gabriel, where an underground restaurant and tasting room are carved out of the hillside. Note that the unusual, strong flavor of the red wine may not be to everyone's taste. ⊠ *Cizre Cad. 333.*

**OFF THE BEATEN PATH**

**Mor Gabriel Monastery.** Twenty-five kilometers (15½ mi) southeast of Midyat is the Mor Gabriel Monastery, built on the site of a church that dates back to 387. The monastery is on the top of a hill in a desolate area, surrounded by fields and vineyards, a peaceful and tranquil setting. Reopened as a monastery in 1952 after having been closed for some time, the building is traditionally a nunnery, though barely a dozen women remain; a few monks and the local patriarch, known as a Metropolitan, are also in residence, as are children sent to boarding school here to help preserve the ancient Syriac language. Two churches and a grotto hold the graves of monks who have lived here throughout the centuries. English-speaking guides—young men who live here as students—are usually on hand to show guests around. ⊠ *25 km (15½ mi) southeast of Midyat* ☎ *482/462–1425* 🎫 *Free* ◷ *Daily 9–11:30 and 1–4.30.*

## WHERE TO EAT AND STAY

*For expanded hotel reviews, visit Fodors.com.*

¢   ✕ **Cihan Lokantası.** This basic steam-table restaurant serves the usual
TURKISH   menu of stews and casseroles but the owners have tried to add some class by hanging white lace curtains and putting pots of plastic yellow flowers on the walls—your call if it's classy or tacky. Either way, the food is tasty, the staff is friendly, and the location, down the street from the Mor Barsaumo Church, makes this one of the few decent options near Midyat's old town. ⊠ *Cizre Yolu Uzeri, Karakol Karş 52* ☎ *482/464–1566* ▭ *No credit cards.*

$   ✕ **Tarihi Midyat Gelüşke Hanı.** This beautifully restored *han* served as
TURKISH   an inn for traveling traders for centuries, and you can eat outside by a fountain in the large courtyard or in one of the small private dining rooms, where you sit on rugs and eat from low tables, reclining on pillows when you're done. The kebabs and other grilled meats are tasty and served with a tangy chopped tomato salad and a refreshing cold yogurt soup that has wheat berries in it. If you call a day in advance, they can prepare the Assyrian speciality, *dobo* (lamb stuffed with rice and pistachios). ⊠ *Eski Midyat Çarşısı* ☎ *482/464–1442.*

$$   ▦ **Kasr-ı Nehroz.** The owners have converted their family home perched
★   on the city walls into a beautiful retreat, where stone-walled, vaulted-ceiling rooms in the old quarters and a new wing are beautifully decorated in a mix of traditional and modern styles and surround an airy courtyard. **Pros:** beautiful old mansion; exotic surroundings; good value. **Cons:** some modern rooms lack the character of rooms in the old house. ⊠ *219 Sok. 14* ☎ *482/464–2525* ⊕ *www.hotelnehroz.com* ⤸ *29 rooms* ⚐ *In-room: Wi-Fi. In-hotel: restaurant, bar.*

$$$   ▦ **Shmayaa.** Shmayaa means "sky" in Syriac, and indeed some of the
Fodor's Choice   rooftop rooms in this beautiful old mansion are open to the sky; in
★   others, furniture is clustered so nothing touches the extraordinary, well-preserved stonework. **Pros:** beautiful surroundings; lovely outdoor spaces; nice locaiton in old quarter. **Cons:** stairs may pose difficulty for some visitors. ⊠ *126 Sok. 12* ☎ *532/457–5838* ⊕ *www.shmayaa.com* ⤸ *18 rooms* ⚐ *In-room: Wi-Fi. In-hotel: restaurant, bar.*

# HASANKEYF

*43 km (27 mi) north of Midyat.*

Just a short drive from Midyat, Hasankeyf makes for a good half-day excursion. This small town has a magical setting, with stone houses on the banks of the Tigris River, lorded over by a cliff topped with the remains of an ancient citadel. A now-ruined bridge was built in 1116 by the Artukid ruler Fahreddin Karaaslan, possibly incorporating parts of a Roman bridge. The best view is from the north end of the modern bridge that now crosses the river; in the background is a magnificent minaret, all that remains of the Artukid Great Mosque, which has collapsed into the waters. Come, explore, have lunch at a string of casual fish restaurants on the banks of the Tigris (at some you can sit in ankle deep water and enjoy a fish as its smaller relatives nibble at your toes) then return to Midyat, Mardin, or even Diyarbakır.

**GETTING HERE AND AROUND**
Hasankeyf is 43 km (27 mi) north of Midyat and 135 km (82 mi) north of Diyarbakır on D955. Minibuses make regular runs between Midyat and Hasankeyf.

**EXPLORING**
**Citadel.** The citadel, which dates back to Roman times, is at the top of a sheer cliff that rises 328 feet above the river. On the back side of the cliff, the citadel looks over a small canyon where several abandoned cave dwellings have been carved into the rock. Excavations and stablization work is ongoing, hence the "No entry" signs that put some of the site off-limits, but the climb up is still worthwhile for the views. ⊠ *Edge of town* ☎ *No phone* 💲 *3 TL* ☉ *Daily 8:30–5:30.*

**Er Rizk Mosque.** Just below the citadel, on the way into town, is the Er Rizk Mosque, which dates back to the 14th century and has a beautiful minaret that has intricate stone carvings on its exterior. ⊠ *Near town center* ☎ *No phone* 💲 *Free* ☉ *Dawn–dusk.*

**Zeynelbey Turbesi.** Across the river from the citadel is another spot worth visiting, Zeynelbey Turbesi, a mausoleum built for a prince who died in battle in 1473. The stylized structure has an onion-dome top and is decorated with still-vivid turquoise-color tiles set in calligraphy-like geometric patterns, reminiscent of Iran and Central Asia. ⊠ *On Batman-Hasankeyf road, near bridge* ☎ *No phone* 💲 *Free* ☉ *During daylight hrs.*

**WHERE TO EAT**
$ ✕ **Villapark.** The mix of kebabs is fairly standard, though they are well prepared, the nice setting includes a terrace with a good view of the town and the Tigris, and there's ice cream for dessert. ⊠ *Burç Sok.* ☎ *488/381–2200.*

> **THE TIGRIS DAM**
>
> For the last several decades a proposed massive dam project along the Tigris has put Hasankeyf in danger of being submerged. A vocal campaign by environmentalists and preservationists has currently succeeded in persuading foreign financial backers to withdraw, temporarily stopping the project. Currently the project is on hold but the Turkish government is said to be pursuing Chinese and Arab money, and there's no telling if the dam will one day be built.

# GAZIANTEP, MT. NEMRUT, AND URFA

Forget about "George Washington slept here"; in this part of Turkey you're more likely to come across places that claim to have been paid a visit by the biblical patriarch Abraham. Cities and monuments in this part of southeast Turkey trace their roots back to biblical times and beyond. Luckily for the traveler, much of that history hasn't been lost to the sands of time, and the ancient cities and historical sites that are part of this excursion are remarkably well preserved and visitor-friendly.

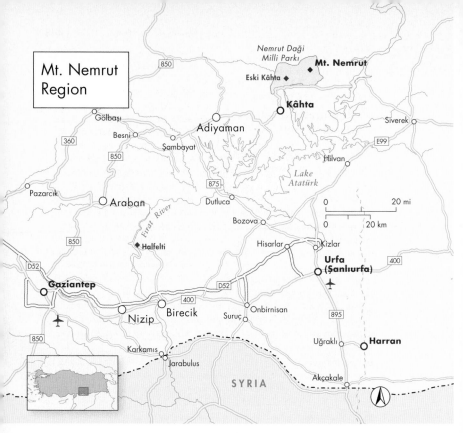

This excursion begins in Gaziantep, not far from Turkey's border with Syria; it's a vibrant, busy town with a fascinating and well-preserved old city and one of Turkey's most authentic bazaars. Gaziantep also has a fantastic museum featuring a stunning collection of Roman-era mosaics from a nearby archaeological dig and is known among Turks as having some of Turkey's best food and certainly its best baklava.

From Gaziantep you will continue on to Mt. Nemrut, where giant sculptures sit improbably at the top of a lonely mountain—a lasting testament to the vanity of the ruler of a local dynasty.

From here you'll head to Urfa, another of the area's ancient cities and a major pilgrimage site for Muslims. There's a tranquil park with mosques, and ponds with sacred fish built on the spot where many Muslims believe Abraham was born. (Abraham also figures prominently into the history of Harran, a fascinating historic site that's a quick side trip from Urfa.) Not far from the quiet of the park is the city's wonderful bazaar, where tailors work on foot-driven sewing machines and the sound of coppersmiths hammering fills the air. The twisting lanes in the city's old neighborhoods are lined with beautiful old stone homes. A short drive from Urfa is Göbekli Tepe, dubbed the world's oldest temple, where a half dozen mini Stonehenge-like structures dot an isolated hill.

# GAZIANTEP

Gaziantep has become the economic and administrative capital of Turkey's southeast, with an inviting mix of modern vitality and ancient tradition. Responsible for a good chunk of Turkey's industrial output, from bulgur wheat and pistachios to car parts and textiles, the city's modern districts are lined with wide boulevards and ever-expanding housing tracts. Only 65 km (40 mi) from the Syrian border, Gaziantep has a distinctive Middle Eastern feel to it, from the historic homes with their large interior courtyards to the red-pepper paste and cumin used in the local dishes. The narrow-laned old town, with graceful stone houses and a bustling bazaar filled with the sound of hammering coppersmiths, has been revived, and the rabbit warren of old streets known as the Bey neighborhood is especially lively these days. This old quarter was once largely Armenian and several old churches survive. A melting pot of many culinary traditions, Gaziantep is also one of Turkey's most important food capitals, and a collection of restaurants and baklava bakeries are considered among the best in the country. In one day you can see the sights but you could easily spend two days exploring and eating.

## GETTING HERE AND AROUND

Turkish Airlines and Onurair fly to Gaziantep from Istanbul and Ankara. SunExpress flies to Gaziantep from İzmir and Antalya.

There are daily buses from Istanbul to Gaziantep: the ride takes about 18 hours and costs about 70 TL.

GUIDED TOURS The knowledgeable Ayşe Nur Arun at Gaziantep's Arsan travel agency can arrange for tours in Gaziantep, around the region, and to Mt. Nemrut.

### ESSENTIALS

**Tour Essentials Arsan** ☎ *342/220–6464* ⊕ *www.arsan.com.tr.*

## EXPLORING

**Bazaar.** The heart of the bazaar is the **Zincirli Bedestan**, with shops selling copperwork, mother-of-pearl inlay, saddles, and Ottoman-style leather shoes. Beyond the *bedestan* is the **Bakırcılar Çarşısı**, the market of the coppersmiths, where an orchestra of craftspeople taps out bowls and coffee cups between customers. From here you emerge at the **Tahmis Coffee House**, one of the most traditional places to try Turkish coffee and where, legend has it, the Sultan Murat IV dropped in for coffee on his way to conquer Baghdad in 1638 (the current shop was built after a fire destroyed the original in the 19th century). The neighboring Sufi lodge, now the **Mevlevihanesi Vakif Museum**, is filled with historic Korans and kilims (free admission). ⊗ *Mon.–Sat. 9–6.*

**Citadel area.** The northern exit of the Zincirli Bedestan brings you out beside the 19th-century Alaüddevle Mosque, with its large dome. From here Hamdi Kutlar Caddesi leads past more coppersmiths and several restored 19th-century caravansaries to the prominent **kale** (castle), built over the layers of the pre-Roman city by the Emperor Justinian in the 6th century and remodeled by the Seljuk Turks in the 12th and 13th centuries. It's a steep walk to the top, but the view over the bazaar district is fantastic. If you need some steam after the excursion, on the far

## Rediscovering Turkish Food in Gaziantep

Turks can be fiercely proud of the food in their region of the country, but even those from other places will easily admit that Gaziantep has perhaps Turkey's best food. Drawing on culinary influences from Turkish and Arab cooking, the earthy cuisine in Gaziantep is assertively spiced and flavorful. If you've grown tired of kebabs during your time in Turkey, be ready to rediscover them in Gaziantep, where kebab making is seen as both an art and a science. Among some of the best kinds of kebabs you can try here are *sebzeli kebab* (a skewer of lamb, tomato, green peppers, parsley, and garlic minced together) and *Ali Nazik* (cubes of grilled lamb taken off their skewer and served on a heavenly bed of smoky roasted eggplant and garlicky yogurt). Other specialties include *mercimek koftesı* (small ovals made out of red lentils mixed with bulgur wheat, fresh herbs, red pepper paste, and spices) and *yuvalama* (tiny dumplings made out of rice flour and ground meat, served in a yogurt broth).

Most of all, though, Gaziantep is famed for its flaky and buttery baklava, which incorporates with great success one of the area's leading crops, pistachios. It is, without a doubt, the preferred ending to any meal in Gaziantep.

Gaziantep is rightfully known as Turkey's baklava capital and there seems to be a shop on every corner, most incorporating the tongue-twister family name "Güllüoğlu."

side of the castle you'll find the recently restored Naib Hamam, dating from 1640 (25 TL).

**Gaziantep Museum.** Gaziantep Museum houses a mix of antiquities from throughout the area's long history. The most interesting exhibits are from the Temple of Zeuz Doliche, north of the city, an important shrine until it was destroyed by the Persians in 253. Other finds range from mammoth bones and prehistoric pottery to Hittite statues and Roman surgical equipment. ⊠ *Kamil Ocak Stat Karşısı 1–2* ☎ *342/324–8809* ⌦ *5 TL* ☉ *May–Oct., daily 8:30–noon and 1–6; Nov.–Apr., daily 8:30–noon and 1–4:30.*

**Hasan Suzer Ethnographic Museum.** While exploring the warren of streets in the Bey neighborhood, step into a traditional Gaziantep house, with dressed-up mannequins filling in as residents. The basement carved out of the rock is a common feature of Antep houses, and the shady courtyard is a welcome retreat from the heat and blazing sun. The surprise exhibit is the captured motorcycle of Lawrence of Arabia, who spied against the Ottomans in World War I. ⊠ *Hanifioğlu Sok. 64* ☎ *342/230–4721* ⌦ *3 TL* ☉ *Tues.–Sun 8–noon, 1–5:30.*

**FodorśChoice** **Zeugma Museum and Conference Center.** What claims to be the largest
★ mosaic museum in the world houses a stunning collection of Roman-era mosaics rescued from a nearby archaeological site called Zeugma, which was submerged under the waters of a man-made lake. The intricate mosaics, some portraying scenes from Roman mythology, others more artistic geometric designs, are dazzling to behold. The fragment of

a mosaic depicting a young woman with an enigmatic gaze (called "The Gypsy Girl") is quickly earning Mona Lisa–like iconic status across Turkey. Many of the mosaics depict less common myths, such as that of Achilles, hidden by his mother before the Trojan War and disguised in women's clothing but tricked into showing interest in a sword, and Parthenope and Metiochus, a Romeo and Juliet of the ancient world. Destruction by illegal excavations is also highlighted, and several of the mosaics on display did time in private collections in the United States before being recovered. Unfortunately, the museum is a bit soulless and cavernous, and the lighting is very low. ⌂ *Sani Konukoğlu Bulvarı* 🖷 *5 TL* ☉ *Tues.–Sun. 9–7.*

## WHERE TO EAT AND STAY
*For expanded hotel reviews, visit Fodors.com.*

¢ ✕ **Baklavacı Güllüoğlu.** This little shop inside a spice bazaar is considered
TURKISH by many Turks nationwide to have the best baklava in the country. Run by a fifth-generation baklava maker, this humble store turns out a delicious version of the classic dessert, as well as other phyllo-and-nut-based sweets. ⌂ *Elmacı Pazarı 4* 🖷 *342/231–2105* ▭ *No credit cards* ☉ *Closed Sun.*

$ ✕ **Bayazhane.** Dining in this warehouse built in 1909 for a tobacco mer-
TURKISH chant is in either a large outdoor courtyard or the cool stone-vaulted chambers at the back. There is a good sampling of such local dishes as smoky eggplant kebabs, as well as meatball and yogurt soup, *yavurma*. This is not only one of the nicest places in town, but one of the few that serves alcohol. ⌂ *Atatürk Bulvarı 119, about 700 m west of İstasyon Cad.* 🖷 *342/221–0212.*

$ ✕ **Imam Çağdaş.** Open since 1887, Imam Çağdaş is certainly doing some-
TURKISH thing right, and the crowds pack this restaurant in the bazaar district
Fodor's Choice day and night. The food is earthy and sublime, from the *Ali Nazik*,
★ minced meat kebab served on puree of roasted eggplant, garlic, and yogurt, to the *sebzeli* kebab, a skewer of lamb minced with garlic and parsley. Finish your meal with the restaurant's terrific syrupy baklava, so widely regarded as the best that orders have regularly been received from Turkish presidents and from as far afield as Fidel Castro. ⌂ *Kale Civarı Uzun Çarşı, behind Bedestan* 🖷 *342/220–4545.*

¢ ✕ **Yörem.** Head here for a break from kebabs and get a taste of classic
TURKISH Gaziantep home cooking. A local woman who returned to Gaziantep
★ after living in Europe for several years rotates her menu on a regular basis, but the food is consistently good. Dishes to try include *yuvalama*, a meat and dumpling stew; *omaç*, a kind of patty made of bread, tomato, onion, and parsley; and *kezan* kebab, eggplant stuffed with meat and poached. For dessert try the local specialty *zerde sutlaç*, rice pudding with a saffron topping. The restaurant is a bit difficult to find—it's one block east of Fevzi Çakmak Caddesi, which runs north from the Gaziantep Museum. ⌂ *Incilpinar Mahallesi 3. Cad. 15, Sokak* 🖷 *342/230–5000.*

$$ 🖫 **Anadolu Evleri.** Down a narrow alleyway, behind a high wall hides
Fodor's Choice this gem, four stylish but comfortable historic Gaziantep stone houses,
★ where rooms have been meticulously restored and are charmingly decorated with quirky antiques like old radios, sewing machines, and

antique telephones. **Pros:** romantic setting; friendly staff; owner speaks fluent English. **Cons:** no swimming pool or hammam, though it's only a few minutes' walk to the best one in town. ⊠ *Şekeroğlu Mahallesi Köroğlu Sok. 6* 🕾 *342/220–9525* ⊕ *www.anadoluevleri.com* ⤣ *10 rooms, 3 suites* ⚲ *In-room: no TV, Wi-Fi* ⍾ *Breakfast.*

$    ⊡ **Kale Evi.** Suites in a restored old building just below Gaziantep's landmark castle are a good value, each with living room, bedroom, and large bath. **Pros:** great value; excellent location. **Cons:** decor can be oppressive. ⊠ *Köprübaşı Sok. 2* 🕾 *342/231–4142* ⊕ *www.kaleevi.com* ⤣ *2 rooms, 6 suites* ⚲ *In-room: Wi-Fi. In-hotel: restaurant.*

$    ⊡ **Zeynep Hanım Konağı.** Rooms in this restored old house on the winding streets of the gentrifying Bey neighborhood are decorated with wooden reproduction furnitue and Turkish carpets, and breakfast is served in an atmospheric old cellar. **Pros:** friendly staff; atmospheric location; nice rooms are a good value. **Cons:** a little lacking in character; can be difficult to find in the backstreets; parking is a short distance from the hotel. ⊠ *Eski Sinema Sok. 17* 🕾 *342/232–0207* ⤣ *12 rooms, 2 suites* ⚲ *In-room: Wi-Fi.*

## HALFETI

*20 km (12 mi) northeast of Gaziantep.*

Halfeti, a small town of honey-color stone houses on the Euphrates, became half-Halfeti with the flooding of the Birecik Dam in 2000. Enough survives for a pleasant excursion, and there are many small restaurants by the water. The only actual landmark is the town's former mosque, so close to the dam that the water now laps around its door. From Halfeti boats take visitors on excursions on the lake, here more like a wide river, to Rumkale, the "Castle of the Romans." The seat of an Armenian Patriarch from the 12th century, the castle is impressive from the outside, but due to ongoing restoration that's all you see. Beyond Rumkale the boats normally continue to another semisunken village, Savaş, where the minaret pokes out of the water. The trips costs about 50 TL for a boat, which can take around 10 people, and last about 90 minutes.

## KÂHTA

*174 km (108 mi) northeast of Gaziantep.*

The quiet and dusty little town of Kâhta is nobody's favorite place in Turkey and is really nothing more than a good base for exploring Mt. Nemrut. There are a few good hotels and places to eat, but nothing to see.

The construction of the large Atatürk Dam and the resulting rising waters have meant that Kâhta is now a lakeside town, and a number of restaurants have taken advantage of this, opening up near the water, which makes for a pleasant setting for a meal.

**GETTING HERE AND AROUND**

From Gaziantep follow D850 to Adıyaman, where it becomes D360, and continue on to Kâhta. Regular minivans make the run from Gaziantep to Urfa and from Urfa to Adiyaman, where you can catch a minivan to Kahta. There's an *otogar* (bus station) in each of the main towns.

**ESSENTIALS**

**Tour Essentials Nemrut Tours** ☎ *416/725–6881.*

**WHERE TO EAT AND STAY**

*For expanded hotel reviews, visit Fodors.com.*

¢ ✕ **Kahta Sofrası.** The pickings might be slim in Kâhta, but this place
TURKISH stands out for its friendly service and well-made food, including freshly baked *pide* as well as kebabs and prepared dishes like roast chicken and lamb stew. The restaurant is decorated with colorful rugs and is bright and open. ⊠ *Mustafa Kemal Cad. 15* ☎ *416/726–2055.*

¢ ✕ **Neşet'in Yeri.** This lakeside restaurant has an outdoor area shaded
TURKISH by an impressive grape arbor where you can eat trout or kebab while looking at the water. It's a nice spot to unwind after a visit to Nemrut. ⊠ *Baraj Kenari* ☎ *416/725–7675.*

$$ ⌂ **Zeus Hotel.** With a pool, quiet garden, and spacious and comfortable rooms, each with a small couch, this well-run hotel is a good base for visiting Mt. Nemrut. **Pros:** pool and nice garden. **Cons:** a little dated. ⊠ *Namık Kemal Cad. 20* ☎ *416/725–5694* ⊕ *www.zeushotel.com.tr* ⌂ *58 rooms, 8 suites* ♿ *In-room: a/c, Internet. In-hotel: restaurant, bar, pool* ⌁*Breakfast.*

## MT. NEMRUT AND ENVIRONS

*228 km (142 mi) northeast of Gaziantep.*

Fodor'sChoice **Mt. Nemrut (Nemrut Dağı).** *See the highlighted feature in this chapter.*
★

**WHERE TO STAY**

*For expanded hotel reviews, visit Fodors.com.*

$$$ ⌂ **Hotel Euphrat.** This low stone building, with spartan but clean rooms and good new bathrooms, is the best of the few places to stay on Mt. Nemrut itself. **Pros:** best rooms on the mountain. **Cons:** tour group central; half board required. ⊠ *Nemrut Dağı, 54 km (34 mi) from Kâhta, Karadut Köyü* ☎ *416/737–2175* 🖷 *416/737–2179* ⌂ *52 rooms* ♿ *In-room: no TV. In-hotel: restaurant, pool, parking* ⌁*Some meals.*

## URFA (ŞANLIURFA)

*143 km (89 mi) southeast of Kâhta; 135 km (84 mi) east of Gaziantep.*

★ With its golden-color stone houses, religious shrines filled with visiting pilgrims, and an authentic bazaar displaying mounds and mounds of the local specialty, crushed red pepper, in various shades and levels of spiciness, Urfa has a timeless quality to it. The city lies at the edge of the Syrian Desert, not far from the border with Syria and, like Gaziantep, also has a strong Middle Eastern flavor—literally as well as figuratively, because the local food has a distinct Armenian influence. Formerly a sleepy and arid frontier town that underwent a huge boom due to

*Continued on page 458*

# MEGALOMANIA ON MOUNT NEMRUT

*"I, Antiochus, caused this monument to be erected in commemoration of my own glory and of that of the gods."*

At the top of remote Mount Nemrut (Nemrut Daği), the monumental tomb of Antiochus (ruled c.69–34 BC), king of the obscure and short-lived kingdom of Commagene on the Euphrates, is one of the world's most extraordinary archaeological sights. Antiochus fancied himself a ruler on par with the gods of antiquity, so he had this grandiose monument to himself erected, to be in the company of his peers.

At 2,150 m (7,053 ft), Mt. Nemrut, not far from the Syrian border, is the highest peak in the area. At the center of the mountaintop site is a huge tumulus, or burial mound of small stones. To the east and west of the burial mound are two great platforms, each with an identical giant statue of Antiochus seated with his fellow gods, overlooking the desertlike landscape and the Euphrates River to the east. Over the years the statues have fallen and now the disembodied stone heads stand separate from their bodies.

Statue heads on West Terrace

# WHAT TO SEE

### 1 The Tumulus
The center of the site is the giant tumulus, 500 feet in diameter and 150 feet high, made of small pebbles. It's believed that the entrance to King Antiochus's tomb is underneath the rocks, but despite several attempts at tunneling, it has yet to be found.

### THE TERRACES
To the east and west of the tumulus, the land was leveled into large terraces where giant statues of Antiochus and the gods were erected. Annual religious ceremonies were performed here.

### 2 The East Terrace
On the east terrace, the stone bodies of the statues are quite well preserved, giving the best idea of what they originally looked like. The heads are more worn, and are now lined up at the feet of their respective bodies. The head of Tyche is said to have sat on her statue's stone shoulders until as late as the 1960s.

### 3 The West Terrace
On the west terrace, the statue bodies have crumbled, but the heads, scattered around the area, are well preserved; these are the now classic images of Mount Nemrut.

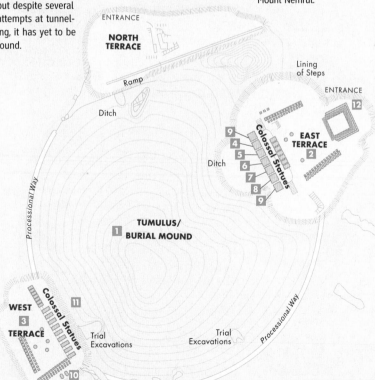

Above: The tumulus

## THE GODS

King Antiochus had himself depicted enthroned with his fellow gods in a matching set of 30-ft-tall stone murals on the east and west terraces. The images of the gods are a mix of eastern and western styles, their faces Greek, their clothes Persian.

**4 Hercules, Artagnes, and Ares** Hercules is bearded, but with a simpler hat than Zeus. Artagnes, or Vahram, was a Persian warrior god, here combined with both the hero Hercules, and Ares, the Greek god of war. On the east terrace, the statue of Hercules bears the symbol of the club.

**5 King Antiochus** In front of the statues stood a smaller stele of Antiochus posing with his fellow gods. The image of the king was on the left, beardless with a long thin, plume-like hat.

**6 Zeus-Oromasdes** Zeus, mixed with his Persian equivalent Oromasdes or Ahura Mazda, stood in the center of the site, his stone throne slightly higher than the rest. His bearded face is hard to distinguish from Hercules, but look for the circle and diamond pattern on his conical hat.

**7 The Tyche of Commagene** Tyche, the goddess of fortune, is the only female figure here and, therefore, the easiest to spot. As an embodiment of fortune and abundance, her headdress is filled with fruit.

Hercules

**8 Apollo, Hermes, Helius, and Mithra** Apollo is another beardless male, with a simpler, more conical, hat than that of Antiochus. The ancients apparently weren't sure who was the Greek equivalent of the Persian Mithra, spirit of light, so his image is a mix of Apollo (the sun god), Helios (the sun itself), and Hermes (the messenger god).

**9 Animal Protectors** On either side of the gods stood a giant lion and eagle, which acted as their protectors. The eagles were built of multiple pieces, as were the gods, and their heads sit together on the west terrace.

**10 The Ancestors** Antiochus had some of the most royal blood in the ancient world. On the back of his throne is carved his royal pedigree: the kings of Persia and Armenia on his father's side, and the Greco-Macedonian kings who ruled the empire of Alexander the Great on his mother's side. Around the great statues are carved reliefs depicting Antiochus with his ancestors. The best preserved are those of him with the great kings of Persia—Darius and Xerxes—on the south side of the west terrace.

**11 The Lion Horoscope** A relief found on the west terrace has been called the world's oldest horoscope. It depicts a lion (representing the constellation Leo), 19 "stars," including the planets Mars, Mercury, and Jupiter, and the crescent moon. Archaeoastronomers have identified the date of this horoscope as either July 109 BC, perhaps the date of Antiochus's father's coronation, or July 61 BC, believed to be that of Antiochus's own coronation. The relief has been removed for restoration and may be replaced with a replica.

**12 The Fire Altar** The sacred fire was a central part of the Persian Zoroastrian religion and the east terrace featured a large fire altar—it's hardly noticed today, although the area is the most popular place for tourists to watch the sunrise.

The Lion Horoscope

**DID YOU KNOW?**

There's no connection
between Mt. Nemrut
and the Biblical Nimrod
(Nemrut in English), creator
of the Tower of Babel.
Somehow the name
got attached and stuck;
Antiochus must be turning
in his monumental grave.

# THE ROAD TO NEMRUT AND WHAT TO SEE ON IT

There are several ancient sites along the road from Kâhta to Nemrut that have become standard stops for visitors to the mountain.

King Antiochus and Hercules at Arsameia

## THE BURIAL MOUND OF KARAKUŞ

A second royal tumulus—it lacks the grandeur of the more famous mountaintop monument—was built by Antiochus's son, for his sister, wife, and daughter. The name Karakuş, or black bird, comes from the statue of an eagle, set on a large column beside the tomb.

## CENDERE BRIDGE

Photos don't do justice to the scale of this huge bridge, a monument to Roman engineering: three large columns once held statues of the Emperor Septimius Severus, his wife Julia Domna, and their son, the future emperor Caracalla. A fourth was probably for the second son, Geta, who was killed by Caracalla, who also tried to erase all trace of his brother's existence.

## ARSAMEIA

Partway up the mountain are the few remains of what is left of Arsameia, the summer home of the kings of Commagene: several carved stelai, the most famous picturing King Antiochus in Persian dress with a very naked Hercules. Above is a long inscription in Greek with a deep tunnel disappearing into the mountain.

## ESKI KÂHTA

The small traditional village of Eski (old) Kâhta is just off the main road where the mountains start. There is a castle here with a view over a dramatic gorge.

### GETTING THERE

Uninspiring Kâhta is the closest town to Mount Nemrut; from here it's a 2-hour drive. The road is good, but steep and bumpy in places, and it can be very windy. You may want to stay in Kâhta and let someone else take the wheel; tours (110-250 TL) also mean the benefit of a guide (there are also multiday tours from Cappadocia). Most tours are timed for sunrise or sunset, when the landscape and its monuments are at their most dramatic—note that in summer, sunrise tours can require a 2 am departure. Dress warmly: even in high summer, nights are chilly atop the mountain. Nemrut can only be visited between about May and October, as snow makes the road to the top impassable in winter. ✈ 7 TL ◷ Daily dawn to dusk.

GAP (the Güneydoğu Anadolu Projesi, or Southeast Anatolia Project, a large-scale damming and irrigation program undertaken by the Turkish government), Urfa is most famous as the supposed birthplace of the biblical patriarch Abraham. A half-dozen mosques crowd around the cave where many Muslims believe Abraham was born, and a pool near the cave is filled with what are believed to be sacred carp.

Urfa is sometimes known as Şanlıurfa; *şanlı,* or "famous," was added by an act of parliament to the city's name in 1984 to commemorate the city's resistance to the French military occupation of the area following World War I. Urfa's old town, at the southern foot of Divan Caddesi, is a remarkable mix of Byzantine, Arab and Ottoman architecture, albeit heavily eroded over the centuries.

Urfa is also the heartland of the unromantically name Pre-Pottery Neolithic Era, a stage of prehistory some 13,500 years ago when humankind was making the first steps toward settlement and agriculture. In the Urfa Museum you can see what is arguably the worlds oldest statue and at nearby Göbekli Tepe see the oldest monumental construction.

### GETTING HERE AND AROUND
Turkish Airlines and Pegasus fly regularly to Urfa from Ankara and Istanbul. By car, Urfa is 135 km (84 mi) east of Gaziantep on E90 and 192 km (120 mi) west of Mardin on E90. Urfa is 143 km (89 mi) southeast of Kâhta on D875. Regular minivans make the run from Gaziantep to Urfa.

### ESSENTIALS
**Guided Tours** Harran-Nemrut tours in Urfa are run by the English-speaking Özcan Aslan, who is friendly and helpful. He can arrange trips to Harran and the surrounding region and also offers one- and two-day tours to Mt. Nemrut from Urfa.

**Tour Information Harran-Nemrut** ☏ *414/215–1575* ✉ *ozcan_aslant_ teacher@hotmail.com.*

**Visitor Information Şanlıurfa** ✉ *Atatürk Bulvarı 4, kiosk on corner* ☏ *414/312–5332.*

### EXPLORING
**Archaeological museum.** Urfa has a small but appealing archaeology museum, covering the area's long history. Especially interesting are sculptures from Göbekli Tepe but the star, unmarked beside the entrance, is a white, alien-looking statue, found in the Gölbaşı Lake in 1993. Nearly 13,500 years old, it is the world's oldest full-size man-made human figure. There are also Hittite sculptures from the area, a collection of exquisite carved antique wooden doors, and classical sculpture in the garden. ✉ *Çamlık Cad.* ☏ *414/313–1588* 💳 *3 TL* ☉ *Tues.–Sun. 8–5.*

**Bazaar.** A short walk east from the park leads to Urfa's bazaar, where in summertime merchants wait patiently in the hot sun for the occasional tour group. The bazaar is filled with small *hans*—a collection of stores and workshops built around a central courtyard—that have tailors, coppersmiths, and other artisans working away, using what seem like ancient machines and tools. At the literal heart of the bazaar is the wonderful *bedestan* and adjacent Gümrük Han, a large courtyard filled with

The gold-color houses of Urfa.

chatting men playing backgammon or chess and sipping tea. Around the courtyard are the small workshops of tailors sewing inexpensive suits. The bazaar is a good place to shop for spices and copper items and you can usually find bargains, especially on carpets and kilims.

**Gölbaşı Parkı.** Gölbaşı Parkı, home of the famed carp pools, is a shady oasis on hot days or summer evenings. According to legend, King Nimrod, angry at Abraham's condemnation of the king's Assyrian polytheism, set about immolating the patriarch. God awakened natural springs, dousing the fire and saving Abraham. The carp, according to the myth, are an incarnation of the wood from Abraham's pyre. Historically the story might not, well, hold water—probably part of a pre-Christian fish shrine, the gorgeous springs remain. The place has a serene and distinctly spiritual feel to it, with groups of visiting pilgrims and families from Turkey and neighboring countries strolling about and feeding what are probably the most pampered fish in the world. Look for the Byzantine era belltower beside the lake. ⊠ *Near center of town* ⌑ *Free* ⊙ *Dawn–dusk.*

**Güzel Sanatlar Galerisi.** Güzel Sanatlar Galerisi, the city's art gallery, right next to the post office, is another restored house that's worth visiting. The art may not be so impressive, but the stone mansion has delightful relief-carving work on its exterior and a lovely indoor courtyard. ⊠ *Sarayönü Cad.* ☎ *No phone* ⌑ *Free* ⊙ *Weekdays 8:30–5, Sat. noon–4.*

**Hazreti İbrahim Doğum Mağarası** (*Prophet İbrahim's Birth Cave*). Local legend has it that Abraham was born in this natural cave hidden behind the Hasan Paşa Mosque in the southeast corner of Gölbaşı Parkı. As is usual, men and women enter through separate doorways. Most people huddled inside this small, dark cavern, darkened by 2,000 years of candle smoke, have come to pray, not to snap photos. There's not much to see, but the atmosphere is reverential. Tourists are welcome (many of the visitors inside are themselves from out of town), but remember that this is a shrine. ⊠ *Göl Cad.* ☎ *No phone* ☐ *Free* ☉ *Daily sunrise–sunset.*

**The Haleplibahçe mosaics.** A recently discovered Byzantine villa in the Haleplibahçe district, just beyond Gölbaşı, has revealed a wealth of mosaics. You enter via what was a long porch, where mosaics depict the life of Achilles, including his mother holding him by the heel and dipping him in the waters of the River Styx. Just beyond is a large hall, with damaged mosaics flanked by the remains of two fountains. At the very rear is a magnificent scene of Amazon queens hunting wild beasts. ⊠ *West side of park beyond Al Ruha Hotel, in the garden of Koruma Amaçlı İmar Müdürlüğü, Haleplibahçe* ☐ *Free* ☉ *Dawn–dusk.*

**İl Özel İdaresi Vali Kemalettin Gazezoğlu Kultur ve Sanat Merkezi.** Urfa's old neighborhoods are filled with lovely stone homes covered with ornamental carving, and several hours exploring will be time well spent. One place worth seeking out is the old Assyrian church complex, İl Özel İdaresi Vali Kemalettin Gazezoğlu Kultur ve Sanat Merkezi—it's a mouthful, but neighborhood locals should be able to point you in the right direction—that has been restored and turned into a cultural center. The hours are unpredictable, but the walk there leads you through narrow alleyways and past several beautiful old houses. ⊠ *Kurtuluş Sok.* ☎ *No phone* ☐ *Free* ☉ *Irregular hrs.*

**Ulu Camii.** Urfa's principal mosque was built in the 12th century by Nur al-Din after he captured the city from the Crusaders. It is a relatively simple long vaulted hall, on the southern end of a long grassy courtyard. The town's cathedral once stood here, and you can see the giant octagonal belltower. ⊠ *Just north of bazaar.*

**Urfa Kale** (*Urfa Fortress*). Apart from the two prominent Roman Columns, the Urfa Kale (castle) is a motley collection of upturned stones, at the top of a lot of stairs. It's impossible to detect any one architectural intent here, probably because the fortress has been razed and rebuilt at least a dozen times since the 2nd century BC. Climb to the summit for a fantastic view of the city. The stairs down are more fun, as they descend through a tunnel cut from the rock. ⊠ *Kale Cad.* ☎ *No phone* ☐ *$2* ☉ *Daily 9–6.*

OFF THE
BEATEN
PATH
Fodor'sChoice
★

**Göbekli Tepe.** Erected around 9,000 BC, 6,000 years before Stonehenge, before even the invention of agriculture, this series of stone circles on a hill 15 km (9 mi) northeast of the town of Urfa have been popularly declared the "World's Oldest Temple." The stones' purpose has been subject to wide interpretation: Some believe this was a burial site; others, a place of ritual initiation, or that each circle belonged to a different tribe that gathered here for ritual and trade. What is clear, though, is that no one lived here, and that it would have taken hundreds of people to transport and erect the pillars. The site is formed by a series of circles and ovals formed by large T-shaped pillars of equal height, usually with two larger pillars inside. The pillars are thought to have held a roof. Many of the outer surfaces are carved, some are anthropomorphic, others depict the savage nightmares of a hunter-gatherer's life, such as snakes, foxes, vultures, scorpions, and wild boar. Most curiously of all, the structures were deliberately buried when the site was abandoned. Four structures have been exposed since excavations began in 1995, and another 16 have been identified by geophysicists; excavations continue in spring and fall. The circles themselves are off-limits and enclosed by low fences, but visitors are welcome to follow pathways from which all is clearly visible. Take the old highway, the D400 east from Şanlıurfa, and look for the marked turning on the left just as you leave the built-up area. This road continues about 15 km (10 mi), crossing over the new highway. Shortly after this is a turn, left for the last few miles up the hill to the site. ⊠ *15 km (9 mi.) northeast of Urfa, Albania* ⊠ *Free* ☉ *Dawn–dusk.*

## WHERE TO EAT AND STAY

*For expanded hotel reviews, visit Fodors.com.*

**$**
TURKISH ✕ **Çardaklı Köşk.** An old Urfa stone house looks out over the city's citadel and the fish-pool complex. Sit on the terrace or in one of the several *çardaks,* small private rooms where you can recline on pillows. The food, the usual mix of kebabs and *pides,* is unexciting, but the location makes up for it. ⊠ *Balıkgöl Civarı Tünel Çıkışı 1* ☎ *414/217–1080.*

**$**
TURKISH ✕ **Urfa Sofrası.** On an outdoor terrace overlooking a small park and the busy streets below, you can order kebabs, *pide,* and *lahmacun* and *kaburga* (lamb stuffed with rice). The dishes come served with a cold and refreshing yogurt soup made with chickpeas and wheat berries. Finish your meal with a small cup of bracing Arab-style bitter coffee, served by a roving waiter who pours the coffee from his copper urn. ⊠ *Karakoyun Işmerkezi Kat 1 No. 226, upstairs in shopping center near tourist office* ☎ *414/315–6130.*

**$$**
★ ▦ **Cevahir Konuk Evi.** Formerly a government guesthouse, this grand old stone home with a great view from its terrace, has hallways lined with colorful rugs and antique furniture, while the rooms have high ceilings, stone walls, and white bedspreads embroidered with flowers. **Pros:** rooms are surprisingly modern and spacious for the price; pleasant patio where breakfast and dinner are served. **Cons:** those looking for peace and quiet may not appreciate the live music most nights. ⊠ *Büyükyol Selahattin Eyyubi Cami, Karşısı* ☎ *414/215–9377* ⊕ *www.cevahirkonukevi.com* ⊗ *6 rooms, 1 suite* ⚲ *In-room: Wi-Fi. In-hotel: restaurant* ¦⊙¦ *Breakfast.*

**$$**
★ ▦ **Hotel El-Ruha.** Built of local stone, in imitation of local houses, this sprawling new hotel tries to mix local character with five-star luxury and offers spacious and comfortable rooms, with large beds, wood furniture, vaulted ceilings, and bathrooms with mosaiclike tiles and bath; most rooms have a view of the fish pool complex. **Pros:** modern design with character; pool; central location. **Cons:** large and rather anonymous; why stay in a fake old building when you can enjoy the real thing at other lodgings? ⊠ *Balıklıgöl* ☎ *414/215–4411* ⊕ *www.hotelelruha.com* ⊗ *71 rooms, 11 suites* ⚲ *In-room: Wi-Fi. In-hotel: restaurant, gym, parking* ¦⊙¦ *Breakfast.*

**¢**
▦ **Urfa Evi.** A series of old houses near the fish ponds, now in the hands of the tourism faculty of the local university, offer an enormous range

**7**

of rooms, some cut out of the rock à la Cappadocia; they are generally large and nicely furnished with wood pieces. **Pros:** good location, nice old building. **Cons:** run by trainees. ⊠ *Göl Cad. 44, Balıklıgöl* ☎ *414/215–5995* ⤵ *10 rooms* ⚒ *In-hotel: restaurant* ⍾ *No meals.*

# HARRAN

*50 km (31 mi) southeast of Urfa.*

A quick ride from Urfa, the ancient city of Harran is well worth a visit. The Urfa region is rife with dubious biblical legends, but there seems to be almost unanimous agreement that this Harran of modern Turkey is quite likely the Harran mentioned in the Old Testament as a place where Abraham spent some time before heading off to the promised land. True or not, today's Harran stands on the spot of a very ancient settlement, with crumbling fortifications surrounding what is now a simple village and the ruins of what was once the world's first Islamic university, built in the 8th century, just on the edge of town. Called the **Ulu Cami,** all that's left is a distinctive square minaret that can be seen from throughout Harran. Indeed, in Harran visitors get the sense that not much has changed here over the centuries, and some of the pastoral scenes around Harran, of shepherds driving their flocks of sheep along seem, well, almost biblical.

Harran's main claims to fame, besides playing host to Abraham, are its beehive-shape houses, wondrous structures built of hay and mud, each topped with a conical roof. The small town is filled with them, although many are no longer family dwellings and are now used as stables or are in the process of collapsing.

## EXPLORING

**The Geleneksel Konik Kubbeli Evi.** The Geleneksel Konik Kubbeli Evi, just down the road from the Harran Evi is another reconstruction of a beehive house built by a rival local family and also worth visiting. The family who lives here is especially friendly and rather exuberant, literally running up to the entrance gate with broad smiles to greet visitors. ⊠ *Ceşme Sok. 23* ☎ *542/337–8512* 🎫 *Free* ☉ *Daily 8 am–10 pm.*

**The Harran Evi.** The Harran Evi is a good reconstruction of a traditional beehive home where you can take a tour of the inside living quarters and hear the guide extol the virtues—cool in summer, warm in winter—of its unique construction. After the tour, you can sit down for tea or a cold drink in the courtyard or in a rug-lined room inside the beehive house itself. ⊠ *Ibni Teymiye Mah* ☎ *414/441–2020* 🎫 *Free* ☉ *Daily 8 am–10 pm.*

# UNDERSTANDING
# TURKEY

---

**BOOKS AND MOVIES**

---

**VOCABULARY**

# BOOKS AND MOVIES

## Books

Whether Homer's *Iliad* should be classified as fiction or nonfiction is up for debate, but it's still the most evocative reading on the Trojan War and the key players of Turkish antiquity.

**Memoirs, Essays and Observations.** For keen insight into the ancient ruins that you may encounter on your trip, try George Bean, author of *Aegean Turkey, Turkey Beyond the Meander, Lycian Turkey,* and *Turkey's Southern Shore.* John Julius Norwich's three-volume *Byzantium* chronicles the rise and fall of one of history's great empires, while Caroline Finkel's *Osman's Dream* provides a comprehensive overview of the history of the Ottoman Empire.

Mary Lee Settle provides a vision of Turkey that is both panoramic and personal in *Turkish Reflections.* The book marks Settle's return to the country that was the setting for her novel *Blood Tie,* a 1978 National Book Award winner. Dame Freya Stark chronicles her visits to Turkey in *The Journey's Echo* and *Alexander's Path.* Only a piece of Mark Twain's *Innocents Abroad* is about Turkey, but it offers a witty glimpse of the country as it used to be. Hans Christian Andersen also wrote a memorable travelogue, *A Poet's Bazaar: A Journey to Greece, Turkey and up the Danube. The Letters and Works of Lady Mary Wortley Montagu* is a significant and entertaining book that delightfully documents life in 18th-century Ottoman Turkey—including its much-quoted passages about the harem—through the eyes of the wife of a British consul.

Irfan Orga's exquisite *Portrait of a Turkish Family* is an evocative memoir weaving personal history with modern politics as it addresses the impact of the upheavals of the early 20th century on his own family. Orhan Pamuk's *Istanbul: Memories of a City* interweaves the novelist's memories of his childhood and youth with black-and-white photographs and vignettes from the city's history; many think this nonfiction is much more readable than his fiction.

**History.** For modern Turkish history and politics, try *Turkey: A Modern History,* by Erik J. Zürcher, or *Turkey Unveiled,* an accessible, journalistic account of Turkish politics by Nicole and Hugh Pope.

More books have been written about Istanbul than about the rest of Turkey. Two of the finest portraits of the city are the excellent *Constantinople: City of the World's Desire 1453–1924,* by Philip Mansel, and *Istanbul: The Imperial City,* by John Freely.

**Literature and Fiction.** For an introduction to Turkish literature, track down a copy of *An Anthology of Turkish Literature,* by Kemal Silay. If you prefer to plunge into a complete novel, look out for *Anatolian Tales* or *Mehmet, My Hawk,* by Yaşar Kemal, one of the country's most famous modern novelists. Of the younger generation of Turkish writers, the best known is Orhan Pamuk, whose dense melancholy prose means that his work is often more highly regarded than it is enjoyed. His novels include *My Name Is Red* and the acclaimed *Snow.* Louis de Bernieres's novel *Birds Without Wings* offers a portrayal of rural life in western Anatolia during the final years of the Ottoman Empire.

Agatha Christie's novel *Murder on the Orient Express* provides the proper atmosphere for a trip to Istanbul, and you can still visit Istanbul's Pera Palas Hotel, the terminus of the famous train, where Christie herself stayed. Harold Nicolson's *Sweet Waters* is usually billed as a thriller although it is more of a love story, and the detail draws heavily on the author's years as a junior diplomat in Istanbul in the years leading up to the outbreak of World War I. If you love spy novels, *Istanbul Intrigues,* by Barry Rubin, paints a vivid picture of real cloak-and-dagger intrigues in the city during World War II.

**Poetry.** *The Penguin Book of Turkish Verse* offers a good selection in English of leading Ottoman and Turkish poets. Nazım Hikmet (1901–63) is generally regarded as Turkey's greatest, if still controversial, poet, and Randy Blasing and Mutlu Konuk have produced excellent English versions of Hikmet's most important poems in *Poems of Nazim Hikmet* and his extraordinary verse epic *Human Landscapes*. (The best English-language biography of Nazım Hikmet is *Romantic Communist*, by Saime Göksu and Edward Timms.)

The poetry of the Sufi mystic Rumi has few rivals in any language, whether for the beauty of his words or for his message of universal love and tolerance. There are several translations of his poetry: the best known include *Rumi: Poet and Mystic*, by Reynold Nicholson, *The Essential Rumi*, by Coleman Barks, and *Rumi: In the Arms of the Beloved,* by Jonathan Star.

## Movies

Western movies filmed in Turkey obviously tend to play up Turkey's exotic aspects, for better or worse. Director Joseph L. Mankiewicz's *Five Fingers* (1952), an Ankara-based spy thriller based on the book *Operation Cicero*, by C.L. Moyzisch, is noteworthy both for its action and for its clever dialogue ("Counter espionage is the highest form of gossip"). Peter Ustinov won an Academy Award for best supporting actor for his performance in the Jules Dassin–directed museum-heist film *Topkapi* (1964), which also stars Melina Mercouri and Maximilian Schell.

Alan Parker directed the film version of *Midnight Express* (1978), about Billy Hayes's days in a Turkish prison following a drug conviction. The film's horrific depiction of Hayes's experiences (some of which were not in his memoir) made the Turkish government gun-shy about allowing Western moviemakers into the country. When *Midnight Express* was finally shown on Turkish TV in the mid-1990s, newscasters interviewed people in the street, who wept over the country's portrayal on-screen and the influence they feared the film may have had on perceptions of Turkey in the West.

Peter Weir's *Gallipoli* (1981) follows the exploits of two Australian soldiers preparing for and fighting in the historic battle in the Dardanelles during World War I. Critics generally praise the film, though some have noted a lack of sensitivity to the Turks.

Turkish movies now regularly feature at international film festivals, and an increasing number are available on DVD (although most on sale in Turkey are Region 2, so you will need a multiregion DVD player to be able to play them in the United States). Notable ones include: Nuri Bilge Ceylan's *Uzak* (2000), a hauntingly beautiful depiction of loneliness, set in Istanbul, that manages to be simultaneously melancholic, humorous, and uplifting; Yılmaz Erdoğan and Ömer Faruk Sorak's *Vizontele* (2001), a charming and often hilarious portrayal of the effect of the arrival of electricity on a rural community; and Fatih Akın's *Head-On* (*Gegen die Wand*) (2004), a stunning, if frequently brutal, love story of a couple who build a relationship out of their shattered lives. Turkey finally took revenge for *Midnight Express* with Serdar Akar and Sadullah Şentürk's *Valley of the Wolves: Iraq* (2006). Poorly scripted, anti-Semitic, and anti-American in tone, the movie nevertheless lays bare some of the many complexes and conspiracy theories that underpin popular Turkish conceptions of current events; it broke all box office records in Turkey on its release.

# TURKISH VOCABULARY

| | ENGLISH | TURKISH | PRONUNCIATION |
|---|---|---|---|
| **BASICS** | | | |
| | Hello | Merhaba | mer-**hab**-a |
| | Yes/no | Evet/hayır | **eh**-vet/**hi**-yer |
| | Please | Lütfen | **lewt**-fen |
| | Thank you | Teşekkür ederim | tay-shake-**kur** eh-day-**reem** |
| | You're welcome | Rica ederim/ Bir şey değil | ree-**jah** eh-day-**reem**/beer shay **day**-eel |
| | Sorry | Özür dilerim | oh-**zewr** deel-air-eem |
| | Sorry | Pardon | **pahr**-dohn |
| | Good morning | Günaydın | goon-eye-**den** |
| | Good day | İyi günler | ee-yee gewn-**lair** |
| | Good evening | İyi akşamlar | ee-yee ahk-shahm-**lar** |
| | Goodbye | Allahaısmarladık/ Güle güle | **allah**-aw-ees-mar-law-deck/ **gew**-leh **gew**-leh |
| | Mr. (Sir) | Bey | by, bay |
| | Mrs./Miss | Hanım | ha-nem |
| | Pleased to meet you | Memnun oldum | **mam**-noon ohl-doom |
| | How are you? | Nasılsınız? | **nah**-suhl-suh-nuhz |
| **NUMBERS** | | | |
| | one half | buçuk | byoo-**chook** |
| | one | bir | beer |
| | two | iki | ee-**kee** |
| | three | üç | ooch |
| | four | dört | doort |
| | five | beş | besh |
| | six | altı | ahl-tuh |
| | seven | yedi | yed-dee |
| | eight | sekiz | sek-**keez** |
| | nine | dokuz | doh-**kooz** |
| | ten | on | **ohn** |
| | eleven | onbir | **ohn**-beer |

| ENGLISH | TURKISH | PRONUNCIATION |
|---|---|---|
| twelve | oniki | **ohn**-ee-kee |
| thirteen | onüç | **ohn**-ooch |
| fourteen | ondört | **ohn**-doort |
| fifteen | onbeş | **ohn**-besh |
| sixteen | onaltı | **ohn**-ahl-tuh |
| seventeen | onyedi | **ohn**-yed-dy |
| eighteen | onsekiz | **ohn**-sek-**keez** |
| nineteen | ondokuz | **ohn**-doh-**kooz** |
| twenty | yirmi | yeer-mee |
| twenty-one | yirmibir | **yeer**-mee-beer |
| thirty | otuz | oh-**tooz** |
| forty | kırk | kerk |
| fifty | elli | ehl-lee |
| sixty | altmış | **alt**-muhsh |
| seventy | yetmiş | **yeht**-meesh |
| eighty | seksen | sehk-san |
| ninety | doksan | dohk-**san** |
| one hundred | yüz | yewz |
| one thousand | bin | bean |
| one million | milyon | **mill**-ee-on |

## COLORS

| | | |
|---|---|---|
| black | siyah | **see**-yah |
| blue | mavi | **mah**-vee |
| brown | kahverengi | **kah**-vay-**rain**-gee |
| green | yeşil | yay-sheel |
| orange | portakal rengi | poor-tah-kahl rain-gee |
| red | kırmızı | ker-muz-uh |
| white | beyaz | **bay**-ahz |
| yellow | sarı | sah-**ruh** |

| ENGLISH | TURKISH | PRONUNCIATION |
|---------|---------|---------------|

**DAYS OF THE WEEK**

| | | |
|---------|---------|---------------|
| Sunday | Pazar | pahz-**ahr** |
| Monday | Pazartesi | pahz-**ahr**-teh-see |
| Tuesday | Salı | sa-**luh** |
| Wednesday | Çarşamba | char-shahm-bah |
| Thursday | Perşembe | pair-shem-beh |
| Friday | Cuma | joom-**ah** |
| Saturday | Cumartesi | joom-**ahr**-teh-see |

**MONTHS**

| | | |
|---------|---------|---------------|
| January | Ocak | oh-**jahk** |
| February | Şubat | shoo-**baht** |
| March | Mart | mart |
| April | Nisan | nee-**sahn** |
| May | Mayıs | my-us |
| June | Haziran | hah-zee-**rahn** |
| July | Temmuz | **tehm**-mooz |
| August | Ağustos | ah-oos-tohs |
| September | Eylül | ey-**lewl** |
| October | Ekim | eh-**keem** |
| November | Kasım | kah-suhm |
| December | Aralık | ah-rah-**luhk** |

**USEFUL PHRASES**

| | | |
|---------|---------|---------------|
| Do you speak English? | İngilizce biliyor musunuz? | in-**gee-leez**-jay bee-lee-**yohr** moo-soo-nooz |
| I don't speak Turkish. | Türkçe bilmiyorum. | **tewrk**-cheh **beel**-mee-yohr-um |
| I don't understand. | Anlamıyorum | ahn-**lah**-muh-yohr-um |
| I understand. | Anlıyorum | ahn-**luh**-yohr-um |
| I don't know. | Bilmiyorum | **beel**-meeh-yohr-um |
| I'm American. | Amerikalıyım | ahm-ay-**ree**-kah-luh-yuhm |
| I'm British. | İngilizim | **een**-gee-leez-eem |

| ENGLISH | TURKISH | PRONUNCIATION |
|---|---|---|
| What's your name? | İsminiz nedir? | ees-mee-niz nay-deer |
| My name is . . . | Benim adım . . . | bay-**neem** ah-duhm |
| What time is it? | Saat kaç? | sah-aht **kahch** |
| How? | Nasıl? | **nah**-suhl |
| When? | Ne zaman? | **nay** zah-mahn |
| Yesterday | Dün | dewn |
| Today | Bugün | **boo**-goon |
| Tomorrow | Yarın | **yah**-ruhn |
| This morning/ afternoon | Bu sabah/öğleden sonra | **boo** sah-bah/**ol-lay**-den sohn-rah |
| Tonight | Bu gece | **boo** ge-jeh |
| What? | Efendim?/Ne? | **eh**-fan-deem/neh |
| What is it? | Nedir? | **neh**-deer |
| Why? | Neden/Niçin? | **neh**-den/**nee**-chin |
| Who? | Kim? | keem |
| Where is . . . | Nerede . . . | **nayr**-deh |
| . . . the train station? | . . . tren istasyonu? | tee-**rehn** ees-**tah**-syohn-oo |
| . . . the subway station? | . . . metro duragı? | metro doo-**raw**-uh |
| . . . the bus stop? | . . . otobüs duragı? | oh-toh-**bewse** doo-**raw**-uh |
| . . . the     terminal? (airport) | . . . hava alanı? | hah-**vah ah**-lah-nuh |
| . . . the post office? | . . . postane? | post-**ahn**-eh |
| . . . the bank? | . . . banka? | **bahn**-kah |
| . . . the hotel? | . . . oteli? | oh-**tel-lee** |
| . . . the museum? | . . . müzesi? | mew-zay-**see** |
| . . . the hospital? | . . . hastane? | hahs-**tah**-neh |
| . . . the elevator? | . . . asansör? | ah-san-**sewr** |
| . . . the telephone? | . . . telefon? | teh-leh-**fohn** |
| Where     are     the restrooms? | Tuvalet nerede? | twah-**let** nayr-deh |

| ENGLISH | TURKISH | PRONUNCIATION |
|---|---|---|
| Here/there | Burası/Orası | **boo**-rah-suh/**ohr**-rah-suh |
| Left/right | sag/sol | sah-ah/sohl |
| Is it near/ | Yakın mı?/ | yah-**kuhn** muh/ |
| far? | Uzak mı? | ooz-**ahk**muh |
| I'd like . . . | istiyorum . . . | **ees**-tee-yohr-ruhm |
| . . . a room | Bir oda. . . | beer oh-**dah** |
| . . . the key | Anahtarı. . . | **ahn**-ah-tahr-uh |
| . . . a newspaper | Bir gazete. . . | beer **gahz**-teh |
| . . . a stamp | Pul. . . | pool |
| I'd like to buy . . . | almak istiyorum . . . | ahl-**mahk** ees-tee-your-ruhm |
| . . . cigarettes | Sigara. . . | **see**-gah-rah |
| . . . matches | Kibrit. . . | **keeb**-reet |
| . . . city map | Şehir planı. . . | shay-**heer plah**-nuh |
| . . . road map | Karayolları haritası. . . | **kah**-rah-yoh-lahr-**uh** hah-ree-tah-**suh** |
| . . . magazine | Dergi. . . | dair-gee |
| . . . envelopes | Zarf. . . | zahrf |
| . . . writing paper | Mektup kagıdı. . . | **make**-toop **kah**-uh-duh |
| . . . postcard | Kartpostal. . . | cart-poh-stahl |
| . . . ticket | Bilet. . . | bee-**let** |
| How much is it? | Fiyatı ne kadar? | fee-yaht-uh **neh** kah-dahr |
| It's expensive/cheap | pahalı/ucuz | pah-hah-**luh**/oo-**jooz** |
| A little/a lot | Az/çok | ahz/choke |
| More/less | daha çok/daha az | da-ha choke/da-ha ahz |
| Enough/too (much) | Yeter/çok fazla | yay-**tehr/choke** fahz-lah |
| I am ill/sick | Hastayım | **hahs**-tah-yum |
| Call a doctor | Doktor çağırın | dohk-toor **chah**-uh-run |
| Help! | İmdat! | eem-**daht** |
| Stop! | Durun! | doo-**roon** |

| ENGLISH | TURKISH | PRONUNCIATION |
|---|---|---|
| **DINING OUT** | | |
| A bottle of . . . | bir şişe . . . | **beer** shee-shay |
| A cup of . . . | bir fincan . . . | beer **feen**-jahn |
| A glass of . . . | bir bardak . . . | beer **bar**-dahk |
| Ashtray | kül tablası | kewl tah-blah-**suh** |
| Beer | bira | **bee**-ra |
| Bill/check | hesap | heh-**sahp** |
| Bread | ekmek | ekmek |
| Breakfast | kahvaltı | kah-**vahl**-tuh |
| Butter | tereyağı | tay-**reh**-yah-uh |
| Cocktail/aperitif | kokteyl, içki | cocktail, **each**-key |
| Coffee | kahve | **kah**-veh |
| Dinner | akşam yemegi | **ahk**-shahm yee-may-ee |
| Fixed-price menu | fiks menü | feex menu |
| Fork | çatal | **chah**-tahl |
| I am a vegetarian/I don't eat meat | vejeteryenim/et yemem | vegeterian-**eem**/eht yeh-**mem** |
| I cannot eat . . . | yiyemem . . . | **yee**-yay-mem |
| I'd like to order . . . | Ismarlamak isterim . . . | us-mahr-lah-**mahk** ee-stair-eem |
| I'd like . . . | . . . isterim | ee-stair-**em** |
| I'm hungry/thirsty | acıktım/susadım | ah-**juck**-tum/soo-sah-**dum** |
| Is service/the tip included? | servis fiyatı dahil mi? | sehr-vees **fee**-yah-tah dah-heel-**mee** |
| It's good/bad | güzel/güzel degil | gew-**zell**/gew-**zell day**-eel |
| It's hot/cold | sıcak/soguk | suh-**jack**/soh-**uk** |
| Knife | bıçak | buh-**chahk** |
| Lunch | ögle yemegi | **oi**-leh **yeh**-may-ee |
| Menu | menü | meh-**noo** |
| Napkin | peçete | **peh**-cheh-teh |
| Pepper | karabiber | kah-**rah**-bee-behr |
| Plate | tabak | tah-**bahk** |

| ENGLISH | TURKISH | PRONUNCIATION |
|---|---|---|
| Please give me . . . | lutfen bana . . . verirmisiniz | **loot**-fan bah-nah vair-**eer**-mee-see-niz |
| Salt | tuz | tooz |
| Spoon | kaşık | kah-**shuhk** |
| Tea | çay | chai |
| Water | su | soo |
| Wine | şarap | shah-**rahp** |

# Travel Smart Turkey

## WORD OF MOUTH

"Before your trip, be sure to check out what other travelers are saying in Talk on www.fodors.com."

# GETTING HERE AND AROUND

The most common way to get around Turkey, for both Turks and tourists, is by bus. If you don't mind the long ride, the extremely popular night buses that connect the major cities inland and on the coast are comfortable and inexpensive. If you are pressed for time or are traveling very long distances—for instance, if you are making an excursion to the eastern part of the country—you may prefer to fly. Once you've arrived at your destination, you can get around by taxi, minibus, *dolmuş* (shared taxi), or rented car. A car gives you more freedom to explore on your own but is more costly and the experience can be a bit stressful at times.

## ■ AIR TRAVEL

Flying time to Istanbul is 11 hours from New York, 13 hours from Chicago, and 15 hours from Los Angeles. Flights from Toronto to Istanbul take 11½ hours. London to Istanbul is a 4-hour flight. In Turkey, security checks for travelers to the United States. mean that you need to be at the airport three hours before takeoff regardless of which airline you are flying, though lines for check-in at Turkish Airlines are generally long regardless.

### AIRPORTS

Turkey's major international airport is **Atatürk Airport,** about 18 km (12 mi) from Istanbul. Sabiha Gökçen Airport serves the Asian part of Istanbul, although it is mainly used by international charters and some domestic flights.

Adana, Adıyaman, Ankara, Antalya, Batman, Çanakkale, Dalaman, Denizli, Diyarbakır, Edremit, Elazığ, Erzincan, Erzurum, Eskişehir, Gaziantep, İsparta, İzmir, Kars, Kayseri, Konya, Malatya, Muş, Nevşehir, Samsun, Siirt, Sinop, Sivas, Şanlıurfa, Tokat, Trabzon, Uşak, and Van all have domestic airports.

**Airports Atatürk Airport** ☎ *212/463–3000* ⊕ *www.ataturkairport.com.* **Sabiha Gökçen**

**Airport** ☎ *216/585–5000* ⊕ *www.sgairport. com.*

### GROUND TRANSPORTATION FROM AIRPORTS

In major destinations such as Adana, Ankara, Antalya, Bodrum, Dalaman, Istanbul, İzmir, Kayseri, Nevşehir, and Trabzon, the Havaş company operates shuttle buses to the airports. These run at regular intervals in the major cities and in the provinces are timed to coincide with incoming and outgoing flights.

An alternative is to take a taxi. From the smaller airports, it is sometimes possible to negotiate with a taxi driver for less than the metered fare. Many hotels will arrange for a driver to collect you from the airport and for someone to take you to the airport. In Cappadocia and other popular tourist regions, it is not unusual for hotels to offer this transportation free of charge, although the driver will still appreciate being tipped a couple of TL.

### TRANSFERS BETWEEN AIRPORTS

If you have a connection between an international flight and a domestic flight in Istanbul, try to ensure that they both use the same airport, which will most likely be Atatürk Airport. While domestic flights to Sabiha Gökçen Airport are usually cheaper than flights into Atatürk Airport (although prices for the latter vary considerably according to the time of day), if you have a connecting international flight from Atatürk Airport, any savings will be more than offset by the time and expense of transferring between airports by taxi (the trip could easily take two to three hours at a busy time of day).

**Contacts Havaş** ☎ *212/465–5656* ⊕ *www. havas.com.tr.*

### FLIGHTS

THY/Turkish Airlines operates nonstops from U.S. and European gateways, though an international carrier based in your home country is more likely to have better connections to your hometown. Third-country carriers (foreign carriers based in a country other than your own or Turkey) sometimes offer the low fares. Air France, for instance often has well-priced flights from the U.S. to Istanbul via Paris.

Turkish Airlines operates an extensive domestic network, with 16 flights daily on weekdays between Istanbul and Ankara alone. In summer many flights to coastal resorts are added. ■TIP➔ Note that at provincial airports it is often necessary for checked luggage to be identified by boarding passengers before it is put on the plane, and all unidentified luggage is left behind and checked for bombs or firearms. If any luggage has not been identified, an announcement will be made on the plane before departure, based on the name on the label on the luggage, but attempts at the pronunciation of foreign names can often mean that they are unrecognizable. Airline staff will always announce whether you need to identify your luggage at some point before boarding but the messages may be difficult to hear or understand. If in doubt, ask a member of the airline staff as they are checking your boarding pass.

# ■ BOAT AND FERRY TRAVEL

In some regions, particularly the Black Sea and greater Istanbul area, ferries are the most efficient means of getting around. On the Aegean and Mediterranean coasts, boats are used mostly for leisurely sightseeing and yachting.

IDO, a subsidiary of Istanbul Metropolitan Municipality, provides regular ferryboat services within Istanbul, as well as to Yalova and Bandirma (both in the Marmara region), and to Bursa. From Bodrum and other Aegean resorts, ferries make frequent runs between Turkey and the Greek islands in the summer.

*For information about sailing trips known as "Blue Cruises" (➪ Tours).*

**Information IDO (Istanbul sea bus and fast Ferry)** ☎ 212/444–4436 ⊕ *www.ido.com.tr.*

# ■ BUS TRAVEL

In Turkey, buses are generally faster than most trains and provide inexpensive service almost around the clock between all cities and towns, and they're usually quite comfortable. Most offer complimentary tea, soda, and biscuits, though with smaller companies you will want to bring your own water in case beverages are not available. All are run by private companies, each of which has its own fixed fares for different routes and, usually more significantly, their own standards of comfort. Most bus companies, such as Varan, Ulusoy, Kamil Koç, Metro, and Pamukkale, which go between major cities and resort areas, can be counted on for comfortable air-conditioned service with snacks. There is often a close correlation between price and comfort, with the more expensive companies such as Varan providing the best amenities. Most of the larger companies have their own terminals and in larger cities run shuttles from locations around the city to the main terminal. *Contact details for the larger companies are listed below.*

Note that *express* buses running between major cities are significantly faster and more comfortable than local buses. By law, all buses are nonsmoking.

## FARES AND SCHEDULES

Buses traveling the Istanbul–Ankara route depart either city every 15 minutes, 24 hours a day, and cost about 30 TL to 60 TL. The Istanbul–İzmir fare ranges from about 30 TL to 45 TL. All buses make periodic rest stops along the way.

The larger companies have their own sales offices as well as Web sites and call centers offering e-tickets. For smaller companies, tickets are sold at stands in a town's *otogar* (central bus terminal); the usual procedure is to go to the bus station and shop around for the best route and price. All seats are reserved. ■TIP➔ When buying your ticket, tell the ticket agent that you would like to sit on the shady side of the bus;

even on air-conditioned buses the sun can feel oppressive on a long trip.

**Information Kamil Koç** ☎ *444–0562 no city code required in Turkey* ⊕ *www.kamilkoc.com. tr.* **Metro Turizm** ☎ *444–3455 no city code required in Turkey,* ⊕ *www.metroturizm.com.tr.* **Pamukkale** ☎ *444–3535 no city code required in Turkey* ⊕ *www.pamukkaleturizm.com.tr.* **Truva Tourism** ☎ *444–0017 no city code required in Turkey.* **Ulusoy** ☎ *444–1888 no city code required in Turkey* ⊕ *www.ulusoy.com.tr.* **Varan** ☎ *212/444–8999* ⊕ *www.varan.com.tr.*

## ■ CAR TRAVEL

In Turkey a driver's license issued in most foreign countries is acceptable. Turkey has one of the world's highest car accident rates. That said, driving is an excellent way to explore regions outside the major cities and having a car allows you the freedom that traveling by bus, train, or plane does not. Turkey has 40,000 km (25,000 mi) of paved and generally well-maintained highways, but off the intercity highways, surfaces are often poor and potholes frequent. A system of four-lane toll roads is now in place around Istanbul, Ankara, and İzmir, but most major highways are two lanes, and cars pass each other with some frequency. △ Sometimes roads have a third lane meant for passing; although the lane is usually labeled with which direction of traffic is meant to use it, drivers don't always follow this rule, so be extremely careful when passing. In general, always expect the unexpected. Don't, for example, assume that one-way streets are one-way in practice or that because you wouldn't do something, such as trying to pass in a dangerous situation, the other driver wouldn't either.

In major cities it's possible to hire a driver along with a car. In some remote places, a driver is usually included in the package with the rental car and will either be the owner of the car or an employee of the agency. If you're particularly happy with the service you may wish to give a tip in addition to the price you pay to the agency. Around 20 TL for a day's driving is reasonable.

△ Driving in Istanbul and other major cities is best avoided. Urban streets and highways are frequently jammed with vehicles operated by high-speed lunatics as well as otherwise sane drivers who constantly honk their horns. In Istanbul, especially, just because a street is marked one-way, you never know when someone is going to barrel down it in the wrong direction. Parking is also a problem in cities and larger towns. In these places it's best to leave your car in a garage and use public transportation or take taxis.

■ TIP➔ If possible, avoid driving on highways after dusk. Drivers often don't use their lights and vehicles may be stopped on the roads in complete darkness. Carts and other farm vehicles are often not equipped with lights.

Highways are numbered or specified by direction (e.g., the route to Antalya). Trans-European highways have a European number as well as a Turkish number (E6 is the European number for Turkish Route D100, for example). △ Note, though, that route numbers may be inconsistent from map to map. Archaeological and historic sites are indicated by yellow signposts.

### EMERGENCY SERVICES

Road rescue service is available on some highways; before you embark on a journey, ask your car rental agency or hotel for contact numbers to use in case of an emergency. Most Turkish gas stations have someone with some knowledge of car mechanics who can diagnose problems and provide "first aid" or advice, such as directions to the nearest mechanic. Make sure to take all car-related documents with you if you leave the car in the shop.

### GASOLINE

Many of the gas stations on the main highways stay open around the clock, others generally from 6 am to 10 pm. Almost all Turkish gas stations provide full service and have unleaded gas. Many attendants will clean your windows while the car's tank is being filled. Tipping is not obligatory though not uncommon if the attendant has been attentive—1 or 2 TL is usually enough. There may be long distances between gas stations in rural areas, so if you're heading off the beaten track, don't allow the tank to run too low. Most gas stations in towns and major highways take credit cards, though you may need cash in rural areas. Many gas stations also have small shops, or just a cooler, where you can buy snacks and chilled drinks.

## RENTING A CAR

In many places, such as Cappadocia and the Turquoise Coast, you may want to rent a car so you can explore on your own. When traveling long distances, however, you may find it easier to take public transportation (either a bus or plane)—unless you plan on sightseeing en route—and renting a car at your destination.

Car rental rates begin at about $50 a day and $250 a week for an economy car with unlimited mileage. Gas costs about 4.4 TL per liter. The majority of rental cars are equipped with manual transmission, though it's possible to get an automatic (usually for a much higher price). Car seats for children are not compulsory and are often difficult to find, although offices of the multinational firms in larger cities may be able to provide them. A wide variety of mostly European car makes are available, ranging from the locally manufactured Tofaş (a subsidiary of Fiat) to Renault and Mercedes.

Check the Web sites of the major multinational companies to see if they have offices at your destination. Many reliable local agencies also operate throughout Turkey. *Only the contacts for the major companies are listed below. Some local car rental agencies are listed in the relevant chapters of this book.*

Hotels often rent cars or have a relationship with a local agency—the local agency is usually anxious to keep the hotel happy by providing a good service, and it's not unusual for the owner of the agency to be a relative of someone at the hotel. The rates for deals done through the hotel, which will include insurance, etc., are often much lower than rates charged by multinational firms.

The rental agency will usually tell you what to do if you have a breakdown or accident and will provide a contact number—often the personal cell number of someone working at the agency—if they don't, ask for one. It's worth remembering that in the case of an accident, Turkish insurance companies usually refuse to pay until they have seen a police report. It is particularly important to obtain a police report if another vehicle is involved, as the driver will need to submit the report when filing a claim with his or her insurance company or with your rental agency. In such a situation, call the contact number for your rental agency and allow a representative to handle all the procedures.

Most likely, agencies will ask you to contact them before attempting to have any repairs done and will usually bring you a replacement car. Most major car manufacturers in Turkey (for example, Renault, Fiat, and Opel/General Motors) also have roaming 24-hour services and rental agencies may ask you to contact one of them.

**Major Agencies Alamo** ☎ 877/222-9075 ⊕ *www.alamo.com.* **Avis** ☎ 800/331-1212 ⊕ *www.avis.com.* **Budget** ☎ 800/527-0700 ⊕ *www.budget.com.* **Hertz** ☎ 800/654-3131 ⊕ *www.hertz.com.* **National Car Rental** ☎ 877/222-9058 ⊕ *www.nationalcar.com.*

## ROAD CONDITIONS

Throughout rural Turkey, roads are often not well marked, lighting is scarce, and roads are sometimes rough. City traffic is generally chaotic. The top speed limit of 120 kph (about 75 mph) is rarely enforced on major highways, although it is not unusual for the Turkish police to set speed traps on other roads. Drive carefully and relatively slowly. Be prepared for sudden changes in road conditions and be alert to the behavior of other drivers.

### ROAD MAPS

Road maps can often be found in tourist areas, and the rental company will usually provide you with one. Remember, though, signposting is erratic and maps are often not very accurate.

### RULES OF THE ROAD

Driving is on the right and passing on the left. Seat belts are required for front-seat passengers and should be used by those in back as well. Using a cell phone while driving is prohibited—but this law is seldom obeyed. Turning right on a red light is not permitted but it is legal to proceed through a flashing red light provided no traffic is coming the other way. Speeding and other traffic violations are subject to on-the-spot fines. Fines for driving under the influence of alcohol are steep and are often accompanied by imprisonment. Most rental companies do not allow you to cross international borders in a rented car.

## ▌ TAXI AND DOLMUŞ TRAVEL

Taxis in Turkey are yellow and easy to spot. Fares are about .90 TL for 1 km (about ½ mi); 50% higher between midnight and 6 am. Be aware that taxi drivers in tourist areas sometimes doctor their meters to charge more (charging the night rate during the day, for example); don't ride in a taxi in which the meter doesn't work. Before setting out, ask at your hotel about how much a ride should cost. Note that saying the word *direkt* after giving your destination helps prevent you from getting an unplanned grand tour of town. In cities it's fairly easy to flag down a taxi, or you can go to a taxi stand where drivers wait for fares. In Istanbul and Ankara many of the larger hotels will find a cab for you, usually with drivers or companies they know and trust. The Web site *Online Taksi* lists taxi companies all over Turkey.

As a tip, it's customary to round up to the next lira. There are no extra charges for luggage. In Istanbul, if you cross one of the Bosphorus bridges, you will be expected to add the 3 TL cost of the toll to the bill regardless of which direction you are going (vehicles only pay going from west to east—the theory is that even if he does not have to pay to take you across, the taxi driver will have to pay to go back). In Ankara, taxi drivers are allowed to charge "night rates" (i.e., 50% higher) for trips to the airport because it's often difficult for them to find a fare for the trip back into town. Particularly in Istanbul and Ankara, taxi drivers are often recent arrivals to the country, with a very limited knowledge of the city and will have to ask bystanders or other taxi drivers for directions.

Dolmuşes (shared taxis) are bright yellow minibuses that run along various routes. You can often hail on the street, at bus stops, or at dolmuş stands marked by the signs "D." The destination is shown either on a roof sign or a card in the front window. The savings over a private taxi are significant. A trip by dolmuş is often just as fast as by taxi, and service extends through the wee hours of the morning. Although dolmuşes only run along specific routes, they generally go to tourist destinations, as well as nightlife hot spots. If you're not familiar with your destination, tell the driver where you are going when you get in; he will usually try to drop you as close to your destination as possible.

It is not customary to tip dolmuş drivers, and they will probably be confused if you try to hand them something extra.

**Taxi Information** **Online Taksi** ⊕ *www. onlinetaksi.com.*

## ▌ TRAIN TRAVEL

Train routes in Turkey tend to meander, meaning that train travel is usually much slower than bus travel—sometimes twice as long. Essentially, the term *express train* is a misnomer in Turkey. The overnight sleeper from Istanbul to Ankara (*Ankara Ekspres*) is the most comfortable and convenient of the trains, with private compartments, attentive service, and a candlelit dining car. There is also daytime service between Ankara and Istanbul, and a high-speed rail connection will connect the two cities in the coming years. The train trip from Istanbul to Ankara currently takes about 6½ hours nonstop, or roughly 10 hours overnight with stops along the way. High-speed service will reduce the travel time to about 3 hours. Trains also run between Istanbul and Edirne and between Ankara and İzmir.

Dining cars on trains between the major cities usually have waiter service and offer decent and inexpensive food. Overnight expresses have sleeping cars and bunk beds. The Istanbul–Ankara run costs about 50 TL for a berth in a two-bed room and about 70 TL for a single-bed room, including tips; although advance reservations are a must, cancellations are frequent, so you can often get a space at the last minute.

Fares are lower for trains than for buses, and round-trip train fares cost less than two one-way tickets. Student discounts are 10% (30% from December through April). Ticket windows in railroad stations are marked "gişeleri." Some post offices and authorized travel agencies also sell train tickets. It's advisable to book in advance, in person, for seats on the best trains and for sleeping quarters.

Long-distance trains offer a number of accommodation options, such as pullman (first-class type, reclining seats), compartments with six or eight seats, reclining or not; couchette (shared four-bunk compartments), and sleeper (private one- or two-bed compartments). In Turkish, pullman is *pulman,* compartment is *kompartımanlı,* couchette is *kuşetli,* and sleeper is *yataklı.*

Most train stations do not accept credit cards, foreign money, or traveler's checks, so be prepared to pay in Turkish lira.

Turkish State Railways (*Türkiye Cumhuriyeti Devlet Demiryolları*) operates train service throughout the country. The Web site is helpful and provides information on how to buy tickets at the station or through travel agencies *(some listed below)* and provides pictures and maps. Seat61.com is another helpful Web site about train travel in Europe and Turkey. Inter-Rail passes can be used in Turkey; Eurail passes cannot.

## THE ORIENT EXPRESS

If you have the time—and money—consider the still-glamorous Venice Simplon-Orient Express. The route runs twice a year from Paris to Istanbul via Budapest and/or Bucharest.

**Contacts seat61.com** ⊕ *www.seat61.com.* **Turkish State Railways** (*Türkiye Cumhuriyeti Devlet Demiryolları*). ☎ *312/311–0602* ⊕ *www. tcdd.gov.tr.* **Venice Simplon-Orient Express** ☎ *800/524–2420 in the U.S.* ⊕ *www.orient-express.com.*

**Authorized Train Travel Agencies Tur-ISTA Tourism Travel Agency** ✉ *Divanyolu Cad. 16, Istanbul* ☎ *212/518–6570* ⊕ *www.turistatravel. com.* **Viking Turizm** ✉ *Mete Cad. 18, Istanbul* ☎ *212/334–2626* ⊕ *www.vikingturizm.com.tr.*

**Train Station Information Ankara Central Station** (*Anakra Garı*). ☎ *312/311–0620.* **Haydarpaşa Station.** The Haydarpaşa Station is on the Asian side of Istanbul. ☎ *216/336–0475.* **Sirkeci Station** ✉ *Istanbul* ☎ *212/527–0051.*

# ESSENTIALS

## ▌ACCOMMODATIONS

Accommodations in Turkey range from international luxury chain hotels to charming inns in historic Ottoman mansions and caravansaries to comfortable but basic family-run *pansiyons* (guesthouses). It's advisable to plan ahead if you'll be traveling in the peak season (April–October), when resort hotels are often booked by tour companies.

Note that reservations should be confirmed more than once, particularly at hotels in popular destinations. Phone reservations are not always honored, so it's a good idea to email the hotel and get written confirmation of your reservation, as well as to confirm again before you arrive.

The lodgings we list are the cream of the crop in each price category. We always list the facilities that are available—but we don't specify whether they cost extra: when pricing accommodations, always ask what's included and what's not. In all but the more luxurious hotels, it's wise to ask to see the room before checking in. It will often be much more basic than the well-decorated reception area. Check for noise, especially if the room faces a street or is anywhere near a nightclub or disco, and in simpler establishments look for such amenities as air-conditioning, as well as such basic amenities as window screens and mosquito coils—small, flat disks that, when lighted, emit an unscented vapor that keeps biting insects away.

*Prices in the lodging charts found in each chapter are for two people in a standard double room in high season, including VAT and service charge.* Private bathrooms, air-conditioning, room phones, and a TV are assumed unless otherwise noted. ▌TIP→ In the low season you should be able to negotiate discounts of at least 20% off the rack rate; it never hurts to try.

### HOTELS

Hotels are officially classified in Turkey as HL (luxury), H1 to H5 (first- to fifth-class); motels, M1 to M2 (first- to second-class); and P (*pansiyons*—guesthouses). These classifications can be misleading, however, as they're based on the number of facilities rather than the quality of the service and decor, and the lack of a restaurant or lounge automatically relegates the establishment to the bottom of the ratings. In practice, a lower-grade hotel may actually be far more charming and comfortable than one with a higher rating.

Though luxury accommodations can be found in many places in Turkey, the standard Turkish hotel room, which you will encounter throughout the country, has bare walls, low wood-frame beds (usually twin beds, often pushed together in lieu of a double bed), and industrial carpeting or kilims on the floor. Less expensive properties will probably have plumbing and furnishings that leave something to be desired.

These are some Turkish words that will come in handy when you're making reservations: "air-conditioning" is *klima,* "private bath" is *banyo,* "tub" is *banyo küveti,* "shower" is *düş,* "double bed" is *iki kişilik yatak,* and "twin beds" is *iki tane tek kişilik yataklar* ("separate" is *ayrı;* "pushed together" is *beraber*). There is no Turkish word for "queen bed" but they will probably use the English (a direct translation is *kraliçe yatağı*). The same is true for "king bed" (they will probably use the English, though a direct translation is *kral yatağı*). Noise-sensitive travelers should ask for a quiet room, *sessiz bir oda.*

*Wherever you stay, keep the following money-saving tips in mind:*

High-end chains catering to businesspeople are often busy only on weekdays and drop rates dramatically on weekends to fill up rooms. Ask when rates go down.

Watch out for hidden costs, including resort fees, energy surcharges, and "convenience" fees for such extras as unlimited local phone service you won't use and a free newspaper written in a language you can't read.

Always verify whether local hotel taxes are or are not included in the rates you are quoted, so that you'll know the real price of your stay. In some places, taxes can add 20% or more to your bill.

If you're trying to book a stay right before or after Turkey's high season (April–October), you might save considerably by changing your dates by a week or two. Many properties charge peak-season rates for your entire stay, even if your travel dates straddle peak and nonpeak seasons.

## PANSIYONS

Outside the cities and resort areas, these small, family-run establishments are generally the most common option. They range from charming old homes decorated with antiques to tiny, utilitarian rooms done in basic modern. As a rule, they are inexpensive and scrupulously clean. Private baths are common, though they are rudimentary—stall showers, toilets with sensitive plumbing. A simple breakfast is typically included. A stay in a *pansiyon* is a comfortable money-saver, especially if you plan on spending most of your time out and about.

# ▌ COMMUNICATIONS

## INTERNET

Most hotels, even basic establishments, provide an Internet connection or Wi-Fi, if not in the rooms at least in public areas; ask when you make a reservation. In most cities and tourist destinations, you'll also be able to find Internet cafés or cafés and other establishments with Wi-Fi hotspots.

Remember that the Turkish electricity supply runs on 220 volts. Many laptops, tablets, and other devices are equipped with built-in converters, but you will need an adapter that allows you to plug into wall outlets, which take European-type plugs, with two or three round prongs.

## PHONES

Telephone numbers in Turkey have seven-digit local numbers preceded by a three-digit city code (toll-free numbers might have fewer or more digits). In Istanbul, European and Asian Istanbul have separate area codes: The code for much of European Istanbul is 212 (making the number look like it's in New York City), and the code for Asian Istanbul (numbers beginning with 3 or 4) is 216. Mobile phone codes are often 534, 533, or 532. The country code for Turkey is 90.

### CALLING WITHIN TURKEY

Within a city you don't need to dial the code for other numbers with the same code, but in Istanbul you need to dial the code (0212 or 0216) when calling from the European to the Asian side of the city or vice versa. All local cellular calls are classed as long distance, and you need to dial the city code for every number.

To call long-distance within Turkey, dial 131 if you need operator assistance; otherwise dial 0, then dial the city code and number.

With the increase in the use of mobile phones very few people now use pay phones, but it's still easy to find them. Directions in English and other languages are often posted in phone booths, along with other country codes. Directory assistance is not terribly efficient and it can be difficult to find an English-speaking operator; you're best off asking the staff at your hotel to help you find a number.

Public phones use phone cards, which can be purchased at post offices and, for a small markup, at most corner stores, newspaper vendors, and street stalls. They come in denominations of 30 (about 5 TL), 60 (about 10 TL), and 100 (about 13 TL) units; buy a 60- or 100-unit card for long-distance calls within Turkey, a 30-unit card for local use. Make sure to ask for a calling card for a public phone, as calling cards for cellular phones are also available, and you cannot use the two interchangeably. A very few public phones (and only in cities) also take credit cards.

To make a local call, insert your phone card or credit card, wait until the light at the top of the phone goes off, then dial the number.

Some kiosks selling newspapers or small stores have phones that you can use to place calls. The cost is usually approximately the same as it would be for a standard pay phone. If you want to use one, say "telefon" (Turkish for telephone), and the proprietor will usually either produce a phone or show you where you can find one.

### CALLING OUTSIDE TURKEY
The country code is 1 for the United States.

For international operator services, dial 115. Intercity telephone operators seldom speak English, although international operators usually have some basic English. If you need international dialing codes and assistance or phone books, you can also go to the nearest post office or Internet café.

To make an international call from a public phone in Turkey, dial 00, then dial the country code, area or city code, and the number. In general, calling from a hotel is almost always expensive, because hotels often add huge surcharges to calls. An inexpensive option is to make international calls from call centers or the post office, and calling cards usually keep costs to a minimum.

Internet cafés typically offer international calling service with prices comparable to a phone card but be sure to ask for rates first.

**Access Codes AT&T Direct** ☎ *0811/288-0001 in Turkey, followed by the area code and number.* **MCI WorldPhone** ☎ *00/8001–1177 in Turkey, followed by the area code and number.* **Sprint International Access** ☎ *00/800–18488 in Turkey, followed by the area code and number.*

### MOBILE PHONES
If you have a multiband phone (some countries use frequencies other than those used in the United States) and your service provider uses the world-standard GSM network (as do T-Mobile, AT&T, and Verizon), you can probably use your phone in Turkey. Roaming fees can be steep, though—99¢ a minute is considered reasonable—and you will probably pay the toll charges for incoming calls. It's almost always cheaper to send a text message than to make a call since text messages have a very low set fee (often less than 5¢).

Renting a phone in Turkey is very expensive, and it's not easy to find shops that rent. The best solution is to buy a SIM card to install in your phone, along with a pay-as-you-go service. There are several mobile phone providers in Turkey. The largest is Turkcell, followed by Vodafone and Avea. Each has a network of clearly marked stores, where it is possible to buy SIM cards and pay-as-you-go cards. Most sales people speak enough English to conduct business and answer basic questions. All stores post easy-to-understand signs that indicate unit packages and prices. Expect to pay about 11 TL for 100 units (*kontör*), regardless of the company. A three-minute conversation within Turkey will generally set you back 4 units, and a three-minute international call will be about 11 units.

# CUSTOMS AND DUTIES

Turkish customs officials rarely look through tourists' luggage on arrival. You are allowed to bring in 400 cigarettes, 50 cigars, 200 grams of tobacco, 1½ kilograms of instant coffee, 500 grams of tea, and 2½ liters of alcohol. Items in the duty-free shops in Turkish airports, for international arrivals, are usually less expensive than they are in European airports or in-flight. Pets are allowed into the country provided that they have all the necessary documentation. Full details can be obtained from the Turkish diplomatic representative in your own country.

⚠ The export of antiquities from Turkey is expressly forbidden, and the ban is rigorously enforced. If you buy a carpet or rug that looks old, make sure to obtain certification that it is not antique. The seller will usually be able to help you. The ban on antiquities extends to historical artifacts, coins, and even pieces of masonry. There have been several recent cases where tourists, some of them children, have tried to take small pieces of stone home as souvenirs and been arrested at the airport on suspicion of trying to export parts of ancient monuments. A genuine mistake is not considered sufficient excuse. Even where the tourists have been ultimately acquitted, they have still had to spend many months either in detention or, more commonly, out on bail but denied permission to leave the country. Turkish antiquities laws apply to every piece of detritus, so don't pick up anything off the ground at archaeological sites.

Visit the Turkish embassy Web site in Washington, D.C., and the Web sites of the U.S. Department of State and the U.S. Embassy in Ankara for more information.

**U.S. Information Turkish Embassy**
☎ *202/612-6701* ⊕ *www.turkishembassy.org.*

# EATING OUT

*For more information about traditional Turkish food and alcohol in Turkey, see the Mezes In-Focus section in Chapter 5.*

The restaurants we list are the cream of the crop in each price category. Prices *on the restaurant chart (at the front of each chapter)* are per main course, or two small dishes, at dinner. A service or "cover" charge (a charge just for sitting at the table, the bread, the water, etc.) of 10% to 15% is usually added to the bill, but you should tip 10% on top of this. If a restaurant's menu has no prices listed, ask before you order—you'll avoid a surprise when the bill comes. *For information on food-related health issues, see Health below.*

## MEALS AND MEALTIMES

Breakfast, usually eaten at your hotel, typically consists of *beyaz peynir* (goat cheese), sliced tomatoes, cucumbers, olives, and yogurt with honey and fresh fruit, with a side order of fresh bread, and tea or Nescafé; the menu varies little, whether you stay in a simple *pansiyon* or an upscale hotel.

Breakfast starts early, typically by 7. Lunch is generally served from noon to 3, dinner from 7 to 10. You can find restaurants or cafés open almost any time of the day or night in cities; in villages getting a meal at odd hours can be a problem. Most Turks fast during daylight hours during the Islamic holy month of Ramadan. If you're visiting during Ramadan, be sensitive to locals and avoid eating on public transportation or other places where you might make mouths water. During Ramadan, many restaurants, particularly smaller ones outside the major cities, close during the day and open at dusk.

Unless otherwise noted, the restaurants listed in this guide are open daily for lunch and dinner.

## PAYING

Most relatively upscale restaurants, particularly those in western Turkey, take major credit cards. Smaller eateries will often accept only cash.

*For guidelines on tipping, see Tipping below.*

## RESERVATIONS AND DRESS

It's a good idea to make a reservation at popular restaurants. We mention when reservations are essential (there's no other way you'll ever get a table) or when they are not accepted. We mention dress only when men are required to wear a jacket or a jacket and tie.

# ■ ELECTRICITY AND ELECTRONICS

The electrical current in Turkey is 220 volts, 50 cycles alternating current (AC). If you're going to be using U.S. appliances, make sure that you have a voltage converter and an adapter, which allows you to plug into wall outlets; in Turkey these take European-type plugs, with two or three round prongs.

Most laptops, tablet, camera, and mobile phone chargers, and some other small appliances are dual voltage (i.e., they operate equally well on 110 and 220 volts) and so require only an adapter. Always check labels and manufacturer instructions to be sure, though. Don't use 110-volt outlets marked "for shavers only" for high-wattage appliances such as hair dryers.

**Contacts Global Electric and Phone Directory.** Global Electric and Phone Directory has information on electrical plugs, accessories, and telephones around the world. ⊕ *www.kropla.com.* **Walkabout Travel Gear.** Walkabout Travel Gear has a good discussion about electricity under "Solving the Riddle of Global Electricity" in its Online Catalogue section. ⊕ *www.walkabouttravelgear.com.*

# ■ EMERGENCIES

If your passport is lost or stolen, contact the police and your embassy immediately. If you have an emergency, you're best off asking a Turk to call an emergency number for you because it's unlikely you'll find an English-speaking person at the other end of the telephone, even at the Tourism Police. Bystanders will almost invariably try their utmost to be of assistance and will usually know of nearby hospitals or doctors. The Turkish words for ambulance, doctor, and police—*ambulans, doktor,* and *polis,* respectively—all sound about the same as their English equivalents, as does *telefon* for telephone. Say whichever is appropriate, and you can feel fairly certain that you'll be understood.

**Embassies Canadian Consulate (Istanbul)** ✉ *Buyukdere Cad. 29, Istanbul* ☎ *212/385-9700.* **U.S. Consulate (Istanbul)** ✉ *İstinye Mahallesi, Şehitler Sok. 2, İstinye, Istanbul* ☎ *212/335–9000* ⊕ *istanbul.usconsulate.gov.* **U.S. Embassy (Ankara)** ✉ *110 Atatürk Bulv., Kavaklıdere, Ankara* ☎ *312/455–5555* ⊕ *www.turkishembassy.org.*

**General Emergency Contacts Ambulance** ☎ *112.* **Emergency (police, etc.)** ☎ *155.* **Tourism Police (Istanbul)** ☎ *212/527–4503.*

# ■ HEALTH

No serious health risks are associated with travel to Turkey, and no vaccinations are required for entry. However, travelers are advised to have vaccinations

# LOCAL DO'S AND TABOOS

Turks set great store in politeness. No one will expect you to have mastered the intricacies of polite speech in Turkish, but a respectful attitude and tone of voice, combined with a readiness to smile, will often work wonders.

Although Turks are a very tactile people, particularly with friends of the same sex, this physical contact is like a language, full of pitfalls for the unwary. Be very careful about initiating physical contact, as misunderstandings are easy. Overt public physical displays of affection between the sexes are more common in younger generations in big cities, but are still are likely to offend people outside the major cities.

Turks shake hands as a greeting, although this is more common between men than between women. It is quite acceptable, and often very appreciated, if a foreign male initiates a handshake with another male when, for example, leaving a carpet shop. For handshakes between the sexes, unless the Turkish woman is obviously highly Westernized, a foreign male should leave it up to her to initiate any physical contact. It is all right for foreign women to initiate a handshake, but be prepared for a very religious Turkish male to pointedly avoid shaking a woman's hand.

A combination of simultaneously shaking hands and kissing on both cheeks is the usual form of greeting between male friends, while women friends more often kiss without shaking hands; this is usually a cheek-to-cheek "air-kiss," and it's unusual for the lips to make contact with the skin. On occasion, a Turk will actually kiss the cheek, but such a kiss is considered very forward when given to members of the opposite sex, particularly those of little acquaintance, and if you are a recipient, you should draw your conclusions accordingly.

Most Turks consider hospitality both a duty and a source of pride. If you visit Turks in their homes, it is expected that you will take off your shoes on entering. You will not be expected to bring gifts, particularly on a first visit, although a small token, such as fresh nuts or dessert, is always appreciated. Chances are the lady of the house will have gone to considerable trouble to prepare food if she has had prior knowledge of your arrival so you, in turn, should go with an empty stomach and at least try the dishes that are offered to you. In appreciation, it is traditional to say *ellerinize sağlık* ("ell-lair-in-izeh sah-luk"), which translates literally as, "May your hands be healthy." No offense will be taken if you don't manage to say it, but it will be much appreciated if you do.

## BUSINESS ETIQUETTE

Business etiquette is a little different from everyday etiquette. In the major cities, many managers of larger companies will have worked or trained abroad, particularly in the United States, and will be familiar with the ways in which Western companies do business. Punctuality is appreciated, but chronic traffic congestion in Istanbul and Ankara means most businesspeople are used to people arriving a little late for appointments. A telephone call to warn of a late arrival is appreciated.

Business negotiations are usually conducted in a relaxed atmosphere, and the business of the day may be padded with friendly conversation and the ubiquitous cups of tea. Provided you eventually get down to business, it is usually a good idea not to force the pace, as the preliminaries are a way for the parties to assess each other and establish mutual trust.

for hepatitis, cholera, and typhoid and to take precautions against malaria if visiting the far southeast. To avoid problems at customs, diabetics and other persons who carry needles and syringes for medical reasons should have a letter from their physician confirming their need for injections. Rabies can be a problem in Turkey, occasionally even in the large cities. If bitten or scratched by a dog or cat about which you have suspicions, go to the nearest pharmacy and ask for assistance.

Even in areas where there is no malaria, you'll want to use something to ward off mosquitoes. All pharmacies and most corner stores and supermarkets stock a variety of oils and/or tablets to burn to keep mosquitoes at bay, as well as sprays and creams you can apply to exposed skin; it's generally easy to identify these products as the packaging usually includes a picture of a mosquito. If you can't find what you want, try asking using the Turkish word for mosquito: *sinek*. It often seems as though mosquitoes favor foreigners, particularly the fair-skinned, so a Turk's assurances that mosquitoes in a particular place are "not bad" can be both sincere and misleading.

Given the high temperatures in summer, dehydration can be a problem in southern and eastern Turkey. Remember to sip water throughout the day rather than waiting until you are very thirsty.

For minor problems, pharmacists can be helpful. Pharmacists at any *eczane*, or pharmacy, are well versed in common ailments and can prescribe some antibiotics and other medications for common travelers' illnesses. Many of the same over-the-counter remedies available in Western countries can be found in Turkish pharmacies, which are usually well stocked. Even a Turkish pharmacist who doesn't speak English will often be able to recognize a specific remedy—particularly if you write the name down—and be able to find an appropriate alternative if that medication is not available.

Doctors and dentists abound in major cities and can be found in all but the smallest towns; many are women. There are also *hastanes* (hospitals) and *kliniks* (clinics). Road signs marked with an "h" point the way to the nearest hospital. Even if doctors cannot converse fluently in English, most will have a working knowledge of the English and French for medical conditions. Turkish dentists, or *dişçi*, are highly regarded.

**FOOD AND DRINK**

Tap water is heavily chlorinated and supposedly safe to drink in cities and resorts. It's okay to wash fruits and vegetables in tap water, but it's best to play it safe and only drink *şişe suyu* (bottled still water), *maden suyu* (bottled sparkling mineral water), or *maden sodası* (carbonated mineral water), which are better tasting and inexpensive. ⚠ **Do not drink tap water in rural areas or in eastern Turkey.** Turkish food is generally safe, though you should still be careful and avoid some types of street food, such as chickpeas and rice (*nohut*) and mussels (*midye*), which can host a number of nasty bacteria.

# ▌ HOLIDAYS

Schools and many offices often close for a full or half day on major Turkish holidays, which are as follows: January 1 (New Year's Day); April 23 (National Independence Day); May 19 (Atatürk's Commemoration Day, celebrating his birthday and the day he landed in Samsun, starting the independence movement); August 30 (Zafer Bayramı, or Victory Day, commemorating Turkish victories over Greek forces in 1922, during Turkey's War of Independence); October 29 (Cumhuriyet Bayramı, or Republic Day, celebrating Atatürk's proclamation of the Turkish republic in 1923—many businesses and government offices also close at midday, usually either 12:30 or 1, on the day before Republic Day); November 10 (the anniversary of Atatürk's death is not a full-day public holiday but is commemorated by a nationwide moment of silence at 9:05 am). Many provincial towns also hold celebrations to mark the anniversary of the date that the Greeks were driven out of the area during the Turkish War of Liberation.

Turks also celebrate the two main Muslim religious holidays each year: the three-day Şeker Bayramı, marking the end of Ramadan and the four-day Kurban Bayramı, which honors Abraham's willingness to sacrifice his son to God. Because the Muslim year is based on the lunar calendar, the dates of the two holidays change every year, both moving earlier by 11 to 12 days each year. The precise timing may vary slightly according to the sighting of the moon. Many businesses and government offices close at midday, usually either 12:30 or 1, on the day before the religious *bayrams*. In 2012, Şeker Bayramı is due to begin at midday on August 18 and last until the evening of August 21. Kurban Bayramı will begin at midday on October 24, 2012, and continue through the evening of October 28; in 2013 it will begin on October 14 and end on the 28th. A word of note: If a religious holiday takes up three or four days of a working week, the government will often declare the rest of the week an official holiday as well. However, such decisions are usually made less than a month before the holiday actually begins.

# ▌ HOURS OF OPERATION

## BANKS AND OFFICES

Banks in Turkey are normally open weekdays from 8:30 until noon or 12:30, and then from 1:30 until 5, but select branches of some Turkish banks, especially those in major cities, now remain open during the middle of the day. Many banks throughout Turkey, even those in small towns, provide 24-hour service from ATMs with service in English.

## GAS STATIONS

Most gas stations are open from early morning until late evening, commonly from 6 am to 10 pm, although there are no fixed rules and there can be considerable variation. In the larger cities and along major highways it is usually possible to find gas stations open 24 hours. Look for the sign "24 saat açık."

## MUSEUMS AND SIGHTS

Museums are generally open Tuesday through Sunday from 9:30 am until 5 or 5:30 pm and closed on Monday—this is not a rule, though, so check the times listed in our individual listings. Palaces are open the same hours but are generally closed Thursday, while during the summer many popular archaeological sites are open seven days a week and close around sunset. Many museums and sites stop selling tickets 30 minutes before the actual closing time. Sometimes this is explicitly stated in the official times, but not always. To be on the safe side, try to ensure that you arrive at least 45 minutes before closing time.

## PHARMACIES

Most pharmacies (*eczane* in Turkish) are open the same hours as shops, and as with shops, there are variations according to the whim of the pharmacist. Typically, they are open 9:30 am until 7 or 7:30 pm, Monday through Saturday. In larger cities, one pharmacy in each neighborhood is open 24/7 and is called the *nöbetçi eczane*. When a pharmacy is closed, there will be a sign in the window or door with details of the location of the nearest *nöbetçi eczane*. Your hotel will always be able to help you find the closest *nöbetçi eczane*.

## SHOPS

Shops and bazaars are usually open Monday through Saturday from 9:30 to 7 with varying open hours on Sunday. Smaller shops often close for lunch between 1 and 2, although all large stores and even most small shops in the major cities remain open throughout the day. In tourist areas, shops may stay open until 9 pm or even 10 pm and all day Sunday.

# ▌ LANGUAGE

English, German, and often French are widely spoken in hotels, restaurants, and shops in cities and resorts. In villages and remote areas you may have a hard time finding anyone who speaks anything but Turkish or Kurdish, though rudimentary communications are still usually possible. According to Turkey's education system, everyone learns English in primary school and may continue into high school and university. Even so, try to learn a few basic Turkish words; your efforts will be appreciated. See the vocabulary list at the back of this book *(⇨ Vocab)*.

# ▌ MAIL AND SHIPPING

The Turkish for "post office" is *postane.* Post offices are painted bright yellow and have "PTT" (Post, Telegraph, and Telephone) signs on the front. The central post offices in larger cities are open Monday through Saturday from 8 am to 9 pm, and Sunday from 9 to 7. Smaller ones are open Monday through Saturday between 8:30 and 5. Turks use franking machines in post offices rather than postage stamps. The latter are still available at post offices but are mainly sold to philatelists and nostalgists. Envelopes and boxes are usually sold in kiosks not far from post offices.

Mail sent from Turkey can take from three to 10 days, or more, to reach a destination in Europe or abroad. Be warned that the mail service is erratic and that you may arrive home long before your postcards do.

Postage rates are frequently adjusted to keep pace with inflation. It generally costs about 50¢ to send a postcard from Turkey to the United States. Shipping a 10-pound rug home via surface mail will cost about $25 and take from two to six months.

If you want to receive mail in Turkey and you're uncertain where you'll be staying, have mail sent to Poste Restante, Merkez Posthanesi (Central Post Office), in the town of your choice.

## OVERNIGHT AND EXPRESS SERVICES

The main couriers (DHL, Federal Express, UPS, etc.) have offices in Istanbul, but it will probably take three days for a package to reach the United States or United Kingdom.

## SHIPPING PARCELS

Some stores and sellers in bazaars will offer to arrange to ship goods for you but where possible, it's better to carry your purchases home with you—even if you have to pay for excess baggage. Most parcels sent from Turkey through the postal service do eventually arrive at their destination, but be aware there is a risk they may become damaged or lost in transit. Other alternatives, such as courier services or shipping companies, are quicker and more reliable but often very expensive.

# ▌ MONEY

Turkey used to be the least expensive of the Mediterranean countries, but prices have risen in recent years. At press time, Istanbul was roughly equivalent to other cities in the Mediterranean in terms of cost, but in the countryside, and particularly away from the main tourist areas, prices are much lower—room and board are not likely to be much more than $50 per person per day.

Coffee can range from about $1.50 to $4.50 a cup, depending on whether it's the less-expensive Turkish coffee or American-style coffee, and whether it's served in a luxury hotel, a café, or an outlet of a multinational chain such as Starbucks or Gloria Jean's. Coffee lovers beware: most coffee listed on menus in a restaurant, unless specified otherwise, is likely to be instant coffee (Nescafé). Tea will cost you about 50¢–$1 a glass, rising to $1–$3 for a cup (the latter is larger). Local beer will be about $4–$6, depending on the type of establishment; soft drinks, $1–$3; and a lamb shish kebab, $5–$8.

Prices throughout this guide are given for adults. Substantially reduced fees are almost always available for children, students, and senior citizens. *For information on taxes, see Taxes.*

## ATMS AND BANKS

ATMs can be found even in some of the smallest Turkish towns. Many accept international credit cards or bank cards (a strip of logos is usually displayed above the ATM). Almost all ATMs have a language key that enables you to read the instructions in English. To use your card in Turkey, your PIN must be four digits long.

In Turkey, as elsewhere, using an ATM is one of the easiest ways to get money. Generally the exchange rate is based on the Turkish Central Bank or the exchange rate according to your bank.

## CREDIT CARDS

Since March 2006, Turkey has started using "chip and PIN" as well as "swipe and sign." The chip-and-PIN system is a more secure method than swipe-and-sign and refers to the chip in the credit card, which contains identifying information. The card is inserted in the POS terminal, which reads the chip and sends the information down the line. The user is then asked to enter his/her PIN and this information is also sent down the wire; if everything matches, the transaction is completed. If you don't have a PIN, check with your bank to get one before you leave the United States.

It's a good idea to inform your credit card company before you travel, especially if you're going abroad and don't travel internationally very often. Otherwise, the credit card company might put a hold on your card owing to unusual activity—not a good thing halfway through your trip. Record all your credit card numbers— as well as the phone numbers to call if your cards are lost or stolen—in a safe place. American Express, Diners Club,

MasterCard, and Visa have numbers you can call (collect if you're abroad) if your card is lost. If possible, you're better off calling the number of your issuing bank, which is sometimes printed on your card.

Although it's usually safer to use a credit card for large purchases (so you can cancel payments or be reimbursed if there's a problem), some credit-card companies and the banks that issue them add substantial percentages to all foreign transactions. Check on these fees before using your card.

Before you charge something, ask the merchant whether or not he or she plans to do a dynamic currency conversion (DCC). In such a transaction the credit card *processor* (shop, restaurant, or hotel) converts the currency and charges you in dollars. In most cases you'll pay the merchant a 3% fee for this service in addition to any credit-card-company and issuing-bank foreign-transaction surcharges.

DCC programs are becoming increasingly widespread. Merchants who participate in them are supposed to ask whether you want to be charged in dollars or the local currency, but they don't always do so. And even if they do offer you a choice, they may well avoid mentioning the additional surcharges. The good news is that you *do* have a choice. And if this practice really gets your goat, you can avoid it entirely thanks to American Express; with its cards, DCC simply isn't an option.

Credit cards are accepted throughout Turkey, especially in larger cities or towns, but many budget-oriented restaurants or hotels in rural areas do not accept them.

Be warned that Turkey has one of the highest rates of credit-card fraud in Europe. Do not let your credit card out of your sight.

**Reporting Lost Cards American Express** ☎ *800/528–4800 in the U.S., 801/849-2124 collect from abroad* ⊕ *www.americanexpress. com.* **Diners Club** ☎ *800/234–6377 in the U.S., 514/877–1577 collect from abroad* ⊕ *www.dinersclub.com.* **MasterCard**

✆ 800/627–8372 in the U.S., 636/722–7111 collect from abroad ⊕ www.mastercard.com. **Visa** ✆ 800/847–2911 in the U.S., 00–800–13/535–0900 collect from abroad ⊕ www.visa.com.

## CURRENCY AND EXCHANGE

The Turkish lira is divided into 100 kuruş, and is issued in denominations of 5, 10, 20, 50, and 100 TL notes, and 5, 10, 25, 50 kuruş, and 1 TL coins.

Your bank will probably charge a fee for using an ATM abroad, and the Turkish bank may also charge a fee. Even so, you'll get a better rate than you will at currency exchanges or at some banks.

Hotels and banks will change money, as will larger post offices, but in Turkey the rates are usually better at the foreign exchange booths (look for signs saying "foreign exchange" or "döviz"). Most are now connected online to the currency markets and there will be little difference between them.

Exchange bureaus are found only in big cities, usually in the center, so if you are heading to small towns make sure you change your money before leaving.

Bureaus in tourist areas often offer slightly less attractive rates—rarely more than 2%–3% difference—than bureaus in other places. Almost all foreign exchange bureaus are open Monday–Saturday. Hours vary but are typically 9:30 am–6:30 pm. In tourist areas it is sometimes possible to find a bureau that is open on a Sunday, but it will usually compensate for the inconvenience by offering a rate 2%–3% worse than those bureaus that close on Sundays.

İş Bankası (İş Bank) is Turkey's largest bank, with many branches in the cities and at least one in each town, usually in the center of town.

## ▮ PACKING

Although Turkey is an informal country, it is often said that Istanbul isn't Turkey—it's Europe. Expect to see the full spectrum in Istanbul when it comes to style and coverage. You may walk down the street next to a girl in a miniskirt, followed by a woman wearing a head scarf or completely covered from head to toe. Istanbul is a cosmopolitan city, so if you plan on a night out on the town, come prepared to dress accordingly. For men, nice jeans coupled with a clean button-down shirt and decent shoes will usually get you in the door; a jacket and tie are only appropriate for top restaurants in Istanbul, Ankara, and İzmir. Women should feel comfortable wearing fashionable styles but, as in any place, consider what kind of attention you want to attract.

Outside major cities, women would do best to avoid overly revealing outfits and short skirts. The general rule is: the smaller the town, the more casual and, at the same time, conservative the dress.

On the beaches along the Mediterranean, topless sunbathing among foreigners is increasingly common. Shorts are acceptable for hiking through ruins, but not for touring mosques. The importance of a sturdy, comfortable pair of shoes cannot be overemphasized. Whether you are in Istanbul, where "everything is uphill," or you're hiking the ruins at Ephesus, you'll be glad you sacrificed style for comfort.

Light cottons are best for summer, particularly along the coast. If you're planning excursions into the interior or north of the country, you'll need sweaters in spring or fall and all-out cold-weather gear in winter. An umbrella is advisable on the Black Sea coast, but as anywhere else in Turkey, as soon as rain begins to fall, people will appear almost magically on the streets to sell cheap umbrellas; so if you don't want to bring one with you, it's almost always possible to find one.

Sunscreen and sunglasses will come in handy. It's a good idea to carry some toilet paper and hand sanitizer with you at all times, especially outside the bigger cities and resort areas. You'll need mosquito repellent from March through October, a flashlight for exploring caves in Cappadocia, and soap if you're staying in inexpensive and moderately priced hotels.

# PASSPORTS AND VISAS

All U.S. citizens, even infants, need a valid passport and a visa to enter Turkey for stays of up to 90 days. Visas can be issued at the Turkish embassy or consulate before you go, or at the point of entry; the cost is $20 and must be paid in American dollars. If you do not have a visa and need to buy one at the airport or other point of entry, look for a sign saying "visas" usually just before passport control.

Even though visas are multiple entry and usually valid for 90 days, they cannot be issued for periods longer than the validity of the passport you present. If your passport has less than a month to run, you may not be given a visa at all. Check the validity of your passport before applying for the visa. Turkish officials may impose stiff fines for an overstay on your visa.

■ TIP➜ If your trip includes a stopover to the Greek side of Cyprus before you come to Turkey, make sure you don't get your passport stamped. Instead, ask for a slip of paper indicating your legal entry to Cyprus. Otherwise, you may encounter difficulties getting through passport control in Turkey. This is not an issue if you're coming from Greece proper, however.

# RESTROOMS

Public facilities are common in the tourist areas of major cities and resorts and at archeological sites and other attractions; in most, a custodian will ask you to pay a fee (ranging from 50 kuruş to 2–3 TL). In virtually all public facilities, including those in all but the fanciest restaurants, toilets are Turkish style (squatters) and toilet paper is often not provided (to cleanse themselves, Turks use a pitcher of water set next to the toilet). Sometimes it's possible to purchase toilet paper from the custodian, but you are well advised to carry a supply with you as part of your travel gear. Alas, standards of restroom cleanliness tend to be a bit low compared to those in Western Europe and America. If you're away from tourist areas, look for a mosque, as many have restrooms as part of the complex of washing facilities for Muslims to perform their ablutions before performing their prayers. Standards of cleanliness at mosque restrooms are usually higher than at public facilities. Most, but not all, restaurants and cafés have restrooms, but, again, the standard of cleanliness is extremely variable. In general, five-star hotels have the best facilities, and the staff rarely raise any objection if restrooms are used by foreigners not staying at the hotel. Many gas stations have restrooms.

# SAFETY

Distribute your cash, credit cards, IDs, and other valuables between a deep front pocket, an inside jacket or vest pocket, and a hidden money pouch. Don't reach for the money pouch once you're in public.

Violent crime against strangers in Turkey has increased in recent years but, when compared with Western Europe or North America, is still relatively rare. You should, nevertheless, watch your valuables, as professional pickpockets do operate in the major cities and tourist areas. Bag snatching has increased in recent years, and women should be careful both when walking and when sitting at open-air cafés and restaurants. Bear in mind that organized gangs often use children to snatch bags.

Though the Kurdistan Workers Party (PKK) has waged an armed campaign in southeastern Turkey, cities and major highways are relatively safe. You should be extremely cautious about visiting more out-of-the-way villages in the region and using unpaved roads or traveling after nightfall. Despite the country's proximity to Iraq, the insurgency there has had no noticeable impact on security inside Turkey. The U.S. occupation of Iraq was deeply unpopular in Turkey, and Turks will often have little hesitation in letting you know how they feel. However, they will invariably distinguish between the actions of the U.S. government and individual Americans. For an up-to-date report on the situation, check with the State Department Web site.

### GOVERNMENT ADVISORIES

As different countries have different worldviews, look at travel advisories from a range of governments to get more of a sense of what's going on out there. And be sure to parse the language carefully. For example, a warning to "avoid all travel" carries more weight than one urging you to "avoid nonessential travel," and both are much stronger than a plea to "exercise caution." A U.S. government travel warning is more permanent (though not necessarily more serious) than a so-called public announcement, which carries an expiration date.

The U.S. Department of State's Web site has more than just travel warnings and advisories. The consular information sheets issued for every country have general safety tips, entry requirements (though be sure to verify these with the country's embassy), and other useful details.

Consider registering online with the State Department (⊕ *https://travelregistration. state.gov/ibrs*), so the government will know to look for you should a crisis occur in the country you're visiting.

**General Information and Warnings** Australian **Department of Foreign Affairs & Trade** ⊕ *www.smartraveller.gov.au.* **Foreign Affairs and International Trade Canada** ⊕ *www. voyage.gc.ca.* **U.K. Foreign & Commonwealth Office** ⊕ *www.fco.gov.uk/travel.* **U.S. Department of State** ⊕ *www.travel.state.gov.*

### LOCAL SCAMS

As Turkey has one of the highest credit card fraud rates in Europe, you should keep your credit cards within sight at all times to prevent them from being copied.

In many restaurants waiters will swipe your card at the table. If a waiter takes the card away, you should either ensure that it remains within eyesight or ask to accompany the waiter to the POS terminal (you can manufacture an excuse, such as telling the waiter that your bank sometimes asks for a PIN).

There have been a few cases of tourists traveling alone being given drugged drinks and then being robbed. The doctored drinks are usually soft drinks such as sodas. Turks are naturally anxious to ply guests with food and drink, and in the vast majority of cases, there should be no cause for alarm. However, if, for example, you are traveling alone and someone is particularly insistent on you having a cold soft drink and comes back with one already poured into a glass, treat it with extreme caution. If the drink is drugged, the person giving it to you will probably be suspiciously insistent that you drink it. If you have any doubts, do not consume it. Someone who is being genuinely hospitable will probably be confused and maybe a little hurt; but both are better than your being robbed.

In crowded areas be aware of a common scam in which two men stage a fight or similar distraction while an accomplice picks the tourist's pocket.

Before taking a private taxi, it can be useful to ask the information desk at your hotel what route (i.e., past what landmarks) the driver will likely drive, how many minutes the ride usually is, and what the average cost is: this way you will avoid an unwanted, and often lengthy, tour of the city. Note that Turkish hospitality is such that if you need directions, someone will often insist on accompanying you part or all the way to your destination.

### WOMEN IN TURKEY

Turkey is a generally safe destination for women traveling alone, though in heavily touristed areas such as Istanbul's Sultanahmet, Antalya, and Marmaris, women unaccompanied by men are likely to be approached and sometimes followed. In rural towns, where visits from foreigners are less frequent, men are more respectful toward women traveling on their own. In the far east of the country, though, you should be particularly careful; women traveling alone have been known to be harassed in this region. As in any other country in the world, the best course of action is simply to walk on if approached, and avoid potentially troublesome situations, such as walking in deserted neighborhoods at night.

Some Turkish men are genuinely curious about women from other lands and really do want only to "practice their English." Still, be forewarned that the willingness to converse can easily be misconstrued as something more meaningful. If you are uncomfortable, seek assistance from a Turkish woman or move to a place where other women are present; when it comes to harassment by males, there really is safety in female solidarity. If a man is acting inappropriately toward you, it is acceptable to be forward and tell him to go away. The phrase *çok ayıp* ("shame on you") will come in handy, as it will also attract attention from passersby. Another phrase, *defol* ("get lost") is more severe and should dispel any persistent men you may encounter. Women who are pregnant or have small children with them are generally treated with such respect as to be virtually immune from harassment.

Turkey, especially outside tourist areas and major cities, is not the place to sport clothing that is short, tight, or revealing. Longer skirts, and shirts and blouses with sleeves, are less likely to attract unwanted attention. Women are expected to cover their heads with scarves when entering mosques.

Many hotels, restaurants, and other eating spots identify themselves as being for an *aile* (family) clientele, and many restaurants have special sections for women and children. How comfortable you are with being alone will affect whether you like these areas, which are away from the action—and you may prefer to take your chances in the main room (though some establishments will resist seating you there).

When traveling alone by bus, you should request a seat next to another woman. If a man sees that you are traveling alone, he will probably offer up his own seat so that you may sit next to a woman.

# ▌TAXES

The value-added tax, in Turkey called Katma Değer Vergisi, or KDV, is 18% on most goods and services. Hotels typically combine it with a service charge of 10% to 15%, and restaurants usually add a 15% service charge.

Value-added tax is nearly always included in quoted prices. Certain shops are authorized to refund the tax (you must ask).

When making a purchase, ask for a VAT refund form and find out whether the merchant gives refunds—not all stores do, nor are they required to. Have the form stamped by customs officials when you leave the country or, if you're visiting several European Union countries, when you leave the EU. After you're through passport control, take the form to a refund-service counter for an on-the-spot refund (which is usually the quickest and easiest option), or mail it to the address on the form (or the envelope with it) after you arrive home—the processing time can be long, especially if you request a credit card adjustment.

Global Blue is a worldwide service with 225,000 affiliated stores and more than 700 refund counters at major airports and border crossings. Its refund form, called a Tax Free Check, is the most common across the European continent. The service issues refunds in the form of cash, check, or credit card adjustment.

**VAT Refunds Global Blue** ☎ *866/706–6090 in the U.S.* ⊕ *www.global-blue.com.*

# TIME

Turkey is 2 hours ahead of London, 7 hours ahead of New York, 10 hours ahead of Los Angeles and Vancouver, 11 hours behind Auckland, and 9 hours behind Sydney and Melbourne. Turkey uses daylight saving time.

# TIPPING

A10%–15% charge is added to the bill in all restaurants except inexpensive fast-food spots. However, since this money does not necessarily find its way to your waiter, leave an additional 10% on the table. In top establishments, waiters expect tips of 10%–15% in addition to the service charge. Although it's acceptable to include the tip with your credit card payment, cash is much appreciated.

In Turkey, taxi drivers are becoming used to foreigners giving them something; round off the fare to the nearest 50 kuruş. *Dolmuş* drivers do not get tipped. Hotel porters expect about 2 TL. At Turkish baths, staff members who attend to you expect to share a tip of 30%–35% of the bill: don't worry about missing them—they'll be lined up expectantly on your departure.

Tour guides often expect a tip. Offer as much or (as little) as you feel the person deserves, usually 5 TL to 7 TL per day if you were happy with the guide. If you've been with the guide for a number of days, tip more. Crews on chartered boats also expect tips.

Restroom attendants will not expect a tip in addition to the charge for using their facilities.

# TOURS

Tours aren't for everyone, but they can be just the thing when making travel arrangements is difficult or too time-consuming. You travel along with a group (sometimes large, sometimes small), stay in prebooked hotels, eat with your fellow travelers (sometimes included in the price of your tour, sometimes not), and follow a schedule. A knowledgeable guide can take you places that you might never discover on your own, and you may be pushed to see more than you would have otherwise. Plus, a package tour to Turkey will often be less expensive than independent travel and you'll be spared the trouble of arranging everything yourself. There are, of course, cons, too, one disadvantage being that you'll have less flexibility in being able to choose your hotel.

Whenever you book a guided tour, find out what's included and what isn't. A "land-only" tour includes all your travel (by bus, in most cases) in the destination, but not necessarily your flights to or even within it. Also, in most cases, prices in tour brochures don't include fees and taxes. And remember that you'll be expected to tip your guide (in cash) at the end of the tour.

New York–based **Heritage Tours** is highly recommended as a higher-end, full-service travel company. Heritage can design a trip start to finish, including great hotels, private drivers, and tour guides.

**Recommended Generalists Cappadoc-cia Tours** ☎ 384/341–7485 in Turkey ⊕ www.cappadociatours.com. **Credo Tours** ☎ 212/254–8175 in Turkey ⊕ www.credo. com.tr. **Heritage Tours** ☎ 800/378–4555 in U.S. and Canada, 212/206–8400 in New York ⊕ htprivatetravel.com. **Istanbul Life** ☎ 212/638–1215 in Turkey ⊕ www.istanbullife. org. **Kirkit Voyage** ☎ 212/518–2282 in Turkey ⊕ www.kirkit.com. **Pacha Tours** ☎ 800/722–4288 in U.S. and Canada ⊕ www.pachatours. com. **Turkey Life Tours** ☎ 212/638–1215 in Turkey ⊕ www.turkeylifetours.org.

## SPECIAL-INTEREST TOUR COMPANIES

**Biblical Tours Turkey** celebrates Turkey's historic richness as a cultivating ground for some of the world's most prominent religions. Different itineraries will take you to historical churches and pilgrimage sites that are awe inspiring, regardless of your religious affiliation. Other tours focus on the country's many other assets. **Bird Paradise** organizes a number of tours that vary in length and region, all geared toward learning about Turkey's indigenous bird species. **Botanical Tours** organizes tours for nature lovers; tours typically start in one major city and end in another, stopping to enjoy Turkey's remarkably diverse scenery and flora along the way. **Breakaway Adventures** leads guided walking tours with stops at archaeological sites, along the Mediterranean coast, and elsewhere. **Kirkit Voyage** has tours featuring everything from hiking to biking, kayaking to canoeing, rafting, horseback riding, and diving. **Peter Sommer Travels** is a UK-based company that provides academic, yet friendly, guided archaeological tours of Turkey on *gulet* cruises. **Runner Tourism and Travel** celebrates slow food, as opposed to fast food, and lets the traveler experience cuisine from the very beginning: from the farmers and producers to the markets, and finally to your plate. The company also runs botany and archaeological tours.

**Biblical Tours Turkey** ☎ *256/618–3268 in Turkey* ⊕ *www.biblicaltoursturkey.com.* **Bird Paradise** ⊕ *www.birdwatchingtoursturkey.com.* **Botanical Turkey Tours** ☎ *542/413–1293 in Turkey* ⊕ *www.wildflowertours.com.* **Breakaway Adventures** ☎ *800/567–6286 in U.S.* ⊕ *www.breakaway-adventures.com.* **Peter Sommer Travels** ☎ *01600/888–220 in U.K.* ⊕ *www.petersommer.com.* **Runner Tourism and Travel** ☎ *242/425-2361 in Turkey* ⊕ *www.runnertourism.com.*

# ▌ VISITOR INFORMATION

## ONLINE RESOURCES

There are hundreds of Web sites about Turkey; these are some of the standouts. For everything you'd want to know about Turkey before your trip, from Atatürk history to religious festivals, to sample authentic music and more, check out ⊕ *www.kultur.gov.tr.* For pictures of what you're about to see live and in-person, try

⊕ *www.balsoy.com/Turkiye/inpictures.* Beat-by-beat news on the city life in Istanbul, Ankara, and elsewhere around the country, as well as details about what's going culturally, can be found at ⊕ *www.mymerhaba.com.*

## VISITOR INFORMATION

There are tourist information offices in most of the main cities in Turkey; *check the listings in the individual chapters.* These offices can provide info on sights and cultural events, and some have accommodation-booking services that can be useful if you arrive in a destination without a hotel reservation.

**Contacts Turkish Culture and Tourism Office** ⊕ *www.goturkey.com.* **Ministry of Culture and Tourism** ⊕ *www.turizm.gov.tr.*

# INDEX

## PHOTO CREDITS

# NOTES

# NOTES

# NOTES

# NOTES

# NOTES